THE ENCYCLOPEDIA OF
DRUG ABUSE

THE ENCYCLOPEDIA OF

DRUG ABUSE

Robert O'Brien and Sidney Cohen, M.D.

Facts On File, Inc.
New York, New York • Bicester, England

EDITORIAL STAFF

Editors
Robert O'Brien   Sidney Cohen, M.D.

Managing Editor
Lynn Prindle

Associate Manager
Gale Toensing

Contributing Editors
Dorothy Cohen, Sophia Dertz, John Harrington,
Joan Harvey, David Merrill, Merrill Noyes,
Joyce O'Brien, Sandy Van Wagner

THE ENCYCLOPEDIA OF DRUG ABUSE

by Robert O'Brien and Sidney Cohen, M.D.

Copyright © 1984 by Green Spring Inc.

Library of Congress Cataloging in Publication Data

O'Brien, Robert.
  Encyclopedia of drug abuse.

  1. Drug abuse — Dictionaries.   2. Drugs — Dictionaries.
I. Title.
HV5804.024   362.2'9   82-5034
ISBN 0-87196-690-5   AACR2

Printed in the United States of America
10 9 8 7 6 5 4 3 2 1

TABLE OF CONTENTS

PREFACE VII
HISTORY OF DRUGS AND MAN IX
DRUG CLASSIFICATION CHART XXIII
ENTRIES A-Z 1
APPENDICES 281
BIBLIOGRAPHY 423
INDEX 447

Sherlock Holmes took his bottle from the corner of the mantelpiece, and his hypodermic syringe from its neat morocco case. With his long, white, nervous fingers he adjusted the delicate needle and rolled back his left shirt cuff. For some time his eyes rested thoughtfully upon the sinewy forearm and wrist, all dotted and scarred with innumerable puncture marks. Finally, he thrust the sharp point home, pressed down the tiny piston, and sank back into the velvet–lined armchair with a long sigh of satisfaction.

—Arthur Conan Doyle,
Sign of the Four (1890)

PREFACE

Since the 1950s, drug abuse has become an increasingly disturbing problem throughout the world. *The Encyclopedia of Drug Abuse* has been designed to give an overall view of the issue, with entries ranging from descriptions of the medical and physical effects of drugs, to psychological factors in drug abuse, to political and legal factors, and, since the problem is international, to how widespread drug abuse is around the world and how it is handled in different countries. Additionally, there are appendices of tabular material concerning use, treatment and traffic and a substantial glossary of street language and slang synonyms for drugs.

The Encyclopedia of Drug Abuse is intended for both the lay person and the professional. We have tried to keep the language simple without becoming simplistic, so that the volume can be used by counselors, educators, and community leaders, as well as by the individual who thinks that he or someone in his family may be facing a drug problem. Whenever a term cannot be simplified, we have tried to define it as clearly as possible.

Drugs and drug abuse are much wider subjects than many people realize, and we have therefore given information about many drugs, not just the "dangerous drugs," such as heroin and cocaine, but substances such as caffeine, nicotine and over–the–counter preparations that have some potential for abuse and can be damaging either physically or psychologically.

Because of the limitations of our format and space, we obviously cannot provide all the information that we would like to. For this reason we have included an extensive bibliography for the reader who needs more information.

While *The Encyclopedia of Drug Abuse* is not the first A to Z volume to appear in the field, it is, to the best knowledge of the editors, the first "encyclopedic" reference. The others are largely devoted to the drugs themselves, without articles on medical and biological aspects, ethnic groups, geographical areas, organizations, laws, and other topics which make up the breadth of the field of drug abuse.

The Encyclopedia of Drug Abuse has been designed as a companion to *The Encyclopedia of Alcoholism,* edited by Robert O'Brien and Dr. Morris Chafetz. It follows the earlier volume in format, approach and presentation of subject matter. Each volume, however, is designed to stand alone. Since alcohol is a drug, and one that is subject to abuse, alcoholism and alcohol abuse are covered in this volume, although not as extensively or in the same depth as in *The Encyclopedia of Alcoholism.*

Another difference between the two volumes is the larger proportion of space devoted to legal aspects in the present volume. Alcohol, while regulated by a variety of laws, is one of the few major drugs of abuse for which the use, possession or sale outside of proper channels is not a criminal act. With drug abuse, the aspect of criminality not only has a significant impact on the problem, it is often a major part of the problem itself.

Research into drug abuse and the extent of the problem continues to accelerate and new information becomes available almost daily. *The Encyclopedia of Drug Abuse* is a "work in progress." Future editions will keep abreast of this all important and continuing issue.

Robert O'Brien   Sidney Cohen, M.D.
Sharon, Conn.   Los Angeles, Cal.

ACKNOWLEDGMENTS

Since projects of this kind are necessarily enormous and cumbersome, they involve the work of many hands including those of the staff members whose names appear on the copyright page.

Any detailed listing of other contributions to this volume would require much more space than is available here. However, some mention should be made of the staffs of the following agencies and organizations: the National Institute on Drug Abuse, the Drug Enforcement Administration, the Federal Bureau of Investigation, the United States Department of Justice, the Alcohol, Drug Abuse and Mental Health Administration, the Food and Drug Administration, the United States Department of Health and Human Services, the Gallup Poll, the Roper Organization, the World Health Organization, the Addiction Research Foundation (Canada), the League of Red Cross Societies, the National Institute on Alcohol Abuse and Alcoholism, the National Clearinghouse for Alcohol Information, the National Clearinghouse for Drug Abuse Information, the National Council on Alcoholism, Alcoholics Anonymous, the various state and provincial (Canadian) agencies, as well as the embassies and agencies of other nations who responded to our requests for information.

Robert O'Brien would like to thank those without whose personal help this book would not have been possible: Dr. Robert Schurtman and Joyce O'Brien.

THE HISTORY OF DRUGS AND MAN

"Pharmacology antedated agriculture."
—Aldous Huxley

The language of drugs has changed considerably over the centuries although the use of drugs, as defined in this volume, predates the use of language itself. Until the 18th century, a "drug" was any substance used in a medicinal, chemical, or even industrial preparation (dyes for fabrics, for example.) We still use the word drugs as a catchall: today it means not only medications, potentially addictive or not, that require a prescription, but also over–the–counter drugs, ointments, lotions, even toothpastes and deodorants—anything, in fact, which may be found in a drugstore or drug department.

"Addiction," as we use the word today, was also slow to develop its present meaning, although the phenomenon was common enough. Addiction was the delivery or surrender of a person or thing ("Did this addiction make him legally a slave?"). Only later, as the word assumed the meaning of "self–addiction," did it take on its modern meaning in connection with drugs. In many ways, this changing vocabulary of drug use and abuse reflects people's ambivalence toward these substances over the centuries.

The history of non–medical drug use is thousands of years old. Man consumed the juice of opium poppies long before there were narcotics such as morphine and heroin. Man chewed coca leaves long before cocaine was extracted from the South American coca plant. Man dried peyote cactus long before hallucinogens were synthesized. Throughout recorded history, drugs have been used for both medicinal and religious purposes. Both uses—to enhance physical well–being and to heighten religious and metaphysical experiences—are closely related to drug use for its own sake. Drug use has always included recreational intoxication and self–induced relief from psychic pain and emotional malady. Distinctions between these various uses are often difficult, and are often arbitrary ones imposed by a particular culture, religion or social group.

The earliest known records of drug use concern the plants that were discovered to have medicinal effects on the body or mind. This practice is, of course, part of folk medicine even today, and the early history of drug use is inseparable from the early history of medicine.

The Sumerian people of Asia Minor, who created the cuneiform alphabet, included references to a "joy plant" in their earliest written records which date from about 5000 B.C. Most experts believe the plant was the opium poppy, and its mention in these tracts suggests medicinal use as a sedative.

In China, *ma-huang,* a species of ephedra *(Ephedra sinica),* a shrub containing the alkaloid ephedrine, was in use as an inhalant by 3000 B.C. A Chinese tract from 2737 B.C. attributed to the Emperor Shen Nung documents how the hemp plant *Cannabis sativa* could be brewed into a tea and used for medicinal purposes. Cannabis was introduced into India by about 2000 B.C.

and the Indians may have been the first people to dry the plant and smoke it. Thus, even at the earliest stage of drug use several methods of administration quickly evolved. There is such a multitude of vegetable remedies and methods of consumption found in early records that is often difficult to distinguish not only the substances used but also the reasons for which they were used.

Although some historians are reluctant to attribute drug use to Semitic people, the Old Testament abounds with references to the cultivation and administration of medicinal herbs. There is, for example, a provocative inventory of favored plants in the Old Testament Song of Solomon (4: 13–14):

> Thy plants are an orchard of pomegranates, with pleasant fruits; camphire, with spikenard,
> Spikenard and saffron; calamus and cinnamon, with trees of frankincense.

Centuries after this was written white men would discover spikenard in use as a cough medicine among the Chippewa Indians in America.

Early records also indicate an awareness of the dangers of drug consumption. Alcoholic beverages must have originated in primitive times by accidental fermentation, and the oldest known legal code, the Code of Hammurabi, inscribed in Babylonia in about 1700 B.C., includes strictures against drunkenness. Ancient Egyptian papyri dating from 1500 B.C. document fears of opium elixirs because of the hallucinogenic delusions they produced. The Egyptians were familiar with the fact that certain drugs produce a stuporous effect and they used them as a kind of primitive anesthetic in order to perform the earliest forms of skull surgery on patients. While many of the apparent references to drugs in the Old Testament remain open to question, there is little doubt that an incident recorded in *Genesis* refers to Noah's drunkenness from alcohol.

In Ancient Greece alcohol and other drugs were used extensively and there are many references to them in classical literature. Homer's epics, the *Illiad* and the *Odyssey* which date from about 800 B.C., contain several references to wine and occasional suggestions that some heroes, perhaps even Achilles, the hero of the Trojan War, suffered from overindulgence. In the *Illiad* Helen is said to have brought a drug–like substance, nepenthe (which some people believe to be marijuana and others opium), with her to Troy; and in the *Odyssey* the "lotus eaters" encountered by Ulysses suffer from a self–induced lethargy and forgetfulness clearly associated with drugs. At the beginning of the fifth century B.C. the Greek historian Herodotus recorded that the Scythians, nomads who lived in part of what is now Russia, cultivated a hemp plant which they burned as a kind of incense in closed rooms. He noted that they inhaled the fumes of the burning hemp and became as intoxicated as Greeks drunk on wine. Around the same time, about 400 B.C., Hippocrates was experimenting with medicinal preparations and using opium as an ingredient. This was also the era when the Greek cult of Dionysus combined wine–drinking with phallic worship, according to debaucheries described by Euripides in the *Bacchae*.

The Roman Empire preserved such wine festivals in its own "baccanalia," which by 100 A.D. had inspired anti–drunkenness laws. Because the Romans, like the Greeks, were conquerors of other lands, they also came into contact with other drug cultures. It was during the Roman conquest of the eastern Mediterranean in the first century A.D. that they became familiar with opium. Dioscorides, a Greek surgeon who traveled with the Roman army on its campaigns, described in *De Materia Medica,* his authoritative medical text, how liquid opium could be prepared by crushing the pod of the poppy plant. Galen, who was appointed court physician to Marcus Aurelius in 164 A.D., had learned his medical lore from the drug–conscious Egyptians and was an ardent proponent of the benefits of opium eating, among other vegetable therapies. Such was his authority that similar preparations were for centuries known as Galenicals.

In the first millenium A.D. the cultivation of cannabis began to spread and well–defined patterns of consumption developed. The *Susruta,* a treatise produced in India in about 400 A.D., documents local use of cannabis at that time and this and other sources provide unusually detailed information of the specific grades of cannabis used by Indians. *Bhang,* the least potent grade, was brewed into a tea by the lowest classes; *ganja,* a stronger grade, was usually smoked by the ''middle'' classes; and *charas,* the most potent preparation (equivalent to hashish), was made into fancy concoctions with nuts and honey and eaten by the most affluent classes in Indian society.

The word *hashish* dates from 11th century Persia where drugs first became associated with criminal activities. This drug preparation takes its name from the Persian cult leader Al–Hassan ibn–al Sabbah, ''The Old Man of the Mountains.'' Hassan led a group of the Isma'ili sect of Shi'ite Muslims called *hashishi* (''hemp–eaters'') who allegedly incorporated the use of hashish into their violent reprisals against political rivals. They are said to have consumed hashish in order to induce ecstatic visions of paradise before setting out to face martyrdom, and in this intoxicated state launched suicidal attacks on challengers to their tribal hegemony. The word ''assassin'' also derives from the cult of Al–Hassan, although in early European usage it meant devotee and only later acquired the meaning of murderer.

The Middle Ages were characterized by increasing contact between Western and Eastern civilizations and the ensuing cultural exchanges included exports from ''drug–rich'' Asia to ''drug–poor'' Europe. The Crusades of the 11th and 12th centuries increased European knowledge of Middle Eastern drug preparations, including hashish and distilled alcohol. Marco Polo returned from expeditions to the Orient not only with the spices and silks usually cited in history books, but also with detailed knowledge of opium cultivation and drug cults such as the *hashishis.*

Much of the lore spread in this era was apothecary in nature and little understood until modern times. Belladonna, for example, was first discovered in Europe in late medieval times, although there are references to it in Greek mythology. This preparation was made from the berries of *Solanum nigrum,* a variety of the nightshade plant known as ''deadly nightshade.'' While modern science has revealed the plant's diaphoretic, narcotic and antispasmodic properties, it was actually used by Italian women to dilate their pupils for cosmetic effect, hence its name belladonna (''beautiful lady''). By the late 1400s, however, Cesare Borgia (thought to be the model for Machiavelli's *The Prince)* had made stronger concentrations of belladonna notorious as a deadly poison. It was not until 1833 that P. L. Geiger isolated the active ingredient of belladonna—the alkaloid drug atropine—which is now used as an antispasmodic.

During these early times, the discovery of drug properties varied in different parts of the world according to the local vegetation. The Indian civilizations of the Americas discovered different drugs from those of the Old World and the Orient. In the Americas one favored drug was derived from a mountain shrub now classified as *Erythroxylon coca.* As long ago as 1000 B.C. the Incas, in what is now Bolivia and Peru, were chewing coca leaves for their stimulant effects. The leaves increased energy, suppressed appetite, and produced short–term euphoria— effects which helped the people endure the rigors of their harsh mountain environment. The drug was also used in the Incas' religious ceremonies and was considered more valuable than gold or silver.

Further north, the Aztec Indians of Mexico had built a culture dating back to 100 B.C. around the magical properties of the peyote cactus, the psilocybin mushroom, and *ololiuqui,* the seeds of a variety of morning glory containing a hallucinogenic chemical similar to lysergic acid amide. In North America the most common kind of drug consumption was inhaling smoke from burning tobacco leaves. All of the drug practices from Indian cultures would fascinate and eventually captivate the earliest European explorers of the New World.

It was through the travels of early explorers that the familiar stimulant, caffeine, came into widespread use. The coffee tree is an evergreen native to Ethiopia. It was cultivated in early times in Arabia and its berries were mixed with liquid to make a stimulating drink. European explorers in the Middle East recorded seeing Mohammedans drinking coffee for energy during long religious pilgrimages and vigils in the 14th century. Coffee was introduced into European countries during the 16th and 17th centuries and the first London coffeehouse was established in about 1652. Frequented by writers and wits, coffeehouses became the rage in late 17th and 18th century London. Coffee's stimulant effect and popularity were ridiculed by Alexander Pope in *The Rape of the Lock* (1714):

> Coffee (which makes the Politican Wise,
> And sees thro' all things with his half–shut Eyes).

It was via England and its global sea trade that coffee cultivation spread to South America, which now produces most of the world supply.

Thus, in their travels to the East, Europeans discovered a variety of drugs that were soon incorporated into their own life–styles. But in their travels to the West, to the Americas, they discovered a veritable trove of drugs ready for export home. The meeting of the Old World with the New stands as the most crucial drug exchange in recorded history. The explorations begun by Columbus discovered, among other resources, cocaine from South America, hallucinogens from Central America and tobacco from North America. These drugs were brought back to European courts and received with as much relish as parrots, gold and furs. The drug exchange became complete when the Europeans introduced into the Americas distilled alcoholic beverages and, in Chile in 1545, cannabis from Asia.

The tobacco revolution of this time was an especially remarkable instance of drug exchange. Indians persuaded to travel to Europe insisted on taking a supply of tobacco with them. They introduced it to European sailors and smoking—with its alternating stimulating and tranquilizing effects—immediately became popular. Ships traveled with supplies of tobacco leaves and seeds, thus insuring the spread of the cultivation of tobacco and the practice of smoking along the world's sea-lanes. Magellan introduced tobacco to Africa, the Dutch carried the plant to the Hottentots, and the Portugese transported it to Polynesia. In England, which controlled the tobacco–rich region of Virginia, the craze for tobacco reached epidemic proportions, despite its high price. Sir Walter Raleigh brought pipe smoking to England and by 1614 tobacco use had spread even to the very poor, and it had become "a commoditie that is now as vendible in every Taverne, Inne, and Alehouse, as eyther Wine, Ale, or Beare. . . ." (Berthold Laufer, *Introduction of Tobacco into Europe,* Anthropology Leaflet 19, Chicago: Field Museum of Natural History, 1924, p. 16). The addictive nature of nicotine, which was named after Jacques Nicot who brought it to France in 1560 claiming that it had great medicinal potential, was quickly apparent. In 1623 Sir Francis Bacon described smoking tobacco as "a certain secret pleasure" and wrote: "those who have once become accustomed thereto can later hardly be restrained therefrom." Earlier, in 1604, James I of England had issued his *Counterblast to Tobacco.* Japan acted to prohibit smoking in 1603, and Papal encyclicals against smoking were published in 1642 and 1650. All proved futile and by the late 1600s most European countries had replaced outright prohibitions on smoking with high and very profitable taxes on tobacco. Tobacco became common in every culture to which it was introduced, the last being the tribes of the Arctic regions in the present century. No social practice matches the virtually universal appeal of smoking, a fact which can only be accounted for by the addictive quality of nicotine and the conditioning established after thousands of nicotine "hits" to the brain.

At the same time that the use of tobacco was becoming so widespread, the use of opium in various forms was also increasing. In 1541 the Swiss alchemist Paracelsus introduced laudanum—opium in liquid form—and it quickly gained great popularity throughout Europe as a medical panacea.

The heaviest national use of opium developed in China. Opium had been used in China since early times but it was not until well after the discovery of America that the practice of *smoking* opium became common. By 1650 opium use was recognized as a serious health problem but nevertheless an organized commerce in the drug developed. The Manchu dynasty attempted to restrict importation of opium to its people but it proved powerless against the economic leverage of the English East India Company, which began shipment of opium from its colony India in 1767. Chinese rulers went so far as to make opium smoking a capital offense in 1776, but this first national effort to control drug abuse failed to curb the appetite for opium. In 1839 the Manchu government escalated its battle by prohibiting the importation of opium; to insure compliance it ordered all ship–borne imports to be confiscated and all vessels involved to be detained. The result was the Opium War between China and England (1839–1842) in which the Chinese were defeated by an England bent on protecting its trade prerogatives. A second Opium War broke out in 1856 and by the subsequent Treaty of Tientsin in 1858 China was forced to permit importation of opium subject to high tariffs. In a pattern that would be repeated in other nations' attempts to curb drug traffic, the tariffs only succeeded in encouraging smuggling and criminal conspiracies.

England's justification during the Opium Wars was that it was also encouraging shipment of opium to its own shores. The drug was, in fact, a common staple in British medicine throughout the 18th and 19th centuries. James Boswell recorded that on March 23, 1783: "I breakfasted with Dr. Johnson, who seemed much relieved, having taken opium the night before." Johnson, however, protested against the use of the drug as a common remedy and thought it should be given only in cases of extreme necessity and then with the utmost reluctance. Despite such fears, the use of opium and opium derivative preparations spread throughout England, Europe and North America, and they were used for their intoxicating effects as well as medicinally. Some of the English Romantics came to associate the effects of the drug with their aesthetics of the sublime and of the suprarational. Samuel Taylor Coleridge's poem "Kubla Khan," with its vision of a "stately pleasure dome," is said to have originated in an opium vision, and Coleridge did indeed suffer progressive physical and intellectual debilitation from his well–documented addiction to opium in the form of laudanum.

The mythology of the inspirational benefits of opium was given its greatest boost at this time by Thomas De Quincey in his book *Confessions of an English Opium Eater* (1822). It was De Quincey who invented the term "tranquilizer" to describe the effect of the drug. De Quincey began taking opium during his student days at Oxford and drug use by writers, part of a mystique still popular today, was further promulgated by the hashish cult surrounding the French poets Theophile Gautier and Charles Baudelaire in the 1840s. It was symptomatic of the times that in the same decade the Swede Magnus Huss invented the term "alcoholism" to describe another, less elitist, form of drug abuse.

Opium use became epidemic in 19th century Europe, particularly England, and America. Tragically, the most widespread use of the drug was in children's medicines which were marketed under names such as Godfrey's Cordial, Munn's Elixir, and Mother Bailey's Quieting

Syrup. The most popular household guide of the time, *Beeton's Book of Household Management,* felt compelled in its 1869 edition to warn that certain "preparations, which are constantly given to children by their nurses and mothers, for the purpose of making them sleep, often prove fatal." But for the poor, especially women who did textile work in their own homes, there were few alternatives. An English survey of 1842 called *The Second Report to the Commissioners* addressed the dilemma that drove poor women to "dope" their children with opium.

One outsider who responded with emotion to this form of drug abuse was the German Frederick Engels. In *The Condition of the Working Class in England in 1844,* he provided a chilling description of increased dosage as infant bodies developed resistance to the drug. Because of the ever–larger doses, "they become pale, stunted and weak, generally dying before they are two years old," he wrote. "The use of this medicine is widespread in all the great cities and industrial towns of the country."

As drug use became more common in the 18th and 19th centuries advances in chemistry and pharmacology were making new and more potent forms of drugs available.

In 1730 the German physician Friedrich Hoffmann introduced Anodyne, a liquid form of ether, as an effective medicine for a variety of ailments. It became popular both as a drink and as an inhalant because it was thought to be an intoxicant free of the addictive qualities of alcohol.

In 1776 Joseph Priestly discovered nitrous oxide (N_2O). It was synthesized a year later by the chemist Humphry Davy, who held "laughing gas" parties in his home.

In 1831 chloroform was simultaneously developed by chemists in several countries. By 1847 it was in use as an anesthetic; it was also used for its pleasurable intoxicating effects, despite the acknowledged danger of fatal overdose.

In 1869 chloral hydrate was developed by Oscar Liebreich as the first synthetic sedative hypnotic. In spite of its objectionable odor, it was widely used recreationally to produce intoxication, especially in combination with alcohol—a possibly lethal combination which earned the nicknames "knockout drops" and "Mickey Finn."

In 1896 mescaline was isolated as the active ingredient in peyote. It would be rediscovered as yet another "risk–free" drug during the LSD era of the 20th century.

One of the most important developments in drug use occurred around 1803 when the active ingredient in opium was isolated. This discovery is usually attributed to the German pharmacist, F.W. Serturner, who named the substance morphine after Morpheus, the Greek god of dreams and sleep. Morphine soon came into common medical use as a pain killer, with the devastating consequence that hundreds of thousands of individuals became addicted to it. In 1853 the hypodermic needle was introduced and used for injecting morphine during emergency surgery. At the time, physicians mistakenly believed that hypodermic administration of morphine was harmless and non–addictive because the drug bypassed the digestive tract.

American medical reliance on morphine reached its apogee during the Civil War, when hideously injured soldiers littered disease–ridden battlefields and prison camps. In 1868 a Dr. Horatio Day wrote that: "maimed and shattered survivors from a hundred battlefields, diseased and disabled soldiers released from hostile prisons, anguished and hopeless wives and mothers, made so by the slaughter of those who were dearest to them, have found, many of them, temporary relief from their sufferings in opium." Day's comments were published in a book called *The Opium Habit* which is significant for its recognition of the danger of addiction and resignation to the necessary use of the drug in desperate circumstances. By most accounts, the Civil War produced about 400,000 morphine addicts in the army alone, who were said to suffer from "the soldier's disease." The lesson was not readily heeded, however, and a large number of morphine addicts were created in Europe during the Franco–Prussian War of 1870–71. By then the results of morphine addiction had been dubbed "morphineomania."

After the Civil War a pattern emerged in American drug consumption of heavy reliance on patent medicines based on opium, often in lieu of professional medical care. The medicines were marketed under names such as Mrs. Winslow's Soothing Syrup, Darby's Carminative and Ayer's Cherry Pectorial. The English import Godfrey's Cordial was also popular. By 1885 a survey of Iowa—a state with a population under two million—documented 3,000 stores that were selling opiate elixirs. Such patent medicines proliferated until the end of the century. There were three reasons for this. First, magazine advertising and mail order sales helped make them known and available in remote parts of the country. Second, self–medication encouraged frequent and increasing dosage. Third, users ran less risk of social criticism than they did if they developed other drug habits, such as alcoholism. As the *Catholic World* observed in September 1881: "The gentleman who would not be seen in a barroom, however respectable, or who would not purchase liquor and use it at home, lest the odor might be detected upon his person, procures his supply of morphia and has it in his pocket ready for instantaneous use. It is odorless and occupies but little space."

Although the use of these "modern" drugs was growing, alcohol was the most abused drug during the 18th and 19th centuries as it continues to be in the 20th century. While alcohol had been used in Europe for centuries, it was not until improved methods of distilling spirits were discovered in the late 17th century that alcohol abuse became widespread. The results were devastating. The English in particular became very concerned about the dangers of alcoholism among the lower classes. In London during the 18th century, gin was available at low cost and rapidly acquired a vast popularity especially among impoverished women, so much so that it was given the nickname "mother's ruin" because so many women could be seen lying in the streets drunk on gin. William Hogarth portrayed the evils of alcohol abuse in illustrations such as *Gin Street* and *Beer Street* and the novels of Charles Dickens are full of warnings against intoxication. These two men took different approaches to the problem: Hogarth showed that abuse of alcohol led to poverty and misery, while Dickens felt that poverty and misery led to the abuse of alcohol. Both approaches probably contain some truth.

In 19th century America, the American Indians suffered from alcoholism in extraordinary proportions after westward–moving white men introduced them to whiskey. In the 1870s the Commanches began to use peyote in their religious practices, a drug whose use was spreading northward from Mexico. Peyote is currently the only hallucinogen whose use is sanctioned by the United States government. In 1964 the California Supreme Court upheld the right of members of the Native American Church to consume peyote during religious ceremonies.

In 1878 cocaine in alkaloid form became readily available as a treatment for morphine addiction among Civil War veterans. It took on another medical use when the pioneering American surgeon William Stewart Halsted began injecting cocaine as a regional anesthetic for surgery in 1886. In that same year, the drug reached the population at large in a surprising form. John Styth Pemberton, a marketer of opiate liver pills from Atlanta, Georgia, mixed coca leaves with wine in what he called French Wine Coca. A year later he added caffeine from the kola nut and called the product Coca–Cola. The company switched to "decocainized" coca leaves in 1906, but it was not until 1982 that it marketed a caffeine–free version of the popular soft drink.

By the 1880s cocaine use was spreading in Europe in the same way, in popular drinks and misguided medical applications. The most notable European cocaine elixir was called Vin Mariani after its Corsican manufacturer Angelo Mariani. Users of the coca leaf and red wine concoction included Pope Leo XIII. In 1883 the German physician Theodor Aschenbrandt began to provide Bavarian soldiers with alkaloid cocaine produced by the pharmaceutical firm of Merck. Aschenbrandt's optimistic publications on the use of cocaine as a stimulant attracted the notice of Sigmund Freud, then a practicing neurologist. Freud began to use cocaine in 1884 as a treatment for depression, and he published his own optimistic accounts of its psychological benefits. Freud appears to have been always able to control his cocaine use, although he would die in 1939 of cancer of the jaw and heart ailments caused by a life–long addiction to cigars.

Freud's cocaine habit was known only to specialists in his own field, but the cocaine addiction of a fictional genius of the same time was the stuff of popular literature. One of the principal characteristics of Sir Arthur Conan Doyle's detective Sherlock Holmes was his use of cocaine injections to counter depression. The first Holmes stories, published in the 1880s, were graphic about this habit: " 'Quick, Watson, the needle!' " But in the later stories in the series, after Holmes was improbably rescued from the Reichenbach Falls to satisfy public demand, he had been cured of his habit.

The resurrection of a "clean" Sherlock Holmes was a significant reflection of changing public attitudes toward drug use. Although the world continued to prize medical pioneering in drug research and to readily accept drugs dispensed by physicians, recreational use of drugs was becoming subject to suspicion, superstition and gross stereotyping.

As we have seen, the Chinese enacted the first drug laws in the modern world in 1796, and the results were unsatisfactory. The Chinese appetite for opium also underlay the first American drug laws. In the 1860s tens of thousands of Chinese immigrated to California to work on railroad gangs; after the tracks had been laid, the laborers drifted back into West Coast cities, where the opium dens to which they were accustomed naturally grew in number. The first U.S. drug law was an 1875 San Francisco city ordinance against "opium houses" which proved unsatisfactory. Nevertheless, the San Francisco law was followed by an identical one in 1876 in Virginia City, Nevada, and by 1914 there were 27 city and state laws against smoking opium. The grade of opium used for smoking, however, was far weaker than the opium that was used in patent medicines which remained legal.

Governments had already responded to alcohol abuse with heavy taxation, thus retaining legal control over trade, and benefiting from accumulating revenues. For a time the same principle was applied to other drugs subject to widespread abuse. In 1883 the U.S. raised the tariff on imported smoking–opium to $10 per pound. It did not raise taxes on the finer grades of opium consumed in other ways and it did not act against American–grown opium. In 1890 the tariff was raised to $12 per pound and then, in 1897, it was reduced to $6 per pound. The government thus found a level of taxation that discouraged the habit without surrendering control of the drug to criminal elements. Opium smoking was still associated in the popular mind with the Chinese subculture, however, and in 1909 Congress bowed to public pressure and made it a criminal offense. Illegal commerce in smoking–opium continued unabated, though, and in 1930 the Federal Narcotics Commission reported that "opium dens could be found in almost any American city." In effect, the law itself had created a drug underground.

The original Pure Food and Drug Act of 1906 was the first U.S. action to protect the safety of drug consumers. It required that the so–called patent medicines containing opium indicate the fact on their labels. The Harrison Narcotics Act which followed in 1914 regularized licensing and taxation of people who dispensed "opium or coca leaves, their salts, derivatives, or preparations." The act also specified that drug prescriptions be issued only by registered physicians. Subsequently courts refused to define addiction as a disease and they banned prescriptions of opium to addicts as not being within the parameters of a doctor's "professional practice." Thus the Harrison Act cut off the legal supply of opium to addicted persons and drove them to seek illegal supplies. This precedent of punishment–without–treatment was emulated by later U.S. drug laws.

At the same time the first international efforts were launched to respond to the problem of world–wide drug abuse. In 1907 India and China entered into a 10–year agreement: China would act to limit domestic opium cultivation and India would end exportation to China within the decade. In 1909, at the urging of U.S President Theodore Roosevelt, the first International Opium Commission met in Shanghai with 13 nations in attendance. This exchange led to meetings in The Hague, Netherlands, from 1912 to 1914 which ratified the first Opium Convention, a treaty to regularize international trade. International discussions on the topic were suspended during World War I but the Treaty of Versailles which ended the war in 1919 also empowered the new League of Nations to restrict commerce in opium to countries indicating consent by formal licensing procedures. Six more international agreements culminated in the Geneva Convention for the Suppression of the Illicit Traffic in Dangerous Drugs signed in 1936. By then the superiority of control over total prohibition had been demonstrated by the failure of U.S. efforts to prohibit alcoholic beverages between 1919 and 1933.

During this time medical researchers increased the kinds of drugs that could be abused or used to support illegal commerce. In 1898 the Bayer company of Germany began commercial production of heroin, which was three times as potent as the morphine from which it was derived. In 1903, also in Germany, barbiturates were introduced, launching a search for profitable variations on barbiturate acid. In 1912 amphetamine, synthesized in 1887, came into use as a substitute for ephedrine in asthma treatment. In 1932 benzedrine inhalers were introduced, also as a treatment for respiratory ailments. A synthesized opioid marketed under the name Demerol was introduced in 1938. The era was rich in new drugs, but there were virtually no significant advances in the as yet ill–defined field of drug treatment.

At the end of World War II, the new United Nations adopted a protocol that brought drug control under the jurisdiction of the World Health Organization (WHO), still the most important international agency in the field. From 1948 to 1964 the agency spearheaded a series of agreements that severely limited international trade in opium, and which restricted legal trade in cocaine and marijuana to supplies necessary for medical and scientific usage. Today WHO continues to collect the most reliable worldwide statistics on drug abuse, including alcoholism.

In the 20th century the governments of the world have played, and continue to play, an increasing role in protecting individual members of society from drug abuse through the control of legal drugs and the elimination of the flow of illegal drugs. In spite of all international efforts, however, the use of illegal drugs (such as marijuana) and legal drugs (such as amphetamines and barbiturates) has become almost commonplace—in some cases even socially acceptable—and, in one way or another, affects almost everyone.

Although it is illegal throughout most of the world, marijuana is the fourth most popular mind–affecting substance used (the first three are caffeine, nicotine and alcohol). The cultivation and use of the hemp plant, from which marijuana is obtained, is documented throughout recorded history. It is perhaps the oldest cultivated nonfood plant and has been valued for its commercial, medical, religious and recreational uses for thousands of years. Marijuana was introduced to the New World in 1545 A.D. when the Spanish brought it to Chile. The Jamestown settlers in Virginia began cultivating hemp for its fiber. It was introduced in New England in 1629 and became a major crop in America until well after the Civil War. Its role in colonial economic policy was so important that in 1762, ''Virginia awarded bounties for hemp culture and manufacture, and imposed penalties upon those who did not produce it.'' (Cited by George Andrews and Simon Vinkenoog, eds., *The Book of Grass: An Anthology of Indian Hemp,* New York: Grove Press, 1967, p.34.)

Cultivation of marijuana continued throughout the 19th century on large hemp plantations in Mississippi, Georgia, California, South Carolina, Nebraska and New York, with the bulk of production centered in Kentucky. Commercial production declined with the invention of the cotton gin and other industrial machinery, and with the competition from cheap imported hemp, but as late as 1937 it is estimated that 10,000 acres of marijuana were still being cultivated in the U.S. During World War II cultivation was increased for a while to meet the demands for hemp.

Throughout this time the hemp plant was used not only for its fiber but also medicinally for a wide–ranging variety of conditions; fluid extracts of marijuana were marketed by leading pharmaceutical companies and sold as low–priced over–the–counter household remedies. Although its medicinal use declined after 1903 with the discovery of more modern and effective drugs, the therapeutic value of marijuana extract remained valid and many doctors continued to prescribe it until medical use of the plant was prohibited in 1937.

During the second half of the 19th century marijuana was also used recreationally, mostly in the form of hashish. From all written accounts, it would seem that its use was largely limited to two groups: the affluent classes who frequented secret hashish houses in the cities; and black farm workers who would load up their pipes in the fields with the flowering tops of the hemp plants. It was not until the 1920s that marijuana came into general use as a recreational drug—and not until the 1960s that its use ''trickled down'' and became so widespread that today some consider it epidemic.

During Prohibition the commercial trade in marijuana for recreational use increased but was still relatively limited to the large cities, especially New York, and to local rural areas where it was grown. In the 1930s marijuana use began to be linked to the crime wave which swept the country and this resulted first in state legislation banning marijuana and then in the passage of the 1937 Marijuana Tax Act which outlawed the possession or sale of it.

In spite of its illegality, marijuana use continued to spread. In the 1950s it was popularized by ''Beat Generation'' author Jack Kerouac. In the 1960s it gained widespread popularity among college and high school students. Since the 1970s the use of marijuana has transcended all social strata and all age groups—the estimated number of *regular* users of marijuana in the United States in the 1980s ranges from 16 million to 30 million.

Because its use is so widespread and far–ranging in our society, and because of the lack of extensive research, the controversy surrounding marijuana continues: Is it an addictive drug? What are its long–term effects? Why do so many people use it? Should it be legalized? Groups such as the National Organization for the Reform of Marijuana Laws (NORML) continue to work toward the legalization of marijuana. They have been instrumental in decriminalizing possession of a small quantity of marijuana for personal use in 11 states; these states now provide a written citation and charge a small fine rather than charging an individual with a criminal offense. Interestingly, as of November 1982, 33 states have enacted legislation authorizing legal access to marijuana for treatment of victims of glaucoma and cancer.

The use of amphetamines began in the 1930s when they were widely prescribed for depression and obesity. During World War II, the U.S., British, German and Japanese armies issued them to their enlisted men for increased energy and wakefulness. The stimulating effect of amphetamines, along with increased self–confidence and euphoria, was soon sought by housewives, truck drivers on long trips, and students studying for exams, among others. They were also widely prescribed by doctors as an anorectic, and there were few problems in obtaining a prescription. The demand for amphetamines soon exceeded supply, resulting in illicit manufacture and amphetamine look–alikes. Commonly referred to as *speed,* they are now often experimented with by high school students.

In 1950 meprobamate was synthesized, introducing the era of minor tranquilizers. Soon members of the benzodiazepine family were in widespread use because their margin of safety was greater than that of the barbiturates. Today minor tranquilizers are among the most widely prescribed drugs, particularly Valium and Librium. When taken in excessive amounts they produce a state of intoxication remarkably similar to that of alcohol. When combined with alcohol they serve as a means of suicide (a method particularly common among women). In great demand, the source of supply may be no further than the family medicine cabinet and, if not, they are readily available on the illicit market. The fully–stocked medicine cabinet and the pattern of use by parents is thought to be one of the reasons for the recent increase in drug use among young people. Polydrug use, the taking or two or more drugs at once, has also developed in the last decade or so and it is common among some users to take a stimulant in the morning and a depressant at night.

The late 1950s and 1960s saw a rash of fad drugs whose popularity quickly waned. In 1959 there was a craze for glue sniffing among young people, particularly boys in the 13 to 15 age group. It has been suggested that nationwide media attention may have alerted potential users and contributed to the abuse.

LSD, used as an adjunct to psychotherapy in the 1950s, was popularized in the 1960s particularly as a result of proselytizing by Dr. Timothy Leary. Use of LSD, easily produced by basement chemists, peaked in the late 1960s and then there was a steady decline. Both glue–sniffing and LSD use were fads that concerned a drug with limited addictive qualities, and each was followed by media scares that abruptly ended their popular appeal.

The United States has the dubious distinction of being the trend–setter in drug abuse patterns around the world. If a drug suddenly becomes popular in the U.S. it is almost a sure thing that it will surface elsewhere in a very short time. A prime example is the use of LSD which gained great popularity in the 1960s and then rapidly declined. The same pattern is reported by authorities throughout the world.

Just as the Civil War produced morphine addicts, and World War II saw extensive use of amphetamines, long–lasting drug problems emerged from U.S. military interventions in Southeast Asia. In Korea, soldiers took advantage of the availability of heroin and often mixed heroin with amphetamines to produce *speedballs.* In Vietnam the military found both heroin and highly potent marijuana readily available and very inexpensive. Alarmed at the extent of the abuse, authorities made a concerted effort to curb the use of marijuana—but their efforts actually had the effect of increasing heroin abuse.

Heroin use in the U.S. has been extensive since the early 1900s when there were an estimated one–quarter million to one million users, mostly among lower and upper socioeconomic groups in urban centers. Since American involvement in Southeast Asia in the late 1960s and early 1970s, when the flow of heroin into the U.S. increased, the use of heroin has spread from metropolitan areas to the suburbs, and from upper and lower socioeconomic groups to the middle class, especially youth. Recent studies estimate that there are now between 400,000 and 750,-000 heroin users in America. When not available from one illicit source, another source materializes: Southeast Asia supplied most of the world's market until the late 1970s, then Southwest Asia emerged as the leading opium producer in the world. It is ironic that when first introduced in 1898 heroin was thought to be a cure for opium and morphine addiction.

Cocaine, which came into use in the late 19th century, did not gain much popularity in the

U.S. until the 1960s; this was due, in part, to the public's acceptance of amphetamines, the stimulating effects of which are similar to cocaine. At first confined to the upper strata of the economic ladder because of its expensive nature, cocaine was referred to as the "drug of the affluent." Perhaps because many people believe that it is not addictive, its popularity has been steadily increasing among the young, particularly college students, and in many blue collar circles as well despite its cost. The use of this drug may become pandemic because supplies are increasing and prices are dropping.

In the 1950s scientists began experimenting with a drug called phencyclidine as an anesthetic. In the 1970s this drug, commonly called PCP or Angel Dust, became so popular among adolescents as a substitute for heroin that in 1978 President Jimmy Carter was forced to enact specific legislation against it. A new sedative, called methaqualone, has come into general use as a "downer"; it is known as "ludes" after its most common brand name, Quaalude. The last legal source of methaqualone has recently been withdrawn. Amyl nitrite has also become popular among those who are seeking an alteration in consciousness.

Amateur athletics was so troubled by drug abuse that in 1976 the Olympic Games authorities required urine analysis of medal winners and other selected entrants. By 1983 more sophisticated tests had been developed and produced mass disqualifications at the Pan American Games in Caracas, Venezuela, for the use of anabolic steroids, a synthesized form of the male hormone testosterone.

Alcohol and tobacco are the most abused mind–altering substances. In the U.S. alone there are an estimated 50 million smokers and an estimated 100 million who drink alcohol (10 million are classified as alcoholics and an additional 10 million are classified as "problem drinkers"). Since the mid–20th century there has been extensive research on both smoking and drinking and numerous educational campaigns have been initiated to combat the problems. The advertising of distilled spirits and cigarettes is prohibited on both radio and television and in 1966 all cigarette packages were required to carry the statement: "Caution: Cigarette smoking may be hazardous to your health." Studies have shown that these two most abused substances are generally used together: heavy drinkers also tend to be heavy smokers.

Treatments for drug abuse which have emerged since the mid–1950s have been based on the principles that blanket legislation against drugs is irresponsible and that therapy is essential to the control of dangerously addictive drugs. This philosophy has permitted rationality in response to the popularity of marijuana among all sections of the American population and a general easing of criminal penalties for personal use of the drug. Most important, this philosophy encourages the scientific study of treatment methods for dangerously addictive drugs, especially heroin. The first viable treatment programs were therapeutic communities. One of the first was Synanon. A treatment center founded by Charles Dederich in California in 1958, its aim was total abstinence and it was designed to provide support during withdrawal. Although plagued by relapses, Synanon influenced other organizations in the 1960s such as Daytop Village, Phoenix House and Odyssey House. The same period saw the development of the first clinical programs to counter addiction to heroin. The Methadone Maintenance program, which began in 1964, substitutes methadone, another narcotic, for heroin in the hope of weaning the addict.

Efforts at treatment helped sensitize the U.S. government to the nature of the nation's drug problem and to design more reasonable legislation to counter it. Among the immediate results was the Drug Abuse Control Amendment of 1965 which moved to regulate stimulants, depressants and hallucinogens not previously recognized by law. A year later the Narcotic Addict Rehabilitation Act legalized civil commitment of addicts for treatment. In 1970 the Controlled Substances Act classified all mood–altering drugs into five categories, or schedules, in order to better define each one's proper medical use and to provide reasonable controls against their abuse. At the same time the power of law enforcement agencies to search and seize were altered to concentrate on dealers rather than users of most drugs.

While these actions have managed to improve treatment and control of dangerous drugs, they have not by anyone's estimation managed to end the problem of drug abuse. New drugs continue to appear and continue to sidestep the legal defenses of even today's modern drug–educated public.

As long as old cultural traditions are maintained, as long as new technology and research produce new products and as along as humankind's curious, experimental nature continues, drug use will probably remain with us. The use and abuse of drugs—for whatever reason—is a major health concern all over the world. It is a complex issue and one that cannot always be stated in simple black and white terms. In this book we have attempted to present the facts, often controversial, for your consideration.

A GLANCE AT THE FUTURE

by Sidney Cohen, M.D.

This glimpse into the past and the present is incomplete unless we attempt to assess the future of drug dependence. It seems clear that many of the taboos against intoxication have been either attenuated or dissolved. The use of the needle to introduce substances of unknown potency and purity into the body has become more frequent. The revolutions in chemical technology and transportation have brought mind alteration within the reach of everyone. What does the future hold?

Alcohol is and will remain man's major intoxicant. It is taking over whole cultures that once used other intoxicating substances; kava in Polynesia, betel nut on the Indian subcontinent and other local inebriants seem doomed to extinction as inexpensive brews displace them. Meanwhile, as civilization becomes more complex, and precision more necessary, alcohol becomes a greater threat to society. One drunk air controller can destroy hundreds of passengers flying in his zone—in fact, this has happened in Yugoslavia. It has been claimed that America is losing its industrial primacy to other countries because of drug and alcohol intoxication in the workplace.

Tobacco is such a poor euphoriant that its popularity is surprising—until we recognize the enormous effects of hundreds of nicotine doses daily to the brain. Will tobacco smoking go away? Thoughtful prevention efforts should be successful and there is evidence that young people can be influenced by accurate information about the consequences of inhaling tobacco fumes.

The illicit use of narcotics and the other depressants of brain activity will never completely disappear. They have a great attraction for the hopeless, the depressed and the anxious as temporary "cures." The long–term consequences are not perceived, and the immediate distancing from a harsh reality is too appealing. The fact that we now have narcotics which are a hundred times more potent than morphine makes their control more problematic.

Cocaine and amphetamine–type drugs will also persist, hopefully in diminished quantity. They, too, have attractions for those who cannot enjoy sober reality and those who are uncertain of their abilities. Cocaine is the most reinforcing (rewarding) drug of all. Animals will work for a cocaine reward until exhaustion or death overcomes them. We are seeing similar behavior in humans.

The hallucinogens such as LSD have risen and fallen in popularity for a long time. For some, the out–of–the–body state is so important that we can predict periodic upsurges in popularity among enclaves attracted to this strange mental alteration.

Marijuana use will probably continue on a widespread scale. As research uncovers additional information about cannabis, it appears to be no less dangerous to the public health than alcohol or tobacco. Whether or not this fact merits its acceptance into this society is dubious. We are at a very early phase of the serious investigation of marijuana, a phase similar to that of our knowledge of tobacco 50 years ago or our knowledge of alcohol a century ago.

We will neither win nor lose the "war against drugs." It will persist, with some battles reducing the social and personal costs and other forays demonstrating again the immaturity and incompleteness of man. It has been repeated *ad nauseum* that each culture needs an intoxicating substance. This is only partly true but, if it were so, it would only be further evidence that man is not yet *homo sapiens*.

DRUG CLASSIFICATION

Antidepressants
Antipsychotic Tranquilizers
Cannabis
Combinations
Hallucinogens
Narcotic Analgesic Agonists
Narcotic Antagonists
Nonprescription Analgesics
Sedative/Hypnotics
Stimulants
Volatile Inhalants

ANTIDEPRESSANTS

MAO Inhibitors
    Isocarboxazid (Marplan)
    Phenelzine sulfate (Nardil)
    Tranylcypromine sulfate (Parnate)

Tricyclic
    Amitriptyline hydrochloride (Elavil; Endep)
    Desipramine hydrochloride (Norpramin; Pertofrane)
    Doxepin hydrochloride (Adapin; Sinequan)
    Imipramine hydrochloride (Janimine; SK–Pramine; Tofranil)
    Nortriptyline hydrochloride (Aventyl; Pamelor)
    Protriptyline hydrochloride (Vivactil)

ANTIPSYCHOTIC TRANQUILIZERS

Butyrophenones
    Droperidol (Inapsine; Innovar)
    Haloperidol (Haldol)

Phenothiazines
    Chlorpromazine (Thorazine)
    Fluphenazine hydrochloride (Permitil; Proloxin)
    Perphenazine (Trilafon)
    Piperacetazine (Quide)
    Prochlorperazine (Compazine)
    Promethazine hydrochloride (Phenergan; Remsed; Synalgos; ZiPan)
    Thioridazine hydrochloride (Mellaril)
    Trifluoperazine hydrochloride (Stelazine)

Reserpates (or Rauwolfia alkaloids)
    Deserpidine (Harmonyl)
    Reserpine (Serpasil)

Thioxanthines
    Chlorprothixene (Taractan)
    Thiothixene (Navane)

CANNABIS

Cannabis derivatives (THC)
Hash Oil
Hashish (charas)
Kief
Marijuana
Sinsemilla

COMBINATIONS

Chlordiazepoxide hydrochloride and amitriptyline hydrochloride (Limbitrol)
Perphenazine and amitripyline hydrochloride (Triavil)
Secobarbital sodium and amobarbital sodium (Tuinal)

HALLUCINOGENS

Dimethoxymethamphetamine (DOM; STP)
Dimethyltryptamine (DMT)
Ditran (piperidyl benzilate)
Lysergic acid diethylamide–25 (LSD)
Mescaline
Methylenedioxyamphetamine (MDA)
Peyote
Phencyclidine (PCP)
Psilocin
Psilocybin

NARCOTIC ANALGESIC AGONISTS

Opiates
  Natural
    codeine
    hydrocodone bitartrate (Dicodid)
    morphine
    opium
      laudanum
      papaverine
      paregoric

  Semisynthetic
    heroin (diacetylmorphine)
    hydromorphone hydrochloride (Dilaudid)
    oxycodone hydrochloride (Percocet–5; Percodan; Tylox)
    oxymorphone hydrochloride (Numorphan)

Opioids (synthetic opiates)
LAAM (levo–alpha–acetylmethadol)
Levorphanol tartrate (Levo–Dromoran)
Meperidine hydrochloride (Demerol)
Methadone hydrochloride (Dolophine)
Pentazocine hydrochloride (Talwin)
Propoxyphene hydrochloride (Darvon)

NARCOTIC ANTAGONISTS

Mixed agonists and antagonists
Buprenorphine Cyclazocine
Lavallorphan tartrate (Lorfan)
Nalbuphine hydrochloride (Nubain)

Pure
Naloxone hydrochloride (Narcan)
Naltrexone

NONPRESCRIPTION ANALGESICS

Acetaminophen (Datril, Tylenol)
Aspirin
Phenacetin

SEDATIVE HYPNOTICS

Alcohol
Beer
Distilled spirits (liquor)
Wine

Antianxiety tranquilizers
Benzodiazepines
clorazepate dipotassium (Tranxene)
chlordiazepoxide hydrochloride (Librium)
diazepam (Valium)
flurazepam hydrochloride (Dalmane)
lorazepam (Ativan)
oxazepam (Serax)
Diphenylmethanes
diphenhydramine hydrochloride (Benadryl)
hydroxyzine hydrochloride (Sedaril)

Meprobamate (Equanil; Miltown)

Tybamate (Tybatran)

Barbiturates
  Ultra–short–acting
    methohexital sodium (Brevital)
    thiopental sodium (Pentothal)

  Short–acting
    hexobarbital sodium (Sombucaps)
    pentobarbital sodium (Nembutal)
    secobarbital sodium (Seconal)

  Intermediate–acting
    amobarbital (Amytal)
    amobarbital sodium (Amytal Sodium)
    aprobarbital (Alurate)
    butabarbital sodium (Buticaps; Butisol Sodium)
    butalbital (Buff–A Comp)

  Long–acting
    barbital (Veronal)
    mephobarbital (Mebaral)
    metharbital (Gemonil)
    phenobarbital (Luminal)

Nonbarbiturates
  bromides
  chloral hydrate and other chloral derivatives
  ethchlorvynol (Placidyl)
  ethinamate (Valmid)
  glutethimide (Doriden)
  methaqualone
  methyprylon (Noludar)
  paraldehyde
  triclofos sodium (Triclos)

STIMULANTS

Ergot alkaloids (Alkergot; Deapril; Hydergine)

Primary
  Amphetamine relatives
    benzphetamine hydrochloride (Didrex)
    clortermine hydrochloride (Voranil)
    diethylpropion hydrochloride (Tenuate; Tepanil)
    mazindol (Sanorex)
    methylphenidate hydrochloride (Ritalin)
    phendimetrazine tartrate (Bacarate; Bontril; Melfiat; Plegine; Prelu–2; Trimtabs; Wehless–35)
    phenmetrazine hydrochloride (Preludin)

Amphetamines
    amphetamine sulfate (Benzedrine)
    dextroamphetamine sulfate (Dexedrine)
    methamphetamine hydrochloride (Desoxyn)

Cocaine and coca

Secondary
    Arecoline
    Caffeine
        coffee
        tea
    Khat
    Nicotine

VOLATILE INHALANTS

Amyl nitrite

Anesthetics (general)
    Gaseous
        nitrous oxide
    Vaporous
        ether
        chloroform

Butyl Nitrite

Hydrocarbons
    chlorinated
        carbon tetrachloride

    fluorocarbons and other aerosol propellants

    ketones and acetates
        acetone

    Petroleum based
        benzene
        gasoline
        naphtha
        toluene

A

absenteeism Absenteeism among drug users is a major problem in industry today. Although absenteeism usually means actually being away from a job, there is another kind of absenteeism, too: on–the–job absenteeism which occurs when a person is physically present but not mentally alert enough to be productive. While there are few statistics available for other drugs, the cost to industry in lost production due to alcoholism was an estimated $19.63 billion in 1975.

absinthe An alcoholic beverage made from the oil of the leaves, stems and bark of the common herb *Artemisia absinthium* (wormwood). Absinthe is habit–forming. It also has a harmful effect on the nerves; can produce convulsions and hallucinations; can cause delirium and, sometimes, a permanent mental deterioration known as absinthism. Though banned in most Western countries (in 1912 in the United States) because of these severe health hazards, absinthe can still be legally consumed in some countries, including Spain. Imitations of absinthe, such as the aperitif wine Pernod, still survive.

absolute alcohol The amount of pure alcohol in a beverage or substance. There is about 1½ ounces of pure alcohol in each of the following, for example: three 1–oz drinks of 100–proof whiskey; a half bottle of wine; four 8–oz glasses of beer. Pure alcohol is obtained by brewing followed by fractional distillation.

absorption The process by which a chemical compound such as a drug or nutrient passes through the body membranes (intestinal lining, etc.) into the bloodstream.

abstainer One who abstains completely from the consumption of alcohol. The term's application can depend on the context in which it is used, though. Many agencies reporting on alcohol abuse group abstainers with moderate and social drinkers, for example. Alcoholics Anonymous, however, insists upon complete abstinence in the strictest sense.

abstinence Complete abstention from the use of alcoholic beverages or other abused drugs at all times. The abstinence syndrome is the pattern of withdrawal symptoms that appears when drugs that produce physical dependence are discontinued.

abuse A general term applied to the misuse of a drug. Usually the term applies to the use of drugs to alter consciousness, or to gratify physical needs. But abuse can also mean using drugs in forms and styles that are illegal; using drugs without appropriate and adequate supervision; or using drugs to the point where the taker loses control of his behavior.

Generally abuse is the use of a substance in such a way that both mental and physical health may be impaired. The Food and Drug Administration defines *drug use* as the "taking of a drug for its intended purpose, in the appropriate amount, frequency, strength and manner"; the FDA defines *drug misuse* as "taking a substance for its intended purpose, but not in the appropriate amount, frequency, strength and manner"; and *drug abuse* as "deliberately taking a substance for other than its intended purpose, and in a manner that can result in damage to the person's health or his ability to function."

abuse potential   A drug's susceptibility to abuse or abuse patterns.

accidents   A person under the influence of a drug is more accident–prone than someone who is not, and the role of drugs in the occurrence of accidents is receiving increasing attention today. Accidents, whether at home, in public places or on the job, are usually a result of the following factors: inhibited coordination; mental confusion; lengthened reaction time; decreased motor performance; risk–taking behavior; paranoid ideas of grandiosity; and impairment of judgment and sensory skill.

Occupational accidents affect a significant portion of the working population. Although many types of drugs are used during working hours, the ones of principal concern are alcohol, cocaine, amphetamines and marijuana. Experiments have demonstrated that alcohol intoxication can alter a normal person's performance up to 18 hours after ingestion, and the use of alcohol prior to and during the work day is widespread. Skills begin to decline at blood alcohol levels as low as 0.05% (a blood level percentage that is considered to be the mark of intoxication in some European countries). Because of a high rate of absenteeism among those who might otherwise have been involved, drinking–related industrial accidents may be lower than expected. Alcohol–related problems, including accidents and lost production due to absenteeism, cost American industry $35 billion in 1982. While the role of alcohol in industrial accidents has not been well documented to date, the problem is unquestionable and readily acknowledged. This is demonstrated by the vast number of EMPLOYEE ASSISTANCE PROGRAMS available.

Cocaine has recently become an on–the–job drug; often because of considerable demands and expectations on the part of employers and feelings of stress and insecurity on the part of employees. Although the action of cocaine is brief, many employees use it because they believe it speeds up the thought process and provides a feeling of competency. However, even small amounts of cocaine snorted just before a period of considerable demand can disturb judgment and the result may be a rapid multi–million dollar loss to a company. Cocaine use in industry is generally confined to white–collar workers simply because of its cost; the use of alcohol and marijuana, on the other hand, is found in all levels of employment. For this reason cocaine–related accidents generally concern costly decisions on an executive level.

Marijuana–related accidents are more apt to occur on the skilled–occupation level. Marijuana intoxication can be as impairing as alcohol intoxication and it particularly affects the memory. Recent studies have shown that free recall is invariably impaired and short–term memory is dulled. Serious skill impairment can be measured for hours after a single marijuana cigarette has been consumed. Along with memory and perception difficulties there is also a decline in psychomotor activities, such as hand steadiness, and in reaction time and attentiveness. These effects become particularly significant when an employee is operating a motor vehicle or a complex industrial machine.

Amphetamines are often used by employees who work night shifts and by truck drivers on long cross–country trips. Both of these groups seek the stimulant effects of amphetamines to relieve sleepiness and fatigue. Adverse reactions can result in accidents, however. Even moderate doses of amphetamine can produce tremors of the limbs, blurred vision and impaired coordination.

A study by the Firestone Tire and Rubber Company suggested that plant accidents were 3.6 times as likely to occur when an employee was under the influence of a drug. The study also revealed that drug users were five times as likely to file a worker's compensation claim and 2.5 times as likely to be absent longer than a week. Drug users also received three times the level of sick benefits as those who did not use drugs, and they tended to be repeatedly involved in grievance procedures. Compared to other employees they were estimated to function at approximately 67% of their work potential.

Drug–related industrial accidents and motor vehicle accidents (see DRUGS AND DRIVING) are the major accident categories. But accidents that occur in the home are also significant. Falls account for the majority of drug–related accidents, both in the home and in public places. A 1978 study of accidental deaths found that almost 50% of those who died from falls had been drinking. There are no comparable figures for falls related to other drugs but because many drugs alter coordination, it can be assumed that statistics would be just as high.

The use of drugs appears to be strongly involved in fires and burns. Compared to the general population alcoholics have been found to be 10 times more likely to die in a fire. Alcohol lowers oxidation in the cells which also increases an individual's risk of being overcome by smoke inhalation. As alcohol is a sedative drug, it follows that other sedative drugs may have the same effect. The involvement of alcoholics and drug addicts in cigarette–related fires is three times that of fires resulting from other causes.

Drug use is also reported to play a significant role in drownings. Such accidents are probably the result of poor judgment, faulty coordination and confusion. In the case of alcohol and other central nervous system depressants, there may also be a depression of the swallowing and breathing reflexes which can turn a normal situation into a dangerous one. There may also be another complication: "risk taking behavior." A person who has taken a depressant may stay in cold water for too long a time because the depressant has a "warming effect."

Although drug–related accidents are un-questionable, they are also occasionally denied or ignored. Further study is needed to promote public awareness of the costs involved to personal life, property and industry.

acetaldehyde   The first step in the metabolism of alcohol results in its conversion to acetaldehyde, which is even more toxic to the body than ethyl alcohol. The second step converts it into acetate, most of which is oxidized to carbon dioxide, but some acetaldehyde still escapes into the bloodstream—particularly with heavy consumption. Acetaldehyde is thought to play a central role in the toxicity of alcohol. Probably because of liver damage, alcoholics metabolize acetaldehyde less effectively than nonalcoholics. The substance has been shown to adversely affect muscles, particularly the heart muscles, and because of its effect on nerve impulses it may be a contributing factor in alcohol addiction. When someone taking ANTABUSE consumes alcohol it can result in a toxic reaction because the person's blood acetaldehyde concentrations increase five to 10 times higher than normal.

acetone   A solvent, commonly found in plastic cements and nail polish removers, which may produce euphoric effects when inhaled. Acetone is a volatile HYDROCARBON.

Ackoff's model   A method of determining the assignment of alcoholic patients to treatment facilities which takes into account alternative courses of action. Usually treatment facilities are determined on the basis of vacancies rather than on the basis of where the patient will receive the best treatment ("uncertainty conditions"). When Ackoff's model is used, alternative courses are researched and uncertainty conditions are changed to "risk conditions."

acne rosacea   Frequently caused by excessive drinking over a prolonged period, acne rosacea is a facial skin condition. It is characterized by a flushed appearance and sometimes also by broken capillaries and puffiness. (See also RHINOPHYMA and GROG BLOSSOM.)

Acquired Immune Deficiency Syndrome (AIDS)

A little understood disease that attacks the body's immune system. Death occurs because the body's immune system fails to function and fight off other diseases. This suggests the possibility that some deaths that are reportedly due to other causes may actually occur because of undiagnosed AIDS.

The first known case of AIDS appeared in the United States in June 1981. By August of 1983 over 2,000 patients with AIDS had been admitted to hospitals. The mortality rate is approximately 50 to 75%. Just under half of the cases have occurred in New York City and about 20% in California. The largest number of victims—approximately 71%—are homosexual or bisexual men who are sexually promiscuous. (There are no reported cases of AIDS in female homosexuals.) Intravenous drug users are the next largest group and constitute about 20% of all cases. About 5% of the victims are Haitians and less than one percent are hemophiliacs. The remaining percentage belongs to none of these categories and the risk factor involved is unknown. Males between the ages of 25 and 45 account for more than 90% of all cases.

At this time the cause of AIDS is not known. Infectious disease experts have suggested that AIDS can be transmitted by blood transfusions; other researchers suggest that AIDS victims have a defect in their blood cells; and others believe that it is due to a virus that affects T–lymphocyte production, impairing immunity on a cellular level. Most experts agree that direct contact with infected blood, feces or semen seems necessary to transmission.

The suggested link to blood transfusions may also supply the link to intravenous drug abusers and the disease: AIDS occurs frequently in the intravenous drug user who shares needles. Intravenous drug users are also known to draw their own blood back into the syringe in order to mix it with the remaining heroin or other substance and prolong the drug's initial effects. The *type* of drug that is injected is irrelevant—it is the administration of a drug in an unsterile manner that could transmit AIDS. AIDS manifests differently in homosexuals and drug abusers. About half of the homosexual cases develop Kaposi sarcomas (a skin tumor of low–grade malignancy) and half develop Pneumocystis carinii pneumonia. Drug users develop Kaposi sarcomas about 10% of the time, and Pneumocystis carinii pneumonia about 70% of the time (with other infections occurring for the remainder). This difference in the way the disease manifests is so far unexplained.

It was thought at one point that there might be a relationship between the use of amyl and butyl nitrites ("poppers") and AIDS but since homosexual men are prone to develop AIDS and they are known to use "poppers," the relationship is now thought to be coincidental.

AIDS researchers have also investigated marijuana, which some believe affects the immune response by acting on the T–lymphocytes. As marijuana is often smoked by intravenous drug users and homosexuals, the investigations have concluded that its use is not a cause but an associated activity.

AIDS has become a worldwide health problem with cases reported in 33 countries and all inhabited continents. In November 1983, 15 European countries, accounting for about 10% of all AIDS cases, reported preliminary results of their studies to the World Health Organization.

Because the disease has reached epidemic levels in such a short time, the U.S. Health and Human Services Department's research funding for AIDS was doubled, from $20 million to $40 million, for the fiscal year beginning October 1, 1983. Hopefully, the work being done by researchers throughout the world will not only discover the cause of this disease and a cure for it, but will also shed some light on the basic nature of the immune process.

active principle   The ALKALOID or other chemical substance in a plant that produces toxic effects on the central nervous system or other organs. For example, the active principle in coca leaves is cocaine (benzyolmethyl ecognine).

actuarial prediction   A method of statistical calculation which uses a large number of subjects. Actuarial prediction is traditionally used in insurance research and population surveys. An insurance research project would study one million people born in the same year in order to predict the probable death rates per year, for example. In the drug abuse field actuarial prediction methods would be used to predict such data as the probability of a tobacco smoker's death at a certain age.

acupuncture   Although its origins are lost in antiquity, acupuncture has been a traditional Chinese medical treatment for over 3,000 years. In recent years it has gained popularity in the United States and other countries around the world. Rooted in Eastern philosophy, acupuncture is a complex system of medicine which involves *ch'i*, the vital life source or energy that the Chinese believe flows through specific pathways in the human body. If the flow of ch'i is blocked or impeded an imbalance—a surplus or deficit—can occur in an organ or area of the body and result in pain or disease. Once the nature of the imbalance has been identified by a variety of diagnostic techniques, the appropriate acupuncture points on the body are selected. These points are then stimulated by acupuncture (the insertion of fine, solid needles), moxibustion (heating with mugwort, a traditional Chinese herb), or acupressure (massage). Modern technology has contributed some new techniques to the ancient practice of acupuncture, including electrical stimulation of the needles, ultrasound and laser beam stimulation.

No single explanation of the phenomenon of acupuncture is presently accepted, but it is acknowledged that the treatment has been effective in many cases, particularly among patients suffering from chronic pain. Despite overwhelming evidence of its effectiveness, however, the Food and Drug Administration and the American Medical Association still consider acupuncture to be an "experimental" form of treatment.

There has been a recent trend in the United States to treat drug addiction, particularly addiction to nicotine, with acupuncture therapy. Although there are patients who claim to have been cured of their smoking habit, very little research has been done on the subject. Acupuncture has also been used to detoxify patients who are dependent on narcotics and sedatives. In light of its effectiveness in China for so many years, and its constructive emphasis on the patient's environment, nutrition and psychological well–being as well as on his physical symptoms, it would seem that in–depth studies on acupuncture should be undertaken.

acute   The term used to describe a condition that quickly develops into a crisis, as opposed to a CHRONIC condition or disease which is characterized by slowly progressing symptoms.

acute alcoholic state   A nonspecific term

for mental or physical disorders associated with and occurring during or immediately following a prolonged drinking bout. More generally, the term is used to refer to alcoholic intoxication.

acute alcohol intoxication   A term used to refer to severe alcohol intoxication, or poisoning, which is the result of a defined episode of intoxication as opposed to a prolonged or chronic state of intoxication.

acute alcoholism   Because alcoholism is usually considered a CHRONIC disease this term is seen as ambiguous. It could refer to intoxication, poisoning, or to temporary disturbances caused by excessive drinking.

adaptive cell metabolism   Tissue cells adapt to constant quantities of a drug: this conditioning leads to increased tissue TOLERANCE, and the consequent onset of WITHDRAWAL. When a drug is not supplied to cells that have adapted to it a CRAVING may develop. In reference to alcohol, adaptive cell metabolism is a factor in GAMMA ALCOHOLISM; in reference to other drugs, when tolerance develops there is the need to consume larger and larger quantities to obtain the desired effects.

Adatuss® (Merchant)   A narcotic, opiate cough suppressant containing the codeine derivative HYDROCODONE BITARTRATE. A proprietary drug, it is slightly more potent than codeine.

addict subculture   See SUBCULTURE, DRUG.

addiction   In the early part of the 20th century the term "drug addiction" simply referred to the illicit use of drugs, and did not distinguish between patterns of drug use and the effects of various drugs. The term "habituation" came into use in the early 1930s. It meant dependence on the effects of a drug was psychological—emotional distress but not physiological illness resulted if the drug ·was stopped. Drug addiction was then distinguished from habituation and came to mean physical dependence on a drug's effects with illness, or withdrawal, occurring if the intake was stopped completely or severely reduced. Although physical dependence is clearly not the only aspect of addiction, the term addiction is still used to refer to physical dependence.

In 1957 the World Health Organization's Expert Committee on Addiction–Producing Drugs defined drug addiction as:

> a state of periodic or chronic intoxication, detrimental to the individual and society, produced by the repeated consumption of a drug (natural or synthetic). Its characteristics include: (1) An overpowering desire or need (compulsion) to continue taking the drug and to obtain it by any means; (2) A tendency to increase the dose; (3) A psychic (psychological) and generally a physical dependence on the effects of the drug.

They further defined *drug habituation* as:

> a condition resulting from the repeated consumption of a drug. Its characteristics include: (1) A desire (but not a compulsion) to continue taking the drug for the sense of improved well–being which it engenders; (2) Little or no tendency to increase the dose; (3) Some degree of psychic dependence on the effect of the drug, but absence of physical dependence and hence of an abstinence syndrome; (4) Detrimental effects, if any, primarily on the individual.

There was still some confusion surrounding these terms, however, and in 1965 a more neutral term, "drug dependence," was adopted by the World Health Organization, and was defined in the following general way:

a state, psychic and sometimes also physical, resulting from the interaction between a living organism and a drug, characterized by behavioral and other responses that always include a compulsion to take the drug on a continuous or periodic basis in order to experience its psychic effects, and sometimes to avoid the discomfort of its absence. Tolerance may or may not be present. A person may be dependent on more than one drug.

(See also DEPENDENCE.)

Addiction Research Foundation   A nonprofit Canadian organization involved in drug abuse prevention and research. The foundation has made notable contributions in the field and produces numerous publications, journals, newsletters, films and other audiovisual materials.

additive effect   The action attained when the combined effect of two drugs taken together is the sum of the two separate effects. Contrast with SYNERGY and POTENTIATION.

Adipex–P® (Lemmon)   An anorectic that contains 37.5 mg of phentermine hydrochloride, it is used for weight control. Tolerance can develop within a few weeks and because its activity is similar to that of AMPHETAMINES it has a high potential for abuse. Psychological dependence and social dysfunction can occur. Overdosage can result in restlessness, tremors, rapid respiration, confusion and hallucinations. It is supplied in white oblong tablets with blue specks.

administration   There are various methods of administering a drug and each has advantages and disadvantages. Sometimes a drug abuser will have to choose between such factors as: time of onset; maximum potency; and duration of effects. For example, an injected drug will produce the quickest onset and usually give maximum potency,

but an orally administered drug will produce longer–lasting effects. The main categories of drug administration are: (1) oral, which includes eating (swallowing), smoking (breathing), and sublingual ingestion (dissolving under the tongue); (2) parenteral or hypodermic injection (intravenously, intramuscularly and subcutaneously); (3) nasal inhalation which includes spraying and snorting (sniffing); and (4) rectal (suppositories). Other miscellaneous methods are sometimes tried but are generally not effective or produce adverse reactions.

In order to exert effects on the body, a drug must be absorbed into the bloodstream and then carried to the CENTRAL NERVOUS SYSTEM. Absorption points in the body are the lungs, the gastrointestinal tract (stomach and intestines), mucous membranes found at natural openings to the body, and the bloodstream itself.

Oral Administration

Oral administration is the most common way of ingesting a drug, whether it involves swallowing a pill, drinking a beverage, placing a drug under the tongue and letting it dissolve (sublingual), or smoking. Drugs which are swallowed are absorbed by the gastrointestinal tract; alcohol is largely absorbed by the stomach, while other drugs are absorbed in the intestines. When a drug is dissolved under the tongue it is absorbed through the mucous membranes and absorption time is unpredictable. When a drug is smoked it is absorbed by the lungs which produces faster effects than a drug absorbed by the stomach or intestines: not all of the drug is inhaled, of course, so a portion of it will be lost through smoke. Smoking a drug is usually associated with the use of tobacco and marijuana but there are numerous other drugs which can be, and are, smoked, such as opium, heroin, DMT, DET, hashish and various herbs. Some drugs, particularly DMT and DET, are sprinkled on tobacco or marijuana in very small quantities and then smoked. Smoking can be done with the substance rolled in cigarette paper or through the use of a water pipe which cools the smoke and makes it less harsh. Some drugs, such as LSD, cannot be smoked because heat breaks them down chemically before they enter the system.

Drugs administered orally will generally produce longer–lasting effects than injected drugs but have less potency and a longer onset time. There are drugs which cannot be taken orally, such as cocaine, because they are not soluble in stomach fluids or they are partially metabolized by digestive juices. Oral administration can produce adverse reactions such as vomiting, but this reaction can also be beneficial if it rids the body of a toxic overdose.

Parenteral Administration

This method is used for the quickest onset of effects. Because the heart pumps 12½ pints of blood a minute (the amount of blood contained in an average adult body) a drug injected directly into the bloodstream (intravenous) will be distributed throughout the body in one minute. The effects, however, will not last as long as a drug administered orally and there are complications and dangers involved in parenteral administration.

The three methods for parenterally administering a drug are: intravenous injection into a vein; intramuscular injection into a muscle (usually the upper arm or buttocks); and subcutaneous injection (also known as SKIN POPPING) under the skin. Injecting a drug into an artery can be particularly dangerous and should never be attempted because it may cause severe damage to the area. This is because a drug injected into a vein is delivered from the tissue to the heart, a drug injected into an artery delivers the blood from the heart to an individual tissue mass—a foot, a hand, and so on—where there is the possibility of centralized damage which can result in gangrene, abcesses or visible tissue poisoning.

The greatest danger of hypodermic administration is infection from germs that may be present on the skin, on the needle, or in the drug itself. TETANUS is generally associated with subcutaneous injection because the anaerobic bacteria have a low oxygen tissue—the fat cells—to grow in. HEPATITIS is most often associated with intravenous injection of the virus and generally is the result of an unclean needle. There is a tendency among addicts to share needles and in some cases needles are rented out to provide income. Addicts are usually so preoccupied with "getting their fix" that little time or thought is given to sterilizing their equipment.

Heroin is the most common drug injected by addicts, although cocaine and some psychedelics are also administered hypodermically. An addict can never be sure what additives have been put in his purchased heroin, as the drug is rarely in pure form and has usually been diluted many times and handled by several people (see CUTTING). Bacteria and viruses found in diluted heroin, which might easily be destroyed by stomach enzymes if the administration is oral, become dangerous when injected into the bloodstream. Heroin is often diluted with quinine or with various sugars, such as lactose. Quinine can, in large amounts, cause blindness and can also affect the central nervous system, the heart and kidneys. Certain tablets (Ritalin, for example) have a talcum powder base that is insoluble in water. It can block small blood vessels in the lungs and cause fibrosis.

The various methods of injection produce varied effects. Intravenous injection produces the quickest onset of effects using the least amount of the drug because it is injected directly into the vein. It takes two–thirds again as much of a drug to produce the same effects when it is injected intramuscularly or subcutaneously. Consequently, intravenous injection is also a thriftier method and this can be of great importance to an addict with an expensive habit. The initial RUSH, or thrill, which is the primary reason for using heroin in the first place, is only satisfied by injecting intravenously.

Some addicts are addicted as much to the act of injecting as they are to the drug they are using. For this reason a person may administer a drug in several small injections just for the joy of injecting. This type of NEEDLE FREAK may even resort to injecting plain water, sugar water or any liquid available.

Other dangers of frequent parenteral administration include collapsed, infected veins (phlebitis), endocarditis and other infections. Abcesses are common in subcutaneous injection.

There is a theory that addicts who administer drugs parenterally are suicide prone and that the act of injecting is really a suicide attempt.

Nasal Administration

Snorting a drug through the nostrils is an effective way of getting the substance into the bloodstream. The drug is absorbed by the small blood vessels located in the mucous membranes of the nose. Frequent snorting, which is the most common method of using cocaine, can result in irritation of the membranes; heavy use can result in a need for nasal surgery because of eroded membranes and, ultimately, deterioration of the nasal cartilage of the septum. Because cocaine acts as an anesthetic, a chronic user may not even be aware of damage being done. The effects of cocaine by snorting are felt within five minutes and the duration can be from 10–30 minutes. The drug is usually snorted from a cokespoon (similar to a small saltspoon) or from a rolled paper or matchbook. One nostril is held closed and the cocaine is sniffed strongly through the open nostril. The process is then repeated with the other nostril.

Volatile drugs are also administered nasally by inhalation. The absorption point in such cases is the lungs rather than the nasal membranes. Among the volatile substances which are inhaled for their intoxicating effects are organic solvents (petroleum derivatives), and vaporous anesthetics such as chloroform, ether and nitrous oxide. Deaths have occurred from the practice in cases where a person has placed a plastic bag over his or her head to enhance the effects; often death is caused by suffocation rather than the effects of the drug (see INHALANTS). Effects produced by inhalation usually have a duration of approximately five minutes, and the person becomes uncoordinated. There are warnings that frequent inhaling of volatile solvents causes brain, heart and kidney damage.

Rectal Administration

Rectal administration is the method used for inserting suppositories, semi–solid substances that contain a drug, and in the case of enemas. The drug is absorbed by the mucous membranes of the anus. Drug abusers rarely administer a drug in this way; it is a method used by doctors when a person is unconscious or cannot swallow.

Topical Administration

Drugs administered topically (placed on or rubbed into the skin) are rare and usually ineffective. People who handle LSD have encountered accidental absorption, however.

adrenochrome   A red (pink adrenaline) derivative of epinephrine which produces hallucinogenic effects.

adulteration   The process by which a drug is made impure or inferior by the addition of an improper substance. Heroin is often CUT to dilute its potency and increase the initial amount. Other drugs are often adulterated with active substances in order to increase the desired effects or to make users think they are getting a more potent drug.

adverse drug reaction   A negative psychological or somatic reaction to drug taking. There has been controversy over what actually constitutes an adverse reaction, just as there has over what constitutes ACUTE versus CHRONIC (long–term) adverse reactions. It has been theorized that "normal well–adjusted" individuals are least likely to experience adverse reactions. Although adverse psychological reactions are generally associated with hallucinogens, they can, in fact, also be caused by the use of amphetamines, barbiturates, alcohol and various other categories of drugs.

advertising   Drug consumption, for both medical and recreational purposes, is influenced both directly and indirectly by the same advertising techniques used to market consumer items such as cars and toilet paper—but with more far–reaching and serious consequences. Drug advertising raises ethical considerations which are difficult to resolve in light of the dual nature of the product in question: manufacturers are obliged by free enterprise to maintain and increase the profit margin on the product they sell, but drugs have the capacity to prolong life (in which instance they are more than a luxury item), or to endanger it (in the case of alcohol and cigarettes and in overdose). Applying the profit motive and powerful, persuasive advertising techniques to chemical substances seems unethical, if not downright dangerous, argue those who oppose such advertising. Their tenacious opposition has resulted in the abolition of TV advertising for cigarettes and distilled spirits but has not affected the equally dubious areas of non–prescription drugs and pharmaceuticals.

Beer and wine ads still appear on television, and advertising for cigarettes and liquor continues in other media, apparently quite effectively. Both advertising and sales of alcoholic beverages have increased steadily since 1950. In 1977 the industry spent $492 million on advertising, employing the slick-est, most successful agencies to develop glossy and persuasive ad campaigns. Ads for alcohol typically appeal to people's fantasies about sex, money, sophistication and youthfulness. Although trade associations maintain advertising codes, their guidelines do not go so far as to limit effectiveness. Rich, beautiful and healthy young people frequently appear on the screen, billboard or magazine page, smilingly and seductively grasping a glass or bottle, creating associations the manufacturer of the product hopes will influence the consumer's behavior at the checkout counter. Sports heroes and (increasingly) ethnic groups figure prominently in alcohol and cigarette advertising. In the last decade or so, manufacturers of these products have recognized women as an important market and have made changes in their product lines as well as in advertising to accommodate and attract the new market. More and more "light" beers and wines and "feminine" cigarettes appear every year and advertising in women's magazines has increased dramatically.

One of the problematical issues most frequently raised is whether such advertising serves to promote a particular brand effectively or the actual acts of drinking and smoking. It is clearly in the manufacturers' interest to increase consumption, but is it in the public interest? This concern has led to counteradvertising by various health groups and sometimes by the manufacturers themselves. Ads warning against smoking, which have decreased since TV and radio cigarette commercials were banned in 1971, have contributed to a decrease in cigarette consumption in recent years and to the increasing popularity of low tar cigarettes over more toxic blends. Television and print media spots encouraging moderation in drinking, and warning especially of the dangers of drinking and driving have been stepped up, with as yet unmeasured results.

Advertisements for non–prescription

"over–the–counter" (OTC) medications flood the media. Manufacturers spend $350 million annually to promote their products and as a group comprise one of the biggest television advertisers. Most of their television efforts are concentrated on the daytime market and are therefore directed mostly at women. As well as being the largest group of television viewers during that time slot, women are also the biggest buyers of OTC preparations.

Ads for non–prescription drugs often illustrate the worst aspects of advertising technique. For example, they try to convince consumers that they need something they really don't. Despite their advertisers' claims, most OTC preparations are relatively ineffective; at best they treat symptoms not an illness itself. Too often the packaging becomes the real product. There was a case recently, for instance, where one manufacturer's larger dose of asprin was being touted as more effective than its lower dose rival. Careful wording, such as "medically proven effective"—which implies much but reveals little real information—is created to prey upon the consumer's ignorance and fears.

Recently, more stringent controls with regard to honesty in advertising have compelled manufacturers to be more forthright in warning about possible side effects and unsafe ingredients. (These controls do not compel manufacturers to justify all their claims, however. The makers of Anacin, for example, do not have to admit that their "more effective" product contains nothing more than an aspirin preparation and caffeine.) Moreover, it may be too late to correct the basic dishonesty that is implicit in manufacturers' attempts to persuade the American people that they should never suffer a moment's discomfort of any kind, and that they need OTC products to ensure that they won't. Encouraging this kind of mentality has helped produce a drug dependent society in which during any 24–36 hour period,

50–80% of the adult population takes at least one medical drug. The casual way in which Americans swallow 50 million aspirin daily doubtless influences young people and contributes to our casual recreational drug habits.

Another group of drugs whose sales depend on advertising and other promotion is pharmaceuticals—prescription drugs which manufacturers market to physicians for eventual use by their patients. The pharmaceutical industry has grown dramatically in the last 40 years, and expenditures for prescription drugs have tripled in the last decade. Clearly, pharmaceutical sales constitute big business and the industry has developed an extensive network through which to promote its products. A key component are sales representatives called "detailmen" who, usually without the benefit of medical or scientific training, visit doctors on a commission basis to convince them of their products' merits. Studies have shown that what detailmen say, and the order in which they describe drugs, definitely influences physicians' ideas about the medicine and, therefore, their prescription practices. Usually the only information doctors receive about a drug is what they hear directly from the manufacturer.

Medical journals, which doctors receive free, depend entirely on advertising dollars from drug companies. Accordingly, about 45% of their content is pharmaceutical advertising. Physicians rely heavily on such advertisements to educate themselves about available medications. Necessarily, they are relying on biased presentations of information, and medical journal advertising is clearly at least partially responsible for the misuse and overuse of prescription drugs in this country. Tranquilizers, for example, are more heavily advertised and prescribed than any other kind of drug. Ads devised to promote them encourage doctors to prescribe them for use in the most mundane anxiety–provoking situations, such as spending an evening with the in–laws. The use of sedatives is also recommended to ease patient management—that is, for the staff's benefit—in nursing homes and other institutions. Repeated implications, if not assertions, that certain groups, such as women or the elderly, for instance, need psychoactive drug X fosters stereotypes that clearly affect doctors' prescription practices. Manufacturers who are reticent in advertising a drug's side effects can doubly harm a patient.

Pharmaceutical advertising is perhaps the most problematical area of drug advertising. Manufacturers incur great losses whenever they introduce new drugs; profits from the existing product line must compensate, therefore. But prescription drugs are not subject to such economic forces as supply and demand which govern the sales of most products. Patients generally have no choice but to trust their doctor's medical expertise to determine what they need to be healthy, and buy the drugs their doctor prescribes for them. Doctors, however, are largely at the mercy of the pharmaceutical companies' inherently biased advertising. Some modification of advertising practices seems called for, whereby the drug manufacturers accept responsibility for providing clear, complete information about their products and—most important—agree not to promote in any way the unnecessary prescription of chemical substances.

aerosol sprays   See INHALANTS.

aftercare   The package of services that are provided for an individual after he or she has been successfully discharged from a drug abuse treatment program. Aftercare activities include involvement in self–help groups, supported work programs, and staff follow–up contacts and interventions. Aftercare is the first line of defense against a return to drug use. (See also REHABILITATION.)

aging   See ELDERLY.

agitation   One of the major symptoms of a non–fatal overdose. It is characterized by excessive restlessness, pacing, hand wringing, fidgeting and other forms of constant motor activity.

agonist   A drug that produces a pharmacological action at a receptor site of a cell. A drug that nullifies or prevents that action is an antagonist. Some drugs have mixed agonist–antagonist actions. Morphine is a narcotic agonist. Naloxone is a narcotic antagonist. Talwin (pentazacine) is a narcotic agonist–antagonist.

AIDS   See ACQUIRED IMMUNE DEFICIENCY SYNDROME.

airplane glue   See INHALANTS.

Al–Anon   An organization designed to provide help for the relatives and friends of alcoholics. It is officially known as the Al–Anon Family Groups. Although the two operate independently, Al–Anon's philosophy, program and structure correspond to the related organization ALCOHOLICS ANONYMOUS (AA). The only requirement for membership in Al–Anon is to have a relative or friend who is an alcoholic. Members are taught that they are not responsible for the actions of the alcoholic; they are responsible only for their own reactions and responses to the alcoholic and to what he or she does. The primary purpose of Al–Anon is not to stop the alcoholic from drinking, but to help his or her family and friends. Members are taught neither to interfere actively with the alcoholic's drinking nor to protect him from the consequences of drinking. The assumption is that the alcoholic will be forced to a point where the effects of drinking have become so severe that he will be motivated to stop voluntarily.

Alateen   Patterned after AL–ANON, Alateen is an organization designed to help teenagers from 12 to 20 who have been affected by someone, usually a parent, with a drinking problem. The person who is drinking does not necessarily have to be a member of ALCOHOLICS ANONYMOUS (AA). The organization was started in 1957 by a boy in California whose father was an alcoholic in AA and whose mother was a member of Al–Anon.

alcohol   For the past 300 years the term "alcohol" has been synonomous with spirituous liquids. There are four major types of alcohol and they have one distinct chemical feature in common: the presence of an oxygen atom and a hydrogen atom bonded together to form a single unit (this single unit is known as a hydroxyl group). A hydroxyl group is more precisely classified by the number of hydrocarbon units that occur in it: methyl alcohol is a one carbon unit; ethyl alcohol has two carbon units; propyl alcohol has three; and butyl alcohol has four. Ethyl alcohol is the type used to make alcoholic beverages and therefore the one that is most abused.

Methyl alcohol (methanol): Commonly referred to as "wood alcohol," it is used commercially in the production of formaldehyde and other organic chemicals, such as antifreeze and industrial solvents. It is now manufactured synthetically because distillation processes can produce only limited amounts of varying purity.

Isopropyl alcohol (propanol): Commonly referred to as "rubbing alcohol," it is now manufactured mostly from a petroleum by–product. It is used commercially in hand and shaving lotions, as an additive in shellac, lacquer and antifreeze, and as a rubbing compound.

Butyl alcohol (butanol): Produced both by fermentation and by synthesizing the petroleum by–product butene, it has perhaps the broadest range of commercial uses. It is used,

in various forms, to produce photographic film, dye, plastic, artificial leather and safety glass.

Ethyl alcohol (ethanol): Produced commercially by fermentation, it is commonly called "grain alcohol" and is used to make alcoholic beverages. Because potable alcohol is heavily taxed, when ethyl alcohol is intended for another purpose, such as an industrial solvent, it is "denatured" and rendered unfit for consumption. Denaturing is accomplished by adding a variety of toxic or nauseous chemicals that cannot be removed.

There are also a variety of high–carbon alcohols that extend beyond these four basic types. They are produced in limited quantities for more specialized uses such as jet fuels, nitroglycerin explosives, etc.

There is no period in recorded history that lacks references to the production and consumption of ethanol. The history of alcohol consumption is inseparable from the history of alcohol abuse, and codes limiting its consumption date back to 1700 B.C. Over the years a pattern of increasing availability of alcoholic beverages has led to concern about resulting alcohol–related problems. After the failure of Prohibition in the United States, the *moral* approach to the problem gave way to a more scientific approach and the *disease* concept of alcoholism was increasingly acknowledged. Since World War II particularly, the scope and depth of research studies have provided a wealth of information about alcohol abuse.

alcohol amblyopia   A rare eye disease that usually occurs in alcoholics who have a lengthy history of severe drinking problems. It is also associated with nutritional deficiency. The disorder begins slowly with a slight vision impairment, then becomes progressively worse. It is believed to be due to a toxic reaction in the orbital portion of the optic nerve, and if not treated adequately may be followed by optic nerve degeneration.

The disease is most common in male alcoholics who are also smokers.

alcohol concentration   The proportion of alcohol in a tissue or fluid expressed as volume or weight of alcohol per volume or weight of fluid or tissue. (See also BLOOD ALCOHOL CONCENTRATION.)

alcohol discharge rate   To get this rate the number of alcohol–related discharges for a given hospital subpopulation or category is divided by the total number of discharges then multiplied by 100,000. The term "discharge" means the formal release of a patient from a hospital. The National Center for Health Statistics defines "alcohol discharge" as a discharge given to a person who has at least one of the following diseases: alcoholic psychosis (delirium tremens, Korsakoff's psychosis, or other alcoholic hallucinosis); alcoholic paranoia; cirrhosis of the liver; alcoholism manifested by habitual excessive drinking or addiction or other unspecified alcoholism; toxic effects of ethyl alcohol; and acute or chronic pancreatitis. The alcohol discharge rate can be used to determine the approximate alcoholic population at any given time and is a significant index of alcoholism and alcohol abuse. There are limitations, however, as only those who have actually sought treatment are counted and there are occasions when a patient may go for more than one treatment.

Alcohol, Drug Abuse and Mental Health Administration (ADAMHA) An umbrella agency that in addition to its own administrative staff, includes the National Institute of Mental Health, the National Institute on Drug Abuse, and the National Institute on Alcohol and Alcohol Abuse. ADAMHA is part of the Public Health Service of the U.S. Department of Health and Human Services.

alcohol pathology   A general term that refers to any morbid physical damage or individual harm caused by the direct or indirect effects of alcohol consumption and abuse.

alcohol poisoning   See ALCOHOLIC POISONING.

alcoholic   Used as a noun, the term refers to a person who manifests signs of ALCOHOLISM. Used as an adjective, the term pertains to the use or presence of alcohol, as in ALCOHOLIC BEVERAGE CONTROL LAWS and ALCOHOLIC TREATMENT CENTER.

alcoholic beverage control laws (ABC laws)   The purpose of ABC laws has always been to prevent the fraudulent sale of alcohol, to assure availability and to secure revenue for the state. ABC laws date back to the Code of Hammurabi almost 4,000 years ago.

After the repeal of PROHIBITION in the United States, emphasis was placed on the promotion of temperance and the prevention of abuse. This concern gradually changed and the primary emphasis of the ABC laws became to maintain an orderly market and collect revenue for government agencies. With an increase in alcohol consumption per capita over the last 30 years, attention is again being given to prevention. There has recently been debate between those who suggest that the control laws are not stringent enough to curtail abuse, and those who believe that strict laws are not very effective anyway and ignore cultural, biological, social and psychological forces involved in problem drinking. Opponents of stricter laws suggest that they will work in opposition to prevention programs based on the promotion of responsible use by individuals. They further suggest that increased control will lead to resentment of the system; increased use of toxic substances; and the growth of illicit alcohol trade.

Supporters of increased legislation, on the other hand, suggest that the increased consumption over the last 30 years seems to contradict the ALCOHOLIC DISEASE concept, which holds that alcoholism only affects those with some particular underlying physical or psychological problem. They point out findings from studies that show a direct relationship between per capita consumption for all drinkers and the proportion of heavy users.

ABC laws vary a great deal from state to state and a large number of federal, state and local level agencies are responsible for making and enforcing regulations. There are two major types of control systems: the monopoly system and the license system. The individual state operates all or part of the wholesale and retail sale of alcohol under the monopoly system. Under the license system the state creates a partial monopoly for private enterprise by restricting competition. Significant conclusions about the comparative effects of the two systems have not been found.

Regulatory controls are exercised through outlets, age restrictions, pricing and taxation regulations, and through miscellaneous controls such as laws concerning PUBLIC DRUNKENNESS and DRIVING WHILE INTOXICATED. Restrictions on outlets—both those where alcohol can be sold and those where it may be consumed—is the most frequent method employed for controlling availability. The age at which alcoholic beverages may be purchased varies from 18 to 21 among the states, with a recent trend toward raising the drinking age. Regulation through pricing and taxation is unpopular with both the public and the liquor industry, but while their impact is inconclusive, there seems to be evidence that they do have some effect. Some states support a doubling of the U.S. government excise tax on liquor ($10.50 per gallon in 1980) and use the additional funds for the treatment and prevention of alcoholism. Federal, state and local taxes on alcohol vary around the country.

alcoholic hepatitis   See LIVER.

alcoholic muscle disease   See ALCOHOLIC MYOPATHY.

alcoholic myopathy   A disease that occurs in several forms and which is associated with changes in muscle tissue. Its cause is unknown but alcohol is a primary factor in its development. The condition has only been recognized in the past 25 years. Even in severe cases the prognosis is good and improvement occurs if the patient stops drinking.

Subclinical Myopathy

A disease indicated by increased levels of the enzyme creatine phosphokinase, considered to be of muscle cell origin, in the blood. Frequently there is also a rise in lactic acid. The condition affects more than one–third of the alcoholic population and is difficult to detect because patients may not complain of muscular symptoms. It may progress to more severe forms of myopathy.

Acute Alcoholic Myopathy

Characterized by severe muscle cramps, particularly in the arms and legs, it generally appears abruptly in chronic alcoholics. If the patient abstains from alcohol recovery is possible.

Chronic Alcoholic Myopathy

A slowly progressive disease, it is characterized by weakness and muscle atrophy, particularly in the legs. This form of myopathy is associated with heavy drinking over an extended period of time but, as with other forms of myopathy, it can be alleviated if the patient abstains from alcohol.

alcoholic poisoning   This condition differs only in degree from a state of extreme alcohol intoxication. Dr. Mark Keller of the Rutgers Center of Alcohol Studies suggests that a BLOOD ALCOHOL CONCENTRATION (BAC) above 0.4% indicates the occurrence of this condition.

alcoholic polyneuropathy   While the origin of this disease has still not been determined, it is thought to be caused by a thiamine deficiency. Characterized by numbness and pain in the lower legs, which sometimes progresses to the upper extremities as well, the condition develops slowly over a number of years. While partial recovery is possible some permanent impairment is frequent.

alcoholic psychosis   Any severe mental disorder caused by the effects of alcohol consumption, generally referable to KORSAKOFF'S PSYCHOSIS and WERNICKE's ENCEPHALOPATHY syndromes.

Alcoholic Treatment Center (ATC) Funded by the National Institute on Alcohol Abuse and Alcoholism, these centers offer treatment for alcoholism in three major settings: hospital, intermediate and outpatient. These different modes of treatment enable a center to fit the particular needs of a client. Most ATC clients receive a combination of treatments, hospital care being quite short and intermediate and outpatient extending over a much longer period.

Hospital setting
Three kinds of care are offered: inpatient, 24–hour service; partial hospitalization, the patient being allowed to go home or to work at appropriate times; and detoxification, which provides a short "drying out" period to handle serious symptoms.

Intermediate setting
This setting also offers three kinds of programs: halfway houses, living quarters along with job counseling, psychotherapy, and other services, for patients who do not require hospitalization but need extensive care; quarterway houses, more intensive care than halfway houses, and often offering physical care; and residential care, living quarters with little or no therapy.

Outpatient setting
This setting offers four kinds of therapy:

individual counseling, sessions given by a paraprofessional; individual therapy sessions given by a professional (someone with a degree in social work, psychology, medicine, etc.); group counseling sessions given by a paraprofessional; and group therapy sessions given by a professional.

Alcoholics Anonymous (AA)   Founded in the United States in 1935, Alcoholics Anonymous is a nonprofessional organization of alcoholics which is international in scope. Its purpose is to maintain the sobriety of its members through self–help and mutual support. The only requirement for membership is the desire to stop drinking. Incorporated as a non–profit organization, AA is supported by the contributions of its members.

Alcoholics Anonymous was founded by Bill Wilson (or as he came to be known, Bill W.), an alcoholic who decided to dry out after attending a meeting of the OXFORD GROUP. This nondenominational group, headed by an Episcopal clergyman, stressed the importance of taking stock of oneself, confessing one's defects, and being willing to make up for past wrongs. These principles form the basis of AA. Wilson believed strongly in the disease concept of alcoholism; as a member of the Oxford Group he tried preaching his theories to other alcoholics but had no appreciable results. Then, during a business trip to Akron, Ohio, Wilson met another member of the group, Dr. Robert Holbrook Smith, an alcoholic who was still drinking. Wilson told his story, this time without preaching, and stressed the disease aspect. Smith sobered up and Wilson started a group, although not formally under the name of Alcoholics Anonymous, in Akron. AA dates its "birth" as June 10, 1935, the first day of Smith's "permanent sobriety." When Wilson returned to New York, where he had once worked on Wall Street, he developed a second group. In 1939 a third group was formed in Cleveland, Ohio, and membership numbered around 100.

In 1938 and 1939 Wilson put together a collection of articles which formed the basis of the growing organization. Entitled *Alcoholics Anonymous,* the volume was published by AA and has become commonly known as "the Big Book." Although it did not do well at first, the Big Book gradually gained in popularity and by the end of 1981 had sold well over three million copies. Along with case histories, it contains the Twelve Steps which Wilson developed for the process of recovery. The Twelve Steps stress faith, disavowal of personal responsibility, passivity in the hands of God or a higher power, confession of wrongdoing and response to spiritual awakening by sharing with others. The idea of despair and admitting one is powerless over alcohol is the first step; the idea of hope is the second step; and in the third step responsibility is shifted from oneself to a higher authority figure. The remaining nine steps involve confessing, making amends, confirming a new image of oneself and redirecting energy to help others. Attempts by AA members to help others who are drinking are known as "twelve-stepping."

Headquarters for AA were set up in New York City and the organization began publishing an international monthly magazine, *The Grapevine,* as well as books dealing with alcoholism. AA is run by two operating bodies: AA World Services, Inc. and the AA Grapevine, Inc., both responsible to a board of trustees.

Because different conflicts were breaking out among AA groups on such questions as organization, religious status and anonymity, tenets known as the Twelve Traditions were formalized in 1946. They specify that the unity of AA is paramount; that leaders serve but do not govern; that all who desire help will be accepted; and that groups are autonomous. They further specify that while the AA message is to be spread, other enterprises are not to be endorsed and no sides are to be taken in controversies; groups are nonprofessional and self-supporting, with as little formal organization as possible; personal ambition is discouraged and anonymity is protected.

Group organization, on the local level, is kept to a minimum. A few officers arrange meeting programs and maintain contact with the General Service Office, and responsibility for leading groups is rotated. New groups are usually started by an experienced member in an area where there is a demand. Group meetings are open to all alcoholics whether or not they have ever attended a previous meeting. Meetings are classified as "open" or "closed." Open meetings are open to everyone, alcoholics and nonalcoholics. Closed meetings are limited to alcoholics only so that members will feel more free to discuss particularly difficult or intimate problems.

The desire to stop drinking is the only requirement for membership in AA. A new member is asked if he has admitted to himself that he is "powerless over alcohol" and is urged to come to 90 meetings in 90 days, a crash program designed to provide maximum support during what is considered a dangerous time. He or she is also urged to select a "sponsor," an experienced AA member in whom they can confide on an individual and continuing basis. The length of a member's sobriety is of major importance in AA and anniversaries are often celebrated. If a member resumes drinking he loses his seniority and his sobriety begins from scratch—regardless of how many years he has attended meetings.

Members of AA are not asked to promise to stop drinking for all time but are encouraged to keep their problems as simple as possible, to "stay away from just one drink for just one day at a time." New members are encouraged to focus their social activity on AA and are urged not to make any major and possibly stressful changes in their life, such as career changes or new relationships with the opposite sex, at the beginning of membership. Regular attendance at meetings is stressed, as is a relationship with a "higher power." In the early days of AA this higher power was identified as God, but as AA has grown to include people with many different religious beliefs, the concept of a higher power has been broadened.

In 1958 there were 6,000 AA groups with approximately 150,000 members. By 1980 the worldwide membership had grown to over one million. Members are primaril middle class, middle aged, married, white and male. However, the percentage of women is rising: from 22% in 1968 to 31% in 1980. Women were also 34% of the new members between 1977 and 1980. During that same period, the number of new members 30 years and younger increased from 11.3% to 14.7%. Since 1977, 27% of new members report dual addiction, indicating a continuing rise in the number of people addicted to a drug besides alcohol.

Because AA views alcoholism as a permanent state that cannot be corrected, only controlled, it encourages and increases its members' dependence on the organization. This dependency has been criticized by some who feel that AA strips members of their identity leaving them with only the label "alcoholic." Critics have pointed out that this ingrown aspect of AA can lead to conflict in the minds of members. AA not only helps maintain sobriety, AA *is* sobriety, and without it, sobriety is unattainable. Because the program encourages dependency and discourages outside interests that would in any way diminish the central place of AA in the life of a member, the individual may not learn to cope with his disease or gain self–reliance.

Critics of AA recognize, however, that the organization has helped to sustain large numbers of alcoholics who would otherwise be without hope or support. Although achievements and failures of AA cannot be proven because there are no membership records to document them, the organization claims a success rate of 75%; 50% on the first approach to AA and half of the first–time failures who later return. Some studies corroborate AA's success claims for 50–60% of the alcoholics who use the organization. Estimates show that 5–10% of the alcoholics in the United States are members of Alcoholics Anonymous

alcoholism   There are a variety of definitions of the term alcoholism but it is generally considered a chronic disorder associated with excessive consumption of alcohol over a period of time. Alcoholism is recognized by most authorities as a "disease," but this position is disputed in some medical circles on the basis that a condition that is self–inflicted cannot properly be termed a disease. The disease concept has been around for a long time, however. References to it have been found in the works of the Roman philosopher Seneca, the English medieval poet Geoffrey Chaucer, and the 18th century American physician Benjamin Rush.

In 1956 the American Medical Association recognized alcoholism as a disease and was followed shortly by the American Bar Association. A landmark resolution, it has had tremendous impact on laws, insurance coverage, program financing (both state and federal) and the legal status of alcoholics.

Certain religious groups, particularly fundamentalist Protestants, continue to oppose the disease concept. They view alcoholism as simple drunkenness and therefore a "sin." Some social scientists view alcoholism as a social dysfunction. They suggest that terming it a disease is to do no more than give it a medical–psychiatric label and that the medical approach is not only constricted but ineffective. These groups tend to have the same approach to people who are dependent on other drugs. There are other arguments against the disease concept, too. One is that as alcoholism has no anatomic structural abnormality it cannot be a disease. Another is that irresponsibile individuals will abuse both legal and medical benefits if they are labeled "sick," and that the disease concept excuses and dignifies drunkenness.

The World Health Organization considers alcoholism or physical dependence on alcohol to consist of the development of tolerance, a withdrawal syndrome (delirium tremens) if the substance is suddenly stopped, and a psychological desire to continue drinking.

alcoholist In Scandinavian countries this term is frequently used to refer to a person whose drinking results in the abuse of alcohol. The definition varies; it is also used to describe a person who uses alcoholic beverages heavily but is not an alcoholic.

alcoolisation The French use this term to describe a pattern of large daily consumption of alcohol, particularly wine, which has harmful effects on health and contributes to a shortened life span, but which does not result in either physical or psychological dependence.

alcoolist A person who follows the pattern of ALCOOLISATION.

alienation An individual's feeling of disassociation or estrangement from the surrounding society. It is a state characterized by feelings of powerlessness, depersonalization, isolation and meaninglessness.

alkaloid A diverse group of some 5000 bitter compounds of plant origin that contain nitrogen in their molecule, as well as carbon, oxygen and hydrogen. They are usually physiologically or pharmacologically active (that is, producing mind–altering or toxic effects). Examples include morphine, nicotine, caffeine, strychnine, atropine and mescaline. The word is often a synomyn for *active ingredient*.

alkyl nitrites Organic nitrites, usually amyl, butyl or isobuytl nitrite. Originally used as coronary vasodilators for angina, the substances were prepared in ampules covered with mesh, and were crushed in the hand and inhaled for anginal chest pains. When inhaled before orgasm, they appear to slow the passage of time and prolong climax. More recently these volatile nitrites have been sold in small, dark bottles and used either for sexual enhancement or to produce a "high." They are said to be favored by male homosexuals because a relaxation of the anal sphincter occurs.

The street term "poppers" comes from the popping sound made when an ampule is crushed.

allergy It has been suggested that an allergy to alcohol may be the cause of alcoholism. The theory, which was published in Alcoholics Anonymous literature, was first presented in 1937 by William D. Silkworth of the Charles R. Towns Hospital, New York. There is no medical evidence to support the theory, however, and the American Medical Association states: "There is no similarity between the signs and symptoms of alcoholism and those of known allergies." There is the possibility that a person may be allergic to some constituent of an alcoholic beverage, though, such as a CONGENER. A hypersensitivity to alcohol, known as pathological intoxication, exists in a small number of individuals. It consists of intoxication and sometimes aggressiveness following ingestion of one or two drinks.

allobarbital An intermediate–acting BARBITURATE.

allopathy The main system of Western medical practice, based on the concept of treating an illness by counteracting its symptoms. It is the opposite of the HOLISTIC approach.

allyl isothiocyanate Oil of mustard. Following the rash of glue sniffing in the 1960s, the largest manufacturer of plastic cement, the Testor Corporation, announced the addition of allyl isothiocyanate to its basic formula as a method of controlling the problem. When oil of mustard is sniffed, it produces severe irritation in the nostrils.

alpha–chloralose An alcohol form of a chloral derivative. It is converted in the body to CHLORAL HYDRATE.

alphaprodine A synthetic analgesic which produces morphine–like effects but is neither as potent as morphine nor as long–lasting in effect. It is a Schedule II drug.

altered state of consciousness (ASC) A broad term that covers a variety of states induced by a variety of drugs and auto–suggestive techniques, including intoxication, delirium, meditative and visionary states and the phases of sleep and dreaming. During such psychological states a person's perception of time and space is somehow influenced and altered.

Alurate® (Roche) A sedative hypnotic, intermediate–acting depressant containing the BARBITURATE aprobarbital. It is used for insomnia and daytime sedation and may be habit–forming. It is available in red and green elixirs with a 20% alcohol content.

American Council for Drug Education (CDE) Formerly the American Council on Marijuana and other Psychoactive Drugs (ACM). The name was changed in 1983 to better reflect the council's aim—that of educating the public about the health hazards associated with the use of psychoactive drugs. Established in 1977, the council believes an educated public is the best defense against drug abuse; consequently, it promotes scientific findings, organizes conferences and seminars, provides media resources and publishes educational materials.

American Council on Alcohol Problems (ACAP) A non–profit organization that provides a medium through which individuals, churches and social agencies can cooperate to find a moral and scientific solution to the alcohol problem in the United States and promote abstinence. It has been in operation since 1895 under different names: the Anti–Saloon League of America, the Temperance League of America and the National Temperance League.

American Indians Drug abuse is a relatively new phenomenon among American Indians, though the use of mind–altering substances dates back to antiquity in their culture. As early as 100 B.C. hallucinogenic psilocybin mushrooms figured prominently in religious observances of the Aztecs and other Mexican Indians, who called them "flesh of the gods." Use of peyote as a spiritual agent which enabled the user to experience transcendental visions also originated in Mexico. It was administered only under the supervision of the tribe's shaman. Religious practices involving peyote spread further north as a result of 19th century raids into Mexico by Indians of the American Midwest.

Peyote is currently the only hallucinogen whose use is sanctioned by the United States government: in 1969 the case of *California v. Woody* established the constitutional right of the 250,000 members of the Native American Church to consume peyote during religious ceremonies.

Because use of psychedelic mushrooms, peyote and other natural drugs (tobacco, morning glory seeds and some substances unknown outside Indian cultures) had always been subject to strict cultural controls which were unquestioningly respected, excessive consumption of intoxicating substances was unknown until European colonists introduced the Indians to "firewater." Until this time, they had used fermented corn and cactus preparations very sparingly in religious ceremonies and did not otherwise consume alcoholic beverages. The Europeans took advantage of this unfamiliarity with alcohol to get the Indians drunk and then cheat them of land and goods. This was done with such unscrupulous regularity that dismayed tribal chiefs finally requested laws which would prohibit the sale of alcohol to Indians. Enacted in 1832, these laws, which also banned public drinking, remained in effect until 1953. The damage had already been done, however, and the laws simply forced the Indians to drink in secret. Because of the laws and the way they were introduced to alcohol, Indians never developed a pattern of moderate social drinking in their culture; in some tribes no word exists for any drinking pattern except quick, heavy consumption intended to get one extremely drunk.

Today the American Indian nation consists of 482 federally recognized tribes totaling one and a half million members who live in cities, in rural areas, and on reservations. Alcoholism is the single biggest health problem facing Native Americans. It has been estimated that at least 60% of the adult population are excessive drinkers, and that 30% of the male population and 15% of the female population are alcoholics. Indians are five times more likely to develop alcoholic cirrhosis than the general population, and cirrhosis, followed by suicide and homicide, is the leading cause of death among them. Alcohol abuse is also reflected in the extremely high rate of arrest among Indians for drunkenness and alcohol–related violence.

Abuse of such drugs as barbiturates, amphetamines and hallucinogens also occurs in the American Indian population, but not extensively. Cocaine and inhalant abuse (the latter especially among adolescents) seem to be fairly widespread. More significantly, a recent study performed at schools on eight reservations showed that marijuana use among Indian youths has reached epidemic proportions and is far more prevalent than among non–Indian youths, particularly in the younger age brackets. Of Indian youths in grades 10–12, 89.3% had tried marijuana at least once as opposed to 52.8% of their non–Indian peers. Among those in grades 7–9, 64.4% had tried it as compared to 24.3% of non–Indian youth; and in grades 4–6, 22.7% had tried it as opposed to 6.6% of non–Indian children. Among eighth graders, 46% classified themselves as users of marijuana, a figure that compares to non–Indian high school seniors.

The investigation found that Indian children are exposed equally to marijuana and alcohol, indicating comparable acceptance of the two drugs in their culture. In non–Indian society alcohol is clearly more widely condoned than marijuana. The alarmingly young age at which Indian children were found to begin smoking marijuana (grades 4–6) may have serious consequences on their development, since THC—the active principle in marijuana—affects testosterone and estrogen levels. Further problems are posed by the likely combination of marijuana and alcohol, which amplify each other's effects (see SYNERGY).

Numerous explanations for the particularly high incidence of alcoholism and, now, abuse of other drugs have been proffered, many of them fairly obvious. As members of a racial and cultural minority, American Indians suffer from social prejudice as well as poverty, unemployment and poor health. Many justifiably feel unrightfully deprived of both territory and tradition. Oppressed and uncomfortable in white America culture, they combat low self–esteem with mind–altering substances. Parental influence and peer pressure seem to be operative. Prohibition laws directed at Indians may also have lead them to fulfill perceived expectations of alcohol abuse.

Rehabilitation programs for drug abusers have not proved particularly helpful because Indians generally resent treatment programs originating in white middle class society. More successful approaches, like the one employed at the Lincoln (Nebraska) Indian Center, have combined mainstream programs such as Alcoholics Anonymous with holistic principles consistent with Indian tradition and belief in the interrelationship of physical, mental, emotional and spiritual existence. Indian women, who in 1975 accounted for almost 50% of Indian deaths from cirrhosis, are especially difficult to help since traditional family and sex roles demand that they remain at home with the children.

American Military   Conditions of military life have traditionally been such that soldiers have often resorted to mind–altering substances, primarily alcohol, to relieve homesickness, loneliness, frustration, boredom, fear, and even hunger and cold. Drinking is also socially conditioned fraternal behavior. Since the American Revolution alcohol abuse has been a problem among enlisted men, though not the only example of drug abuse. Drug problems have not resulted solely from enlistees' efforts to intoxicate themselves. The American Civil War broke out shortly after the invention in 1853 of the hypodermic syringe. Many of the physicians serving both Union and Confederate troops mistakenly believed, along with the rest of the medical profession, that intravenous administration of morphine circumvented the danger of addiction to the drug since it bypassed the stomach. Consequently, they administered morphine freely to wounded soldiers and often provided them with their own personal drug supplies and syringes. Doctors also routinely distributed other opium preparations to relieve dysentery and diarrhea. In the years following the war, their error in judgment became apparent. Some 400,000 ex–soldiers showed evidence of morphine addiction: it came to be known, in fact, as "the army disease."

In the early 20th century, when American military forces occupied the Panama Canal Zone, government authorities became concerned about heavy and widespread marijuana smoking among military personnel stationed there. Up to 20% of enlisted men admitted a marijuana habit consisting of an average of five cigarettes a day over the previous 14 months. A military investigation into the matter concluded that such individuals were "constitutional psychopaths and morons." Later studies confirmed there were underlying personality deficiencies involved but found they had little effect on military performance.

Marijuana use in the ranks persisted during World War II, by which time it had also gained significant popularity among civilians, but it received little attention and was not considered a serious problem. During the Korean conflict, military personnel in the Far East took advantage of local availability to experiment with heroin and other narcotics, but few addictions or other problems developed.

Recent history has shown that drug trends in American society are reflected in even the strictest military environments and may be exacerbated by factors unique to wartime circumstances. Drug offenses at the military and naval academies (West Point and Annapolis) have increased markedly in the last few years, as have court martials and dishonorable discharges for such infractions. Moreover, during the recent unpopular war in Vietnam the scope of military drug abuse and addiction enlarged dramatically, shocking authorities (after their rather late recognition of the problem) into establishing educational, treatment and rehabilitation programs. These programs, which included surprise urinalysis to test for drugs, met with some success.

American soldiers stationed in Vietnam, particularly those involved in heavy combat, found themselves in an ambivalent situation which made them especially prone to develop drug habits. They fought in a dubious war, which their civilian peers outspokenly opposed, and many undoubtedly questioned their own participation. Combat duty naturally increased their stress. Many of those men who enlisted late in the war had already developed patterns of drug use in civilian society, where drug popularity continued to spread. Finally, these men were stationed in a place where extremely potent marijuana and pure heroin were available very inexpensively. Abuse of these drugs was less obvious than alcohol intoxication, which was subject to severe penalties. In light of these factors, the development of heavy drug consumption among enlisted men is not surprising.

Alcohol and marijuana were the drugs most commonly used by servicemen in Vietnam combat zones, and most men who indulged in drugs used a combination of several. On their return home, almost all veterans said they drank while in Vietnam, and about 11% admitted drinking problems; 69% said they had smoked marijuana during their tours of duty and most consumed very large doses. One-third of these men quit smoking marijuana after their return. Many complained that they were unaffected by the marijuana available in the United States because the THC content of the marijuana available in Vietnam reached 10–14% making it even stronger than hashish.

The years following 1970 saw a dramatic increase in heroin use. In a study of soldiers returning to the United States in September, 1971, 34% admitted heroin use during their stay in Vietnam. Since easy availability made economic considerations (the usual impetus for injecting) unnecessary, most smoked or sniffed the heroin. It was 92–94% pure. Although reported average daily consumption exceeded an astounding 1000 mg, the method of administration and the relatively short duration of regular use (most men were in Vietnam for only a year) limited the development of heroin addictions. Upon their return home, two–thirds of the narcotic users quickly discontinued their habits.

Despite the severity of the drug problem in Vietnam, a higher percentage of nonveterans than veterans currently use drugs. The armed forces tend to reflect drug use in American society at large, and soldiers generally exhibit no more tendency than the rest of the American people to abuse drugs, except perhaps under extraordinary conditions such as those found in Vietnam. Nevertheless, drug abuse in the military, especially in combat situations, presents a more serious problem than in the general population. Combat fighting demands that soldiers, who represent and defend an entire nation's interests, be alert, attentive and fully responsive in order to achieve full mission effectiveness.

Recent regulations include irregular urine testing and Breathometer tests for alcohol. The presence of marijuana and other drugs, including alcohol in intoxicating amounts, can lead to discharge if rehabilitation fails.

amethystic   A descriptive term for a treatment method or substance that can offset the effects of alcohol on the body or accelerate the normal sobering process. Researchers have for some time been looking for an agent to counteract the effects of alcohol on the central nervous system but, unfortunately, there are no antidotes at present. Of primary concern to researchers are the potential possibilities of such an agent in treating medical emergencies caused by overdose and in the prevention of automobile accidents caused by intoxication. Recent findings do indicate that a chemical stimulation of noradrenalin (a neuro–transmitter substance in the brain) can reverse some of the depressive effects of alcohol.

ammonium chloride   The administration of ammonium chloride in a 1 or 2% solution is a method of treatment for PCP overdose. PCP is readily excreted in acid fluids, and ammonium chloride increases the acidity of the urine.

amnesia   A temporary loss of memory, a period during which a person is conscious but later cannot recall what transpired. It is one of the typical warning signs of alcoholism. (See also BLACKOUT.)

amobarbital   An intermediate–acting BARBITURATE which is commonly sought by drug abusers. (See AMYTAL.)

amotivational syndrome   A term used to describe a condition associated with regular marijuana use. The syndrome is characterized by loss of effectiveness and apathy; and by a reduced capacity to carry out long–term plans, endure frustrations, follow routines or concentrate for long periods.

amphetamines   A(lpha) + M(ETHYL) + PH(ENYL) + ET(HYL) + AMINE. Amphetamines are central nervous system STIMULANTS with actions that resemble those of the naturally–occurring substance, adrenaline. Up until recent years amphetamines were widely prescribed by physicians for conditions such as obesity, depression, certain types of hyperactivity in minimal brain damaged children, and narcolepsy (uncon-

trolled fits of sleep). Amphetamines have also been widely used non–medically—by students studying for examinations, for instance, and truck drivers on long trips. Others have used amphetamines for purely hedonistic reasons, enjoying the euphoria and sense of self–confidence the drugs produce. In the United States during the 1960s some users began to inject massive doses of amphetamine (usually methamphetamine). Such chronic abusers are known as "speed freaks." This abuse pattern was common in Japan and Scandinavia following World War II, when doses of amphetamine supplied to service personnel were dumped onto the civilian market.

Amphetamine was first synthesized in 1887. Over the past 40 years it has been manufactured in two chemical forms. Its clinical use as a decongestant under the trade name of Benzedrine began in the early 1930s. Soon after, the drug's central nervous system stimulating properties became widely known and by the end of the decade it was used primarily as an analeptic or stimulating drug. Later, dextro–amphetamine (DEXEDRINE) was marketed as a more potent form (on a weight basis) of amphetamine. The pharmacological effects of both are identical.

Methamphetamine, commonly called "speed" and "crystal," is an amphetamine derivative. Manufactured under the trade name Desoxyn, it is more potent as a central nervous system stimulator. Amphetamine appears in a variety of forms; tablets and capsules are the most common. Methamphetamine usually appears in powder or crystal form and is usually illicitly made. Pharmacologically similar drugs with different chemical structures include benzphetamine (DIDREX), phenmetrazine (PRELUDIN), phendimetrazine (PHENAZINE, PLEGINE), methylphenidate (RITALIN), diethylpropion (TENUATE), and chlorphentermine (PRE–SATE).

Effects: When taken orally at low doses (usually those prescribed therapeutically), physical effects include increased breathing and heart rate, rise in blood pressure, reduction of appetite, and dilation of pupils. Reflexes are brisk and fine tremors of the limbs may be exhibited. At higher doses, dry mouth, fever, sweating, blurred vision and dizziness may occur. There may be teeth–grinding movements. Very high doses may cause flushing, pallor, very rapid or irregular heartbeat, tremors, loss of coordination, and collapse. Although few deaths have been reported as a direct result of amphetamine use, those which have occurred were the consequence of burst blood vessels in the brain, heart failure, or very high fever.

Psychological effects of short–term use typically include feelings of euphoria, enhanced self–confidence, heightened alertness, greater energy, and an increased capacity for concentration. Users become more talkative and sometimes more irritable. They are restless and move about frequently. Although the reason is not yet fully understood, in hyperactive children these drugs often produce a calming effect.

As the drug effects wane, feelings of fatigue, "let down" and drowsiness occur and some users may be depressed emotionally. Most users then fall asleep for a relatively normal length of time. With mild amphetamine use there is generally no hangover on awakening; however, if there is a pattern of oral abuse, hangovers do occur and often grow more severe as use continues.

Injection of amphetamine, usually methamphetamine, results in higher drug concentration in the blood and often a different pattern of abuse. For most who use the drug intravenously the sensations experienced almost instantly on injection (the "rush" or "flash") are the effects most sought after. Most users compare this initial sensation to a sexual orgasm or to an electrical shock. Often there is a very short interval between injections, less than two hours in some cases, because users are eager to reexperience the initial sensations. After shooting up users feel energetic and self–confident and are generally sociable. They may have feelings of enhanced sexuality; orgasm is delayed in both men and women, prolonging and intensifying sexual intercourse. Dry mouth and difficulty eating and urinating are also experienced.

One pattern of abuse is known as a "run"; a period of continuous amphetamine use for from three to five days. On the first day of a run a user is generally euphoric, with typical feelings of sociability and enhanced self–confidence. By the second day, concentration on one particular thing is difficult and abrupt changes in mood occur. The user may experience frightening visions or feel that bugs are crawling on his skin. Paranoid symptoms invariably follow prolonged heavy injection of methamphetamine. A combination of this suspicious, anxious state with feelings of great energy may lead to outbursts of violence. Speed freaks have a persistent desire to be sociable, but as they are known for their aggressive behavior they are often only tolerated by other speed freaks.

As the run progresses the user is less and less able to cope with the outside world. Behavior may become repetitive and useless. Eventually the run ends and the user sinks into an exhausted sleep (crash). The period of sleep may last several days and is said to be proportional to the duration of the run. The crash may occur because the user runs out of drugs or because they no longer produce the desired effect. On awakening after crashing the user generally experiences great psychic discomfort including anxiety, emotional depression, and irritability. He or she usually has a large appetite and feels lethargic and fatigued.

Fatalities due to an overdose of amphetamine are fairly rare. The symptoms are convulsions, coma and cerebral hemorrhage. The size of a lethal dose varies from individual to individual; a habitual user can ingest much more than a non–user. Death may also result from infectious diseases caused by non–sterile needles.

A chronic speed user may have a number of symptoms. Weight loss of 20 to 30 pounds or more is a common finding. Nonhealing ulcers and brittle fingernails may develop, possibly due to malnutrition. Teeth grinding occurs frequently during runs. Violent behavior and the onset of a psychotic state are two of the most common negative symptoms that can occur.

The speed user typically has paranoid suspicions and an essentially clear state of consciousness. He or she is more likely to act successfully on violent impulses than someone who may be uncoordinated and more easily distracted, such as a drunkard or someone on LSD.

Amphetamine psychosis is a paranoid psychotic state that may develop after the ingestion or injection of large doses of amphetamine. After drug usage is stopped the psychosis usually subsides within a week; however, 5 to 15% of patients fail to recover completely and continue to exhibit disturbances for months or years after the last episode of drug abuse. Other psychological changes have been observed in speed users, including greatly increased suspicion (toward everyone), reduced ability to concentrate, and an impairment of memory.

According to the National Institute of Drug Abuse, 3% of Americans over the age of 14 surveyed in one study reported having used stimulants within the previous six months. In 1980 the Institute for Social Research reported that 26% of high school seniors had used stimulants at some time and 12% considered themselves current users.

Addictive aspects: While it is generally believed that no physical DEPENDENCE on the effects of amphetamines develops regardless of the pattern of usage, there are a number of investigators who believe that the amphetamine hangover and depression are actually symptoms of WITHDRAWAL. Psychological dependence on amphetamines does occur. Experiments with animals have shown that those addicted to amphetamines and then withdrawn will work very hard to get more of the drug, and will keep trying approximately twice as long as similar animals who are addicted to heroin and then withdrawn.

Tolerance: Tolerance appears to develop to the euphoric effects of amphetamines. Users increase dose size considerably as a run progresses and there is a tendency to increase the amount of the drug used over a period of weeks or months. Tolerance to the cardiovascular effects of amphetamines is suggested by the fact that habitual users can survive single intravenous doses of 1000 mg or more with only occasional negative physiological effects, while a non–user would be at considerable risk at this dose. No tolerance seems to develop to the awakening or anti–sleep action of these drugs.

Amphetamines with alcohol: Amphetamine users have been known to use alcohol as an aid to induce sleep or to counter the wired–up feeling produced by a large amount of amphetamines. On the other hand, alcohol users have been known to take amphetamines to counter the depressant effects of alcohol. Although there is possible antagonism of the depressant effects of alcohol on the central nervous system, there is no improvement of impaired motor coordination. Not only can the combination of alcohol and amphetamines produce gastrointestinal upset, there is also the danger of producing a false sense of security which can lead to carelessness and accidents. Amphetamines can be dangerous when combined with alcohol because the safeguard against overdosing with alcohol—unconsciousness—is evaded. Some alcoholic beverages, Chianti wine for example, contain tyramine, a white crystalline base derived from the amino acid tyrosine. The combination of tyramime and amphetamine can cause an excessive rise in blood pressure. The belief that amphetamines will increase the brief high produced by alcohol is false.

Sources: Amphetamines are commercially produced, but are limited by the CONTROLLED SUBSTANCES ACT as of 1972. Amphetamines are also smuggled in from Colombia and Mexico and sold on the black market. They are also illicitly manufactured in this country. Demand greatly exceeds supply and a large number of amphetamine look–alikes have appeared on the market.

Traffic and control: Amphetamines and amphetamine–BARBITURATE preparations are Schedule II drugs under the Controlled Substances Act.

Synonyms: speed, crystal, meth, bennies, dexies, uppers, pep pills, diet pills, hearts, footballs, cranks, splash, and many others.

amyl alcohol   The chief constituent of fusel oil, amyl alcohol is used as a source of amyl compounds, such as AMYL NITRITE. It is a colorless liquid with a burning taste. The term should not be confused with ETHANOL which is the principal chemical in alcoholic beverages.

amyl nitrite   An inhalant used for vasodilation and to lower blood pressure, and occasionally in the treatment of asthma and

---

History of Amphetamines

1887	Amphetamines first synthesized.
1927	First medical use of amphetamines as a stimulant and as a nasal decongestant.
1932	Marketed as Benzedrine tablets and inhalers.
1937	First used medically to calm hyperactive children.
1940s	American, British, German and Japanese governments issue amphetamines to soldiers to counteract fatigue, elevate mood and increase endurance.
	Use of amphetamines by athletes and businessmen reported as early as 1940.
	Black market begins—"pep pills" used by students and truck drivers.
1949	Manufacture of Benzedrine inhalers discontinued because of danger of overdose.
1950s	First wave of abuse. American soldiers in Korea and Japan mix amphetamines with heroin to create the first "speedballs" and use intravenously.
	Amphetamines prescribed for narcolepsy, chronic fatigue and as an anorectic. American housewives begin abuse of "diet pills."
	Amphetamines combined with barbiturates or tranquilizers (Dexamyl) and prescribed for depression.
1960s	Widespread abuse begins. "Speedfreaks" inject massive doses of methamphetamine (Methedrine). FDA begins anti-speed campaign with slogan "Speed Kills." Methedrine withdrawn from distribution through retail pharmacies (remains in distribution to hospitals) and black market manufacture booms.
1970s–1980s	Widespread abuse continues and increases in the U.S. Studies show 12% of youth (aged 18-25) in 1972 used amphetamines; in 1982 this figure had risen to 18%. Similar patterns of abuse are seen worldwide.

convulsions. Discovered in 1857, it was first used to treat angina pectoris. Amyl nitrite causes a sudden lowering of the blood pressure by dilating blood vessels; the lowering of blood pressure causes the heart to pump rapidly. The substance is supplied in glass vials (ampules) which are broken open and inhaled; amyl nitrite is only active when inhaled. A very quick–acting drug, it takes effect in 15 to 30 seconds and its duration is approximately three minutes. It is prized among drug abusers for its purported sexual stimulation and ability to intensify orgasm. It is also used to produce an intense brief euphoric high. Tolerance can occur but dependency is rare. It can have unpleasant side effects—vomiting and nausea—and can be dangerous for anyone with a heart problem. Synonyms: pearls, poppers, snappers. (See also ALKYL NITRITES.)

Amytal® (Lilly)   A sedative hypnotic DEPRESSANT containing the moderately rapid–acting BARBITURATE amobarbital. It is used for insomnia, daytime sedation and as a preanesthetic medication. Overdosage can cause central nervous system depression: symptoms are respiratory depression, reduction in reflexes, pupil dilation or constriction, decreased urine formation, reduced body temperature and coma. When used with alcohol or other CNS depressants it can have a potentiating effect. It is occasionally used non–medically. It is available as an elixir containing 34% alcohol and is also available in tablet form: 15 mg are light green; 30 mg yellow; 50 mg orange; and 100 mg pink.

Amytal Sodium® (Lilly)   A sedative hypnotic DEPRESSANT containing the short–acting BARBITURATE amobarbital, which is used for the control of convulsions and as a diagnostic aid in schizophrenia. It can be administered intravenously or intramuscularly but administration should be closely supervised. It is occasionally used non–medically. Amytal Sodium is available in ampules to be mixed with sterile water before injection, and in 65 mg and 200 mg blue capsules.

anal administration   See ADMINISTRATION.

analeptics   A class of drugs that act as stimulants on the central nervous system, such as caffeine and amphetamines.

analgesic   A drug used for the relief of varying degrees of pain without the loss of consciousness. Some of the more potent analgesics will produce sedation.

anesthetics   Substances, usually gases, which are used to produce anesthesia (coma) for surgical procedures. Along with their use in medicine, anesthetics have a long history of abuse. (See NITROUS OXIDE, ETHER, CHLOROFORM and INHALANTS.)

Anexsia–D® (Beecham Lab)   A narcotic opiate containing the CODEINE derivative hydrocodone bitartrate, which is used as an analgesic. Its habit–forming potential is greater than codeine and less than morphine. It also contains aspirin, caffeine and phenacetin. A Schedule III drug, it is available in white uncoated compressed tablets.

angiitis, necrotizing   A disease characterized by inflammation of small and medium sized arteries and segmental necrosis (death of living tissue in a localized area). It has been associated with viral infections such as hepatitis and the intravenous use of such drugs as methamphetamines and heroin. The disease usually terminates in the failure of vital organs and is generally fatal.

anileridine   A synthetic NARCOTIC whose activity is similar to meperidine and which produces morphine–like effects. It is a Schedule II drug.

anorectics   Drugs used as appetite suppressants in cases of obesity and for weight control. In recent years a number of anorectics have come on the market to replace AMPHETAMINES, and though they are less potent they produce many of the effects of amphetamines and have a very high potential for abuse. Some of the more common anorectics are benzphetamine, chlorphentermine, diethylpropion, fenfluramine, mazindol, phenmetrazine, phendimetrazine and phentermine.

Anstie's Law   Sir Francis Anstie made public Anstie's Law of Safe Drinking in 1862: the law stated that 1½ ounces of absolute alcohol per day was the upper limit of safe drinking. Anstie was a British psychiatrist who established the first women's medical school in England. Even today after years of research, his law is viewed as a good general guideline for the average drinker. One and a half ounces of absolute alcohol is equivalent to four 8–oz glasses of beer, a half bottle of wine, or three 1–oz drinks of 100 proof liquor. It must be remembered, of course, that some individuals cannot tolerate any alcohol so the law does not apply to everyone.

Antabuse®   (Ayerst)   A drug used to stop people from drinking while they are being treated for alcoholism. Antabuse alone has little effect on the body, but if a patient combines it with alcohol he will have severe reactions, including headache, flushing, vomiting, breathing difficulty, and sometimes collapse and coma. Reaction begins 5 to 10 minutes after ingesting alcohol and may last from 30 minutes to several hours, depending on the amount drunk. The reaction occurs because Antabuse interferes with the metabolism of alcohol in the liver by causing a toxic buildup of acetaldehyde by inactivating aldehyde dehydrogenose. Its real value is in the knowledge of what will occur if a drink is taken, and though far from a complete answer, it can be a major aid in the treatment of alcoholics. The brand name of the generic drug disulfiram, it is supplied in white scored tablets of 250 and 500 mg. It should never be administered to a patient in a state of alcohol intoxication or without the full knowledge of the patient.

anticholinergic   A drug that blocks cholinergic (or parasympathetic) nerve transmission. Therefore anticholinergics will dilate the pupils, cause dry mouth, cause the gastrointestinal tract to stop its movements, and sometimes produce delirium. Many drugs used in medicine have anticholinergic properties: examples are anti–Parkinsonian agents, antispasmodics, some antihistamines, antidepressants and antipsychotic drugs. Atropine is a classic example of an anticholinergic drug.

antidepressant   A major classification of drugs developed in recent times to medically improve mood in severely depressed patients. Antidepressant drugs are rarely used recreationally because although they seem to have a stimulant effect in cases of pathologic depression, they appear to have little immediate pleasurable effect on normal mood states. In fact, amitriptyline (Elavil) is occasionally abused for its sedative effect. Antidepressants are subdivided into tricyclic antidepressants (TCA) and monoamine oxidase (MAO) inhibitors .

antihistamines   Drugs used as histamine antagonists. They are usually prescribed for allergies, runny nose, sneezing, and motion sickness. They have central nervous system DEPRESSANT properties and when used with alcohol or other CNS depressants (narcotics, barbiturates, tranquilizers) they can have an additive effect. Some antihistamines are combined with codeine or pentazocine (Talwin) and are sought after by drug abusers for their sedative effects. Alcohol, found in some antihistamines, produces a synergistic effect which increases the sedative properties of both the alcohol and antihistamine.

Antilirium® (O'Neal, Jones & Feldman) A drug containing physostigmine, a salicylic acid derivative of an alkaloid extracted from the seeds of the calabar bean (Physostigma venenosum). It is used to reverse toxic effects on the central nervous system (hallucination, delirium, disorientation, coma, and so on) caused by drugs which produced anticholinergic poisoning. It is supplied in 2 ml ampules for injection.

antipsychotics Also referred to as major TRANQUILIZERS and neuroleptics, drugs in this category are rarely used nonmedically because they do not produce euphoria and can produce unpleasant side effects.

antitussive A drug used to relieve or prevent coughing, such as codeine or dextromethorphan.

anxiety A state of overwhelming and abnormal apprehension or fear often characterized by tension, increased pulse and sweating. Anxiety is a primary cause of drug dependence. When someone learns that a drug can have an immediate effect in the management of these disturbing feelings, a pattern of drug abuse can be quickly established. But abuse and heavy consumption may increase rather than decrease anxiety, particularly in the case of alcohol.

anxiolytic A minor tranquilizer that reduces anxiety.

aphrodisiac A substance that enhances or heightens sexual arousal or activity. (See SEX.)

apomorphine A chemical derivative of morphine that is used to induce vomiting. Unlike morphine it does not produce dependency and has no euphoric effects. It is also used in AVERSION THERAPY, in the treatment of alcoholism.

approval See PEER PRESSURE.

aprobarbital An intermediate–acting BARBITURATE generally used for sedation and to produce sleep. (See ALURATE.)

arecoline An alkaloid found in the nut of the betal palm, *Areca catechu,* native to Malaya. It has mild stimulant effects when chewed or sucked.

asarone A drug found in the roots of the marsh herb sweet flag which grows wild in the United States. It is purported to have hallucinogenic effects similar to MESCALINE.

Ascriptin with Codeine® (Rorer) A narcotic opiate containing CODEINE and aspirin. An analgesic used for moderate to severe pain, Ascriptin also contains Maalox, an antacid medication, which keeps aspirin–induced gastric distress at a minimum. It is often used for arthritic conditions and can be habit–forming. It is also available without codeine.

aspergillosis A number of samples of marijuana are contaminated by the fungus aspergillus. Only a very few instances of pulmonary aspergillosis have resulted from smoking marijuana, however, because heat destroys most or all of the fungus, and the healthy human is unlikely to become ill from a minor invasion of aspergillus fungi.

Asthmador A cigarette containing stramonium and atropine and once used by asthma sufferers. It is now obsolete. Along with relieving bronchial spasms, in large doses it also produced hallucinogenic effects.

ataraxic drugs Drugs used as TRANQUILIZERS. Also called ataractics.

at–risk populations Among the general population subgroups have been identified as being particularly susceptible to drug abuse. At–risk populations include adolescents, the elderly, and certain minority groups such as blacks and Puerto Ricans. Such subgroups have been targeted by drug misuse and prevention organizations.

Atropa belladonna See BELLADONNA.

atropine A belladonna (deadly nightshade) alkaloid that has also been synthesized. While generally used as an antispasmodic because it relaxes smooth muscle, it is also used as an antidote to certain poisons. In large doses it is toxic and since ancient times has been used as a sedative and poison. There have been fatalities among children who have eaten deadly nightshade.

attack therapy A group therapy in which individuals are verbally (never physically) attacked in the expectation that their defensiveness, rationalizations and denials will be broken down. They are vigorously confronted with their inappropriate or "junkie" thinking and behavior, so that they are compelled to examine themselves stripped of their defensive armor. Some therapeutic communities place the person under attack on a "hot seat" at the center of the group for greater focus.

Following the attack the individual is given considerable group support and understanding so that he can reconstitute his shattered psychological defenses into something more honest, realistic and resilient.

Australia Aside from excessive drinking which is the major drug problem in Australia, government surveys clearly show that marijuana is the illegal drug most often used in the country's various states. Not only is its use widespread, it is also increasing. Heroin use is also on the increase but in comparison to marijuana it is small in volume. There has been an increase in the use of methaqualone, too, particularly Mandrax (a British trade name). These trends are also clearly illustrated in statistics on drug charges prepared by the Australian Federal Police. Although barbiturates and amphetamines were popular in the late 1960s and were much abused, their use has declined. LSD, also popular in the 1960s, now enjoys minimal abuse. A survey in the late 1970s showed relatively minor use of cocaine, though if overseas trends affect Australia this could become a major problem.

Evidence presented to the Royal Commission of Inquiry into Drugs in the early 1970s showed illegal drug use was confined to certain community groups; by 1979, surveys showed a spread to almost every social, economic, cultural and age group, with the exception of the state of Tasmania. The latter was probably due to Tasmania's small population and its isolation from the mainland. The Royal Commission of Inquiry into Drugs is sponsored by the federal government. In Australia the responsibility for drug prevention is shared by the federal and state governments; the federal government acts primarily as a coordinator and adviser while the state governments are responsible for implementing policies and programs in their areas.

Government surveys carried out during the 1970s indicate certain trends among drug abusers in Australia. The majority are between the ages of 16 and 35 and within this range the 18–24 age group predominates. The predominance of young users is particularly noticeable in relation to heroin. It was found that use was far more prevalent among persons who had left school than those still attending, however. The same is true of marijuana use, though there has been a recent increase in use among older high school students. Although the 18–24 age group predominates, surveys showed that use of marijuana by well–educated people over the age of 30 is not uncommon. Regardless of whether the surveys investigated illegal use of drugs in general or specific drugs, the results showed that more males than females are abusers. The male to female ratio was, generally, three to two and two to one. It should be noted, however, that more males were involved in answering the surveys than females.

Few surveys have attempted to determine a connection between drug use and socio–economic background and the few that have are generally inconclusive. Inconclusive as they are, though, findings did indicate a higher rate of drug use among middle class children than working class children. One survey (Melbourne, 1973) found that the percentage of middle class fathers decreased in proportion to the intensity of drug use. Children of unskilled workers were more likely to become intravenous users than their middle class counterparts. There was also a trend of drug abuse among the unemployed.

Although few surveys have considered ethnic background and nationality, a 1972 study showed that the highest rates of abuse were among those who came to Australia from the British Isles and western Europe. Immigrants from southern and eastern Europe and Asia reported using drugs nearly three times less frequently. Midway between the two groups were those born in Australia. It should be noted, however, that the survey did not discriminate between tourists, newly–arrived settlers, and people who had lived in Australia for a number of years.

Although there was an indication that illegal drug use is more common among those who profess no religion than among those of

a particular faith, again the surveys are inconclusive.

In recent years Australia has approached the drug situation with greater emphasis on abuse as a medical problem. Government programs now focus on education, treatment and rehabilitation along with continued law enforcement. Drug abuse treatment is provided, in one form or another, at all public hospitals. There are also voluntary community organizations in all states and territories which give additional help that the more rigid federal government is unable to provide.

In 1969 the government established a nationally coordinated approach to drug abuse control; the National Standing Control Committee on Drug Dependence, comprised of federal and state members. In 1970 the Drug Education Sub–Committee was established. It is made up of state and territorial health education administrators and non–government members with expertise in education, law enforcement and management fields, and has developed a National Drug Education Program aimed at incorporating drug education into the wider concept of health education in the community.

Federal hospital and treatment services are funded on a cost–shared basis with state governments. Many private organizations and hospitals also receive financial support from the government. As no single form of treatment is appropriate to all forms of drug dependence, a variety of programs and treatments are offered by the various institutions: (1) counseling and consultation; (2) detoxification with both chemical and psychological support; (3) controlled maintenance through methadone with the support of therapy; (4) psychiatric treatment; (5) participation in therapeutic communities; and (6) attendence at "drop–in" centers with advisory service. There is also continuing rehabilitation in the form of vocational guidance and counseling.

Law enforcement with respect to drugs in

Australia is handled mainly by the following three bodies: the Australian Federal Police who police Commonwealth laws; state and territory police who work in conjunction with Commonwealth authorities; and the Bureau of Customs which has the responsibility of enforcing regulations on the importing and exporting of drugs. All state governments have agreed to a uniform code of penalties based on those applicable under Commonwealth government legislation. The Australian Federal Police serve as the national

Drug and Drug–Related Offenses:
Number of Charges* Involving Specific Drug Types: Australia 1978 to 1980

Year	Possess	Import	Use/ Administer	Traffic	Steal	False Pretenses	Forged Scripts	Other	Total
Narcotics									
1978	1,394	30	1,469	483	222	89	257	318	4,262
1979	1,068	73	1,009	414	137	73	379	367	3,520
1980	877	36	783	352	85	114	136	228	2,611
Cannabis									
1978	8,589	126	3,263	780	15	–	–	1,476	14,249
1979	10,688	102	3,472	862	23	2	–	2,352	17,501
1980	12,269	95	4,027	1,266	37	–	–	2,584	20,278
Amphetamines									
1978	46	–	46	5	–	5	18	3	123
1979	94	1	57	12	12	20	37	12	245
1980	85	–	49	25	–	22	14	6	201
Barbiturates, hypnotics									
1978	200	–	156	46	12	8	51	30	503
1979	359	–	263	53	45	32	104	51	907
1980	224	–	197	59	11	30	65	44	630
Tranquilizers									
1978	54	–	50	10	29	10	32	8	193
1979	79	–	40	29	34	12	36	18	248
1980	64	1	66	30	11	19	12	17	220
Hallucinogens									
1978	191	–	46	45	1	–	–	3	286
1979	186	–	40	33	–	–	1	18	278
1980	183	3	32	58	–	–	2	12	290
Other									
1978	53	–	14	10	32	2	212	9	332
1979	46	–	12	48	30	8	14	14	172
1980	50	–	23	51	24	74	41	22	285
Total									
1978	10,527	156	5,044	1,379	311	114	570	1,847	19,948
1979	12,520	176	4,893	1,451	281	147	571	2,832	22,871
1980	13,752	135	5,177	1,841	168	259	270	2,913	24,515

* Charges arising from offenses involving a number of different drug types have been counted under each drug type involved.

Source: *Drug Abuse in Australia, 1980.* Australian Federal Police.

agency for the systematic collection, collation, evaluation and dissemination of information concerning illicit drug traffic and use in the country. The 1980 chart included in this article is an extract from the detailed statistics published in their annual report, *Drug Abuse in Australia.*

Excessive drinking is the major substance abuse problem in Australia. This was acknowledged in the country's Alcohol and Drug Addicts Treatment Act of 1961. According to several government studies, the most important cause of the alcohol problem is that excessive consumption—usually of beer—is not only accepted by most of the population but is actually expected and encouraged. Though there is some variation in the drinking pattern in urban and rural areas, the country as a whole is prone to associate heavy drinking with civil liberty, a pioneer identity, and other images of pride and freedom embedded in the Australian concept of "mateship." Between 1962 and 1972 there was a 25% increase in per capita consumption of beer. Extrapolations from limited surveys suggest that 5% of the male population (215,000) and 1% of the female population (43,000) are alcoholics. Surveys in Perth indicate that 11.4% of the aboriginal population suffer from "chronic" drinking problems and another 29% suffer indirectly from "environmental" problems associated with alcoholism. Adolescents are a particularly vulnerable group in Australia. A 1974 survey by the Department of Education and Health reported that by age 11 nearly half the boys and a third of the girls in the survey had been introduced to alcohol, usually by their parents.

The cost of alcoholism to the country is shown in traffic fatalities and injuries; hospitalization costs; and productivity losses by the labor force. Treatment is complicated by the difficulty of operating a centralized program in a country of continental proportions. One major detoxification unit, three clinics, and various social work centers are operated by the Alcohol and Drug Addicts Treatment Board. The board also coordinates the work of various volunteer organizations. Beyond these efforts, establishment of treatment centers is the responsibility of individual states, and it should be noted that facilities and treatment philosophies vary considerably throughout the country.

aversion therapy   Based on experiments by the Russian scientist Ivan Pavlov (1849–1936), it is a behavior therapy based on conditioned reflexes and is used in the treatment of alcoholism. In aversion therapy a patient is detoxified and given a nausea–producing drug, such as APOMORPHINE, and then a shot of liquor. The nausea produced by the apomorphine subsequently becomes associated with the alcohol. Electric shock and verbally induced aversion are variations of this therapy. It has been stressed that alcoholics in such aversion programs must be provided with alternative ways of securing gratification while sober.

Disagreements have occurred as to whether aversion therapy provides a long–lasting cure and many patients drop out of this type of treatment because of its unpleasant effects. Popular in some Eastern European countries, it is not a type of therapy that is widely used in the United States.

aversive conditioning   See AVERSION THERAPY.

ayahuasca   A psychedelic beverage brewed by the Chama Indians of Peru. It is prepared from the vine and sometimes the leaves of *Banisteriopsis caapi.* The active alkaloid is HARMALINE. Synonyms: caapi, natema, yage.

B

BAC   See BLOOD ALCOHOL CONCENTRATION.

Bacarate® (Tutag)   A brand of phendimetrazine tartrate which is used as an anorectic for weight control. The drug elevates blood pressure and stimulates the central nervous system. Its activity is similar to that of AMPHETAMINES and tolerance to its effects can build up within a few weeks. Overdosage results in rapid respiration, restlessness, tremors and hallucinations. It is available in 35 mg pink tablets.

BAL   Blood alcohol level. (See BLOOD ALCOHOL CONCENTRATION.)

balloon effect   A term which refers to the substitution of one type of drug for another when authorities clamp down on the original drug of choice: the crackdown on Mexican marijuana in southern California, for instance, resulted in an increase in heroin use. The phenomenon is likened to the squeezing of a balloon which, when squeezed in one direction, will expand in another.

banana smoking   In the mid–1960s there was a widespread rumor that smoking the scrapings of the inside of a dried banana peel would produce a marijuana–like high. It was a hoax played on narcotics authorities, who would have found it impossible to prohibit the sale of bananas.

Bancap® (O'Neal, Jones & Feldman)   A narcotic opiate containing CODEINE which is used as an analgesic for minor pain. It may be habit–forming. and overdosage can cause excitability.

Banisteriopsis caapi   See AYAHUASCA.

bar drinker   A person with a pronounced habitual tendency to consume alcoholic beverages in bars, saloons and other public establishments rather than at home or at social functions. A tendency to drink in bars can be caused by several reasons: because the person wants to hide a drinking problem; because of parental disapproval (particularly if the drinker is a minor); because drinking at home or at social functions is discouraged or disapproved of for religious reasons; or for other reasons. Convivial anonymity is characteristic of bar drinking, of course. There is little peer pressure; transient relationships are conducted in an atmosphere of at least mild intoxication; and alcohol is central to all involved. Alcoholics Anonymous, which stresses anonymity, group support and a preoccupation with alcohol, suggests that recovering alcoholics with past patterns of bar drinking are most receptive to their type of self–help group.

barbital   A long–acting BARBITURATE with an onset time of up to one hour and a duration of up to 16 hours.

barbiturates   Sedative (calming), hypnotic (sleep inducing) drugs that act as central nervous system (CNS) depressants. They slow down or decrease the activity of the nerves that control the emotions, breathing, heart action and a number of other body functions.

The first barbiturate was synthesized in 1864 from barbituric acid (malonylurea). It was first manufactured and used in medicine in 1882 as barbital and released under the trade name Veronal in 1903. Initially, barbiturates were used to induce sleep, replacing such aids as alcohol, bromides and opiates such as laudanum. Since the appearance of Luminal (a phenobarbital) in 1912, several thousand barbituric acid derivatives have been synthesized. Each of the 80–or–so brand names manufactured come in a variety of forms: tablets, capsules, suppositories, liquids for injection, and in combination with many other drugs. However, the medical profession considers five or six types sufficient for clinical use.

Classification: Barbiturates are metabolized (broken down chemically) in the liver and eliminated by the kidneys at varying speeds according to their types: slow- or long-acting (mostly phenobarbital and barbital); intermediate and short-acting (mostly secobarbital and pentobarbital); and ultra-fast (thiopental).

Slow- or long-acting barbiturates take one to two hours to reach the brain through the bloodstream. Their effects last six to 24 hours with a half-life of 48 hours for phenobarbital and 24 hours for barbital brands. They are used medically to induce sleep, to provide day-long sedation in the treatment of tension and anxiety problems, and in combination with other drugs in the treatment of epilepsy and other convulsive and neurological conditions. They are also used in withdrawal treatment for alcoholism and addiction to other central nervous system drugs. Long-acting barbiturates are metabolized slowly and pass through the liver unchanged, leaving most of the work of detoxification to the kidneys. They are the preferred type for patients with liver problems. Because barbiturate users want quick action they are seldom attracted to slow- or long-acting brands and this group of drugs rarely makes its way into the black market.

Intermediate and short-acting barbiturates take effect in 20 to 45 minutes and are very much alike. They are metabolized rapidly by the liver, placing much less strain on the kidneys and are consequently preferred for patients with kidney problems. Short-acting barbiturates are the type commonly known as "sleeping pills." Their effects last only five or six hours and they produce little or no hangover when not abused. They are used medically as sedatives in ob-stetrics, in the treament of insomnia, anxiety neuroses, high blood pressure and coronary artery disease and for various diagnostic procedures. Because of the speed with which they take effect, short-acting barbiturates are invariably the choice of abusers and are most likely to produce dependence. The four most in demand, according to the Drug Enforcement Agency, are Nembutal (pentobarbital), Amytal (amobarbital), Seconal (secobarbital), and Tuinal (secobarbital and amobarbital combined). They are most like alcohol in the speed with which they take effect, in the kind of intoxication produced by their abuse, and in the addiction which can result. These are the sleeping pills most in demand by would-be suicides.

Ultra-fast-acting barbiturates produce unconsciousness in a very few minutes. The best known type is sodium pentothal (thiopental). It is used almost exclusively in hospitals as an anesthetic in minor surgery and to induce anesthesia before the administration of a longer-acting anesthetic such as nitrous oxide. Ultra-fast-acting barbiturates are rarely found outside of medical channels and present no abuse problems.

Effects of Abuse: The effect of these drugs varies with the strength of the dose, individual tolerance depending on previous use, and when and where taken. A prescribed dose at bedtime will merely induce sleep. Intoxication results when they are taken in larger doses in a social setting such as a party or at a bar, especially when combined with alcohol. With mild intoxication there is a feeling of well-being (euphoria); there is a heightening of self-esteem and a lowering of inhibitions. Increasing intoxication produces reactions exactly like those of alcohol intoxication—staggering due to loss of muscular control, short temper, the "fighting drunk" syndrome of aggressiveness and violence or, in some individuals, depression and withdrawal. Barbiturate abusers suffer the same morning-after hangover miseries as alcoholics including headache, nausea, dizziness, depression and drowsiness that may persist for hours. Impairment of judgment, poor motor control and mood swings may last many more hours, making chronic users unfit to drive or operate machinery. Very high doses increase blood pressure and depress respiration so that less oxygen reaches the heart and brain. Such doses may result in acute poisoning with all the classic signs of shock: shallow breathing, weak pulse, cold and clammy skin, depressed reflexes. Coma and finally death—usually from respiratory failure—may occur unless hospital care is available in time.

Tolerance: With regular use the body gets so accustomed to the presence of the drug that ever larger or more frequent doses are needed to get the desired effects. Unfortunately, tolerance to the lethal level does not develop and as time goes on chronic users may find themselves close to a fatal dose before they get any effect at all. Accidental death may occur when the user is not certain about how much to take because of his increased tolerance, or because he becomes confused and does not remember taking a previous dose or how much of a dose was taken.

Dependence: Two kinds of dependence (addiction) may develop with abuse. Psychological (psychic) dependence, which can develop very quickly, occurs when there is a compulsive desire for the relaxing or hypnotic effects of the drug—a feeling that well-being or sleep is not possible without it. Physical dependence takes longer to develop and is far more dangerous. It occurs when the body has grown so used to the presence of the drug that it reacts violently if the drug is suddenly withdrawn or sharply reduced. Physical dependence on barbiturates and other sedative hypnotic drugs is one of the most dangerous of all drug dependencies.

Barbiturates and pregnancy: A woman who uses barbiturates regularly during pregnancy, especially in high doses, may endanger her baby. Congenital defects and abnormal behavior have been observed in such children. The drug is carried from the mother's bloodstream into the child's through the placenta and after birth the baby suffers the same withdrawal symptoms that are produced by all central nervous system depressants. These may include feeding difficulties, disturbed sleep patterns, breathing problems, irritability and fever.

Withdrawal symptoms: Once physical dependence has developed, suddenly stopping or sharply reducing daily barbiturate doses causes very severe withdrawal symptoms— worse than those that follow morphine or heroin withdrawal. They include anxiety, progressive weakness and restlessness, dizziness, visual distortion, nausea, vomiting, delirium and severe convulsions. With fast-acting barbiturates, reactions come to a peak in about two to three days. Reactions to withdrawal of slow-acting types take seven or eight days to reach their height. When dependence on barbiturates has been very deep, symptoms can last for several months. Treatment consists of slowly reducing the daily intake. While this does not eliminate suffering, it at least decreases the severity of the more serious reactions and lessens the danger of death while the body slowly adjusts. Death occurs in about 5 to 7% percent of those attempting withdrawal without treatment.

Interaction with other drugs: Barbiturate users often take other drugs as well. A common abuse pattern is to take AMPHETAMINES to wake up and to offset the morning-after barbiturate hangover. Then more barbiturates are needed to fall asleep and as the dose increases so does the need for more amphetamines until a vicious cycle develops. Alcohol and barbiturates are another common and dangerous mixture: each one enhances the effect of the other so that a dose of either one—not normally fatal taken alone—can cause death (see SYNERGY). Other drugs which interact with barbiturates are tranquilizers, antihistamines, and opiates which also depress the brain's control over breathing and increase the risk of respiratory failure.

Who uses barbiturates? According to one study, the elderly (especially women) received the most prescriptions for sedative hypnotics. Since age decreases the speed with which drugs are metabolized, people over 65 are particularly vulnerable to their toxic effects and to the development of dependence. In addition, some of the effects of these drugs are often mistaken for senility.

There has been a marked increase in abuse of barbiturates and other sedative hypnotic drugs among young people—even down to the grade school level. One Canadian study revealed that 12.8% of students in grades 7 to 12 had used prescribed barbiturates and 6.8% had used unprescribed pills.

Sources: Barbiturates are legitimately available only by prescription. Their manufacture is strictly controlled by the Drug Enforcement Administration under Schedule II of the Controlled Substances Act. Unlike amphetamines and narcotics, barbiturates are not illicitly manufactured in clandestine laboratories. The supplies that reach the black market are generally stolen or smuggled in from Colombia or Mexico. Government agencies estimate that about 20% of legally produced barbiturates are diverted through illicit channels.

Traffic and control: As with other dangerous drugs, illegal possession of barbiturates is a criminal offense. The charge is "possession" and the offender is subject to arrest. Without proof of intent to sell, however, sentences are often light.

Synonyms: Goof balls, barbs, downers, block busters, and numerous others. Terms tied in with the color of the capsules include: blues or blue devils (Amytal); Mexican reds, red birds or red devils (Seconal); yellow jackets (Nembutal); rainbows or Christmas trees (Tuinal); and purple hearts (Luminal).

History of Barbiturates	
1864	Two German scientists, von Mering and Fischer, synthesize barbital, a derivative of barbituric acid.
1903	Barbital is introduced to medicine under the trade name Veronal.
1912	Phenobarbital, a second derivative, is introduced under the trade name Luminal.
1930s	Barbiturates are widely prescribed in the U.S.
1940s	Studies show that barbiturates are intoxicating and addictive, and that withdrawal symptoms appear when use is stopped.
1942	First major campaign against nonmedical use of "thrill pills" is launched.
	States begin passing laws against nonprescription barbiturates, and black market becomes profitable.
1950s	Barbiturates become one of the major abused drugs in U.S.
1960s	Abuse spreads to youth.
1970s-1980s	Barbiturates still widely prescribed and abused. Government estimates that 20% of legally manufactured barbiturates is diverted into illicit channels.

behavioral learning theory   A psychological theory of alcoholism based on the assumption that alcoholics drink because alcohol consumption is followed by a reduction in anxiety and tension. Since alcohol is a sedative drug, this theory may also apply to the abuse of other sedative drugs. As more is understood about alcoholism, so the theory has become broader in concept. A number of behavior theorists now recognize that factors other than tension reduction may play an important role in the development of alcoholism, including peer pressure, heredity, family drinking styles, specific situational cues such as bars and cocktail parties, and so on. Because behavioral models propose that alcoholism is a conditioned behavioral response, it is suggested that alcoholism or other sedative drug abuse can be helped through modification of stimuli and reinforcement.

behavioral toxicity   Behavior that is destructive to the individual or those around him. When aberrant, damaging behavior is due to drug intoxication, withdrawal or overdose, it is more obvious than the impaired perceptions or mood changes caused by chronic use of a drug. If a person has hallucinations and does not act upon them, they would not be detected. If he responds to the hallucinatory event, the behavior becomes evident to others and may culminate in injury or incarceration.

beinsa   *Mitragyna speciosa,* a plant native to Burma. There are claims that it can produce sedative effects when chewed or brewed into a tea.

belladonna   A plant, *Atropa belladonna,* also called deadly nightshade, that has been known since the Middle Ages as a sedative and a poison. The Romans considered the pupil dilation caused by belladonna a mark of beauty. It can produce hallucinations with severe adverse reactions, and sometimes even extremely small doses can prove toxic. As little as 120 mg of plant material (less than the amount of material in a marijuana cigarette) may result in coma or death. There have been fatalities among children who have eaten deadly nightshade. It contains the alkaloids ATROPINE, HYOSCYAMINE and SCOPOLAMINE and these extracts are used today as ingredients in proprietary drugs. Other plants containing belladonna alkaloids are DATURA, HENBANE, MANDRAKE, PITURI and SCOPOLA.

Benzedrine® (Smith, Klein & French)   A brand of AMPHETAMINE sulfate. Generally used for weight control, it has a high potential for abuse and tolerance and extreme psychological dependence often occurs. Overdosage can result in insomnia, irritability and personality changes. It is available in 15 mg transparent capsules containing red and white grains, and in 5 and 10 mg peach–colored tablets. Synonyms: bennies, benz, peaches, roses, whites.

benzene   A toxic volatile hydrocarbon found in paint and varnish removers, gasolines and pesticides. It has an intoxicating effect when inhaled, and has consequently been abused. Prolonged inhalation can result in acute poisoning and liver damage. It is being decreasingly used in industry.

benzine   A volatile petroleum distillate used in motor fuels and numerous cleaning fluids. It produces intoxicating effects when inhaled. Acute poisoning can result from prolonged inhalation.

benzodiazepine   The chemical source of the class of DEPRESSANT drugs known as minor tranquilizers (or anxiolytics) which includes chlordiazepoxide (Librium), diazepam (Valium), oxazepam (Serax), clorazepate dipotassium (Tranxene) and others. Flurazepam (Dalmane), which is a sedative hypnotic, is also a benzodiazepine derivative. Stronger than meprobamate and tybamate, the benzodiazepine derivatives have gained popularity as safer substitutes for BARBITURATES. Australian authorities credit the replacement of barbiturates with benzodiazepine derivatives for the fall in the Australian suicide rate between 1962 and 1973.

Activity in the body: The benzodiazepine derivatives are readily absorbed in the gastrointestinal tract and quickly though unevenly distributed in the body. Metabolized in the liver and slowly excreted in the urine, they are central nervous system (CNS) depressants and act on the brain's limbic system, the center of emotional response. The usual half life is about one day.

Dosage: The usual dose in the treatment of mild to moderate anxiety is 5–10 mg from two to four times daily; 20–25 mg from three to four times daily is suggested for more severe cases. Daily doses of 300–600 mg over a period of five months are likely to produce physical dependence. No lethal dose has been established and the preference for the minor tranquilizers over barbiturates is largely due to their wide safety span. Overdose of a minor tranquilizer alone rarely causes death,

and for this reason they are considered suicide–proof drugs except when combined with other depressants.

Effects: The effects of the benzodiazepine derivatives closely resemble those of the barbiturates, though they produce less euphoria. Their effects manifest more slowly than barbiturates but they have a longer duration. The drugs relieve tension and anxiety due to emotional stress. They also relax muscular tension caused by anxiety, and have some muscle relaxant activity. They have very little effect on REM sleep in ordinary amounts.

Adverse reactions are rare but can include drowsiness, loss of coordination, confusion, constipation, depression, double vision, headache, rash, jaundice, tremors and—in large doses—fainting. Paradoxical hostility has also been reported.

Use of benzodiazepine derivatives involves a low risk of tolerance or the development of physical or psychological dependence, though these can occur with very high

Benzodiazepines

Generic name	Trade name	Special indication
Short half life (4–20 hours)		
Oxazepam	Serax	
Lorazepam	Ativan	
Temazepam	Restoril	Hypnotic
Alprazolam	Xanax	
Triazolam	Halcion	Hypnotic
Long half life (24-72 hours)		
Chlordiazepoxide	Librium	
Diazepam	Valium	Status Epilepticus
Clorazepate	Tranxene, Azene	
Flurazepam	Dalmane	Hypnotic
Clonazepam	Clonopin	Petit Mal
Prazepam	Verstram Centrax	
Haalzepam	Paxipam	

doses. This is another factor in doctors' preference for these drugs over barbiturates. When dependence does occur and the drug is stopped, cessation of administration is accompanied by withdrawal symptoms similar to but less severe than those seen in barbiturate and alcohol addicton: convulsions, tremors, muscular and abdominal cramps, vomiting, sweating, insomnia, loss of appetite, and the recurrence and aggravation of the patient's neurosis. These symptoms can last 7–10 days.

The mild tranquilizers are additive with alcohol and other CNS depressants (see SYNERGY), and should be administered very carefully, if at all, in combination with these drugs.

Usage: Medical applications of the benzodiazepine derivatives cover a wide range. Their most common use is as anxiolytics in the relief of symptoms of tension and anxiety resulting from neurosis or stressful circumstances. Other applications include treatment of convulsive disorders, neuromuscular and cardiovascular conditions, and gastrointestinal distress related to anxiety.

Knowledge of the advantages of the minor tranquilizers over barbiturates has spread beyond the medical community to drug abusers, and many of these drugs are available illicitly. Because they produce less euphoria and intoxication than barbiturates, abusers often take them in dangerous combination with other drugs, particularly alcohol; 10% of drivers arrested for DRIVING UNDER THE INFLUENCE have both alcohol and minor tranquilizers in their systems. Similarly, the minor tranquilizers have been used successfully in suicides (and accidental deaths) when ingested with alcohol.

benzoylecgonine   A cocaine metabolite which is looked for when testing an individual for drug use. Benzoylecgonine is invariably found in the urine of a cocaine user whether or not cocaine itself is present.

benzphetamine   A sympathomimetic amine with pharmacological activity similar to AMPHETAMINES. It is used as an anorectic for weight control and in the treatment of narcolepsy and has a significant potential for abuse. (See DIDREX.)

benzpyrene   A carcinogen in MARIJUANA and TOBACCO.

Beta Alcoholism   See JELLINEK.

biofeedback   A treatment method used in addict withdrawal and rehabilitation. It's aim is to increase motivation to tolerate withdrawal and decrease tension after physical withdrawal is complete. The patient is presented with his ongoing biological information (such as heart rate) by means of biofeedback machines using meters, lights, auditory signals, etc. The treatment then centers on the patient using this information to self–regulate the biological process and control certain autonomic functions. This method of self–regulation is similar to the ancient practice of yoga. The technique is not completely understood and the Biofeedback Society of America, founded in 1969, along with other medical organizations, is continuing to research the subject.

biological models   See PHYSIOLOGICAL ETIOLOGICAL MODELS.

Biphetamine® (Pennwalt)   A central nervous system stimulant that contains AMPHETAMINE and DEXTROAMPHETAMINE. It is used as an anorectic for weight control. Tolerance can develop within a few weeks and it has a high potential for abuse. Psychological dependence and social disability can occur. Overdosage can result in restlessness, tremors, hallucinations and coma. It is available as Biphetamine 7½ mg in white capsules; Biphetamine 12½ mg in black and white capsules; and Biphetamine 20 mg in black capsules. Synonyms: black beauties, blackbirds, black mollies.

black Americans   According to the National Institute on Drug Abuse, 61.2% of black males admitted to federally–funded drug abuse treatment programs in 1980 were admitted for heroin abuse, as opposed to 21.3% of white males. As with other available statistics, however, this figure may be the result of several factors unrelated to actual usage. There is a greater likelihood that a black addict will be arrested or otherwise become *known,* for instance. If there is indeed a higher proportion of heroin addicts among blacks it may well be the result of a difference in heroin distribution channels in recent years, and may not mean that there is a predilection for heroin among blacks. Primary heroin distribution centers for urban areas are often located in black sections. Because of this illicit drug traffic pattern, narcotic agents often follow traffickers into black ghettos and this may account for a heavy overrepresention of black addicts.

Treatment programs for black addicts have encountered difficulties in cases where METHADONE maintenance is suggested. It appears there is a general feeling that methadone maintenance is a conspiracy against the black community. It is widely believed, for instance, that methadone renders males impotent and causes both males and females to become sterile. Although these beliefs have been proved false, there is still concern among black community leaders that those who control methadone programs are misusing the programs to repress the communities.

In the case of alcoholism rates, there are no significant differences in those for black males and white males, though the latest government report shows there has been an increase in the problems and consequences of alcoholism in the last 10 years. As with the white community, alcoholism is a serious problem. Among blacks it is particularly se-

rious, however, because the mortality rate for CIRRHOSIS is nearly twice as high as it is for whites. Studies have suggested that blacks are also more susceptible to CANCER of the upper digestive tract. Blacks suffer as well from a significantly higher rate of hypertension, which is further complicated by drinking. The black community also has a significantly higher rate of alcohol–related homicides.

Theorists suggest that drinking problems among blacks may date back to the "slave era": blacks were sometimes encouraged to drink on weekends as a way of keeping them pacified and under control. This pattern of weekend drinking exists today in some black communities where many liquor stores only open on weekends. Economic frustration and racism no doubt account for many cases of drug use and drinking, especially in black ghettos where living conditions may be intolerable and life pervaded by a general sense of powerlessness. There is also the question of status. Drinking certain kinds of liquor and buying rounds for friends may provide social status. Black Americans buy 30% of the nation's scotch, for example.

Among black adolescents there is reported to be a higher abstention rate and a lower rate of heavy drinking than among whites. Due to social, economic and family problems this tendency changes and there is a higher rate of alcoholism among young black adults.

There is a high rate of heavy drinking among black women (11% compared with 4% of white women) and it has increased over the last 10 years. This fact is supported by studies that show black women to have lower expectations about life than white women. There is also a higher rate of abstainers among black women—51% compared with 39% of white women. Economic and domestic problems drive some black women to heavy drinking, while the same stresses cause others to abstain from alcohol altogether and focus on a "happier hereafter."

As is the case with drugs, treatment programs for alcoholism are not recognized or accepted in many black communities, probably because there is often more tolerance for drunks than in white communities. Alcoholics Anonymous (AA) groups, for instance, are sometimes perceived by blacks as being strictly white middle–class institutions. Blacks are also less likely to have insurance to pay for alcohol treatment services, and they may lack knowledge about free social services. It should be noted, however, that blacks who are admitted to hospitals and clinics show a stronger motivation to abstain and cooperate more fully in treatment than do white alcoholics.

blackout' A memory disturbance commonly suffered by chronic alcoholics and not uncommonly by nonalcoholics in conjunction with bouts of extremely heavy drinking over a short period of time. Blackout consists of an individual's inability to recall entire blocks of time during which he was fully conscious, and seems related to the impairment of the brain's information transfer facilities to long–term memory stores. An early sign of progressive alcoholism, the risk of blackout is increased by factors such as fatigue and stress and by the combination of alcohol with such drugs as sedatives, tranquilizers and marijuana. Blackouts are called alcohol amnestic disorder in DSM III (Diagnostic and Statistical Manual, Third Edition).

blood alcohol concentration (BAC)

The degree of a person's intoxication can be measured by the concentration of alcohol in his bloodstream. Blood alcohol concentration (BAC), also referred to as blood alcohol level (BAL), measures the weight of the alcohol in a fixed volume of blood.

BAC tests are most often given to motorists suspected of DRIVING WHILE INTOXICATED (DWI), but they are also used in alcohol treatment centers and medical facilities as guides for the treatment of inebriated patients. The percentages of BAC are expressed differently throughout the world: in the United States, for example, BAC for seven parts of alcohol per 10,000 parts of blood is expressed as .07%; in Canada the equivalent would be 70 milligrams per 100 milliliters of blood and would be expressed as 70 mg%; in Sweden it would be recorded as 0.7 promille.

In DWI tests, the percentage necessary for a person to be considered legally intoxicated varies from state to state; from .08% in Idaho and Utah to .10% in the District of Columbia and most other states. A person's BAC can be determined by testing his breath or urine as well as by giving a blood test. Breath analyzers have come into common use, particularly for on–the–spot analysis.

A number of factors contribute to a person's BAC:

(1) Weight: The larger and heavier a person is, the greater his or her blood supply, thus more alcohol can be accommodated. Fatty tissue is a major determinant of a BAC level. Since excess weight is stored in the form of fat, an overweight person's blood supply is not increased in proportion to the additional weight. Therefore a fat person can have a higher BAC than a lean person of the same weight from a given amount of alcohol.

(2) Sex: BAC is generally higher for women because women usually have a larger percentage of fatty tissue than men.

(3) Time of consumption: Unless alcohol consumption is limited to less than one full drink an hour, BAC will generally continue to climb. Alcohol is slowly excreted by the body in the following way: oxidization by the liver 95%; breath 2%; urine 2%; perspiration 1%.

(4) Food consumption: Although the effect of food on BAC varies from individual to individual, in general a full stomach will help to retard the absorption of alcohol.

(5) Quantity: Drink equivalents vary from 1½ ounces of "hard" liquor (gin, scotch, etc.) to 5 ounces of table wine to 12 ounces of normal–strength beer. Two to four 1½–ounce shots of hard liquor, and the equivalent in wine or beer, are close to the danger limit for drivers.

blood alcohol level (BAL)   See BLOOD ALCOHOL CONCENTRATION (BAC).

blood sugar   An alcoholic will sometimes suffer from hypoglycemia, a low concentration of sugar in the blood. The condition is apparently due to the interference of alcohol with the normal conversion of carbohydrates into sugar. Alcohol may also indirectly stimulate the hormone insulin, which works to lower blood sugar. Inadequate food intake, common in alcoholics, can also contribute to hypoglycemia. Low blood sugar is also thought to be a possible cause of the HANGOVER effect.

B'nai B'rith International   An international service organization established in 1843 to unite world Jewry for the advancement of the Jewish people and to help create a better world for all. CVS, the Community Volunteer Services of B'nai B'rith, suggests that alcoholism is probably a greater problem than other areas of drug abuse and has begun a concentrated program of prevention. Focusing on a mass media information campaign, the program includes the distribution of literature directed at both the Jewish and general communities.

BNDD   The Bureau of Narcotics and Dangerous Drugs, now called the Drug Enforcement Administration (DEA).

B & O Supprettes® (Webcon)   A narcotic analgesic containing powdered OPIUM and BELLADONNA extract. It is used rectally for minor to severe pain, and can be habit–forming. Overdosage results in respiratory depression.

Boggs Amendment   An amendment to the HARRISON NARCOTICS ACT of 1914, the NARCOTIC DRUGS IMPORT AND EXPORT ACT of 1922, and the MARIJUANA TAX ACT of 1937. Enacted in 1951, the amendment increased the penalties for all drug violations. Reflecting the increased concern over drug addiction after World War II, it lumped together—for the first time—marijuana and narcotic drugs and established uniform penalties for offenses: a mandatory minimum sentence of two years for first "narcotic" violators and up to 10 years' imprisonment for repeat offenders. These penalties were raised in 1956 by the Narcotic Drug Control Act.

BOL–148   A congener of LSD–25, d–2–bromolysergic acid tartrate. It is a hallucinogen.

Bolivia   Coca cultivation and consumption have been traditional for centuries in Bolivia, but licit demands for coca account for only 12,000 of the estimated 50,500 metric tons that are produced annually. Along with Peru and Colombia, Bolivia is responsible for the majority of cocaine on the world market (see Appendix 3, Tables 39, 43 and 44). Most of the coca cultivated in Bolivia is processed and distributed by Colombia.

Bolivia has averaged more than one government per year since the republic was founded in 1825, and after each change attempts by the U.S. government to resume coca control must begin all over again. Narcotics assistance programs were begun in Bolivia in 1972, for instance, and in 1977 there was an agreement that provided for narcotics control assistance and a study of alternate crops. But a coup by General Garcia Meza in 1980 halted these activities; allegedly Meza had the support of a Mafia group who dominated the cocaine trade. Currently, the Bureau of International Narcotics Matters (INM) is discussing an eradication program which would reduce Bolivia's coca cultivation to a licit level. The program includes both voluntary and mandatory crop eradication and controls. There are an estimated 23,000 farm families growing coca, usually on small holdings of one hectare (2.47 acres) or less. The large number of landowners complicates the eradication problem.

Bontril PDM® (Carnrick)   A brand of phendimetrazine tartrate; a stimulant used as an anorectic for weight control. Its activity is similar to that of AMPHETAMINES and tolerance to its effects develops within a few weeks. It has a potential for abuse and can cause personality changes, insomnia, irritability and hyperactivity. Overdosage can result in rapid respiration, hallucinations, restlessness and tremor. It is available in three–layer green, white and yellow tablets.

booting   Attempting to prolong the initial effects of a HEROIN injection by injecting a small amount, then withdrawing blood back into the syringe and repeating the process.

booze   As a verb it means to guzzle or drink to excess, usually to get drunk quickly. As a noun, it is an alcoholic beverage, often whiskey, such as that made around 1840 by a Philadelphia distiller named E. G. Booze. Both the verb and the noun predate Mr. Booze by many centuries. It was formerly spelled "boose" from early Germanic sources. From booze comes other terms: "boozing it up," "boozer," and so on.

Bowery   A section and street in lower Manhattan, populated largely by derelicts. Although it has been partially rehabilitated, it is still an impoverished area and contains a large SKID ROW secton. Its inhabitants are the source of the term "Bowery bum." The area was formerly notorious for its cheap theaters, dance halls and drinking gardens.

brain   A part of the CENTRAL NERVOUS SYSTEM (CNS), which is made up of the brain and spinal cord. The brain controls almost all the functions of the body through its nerve cell network which reaches all the tissues, and through its regulation of the endocrine hormones.

The brain consists of some 12 billion cells, and has a complex chemistry that is only now being explored. Stimulation of a neuron results in an electrical transmission through the long cell axons that extend from the nerve cell. Transmission from one neuron to another is a chemical process across a microscopic gap (or synaptic cleft) between the cells. We are aware of numerous neurotransmitters (also called biogenic amines) that carry the signal across the gap. They include dopamine, norepinephrine, serotonin and acetylcholine. It is suspected that hundreds of neurochemicals are present in various parts of the brain.

Not all substances in the bloodstream enter the neuron. A blood–barrier exists that keeps certain molecules out—proteins, for example. All drugs that have an effect on brain function will, of course, pass the blood–brain barrier. The drugs that are abused usually affect synaptic transmission, others impact on cell membrane permeability.

Alcohol

Ethanol affects the neuronal membrane, delaying the exchange of ions and thereby diminishing its electrical excitation. Alcohol interferes with the cell's ability to utilize oxygen and glucose which leads to malfunction and eventually death of the neuron. This explains the brain atrophy seen in chronic alcoholics. A certain amount of function can be regained if the alcoholic becomes abstinent: in this case the remaining neurons take over the lost cell's functions.

Marijuana

The precise way in which cannabis affects the brain is not known. Many mental functions are affected by marijuana intoxication, including immediate recall, sensory perception, tracking, attention span, etc. The heavy, consistent ingestion of marijuana produces a chronic cannabis syndrome (amotivational syndrome) in certain people. Since it is LIPID SOLUBLE and the nerve cell membrane is lipid, the drug seems to be retained in the brain for longer periods than alcohol. Studies that show distortions of synaptic structure are suggestive of marijuana's effect, but further work is needed.

Cocaine and amphetamines

Both drugs make dopamine available at the pleasure centers of the brain in excessive quantities, leading to euphoria, and later paranoid psychosis and depression.

LSD and other hallucinogens

Serotonin antagonism may account for the unusual mental effects of these drugs.

Heroin

Heroin is locked into specific opiate binding sites and exerts its euphoriant, analgesic and sleep–inducing activity on that basis.

Benzodiazepines

A specific benzodiazepine receptor site has been identified. When occupied by a benzodiazepine, reduction of anxiety and tension results.

Barbiturates

Like alcohol, barbiturates appear to act on the cell membrane. They have effects similar to alcohol on brain cell transmission and the withdrawal syndrome (the DTs) is identical to alcohol withdrawal symptoms which confirms the idea that both drugs have similar mechanisms.

(See also individual drug categories and CENTRAL NERVOUS SYSTEM.)

breathalyzers   Machines which detect and measure the blood alcohol concentration (BAC) of a person. They have been used for a number of years by law enforcement agencies in an effort to crack down on drunk drivers. The readings are based on a solid state, semi–conductor reaction to alcohol present in the breath. Recently a portable, handheld breathalyzer has begun to gain popularity in high schools. A number of schools which have purchased them admit that they are reluctant to use them but they hope the presence of a breathalyzer at the school and the students' awareness of the fact will deter alcohol use during school hours. Although there have been no major complaints, it has been hinted that the use of breathalyzers in schools may be the source of potential conflicts over constitutional rights. Breathalyzers are being utilized increasingly by the military, and in areas where the public is at risk.

Breath alcohol has a constant ratio to blood alcohol levels. Breath alcohol levels are multiplied by a factor of 2,300 to obtain blood alcohol levels.

breech births   Studies have shown that breech births, in which a fetus emerges with the buttocks, knees or feet appearing first, are significantly higher among mothers addicted to narcotics. (See PREGNANCY for other effects of narcotic use among pregnant women.)

Brevital Sodium® (Lilly)   An intravenous anesthetic containing methohexital sodium. A rapid, ultra–short acting BARBITURATE, it is used for short surgical procedures. It may be habit–forming but the rapid onset of effects and brief duration of action makes it less desirable for purposes of abuse.

British System, the   In Great Britain the treatment of opiate users is medically oriented and addicts are allowed to obtain and use opiates legally. Widely praised by advocates of heroin maintenance, the system has been recommended as a model for implementation in the United States. The British

System has been credited with limiting the use of heroin, preventing the development of a black market, reducing drug–related crimes, and enabling addicts to lead more useful lives.

Before 1967, the system was simply a policy that allowed private physicians to prescribe maintenance doses to opiate users. As heroin abuse increased during the 1960s, however, the approach was altered and in 1967 a government–sponsored program was established. The new program imposed stricter controls on the manufacture, sale and possession of opiate drugs, and required addicts to be registered and treated through clinics or through specially licensed physicians.

It is of interest that the British System of heroin maintenance has become a methadone maintenance system. In 1980, 2,095 of the 2,846 patients in treatment received methadone alone; others received methadone in combination with other drugs; and only 53 patients were given heroin alone.

The British System remains highly controversial, and while some observers view government clinics as a sensible and humane approach to the problem, others maintain that the clinics are not abstinence–oriented and do not handle the problem of addiction. (See also UNITED KINGDOM.)

bromides   A group of synthetic sedative hypnotic DEPRESSANTS derived from bromine. Introduced to medicine in 1857 as a treatment for epilepsy, bromides were later widely prescribed as sedatives, though rarely used as hypnotics. Bromides are now considered obsolete and have been replaced by BARBITURATES and BENZODIAZEPINES.

Activity: Bromides are readily absorbed into the bloodstream and have a 12–day half–life. They appear in mother's milk and cross the placental barrier.

Effects: Bromides depress the central nervous system but, like paraldehyde, have little or no effect on the medullary centers

and thus do not affect breathing or circulation. In low doses bromides have a typical sedative effect, causing drowsiness and loss of muscular coordination. The substance is cumulatively toxic, however, and larger doses can, paradoxically, cause confusion and agitation.

Dependence can occur, resulting in a disease similar to alcoholism called bromism. Symptoms include tremors, skin rashes, dizziness, delirium and lethargy. Coma and death can result.

Usage: Bromides have been used medically as antiemetics (to suppress vomiting), aphrodisiacs, anticonvulsants and sedatives but they are rarely used nowadays. They are not often used for recreational purposes.

Bromides are not subject to the Controlled Substances Act.

Brompton Cocktail   A variable mixture of drugs used in British and American hospices to control terminal pain associated with cancer. Traditionally, it contained heroin, cocaine and an antiemetic like Thorazine. Morphine is equally effective as heroin when given orally after dosage adjustment. Cocaine has been dropped from the formulation in many hospices.

bruxism   See TOOTH GRINDING.

Buff–A–Comp® (Mayrand)   A buffered analgesic containing aspirin, caffeine, phenacetin and the intermediate–acting BARBITURATE, butalbital. It may be habit–forming and has the potential for abuse. It is also available in capsules and tablets containing 30 mg of codeine in additon to the above ingredients.

bufotenine   A HALLUCINOGEN found in the skin glands of certain toads, as well as in several plant species. In Haiti and parts of Central and South America, natives use a snuff, Cohoba, which contains bufotenine as

well as DMT and other hallucinogenic substances. Bufotenine produces an LSD–like
experience though the illusionary disturbances are less complex. Physical effects are
pronounced. The user experiences walking
difficulties and paralysis and the face may
swell and redden. Typically, the physical effects of the drug appear first. As the effects
wane, the user falls into a stupor–like sleep.
Synonym: Yopo (for Cohoba).

buprenorphine   A NARCOTIC ANTAGO-
NIST.

**Bureau of Narcotics and Dangerous
Drugs (BNDD)**   A law enforcement
agency in the U.S. Department of Justice
which was created in 1968. It was replaced
in 1973 by the Drug Enforcement Administration (DEA).

Bureau of Narcotics, Federal   A government agency within the Treasury Department created in 1930. Its goal was to investigate, detect, and prevent violations of laws
prohibiting unauthorized possession, sale or
transfer of opium, opium derivatives, synthetic opiates, cocaine and marijuana. Transferred in 1968 to the Department of Justice,
it was merged with the Bureau of Drug Abuse
Control to form the Bureau of Narcotics and
Dangerous Drugs. This bureau, in turn, was
replaced by the Drug Enforcement Administration (DEA).

business   Drug abuse is having an astro-
nomical effect on American business and the
American economy. Not only is drug abuse
causing lost productivity, its effects are
mushrooming throughout other areas of
business. A government–sponsored survey
by the Research Triangle Group in 1977
showed that the total cost to the economy
(adjusted to reflect 1983 dollars due to inflation) is conservatively estimated at $25 bil-

lion. A breakdown includes the following
categories:

Lost productivity: Absenteeism, nearly $5
billion; drug–related deaths, $1.3 billion;
imprisonment, $2.1 billion; and the loss of
employees who left the job to find more lucrative methods (often criminal) to support
their habits, $8.3 billion.

Medical expenses: Treatment in hospitals,
by private doctors, and in rehabilitation centers, $1.9 billion; Employee Assistance Pro-
grams research and training, and the administration of other programs, $367 million.

Crime: Court, police, and prison costs on
all levels (federal, state and local), $5.2 bil-
lion; crime prevention methods (locks, alarm
systems, etc.), $1.6 billion; and the destruc-
tion of property during drug–related criminal
acts, $113 million.

It has been suggested that these incredible
costs to business reflect the fact that previous
high school age drug abusers are now a part
of the U.S. work force. This additional population compounds the loss in productivity
created by older drug users on the work
force.

Alcohol, the most abused drug, was recognized as a problem in industry as long ago
as the 1930s and 1940s, and steps were taken
to deal with it (see EMPLOYEE ASSISTANCE
PROGRAMS). Today the problem of abuse
also includes illicit drugs, such as cocaine,
marijuana, and prescription drugs (particularly amphetamines). They present an entirely different problem. Because these drugs
are illegal, they are usually used secretly and
identifying employees involved in such drug
abuse is more difficult. There is also the expense factor. While alcohol is relatively inexpensive, an illicit drug habit can easily become more than a person can handle on his
or her salary. The cocaine habit, in particular, can cost hundreds of dollars a day to
support.

Drug abuse is not centered around a particular level of employment; nor are actual

working hours particularly relevant. Secretaries will use drugs (particularly marijuana) on a lunch break; nightshift workers will take amphetamines to stay awake; high–level executives will snort cocaine in the morning to "get going" and will continue to snort the drug during the day to "stay on top." Drug abuse is also becoming common practice in *all* occupations. Even the medical profession is not exempt, although doctors see the consequences of abuse more than anyone. Perhaps the pressure, stress and long hours involved in medical practice are responsible, perhaps it is the availability of drugs. Whatever the reason, it has been suggested that nearly 4% of doctors and nurses are drug dependent. The consequences of drug use by members of the medical profession could be staggering when one considers the importance of clear judgement in saving lives.

In the area of car production, one of the biggest industries in the U.S., it has been suggested that the poor quality and low sales of American cars are related to the problem of drug abuse among employees and that this problem accounts for the success of imported cars. The problem is not always limited to employees on the assembly line but extends to office personnel; they may cost a company money because of poor bookkeeping. Surveys have shown that drug abusing employees perform at only 67% of their ability. In order for the American car industry to remain in business, it has been suggested that these employees be weeded out or rehabilitated.

Companies are increasingly employing drug detection tests, usually blood and urine tests. These tests are generally performed on employees who exhibit the following symptoms: requests for late arrivals and early departures; requests for time off; numerous sick days; and those who are more likely to file a workmen's compensation claim in case of accidents. Companies also are looking for other tell–tale signs among drug abusers:

pupil changes, odors, chain smokers who do not use filter tips, and constant licking of the lips. Investigations are also often instigated by other employees who complain about the performance of fellow employees because they are tired of "covering" for them.

The implementation of Employee Assistance Programs can save billions of dollars annually among large corporations. Dr. Robert G. Wiencek, associated with General Motors, states that "for every $1 invested in treatment, General Motors can identify $3 in return for full–time employees who recover completely."

Unless a worker has union backing, or an employment contract that will help defend him, he has little legal protection against drug tests or "the right to search." Workers have occasionally sued for "invasion of privacy" and "defamation of character"; court battles are time–consuming and corporation practices have often been found negligent.

The biggest problems to American industry are loss of productivity and accidents, but there is also the additional problem of theft. Drug habits are expensive and there is a clear relationship between heavy drug use and crime. Employees not only embezzle money, they also take company property and are often involved in "company kickbacks."

Employee Assistance Programs seem to be one of the best answers to industry's drug–related problems. The General Motors program is well known; the company set up its original alcohol–based programs in 1972 and in 1975 expanded them to include the abuse of other drugs. Unfortunately, despite widespread reports of success and many fully recovered drug abusers, many companies do not want to get involved in treatment programs—possibly because the monetary value of treatment programs is sometimes difficult or impossible to evaluate, or because the company feels it is too small to take on such projects. Small– to medium–sized industries are often the most difficult to reach because of monetary considerations. (See also AB-SENTEEISM and ACCIDENTS.)

butabarbital   An intermediate–acting barbiturate which produces mild sedation and has muscle–relaxing properties. (See BARBI-TURATES.)

butalbital   An intermediate–acting barbiturate used as a sedative hypnotic. (See BAR-BITURATES and BUFF–A–COMP.)

Buticaps® (McNeil)   A central nervous system depressant containing the intermediate–acting BARBITURATE sodium butabarbital. It is used for sedation and hypnotic purposes and psychological dependence can occur. Overdosage can result in severe respiratory depression. It is available in 15 mg lavender and white capsules; 30 mg green and white capsules; 50 mg orange and white capsules; and 100 mg pink and white capsules.

Butisol Sodium® (McNeil)   A central nervous system depressant that contains the intermediate–acting BARBITURATE sodium butabarbital. It is used for sedation and hypnotic purposes and may be habit–forming. Psychological dependence can occur. Overdosage can result in severe respiratory depression. It is available in green elixir, 30 mg per 5 ml with 7% alcohol, and in tablets: 15 mg lavender; 30 mg green; 50 mg orange; and 100 mg pink.

butyl alcohol   A solvent made by the fermentation of glucose. It should not be confused with ETHANOL, the principal chemical in alcoholic beverages.

butyl nitrite   An inhalant drug that first appeared in 1969 and which is similar to AMYL NITRITE. Classified as a volatile inhalant, butyl nitrite inhalation produces a brief but intense lightheaded feeling, the result of

lowered blood pressure and relaxation of smooth (involuntary) muscles of the body.

C

caffeine (1, 3, 7–trimethylxanthine)   A naturally occurring alkaloid found in many plants throughout the world, caffeine was first isolated from coffee in 1820 and from tea leaves in 1827. Both "coffee" and "caffeine" are derived from the Arabic word *gahweh* (pronounced "kehveh" in Turkish).

Caffeine is a STIMULANT of the CENTRAL NERVOUS SYSTEM. When taken in beverage form, it begins to reach all the body tissues within five minutes; peak blood levels are reached in about 30 minutes. Caffeine has a half–life in the body of about three and a half hours. Normally caffeine is rapidly and completely absorbed from the gastrointestinal tract. Little can be recovered unchanged in urine and there is no day–to–day accumulation of the drug in the body.

Caffeine increases the heart rate and rhythm, affects the circulatory system and acts as a diuretic. It also stimulates gastric acid secretion. There may be an elevation in blood pressure, especially during stress. Caffeine inhibits glucose metabolism and may thereby raise blood sugar levels.

A behavioral stimulant which interferes with sleep and may postpone fatigue, caffeine appears to interact with stress—improving intellectual performance in extroverts and impairing it in introverts. When taken before bedtime caffeine usually delays the onset of sleep, shortens sleep time and reduces the average "depth of sleep." It also increases the amount of dream sleep (REM) early in the night while reducing it overall.

Fatalities resulting from caffeine poisoning are rare: only seven deaths have been recorded to date. The lowest known fatal dose is 3.2 grams administered intravenously. The fatal oral dose appears to be of the order of 10 grams.

While caffeine in moderate doses can increase alertness and talkativeness and decrease fatigue, regular use of 350 mg or more a day results in a form of physical dependence. Interruption of such use can result in withdrawal symptoms, the most prominent of which is sometimes quite severe headache—which can be relieved by taking caffeine. Irritability and fatigue are other symptoms. The regular use of caffeine produces partial tolerance to some or all of its effects.

Regular use of over 600 mg a day (approximately eight cups of percolated coffee) may cause chronic insomnia, breathlessness, persistent anxiety and depression, mild delirium and stomach upset. It may also cause heart disease; researchers at Johns Hopkins University School of Hygiene and Public Health found a modest association between heavy coffee drinking (considered to be five cups or more per day) and myocardial infarction in young women (a condition in the heart muscle resulting from the formation of a blood clot in the coronary arterial system.) Excessive use of caffeine has been suspected as a factor in cancer of the bladder and renal pelvis, but the evidence is inconclusive. In addition, caffeine consumption has been linked to fibrocystic disease in women, but, again, the evidence so far is inconclusive.

Studies have also indicated that heavy use of caffeine in amounts equivalent to eight or more regular cups of coffee a day is responsible for an increased incidence of spontaneous abortions and stillbirths, breech deliveries, and cyanosis at birth.

Caffeine is probably the most popular drug in the world. It is primarily consumed in tea and coffee but is also present in cola drinks, cocoa, certain headache pills, diet pills, and patent stimulants such as Vivarin and Nodoz. Caffeine belongs to the family of methylxanthines. Theophylline and theobromine are closely related compounds but caffeine is the most potent of the group.

The following chart shows the caffeine content of various products:

Product	Caffeine (mgs)
Coffee (5 oz.)	
Regular Brewed	
percolated	110
dripolator	150
Instant	66
Decaf Brewed	4.5
Instant Decaf	2
Soft Drinks (12 oz.)	
Dr. Pepper	61
Mr. Pibb	57
Mountain Dew	49
Tab	45
Coca–Cola	42
RC Cola	36
Pepsi–Cola	35
Diet Pepsi	34
Pepsi Light	34
Instant/Brewed Tea	
(5 min. brew)	45
Cocoa (5 oz.)	13
Milk Chocolate	6
(1 oz.)	
Drugs	
Vivarin Tablets	200
Nodoz	100
Excedrin	65
Vanquish	33
Empirin Compound	32
Anacin	32
Dristan	16.2

Sara J. Carrillo, "Caffeine Versus the Body," *PharmChem Newsletter*, Vol. 10, No. 3 (April 1981).

"Facts About Caffeine" (Toronto, Canada: Addiction Research Foundation of Ontario, January 1980).

M.B. McGee, "Caffeine Poisoning in a 19–Year–Old Female," *Journal of Foren-*

sic Sciences, Vol. 24, No. 1 (January 1980).

Mark Wenneker, "Breast Lumps: Is Caffeine the Culprit?" *Nutrition Action* (August 1980) (Publication of Center for Science in the Public Interest).

Caines   A group of synthetic local anesthetics that are sometimes used as adulterants of cocaine. They include Novocaine, Pontocaine and Lidocaine and provide the numbness, and perhaps a little of the euphoria of cocaine. They are to be found in the "legal cocaines" advertised in publications that specialize in drug paraphernalia. They are cocaine look–alikes and sound–alikes with names like "cococaine," "snowcaine," etc.

calabar bean   Seeds of the plant *Physostigma venenosum,* which is native to the West Indies. The seeds contain physostigmine, an inhibitor of the enzyme that breaks down acetylcholine, and therefore cause severe adverse reactions.

California poppy   There are unconfirmed claims that smoking the poppy *Eschscholtzia californica* can produce narcotic–like effects.

calorie   A unit of measure used to express the heat– or energy–producing value of food when it is metabolized in the body. Absolute alcohol, on the average, contains about 150 to 200 calories an ounce. Calories contained in alcohol are so–called empty calories because they cannot be stored and do not produce essential vitamins for the body's nutritional needs. The body burns alcohol before it burns food which is stored and used as fat. Prolonged consumption of heavy amounts of alcohol while cutting down on food can lead to malnutrition and avitamenosis, a condition frequently seen in alcoholics.

Canada   The patterns and trends of drug abuse in Canada tend to follow those of the United States, probably because of the geographical proximity, but to a much lesser extent. As in the U.S. smoking and drinking are the two major health problems; but there has been increasing use of marijuana, heroin and methaqualone.

It is estimated that 1.5 million Canadians (out of a total population of 20 million) have used marijuana at some time; a government survey in 1973 reported 45,000 *known* users and over 10,000 convictions on marijuana–related charges. Regarding heroin, the survey reported 7,719 *known* users. The survey also reported 10,000 known users of other hallucinogens, particularly LSD, PCP and MDA. The use of inhalants was also reported but to a far lesser degree. An earlier survey had shown an increase in the abuse of methaqualone which led to the establishment of a methaqualone treatment program in 1971.

There was a movement in Canada, as there is in the United States, toward the legalization of marijuana. The federal Commission of Inquiry into the Non–Medical Use of Drugs (commonly called the Le Dain Commission) which is conducting a continuing study, suggested that while marijuana should not be legalized, penalties for possession cases should be reduced—no jail sentences for first offenders—and that research on the subject be continued and expanded. As a result of the study, considerable discretion is now used in possession cases. However, convictions for trafficking, importing, exporting and growing marijuana can result in prison terms of up to seven years. If the charges concern narcotics or other dangerous drugs, the penalty can be seven years to life imprisonment.

Treatment programs in Canada generally center around the problem of heroin addiction; methadone maintenance is generally used. It should be noted, however, that there has been an increase in methadone abuse recently.

Attitudes toward alcohol consumption, which is one of the country's major health problems, are becoming more liberal as they are in most other developed Western countries. Between 1950 and 1980 there was an increase in drinking among youth and women—groups that in the past did not generally drink—and the number of abstainers may have dropped by 50%. Canada's drinking pattern is one of increased consumption on weekends and holidays, though only one–sixth of the consumption takes place in public places. Beer is the most popular drink. Proportions of alcoholic beverages consumed breaks down to 50% beer, 40% distilled spirits, and 10% wine, with the latter two on the increase. Per capita consumption, on a national level, rose 34% between 1966 and 1974. Between 1975 and 1979 sales of alcoholic beverages by value rose 46%, from $2.9 billion to $4.37 billion.

There are no estimates of the national alcoholism rate in Canada, but a survey in Ontario—the most populous province—in 1976 suggested that alcoholics numbered 2.7% of the province's total population. A conservative estimate of the entire country put the total of alcoholics at 617,000. There is an acknowledged need for comprehensive training programs to deal with the problem and there are agencies responsible for combating abuse on both the federal and provincial levels. But while most of the provinces maintain research foundations, health facilities and education programs, formal policies aimed at reducing abuse appear to be lacking. In many provinces voluntary and charitable organizations, such as the Salvation Army and Alcoholics Anonymous, have been the most successful in addressing the problem.

Canary Island Broom   *Genista canariensis.* There are claims that when smoked or taken orally, this plant can produce narcotic–like effects. It is poisonous even in low doses.

cancer   The primary drugs of abuse which seem to be directly related to cancer are alcohol and tobacco—the two most abused drugs in the United States. Recent studies have shown that heavy drinkers who also smoke have a higher incidence of cancer than drinkers who do not smoke or smokers who do not drink. Compared to the rest of the population, alcoholics and heavy drinkers show a high incidence of mortality from cancer of the mouth, pharynx, larynx, esophagus, liver and lungs. Cancer associated with alcohol accounts for 6.1% to 27.9% of the total incidence of all cancer. It has been difficult to separate the effects of drinking from the effects of smoking because most heavy drinkers are also heavy smokers. Alcohol itself has not been shown to be an independent carcinogen, but it is thought to act as a co–carcinogen—a substance that promotes cancer in conjunction with a carcinogen. Studies have indicated that alcohol and cigarettes act synergistically to increase carcinogenic potential, particularly in cancers of the mouth and throat. It has been suggested that the combination of drinking and smoking increases the risk of throat and mouth cancer 15 times above that of the non–smoking non–drinking population.

Studies of marijuana smokers and the incidence of cancer are few and inconclusive; in fact, THC (the active ingredient in marijuana) is sometimes prescribed for cancer patients as a treatment for the nausea and vomiting caused by chemotherapy.

During the 1950s and 1960s extensive studies provided conclusive evidence that cigarette smoking was directly related to lung cancer, heart disease, emphysema and chronic bronchitis. It was further shown that cigarette smoking during pregnancy was hazardous to the unborn child. (See NICOTINE.)

Hepatoma (primary liver cancer) is often accompanied by and probably preceded by CIRRHOSIS. Studies have shown that 64% to 90% of victims suffer from both conditions.

It has been suggested that liver cancer proceeds in two stages: liver damage due to alcoholism, followed by intervention of a secondary agent which sets off the actual malignancy.

A number of theories seek to explain the increased incidence of cancer in alcoholics and/or smokers. Inadequate nutrition is one of them: lack of nutritious food weakens the body's immune defense system, leaving it vulnerable to cancer–causing agents. Another theory suggests that alcohol itself causes cancer. Known carcinogens have been found in many alcoholic beverages; beer, for example, has been found to contain asbestos fibers from the filters used in its manufacture. Alcohol has also been shown to have an effect on the cell membranes, possibly increasing the ability of carcinogens to affect the cells themselves. Alcohol may also dissolve water–insoluble carcinogens making them more available to various organs.

cannabinoids   Derivatives of CANNABIS. Cannabis contains some 60 cannabinoids.

cannabis   The Indian hemp plant, *Cannabis sativa.* The resin, flowering tops, leaves and stems contain the psychoactive substance delta–9–TETRAHYDROCANNABINOL (THC).

Cannabis sativa, which probably originated in Central Asia, grows wild practically anywhere but flourishes in temperate and tropical climates. The resin contains the highest concentration of THC; plants grown in very hot, dry climates produce the most resin and are therefore most potent. An herbaceous annual with palm–like leaves, male and female plants occur separately. The female plant is taller, broader and longer–lived than the male and produces more leaves and resin. Although the plant can reach 30 feet, average height is four to eight feet, and it has a hollow, six–sided base that is at least two inches in diameter at maturity.

Cannabis occurs in a variety of grades, depending on climate and method of cultivation, and can be processed to yield several different forms of graduated strength. Plants cultivated for the hemp fiber contain only .05% THC. The name marijuana refers to the leaves and flowering tops which are dried and shredded and usually consumed orally— either smoked in cigarettes or pipes, or prepared in foods or beverages such as tea. It typically contains 0.5–5% THC. Ghanga, which is cultivated and consumed primarily in Jamaica, is made from the flowering tops, leaves and top stems of a specially cultivated female plant and contains about 5–8% THC. Hashish (or charas) consists of the resin of the plant mixed with a binding agent and contains about 10% THC. Hash oil is the most potent form of cannabis with a THC content of 20%.

The cannabis family, *Cannabinaceae,* has one other member, *humulus lupulus:* the hops of this plant are used to flavor beer and ale.

Cannabis has been not quite appropriately classified as a HALLUCINOGEN. Although it is true that it *can* produce psychedelic effects in very high doses, it also exhibits some of the characteristics of depressants (sedation), narcotics (analgesia) and even stimulants (enhanced perception). Its defiance of previously established categories seems to merit its being classified in a category all its own. It is currently a Schedule I drug under the CONTROLLED SUBSTANCES ACT.

The hemp plant has long been cultivated for a variety of commercial, medical, recreational and religious purposes. First documented as early as 2700 B.C. (by the Chinese emperor Shun Nung) as a pharmacologically useful herb, it is probably the oldest cultivated nonfood plant. As a source of fiber for cloth and rope, hemp was a principal crop in 18th century Virginia (one of George Washington's plantations produced it). Its legitimate cultivation in the United States peaked during World War II when Asian sources were cut off by Japanese military conquests. Today hemp fiber has been largely replaced in commercial use by nylon. Other commercial cannabis products include oil for soap and cooking. The seeds are used in bird seed, fish bait and fertilizer.

Cannabis has also been used medicinally for centuries. Its primary use has been as an analgesic, to treat such conditions as open wounds, scorpion bites and skin inflammations. It has also been used as a sedative in cases of mania and hysteria, and as an anticonvulsant. In the U.S., public misconceptions and fears about the ''killer weed,'' and consequent legislation, limited the exploration of its usefulness. But with the first production of synthetic THC by Mechaulam at the Hebrew University in 1966 medical research progressed rapidly. Recently discovered possible medical applications include relieving pressure on the eyeballs in the treatment of glaucoma, and opening contricted bronchial airways in the treatment of asthma. Its most widespread use has been as an antiemetic for the nausea and vomiting of cancer chemotherapy. Cannabidiolic acid, a cannabis alkaloid, is a topical antibiotic. (See also MARIJUANA and HASHISH.)

Capital with Codeine® (Carnrick)   A narcotic opiate containing 325 mg of acetaminophen and 30 mg of codeine, that is used as an analgesic for mild to moderate pain. It can produce effects similar to morphine and therefore has a potential for abuse and for the development of dependency. When used with alcohol or other central nervous system depressants it can have an additive effect. Overdosage can result in respiratory depression, cold and clammy skin, muscle flaccidity and extreme somnolence leading to stupor or coma. It is available in pale blue tablets.

carbohydrate   Carbohydrate metabolism is affected by the consumption of alcohol, and the blood sugar level may increase or decrease depending on the state of nutrition in the body. When carbohydrate stores are high, alcohol induces hyperglycemia (high blood sugar); when carbohydrate stores are low, hypoglycemia results (low blood sugar). Most distilled liquors have almost no carbohydrates, wine contains some, and beer is very high in carbohydrates. A popular fad diet, the ''drinking man's diet,'' is based on the fact that there are very few carbohydrates in hard liquor. However, liquor does contain a lot of ''empty calories,'' so if someone eats and at the same time drinks large amounts of alcohol, he or she is likely to gain rather than lose weight simply because the calories in liquor will be metabolized before the food calories which are stored as fat.

carbon tetrachloride   A toxic hydrocarbon that was a common ingredient in many cleaning fluids. Although it was sometimes inhaled for the intoxicating effect produced, it is extremely dangerous: inhalation can result in headache, confusion, vomiting, and coma or death. Inhaled in large quantities it can cause damage to the nervous system, heart, liver and kidneys. It is especially dangerous when combined with alcohol. Carbon tetrachloride has been barred from consumer products because of its toxic effect.

Carbrital® (Parke–Davis)   A sedative hypnotic containing the BARBITURATE pentobarbital sodium along with carbromal, that is used for insomnia. Tolerance can develop along with physical and psychological dependence. It has a significant potential for abuse. Overdosage can result in shallow respiration, coma and possible death. It is supplied as Elixir Carbrital, each fluid ounce containing 2 grains (120 mg) pentobarbital; Carbrital Kapseals with 1½ gr pentobarbital; and Carbrital Kapseals Half Strength with ¾ gr.

cardiac arrhythmia   See HEART.

catnip   A herb, *Nepeta cataria*. There are claims that when it is smoked it can produce marijuana–like effects, but the likelihood of this is doubtful.

causes   See ETIOLOGY.

cement, household   See GLUE SNIFFING.

central nervous system (CNS)   The network of neurons (nerve cells) concentrated in the BRAIN and spinal cord which conduct electrical sensory and motor impulses to and from all parts of the body, via the peripheral nervous system (PNS). The PNS also includes the autonomic nervous system which is divided anatomically and functionally into the sympathetic and parasympathetic branches.

Nerve fibers called axons lead away from neurons and produce and store neurohormones such as norepinephrine, serotonin and acetylcholine. Transmission of an impulse occurs when neurohormones cross the synaptic gap to a neuron or its attached dentrite (a nerve fiber which carries impulses toward a neuron).

The brain is divided into a number of areas which exert control over specific functions: in the brainstem, the medulla oblongata is the center of respiratory, cardiac and vasomotor functions. The reticular activating system, a network of specialized nerve cells within the brainstem, controls alertness. The brainstem also includes the pons and mesencephalon (midbrain), collections of nerve fiber bundles which relay impulses.

Located above the brainstem, the thalamus acts as a central switchboard, directing impulses between the body and brain and within the subcortical area. Projecting from the thalamus, the hypothalamus affects emotional balance, regulates the autonomic nervous system, body temperature and water balance, and controls the dichotomous pleasure/pain and hunger/satiety reactions. Attached to and behind the brainstem, the cerebellum controls coordination, equilibrium and muscle tone. The most highly evolved part of the human brain is the approximately 6 mm outside layer called the cerebral cortex. It controls intellectual functions (including memory), certain motor functions, language and speech, auditory, visual, and other sensory skills.

Drugs and other toxic substances can alter nervous system function by inhibiting, stimulating or imitating neurohormones, by disturbing their metabolism, or by affecting structures involved in the neurological process. Drugs also specifically affect different parts of the brain and therefore predictably impair certain functions. Drug abuse can cause permanent organic damage.

Depressant drugs, including alcohol and the opiates, interfere with neurohormonal production and absorption by the postsynaptic membrane and exert their principal effect on the medulla. This action explains the danger of respiratory failure that accompanies abuse of these drugs. They also affect the reticular activating system, including sleep, and other areas of the cerebral cortex.

One of the best documented categories of drug abuse pathology is that of brain damage related to alcoholism, though the mechanisms of many of these disorders are not fully understood.

Alcoholics commonly suffer from impairment of judgment, concentration and memory. In their early stages these symptoms can disappear with abstinence, which does not, however, always reverse brain atrophy which occurs as more and more brain cells are destroyed by alcohol.

Factors associated with alcoholism, such as malnutrition, also contribute to the development of both reversible and irreversible brain damage; thiamine deficiency in particular is at least partially responsible for a number of common alcoholic brain disorders. Victims of WERNICKE'S ENCEPHALOPATHY and KORSAKOFF'S PSYCHOSIS, for example, exhibit delirium, tremors, visual impairment, inability to maintain balance and memory failure. Thiamine deficiency also contributes to alcoholic polyneuropathy, another relatively common condition which involves numbness, pain, wasting and impaired function of the limbs, beginning with the legs. Alcoholic amblyopia provides another example. This disorder consists of visual impairment which sometimes involves degeneration of the optic nerves.

Structural damage, such as cerebral edema, congestion and hemorrhage, also occurs with abuse of depressant drugs. Brain injuries also result from accidents attributable to intoxication.

Stimulant substances generally accelerate production and release of neurohormones. Nicotine overloads the nerve cells and blocks synapses by mimicking acetycholine. Stimulants seem to focus on the autonomic nervous system, increasing heartbeat and blood pressure. Hypertension and tachycardia leading to cerebral hemorrhage are risks associated with the abuse of amphetamines and other stimulants. These drugs also keep the user awake by stimulating the reticular activating system, and appear to stimulate the pleasure and satiety centers located in the hypothalamus. Altered patterns of thinking, such as the exaggerated attention to insignificant detail that often occurs on an amphetamine binge, may indicate that there is an effect on the cerebral cortex as well. Cumulative nervous system degeneration has been associated with chronic stimulant abuse.

Heroin and other opiates act primarily on the thalamus, medulla and cerebral cortex. Large doses stimulate the hypothalamic pleasure center to produce immediate euphoria which is often likened to a "complete body orgasm." Opiates also appear to stimulate or mimic activity of the parasympathetic division of the autonomic nervous system and generally depress the function of affected areas. Opiate overdose sometimes involves coma and cerebral edema.

Hallucinogens, such as LSD, excite a collection of structures known as the limbic system which plays a large role in emotional response and is closely connected to the thalamus and hypothalamus. They also seem to affect those areas of the brain which control auditory and visual reflexes and speech skills. Psychedelics may inhibit nerve impulses by antagonizing the neurohormone serotonin and possibly by mimicking norepinephrine. Reports of permanent brain damage resulting from the use of LSD have been largely unsubstantiated, but long–term psychotic reactions are known.

Many studies have been conducted to determine the relationship of chronic marijuana use to the loss of short–term memory, but none has sufficiently explained this phenomenon. It has been postulated that chronic marijuana smoking inhibits production of DNA which chemically stores information. To date there has been no conclusive evidence that structural brain damage, including cerebral atrophy, can result from chronic cannabis consumption.

central pontine myelinolysis   A disease characterized by a progressive weakness in the muscles extending from the medulla to the spinal cord. Other symptoms include an inability to swallow and an absence of the gag reflex. A rare disease that is difficult to diagnose, it is most often found in long–time alcoholics suffering from malnutrition. As the disease progresses the patient becomes drowsy and, finally, comatose.

cephalotropic   See PSYCHOTROPIC.

charas   The Indian term for the resin produced by the flowering top of the female plant of *Cannabis sativa*. It is far more potent than GHANGA in which the leaves, stems and twigs are ground up along with the flowering top.

chia seeds   The term is applied to seeds from any plant which belongs to the genus *Salvia*. There have been claims that they produce a marijuana–like effect when smoked.

child abuse   See CHILDREN OF DRUG DEPENDENT INDIVIDUALS.

children of drug dependent individuals   Most studies in this area deal with children of alcoholics. Unfortunately, the best way to predict the future drinking habits of a child is to study the drinking pattern of his or her parents. One of the most negative effects of having an alcoholic parent is that it predisposes a child to alcohol abuse. Daughters of alcoholics become alcoholic 20–50% of the time and alcoholic mothers seem to exert more influence in this way than alcoholic fathers. Studies have also shown that even if a daughter of an alcoholic parent escapes becoming an alcoholic, she is likely to marry one (see PARA–ALCOHOLIC).

Alcoholic parents often vacillate between being overly affectionate and being abusive and neglectful. This type of treatment is not understood by children and, along with becoming anxious and frightened, they often become confused about their own responsibility for their parents' behavior.

Although some children may seem to cope with the problems of having an alcoholic parent, they run a high risk of developing problems later in life. For instance, some children assume a responsible role and attempt to take care of parents and other siblings; this can lead to the inability to depend on others in later life and the need to always be in control of a situation. The child who always tries to smooth over conflicts and help others in an alcoholic household may

deny his or her own feelings of anger and hurt and later in life will be constantly trying to please others. In addition, a child who constantly adjusts to the moods of an alcoholic parent may find himself going through life being manipulated by others. Even if an alcoholic parent stops drinking, the child's problems may not end. He can then no longer use the parent as a scapegoat for misbehavior; he may also feel resentment or hostility because he has become accustomed to handling situations and having responsibilities (these feelings have also been noted in spouses of alcoholics).

Most of the studies concerning other drugs have centered around the effects on an unborn child and the consequent symptoms of withdrawal at birth (see PREGNANCY). However, it would follow that the negative effects of having an alcoholic parent would also be true of having a parent addicted to heroin, amphetamines, barbiturates or any mind–altering substance. In a situation where a parent is not rational at all times, the same neglect, instability of home life, and abusive treatment will be present.

There are an estimated one million cases of child abuse and neglect each year in the United States. It has been suggested that one–third of these cases are alcohol–related. How many are attributable to other drug use is not known. Child abuse in the family can be a vicious circle. It is not always the alcoholic parent who abuses a child; often the alcoholic will abuse the spouse who, in turn, will abuse the children as a means of releasing frustration. When a parent is undergoing WITHDRAWAL symptoms from any drug, his or her irritability threshold is very low and this may also lead to child abuse.

The exact connection between child abuse and drug use is not known but studies have shown repetitive cycles from generation to generation. If an adult has been abused as a child, he or she will be more apt to continue the abuse pattern. In regard to alcohol, it was found that nearly one–third of all reported cases of father–daughter incest were attributed to alcohol dependence. Even when drug abuse is not considered the major factor in child abuse, it may aggravate the problem.

As the incidence of child abuse grows, so does public awareness of the problem. Adults who were abused children are now more open about discussing their childhood, both as a way of helping others who have suffered child abuse and as a way of dealing with their own emotional problems. Neighbors and relatives of battered children are also more forthcoming with reports, and school officials, law enforcement agencies and hospitals are now more conscious of the problem. The number of cases reported, however, is still thought to represent only the tip of the iceberg.

China   The cultivation and use of opium has been a tradition in China for centuries. The Chinese and British fought two Opium Wars during the 19th century because Britain was bringing opium into China from India and undercutting the local competition. The Chinese government, however, contends that the Opium Wars were fought to combat the consumption of opium. In the 1850s and 1860s, when Chinese laborers were brought to the United States to work on the railroads, they were said to have brought the practice of opium smoking with them. Opium smoking rapidly gained popularity in the U.S. and it was the prevalence of ''opium dens'' that prompted San Francisco to enact the first narcotics ordinance in 1875.

The cultivation of the opium poppy is a laborous undertaking (the labor involved in the short 10–day harvest season can amount to hundreds of hours) and this accounts for the fact that commercial production flourishes mainly in economically deprived countries that have cheap sources of labor available on short–term notice. While opium is cultivated in rural China, the involvement of the Chinese in opium exported from the GOLDEN TRIANGLE has all but ceased to exist. Until the late 1970s the Chinese were regularly involved in smuggling but government regulations, along with internal competition among traffickers, greatly reduced their activities.

In recent years opium intoxication and addiction have been considered political offenses. Although statistics are unavailable, it is thought that drug abuse in China is not a major problem. However, opium is still grown and smoked in remote areas, and control over individual consumption is strong in urban areas.

An alcohol problem in China is acknowledged to exist but to what extent is unknown.

chloral alcoholate   A chloral derivative that is converted to CHLORAL HYDRATE in the body.

chloral betaine   A synthetic chloral derivative that is similar to CHLORAL HYDRATE but is said to cause less gastric distress. It is used as a sedative.

chloral derivatives   CHLORAL HYDRATE, CHLORAL BETAINE, CHLOROBUTANOL, TRICLOFOS SODIUM, and CHLORAL ALCOHOLATE. (See CHLORAL HYDRATE for characteristics.)

chloral hydrate   A nonbarbiturate sedative hypnotic which acts as a depressant on the central nervous system. It is produced by passing chlorine gas through ethyl alcohol. The first synthetic sedative hypnotic, it was introduced in 1869 by Oskar Liebreich and was widely used both medically and recreationally. Today it has been largely replaced by newer drugs.

Appearance: Chloral hydrate appears as colorless or white transparent crystals which are soluble in water, olive oil and alcohol. It is available in liquid, capsule or tablet form for oral use, and in suppositories and olive oil enemas for rectal use. The substance decomposes quickly when exposed to light and, in liquid form, quickly develops mold. It has a bitter taste and unpleasant odor.

Activity in the body: Chloral hydrate is absorbed into the bloodstream from the intestinal tract and evenly distributed through the body. It appears in breast milk and crosses the placental barrier; like the barbiturates, it is not advised for use during pregnancy and nursing. The drug's half–life is four to eight hours.

Dosage: The average lethal dose of chloral hydrate is 10 grams. As little as 3 grams have proved fatal, and up to 30 grams have been survived. The recommended sedative dosage is 250 mg three times a day after meals. The usual hypnotic dose is .5 to 1 gm approximately 15–30 minutes before bedtime.

Effects: Like other DEPRESSANTS, chloral hydrate inhibits the transmission of nerve impulses in the ascending reticular formation of the brain, thereby affecting such functions as breathing. As a hypnotic it acts very quickly, producing immediate drowsiness and—within 15–30 minutes—a sound sleep which lasts four to eight hours. Chloral hydrate is considered safer than other hypnotics, particularly BARBITURATES, because it interferes very little with REM sleep, and because it has less effect on the respiratory center in the brain.

In sedative doses, chloral hydrate's effects are similar to those of alcohol and barbiturates: euphoria leading to intoxication and usually resulting in a slight hangover. Common side effects include gastrointestinal irritation and loss of muscular coordination. Overdoses can result in falling temperature, pupil constriction followed by dilation, irregular pulse, delirium, coma, and death within five to 10 hours. Tolerance, along with physical and psychological dependence, can develop; consequently the drug is not recommended for long–term use, especially for patients with histories of drug addiction or abuse. However, the abuse risk for chloral hydrate is only low to moderate. Probably because of its bad taste and gastric effects it is not favored by drug abusers; they generally prefer barbiturates and the newer nonbarbiturates, such as glutethimide and ethclorvynol.

The combination of chloral hydrate and alcohol increases the depressant activity of both drugs (see SYNERGY), intensifying the euphoria and intoxication as well as slowing the breathing and accentuating loss of muscular coordination. Coma can result. This possibly lethal combination has earned chloral hydrate preparations the nicknames "knockout drops," "Mickeys" and "Mickey Finns."

Chloral hydrate also interferes with anticoagulants and should be used cautiously in combination with other drugs.

Usage: Chloral hydrate is used medically as a post– and pre–operative sedative and hypnotic, particularly in combination with barbiturates. It is used in the first stages of labor, as a nocturnal sedative in the treatment of insomnia, and in the treatment of certain convulsive disorders. Like other sedatives, it is also frequently used in treating withdrawal from other drugs, such as alcohol, barbiturates and narcotics.

Recreationally, it is used to produce the same euphoria and intoxication derived from the use of alcohol and barbiturates, although its use in this regard is infrequent. Morphine and heroin addicts use it as a substitute when their habitual drugs are unavailable.

Chloral hydrate is a Schedule IV drug under the Controlled Substances Act.

chlordiazepoxide   A minor tranquilizer, best known under the tradename LIBRIUM, and one of the most commonly prescribed tranquilizers in the United States. Chlordiazepoxide hydrochloride is a benzodiazepine derivative and is very similar to diazepam and oxazepam. It is used to relieve symptoms of tension and anxiety. It is prescribed in large doses for pre–operative anxiety and for the relief of panic associated with agitated psychotic states such as phobias and obsessive compulsive states. It is used extensively to relieve alcoholic anxiety and in alcohol detoxification programs.

Appearance and activity: Chlordiazepoxide hydrochloride appears as a colorless crystalline substance which is water soluble. It is absorbed in the gastrointestinal tract, and depresses the limbic system—the center of emotional response. Metabolized chiefly in the liver, it is excreted in the urine and crosses the placental barrier. After oral administration, its effects manifest in about half an hour and peak in two to four hours. Onset after intramuscular injection occurs in 15–30 minutes, and in 3–15 minutes after intravenous administration. The substance has a 24–48 hour half life.

Dosage: In the form of Librium, it is prescribed in two or four daily doses of 5–50 mg. Daily doses can range as high as 100 mg but should not exceed 300 mg. A daily dosage of 300–600 mg can produce physical dependence. No lethal dose has been specified in humans, but 50% of mice fed 620 mg per kilogram of body weight died.

Effects: Like the other minor tranquilizers, Librium calms symptoms of anxiety and tension resulting from emotional stress. It is possibly more effective than other drugs of its class in relieving anxiety–induced gastrointestinal distress. One of its principal applications is the treatment of alcohol withdrawal symptoms, especially delirium tremens.

Chlordiazepoxide produces less euphoria than meprobamate, opiates or barbiturates, so psychological dependence may be less of a risk. But as high doses produce the kind of intoxication induced by barbiturates, physical dependence is likely with doses 10 times larger than the recommended therapeutic dose.

Withdrawal symptoms for physical dependence are convulsions, insomnia, loss of appetite, tremors and the recurrence of previous symptoms of anxiety. Like other benzodiazepine derivatives, it is additive to other depressant drugs (see SYNERGY), and their combination can result in fatal respiratory depression.

The euphoria produced by large doses makes the drug attractive to drug abusers. It has also been used in enormous amounts in suicide attempts.

It is a Schedule IV drug under the Controlled Substances Act.

chlormezanone   A DEPRESSANT drug used as a tranquilizer in the treatment of mild anxiety and tension. It acts without impairing the patient's clarity of consciousness. (See TRANCOPAL.)

chloroform   A vaporous ANESTHETIC, more potent than ether, but no longer used therapeutically because it produces serious adverse effects on the liver.

chlorphentermine hydrochloride   A sympathomimetic amine with pharmacologic activities similar to AMPHETAMINES. (See PRE–SATE.)

chlorpromazine   A DEPRESSENT which has actions at all levels of the central nervous system and is used as a major tranquilizer. (See THORAZINE.)

chocolate   A very mild stimulant (containing 1.0% CAFFEINE) made from cacao beans.

chromatography   A technique used for urine testing for drugs. Both thin–layer and gas chromatographic methods of urine testing are considered the most useful techniques for detecting drugs with the exception of LSD. (Methods for detecting LSD in both blood and urine are presently restricted to research laboratories.) Gas or gas liquid chromatography (GLC) is more sensitive for detecting a wide variety of drugs than thin–layer chromatography (TLC), but TLC is a much simplier method that is fast and inexpensive. GLC testing is more sophisticated and usually performed only in laboratories and large hospitals because of the expense of the equipment needed.

chronic   A descriptive term for a condition or disease that is characterized by slowly progressing symptoms and which continues for a long time, as opposed to an ACUTE disease or condition which quickly develops into a crisis.

chronic alcohol intoxication   Continuous intoxication maintained by repeated consumption of alcohol. The term is also used generally to refer to alcoholism, although many alcoholics are not continually intoxicated.

chronic alcoholic   See CHRONIC ALCOHOLISM.

chronic alcoholism   As alcoholism is a chronic disorder the term chronic alcoholism is superfluous. It is used, however, to distinguish a long–lasting condition from ACUTE ALCOHOLISM, which is generally used to refer to alcohol intoxication or alcohol poisoning which may be a temporary disturbance.

cigarettes   See NICOTINE.

cirrhosis   A liver disease that occurs frequently, but not exclusively, in association with alcohol abuse. The word comes from the Greek ''kirrhos,'' meaning orange–colored—the color of a cirrhotic liver. The disease is characterized by scarring and severe dysfunction. (See LIVER.)

citronella   An oil with a lemonish odor made from citronella grass. There are unconfirmed claims that it can produce intoxicating effects when inhaled.

cleaning fluids   Although toxic, with the potential to produce brain, liver and kidney damage, cleaning fluids are sometimes inhaled by those seeking an intoxicating effect. (See INHALANTS.)

clonidine   A non–narcotic drug used in the treatment of hypertension. This drug also has the ability to diminish withdrawal symptoms during detoxification from methadone, heroin or other opiates. Its trade name is Catapres and it acts as a central adrenergic agonist. Other drugs of this class have been developed that may be superior to clonidine for narcotic detoxification.

Clonopin® (Roche)   An anticonvulsant, containing clonazepam, that is used for the control of seizures. Because it is a BENZODIAZEPINE, tolerance can develop and it has the potential for abuse. When taken with alcohol or other central nervous system depressants it can have an additive effect. Overdosage can result in somnolence, diminished reflexes, confusion and coma. It is supplied in tablet form: 0.5 mg orange; 1 mg blue; and 2 mg white.

clorazepate dipotassium   A synthetic BENZODIAZEPINE used in the treatment of anxiety. (See also TRANXENE.)

clortermine   A sympathomimetic amine with pharmacologic activity similar to that of AMPHETAMINES. It is used as an anorectic. (See VORANIL.)

co–alcoholic   See PARA–ALCOHOLIC.

coca   *Erthroxylon coca,* a bush which grows in South America. From 0.65% to

1.25% (by weight) of the alkaloid COCAINE is found in its leaves. South American Indians mix the leaves with lime to release the cocaine, then chew them for a stimulant effect. Coca was an ingredient of Coca Cola until the U.S. government prohibited its use in 1906. Now the coca leaves are decocainized before being used as a flavoring in cola drinks.

coca paste   The first extract produced during the manufacture of cocaine from coca leaves. It is made by adding sulfuric acid and kerosene to the leaves. In South America cocaine is not processed into FREEBASE before smoking; it is smoked in the form of coca paste which is dangerous because of the impurities it contains and its high cocaine content.

cocaine   An alkaloid found in the leaves of the coca bush, *Erthroxylon coca*. Cocaine affects the central nervous system and induces feelings of euphoria. Used since the time of the Inca Empire, which flourished for hundreds of years in the Andean Mountain region of Peru until the arrival of the white man in the 1500s, Inca priests and nobles chewed coca leaves in order to achieve and enhance their understanding of religious experiences. Using coca leaves was originally a mark of the aristocracy, but gradually other members of the male Inca population took up the habit. The Indians discovered that besides helping to resolve religious truths, the magical leaves would prolong physical endurance, retard fatigue and hunger and give a pleasurable feeling of euphoria. Coca was widely used by the men who worked in mines which were located at very high mountain altitudes. Today it is estimated that fully 90% of the adult male Indian population of the region regularly chews coca leaves.

The Indians chew coca leaves along with an alkali, such as bird lime: when mixed with saliva, it acts as an agent to release the cocaine from the leaves. Someone chewing two ounces of coca a day would be taking in 0.7 grams of pure cocaine. Someone taking several doses of "pure" cocaine—actually only 5–35% pure—sold on the street, on the other hand, would be ingesting 6–8 grams.

The pure cocaine substance benzoylmethylecognine was first identified and extracted from the leaves of the coca bush in the 1850s by the German chemist Albert Niemann.

The use of cocaine in its pure form began in the 1880s. Bavarian soldiers were given it to help them gain endurance and to retard fatigue. Shortly afterward, cocaine was touted in medical circles as a highly effective local anesthetic for certain operations. Experiments were conducted to discover what other disorders and maladies cocaine could cure or sooth, and a small circle of professional people began taking the drug themselves. Sigmund Freud insisted it helped him in his work. He even went so far as to praise cocaine in a series of papers to the public in which he commented favorably on the drug's beneficial properties as a cure for morphine addiction, depression, overeating and alcoholism. But when reports of cases of cocaine addiction and death by overdose began surfacing, Freud immediately ceased taking the drug.

By the early 1900s cocaine had found its way, through patent medicines like Vin Mariani, into the lives of many people. A great deal of cocaine was produced for use in potions and beverages. Coca Cola contained cocaine until 1906 when the company, at the insistence of the U.S. government, removed the ingredient from its recipe.

Both the Canadian government (in 1911) and the U.S. government (in 1914) put legal restrictions on the sale of the drug. Cocaine diminished greatly in popularity and it wasn't until the 1960s that it made a comeback. Its appeal was due in part to the public's acceptance of amphetamines, the effects of which are remarkably similar to cocaine.

There are several methods of taking cocaine. The most common is by "snorting" it into the nostrils through a straw, a rolled paper, or from a tiny "coke spoon." Another method, favored by some heavy users, is to inject the substance directly into the bloodstream—sometimes following it up with a shot of heroin. Cocaine can also be taken by applying it to the mucous lining of the mouth, rectum or vagina. Oral ingestion of the drug decreases its potency. For a more recent method of using cocaine see FREEBASE.

Because of the expensive nature of cocaine, its use until recently was confined primarily to the upper strata of the economic ladder, particularly to people in the sports and entertainment fields. But cocaine has been steadily gaining acceptance among the young, among college students, and in many blue and white collar circles as well. Although expensive, its popularity may stem from the fact that people believe it to be nonaddictive.

Classification: The effects of cocaine are similar to the effects of the natural substance adrenaline as well to the manufactured stimulants, amphetamines. In its pure form cocaine is a white powder but it is often cut with other drugs or similar looking substances, such as talcum powder or sugar, and very little street–purchased cocaine is in pure form. The Federal Bureau of Narcotics once mistakenly classified cocaine as a narcotic but it is presently classified as a STIMULANT. It is also classified as a legal, though tightly regulated (Schedule II) anesthetic, and used in some surgical operations on the mouth, eyes and throat because of its ability to constrict blood vessels and to be rapidly absorbed by the mucous membranes.

Effects: Cocaine directly affects the central nervous system, causing a definite stimulative sensation. The effects, which only last a very short time, depend on the size of the dose. Small doses will bring about sensations of extreme euphoria; illusions of increased mental and physical strength and sensory awareness; and a decrease in hunger, pain and the need for sleep. Large doses significantly magnify these effects, sometimes causing irrational behavior. For heavy users, the heightened euphoria is often accompanied by intensified heartbeat, sweating, dilation of the pupils and a rise in body temperature. Euphoria can be followed by irritability, depression, insomnia and an extreme condition of paranoia. These effects are similar to those felt by heavy amphetamine users. Formication, the belief and feeling that ants or other insects are running up and down the skin, is also common. In some cases, a condition similar to amphetamine poisoning may occur and the user will not only appear extremely restless and nervous, but will experience delirium, hallucinations, muscle spasms and pain in the chest. Male users may become impotent or incapable of ejaculation. If the drug is injected, abscesses may appear on the skin. Malnutrition and anemia may be experienced because of a decrease in appetite. Many of these symptoms can be reversed simply by halting the drug.

Both heavy and light users will eventually develop some of the same physical side effects: runny nose, eczema around the nostrils, and gradual deterioration of the nasal cartilage. Death from cocaine overdose is rare, although such instances are on the increase. An overdose usually results in respiratory arrest. Death may also be caused by heart rhythm disturbances, high fever or convulsions.

Addictive aspects: Outside of heavy use, physical dependence is rare. When it does occur, withdrawal symptoms are reported to be great hunger, irritability, extreme fatigue, serious depression and prolonged periods of restless sleep. Psychological dependence is more common. Many users become "hooked" on the feeling of euphoria induced by cocaine and their entire being begins to revolve around the next dose. If dependence is severe, a user will experience a deep depression when the effects of a dose wear off.

Tolerance: Tolerance to cocaine has not been firmly established, but there is evidence that the same dose frequently repeated will not produce similar symptoms over a period of time. Many cocaine users do find a need to increase the dosage frequently. A lethal dose can be as small as 1.2 grams intravenously, but a heavy user may, through frequent small doses, ingest as much as 10 grams in a day.

Sources: Approximately 70% of the cocaine entering the United States comes from COLOMBIA, and passes through South Florida. Colombia is also responsible for 50% of the world's supply. (See Appendix 3, Tables 39 and 44.)

Synonyms: coke, snow, blow, leaf, stardust, flake, C, girl, and many others.

cocaine freebase   See FREEBASE, COCAINE.

History of Cocaine

c.1532 Pizarro discovers Incas chewing coca leaves in Peru.

1750 Coca specimens classified as *Erythroxylon coca.*

1844 Cocaine, the principal alkaloid in coca leaves, is isolated.

1863 A preparation of coca leaves and wine called "Vin Mariani" gains popularity in Europe.

1878 Cocaine used for morphine addiction.

1883 Bavarian soldiers use cocaine to combat fatigue.

1884 Sigmund Freud studies cocaine as a psychoactive drug to treat depression and fatigue.

Karl Koller uses cocaine as a topical anesthetic in eye operations.

William Halstead injects cocaine into nerve trunks as a regional anesthetic.

1885 Dr. Albrecht Erlenmeyer warns against the use of cocaine to cure morphine addiction.

1886 Coca-Cola, containing coca extract, comes on the market.

1902 Richard Willstatter synthesizes cocaine.

1906 Pure Food and Drug Act prohibits interstate shipment of food and soda water containing cocaine.

Coca-Cola Company switches to "decocainized" cola leaves.

1914 Harrison Narcotics Act lists cocaine as a narcotic.

1922 Congress prohibits most importation of cocaine and coca leaves.

1932 Uniform Narcotic Drug Act requires licensing for manufacture and imposes criminal penalties for illegal possession.

1956 Narcotics Drug Control Act imposes severe penalties for offenses.

1970 Controlled Substances Act classifies cocaine as a Schedule II drug.

1970s-1980s Use of cocaine spreads to all segments of society. An estimated 30-60 tons are smuggled into the U.S. annually.

cocktail   A drink which is a mixture of a distilled spirit and an aperitif or other flavoring. A cocktail is usually shaken or stirred with ice and then strained into a glass. Although there are various theories, the origin of the term is unknown. It came into popular usage in the United States in the 1920s and although the word is now widely used throughout the world it is considered an American term. Probably the most common cocktail is the martini, a mixture of gin and vermouth. The term has been extended to include COCKTAIL HOUR.

cocktail hour   A term referring to the time when COCKTAILS are usually served, either at a social gathering (a 4–6 p.m. cocktail party) or a designated hour at a restaurant, bar or lounge. The term "happy hour" has become popular in recent years.

cocoa   *Theobroma cacao,* a bush that grows in Central and South America. The seeds are used to make cocoa powder and chocolate. Cocoa is a mild stimulant containing 1.0% CAFFEINE by weight.

Codalan® (Lannett)   A narcotic opiate that contains CODEINE. It is used as an analgesic for degrees of pain that would require less analgesia than morphine. It may be habit–forming. It is available in three varieties: No. 1, orange tablets containing ⅛ gr codeine; No. 2, white tablets with ¼ gr; and No. 3, green tablets with ½ gr. All three varieties contain caffeine, salicylamide and acetaminophen.

CODAP (Client Oriented Data Acquisition Program)   This reporting system provides demographic, diagnostic and outcome data on patients in federally supported drug treatment facilities. The reporting forms can be found in National Institute on Drug Abuse (NIDA) Research Issue Series 12, "Drug Abuse Instrument Handbook."

codeine   (morphine 3 – methyl ether). A narcotic analgesic, codeine was discovered in 1832 and gets its name from the Greek word *kodeia* meaning "poppyhead." Like morphine, it is an opiate, a natural opium alkaloid, and appears in the juices of the unripe white poppy pod. The natural yield is rather small (about .5%) so codeine is also synthesized through the methylization of morphine (and is sometimes called "methyl morphine").

Appearance: Codeine appears in two forms. The first, codeine phosphate, is an odorless white crystalline powder soluble in water and slightly soluble in alcohol. The second, codeine sulfate, appears as white crystals which are slightly soluble in water and freely soluble in alcohol. Being more soluble in water, codeine phosphate is used most often in elixirs and in injectable form. Codeine sulfate appears in pill form.

Activity in the body: Taken orally, codeine is absorbed (more rapidly than morphine) from the gastrointestinal tract. It is biodegraded in the liver and appears in the urine. Codeine's effects peak in 30–60 minutes and last three to four hours. Its half life is three to five hours. About 10% of the substance converts to morphine in the body. Codeine crosses the placental barrier and therefore can affect unborn babies.

Dosage: Codeine can be taken orally, subcutaneously or intramuscularly. As an antitussive, it is prescribed in doses ranging from 5–10 mg; the usual analgesic dose is 15–60 mg. Doses over 60 mg can have stimulatory rather than sedative effects. In hypodermic administration 120 mg of codeine is equivalent to 10 mg of morphine. Death from codeine is very rare and the lethal dose has not be determined.

Effects: Codeine's analgesic effects are very similar to morphine's, although it has only about one–sixth to one–tenth of morphine's potency. It relieves minor pain, producing a mild euphoria and drowsiness.

Codeine also dries the respiratory mucosa and affects the autonomic nervous system. Large doses intensify these effects. Tolerance to the drug's sedative effects does develop, but codeine is considered only moderately physically addictive. Psychological dependence is more common: in addition to the desired euphoria, addicts experience loss of appetite, depressed sexual drive, itchiness and, most often, constipation and nausea. Withdrawal symptoms are relatively mild.

Usage: Codeine's most common medical use is as an antitussive in cough syrups, often in combination with non–narcotic pain relievers such as aspirin or Tylenol. Codeine is used for this purpose more than any other drug and is thus widely prescribed. Other medical applications include relief of minor pain of various kinds and relief of constipation, though large doses can cause the latter problem.

Codeine is subject to abuse but the problem is not a big one. Since large doses are required to achieve and maintain the kind of "high" abusers seek, brand name codeine products, which often contain other drugs, are not satisfactory for this purpose. In the 1960s, however, many teenagers drank codeine cough syrups in large quantities for their euphoric effects, and studies have shown that many addicts of harder drugs began their pursuit of artificial euphoria with codeine syrups. The discovery of this abuse led to tighter control over the drug's prescription; consequently recreational use of codeine is no longer such a big problem. Codeine is a Schedule II drug under the Controlled Substances Act. Street terms for codeine tablets are "schoolboys" and "pops."

Codeine and alcohol: The combination of codeine and alcohol can be dangerous and can result in respiratory arrest and depressed brain activity.

coercive therapy When a drug dependent person is forced into a treatment situation, it is considered coercive therapy. The pressure may arise from a court, "Get into treatment or go to jail"; from one's employer, "If you don't stop drinking, you will be fired"; or from other sources. Since the entry into treatment is not voluntary, the person may have little or no motivation to change and the therapist must induce the desire. It has been found in some cases that if the threat of punishment is maintained, the results of coercion are as good as those for voluntary participation in treatment programs.

coffee See CAFFEINE.

cola An African tree belonging to the Sterculiaceae family. The seeds, kola nuts, contain 2% CAFFEINE and are used to make a mildly stimulative beverage. Kola nuts are an ingredient of the carbonated soft drink Coca Cola.

collapsed veins A common condition among HEROIN addicts caused by frequent injections over a long period of time. When a vein beomes swollen and blocked (collapsed), an infection known as thrombophlebitis or venous thrombosis, an addict will start using another vein. Long–term addicts have been known to use veins in the neck, the penis, between the toes and even under the tongue.

Colombia Colombia has the dubious distinction of being the world's principal drug source, a fact which may be attributed to its strategic location on the South American continent and its geographic makeup, as well as to its experience as a well–ordered trafficking community. The major processing and transshipment center for Peruvian and Bolivian coca, Colombia is responsible for 70% of the cocaine entering the United States and for 50% of the world's supply. U.S. drug enforcement officials estimate that 44 tons (with a street value of $29 billion) is annually smuggled into the U.S. from Colombia. The country also cultivates coca on some 7,200 acres that yield an estimated 4 tons of cocaine annually. Colombia is also the major exporter of marijuana to the U.S., supplying 75% of the market (see Appendix 3, Tables 38, 39 and 44). An estimated 80% of other dangerous drugs entering the U.S., particularly methaqualone, are supplied through Colombia. Most of the illicit drug traffic passes through South Florida, the Gulf of Mexico and East Coast port areas.

Trafficking in cocaine and marijuana, the top two money–producers, has a value to the Colombian economy of an estimated $1 to $1.5 billion, perhaps $500 million of which stays in the country and—untaxed and inflationary—undermines the legitimate economy.

While cocaine processing is big business in Colombia, it is interesting to note that three of the chemicals considered essential to the processing of coca into cocaine—ether, hydrochloric acid and acetone—are not produced in the country. Until recently Colombia's principal suppliers for these chemicals were the Netherlands, the Federal Republic of Germany, and the United States. Colombia in turn supplies these three countries with the majority of their cocaine. On January 4, 1983, the Colombian Minister of Economic Development banned the importation of these chemicals in an effort aimed at curbing cocaine smuggling into the U.S.

Although the Colombian government and public do not perceive drug abuse as a major problem, it has been suggested by outside observers that there has been an increase in the use of cocaine, marijuana and methaqualone among Colombian youth. If true, it is certainly not surprising considering the availability of these drugs. In 1981, after two years of inactivity, the National Council on Dangerous Drugs in Colombia initiated a program to reduce the domestic demand for narcotics. With the recent political unrest in

the country it is difficult to foresee what government efforts and actions will be effective. There have been reports that guerrilla groups are trafficking drugs as a source of income to pay for arms shipments. Drug control assistance programs with the U.S. are difficult to implement at this time, not only because of the political unrest but also because many Colombians consider drug trafficking a problem created by and pertaining solely to the U.S.

colorines   *Erythrina flabelliformis,* a tropical shrub of the Leguminosae family. There are claims that the seeds are a hallucinogen. In fact, they are toxic.

coma   A state of unconsciousness. A person in a coma cannot be aroused even by powerful stimulation.

Compazine® (Smith, Kline & French)   A brand of prochlorperozine used as a major tranquilizer for severe neuropsychiatric conditions. The drug is rarely abused as its effects do not produce euphoria.

compulsion   A psychological term used to refer to a force that compels a person to act against his own will. The term is often used interchangeably with the word CRAVING. Compulsion is different from the type of behavior exhibited during withdrawal when the need for a drug is physical.

confidentiality   In drug abuse treatment programs, confidentiality—the assured anonymity of participants—is protected by federal and state regulations. Records may only be disclosed with the prior written consent of the person involved.

congener   When used in reference to drugs, the term means a chemical relative; a derivative. In reference to alcohol, congeners are the organic alcohols and salts formed in the manufacture of alcoholic beverages. They provide the distinctive flavor and pungency of various beverages; vodkas contain the least congeners and bourbons and brandies the most.

consumption   Alcohol consumption is estimated in one of two ways: self–reported consumption which is derived from individual responses to surveys; and apparent consumption which is derived from tax records, official state reports and reports of sales by the alcoholic beverage industry.

Since 1938, apparent consumption of alcoholic beverages in the United States has increased; the largest rate of increase took place between 1960 and 1970 (25%). The rate of growth slowed to 8% in the 1970s. For each person in the U.S. 14 years of age or over, the apparent consumption now averages about 1 ounce of 100% ethanol per day (approximately two drinks). This average is somewhat misleading, however, because one–third of the adult population reports abstaining. Consequently daily average consumption for those who drink is higher: 1.5 ounces of 100% ethanol, or three drinks a day. Even this average is misleading, though, because a small proportion of adults drink far more than the average and the majority drink less. It has been estimated that 11% of the adult population (16 million adults 18 years and older) consume about half of all beverages.

In a 1979 survey the one–third of adults who reported abstaining from drinking was broken down into 40% female and 25% male. In the heavier drinking category (1 or more ounces of 100% ethanol a day), males outnumbered females 14% to 4%. The percentage of drinkers showed a decrease with age except for a rise in the proportion of female drinkers from ages 18 to 20 and ages 21 to 34. Among males, heavier drinking appeared to peak at ages 21 to 34. Among females, heavier drinking peaked during the years between age 35 and 49. When the 1979 survey figures were compared to 1977, they revealed a decrease in the number of abstainers and an increase in the number of drinkers in the lighter category (0.01 to 0.21 ounces of 100% ethanol per day).

Beer is by far the most popular alcoholic beverage consumed; per capita consumption is nearly 30 gallons a year for the population aged 14 and over. Per capita consumption of distilled spirits is approximately 2.4 gallons and wine is approximately 2.2 gallons. Wine consumption showed a steady increase through the 1970s while the consumption of distilled spirits showed a small decrease. Per capita consumption of alcohol in the U.S. is lower than in many other countries. A 1976 World Health Organization survey ranked the U.S. 22nd out of 26 countries surveyed. The U.S. per capita consumption of 100% ethanol was 8.1 liters; France ranked first (16.5), and Portugal ranked second (14.1). The United Kingdom ranked 18th with a per capita consumption of 8.4 liters.

contingency   A behavior modification procedure frequently used in residential drug abuse treatment settings. Specifically agreed upon behavior and activities are rewarded; failure to act in the way agreed upon is punished. Under this system, the continuation of specified rewards is contingent upon continuation of agreed upon behaviors.

controlled drinking   A concept whereby someone deliberately sets a limit on the number of drinks he or she will take, and when he reaches it, stops drinking. In the case of alcoholics, this concept runs directly contrary to the traditional belief that abstinence is the only course to recovery. The authors of the RAND REPORTS are among those who have suggested that alcoholics may resume "controlled" drinking. Their findings show that patients with a relatively short history of problem drinking will have a greater likelihood of success than those with a long history of alcoholism. Generally, patients who are able to control their drinking are younger and have a lower consumption rate than those who are not able to exercise control. The authors point out that with the wider range of treatment possibilities today, therapists can gear treatment to suit the patient rather than impose a uniform abstinence program upon all.

Opponents see the idea of controlled drinking as a tempting illusion presented with scientific authority. They believe that the concept will be most tempting to those alcoholics who are least able to cope with it. They also suggest that the Rand Report studies are faulty; that the time span of the study was too short and that many of the controlled drinkers in the sample were not really gamma alcoholics in the first place.

In 1970, Mark and Linda Sobell of the University of California began what was to become one of the most controversial studies to date on controlled drinking. Their study compared two different treatment methods: 20 patients were assigned to a behavior–modification program whose goal was to produce moderate drinkers, and another 20 patients received regular hospital treatment aimed at total abstinence. The Sobells published the results of their research, including one– and two–year follow-ups, and claimed that the patients in the controlled–drinking group were able to function better than those who abstained. In 1973, Mary Pendery, a psychologist and alcoholism counselor at the University of California at Los Angeles, began to investigate the Sobells' findings. In an article in the July 9, 1982, issue of *Science,* Pendery and her colleagues attacked the Sobells' results and were highly critical of the Sobells themselves. Pendery stated that the reexamination of the 20 patients who had undergone behavior–modification indicated failure to achieve controlled drinking in all cases ex-

cept one. The controversy continues between those who see alcoholism as irreversible and those who see controlled drinking as a viable treatment method.

controlled drugs   Drugs that are strictly controlled by the CONTROLLED SUBSTANCES ACT. Although alcoholic beverages are sometimes said to be controlled, they are only "regulated" by federal and state laws which govern their sale and purchase. Unlike other controlled drugs, the manufacturers and suppliers of alcoholic beverages are not held accountable for every ounce of the substances involved.

Controlled Substances Act   The Comprehensive Drug Abuse Prevention and Control Act of 1970 (Public Law 91–513), Title II, more familiarly known as the Controlled Substances Act (CSA). It is the legal foundation of a federal strategy aimed at reducing the consumption of illicit drugs. The Controlled Substances Act brought up to date and consolidated all federal drug laws since the nation's first law regarding narcotics regulation was passed in 1914 (the HARRISON NARCOTICS ACT). The Drug Enforcement Administration (DEA) of the Department of Justice is responsible for enforcing the provisions of the act. The following material is quoted from *Drugs of Abuse* (Vol. 6, No. 2, July 1979), published by the DEA:

Criteria by which Drugs are Scheduled. The CSA sets forth the findings which must be made to put a substance in any of the five schedules. These are as follows (Section 202b):
SCHEDULE I
(A) The drug or other substance has a high potential for abuse.
(B) The drug or other substance has no currently accepted medical use in treatment in the United States.
(C) There is a lack of accepted safety for

use of the drug or other substance under medical supervision.

SCHEDULE II

(A) The drug or other substance has a high potential for abuse.

(B) The drug or other substance has a currently accepted medical use in treatment in the United States or a currently accepted medical use with severe restrictions.

(C) Abuse of the drug or other substance may lead to severe psychological or physical dependence.

SCHEDULE III

(A) The drug or other substance has a potential for abuse less than the drugs or other substances in Schedules I and II.

(B) The drug or other substance has a currently accepted medical use in treatment in the United States.

(C) Abuse of the drug or other substance may lead to moderate or low physical dependence or high psychological dependence.

SCHEDULE IV

(A) The drug or other substance has a low potential for abuse relative to the drugs or other substances in Schedule III.

(B) The drug or other substance has currently accepted medical use in treatment in the United States.

(C) Abuse of the drug or other substance may lead to limited physical dependence or psychological dependence relative to the drugs or other substances in Schedule III.

SCHEDULE V

(A) The drug or other substance has a low potential for abuse relative to the drugs or other substances in Schedule IV.

(B) The drug or other substance has a currently accepted medical use in treatment in the United States.

(C) Abuse of the drug or other substance may lead to limited physical dependence or psychological dependence relative to

the drugs or other substances in Schedule IV.

There are eight specific factors which the DEA and the Department of Health, Education and Welfare (HEW) are directed to consider when including a drug or other substance in a particular schedule, or when transferring or removing a substance entirely from the schedules. These criteria, as published by the DEA in *Drugs of Abuse* (Vol. 6 No. 2, July 1979), are:

1. Its actual or relative potential for abuse.
2. Scientific evidence of its pharmacological effect, if known.
3. The state of current scientific knowledge regarding the drug or other substance.
4. Its history and current pattern of abuse.
5. The scope, duration and significance of abuse.
6. What, if any, risk there is to the public health.
7. Its psychic or physiological dependence liability.
8. Whether the substance is an immediate precursor of a substance already controlled under this title.

Under the Controlled Substances Act nine major control mechanisms are imposed on manufacturing, purchasing, and distributing controlled substances:

1. Registration of handlers. Any person who handles or intends to handle controlled substances must obtain a registration issued by the DEA. A unique number is assigned to legitimate handlers: importers, exporters, manufacturers, wholesalers, hospitals, pharmacies, physicians and researchers. Prior to the purchase of a controlled substance the number must be made available to the supplier by the customer, thus diminishing the opportunity for unauthorized transactions.

2. Recordkeeping Requirements. Full records must be kept of all quantities manufactured, and of all purchases, sales and inventories of all controlled substances regardless of the schedule in which they are placed. Limited exemptions are available to physicians and researchers. Because they are highly abusable substances, records for Schedule I and II drugs must be kept separate from all other records by the handler for expeditious investigations if called for. The system of control makes it possible to trace the flow of any drug from the time it is first manufactured or imported to the actual person who receives it. It also serves as an international check for large corporations who must be concerned about employee pilferage. The mere existence of this requirement can discourage forms of abuse.

3. *Quotas on Manufacturing.* The DEA limits the quantity of controlled substances listed in Schedules I and II which may be produced during any calendar year. Although the statute speaks exclusively in terms of Schedules I and II, certain drugs in Schedules III, IV and V derive from materials listed in Schedule II. Codeine syrups, for example, are made by combining codeine (a Schedule II drug) with other ingredients in a special diluted form. Therefore many narcotic products in Schedules III and V, as well as certain barbiturate combination drugs in Schedule III, are in fact subject to quotas as well. The DEA uses available data on sales and inventories of Schedule I and II substances, and taking into accouunt Food and Drug Administration (FDA) estimates of drug usage, it establishes aggregate production quotas which set the national limits of production. The overall production limits are subdivided into manufacturing quotas which are granted to the registered manufacturers. To set manufacturing quotas it is necessary to determine how much bulk controlled substance will be purchased by those companies engaged only in the formulation of dosage units. Formulating companies are granted procurement quotas, based on their past usage.

4. *Restrictions on Distribution.* Record-keeping is required for the distribution of a controlled substance from one manufacturer to another, from manufacturer to wholesaler, from importer to wholesaler, and from wholesaler to dispenser. In the case of Schedule I and II drugs, the supplier must have a special order form from the customer. This form is issued only by the DEA (form 222) to those who are properly registered and is preprinted with the name and address of the customer. The drug must be shipped only to that person. This reinforcement of the registration requirement makes certain that only authorized persons may receive Schedule I and II drugs. For Schedule III, IV, and V drugs, no order form is necessary but the supplier is held fully accountable for any drug shipped to a purchaser who does not have a valid registration.

5. *Restrictions on Dispensing.* There are also restrictions on the dispensing or delivery of a controlled substance to the ultimate user, who may be a patient or research subject. Schedule I drugs may be used only in research situations as currently they have no accepted medical use in the U.S. A prescription order is required for Schedule II, III, and IV medications under the Federal Food, Drug and Cosmetic Act. The determination to place drugs on prescription is within the jurisdiction of the FDA. Schedule II drugs are subject to additional special restrictions: prescription orders must be written and signed by the practitioner and may not be telephoned in except in an emergency. In addition, these prescriptions may not be refilled; the patient must see the doctor again in order to get more drugs. Schedule III and IV drug orders may be either written or oral and with the doctor's authorization may be refilled up to five times within six months of the initial dispensing. Schedule V drugs include many over–the–counter (OTC) narcotic preparations, including many antitussives and antidiarrheals, and here too restrictions are im-

posed. The patient must be 18 years old, have some form of identification, and have his name entered into a special log maintained by the pharmacist.

6. *Limitations on Imports and Exports.* International transactions involving any drug in Schedules I or II or a narcotic drug in Schedule III must have prior approval of the DEA; international transactions involving a non–narcotic in Schedule III or any drug in Schedules IV or V do not need approval but prior notice must be given to the DEA. Approval to import a Schedule I or II drug is not given unless an importer can show that there is an insufficient domestic supply with no adequate competition. Similarly, exportation of Schedule I and II drugs and narcotic drugs in Schedule III is severely limited: exporters must demonstrate that the drugs are going to a country where they will actually be used and will not be re–exported.

7. *Conditions for Storage of Drugs.* The DEA sets requirements for the security of premises where controlled substances are stored. Among the requirements for Schedule I and II drugs are specially constructed vault and alarm systems. For Schedule III, IV and V drugs a vault is optional and the handler may segregate the controlled substance in a secure area under constant supervision. These requirements do not apply to qualified researchers, physicians, exporters and wholesalers who handle small quantities of controlled substances. The DEA is presently reviewing requirements for shippers as well as for employees who have access to controlled drugs.

8. *Reports of Transactions to the Government.* The monitoring of all drugs in Schedules I and II and narcotic drugs in Schedule III is carried out by the Automation of Reports and Consolidated Orders System (AR-COS), established in January 1974. Manufacturers, wholesalers, importers and exporters of these drugs must report all manufacturing activities, importations, exportations and all other distributions to the DEA. Inventories must also be filed annually.

9. *Criminal, Civil and Administrative Penalties for Illegal Acts.* Trafficking is defined as the unauthorized manufacture, distribution (that is, delivery whether by sale, gift or otherwise), or possession of with intent to distribute any controlled substance. For narcotics in Schedules I and II, a first offense is punishable by up to 15 years in prison and up to a $25,000 fine. For trafficking in a Schedule I and II non–narcotic drug or any Schedule III drug, the penalty is up to five years imprisonment and a $15,000 fine (except phencyclidine and certain related drugs for which there is a penalty of not more than ten years and $25,000). Trafficking in a Schedule IV drug is punishable by a maximum of three years and up to $10,000. Trafficking in a Schedule V drug is a misdemeanor punishable by up to one year and up to $5,000. Second and subsequent offenses are punishable by twice the penalty imposed for the first offense.

The CSA carefully distinguishes between trafficking offenses (by those who supply illicit drugs to abusers) and use offenses (by those possessing drugs solely for personal use). A use offense is always a misdemeanor on the first offense, punishable by one year and up to $5,000.

Procedures for Controlling Substances

The various procedures for controlling a substance under the CSA are set forth in Section 201 of the act. Proceedings may be initiated by HEW, by the DEA, or by petition from any interested person or group: the manufacturer of a drug; a medical society or association; a pharmacy association; a public interest group concerned with drug abuse; or a state or local government agency. When a petition is received by the DEA the agency begins its own investigation of the drug. In most cases this process has led to a report and recommendation to HEW.

International Obligations

The CSA further provides that if control of any drug is required by U.S. obligation under international treaty arrangements, the drug shall be placed under the schedule deemed most appropriate to carry out these obligations. As cited in the CSA, the U.S. is a party to the Single Convention on Narcotic Drugs of 1961, designed to establish effective control over international and domestic traffic in narcotics: coca leaf, cocaine and cannabis are included within the legal definitions. A second treaty, the Convention on Psychotropic Substances of 1971, which became enforceable in 1976, is designed to establish comparable control over such drugs as LSD, amphetamines, certain barbiturates and other depressants. Legislation has been passed by Congress authorizing the U.S. to become a signatory to this treaty, and ratification is expected shortly.

convulsions   Involuntary spasmodic contractions of muscles. Convulsions can occur in cases of stimulant OVERDOSE and during CNS depressant WITHDRAWAL. (See also DELIRIUM TREMENS.)

cough medicine   Cough medicines are often abused because of their high alcohol content. Some nighttime cough medicines have more than twice the amount of alcohol found in wine and only 15% less than the amount found in some hard liquors. Comtrex Nighttime and Vick's Nyquil Cold Medicine both contain 25% alcohol; Vick's Formula 44D has 10% alcohol; Pertussin Cough Syrup for Children, 8% alcohol; Chlor–Trimeton Allergy Syrup, 7%; and Robitussin Cough Formula, 3.5%.

Many cough medicines are also abused because of the CODEINE they contain. An effective antitussive, codeine resembles MORPHINE but its effects are milder. Although it is considered only mildly addictive and instances of addiction are rare, it is often abused

for its mild euphoric and sedative properties. Codeine is a Schedule II drug and it is more difficult to obtain a cough medicine containing codeine than it is an over–the–counter (OTC) cough medicine with a high alcohol content, although both can be and are abused. Dextromethorphan, contained in Ramilar and most other OTC cough preparations, has a lower abuse potential than codeine. It has been taken infrequently in large quantities for abuse purposes.

counseling   See TREATMENT, REHABILITATION and GROUP THERAPY.

counterculture   A culture which rejects key norms and values of the general society at large. The term was coined in the 1960s and was used to describe those who were in favor of the use of such drugs as LSD and marijuana. Many of these individuals were also anti–government, anti–police and anti–war. It was particularly applied to the young adults living in HAIGHT–ASHBURY.

craving   An overwhelming desire or need for a drug that can be either physical or psychological in origin. (See also DEPENDENCY.)

crime   A drug user needs a vast amount of money in order to support a habit—usually more than he has access to by legal means. The usual categories of crime indulged in by drug users to support their habits are: theft, drug dealing (buying and selling), confidence games, pimping, prostitution, gambling and forgery.

Studies conducted by the National Institute of Drug Abuse (NIDA) found that many drug users commit more than one type of crime to maintain their habits, although they tend to focus on a particular activity. It was also found that those addicted to drugs at a younger age tend to commit crimes more frequently later on. The following table identifies the types and frequencies of crimes committed by heroin addicts in an NIDA study. The survey, which covered 11 years, followed 243 male heroin addicts in Baltimore, Maryland. In total, the men committed more than 473,738 crimes during their years on the street (they were not incarcerated). The study is based on "crime days per year at risk."

A second study by NIDA in Miami, Florida, covered 1,007 drug– and non–drug–using criminals. In the year prior to being interviewed, the individuals committed 355,699 crimes: heroin users were more heavily involved in criminal activities than other drug users or non–users, not a surprising fact considering the expense of a heroin habit. Employed heroin users committed crimes considered less serious than those committed by unemployed users. Of the total crimes committed, 122,484 were drug sales; 8,144 were assaults and robberies; 87,795 involved burglary and other types of theft; 9,514 were forgeries. Only a small portion of the crimes committed resulted in arrest: 248 crimes to one arrest. The ratio of crimes to arrest varied according to the type of illegal activity: 35:1 for assaults and robberies; 102:1 for forgeries; 148:1 for burglaries and other thefts; 761:1 for drug sales.

The seriousness of the crimes involved grows greater with age. Among youthful addicts there are more muggings and purse snatchings; older addicts commit robberies. Because of black market prices, an addict only realizes one–fourth of the value of stolen merchandise, a fact that accounts for the cost of addiction in relation to the criminality involved. Unfortunately, many members of the public welcome the opportunity to buy black market items at bargain prices and thus

Crime–Days Per Year at Risk by Type of Criminal Career and Addiction Status				
			Crime–Days Per Year at Risk	
Crime Career Type	Number of Subjects	Crime–Days Per Year at Risk	When Addicted	When Not Addicted*
Theft Daily	41	330.3	347.7	109.7
Sale of Drugs Daily	13	328.0	353.2	88.3
Other Crimes Daily	7	319.4	341.4	151.0
Weekly** Theft	58	189.6	280.9	23.3
Weekly Sale of Drugs	18	181.1	284.0	27.6
Weekly, Other Crimes	7	201.9	297.0	70.1
Infrequent Theft	57	72.4	140.7	7.4
Infrequent Sales	14	102.4	260.9	10.5
Infrequent, Other Crimes	22	46.8	108.2	2.3
No Crime	6	—	—	—
Total	243	178.5	248.0	40.8

*Addicted refers to regular use of opiates at least four times per week for a period lasting at least one month. Not addicted refers to usage less than this.

**Weekly refers to more than once a week but less than daily.

Source: Department of Health and Human Services, National Institute of Drug Abuse, Rockville, Md.

provide a ready market for stolen goods. The business community is also affected by criminality. Not only does business suffer from on–and–off–the–job absenteeism because of drug abuse, it also suffers substantial losses due to theft. Thefts are committed both by low level employees, and high level employees with $100–a–day habits.

In crimes that involve drug abuse everyone is a victim: the business community, the addict and the non–addict are all hurt. Still, it cannot be generalized that all addicts are criminals. While there is an undeniable connection between crime and addiction, there are a great many people who were engaged in criminal activity before they became addicted, and an equally great number would be involved in criminal activity whether or not they are addicted. There are still others who prefer to give up drugs rather than indulge in criminal activity. Although crimes connected with addiction are usually perpetrated against property, and do not generally involve serious crimes against individuals, such as murder, addicts should not be excused from responsibility. Supportive measures by the courts, treatment and rehabilitation, along with correction, parole and probation would certainly help to reverse the criminal trend.

Although it has been suggested that METH-ADONE maintenance will reduce criminal activity among heroin abusers, the theory has been challenged by those who offer overwhelming evidence of clinic drugs being bought and sold illegally on the streets. Some addicts have even been known to support their habits by selling their take home supplies or methadone that has been smuggled out of clinics.

As to the involvement of alcohol in criminal activity, it is not clear whether drinking leads to criminal activity or whether involvement in criminal activity leads to drinking. Statistics involving alcohol–related crimes vary widely. In the case of rape offenders,

alcohol involvement was from 13% to 50%; in the case of rape victims, alcohol involvement was 6% to 31%. In studies of homicides it was found that from 28% to 86% of the offenders used alcohol and 14% to 87% of the victims used alcohol. There have been a number of theories which have attempted to explain the role of alcohol in criminal and violent behavior. It has been suggested that alcohol releases inhibitions and intensifies certain mental states: the release of anger may enhance the likelihood of violence and aggression. The synergistic combination of alcohol and another drug may result in increased violent behavior.

The relationship of crime to drug abuse is generally confined to the study of those addicted to heroin or alcohol, and much less to those addicted to other drugs. This is probably because of the high cost involved in heroin addiction and the greater incidence of violence related to alcoholism. This is not to say that there is no incidence of crime among those addicted to drugs such as marijuana. Studies of marijuana are generally related to its effects on the body but it has been suggested that it should not be given a clean bill of health in relation to crime. The same holds true for amphetamines and hallucinogens. Excessive indulgence can result in mental disorder and confusion leading to intellectual impairment; the resulting relaxation of moral sense can lead to criminal and violent acts. The susceptibility of an individual when he takes a drug, along with the dosage, can also account for criminal involvement. Because there are no conclusive criminal studies of marijuana and other drugs, it is hard to estimate how many crimes would be committed if they were not available.

There is less chance of violent aggressive behavior in heroin addicts than in other drug addicts because heroin tends to diminish aggressiveness. This does not hold true for alcoholics because alcohol tends to evoke aggressiveness; nor is it true of barbiturate users.

One would think that because barbiturates are sedative hypnotic drugs, abusers would simply fall asleep. In fact, they become argumentative, overactive and irritable. Studies have found, for example, that members of motorcycle gangs will take "downers" before engaging in street fights and confrontations; this kind of reaction is similar to the aggressive behavior that alcohol often produces. Drug use can produce false feelings and ideas of suspicion and persecution. It can also produce feelings of omnipotence and bravado. These paranoid thought disorders can lead to bursts of violence and hyperactivity which, in turn, can lead to criminal behavior. Ordinarily it is only moderate doses of a drug that lead to violence and criminality. Small doses do not generally lead to aggressiveness, and large doses are usually incapacitating. The setting in which someone takes a drug, along with his mood and personality, can also alter a drug's action. In other words, no drug is invariably criminogenic.

crime, organized   There is a massive involvement of organized crime in drug trafficking largely because it is extremely lucrative. Illicit retail drug sales in 1980 were estimated by the U.S. government to total more than $79 billion, a figure that nearly equals the combined profits of the largest 500 industrial corporations in America.

Organized crime reaped the bulk of these profits, a 50% increase from 1977, through large-scale highly sophisticated drug operations. "Big time" drug dealers have to obtain the illicit substances (usually overseas), arrange for the processing of the drugs (coca into cocaine, and so on), smuggle them into the country, arrange for the cutting of pure drugs, and then distribute them over a wide geographical area in elaborate trafficking networks. Drug money is often "laundered" or passed through legitimate businesses, some

of which are "fronts" in major enterprises, before it is put back into the drug trade.

Two new non-traditional groups have emerged in organized crime in the last two decades—prison gangs which operate inside and outside prison, and outlaw motorcycle gangs. Other drug cartels that have recently appeared are Colombian groups known as "Cocaine Cowboys," and Southeast Asian groups. The common objective is money and the primary tactic is violence. The use of violence is a major problem. In 1981, for example, 25% of all homicides in Dade County, Florida, were the result of drug groups carrying out machine-gun assassinations in public places. Organized crime also engages in weapons trafficking, prostitution, gambling, pornography, and other activities that directly or indirectly involve many innocent people and institutions. There are also reports of public officials at all levels who are being corrupted by drug money, particularly rural police officers who accept large sums to "look the other way" during smuggling operations.

To combat organized crime, the number one crime problem, the Drug Enforcement Administration (DEA) has recently been reorganized; and for the first time the FBI has been brought into the fight to work with the DEA. The Navy and Coast Guard are also cooperating in interdicting smuggling operations.

crisis intervention   The process of diagnosing and arresting such conditions as overdose, suicide attempts and panic reaction in drug crisis situations. Unconsciousness, low breathing rate, respiratory arrest, fever, extreme high or low pulse rate, muscle rigidity and vomiting in a semi- or unconscious state are signs indicating overdose and the need for immediate drug crisis intervention.

cross-addiction   Addiction between drugs within the same group can be mutual or interchangeable. For example, a person addicted to a sedative will in some degree be addicted to all other sedatives, including alcohol. Therefore a person addicted to Librium could prevent WITHDRAWAL SYMPTOMS by taking alcohol and vice versa. The same does not apply to drugs from other groups: if someone is addicted to a sedative, a narcotic would not be completely effective.

cross–dependence   The term is used in much the same way as CROSS–ADDICTION, meaning that dependence between drugs of the same group is mutual or interchangeable.

cross–tolerance   If tolerance has developed to one drug it will carry over to another in the same group. For example, alcoholics are more difficult to anesthetize than nonalcoholics. The increased ability to metabolize another drug may be a cause of cross–tolerance, or it may be caused by changes in the tissues of the central nervous system (CNS) which make the system less responsive to the other drug.

cultural stress etiological theories   See SOCIOCULTURAL ETIOLOGICAL THEORIES.

cut   The act of diluting HEROIN (usually with milk sugar) so that the pusher can make a larger profit. A mixture containing only 5% heroin is the usual product sold to the consumer.

cyclazocine   A narcotic antagonist used in the treatment of heroin addiction. An addict who has been withdrawn from heroin and then treated with cyclazocine will not feel the effects of an ordinary dose of heroin. The drug can cause dependence but withdrawal is milder than heroin withdrawal. Cyclazocine has not been used since naltrexone, a more effective and longer lasting antagonist, has become available.

cyclobarbital   A short–acting BARBITURATE that is mainly used in hypnosis. Because of the rapid onset of its effects and their short duration it is found undesirable by most drug abusers.

Cylert® (Abbott)   A STIMULANT of the central nervous system that is generally used for children with Minimal Brain Dysfunction (Attention Deficit Disorder). It is a brand of pemoline. Although it is pharmacologically similar to other CNS stimulants (AMPHETAMINES), it does not have a high potential for abuse. Overdosage can result in agitation, restlessness and hallucinations. It is available in 18.75 mg yellow tablets; 37.5 mg orange tablets; and 75 mg tan tablets.

Cystospaz–SR® (Webcon)   A depressant containing the intermediate–acting BARBITURATE, butabarbital. It is used as an antispasmodic–sedative and may be habit–forming. It is supplied in blue opaque and clear yellow capsules.

cytisine   An extremely poisonous alkaloid found in many plants of the pea family. It was once used as a cathartic and diuretic. Canary Island broom, Spanish broom and Scotch broom, which are sometimes smoked or taken orally, all contain cytisine.

D

Dalmane® (Roche)   A DEPRESSANT, benzodiazepine flurazepam hydrochloride, used as a hypnotic agent in the treatment of insomnia. It is in widespread use. When used with alcohol or other central nervous system depressants, it can have an additive effect. Overdosage can result in somnolence, confusion and coma. It is available in 15 mg orange and ivory capsules, and in 30 mg red and ivory capsules.

damiana   *Turnera diffusa*, a tropical American plant of the Turneraceae family. There are claims that smoking the leaves can produce a marijuana–like effect. It is also purported to be a mild aphrodisiac.

Darvocet–N® (Lilly)   See DARVON–N.

Darvon® (Lilly)   An analgesic that is widely used for mild to moderate pain, Darvon has the pharmacological properties of a NARCOTIC but does not compare with narcotics in analgesic potency. It contains propoxyphene hydrochloride. The use of Darvon with alcohol or other central nervous system depressants can result in additive depressant effects. The drug can produce psychic dependence, and its potential for abuse is similar to codeine. Overdosage can result in respiratory depression, convulsions, circulatory collapse, pupil constriction, and extreme somnolence leading to stupor and coma. Cardiac arrest and death have occurred. Darvon is supplied in 32 and 65 mg light pink opaque capsules. It is also available mixed with other drugs: Darvon Compound and Darvon Compound–65, each with aspirin, caffeine, and phenacetin; and Darvon with A.S.A. which is aspirin. The combination of propoxyphene with aspirin, or a mixture of aspirin, caffeine and phenacetin, will produce greater analgesia than that of propoxyphene alone. Darvon Compound is supplied in capsules with a light pink opaque body and light gray opaque cap. Darvon Compound–65 is supplied in capsules with a red opaque body and light gray cap. Darvon with A.S.A. is supplied in capsules with a red opaque body and light pink opaque cap.

Darvon–N® (Lilly)   A drug that contains propoxyphene napsylate, which is similar to propoxyphene hydrochloride (see DARVON),

but differs in that it allows more stable, longer–acting liquid and tablet dosage forms. Like Darvon, it is a mild analgesic and is structurally related to the narcotics but it does not compare in potency. Psychic dependence can occur and there is potential for abuse. Overdose symptoms are the same as those for Darvon. Darvon–N has been used to detoxify patients from opiate dependence. Darvon–N is supplied in buff–colored oval tablets; Darvon–N with A.S.A. (aspirin) are oval–shaped orange tablets. Darvocet–N 50, and Darvocet–N 100 (which are propoxyphene napsylate and acetaminophen) are dark orange capsule–shaped tablets.

datura   A HALLUCINOGEN found in the poisonous Jimson weed plant, *Datura stramonium*, which is a member of the potato family (Solanaceae). The active ingredients in the substance are the BELLADONNA alkaloids, atropine, scopolamine and hyoscyamine. Leaves and seeds of this extremely dangerous plant have been used as poisons and hallucinogens for centuries. Users smoke the dried leaves. The leaves have also been used in asthma powders and in the anti–asthma cigarette, Asthmador.
   Synonyms: angel's trumpet, devil's apple, devil's weed, Jamestown weed, Jimsonweed, stinkweed, stramonium, thorn apple.

dawamesk   A green cake popular in North Africa, made from sugar, spices, orange juice and the tops of the CANNABIS plant. It is eaten for its hallucinogenic effects and it was in the form of dawamesk that cannabis was first introduced to Europe in the mid–1800s.

DAWN   See DRUG ABUSE WARNING NETWORK.

Daytop   See THERAPEUTIC COMMUNITIES.

DEA   See DRUG ENFORCEMENT ADMINISTRATION.

deadly nightshade   See BELLADONNA.

decriminalization   See LEGAL ASPECTS.

delirium   Many drugs, including some which do not have a mental effect, can cause a delirium in large doses or in average amounts in people who are sensitive to them. A delirium, also called a toxic psychosis, is marked by confusion, disorientation, clouding of consciousness, hallucinations and delusions. Distractibility, inability to concentrate and agitation are often observed.

delirium tremens   A serious condition of WITHDRAWAL from barbiturate–type drugs and alcohol, commonly referred to as the D.T.'s. This condition is considered a medical emergency and the patient should be hospitalized immediately. Symptoms may include vivid and terrifying auditory, visual and tactile hallucinations; profound confusion; disorientation; severe agitation and restlessness; insomnia; fever; and abnormally rapid heartbeat. Sedation may be required, but extreme caution should be used in order to avoid oversedation, for a drug dosage that would suppress all symptoms would also seriously depress the patient's respiration. The D.T.'s can last for three to four days, or can persist intermittently for several weeks.

delta alcoholism   See JELLINEK.

delusions   A belief or firm fixed idea that is not amenable to reason, rationality or evidence to the contrary. Delusions are common among those who are under the influence of a hallucinogen or large doses of stimulants, and can be dangerous. During the "LSD era" several deaths were reported because some users were under the delusion that they could walk on water or fly. Delusions may be persecutory or grandiose in quality.

dementia   A condition described by the Diagnostic and Statistical Manual (see DSM III) as "a loss of intellectual abilities of sufficient severity to interfere with social or intellectual functioning." The deficit is multifaceted and involves memory, judgment, abstract thought and other cortical functions. Changes in personality and behavior also occur. Alcoholism, or nutritional deficiencies associated with alcoholism, are two of its many possible causes. Early symptoms, which can vary, include a slow deterioration of personality and intellect. Judgment, insight, speech and motor activity are affected. Personal habits deteriorate and eventually the patient requires total nursing care.

Demerol® (Winthrop)   A narcotic (a brand of MEPERIDINE hydrochloride) used as an analgesic for moderate to severe pain and as a sedative. Its activity is similar to that of morphine: it can produce the same type of dependence, and it has a high potential for abuse. Respiratory depression and coma may result from overdosage, and if Demerol is combined with alcohol or other central nervous system depressants an additive effect can occur. It is available in white scored tablets of 50 and 100 mg, and as a banana–flavored syrup (nonalcoholic) of 50 mg per ml. For parenteral use it is available in vials, ampules and disposable syringes.

denial   An addicted person's refusal or inability to admit the existence of a drinking or drug problem. It is one of the main defense mechanisms alcoholics employ to deal with life and this posture distinguishes them from social drinkers. Relatives and friends will also often "deny" an alcoholic's problem to protect him. Denial should be dealt with quickly in alcohol treatment: by recognizing his denial for what it is, an alcoholic becomes more aware of his problem and his role in its creation.

Denmark Drug abuse began to be noted as a problem in Denmark early on in World War II, around 1940. As the problem increased, particularly morphine abuse, the government took action and passed the Euphoric Drugs Act of 1955. It empowered the Minister of the Interior to limit the use of certain drugs to medical purposes. In the 1960s, as abuse grew more widespread and included the use of cannabis and amphetamines along with morphine, the government switched its attention to peddlers and stiff penal rules for drug offenses were introduced in 1965. A 1968 study revealed that out of 350,000 school–age youths, 42,000 had used drugs (90% of the cases involved the use of marijuana). A follow–up study in 1970 showed that while the use of marijuana and other drugs showed a steady increase it was on a smaller scale than before. Despite a new wave of legislation and increased penalties, the Danish attitude toward drug abuse (similar to that of Great Britian) is that addiction is first and foremost a medical problem and is a manifestation of disease.

Since the mid–1970s the number of addicts seems to have stabilized at around 6,000 to 10,000, out of a total population of five million. Abuse is dominated by heroin—most of which is brought in from Southwest Asia—but also includes the use of barbiturates, amphetamines and cannabis. Although the abuse of LSD was once pronounced it is now negligible. Today the average age of drug abusers is 26–27 (70% of the addicts being over 25). As most addicts make their debut around the age of 18, this means an abuse career of from six to 10 years. The incidence of new addicts each year is not known but is estimated to be around 500 to 800 per year. The rising age of addicts reflects the fact that few are able to stop their abuse—only 5% a year.

Although the number of addicts has stabilized somewhat, the consequences of abuse have increased considerably. Along with the strain on penal institutions because of growing offenses against property, there is also an increase in organized crime—a relatively new development in Denmark. The number of deaths from drug abuse in the 26–27 age group is second only to vehicle fatalities, although it is possible that some of the deaths—particularly those attributed to heroin—are actually the result of other complications (see SYNDROME X).

Drug addicts in Denmark can receive treatment in two ways, from general practitioners or from publicly financed treatment centers (youth centers). Treatment in youth centers is generally on an outpatient basis and includes the use of therapeutic communities. There is, however, relatively little use of prescribed drugs in the treatment of heroin abuse, and methadone treatment of long duration is limited. The program includes counseling, social and psychological support, and vocational rehabilitation. There is now a plan to rapidly expand facilities for youth centers.

A relatively large number of addicts seek treatment from general practitioners. This is partly a result of lack of places in treatment centers, and partly because many addicts prefer the more medical type of treatment.

A majority of drug addicts are not in contact with either general practitioners or treatment centers. A total of 2,000 addicts were in touch with a treatment institution in 1981, but only a small portion received prolonged treatment. Because of this fact, there is a growing trend toward strengthening established social institutions and training more social workers. There are also plans to set up more youth centers to house drug abusers within the penal system.

In Denmark there has always been a liberal attitude toward alcohol consumption; the national drinking pattern has been one of frequent but temperate consumption. The majority of consumption takes place in the home and mostly beer is involved. Although there has been some increase in preference for distilled spirits during recent years the basic pattern remains unchanged.

Because the Danish government believes that the regulation of alcohol consumption is suitable only if agreed to by the majority, it limits control to the taxation of alcoholic beverages. There is a National Commission on Alcohol, but its purpose is advisory; public responsibility for prevention and control of alcohol–related problems is left in the hands of county–level government. Because the consumption of both wine and distilled spirits rose twice as fast as beer between 1967 and 1977, there is a growing number of problem drinkers in the country. It is responsible for an increase in alcohol–impaired driving offenses and in admissions to psychiatric hospitals for alcohol–related problems. Mortality rates for alcoholism and the incidence of liver cirrhosis have also increased in the last 10 years.

dentistry   Alcoholism and the abuse of other sedative drugs can complicate dental surgery. Dentists should, therefore, be informed or be on the lookout for warning signs of drug abuse. Care should be taken in the use of anesthetics since both cross–tolerance and synergistic effects can result from alcohol–sedative drug–anesthetic combinations. If a patient has a sedative drug in his system while undergoing dental surgery, the initial phase of anesthesia will be followed by a synergistic reaction that can produce a potentially dangerous situation.

Routine dental examinations can frequently disclose symptoms of alcoholism, such as long–term neglect; enlarged parotid glands (the largest salivary glands); and general deficiencies in oral hygiene. Alcoholics have a rate of permanent tooth loss that is three times that of the general population and they are more likely to consult dentists for emergency treatment than for routine care. The abuse of any drug is likely to lead to the

neglect of oral care. Poor nutrition, which is common among drug abusers, can also lead to tooth decay and loss.

dependence   There are two aspects to dependency: physical and psychological. A person can be dependent in either one of these ways or in both. Dependency can occur after periodic or prolonged use of a drug and its characteristics vary according to the drug involved. In 1964 the World Health Organization recommended that the term "drug dependence" be substituted for the term "drug addiction" because the latter term was too general. (See also ADDICTION, PHYSICAL DEPENDENCE and PSYCHOLOGICAL DEPENDENCE.)

depressants   Drugs which act on and slow down the action of the CENTRAL NERVOUS SYSTEM (CNS), diminishing or stopping vital body functions. OPIATES, BARBITURATES, ALCOHOL and INHALANTS are depressants. Alcohol and sedatives (tranquilizers) are the most commonly used and abused depressant drugs. Their action is irregular because they do not depress all parts of the CNS at once. They work primarily on the brain, depressing psychomotor activity and relieving tension and anxiety. When the sedative level in the blood begins to fall, psychomotor activity increases, producing agitation. The term "depressant" may be misleading because such drugs actually elevate a person's mood initially. The word "depressant" has no direct relationship to "depression" except that consistent use of CNS depressants can result in psychological depression.

depressed communities   Unlike boom towns, depressed communities show a decline in economic growth and/or population. They are generally long–established stable areas that have declined over a period of time. Because employment opportunities are limited, young people generally leave such communities and the population therefore tends to be older than average. Although increases in drug abuse are usually low, alcohol abuse tends to be higher—probably a reflection of individual rather than mass reaction, and of differences in the ethnic and religious make–up of communities. Although there is less money to be spent on alcohol it is still a ready sedative for problems and is often cheaper than other forms of recreation. It can also be indulged in at any time of day. (See also ELDERLY.)

depression Depression is a mood or state of despondency which, in normal individuals, is characterized by feelings of inadequacy, pessimism (particularly about the future) and lowered activity. In pathological cases, depression is an extreme state of unresponsiveness to stimuli, along with feelings of hopelessness, delusions of inadequacy and self–depreciation.

Drugs are often prescibed as a treatment for depression but they can also be the cause of depression. Individuals suffering from mild or temporary depression have found small prescribed doses of amphetamine effective. Long–term use or large doses are generally followed by depression, however. Consequently, amphetamines are worthless and possibly harmful in many cases. Abusers of illicit amphetamines are usually depressed individuals who seek the feeling of self–worth and added energy that the drug will produce.

Cocaine is another stimulant drug often used to overcome depression because it produces feelings of euphoria, increased alertness and great power. When cocaine is used regularly and for a long period of time and then discontinued, depression will return and generally in a more severe form. More cocaine is then needed to combat the depression which leads to a perpetuation of the habit. This vicious circle is also true of amphetamine use.

Depression tends to be a major withdrawal symptom of most drug use. In the case of heroin addiction, depression, along with craving and anxiety, is not just a short–term symptom but may continue for years and oftens leads to a relapse. Depression is also a frequent symptom of withdrawal from caffeine and nicotine.

Depression is a disorder often associated with alcoholism. It may be a reason for drinking or it may be a result of drinking. Alcohol is often consumed for its euphoric effects and the feeling of self–confidence that it induces. These pleasant feelings, however, are quickly followed by depression and prolonged drinking almost always leads to a deterioration of mood.

Suicide attempts are common among individuals who experience depression in post-withdrawal states. Doctors sometimes prescribe tranquilizers in an attempt to calm the patient but they usually worsen the depression.

Depressive states are commonly found among the elderly, perhaps because they often feel of little use to society and wonder what they have to live for. ANTIDEPRESSANTS, a major classification of recently developed drugs, are often prescribed to improve mood in severely depressed patients. Antidepressants are generally divided into two categories: the tricyclic compounds (amitriptyline hydrochloride and imipramine hydrochloride), and the MONOAMINE OXIDASE (MAO) INHIBITORS. Antidepressants are rarely used for nonmedical purposes since they have no immediate pleasurable effect on normal mood states. In cases of pathological depression, however, they seem to have a stimulant effect.

deprivation A psychological theory that suggests alcoholism is caused by disturbance and deprivation in early infancy. If deprived of a significant emotional relationship during his or her early years, so the theory goes, an individual will later develop primitive, excessive and insatiable demands which will result in the failure of interpersonal relationships. Long suppressed feelings of loss and rejection will reawaken and, rather than destroy another, the person will turn his anger inward or obliterate it by drinking. As alcohol is a sedative drug, this theory can be extended to include the use of other sedative drugs.

Deprol® (Wallace) A depressant that is a combination of MEPROBAMATE (for tranquilizing action) and benactyzine hydrochloride (for antidepressant action). Psychological and physical dependence can occur and its combination with alcohol or other central nervous system depressants can have an additive effect. There has been a relatively high incidence of suicide attempts with Deprol. In the case of overdosage, sleep ensues rapidly; respiratory rates, pulse and blood pressure are reduced. It is supplied in pink tablets of 400 mg meprobamate and 1 mg benactyzine.

desensitization A technique employed to decrease tension in situations that can lead to the use of drugs. Clients are asked to visualize a scene that would ordinarily make them tense and reduce their self–control, such as being offered a "fix" by an old friend. They are then taught relaxation methods and how to make a deliberate shift to calming mental imagery.

Desoxyn® (Abbott) A central nervous system stimulant containing methamphetamine hydrochloride, that is used primarily as an anorectic for weight control. A member of the AMPHETAMINE group of sympathomimetic amines, it has a high potential for abuse. Tolerance and severe psychological dependence, along with social disability, can occur. Overdosage can result in restlessness, tremors, rapid respiration and hallucinations. It is supplied in 2.5 and 5 mg white tablets, and in gradumet (long–acting) tablets (inert, porous, plastic matrix which is impregnated with Desoxyn) of 5 mg white, 10 mg orange and 15 mg yellow.

DET (diethyltryptamine) A completely synthetic HALLUCINOGEN similar to DMT. Like DMT, the drug is easily produced in home laboratories. DET produces an experience similar to a DMT trip except that it is milder and of even shorter duration.

detoxification A treatment process by which a patient is slowly withdrawn from a drug to which he has become addicted. After detoxification the patient is no longer *physically* dependent on the drug and is able to abstain from using it without physical discomfort. The symptoms that occur during the process depend on the type of drug involved. Decisions concerning where and how a patient should be detoxified depend on a number of factors: the drug concerned, the length of use, and the degree of tolerance that has developed.

In the case of HEROIN addiction, the alternatives are: (1) the immediate goal of complete opiate abstinence; (2) opiate abstinence in preparation for antagonist therapy; or (3) abstinence with substitution therapy (METHADONE maintenance). Based on individual motivation, opiate abstinence is generally only chosen in the case of a short–term, low–dose habit, and only for an addict who does not have a history of relapse after detoxification. This is because relapse is probable with this program unless the addict is removed from his previous life situation where the drug is available and its use is reinforced by his friends. Therapeutic communities such as SYNANON houses, often follow this type of detoxification. Drug–free outpatient treatment is another alternative.

The second method, programs which use narcotic antagonists, are not as widely available as those which use substitution therapy. A narcotic antagonist, such as NALTREXONE, blocks the euphoric effects of opiates if they are injected and there is no dependence or tolerance. Antagonists do not block the effects of alcohol and other non–opiate drugs, however. There are two major drawbacks to the use of an antagonist. First, because it is not addictive, a patient may stop using it and return to his or her old drug habits. And, second, it does not suppress the anxiety and craving that occurs after detoxification as a substitute substance does.

Although abstinence is obviously the most desirable program *if* it is effective, the most widely used program is that of substitution therapy. Methadone, a synthetic opiate developed in Germany at the close of World War II because of a shortage of morphine, was first tried in the United States in the treatment of narcotic addicts during the late 1940s. Methadone has two distinct advantages—it is legal and it is inexpensive. It also has disadvantages; it is just as addictive as heroin and it must be continued until the patient has reconstructed his entire life–style. The use of methadone is three–fold: it prevents the patient from suffering withdrawal symptoms (detoxification); it satisfies craving (maintenance); and with proper dosage it prevents the patient from experiencing the euphoric effects of heroin (maintenance).

Self–treatment attempts by heroin addicts are common. COLD TURKEY approaches undertaken at home, in some therapeutic communities, or in the company of friends, are sometimes unsuccessful.

Non–narcotic detoxification is practiced with sedatives and antispasmotics or with CLONIDINE.

Detoxification from MARIJUANA and HALLUCINOGENS can usually be achieved in a relatively short time and without hospitalization. The severe symptoms felt during narcotic withdrawal are not present.

Withdrawal from AMPHETAMINES can take several days and is usually accompanied by increased sleeping, ravenous appetite,

uneasiness, perspiration, twitching of limbs and severe depression. The same is true of COCAINE withdrawal. Because of the depression, detoxification programs for amphetamines and cocaine involve constant medical attention to combat suicide attempts.

Withdrawal from ALCOHOL and BARBITURATES is much more difficult and dangerous than withdrawal from amphetamines. The detoxification process should be undertaken with medical supervision. In the case of barbiturates withdrawal symptoms may not occur until a few days after the last dose is taken. Weakness, dizziness, anxiety and tremors may be followed by hallucinations and delusions. The patient may exhibit hostile and violent behavior. Detoxification is usually accomplished by the doctor administering smaller and smaller doses of the drug, beginning with the amount the patient has developed a tolerance to. This system usually wards off severe withdrawal symptoms. (Alternatively, a drug that is cross–tolerant to the abused substance may be substituted. For barbiturates it is customarily phenobarbital or pentobarbital.) As in the case of heroin addiction, once physical dependency has been overcome, the patient must undergo psychological rehabilitation.

Alcohol detoxification can generally be accomplished during a short confinement (five to ten days) in a general hospital. Although hospitalization has advantages, patients with mild or moderate withdrawal symptoms and no medical complications may be able to undergo detoxification in a more social setting. For severe cases hospitalization has several advantages, including removing the alcoholic from his drinking environment; emphasizing that he is suffering from a disease; protecting him from the sometimes fatal effects of withdrawal; and giving him the chance to start rehabilitation.

Withdrawal symptoms during alcohol detoxification tend to appear in three stages. The first symptoms include weakness, tremulousness, headache, anxiety and sometimes abdominal cramps and appear in a matter of hours. During the second stage, tremors become more marked and the patient may begin to "see" or "hear" things. Convulsive seizures known as RUM FITS may occur on the second or third day of detoxification; the number of seizures vary depending on the individual. In the third stage, withdrawal involves delirium tremens and alcoholic hallucinosis, commonly accompanied by loss of insight. During this stage the patient is in a severe state of agitation and disorientation, and sleeps little. The delusions can be terrifying and there is often violent behavior. After the patient passes through this third stage, detoxification is usually complete.

LIBRIUM or a similar tranquilizer is usually prescribed upon admission to a hospital (50 to 100 mg on a three–hour basis). This dosage is tapered down and an attempt is made to keep the patient alert but not tremulous. Before discharge all medications are discontinued. A plan for rehabilitation (ALCOHOL-ICS ANONYMOUS, ANTABUSE therapy or group therapy) is generally set up before the patient leaves the hospital. There has recently been some interest in the possibility of limited use of ambulatory detoxification for patients who have been carefully screened. Under such a program the patient attends a clinic on a daily basis and receives medication and counseling. Family and friends of a patient are encouraged to participate in this type of program.

Detoxification is just the beginning of a treatment that lasts a long time, perhaps a lifetime. Generally the physical dependency is the easiest to overcome; the patient is then faced with psychological REHABILITATION.

Dexedrine® (Smith, Kline & French)   An AMPHETAMINE (a brand of dextroamphetamine sulfate) usually used as an anorectic for weight control. It has been extensively abused and extreme psychological dependence and social disability can occur. It is a Schedule II drug. It is supplied in elixir; in 5 mg orange tablets; and in orange and brown Spansule capsules of 5 and 10 mg.

Synonyms: copilots, dexies.

dextroamphetamine   A synthetic AM-PHETAMINE. A central nervous system stimulant, it is used in the treatment of narcolepsy, Minimal Brain Dysfunction in children and as an anorectic. (See DEXEDRINE.)

dextromoramide   An analgesic with a potency greater than morphine. It is a synthetic OPIATE and classified as a Schedule II drug.

diabetes   The principal manifestation of diabetes is hyperglycemia (high blood sugar) and there has been some controversy about whether diabetics should be allowed to consume alcoholic beverages. Although small amounts of alcohol taken close to or with a meal generally produce little change in blood sugar levels, excessive consumption during a time of fasting can cause problems, and so can the consumption of sweet dessert wines, ports or liqueurs. When taken during a fasting state, alcohol can enhance the blood sugar–lowering action of insulin and interfere with the body's ability to produce its own glucose. Alcohol should not contribute more than 6% of the total calories consumed each day by a diabetic, because it can, on the simplest level, disrupt diet control, stimulate the appetite and provide extra calories. It is best for diabetics to consult their physicians about including alcohol in their diets. Alcoholics can develop diabetes because of destruction of insulin–producing cells in the pancreas.

diacetylmorphine   The semisynthetic opiate derivative HEROIN, first produced in 1898.

diazepam   A minor tranquilizer, diazepam is best known under the brand name VALIUM, which was until recently the number one prescribed drug in the United States. In 1974 Americans spent $500 million on 50 million prescriptions. Valium's liberal dispensation for anxiety and as a sleeping aid has made it a socially acceptable drug of abuse: it has been known to play as large a role in middle class American life as cocktail parties and little league baseball.

Diazepam appears as a colorless crystalline powder which is insoluble in water and slightly soluble in alcohol. After oral administration it is quickly and completely absorbed by the gastrointestinal tract, with effects manifesting in 30 minutes to one hour. The onset of effects from intramuscular injection is 15–30 minutes and there is even quicker onset of effects by intravenous injection. Diazepam is detoxified in the liver and metabolites are excreted in the urine and feces. The drug acts on the brain's limbic system, but does not interfere with the peripheral autonomic system. It has a half life of 20–50 hours and crosses the placental barrier.

Diazepam is prescribed to alleviate neurotic tension and anxiety which prevent a person from coping with daily life. It is also an effective sleeping pill. Its anticonvulsive properties warrant its use, alone and in conjunction with other drugs, to control muscle spasms in such conditions as cerebral palsy, paraplegia, petit mal and myoclonic seizures. It is also used to treat the symptoms of alcohol withdrawal. Both physicians and "street drug users" use diazepam to calm anxiety and panic induced by hallucinogenic drugs.

For mild to moderate neuroses it is prescribed in two or three daily doses of 2–5 mg, and in severe anxiety three or four daily doses of 5–10 mg are prescribed. A lethal dose of diazepam in humans has not yet been specified, but 50% of mice fed 758 mg per kilogram of body weight died. Therefore, it can hardly be used for suicidal purposes except in combination with other central nervous system (CNS) depressants.

A benzodiazepine derivative, diazepam's common side effects include initial drowsiness, unsteadiness and weakness. High doses cause intoxication similar to that produced by alcohol and barbiturates. When taken with alcohol or other central nervous system depressants it can have an additive effect. Tolerance, along with physical and psychological dependence can also occur. Withdrawal symptoms include convulsions, tremors, cramps and sweating.

Valium, a brand name of diazepam, is a favorite drug of minor abusers. It is available illicitly but probably a bigger problem is the fact that it is overprescribed for minimal anxiety. Doctors have been known to prescribe it freely to patients who insist they require a tranquilizer. Matters are complicated when a prescription is not limited to a certain number of refills, and Valium users have been known to take them freely when they know they will be well supplied. Supervision of the patient on diazepam or other benzodiazepines is essential despite their safety insofar as overdose is concerned. Situational anxiety does not seem to warrant constant tranquilization. Another question in the Valium controversy is whether, in the absence of Valium, a patient would resort to barbiturates or alcohol—which are much more dangerous—or not use any drug at all.

Illicit Valium (sometimes known as "the big V") is used by abusers who take large quantities to achieve intoxication. It is also frequently used to ease the crash experienced after amphetamine abuse.

Although over two hundred times the normal dose of Valium has been survived, the drug is still often used in suicide attempts. Some of these attempts have been successful, particularly in cases where alcohol was taken with the Valium.

Diazepam is a Schedule IV drug under the Controlled Substances Act.

Didrex® (Upjohn)   A central nervous system stimulant that contains benzphetamine hydrochloride, and which has a pharmacological and chemical activity similar to that of the AMPHETAMINES. It is used as an anorectic for weight control. Psychological dependence and social disability can occur and the drug has a potential for abuse. It is supplied in 25 mg yellow and 50 mg peach press–coated tablets.

diethylpropion   A synthetic drug similar to the AMPHETAMINES in its activity but with less central nervous system stimulation. It is usually used as an anorectic. See TENUATE.

diethyltryptamine   See DET.

digestion   Alcohol, particularly wine when taken in small quantities, may aid digestion. It allows freer salivation in "dry mouth" associated with stress, which in turn triggers increased gastric motility, the gentle motion which is beneficial to digestion and empties the stomach. Heavier doses, however—more than a glass or two of wine—can result in increased acid secretion causing gastritis and peptic ulceration.

dihydrocodeine   A semisynthetic narcotic analgesic that is related to codeine and has a similar activity. (See SYNALGOS.)

dihydrocodeinone   A synthetic codeine derivative, also oxycodone. (See PERCODAN.)

dihydromorphinone   An opium derivative that is used as an analgesic; also called hydromorphone. (See DILAUDID.)

Dilaudid® (Knoll)   A narcotic analgesic that contains hydromorphone, a MORPHINE derivative. It is used for moderate to severe pain and is habit–forming. Physical dependence can occur. Although it has the same activity as morphine, Dilaudid is much more potent and does not produce such adverse reactions as nausea and vomiting. It is available in ampules for injection and in rectal suppositories. In tablet form it is supplied in 1 mg green tablets; 2 mg orange tablets; 3 mg pink tablets; and 4 mg yellow tablets.

dill   There are claims that when they are dried and smoked dill seeds can produce a mild high. This is extremely doubtful.

dimethyltryptamine   A psychedelic drug that is manufactured synthetically in England. (See DMT.)

diphenoxylate   A Schedule V drug that is chemically related to the narcotic MEPERIDINE and may be habit–forming. Used in the management of diarrhea, it slows intestinal motility. (See LOMOTIL.)

dipipanone   A synthetic OPIATE that is used as an analgesic. Its potency is less than morphine but dependency can develop. It is a Schedule II drug.

dipsomania   A term that refers to an uncontrollable craving for alcohol, it is sometimes improperly used as a synonym for alcoholism. The term is obsolete in the United States.

disease concept of alcoholism   Despite the misconception that the disease concept of alcoholism is of recent origin, studies point out that as early as the first century the Roman philosopher Seneca distinguished between a man "who is drunk" and a man "who has no control over himself." Benjamin Rush, an 18th century American physician, expounded further on the theory. By the 19th century the disease concept was widely accepted by the medical community, and in 1952 JELLINEK elaborated further on the developments of alcohol addiction. Although Jellinek's theories on the progression of the major symptoms are seriously questioned, the disease concept itself is backed today by the World Health Organization and the American Medical Association.

Because alcoholism is designated as a disease, the guilt stigma—often in itself a stimulus for further drinking—is lifted from the patient, and social support rather than punishment is emphasized. Opponents of the concept argue that alcoholism may be a symptom of a number of separate problems and that to be classified as a disease there should be some abnormality of the anatomic or biologic structure. Under this definition all behavioral disorders would be eliminated from the classification of disease. Opponents further suggest that too little account is taken of sociocultural factors, and that calling alcoholism a disease fosters irresponsibility and passivity in the patient. Proponents of the concept, on the other hand, argue that along with lifting the "guilt stigma," making alcoholism a medical disease problem means that some of the personal economic costs are handled by insurance, disability payments and workmen's compensation. Although proponents feel the disease concept may not be completely adequate, they generally believe it to be the most sound basis for a 20th century approach to the problem.

diseases   There are numerous diseases which are caused by extended, heavy use of drugs, and others in which drug abuse may play a significant role. The use of alcohol and tobacco are major contributors to various diseases of the HEART, LIVER, LUNGS, PANCREAS and STOMACH. Heavy drug use can also damage the BRAIN and CENTRAL NERVOUS SYSTEM, and TETANUS and HEPATITIS are common among heroin addicts. Diseases attributable to poor NUTRITION are common among drugs users in general. Not only can drug use be harmful to the individual, it can also be harmful to the fetus. (See also PREGNANCY and CANCER.)

disorientation   A state of mental confusion in which the person has no concept of time, place, situation or identity. A variety of drugs—stimulants, depressants, hallucinogens—can produce this effect. Accidental deaths may result from cases of disorientation where the individual has no idea when, or even if, he took a previous dose of a drug.

distillation   The process of heating fermented mash, collecting the alcohol content that vaporizes, and then collecting the recondensed alcohol as a distillate. Using the distillate as a base, any number of potable spirits can be produced by aging and flavoring techniques. Thought to have been a discovery of the Arab cultures, distillation became common practice in Europe around 1000 A.D.

diviner's sage   *Salvia divinorum,* a plant belonging to the mint family. The Mazatec Indians of Mexico chew the leaves or brew them as a beverage for their hallucinogenic effects.

d–lysergic acid diethylamide tartrate 25   LSD–25.

DMT   (N–dimethyltryptamine)   A fast–acting HALLUCINOGEN similar in structure to PSILOCIN, the hallucinogenic substance to which PSILOCYBIN is converted in the body. Organic DMT is found in the seeds of the shrubs *Piptadenia,* in the flesh of the climbing vine *Banisteriopsis caapi,* and in the roots of *Mimosa hostilis.* It can also be easily synthesized. DET and DPT are close chemical variants.

Effects: Within five to 10 minutes after ingestion, DMT produces an LSD–like experience which lasts from 30 to 60 minutes. Because the effects do not last long, DMT is sometimes referred to as the "businessman's LSD" or the "businessman's lunchtime high." Unlike LSD, it affects only visual perceptions, not auditory and tactile ones. It can cause lack of coordination and spasticity, physical effects which are not associated with LSD. Physical and psychic effects appear simultaneously. The DMT experience can be quite intense and, for many who try it, frightening and nightmarish.

Addictive aspects: As is the case with all of the hallucinogens, DMT does not produce physical DEPENDENCE.

Tolerance: Users of DMT can develop tolerance to the drug.

Sources: Easily synthesized, DMT is produced in "basement" laboratories and sold illicitly. Its popularity seems to be on the increase in the United States but it is most widely used outside the U.S. It is an important component of COHABA, a snuff used in Haiti and parts of Central and South America, which also contains BUFOTENINE.

Synonyms: businessman's LSD, businessman's lunchtime high.

DNA   Deoxyribonucleic acid, an organic substance found in the chromosomes of living cells. It is vital in the storage and replication of hereditary information, and also plays an important role in protein synthesis. RNA is the other main type of nucleic acid. Drugs like the cannabinoids may interfere with DNA–RNA synthesis.

Do It Now Foundation (DIN)   A non–profit publisher of low–cost drug, alcohol, and health education materials which are distributed nationally and internationally. Founded in 1968 and supported entirely by its sales, DIN distributes approximately seven million pieces of literature a year. The foundation believes that ignorance about drugs can be as dangerous to an individual as drugs themselves, and consequently publishes materials in both primary and secondary prevention as well as general information.

Dolene® (Lederle)   A mild analgesic, containing propoxyphene hydrochloride, that is similar to a NARCOTIC in pharmacological properties but is less potent. It can produce psychic and physical dependence and has some potential for abuse. Taken with alcohol or other central nervous system depressants, it can have an additive effect. It is supplied in 65 mg pink capsules. Dolene Compound–6, which also contains aspirin, caffeine and phenacetin, is supplied in pink and brown capsules. Dolene AP–65, which contains propoxyphene and acetaminophen, comes in pink oval–shaped tablets.

Dolonil® (Parke–Davis)   A depressant that contains phenazopyridine hydrochloride, hyoscyamine hydrobromide, and the short–to–intermediate acting BARBITURATE, butabarbital. It is used for inflammation of the lower urinary tract, and may be habit–forming. Dolonil is supplied in dark maroon coated square tablets.

Dolophine Hydrochloride® (Lilly)   A synthetic narcotic analgesic that contains METHADONE hydrochloride, and has multiple action similar to MORPHINE. It is used for severe pain and for detoxification and maintenance in the treatment of narcotic addiction. Drug dependence, similar to morphine dependence, can occur and Dolophine has the potential for abuse. It is supplied in ampules for injection and in 5 and 10 mg tablets.

DOM (STP) (2, 5–dimethoxy–4–methyl amphetamine)   A synthetic HALLUCINO-

GEN with a structural resemblance to both AMPHETAMINES and MESCALINE, DOM is sometimes classified as an adrenergic hallucinogen because it produces physiological changes typical of such adrenergic agents as epinephrine.

The synthesis of DOM was reported in chemical literature in 1964 and first came to public attention in 1967 when FDA chemists identified it as one of the active constituents of STP. Today STP is a common synonym for DOM, although the original STP was a variety of drug mixtures and not all of them contained DOM.

DOM is considerably more potent than either amphetamines or mescaline which it resembles in its chemical structure. On a weight for weight basis it is less potent than LSD but the effects last somewhat longer: effects are perceptible about one hour after ingestion and reach their highest intensity three to five hours after ingestion. They subside in seven to eight hours. Psychological effects the next day are only rarely reported.

It is difficult to know how much DOM is available today. Users may buy DOM and receive some other drug, or they may receive DOM when they think they are buying something else.

Effects: Physiological changes include an increase in heart rate and systolic blood pressure, dilation of the pupils, and a slight rise in body temperature. Other changes that may occur include nausea, tremors, and perspiration. The intensity of these changes appears to be a result of the dose. Psychological effects also vary with the dose. Doses of approximately 3 mg produce euphoria and "enhanced self–awareness," while doses above 5 mg produce hallucinations. Some users may experience vivid visual imagery on closing their eyes along with a change in their perception of time. Eventually images may be seen with the eyes open. The predominant emotional state of the user is usually one of happiness. The experience is clear to the user after it is over and insight is retained throughout.

Addictive aspects: Physical dependence probably does not develop to DOM.

Tolerance: Little is known about tolerance to the effects of DOM. It is probably similar to other hallucinogens in that tolerance to at least some of its effects develops with regular use.

Sources: DOM is produced by "basement" chemists who supply the illegal drug market.

Frederick G. Hofman, *A Handbook on Drug and Alcohol Abuse* (New York: Oxford University Press, 1975), pp. 171–173.

Richard R. Lingeman, *Drugs from A to Z* (New York: McGraw–Hill Book Company, 1974), pp. 236–238.

Dona Ana A cactus, *Coryphantha macromeris,* native to Texas and Mexico, which contains the psychedelic alkaloid macromerine. It is eaten or brewed into a tea and has about one–fifth the potency of mescaline.

dopamine The immediate precursor of norepinephrine in the body, dopamine is found especially in the adrenal glands and exhibits adrenergic effects. It is a neurotransmitter and is important in the action of amphetamines and cocaine. Dopamine deficiency is thought to be a primary defect in Parkinson's disease. Dopamine hydrochloride is a synthetic drug which affects the autonomic nervous system and is used in the treatment of shock syndrome and congestive heart failure.

Doriden® (USV Pharmaceutical) A nonbarbiturate HYPNOTIC that contains glutethimide and is used for insomnia. Because it does not cause respiratory depression it is also used as a preanesthetic. Physical and psychological dependence can occur. Overdosage can result in central nervous system depression, coma, pupil dilation and loss of tendon reflexes. Taken with alcohol or other CNS depressants, Doriden can have an additive effect. It is supplied in white scored tablets of 0.5 gm and 0.25 gm; and in 0.5 gm blue and white capsules.

Dover's powder   An obsolete remedy which contained 10% opium and ipecac. It was given to induce sweating during a febrile illness.

doxepin   A tricyclic ANTIDEPRESSANT that is manufactured as Apapini and Sinequani.

DPT (dipropyltryptamine)   A little–known synthetic HALLUCINOGEN related to DMT and DET.

dram   In fluid measurement, 1 dram is equal to ⅛ of an ounce. There are 1⅓ drams in a teaspoon. In terms of alcohol, the word dram is often used interchangeably with the word "shot." "Dram–drinking" and "dramming" were used in the 17th century to refer to habitual drinking. A dramshop was a barroom.

dram shop law   A law which imposes legal liability upon a person, usually a tavern keeper, who supplies alcoholic beverages to a person who becomes intoxicated and causes injuries or damages to himself or another as a result.

Drinamyl®   A drug manufactured in England, which combines amphetamine sulfate and amobarbital. See DEXAMYL. It is supplied as purple tablets which are often referred to by abusers as "purple hearts" or "French blues."

driving and drugs   Although there have been numerous studies on the effects of alcohol on driving skills, there is little information available concerning the effects of other drugs.

One 1981 study, by Dr. Kenneth W. Terhune and James C. Fell for the National Highway Traffic and Safety Administration, covered 497 drivers injured in motor vehicle accidents and treated at a hospital. The sample was considered conservative because only drivers who consented to blood analysis were included. The results of the study showed 38% of the drivers had alcohol or some other drug in their system: alcohol was found in 25% of the drivers; tetrahydrocannabinol (THC—the active principle in marijuana) in 9.5%; and tranquilizers in 7.5%. Two or more drugs had been ingested by 10% of the drivers. A negligence rate of 74% was found in drivers who were legally intoxicated (BAC of .10%). Drivers with lower alcohol levels had a negligence rate of 54%, and those with THC in their system had a rate of 53%. In comparison, drug–free drivers had a negligence rate of 34%. Drivers with tranquilizers in their system were considered negligent in 22% of their accidents. This evidence, along with the results of similar studies, strongly suggests that marijuana interferes with driving skills, perception, coordination, attention, visual awareness, reaction time, and so on. Another danger is that performance decrements may persist for some time, possibly several hours beyond the time that someone actually feels "high" and he may drive without realizing that his ability is still impaired.

When drugs are combined there can be an additive effect on driving skills; even when drugs are used in therapeutic doses and not in the amounts used by abusers. Even over–the–counter sleeping aids can have more of a depressant effect on the central nervous system when combined with alcohol. In highway accidents where the driver has taken more than one drug, alcohol is almost always found to be one of the drugs.

Each year nearly 50,000 people die on U.S. highways and over half of these fatalities are alcohol related. Accidents involving alcohol also result in injuries to more than a half million people, more than $1 billion in property damage, insurance costs and medical services and several hundred thousand arrests.

The majority of alcohol–related accidents occur at night and a larger proportion of men than women are involved (perhaps partly because of drinking patterns as women tend to drink at home). One of the biggest menaces on the highway is the problem drinker who has previous arrests for offenses involving alcohol. Studies indicate that people with severe drinking problems are disproportionately involved in all kinds of crashes. Single vehicle accidents are alcohol or drug related in 75% of the cases.

About 50% of all fatally injured drinking drivers are less than 30 years old. From 40–60% of all fatal crashes involving young people are alcohol related. Not only are they inexperienced in both drinking and driving, they are more likely to combine alcohol with another drug. (See also BLOOD ALCOHOL CONCENTRATION and MOTHERS AGAINST DRUNK DRIVING.)

dropper   A medicine dropper which is used for injecting heroin when a needle is attached to its tip. The bulb acts as a plunger and the glass portion acts as the barrel. A dropper is sometimes favored over a regular hypodermic because it gives an addict more control over injecting the heroin.

Drug Abuse Warning Network (DAWN)   A network started in 1972 by the Bureau of Narcotics and Dangerous Drugs to provide information on medical and psychological problems associated with the effects of drug use. The network's aim is to identify patterns and trends in drug use and to pinpoint those drugs that are bringing users into emergency facilities. Data is received from such sources as general hospital emergency rooms, medical examiners and coroners, and crisis intervention centers and fed into DAWN; there are approximately 15,000 new case descriptions a month. The network issues quarterly reports describing current drug emergencies and whether or not the people concerned are in treatment. Presently funded and administered by NIDA, it derives information from 26 metropolitan areas and detects trends in which drugs are being used for their psychic effects, suicide, dependence, and so on.

drug addiction   See ADDICTION and DEPENDENCE.

drug automatism   Taking drugs without being aware of the amounts; a state that often occurs with heavy barbiturate use when tolerance has developed. In order to produce sleep, the user takes more of the drug because of an amnesia about the amount previously taken.

drug culture   See SUBCULTURE, DRUG.

Drug Enforcement Administration (DEA)   The lead agency in narcotic and dangerous drug suppression programs at the national and international levels and in federal drug law enforcement. Established in 1973 to replace the Bureau of Narcotics and Dangerous Drugs, the DEA was created to enforce the Controlled Substances laws and regulations. To this end, it investigates and prosecutes organizations and individuals involved in the growing, manufacture, or distribution of controlled substances destined for illicit traffic in the United States. In order to expand its facilities and become more efficient, the DEA began working with the Federal Bureau of Investigation (FBI) in January 1982. (See FEDERAL BUREAU OF INVESTIGATION.)

drug interaction   See SYNERGY.

drug trafficking   See TRAFFICKING, SMUGGLING, GOLDEN TRIANGLE, GOLDEN CRESCENT and FRENCH CONNECTION.

drunk   The term for a person under the influence of alcohol or in a state of intoxication. The term is also used to describe a drinking spree.

dry drunk   A person who has stopped drinking but continues to crave alcohol. As used by Alcoholics Anonymous, it refers to someone who has not attained true SOBRIETY but exists in a state of "white–knuckled sobriety," and is usually irritable and depressed because of his or her effort not to drink.

DSM III   The third edition of *Diagnostic and Statistical Manual* of mental disorders, including substance use disorders. It is currently in use and contains the criteria for diagnosing a variety of substance abuse conditions.

DUI   Driving under the influence. See DRIVING AND DRUGS.

Duradyne DHC® (O'Neal, Jones & Feldman)   A NARCOTIC analgesic, containing dihydrocodeinone bitartrate along with aspirin, caffeine and acetaminophen, that is used for moderate to severe pain. It may be habit–forming and repeated administration can produce drug dependence. If used with alcohol or other central nervous system depressants, an additive effect can occur. A Schedule III drug, it is supplied in green scored tablets.

DWI   Driving while intoxicated. See DRIVING AND DRUGS.

dynorphin   A potent ENDORPHIN found in the cow's pituitary gland. It is about two hundred times more powerful than morphine and one of the most potent endorphins yet discovered.

dysphoria   A generalized feeling of discomfort, malaise or unhappiness that often accompanies WITHDRAWAL. All abused drugs can occasionally produce a dysphoric state. Antonym: euphoria.

E

---

ebriate   To intoxicate or inebriate.

ebriety   See INEBRIETY.

economic impact   See BUSINESS, EMPLOYEE ASSISTANCE PROGRAMS and ABSENTEEISM.

Ectasul (SR, JR, & III)® (Fleming)   A drug used for sinusitis and hay fever that contains ephedrine and AMOBARBITAL. It may be habit–forming. Ectasul SR contains 60 mg ephedrine and 60 mg amobarbital; Ectasul JR contains 30 mg ephedrine and 30 mg amobarbital; and Ectasul III contains 15 mg ephedrine and 9 mg amobarbital.

ED50   See EFFECTIVE DOSE OF A DRUG.

effective dose of a drug (ED50)   This term refers to the dosage of a drug which produces a certain effect in 50% of the people tested, whereas 25% of those tested require a higher dosage and 25% require a lesser dosage to produce the same effect.

Eighteenth Amendment   The amendment under which the manufacture, transportation and sale of intoxicating beverages were banned, beginning Prohibition on January 17, 1920. It was repealed by the Twenty–first Amendment in 1932.

Elavil® (Merck, Sharp & Dohme)   An AN-TIDEPRESSANT with sedative effects that contains amitriptyline. While the mechanism of its action is not known, Elavil is more likely to alleviate endogenous depression than other depressive states. When used with central nervous system depressants it can have an additive effect. Although abrupt cessation can result in nausea, headache and malaise, these withdrawal symptoms are not indicative of addiction. Patients who are potentially suicidal should not have access to large quantities of the drug as severe overdosage can result in convulsions, congestive heart failure, coma and death. It is supplied in 10 mg round blue tablets; 25 mg yellow tablets; 50 mg beige tablets; 75 mg orange tablets; 100 mg mauve tablets; and 150 mg capsule–shaped blue tablets. It is also available in 10 mg vials for injection.

elderly   Current statistics reveal that "senior citizens," individuals over 65 years of age, comprise 10% of American society. By the year 2000 the number will have doubled to 20% of the population. In view of this increase and the fact that most of us will one day belong to this age group, it is important to recognize the special substance abuse problems facing the elderly.

Misuse and abuse of medications and other drugs is pronounced among people over 65 for several reasons. Many older people suffer from a variety of physical ailments for which they receive prescription medications and for which they also buy non–prescription, over–the–counter drugs. Old age is also often fraught with emotional problems which may prompt further medication. In addition to experiencing frustration as a result of physical deterioration, older people frequently have a new life–style forced on them by retirement and react, not unnaturally, with feelings of loneliness, boredom and uselessness. Lowered incomes and the acute awareness of mortality that comes when more and more of one's friends and relatives die add to their distress. As a result, many older people request and receive tranquilizers and other sedative medicines as well as resort to alcohol to alleviate their feelings. People over 65 consume more than 25 percent of all prescription drugs, at a cost of more than $2.5 billion a year, and even more non–prescription, over–the–counter preparations.

Many older people, then, regularly ingest significant quantities of several drugs. Unconscious, habitual drug taking can have seriously debilitating effects, especially in old age when the system is more sensitive. People over 60 experience adverse drug reactions twice as frequently as the rest of the population. Because the body of an elderly person has a higher fat content than that of a younger person, fat soluble drugs remain in the system longer. Less effective metabolism in old age also contributes to the accumulation of such substances, making the elderly particularly vulnerable to drug interactions. Lack of communication between older patients and their doctors (and, often, they have several doctors) can result in the prescription of contradictory medication—sometimes with serious results. Doctors often fail to explain adequately the purpose and effects of the drugs they prescribe, and it has been suggested that older patients may also self–prescribe over–the–counter medications and experiment with friends' and neighbors' medications which do not complement their prescribed drugs. Forgetfulness may also lead them to take larger than safe quantities of drugs or fail to take doses of an essential drug.

One of the most dangerous effects of drug interaction arises with the use of alcohol, the foremost form of substance abuse among older people. To numb the feelings of loneliness and uselessness, many elderly people increase their alcohol intake, while some others have longstanding problems with alcohol. About 10–15% of people over 65 have drinking problems, and 1–5% of the elderly population is estimated to be alcoholic.

As with other drugs, alcohol's effects intensify in old age. The combination of alcohol's solubility in fat and the increased fat content of the body may produce higher concentrations of acetaldehyde in the blood and brain, and therefore more prolonged and toxic effects than in younger individuals. Slower metabolism may induce WITHDRAWAL symptoms and prompt the older drinker to increase his drinking to alleviate them.

This lowered tolerance magnifies the addictive effects of alcohol and of the CNS depressants which are so commonly used by older people, and so greatly increases the risks of taking the drugs together. Another common and dangerous practice is combining alcohol with medication for heart conditions, since alcohol acts as a cardiac muscle toxin in large amounts.

The diagnosis and treatment of alcoholism also presents special problems. Some of the symptoms of alcoholism, such as forgetfulness and incoherence, may be interpreted as signs of senility; thus the real problem may go undetected. Alcohol can also mask pain and other symptoms of physical illness.

Older chronic drinkers, who are predominantly male, are more likely to deny their problem than younger alcoholics, possibly because of culturally derived prejudices common to the generation. Some professionals in alcohol rehabilitation methods have suggested that social activity programs which break the pattern of lonely solitary drinking is a relatively easy way to treat alcohol problems in older people, especially if the problems have developed only since the onset of old age. The comparative ease of this kind of treatment should not be assumed, however.

Chemical abuse in nursing homes is a particularly sensitive issue for the elderly. Less than 5% of the elderly are currently confined to such institutions; two–thirds are women, and their average age is 82. Recent years have produced reports of overmedication of nursing home patients with high–power tranquilizers and antidepressants, even when their use is not necessary. Constant tranquilization can seriously incapacitate a patient as well as simulate symptoms of senility or physical ailments from which he has not previously suffered. The tranquilizer Thorazine, for example, induces symptoms of Parkinson's disease. Such deceptive symptoms may prompt attending physicians, insufficiently aware of the medication's effect or of the patient's condition, to prescribe more medication. Routine administration of sedatives makes life easier for nursing home *staff*. Advertisements for some drugs promote this misuse of medication by stressing the product's value in "patient management," rather than patient care. In *The Tranquilizing of America*, Richard Hughes and Robert Brewin labeled this practice "the chemical pacification of the elderly." They blamed doctors for their negligence, irresponsibility and general lack of knowledge about geriatric medical problems. Geriatric specialists are few in the United States, and doctors who treat all age groups sometimes exhibit impatience with their older patients, who generally have numerous complaints and demand a great deal of time and attention. The elderly frequently have little chance of recovery and little money. Sometimes doctors terminate the visits and silence the complaints of what they consider a cantankerous group by simply writing prescriptions which are not really necessary. Hopefully, with increasing postgraduate education in geriatrics, this practice may be on the decline.

electric shock   In the treatment of alcoholism, conditioning with electric shock was once used in AVERSION THERAPY. It is currently used to treat patients suffering from depression, especially those who are unresponsive to antidepressant medication.

elemicin   An alkaloid found in NUTMEG and believed to produce mild hallucinogenic effects.

emetine   An emetic drug which induces nausea. It is used in AVERSION THERAPY.

Empirin Compound with Codeine®
(Burroughs Wellcome)   An analgesic used for moderate pain. It could be habit–forming. A Schedule III drug, it contains aspirin, caffeine and phenacetin, along with codeine. No. 1 has ⅛ grain codeine; No. 2 has ¼ grain; No. 3 has ½ grain; and No. 4 has 1 grain (65 mg).

Employee Assistance Programs (EAPs)
First begun in the 1930s and 1940s by such companies as Kodak and DuPont, EAPs are now an established part of today's alcohol and drug abuse programs. Between 1950 and 1973 the number of EAPs grew from 50 to 500; in the last nine years the programs have grown to 5,000 (covering 400 major U.S. companies). Most of the original programs dealt only with alcoholism but the increase in drug abuse has forced them to expand.

The National Institute on Alcohol Abuse and Alcoholism estimates that 50% of people with job performance problems suffer from alcoholism; this results in a loss of production to companies estimated at $20 billion a year. When absenteeism and medical care estimates are included, this figure jumps to $50 billion. Because alcoholism is a progressive disease, often taking 10 to 15 years to

reach its middle stages, the worker suffering from alcoholism has often reached a position of responsibility in his or her company. The Stanford Research group has estimated that by treating workers with a drinking problem industry saves about $6,000 annually for each alcoholic employee. A rehabilitated high–level executive could alone save a company millions of dollars on a project no one else is equipped to handle. Although employers once sought to weed out "troublesome" employees, they now realize the need to provide help.

Voluntary associations, labor unions and organizations for employees in both public and private sectors are among the sources that provide EAPs. Labor unions are the most recent supporters of these programs, probably because initially they were suspicious that companies were trying to "spy" on drinkers in their ranks. The success of the programs in restoring their members to good health has obviously changed their minds, and most successful programs often depend upon labor union support.

The U.S. Department of Health and Human Services has found that the highest rate of recovery from alcoholism occurs in the office or factory rather than the clinic or hospital program. Perhaps EAPs have greater leverage because while problem drinkers are generally not intimidated by threats of losing family, possessions, reputation or pride, they are usually deeply concerned about losing their jobs.

A person's place of work provides helpful structures for early intervention and confrontation. Deterioration of job performance is usually apparent before physical signs of alcoholism appear. Managers and supervisors are trained to look for unsatisfactory performance and at this time an employee is generally sent off to an EAP where a variety of counseling services are available. The basic orientation of most programs is alcoholism identification and intervention, but actual treatment methods differ from company to company. While some care for their employees in–house, others refer them to community–based agencies that are more professionally equipped to handle the problem. Other companies refer employees to Alcoholics Anonymous or other self–help groups.

Public opinion about EAPs differs widely. In the case of airlines, some people say they will not fly with a company that has admitted an alcoholism problem among its employees. On the other hand, there are people who say they won't fly with a company that *doesn't* have an EAP. Regardless of how public opinion sways, companies have found that they have at least a 50% recovery rate among employees who had to choose between getting treatment and losing their jobs. In some cases between 70% and 80% of employees return to their jobs "recovered."

Despite the success rate of many programs there are numerous companies that evaluate on a cost–benefit analysis basis, and because the monetary value of benefits is sometimes difficult or impossible to evaluate, EAPs are not implemented. This prevents many small and medium–sized businesses from participating in such programs. There is also a strong need to reach women, minorities and those in high–income levels. High–level employees, in particular, often work in isolated conditions with minimal supervision and if approached may feel that EAPs are only for low–level employees.

Alcoholism is still the cause of most cases of poor job performance related to drugs. This is probably because, unlike heroin and cocaine, alcohol is not only legally available, it is socially respectable.

enabling   A term that refers to attempts (usually made by relatives and friends) to protect an alcoholic from the consequences of drinking. Although aimed at helping the alcoholic, such attempts "enable" the person's drinking pattern to continue unchecked. (See also PARA–ALCOHOLIC.)

encounter groups   See GROUP THERAPY.

endocrine etiological theories   A theory which suggests that dysfunction of the endocrine system may lead to the development of alcoholism. Hypoglycemia, a result of a pituitary–adrenocortical deficiency, is thought to cause symptoms that can stimulate drinking. Alcohol can temporarily elevate blood sugar and relieve the hypoglycemia, but it eventually intensifies the condition and can cause a dependence on increasingly larger amounts. Because alcohol is a sedative drug it is likely that this theory can also be applied to the use of other sedative drugs. Up to now there has been no strong evidence to support this physiological approach to the cause of alcoholism.

endorphins   OPIOID biochemical compounds that are produced by the body and resemble the opiates in their ability to promote a general sense of well–being and induce analgesia. The term is used generically to refer to all endogenous opioid compounds and it implies a pharmacological activity as opposed to a specific chemical formulation. Endorphins have thus far been found only in vertebrate animals.

enkephalins   Short chain amino acids that have opioid actions. Endorphin is becoming a collective name for the long chain and short chain endogenous opioids.

enzyme multiplied imminoassay technique (EMIT)   A method used for rapid urine screening for drugs of abuse produced by Syna Corporation.

epena   The Waika Indians of Brazil grind up the bark of the epena tree to make a snuff that produces hallucinogenic effects.

ephedrine   A synthetic cardiac and central nervous system stimulant that is used for asthma and other allergies, hypotension and narcolepsy. It is used mainly as a bronchial dilator and vasoconstrictor of the nasal membranes.

epidemiology   The medical study of the occurrence and prevalence of disease. The term is often applied to the study of a disease that affects large numbers of people in a community, such as alcoholism.

Epsilon Alcoholism   See JELLINEK.

Equanil® (Wyeth)   A minor tranquilizer that contains MEPROBAMATE. It has a potential for abuse and may produce physical and psychological dependence. Excessive doses can cause the rapid onset of sleep, with pulse, blood pressure and respiratory rates being reduced to basal levels. Equanil is supplied in white scored 200 and 400 mg tablets; 400 mg red and white capsules; and 400 mg yellow coated tablets called Equanil Wyseals.

Erthroxylon coca   The coca bush containing the alkloid COCAINE.

erogenics   Synonymous with STIMULANTS; drugs that increase the capacity of physical and mental functioning.

Esgic® (Gilbert)   An analgesic with a mild sedative effect that contains caffeine, acetaminophen, and the BARBITURATE butalbital. It is generally used for headache pain and may be habit–forming. Esgic is supplied in yellow compressed tablets containing 50 mg of butalbital.

esophagus   In comparison with the general population, smokers, heavy drinkers and alcoholics show a high incidence of esophageal CANCER. Patients with cirrhosis of the liver have blockages of the veins returning blood from the abdominal cavity to the heart. In an effort to overcome the obstruction, esophageal varicosities develop. These are enlarged veins that can easily rupture causing bleeding that can be profuse.

ethanol   Ethyl alcohol, the principal chemical in distilled spirits, wine and beer. An inflammable liquid, it is produced by the reaction of fermenting sugar with yeast spores. Distillation can produce 96–100% ethanol, also called ABSOLUTE ALCOHOL. (See also ALCOHOL.)

ethchlorvynol   A nonbarbiturate sedative hypnotic. Its overdose symptoms are similar to BARBITURATES and dependency can occur. (See PLACIDYL.)

ether   A volatile anesthetic obtained by the distillation of alcohol with sulfuric acid. Its medical usage began in the early 1800s and because of its intoxicating effects (similar to alcohol), ether sniffing became quite popular. It was also taken orally for a quicker onset of effects and less expensive intoxication than alcohol. Ether is seldom used today as an anesthetic or a euphoriant.

ethinamate   A nonbarbiturate mild sedative hypnotic that is effective when deep hypnosis is not needed. (See VALMID.)

ethnopharmacology   The study of human beings in relation to drug use, with special emphasis on the social, cultural and historic aspects of the subject.

ethyl alcohol   See ETHANOL.

ethylmorphone hydrochloride   An OPIUM derivative.

etiology   The science of causes, particularly the investigation of the causes and origins of disease and abnormal conditions.

euphoria   A feeling of elation and extreme well–being that can be achieved with a variety of psychoactive drugs.

ex–addict   The term is generally applied to someone who is no longer addicted to a drug. It usually implies abstinence for some minimum length of time (six months, one year, two years, etc.), rather than detoxification alone. It also implies a change in life–style, characterized by such measures as employment, lack of arrests, school enrollment, improved relationships and continuing or completing treatment.

experimental drug use   A short–term nonpatterned trial period of drug use, usually motivated by curiosity or by the desire to assess anticipated drug effects. Experimental use of drugs most often occurs in the company of one or more friends or social acquaintances. It can lead to a heavier involvement in drug use.

eyes   Traditionally considered the "windows to the soul," the eyes can also reveal a good deal about a person in relation to drug abuse. Bloodshot eyes, for example, consistently betray the use of marijuana or of heavy alcohol consumption, while dilated pupils are the classic telltale sign of LSD and stimulant ingestion. Although most types of drugs exert some effect on the eyes, no ocular diseases or other damage to the eyes seems to be precipitated by short or long–term use of any recreational drug, with the exception of alcoholic amblyopia. This rare disease occurs most commonly in male alcoholics who also smoke. It involves painless, progressive blurring of the vision which is thought to be the result of a toxic reaction in the orbital portion of the optic nerve. If unchecked, the disease may progress to include degeneration of the optic nerve, but it is otherwise reversible with abstinence and a vitamin and mineral treatment program.

By affecting areas of the brain which control sensory perceptions, large doses of alcohol disturb the vision and other senses. Alcohol congests blood vessels in the eyes, causing "red eye." It also relaxes certain eye muscles, thereby interfering with the eyes' ability to focus, and slows adjustment reactions. These two effects result in double vision—common in those who are intoxicated. Nystagmus, involuntary oscillation of the eyeball, may also be present in cases of extreme intoxication. Horizontal nystagmus is most common in alcohol and other intoxications, but PCP can also cause vertical nystagmus.

Constricted pupils accompany opiate use, but extreme tearing, dilated pupils and double vision occur during withdrawal. Dilated pupils are also a part of the experience of using hallucinogens, certain solvents and stimulants, and can cause photophobia.

Psychedelic drugs produce intense visual hallucinations, often consisting of brightly colored geometric designs which are seen especially when the eyes are closed. These hallucinations, prolonged afterimages, and sensory interaction such as hearing colors and seeing sounds (synesthesis), all seem to be manifestations of the drug's effect on the central nervous system.

Cocaine gained international recognition in the nineteenth century after Freud and his colleague Koller endorsed it as a local anesthetic for eye surgery. The drug acts directly to anesthetize the corneal sensory nerve, but it is rarely used medically any more. THC (the active ingredient in marijuana), however, is beginning to enjoy professional approval in the treatment of open angle glaucoma, which it relieves by lowering pressure within the eyeball.

F

fake coke In 1982 the Food and Drug Administration (FDA) issued a warning against fake coke—or cocaine substitutes—white powders that look like cocaine and are sold openly to members of the drug culture through the U.S. mail and in HEADSHOPS. Many of these substitutes contain local anesthetics such as lidocaine, procaine and tetracaine, and can be as hazardous as cocaine itself. Although they are not controlled substances, these substitutes are subject to FDA regulation and the FDA has asked all manufacturers and distributors to help stop their dissemination. Adverse reactions can include collapsed blood vessels, lowered blood pressure and depressed heart muscle strength. Some of the trade names for these cocaine substitutes are: Toot, Florida Snow, Supercaine and Ultracaine.

false negative, false positive Terms used to indicate erroneous results in tests which measure the presence (positive) or absence (negative) of something. In a screening for drugs, for example, *a false positive* means that the test indicated the presence of a drug when in fact none was there, and a *false negative* means just the reverse. Whether a result of personal or computer error, or of errors associated with the collection or transportation of specimens, or improperly performed tests, nearly all drug–testing techniques are susceptible to false or erroneous test results, especially when improper techniques, identification or storage occurs.

familial etiological theories Sociocultural theories on the cause of alcoholism that emphasize the important role the family plays in the development of drinking patterns. Some studies have shown that among siblings of alcoholics there is two to 14 times more alcoholism than among siblings of nonalcoholics. It has been suggested that children will tend to follow parental modes of coping with stress, tension and anxiety. Because alcohol is a sedative drug, it is also possible to apply familial etiological theories to the abuse patterns of other sedative drugs. (See also CHILDREN OF DRUG DEPENDENT INDIVIDUALS.)

Families in Action (FIA) The nation's first community–based parents' group formed to prevent drug abuse among children and teenagers. Founded in De Kalb County, Georgia, in 1977, it now has over 3,000 members. The group collects and distributes relevant information about young people and drugs and conducts research on the effects of drugs. FIA has established the Drug Information Data Base of over 70,000 documents and the U.S. Library of Congress lists the group as a national referral center.

family problems See FAMILIAL ETIOLOGICAL THEORIES, YOUTHS, CHILDREN OF DRUG DEPENDENT INDIVIDUALS, ORAL FIXATION and SPOUSE ABUSE.

family therapy See TREATMENT and REHABILITATION.

Fastin® (Beecham Laboratories) An anorectic used for weight control that contains phentermine hydrochloride and has a pharmacological activity similar to that of AMPHETAMINES. Because of this similarity Fastin has a significant potential for abuse and tolerance develops quickly. Overdosage can result in restlessness, rapid respiration, confusion and hallucinations. It is supplied in blue and white capsules.

fatty liver A reversible condition of the liver that results from heavy drinking. It is characterized by an excessive accumulation of fat in the liver and liver dysfunction. (See also LIVER.)

FBI   See FEDERAL BUREAU OF INVESTIGA-
TION.

Federal Bureau of Investigation (FBI)

On January 21, 1982, the U.S. Attorney General announced that the FBI and the Drug Enforcement Administration (DEA) would have concurrent jurisdiction over violations of the federal drug laws. The announcement was a result of the serious drug trafficking problem in the United States and the need for a more concentrated effort at all levels. Under the new alliance, the DEA will report to the Director of the FBI and the FBI will then be given concurrent jurisdiction with the DEA for investigations of violations of the Controlled Substances Act. The DEA will continue to be the lead organization in the federal government's efforts to direct the assault on traffickers and to assist state and local enforcement, but the alliance will serve to open new fronts in the war on drugs and insure that the skills and resources of both agencies will be used to the best advantage. Drug enforcement investigators now have the backing of 1,200 trained FBI agents. They also have access to ISIS, the Investigative Support Information System of the FBI, and to OCIS, the Organized Crime Information System which retrieves, organizes and analyses information developed in organized crime investigations.

In the first few months of the alliance, FBI narcotics investigations increased from 100 to over 800, and joint FBI/DEA investigations increased from a handful to about 200.

fenfluramine hydrochloride

A synthetic drug chemically related to the AMPHETAMINES. It is used as an anorectic. (See PONDIMIN.)

fentanyl

A narcotic analgesic and opium derivative. Fentanyl is about one hundred times more potent than morphine. It is generally used intravenously as a pre–operative anesthetic, for brief anesthesia or for post–operative pain. In terms of drug abuse, anesthesiologists and nurse anesthetists have been known to self–administer the drug to provide sedation and sleep. Compulsive use becomes a possibility. Fentanyl is also the basis for the manufacture of CHINA WHITE (methylfantanyl) which is even more potent, and is a street drug. Because it is so potent overdose is a possibility. (See SUBLIMAZE.)

fetal alcohol syndrome (FAS)

Identified in 1973 by Kenneth L. Jones and David W. Smith of the University of Washington in Seattle, fetal alcohol syndrome is the name applied to alcohol–related birth defects. Jones and Smith replicated studies done a few years earlier by Christie Ulleland, also of the University of Washington.

Born to mothers who have used alcohol excessively during pregnancy, children with fetal alcohol syndrome exhibit a number of characteristics, including growth deficiencies, mental retardation and physical malformations. FAS is the third leading cause of congenital mental disorders, ranking behind Down's Syndrome and Spina Bifida, and is the only one which is preventable.

Certain features are commonly found in cases of FAS. The victims usually fail to reach normal length both before and after birth; they are below normal weight and have a tendency to remain thin and small as they grow older; and they tend to have elongated folds in their eyelids, causing eye slits. A short nose, low nasal bridge, narrow upper lip, small chin and flat midface, and indistinct philtrum (the vertical groove between nose and mouth) are among the other physical abnormalities that occur. Approximately 30% of children with FAS have heart defects. Central nervous system effects of FAS include retarded mental and motor development, hyperactivity, tremulousness and a poor attention span. Mental deficiency is the most common sign of fetal damage and even when placed in supportive atmospheres, such children show no improvement with time.

Alcohol consumed by a pregnant woman passes freely across the placental barrier into the baby's bloodstream. The concentrations are at least as high as those in the mother and the fetus is not equipped to handle such amounts. (See PREGNANCY.)

Mineral and vitamin deficiencies resulting from maternal drinking may also be harmful to the fetus. Although research in this area is still in its early stages, it is known that insufficient amounts of calcium, magnesium and zinc all play an important role in fetal development. Fetal malformations may also be caused by a deficiency of vitamins, particularly folic acid, which is common in alcoholics.

It is not yet known exactly how much alcohol is harmful to a fetus, and it should be noted that most documented cases of FAS have been children of women whose drinking meets the criteria of alcoholism. Many organizations, such as the National Institute on Alcohol Abuse and Alcoholism, and the American Medical Association Panel on Alcoholism, recommend complete abstinence from alcohol during pregnancy. They consider this the wisest course because the effects of even a small amount of alcohol are still unknown. The March of Dimes, along with some other organizations, do not emphasize complete abstinence since they feel the suggestion may unnecessarily frighten a woman whose custom is to have a drink or two in the evening during pregnancy. Organizations who take this view, point out that millions of social drinkers have healthy babies and they feel it is better to raise the consciousness of drinkers by alerting them to the dangers instead of counseling complete abstinence. Unless complicated by other factors, some organizations suggest that as long

as normal daily consumption falls below the level of 3 ounces of ABSOLUTE ALCOHOL, adverse effects are rare.

Until more is known, caution or abstinence is the recommendation of most agencies and organizations.

Finland   The use of cannabis, LSD and amphetamines was first detected in Finland during the late 1960s. At this time, too, the use of barbiturates and minor tranquilizers increased. In 1968 the National Board of Health withdrew amphetamines from the market and doctors were required to obtain a special license in order to prescribe their use in individual cases. These legal restrictions, however, led to illicit smuggling and illegal manufacture. Cannabis became popular, particularly among youths, and was often combined with the use of alcohol. These increases in drug abuse led to an extensive study by the National Board of Health in 1971. As a result, rules for prescribing drugs were re–evaluated and a permanent system to monitor drug use was established.

A follow–up study was done in 1977 which showed a decrease in the use of barbiturates and minor tranquilizers but a compensatory use of antidepressants and neuroleptics (major tranquilizers). From 1979 to 1980 the use of neuroleptics once again showed an increase.

There is a high incidence of respiratory ailments in Finland due to the cold moist climate and treatment has centered on codeine— the traditional ingredient in most analgesics and cough medicines. Codeine accounted for 80–90% of narcotic use in Finland until 1972 when the Board of Health revised the control of codeine and consumption decreased significantly. As the use of methaqualone increased, it too was placed under the same sort of control, and doctors had to follow certain rules in prescribing the drug and keep detailed records of the patients concerned. In

1977 methaqualone use was restricted to hospitals only. The government's concern and actions have led to a decrease or leveling off in the abuse of most drugs and it continues to monitor the situation closely.

Alcohol problems are a concern in Finland, although the per capita consumption is far less than in other European nations. The pattern of abuse which prevails today is one of occasional but heavy consumption, and more than half of the alcoholic beverages consumed are strong liquors rather than wine or beer. The State Alcohol Monopoly controls distribution, and restricted centers where alcohol is available are mainly in cities. Because of this, illegal distilling is popular in rural areas and it has been suggested that 10% of alcohol consumed in Finland is illegally distilled. At present, the government's emphasis in trying to control alcohol consumption is placed on increased supervision of public drinking places—places where cultural trends and habits are likely to form.

Fiorinal® (Sandoz)   An analgesic used for tension (or muscle contraction) headache. It contains aspirin, phenacetin, caffeine and Sandoptal (the BARBITURATE, butalbital). It may be habit–forming and psychological dependence can occur. Overdosage can result in respiratory depression, confusion, hypotension and coma. It is supplied in two–tone green capsules, and white compressed tablets. Fiorinal with Codeine® is used for more severe pain. It is supplied in capsule form: No. 1, ⅛ grain codeine, red and yellow; No. 2, ¼ grain codeine, gray and yellow; No. 3, ½ grain codeine, blue and yellow.

flashback   A little understood phenomenon of the MEMORY that occurs in a small percentage of users of hallucinogenic drugs, whereby the individual reexperiences the drug state days, weeks or months after the original experience. Stressful or other dissociative states, such as falling asleep or waking up,

usually precipitate flashback. They may represent a form of state dependent learning: when the nervous system is aroused and ego functioning is diminished, the physical and psychological state induced by LSD or other hallucinogens is reproduced and intensified visual and other perceptions experienced and stored during the drug "trip" surface. Since the body eliminates LSD within 24 hours after ingestion, prolonged retention of the substance cannot explain flashback. Nor does the drug affect the brain's structure in any way.

Flashback has been known to occur with large doses of amphetamines and may be provoked by marijuana and such substances as antihistamines, nitrous oxide and even caffeine.

fluorocarbons   A group of hydrocarbons, chlorinated or fluorinated, that are now used chiefly as refrigerants. They were widely used as aerosol propellants prior to 1978 and were subject to abuse because of their intoxicating effects when inhaled. In 1978 the U.S. Environmental Protection Agency under the Toxic Substance Control Act banned fluorocarbons and chlorofluorocarbons from use in household consumer products.

flurazepan   A BENZODIAZEPINE derivative that is a central nervous system depressant. (See DALMANE.)

fly agaric   A HALLUCINOGEN which is obtained from the *Amanita muscaria* mushroom. The mushroom is also used as a fly poison, which explains the origin of the drug's name.

Effects: Fly agaric produces various PSYCHOTOMIMETIC reactions which are similar to but less intense than those produced by LSD and PSILOCYBIN. As mentioned in the entry on HALLUCINOGENS, it is suspected that the Norse tribesmen used this drug to stimulate warlike rage before going into battle.

The mushroom is consumed whole or mixed with milk or water. As the hallucinogen passes through the system, it remains chemically unchanged. Thus, it is a practice among some users to "recycle" the urine of a person who is intoxicated.

formaldehyde   A pungent gas formed in the body in small amounts by the oxidation of methyl alcohol. It is toxic but is usually broken down into nontoxic units by the liver. When a large amount of alcohol has been consumed the liver works first to break down and metabolize the ethyl alcohol. Methyl alcohol builds up and when it is finally metabolized, a modest amount of formaldehyde is produced. Formaldehyde is thought to be partially responsible for the hangover effect and may also be responsible for certain withdrawal symptoms.

France   Until recently, recreational drug use in France consisted primarily of the use of alcohol, particularly wine, and tobacco. Changing cultural habits, however, are altering the pattern to include a broad range of narcotics, marijuana, amphetamines and barbiturates. This is not to say that drugs were not previously used (hashish was introduced in the 19th century), only that they have recently gained in popularity.

In a country where approximately one–tenth of the population derives its income directly or indirectly from the production and sale of alcoholic beverages, particularly wine, alcohol has understandably been the object of strong economic, as well as cultural, emphasis. In 1976 a World Health Organization survey of 26 countries ranked France first in per capita annual consumption of 100% ethanol (16.5 liters), twice the consumption rate in the United States. Wine, which is generally less expensive than such non–alcoholic beverages as soft drinks or fruit juices, is regularly consumed with meals and is viewed as a natural part of the daily diet. According to 1983 statistics, 46% of the French population drinks wine on a daily basis; 31% imbibes occasionally; and 23% abstains. Although there has been a recent increase in the consumption of beer and distilled spirits, wine is still the most popular beverage.

Recent statistics indicate, however, that per capita wine consumption is on the decline: in 1960 the average French citizen drank 120 quarts of wine annually; in 1982 the annual consumption had dropped to 80 quarts. While the study claims that the majority of French people have replaced wine with non–alcoholic beverages, the statistical decline may, in fact, simply reflect the rising popularity of beer and hard liquor, the consumption of which has increased threefold since 1960.

Statistics on alchohol–related physical and mental illnesses reflect the important role wine and other alcoholic beverages traditionally assume in French culture. In a country of some 53 million, roughly two million individuals (2.6% of the population) suffer from alcoholism. The consumption of red wine accounts for 70% of these cases. Another three to five million people are considered problem drinkers. Alcohol consumption is the third leading cause of death in France after cardiovascular diseases and cancer. In 1978 there were approximately 30.2 deaths per 100,000 people from cirrhosis and 6.6 deaths per 100,000 people from alcoholism and alcohol psychosis. It has been estimated that alcohol abuse also accounts for half the country's murders and a quarter of its suicides. The overall cost of alcoholism to the French government in 1977 was estimated at over $4 billion; of this amount taxes on alcoholic beverages compensated for only a third.

Nearly all drugs of abuse are found in France, particularly in the metropolitan areas and around the southern ports. Marseilles, in particular, achieved worldwide notoriety during the days of the FRENCH CONNECTION, and there is reason to believe that heavy trafficking and clandestine laboratories still exist in the area. France's long Mediterranean coastline and its proximity to Southwest Asia facilitates smuggling and provides almost ideal conditions for the illicit drug trade. During the 1960s and 1970s most of the heroin for the U.S. market came through France—an estimated 10 tons annually. Morphine base and opium from Turkey and other Middle Eastern countries was converted to heroin in French laboratories and then shipped on. At the time, most of the heroin was exported and little was consumed in France itself. This pattern has now changed and heroin use is appearing with increasing frequency in France. Over the last decade heroin has played an increasingly important role as a drug of choice among abusers.

The pattern of drug use in France generally closely resembles the pattern in other Western countries. In addition to heroin, cannabis use (especially hashish) has spread to all ages and social groups. The use of cocaine is also increasing; not only is France one of the primary points of entry to Europe for cocaine traffickers (generally arriving by way of commerical airliner from South America), much of the cocaine passing through French airports actually stays within the country. From 1980 to 1981, cocaine seizures increased 150%.

Hallucinogens and psychedelic drugs are not used frequently in France. PCP, which has been a problem in the United States, has barely made an appearance on the illicit market. The pattern of amphetamine and barbiturate abuse follows the steady increase found in other European countries but has not reached the magnitude seen in the U.S.

In 1970 and 1971 the French government initiated new treatment programs for drug abusers and severe penalties for use and possession. The legislation of the early 1970s

also increased official awareness of drug abuse and addiction as a medical rather than behavioral problem. It provided more possibilities for effective treatment and made treatment compulsory for addicted criminal offenders. The legislation did, however, provide clemency for individuals who sought treatment voluntarily.

The French government has not been trying to handle its problem alone. In 1971 the United States and France signed a protocol agreement which sought to stop the flow of heroin from France into the U.S. French authorities were stationed in the U.S. and the U.S. Bureau of Narcotics and Dangerous Drugs maintained an office in France. This agreement was renewed in 1976, and in 1981 it was extended for an additional five years. France has also become active in worldwide organizations aimed at stemming drug abuse, particularly the United Nations Commission on Narcotics.

Although drug use in France has continued to increase in recent years, particularly in the over–25 age group, there has been a decrease in the likelihood of teenagers to indulge in heavy drug use—an encouraging sign for the future. If, however, the recent heroin seizures in France (see FRENCH CONNECTION) are an indication of increased trafficking, these encouraging signs are likely to be reversed.

freebase, cocaine   In its normal street form cocaine hydrochloride is not effective when smoked; an alkali and solvent is required to convert it to cocaine alkaloid, called "freebase." The process involves heating ether, lighter fluid, or a similar flammable solvent with cocaine—a potentially dangerous process that could lead to burns. It can also be produced by adding bicarbonate of soda (baking soda) and ether to street cocaine and smoking the mixture. The result is a purified cocaine base which is smoked in a special pipe with wire screens, or sprinkled on a tobacco or marijuana cigarette. When smoked it produces a sudden and intense high that lasts for less than two minutes.

Freebase has a lower vaporizing temperature than cocaine hydrochloride, therefore smoking does not destroy it. It is rapidly absorbed by the lungs and carried to the brain in a few seconds. The brief euphoria that results is quickly replaced by a feeling of restless irritability. The posthigh after freebase can be so uncomfortable, in fact, that in order to maintain the high, users often continue smoking until they either run out of cocaine or until they are completely exhausted.

The custom of smoking cocaine originated in the 1970s in Peru, and quickly spread through the South American countries and into the United States. In South America cocaine is not processed into freebase before smoking; it is smoked in the form of coca paste, the extract produced during the manufacture of cocaine from coca leaves. Smoking coca paste is extremely dangerous because of the impurities it contains.

Synonyms: white tornado, freebase, baseball, snowflake.

French Connection   Led by Jean Jehan, the French Connection was a group of French underworld figures who were the major suppliers of heroin to the U.S. from the 1930s until 1973 when a concentrated international law enforcement effort smashed the ring. Jehan was later arrested in France but was held only briefly, then released.

While it was flourishing, the French Connection dominated heroin trafficking; it had control of smuggling and a monopoly on heroin laboratories. It also had a working relationship with Italian criminals that guaranteed the American market to the French: apparently the agreement was to the effect that if the French sold only to the Italians in America, the Italians in Europe would stay out of the traffic. Of necessity, this agreement required the closest understanding between the highest level of the criminal underworld in Italy and its counterpart in the U.S.

Although the French Connection was wrecked, it has been suggested that it is not really dead. Heroin laboratories were found in France in February of 1978 and September of 1979; two months later a French chemist was arrested at a clandestine heroin laboratory in Italy. In March 1980, another small lab was seized outside Marseilles, France. Among those who were in contact with the people managing the laboratory was Jean Jehan. In June 1980, three laboratories were seized in and near Milan, Italy; following the raids the French police arrested Jehan at Marseilles. Jehan was released in September of 1980, at the age of 82, for reasons of ill health.

The U.S. government considers these events warning signals that the French Connection may be showing signs of life. If this is true, they suggest it will resurface as the Franco–Italian Connection.

Freon   A FLUOROCARBON. It was frequently used as a propellant for aerosols prior to 1978 when fluorocarbons were banned from use in household consumer products.

fructose   It is thought that fructose, a natural sugar in fruits and honey, may speed up the rate at which ethanol is metabolized. The degree of acceleration involved is not known but is thought to be small. The addition of fructose to one's diet is not a practical sobering agent but may slightly reduce hangover effects.

fumo d'Angola   Brazilian for CANNABIS. This Brazilian reference to Angola, a Portugese colony in Africa, supports the theory that African slaves may have been the first to bring cannabis to South America.

G

Gamma alcoholism   See JELLINEK.

gaseous anesthetics   See NITROUS OXIDE.

gasoline   Inhaling gasoline fumes can produce an intoxicating effect similar to alcohol. Extensive inhaling can produce hallucinations, confusion, delirium and coma. Lead poisoning is a possible outcome. (See also INHALANTS.)

gastrointestinal tract   The gastrointestinal tract is the term applied to the part of the digestive system which includes the stomach and the small and large intestines. (The digestive tract includes the complete food canal from the mouth to the anus.)

Food is converted into soluble or emulsified material that can be absorbed by the blood and circulated for distribution and utilization by the various tissues of the body. This conversion is achieved by the secretions and enzymes of the gastrointestinal tract. Digestion begins in the mouth, where chewing reduces the food to a fine texture and where the action of the saliva begins the alteration of starch. The juices and enzymes of the stomach then continue the process as hydrochloric acid, pepsin and rennin act upon the protein components of the food. When the partially altered mass enters the small intestine there is further enzymatic action by the bile and the pancreatic secretions, and the conversion of starch, sugar, fat and protein is completed. The residue that cannot be utilized by the body passes into the large intestine and is excreted as waste from the rectum.

Drugs taken by mouth begin to enter the blood through the walls of the stomach or through the upper portion of the small intestine.

Alcohol passes through the mouth to the stomach where about 20% of it is absorbed. The rest is absorbed in the upper small intestine. The ingestion of alcohol has been widely associated with inflammation of the stomach, particularly inflammation of the stomach's mucous membranes. Although small amounts of alcohol (a glass or two of wine) can stimulate the appetite, high concentrations of alcohol depress the appetite and produce hypersecretion and gastric irritation which cause nausea and vomiting. In addition, alcohol delays the emptying time of the stomach. Consistent drinking impairs pancreatic enzyme function producing diarrhea. Prolonged and excessive use of alcohol may result in more serious erosion of the stomach membrane, ranging from inflammation to ulceration and hemorrhage. In addition, many alcoholics suffer from malnutrition because their main caloric intake consists of alcohol.

Barbiturates and other sedative and hypnotic drugs are rapidly absorbed into the body through the upper portion of the small intestine. The presence of food in the stomach slows down the absorption of these drugs, as it does with alcohol. The moderate, medically prescribed use of barbiturates seems to have little or no direct adverse effect on the gastrointestinal tract. The abuse of these drugs, however, can produce symptoms like those of alcohol intoxication—nausea and vomiting. Unlike alcoholics, barbiturate addicts are not likely to suffer serious malnutrition or gastric irritation.

The popular stereotype of a heroin addict is someone who is emaciated, sallow–complexioned and obviously unhealthy. The most authoritative studies have shown that addiction to opiate derivative drugs "is not characterized by physical deterioration or impairment of physical fitness aside from the addiction per se. There is no evidence of change in the circulatory, hepatic, renal or endocrine functions." (Arthur B. Light and Edward G. Torrance, in *A.M.A Archives of Internal Medicine*, 44, [1929]:876.)

In terms of the effects on the digestive system, and on the gastrointestinal tract in particular, the opiates are sometimes constipating (in fact, codeine and opium itself have been used as treatments for diarrhea). Some addicts must use laxatives to aid elimination. "Street" heroin is sometimes cut with mannite, a mild laxative that counteracts the constipating effect of the heroin.

Cocaine is easily absorbed by the mucous membranes and is usually sniffed; it is not taken orally because it is hydrolyzed by the gastrointestinal secretions. Perhaps because cocaine is absorbed and eliminated by the body so quickly it does not seem to have any adverse effects on the gastrointestinal tract. Freud is said to have successfully prescribed cocaine for a patient with gastric distress probably because of its local anesthetic action.

In the case of cigarette smoking, Dr. Vincent P. Dole of Rockefeller University made an interesting comparison: "Cigarette smoking is unquestionably more damaging to the human body than heroin." He made this statement after examining and testing many heroin addicts who had been addicted for a long time. Most of the nicotine in cigarettes is absorbed through the buccal membranes of the mouth and the lungs, but nicotine is also readily absorbed through the stomach and is quickly distributed to the brain, body organs and all the body fluids. It is a stimulant to both the central and peripheral nervous systems and, as is the case with amphetamines, caffeine and other stimulants, even moderate doses can result in prolonged gastric secretions which can lead to the formation of peptic ulcers.

Very heavy use of cannabis has been as-

sociated with temporary intestinal disorders such as diarrhea, abdominal cramps and inflammation, but it does not seem to have any long–term effect on the gastrointestinal tract. The synthetic psychedelic drugs, such as LSD, seem to have no effect on the gastrointestinal tract but organic psychedelics, such as peyote or "sacred mushrooms," sometimes cause nausea and vomiting at the beginning of a "trip." Again, these drugs do not seem to have any long–lasting effects on the digestive system.

gay drug users   See HOMOSEXUALS.

Gaysal® (Geriatric)   An analgesic (generally used for arthritis) and a sedative. It contains sodium salicylate, acetaminophen, aluminum hydroxide and the BARBITURATES, phenobarbital and secobarbital. It may be habit–forming and dependence can occur. Gaysal-S has the same formula minus the barbiturates.

Gemonil® (Abbott)   An anticonvulsant that contains metharbital (a synthetic derivative of barbital) and is used for the control of seizures. It is a BARBITURATE of long duration and slow action and may be habit–forming. Physical and psychological dependence can occur and, when taken with alcohol or other central nervous system depressants, it can have an additive effect. Overdosage can result in drowsiness, irritability, dizziness and coma. It is supplied in 100 mg tablets.

generics   When applied to drugs, the term means the chemical description of the drug's class as opposed to a commercial brand or trade name for the same compound. For example, Valium is a trade name for diazepam, the generic name.

genetics   See HEREDITY.

genetotropic etiological theory   A theory that the satisfaction of all nutritional needs will end the desire for alcohol. The theory was first advanced by R. J. Williams, who suggested that alcoholism is related to a genetically determined biochemical defect. Although Williams' theory has been criticized, it is known that nutrition may well play a role in the cause of alcoholism. (See also NUTRITION.)

Germany (West)   The pattern of drug abuse in West Germany has changed drastically in the past two decades. Initially, the country was troubled by the abuse of LSD, other psychedelic drugs, and hashish. Today the main problem is heroin.

In 1980 the number of heroin addicts was estimated at between 80,000 and 100,000 and it has been suggested that one out of every 20 Germans has experimented with various dangerous drugs. Of particular concern is the fact that government surveys show an increase in the number of heroin abusers under the age of 21. The increase in abuse tends to go along with an increase in illicit drug trafficking and smuggling (a 7% increase between 1977 and 1980 in recorded cases). Government surveys show there is an excessive supply of heroin and cocaine at extremely low prices despite increased police seizures. In 1980, 95% of heroin seizures came from Southwest Asia; preliminary figures for the first few months of 1981 indicate that Southeast Asia heroin accounted for 30% of the seizures. It is thought that much of the increase in heroin abuse is due to West Germany's geographical position as a supply route for illegal drug smuggling across Western Europe.

Recently officials have expressed concern about a renewed wave of cocaine abuse.

Early in 1970 the government initiated a crash program to deal with drug abuse. In-depth surveys were begun and funding was made available for research into the reasons behind the increase. Law enforcement was strengthened to try to halt illegal trafficking; a system of public education on the dangers of narcotics was set up; and improvements were made in the medical assistance available to addicts. In the late 1970s the program was further expanded; international contacts were beefed up and cooperation with neighboring countries on border control was greatly increased.

Since the initial crash program of the early 1970s, 50 institutions are now available to abusers for long–term therapy. Former addicts have access to vocational rehabilitation institutions, and under federal law employers can now be reimbursed for 60–80% of salary for up to two years if they employ a former addict.

Educational programs aimed at combating drug abuse take the form of government booklets and pamphlets, and public media education through television. These informative and educational efforts are carried out by the Federal Center for Health Education, an agency subordinate to the Federal Ministry for Youth, Family Affairs, and Health. Future government programs call for an intensification of these existing programs, particularly with regard to epidemiological research. A recent government study revealed that the increase in drug abuse coincides with the German people's search for solidarity, autonomy, hedonism and spirituality. It was suggested that those particularly liable to addiction are those who feel they do not belong to any society and believe they are getting "too little from life." This theory would demonstrate why it is so difficult to identify these people at an early age and why it is so important to educate them at an early age. Consequently, the government has concentrated its public health education measures on the following target groups: children prior to at–risk age (8–12 years); young people in high–risk groups (13–17 years); parents with children in these two age groups; "mediators'' who work with these age groups and parents; and representatives and decision–makers of institutions responsible for structuring and implementing preventive measures.

The problem of alcohol abuse is also serious in West Germany and the country reports one of the highest levels of consumption of absolute alcohol in the world. The annual level of consumption, according to a 1974 report, was approximately 14.8 liters per person aged 15 and over. Although a very high level, it was still below those of Portugal (23.4) and France (22.4) during the same period. The high consumption in West Germany is not surprising in view of the fact that almost all meals and social occasions are accompanied by beer, wine and other alcoholic beverages. A slight decline in consumption was reported from 1975–78 (a drop of 0.3 liters); this drop was significant because until 1975 the level had been steadily rising.

Based on reports from Frankfurt and Hamburg, the following types of programs for alcoholics are available: self–help groups; treatment centers; and advice bureaus. The best known of the self–help groups is Anonymen Alkoholiker, modeled after AA in the United States, which has approximately 800 groups throughout West Germany. Self–help groups with religious affiliations are sponsored by Protestants, Catholics and Jews. Advice Bureaus are numerous throughout the country and are usually located in clubs, health services, churches and various other organizations. The first centralized center for the intoxicated opened in Hamburg in the mid–1970s and was primarily designed to provide a place where individuals suspected by the police of being drunk could sober up overnight. The center was considered necessary because there were reports of people dying in police "coolers" because they were in need of medical attention. At the center a doctor examines each person and those in need of medical care are sent on to a hospital; those who are merely drunk are kept in the center overnight at their own expense. Other cities throughout the country are considering opening such centers.

glue sniffing   See INHALANTS.

glutethimide   A nonbarbiturate hypnotic usually prescribed for insomnia. It has a rapid onset. (See DORIDEN.)

Golden Crescent   In the late 1970s, following a drop in illicit opium from the GOLDEN TRIANGLE, three Southwest Asian countries emerged as the leading opium producers in the world: Pakistan, Afganistan and Iran. Most of the trafficking of Southwest Asian heroin is carried on by Turkish nationals who smuggle heroin which has been converted from opium grown in Southwest Asia and processed in illicit laboratories in eastern Turkey and western Iran. Current trends indicate that increasing numbers of other Southwest Asian nationals (Lebanese and Syrians) are moving into the European heroin market. Southwest Asian heroin has enjoyed great success in Europe because it is less expensive and of higher quality than Southeast Asian heroin.

The Federal Republic of Germany has become the major market for Turkish traffickers (partly because of the large number of Turkish guest workers there) although the Netherlands has also experienced a recent influx of smuggled heroin. Italy is also beginning to play an increasingly important role in international heroin trafficking. Being a key transit point for Southwest Asian heroin reaching other Western European nations, Italy is also a location for heroin conversion laboratories and a major source area for the increasing quantities of heroin reaching the U.S. Italy has become an important consumer country for heroin, too. Italian authorities estimate that between 40,000 to 50,000 Italians may use heroin on a daily basis.

For years the governments of Southwest Asian countries have viewed the abuse of heroin as an American problem. Although narcotics have been used in Asia throughout history, there are now more addicts in Asia than there are in the U.S. and heroin addiction is quickly becoming epidemic. The trend is troubling local governments and making them take a closer look at the international war on narcotics.

Three consecutive bumper opium harvests, beginning in 1980, have produced a stockpile, and officials believe there is little hope of controlling the supply soon. Because of the excess supplies, dealers are cutting prices—the price of street heroin has halved since 1980—and are looking for new markets. It is estimated that Asia already accounts for 60% of world heroin use, and addiction among people under 21 is growing at an alarming rate.

There are several reasons for the increase in heroin abuse in the area. In addition to excess supplies and cheap prices, Asians have become more open to drug use in recent years: there has been a shift in population from rural to urban areas; people have started to earn more money and have become alienated from traditional ways; and in many households both parents now work, leaving children unsupervised. In Burma, Thailand,

Pakistan and Afganistan traffickers are often government insurgents or independent tribal leaders who are almost impossible to control. Furthermore, the process of refining heroin is increasingly taking place in Asian laboratories.

Golden Triangle An area that includes regions in eastern Burma, northern Laos and Thailand. It emerged in the 1960s and 1970s as the largest producer of illicit opium in the world and, until recently, dominated the heroin market in Western Europe. The growing of opium poppies is thought to have been introduced to the region by Chinese political refugees and further encouraged by Europeans as a source of revenue. Chinese traffickers, using the Netherlands as the main importation and distribution area, virtually controlled the heroin market; arranging for the purchase of raw opium, overseeing its conversion (usually in laboratories in and around Bangkok and Hong Kong), and managing an international smuggling network. In the late 1970s there was a reduction in trafficking due to several factors: rivalry among the various Chinese groups of crime syndicates, law enforcement efforts against major Oriental traffickers, and a drop in opium production due to poor crops.

Major Areas of Heroin Addiction in Asia			
Country	Addicts (in thousands)	Population (in millions)	Percentage
Burma	60	35	0.17
Hong Kong	50	5.5	0.9
Iran	300–500	40	1.0
Malaysia	250	14	1.8
Pakistan	120	87	0.14
Singapore	7	2.5	0.28
Thailand	400–600	48	1.0
These figures are based on Asian and U.S. government estimates.			

Source: *The Wall Street Journal*, Thursday, January 12, 1984. Reprinted by permission.

With the decrease in heroin from Southeast Asia, the European market was successfully challenged by other traffickers, mostly Turkish nationals smuggling heroin converted from opium grown in Southwest Asia (see GOLDEN CRESCENT) and processed in western Iran and eastern Turkey. Since the late 1970s Southwest Asian heroin has enjoyed great success because it is less expensive and generally more potent than heroin from the Golden Triangle.

grand mal convulsions   Convulsive seizures that can occur during WITHDRAWAL from barbiturates or alcohol (there have only been extremely rare instances of such convulsions occurring during narcotic withdrawal). They generally occur 24 to 48 hours after cessation of drinking and a third of those who experience convulsions also go on to have DELIRIUM TREMENS. Grand mal convulsions are less common in barbiturate withdrawal and do not occur as quickly as they do in the case of alcohol withdrawal. Convulsions can also occur in drug OVERDOSE.

grog   A mixture of rum and water, sometimes served hot. It was named for Edward Vernon (1684–1757), a British admiral, who ordered his men's daily ration of rum to be diluted with water because he feared they were becoming habitually intoxicated. The name given to the mixture came from the admiral's sobriquet, "Old Grog." This term referred to Vernon's habit of wearing a coat made of grogham (a wool–silk–mohair combination) in inclement weather. The term is also extended to refer to any liquor.

group therapy   A drug treatment and rehabilitation technique which involves group rather than individual treatment as a way of emphasizing that a patient's problems are not unique. Usually fewer than a dozen patients are involved in a group, which allows for maximum participation, and the group is generally led by a psychiatrist, a psychologist or a social worker. Members open up their problems to the scrutiny of others and discuss them as a group. This communal type of therapy also allows members to benefit vicariously from the resolution of other members' problems. The technique is sometimes preferred over large group meetings, such as Alcoholics Anonymous or Narcotics Anonymous, where extensive and intimate exploration of a problem is limited.

gum opium   Raw OPIUM.

H

habit   Dependency on drugs. (See ADDICTION.)

habit–forming   Manufacturers of drugs use the term "Warning: May be habit–forming" if there is a possibility that tolerance can develop and physical or psychological dependency can occur.

habituation   The process of forming a habit; also, a synonym for TOLERANCE. Tolerance or ADDICTION are preferable terms because they are more specific.

Haight–Ashbury, the   A district in San Francisco, California, which during the mid–1960s was a gathering spot for counterculture youths whose lives centered around hallucinogenic drugs, particularly LSD.

Haldol® (McNeil)   A major TRANQUILIZER that contains haloperidol and which is used in the treatment of acute or chronic psychosis. When taken with alcohol or other central nervous system depressants it can have an additive effect. Overdosage can result in respiratory depression and hypotension. It is supplied in 0.5 mg white tablets; 1 mg yellow; 2 mg pink; 5 mg green; 10 mg aqua; as a concentrate of 2 mg per ml; and in ampules for injection.

half–life of drugs   The amount of time it takes for the body to remove half of a drug dose from the system. For drugs with a half–life of 24 hours or more, such as Valium, half of the first dose may still be in the body when the next dose is taken 24 hours later. After several days the cumulation in the body can be fairly large, and if alcohol or another central nervous system depressant is taken the result can be additive. Cumulation levels off within a week. (See also SYNERGY.)

halfway house   A home for formerly institutionalized individuals, such as alcoholics, drug addicts, mental patients or ex–prisoners. It is a transition point as they move from inpatient care to outside life. The halfway house movement developed in the 1970s. It is based on the belief that to be effective such houses should have only a small number of residents and maintain an informal "homelike" atmosphere. Primarily for the homeless who need support and protection, rather than medical care, until they can again take their place in the community, halfway houses are generally staffed by non-professionals and provide residents with food, shelter and a therapeutic environment. Professionals are available for any needed medical care.

hallucinogens   (From *hallucination*—a sensory experience that does not relate to external reality.) Hallucinogens are drugs that act on the central nervous system and produce mood changes and perceptual changes varying from sensory illusion to hallucinations. Because some of these drugs have the ability to "mimic" psychotic reactions—loss of contact with reality, hallucinations, mania, and schizophrenia—they are sometimes called psychotomimetic drugs. The term psychotogenic, which refers to the production of a psychotic–like state, is also applied. In addition, because of their mind–expanding qualities, the hallucinogens are sometimes called psychedelics.

Hallucinogens are classified as Schedule I drugs under the CONTROLLED SUBSTANCES ACT, and include LSD, MESCALINE, PEYOTE, DMT, PSILOCYBIN (PSILOCIN), MARIJUANA, and TETRAHYDROCANNABINOLS, among others. Apart from marijuana (which has not quite appropriately been placed in this classification although it can produce some psychedelic effects) the most widely used of the hallucinogens are LSD, mescaline, DOM (STP), and psilocybin (psilocin). LSD and DOM (STP) are synthetic compounds, as are other hallucinogens such as MDA, PCP, and TMA. Mescaline and psilocybin are naturally–occurring substances which can also be synthesized. Some of the less widely used hallucinogens occur only in natural materials such as MORNING GLORY SEEDS, NUTMEG, and certain varieties of mushrooms.

Numerous pharmaceuticals and other drugs can produce hallucinogenic reactions. Such drugs are not classified as hallucinogens, however, since the primary reaction sought from them is not a hallucinogenic one.

Hallucinogenic drugs have been in use at least 5000 years. In many parts of the world they have traditionally been used on religious and ceremonial occasions and continue to be so used today. The peyote cactus (containing mescaline) was first used by the Aztec Indians of Mexico and is still used by the American Indians of the Native American Church as a sacrament in religious ceremonies.

The Indians of Central America and Mexico have long used *Psilocyba mexicana,* a mushroom which contains the hallucinogens ocybin and psilocybin. They call it "food of the gods." It is believed that Norse tribesmen used *Amanita muscaria* mushrooms to bring on a feeling of rage before going into battle. This mushroom, also known as FLY AGARIC, contains hallucinogenic agents which produce effects similar to those induced by LSD. The word berserk comes from the bearskin shirt which these warriors wore in battle.

More recently, because many of these drugs mimic psychoses, it has been hoped that they could be beneficial in the research and treatment of various mental illnesses. But while many therapeutic claims have been made for these drugs, as yet none have proven safe or effective in the treatment of mental disorders.

Effects: Most drugs affect individuals differently depending on the amount taken, the past experience of the user, the method of administration, and whether or not the drug is used concurrently with another substance. Reactions to the hallucinogens are particularly variable and often depend on the context in which the drugs are taken and the mental condition of the user. Variations in composition and purity also contribute to the idiosyncratic effects of these drugs.

In low doses the drugs commonly alter moods and perceptions, though they do not necessarily produce hallucinations or other psychotic–like reactions. Mood changes may range from euphoria to depression. Perceptual changes may be pleasant and quasi–mystical or frightening and unpleasant. Typically, sensory perceptions are heightened. In high doses the drugs may also produce hallucinations.

The onset of the hallucinogenic experience may be fast or slow depending on the drug itself and the manner in which it is used. Duration is also variable. Occasionally the user will experience a prolonged reaction or a recurring reaction to a hallucinogen. In such cases, the effects may continue for an extended period after the drug is taken or there may be a spontaneous recurrence of the original experience weeks or even months later. The latter experience is sometimes called a FLASHBACK.

Interestingly, a user is generally aware that his experiences are distortions of reality. With some of the more powerful hallucinogens, however, he may lose all sense of reality. Though this state usually passes quickly, cases exist where individuals have become permanently psychotic either from the stress of the experience or from the precipitation of a schizophrenic reaction.

Physical effects of the hallucinogens are also wide ranging. Adverse effects such as headache, nausea, blurred vision, sleeplessness and dilation of the pupils are all common. Other effects include loss of appetite, increased body temperature, vomiting, lowered or raised blood pressure, decreased or increased heart or respiratory activity, trembling, dizziness, profuse perspiration and numbness of extremities. Some of the hallucinogens are also known to produce convulsions on occasion.

Though hallucinogens are relatively nontoxic—there are no known cases of death caused by heavy doses—individual psychological reactions to them can be life–threatening. BAD TRIPS and prolonged or recurring reactions have brought on delusions which have caused serious accidents, even suicides and homicides. And though not confirmed conclusively, research suggests that LSD increases the risk of spontaneous abortion among pregnant women. Use of the drug may also be linked to a higher incidence of congenital birth defects among the offspring of LSD users.

Among drug users, it is a common belief that the mind–expanding qualities of LSD and other hallucinogens stimulate creativity.

This has not been confirmed by objective studies.

Addictive aspects: Chronic users of hallucinogens can become psychologically dependent on these drugs, but it is generally agreed that no physical DEPENDENCE develops. Even after long use no WITHDRAWAL symptoms are known to develop when the drugs are given up. Psychological dependence is manifested by a compelling need to use the drug involved. The mental state induced by the drug becomes so much a part of the user's life that to be without it seems abnormal. Thus the user craves the mental state induced by the drug.

Tolerance: Regular use of certain hallucinogens, such as LSD, will rapidly produce tolerance but it disappears after a few days abstinence. Tolerance is not generally an issue as few people would use a drug such as LSD or mescaline on a daily basis. However, users tolerant to the effects of LSD exhibit CROSS–TOLERANCE to mescaline and to psilocybin. Tolerance to hashish develops to a slight degree over a long period of time, but as a general rule the same dose of marijuana—no matter how frequently taken—will have the same effects.

Sources: Only limited amounts of certain hallucinogens are produced commercially in government–authorized laboratories for research or treatment. Most of the synthetic hallucinogens can be readily manufactured and these along with the naturally occurring hallucinogens are sold illicitly.

Traffic and control: Because they have a potential for abuse and no accepted medical benefits, most of the hallucinogens are federally regulated under Schedule I of the CONTROLLED SUBSTANCES ACT (CSA). The drugs under Schedule I are basically research substances for which there is no known or accepted medical use in the United States. They can be manufactured only in federally-regulated laboratories for research purposes.

They cannot be sold by prescription. Researchers using the drugs must administer the substances directly to their subjects, although small amounts of THC have been given to cancer patients to take home for the treatment of nausea from chemotherapy.

Morning glory seeds, nutmeg, jimson weed and the like are not subject to any specific legal regulations. PEYOTE is used legally by the Native American Church.

Synonyms: illusionogenics, psychedelics, psychotomimetics, psychotogenics, mind–expanding or mind–manifesting drugs, acid (refers mainly to LSD).

Samuel M. Levine, *Narcotics and Drug Abuse* (Cincinnati: The W.H. Anderson Company, 1973).

Robert J. Wicks and Jerome J. Platt, *Drug Abuse: A Criminal Justice Primer* (Beverly Hills, Cal.: Enziger Bruce & Glencoe, Inc., 1977).

hangover   A condition that follows alcohol intoxication by eight to 12 hours. It is characterized by general malaise; nausea and vomiting; dizziness; dry mouth and thirst; sensitivity to movement, bright lights and loud sounds; a splitting headache; anxiety or depression. A person who is "hung over" may experience one, several, or all of the above symptoms. There are probably a number of factors involved in the cause of a hangover, but they are not completely understood. Because many of the symptoms are similar to those of hypoglycemia it is believed that lowered blood sugar may be a factor (blood glucose levels are at their lowest during a hangover). Another element may be stress reaction: the stress of intoxication is often heightened by guilt resulting from uninhibited behavior, lack of sleep, and heavy smoking. Dehydration and acidosis are also contributors to the post–intoxicated hangover state.

There is speculation that the hangover syndrome is a symptom of early withdrawal—that overdrinking has established a dependency and the body is reacting because of a need for more alcohol. There is evidence that consuming alcohol (hair of the dog that bit you) will alleviate or reverse hangover symptoms and this fact supports the theory that a hangover may indeed be early withdrawal. But while drinking a small amount of alcohol to correct metabolic rebound may be justified, there is the danger that it will lead to another bout of excessive drinking.

hard drugs, hard narcotics   Opium, morphine, and cocaine, along with their derivatives, are considered by addicts to be hard narcotics. Marijuana and non–opiates, on the other hand, are called soft drugs. This dichotomy is not realistic or scientific. Soft drugs like alcohol and tobacco are likely to be more harmful over a period of time than hard drugs.

harmal   *Peganum harmal*, an herb containing the psychedelic alkaloids HARMINE and HARMALINE. The plant is native to India and countries of the eastern Mediterranean.

harmaline   A psychedelic alkaloid found in the herb HARMAL. It is also the active alkaloid in *Banisteriopsis caapi*, native to Peru. (See also AYAHUASCA.)

harmine   A psychedelic alkaloid found in *Banisteriopsis caapi*, a plant native to the Amazon River basin. The substance is extracted by boiling pieces of the vine in water. Harmine produces reactions similar to those induced by LSD and mescaline. South American Indians use the substance in religious ceremonies and as a healing agent. (See AYAHUASCA.) Harmine is also found in the herb HARMAL, native to India and countries of the eastern Mediterranean.

Harris–Dodd Act   A drug abuse control act passed in 1965 that has since been superceded. (See CONTROLLED SUBSTANCES ACT.)

Harrison Narcotic Act   The first law in the United States to regulate narcotics. Passed in December 1914, it became effective in 1915 and was designed primarily to channel the flow of opium and coca leaves and their derivatives and to make their transfer a matter of record. Forms issued by the Collector of Internal Revenue were required for all transfers of the drugs between manufacturer, wholesaler, retailer and doctor. A tax was also levied on the narcotic. The act also required the registration of all those who dealt in the production or transfer of narcotics, with the exception of warehousemen and common carriers, nurses who were under a doctor's supervision, and government officials who had drugs in their possession for official duties. The Federal Bureau of Narcotics was not in existence in 1915 and enforcement of the act was carried out by the Collector of Internal Revenue and the Narcotic Unit of the Bureau of Prohibition, both agencies of the Treasury Department. Under the law the only way an unregistered person could legally possess one of these drugs was when he had obtained it through a doctor's prescription.

haschischins, Le club des   A French club attended by literary men with the purpose of experimenting with hashish. It was founded in 1844 by the French novelist Theophile Gautier.

hashish   From the Arabic *hashish*, "dry grass," the word "hashish" is also associated with a semi–legendary religious cult in 11th century Persia. The cult was headed by Al–Hasan ibn–al Sabbah, the so–called "Old Man of the Mountain," who led a branch of the Isma'ili sect of Shi'ite Muslims in a number of terrorist murders committed for political and religious reasons. Known as the Hashishi, the sect has been linked to the use of hashish, though there is no concrete evidence of this. Our word "assassin" comes from the name of this sect.

Hashish is the resinous extract of the hemp plant, CANNABIS SATIVA. It is obtained by boiling the parts of the plant that are covered with resin in a solvent, or by scraping the resin from the plant. The resin, which contains the active principal TETRAHYDROCANNABINOL (THC), is then formed into cakes or lumps that range from brown to black. Hashish is a very potent form of cannabis: its THC content may range from 5–12% by weight compared with 5–10% for the most potent forms of MARIJUANA, and 1% for Mexican marijuana. An even more potent form of cannabis with a THC content of about 20–80% is known as LIQUID HASHISH (Hash Oil).

In America hashish is usually smoked, sometimes in a waterpipe which regulates the intake and cools the smoke. In North Africa hashish is smoked or eaten in a confection known as *majoon* or DAWAMESK, a sort of cake made of sugar, vanilla, almonds, pistachios, and spices, along with the hashish. In India hashish is known as *charas*.

The effects of hashish, like those of marijuana, depend a great deal on the user, on the dosage, and—in particular—on the potency of the drug. In the 19th century a group of French literary figures, including Gautier, Baudelaire, Hugo, Balzac, and de Nerval, formed a group known as LE CLUB DES HASHISHCHINS. They ingested hashish in the dawamesk form, a more unpredictable way of consuming it than smoking because it is difficult to control the dose. The effects which these men describe in their writings vary a great deal and were almost certainly linked to their individual imaginations and person-

alities and the atmosphere in which they took the drug. Gautier had hallucinations of "hybrid creatures, formless mixtures of men, beasts, and utensils; monks with wheels for feet and cauldrons for bellies," while Baudelaire saw "an exquisite harmony of proportion . . . through space." The effects experienced by most users are quite similar to those produced by smoking potent marijuana. Large amounts of ingested hashish, on the other hand, can lead to such a degree of intoxication that extreme perceptual distortion and anxiety may result. Psychotic episodes rarely last for more than 48 hours after the hashish has been ingested. While it is true that hashish may bring on psychotic episodes, it may also be the case that it does so only in those who already have shown signs of potentially psychotic behavior (antecedent psychopathology) before taking any drugs.

A typical American hashish user is white, male, aged 18–25, with some college education. Use is limited almost exclusively to those who also use marijuana. In spite of its relative scarcity, use of hashish is increasing in the U.S. because of a growing preference for higher potency cannabis.

Classification: Hashish is a very potent form of CANNABIS SATIVA. Marijuana and all other cannabis drugs come from this one species, but different varieties and different growing climates affect the potency. Hashish, which is the resin of the upper leaves and flowering tops of the female plant, is usually produced from plants grown in areas of fairly high altitude and high temperature because they tend to produce a greater amount of resin. The principal psychoactive ingredient in all forms of cannabis is Delta–9 Tetrahydrocannabinol, or THC, found in the resin on the undersurface of the flowers and leaves. Hashish is classified as a hallucinogen (a Schedule I classification under the CONTROLLED SUBSTANCES ACT).

Effects: The effects may include distorted

perception, depersonalization or "double consciousness," spatial and time distortions, intensification of scents, tastes, colors and sounds, and visual hallucinations. The effects are similar to those produced by marijuana, but usually they are more intense because of the higher potency of hashish.

Addictive aspects: Hashish is not physically addictive, and withdrawal symptoms are non–specific. Psychological dependence is a danger; this has been seen primarily in North Africa and India where use is quite heavy but infrequently in the U.S.

Tolerance: Tolerance to hashish develops at a moderate rate. Someone who has smoked hashish regularly will usually need a larger dose to achieve the same "high."

Sources: Most of the hashish in the U.S. is smuggled in from Morocco, Nepal, Pakistan, Afghanistan and Lebanon. The principal suppliers of marijuana to the U.S. market, Colombia, Mexico and Jamaica, do not produce significant quantities of hashish. This is probably due to differences in the amounts of resin produced by the plants in different climates (more resin is produced in dry areas at high altitudes) and to cultural and traditional practices.

Traffic and control: The use of hashish in the U.S. is apparently on the rise but it is difficult to estimate how much is being used because seizures by the authorities fluctuate widely from year to year: from 700 pounds in 1970 to over 50,000 pounds in 1973–74, for example. Although most seizures are relatively small, one large seizure will completely change the figures for a given year. In 1978, for instance, 2,999 pounds were seized; but in 1979 a total of 43,233 pounds were taken which included one huge seizure of 41,676 pounds of suspected Lebanese hashish from a ship off Sandy Hook, New Jersey. During the first half of 1980, on the other hand, only 45 pounds of hashish were seized.

Synonyms: hash, Goma de Mota, soles, charas.

Hawaiian wood rose, baby   A plant, native to Hawaii and Asia, whose seeds contain lysergic acid amide. When eaten they produce psychedelic effects similar to but milder than LSD.

Hawaiian wood rose, large   Similar to HAWAIIAN WOOD ROSE, BABY but only half as potent.

head shop   Head shops, which have sprung up across the country in recent years (there are an estimated 15,000 to 30,000), sell assorted drug paraphernalia. Their stock includes everything from roach clips and water pipes to hypodermic syringes and cocaine spoons. They also carry publications which give advice on drugs to buy and how much to pay, and others that provide gardening tips on how to grow your own marijuana and mushrooms. They sell kits to convert street cocaine to FREEBASE that can be smoked and that will produce a more intense high than when it is snorted. Not only are head shops a place to make contacts for the purchase of an illicit drug, they also sell certain uncontrolled drugs. Butyl nitrite, which is technically not a drug and is usually sold as a room deodorizer, is sold as an inhalant. It is a vasodilator which expands blood vessels and produces a three to five minute "high." The Food and Drug Administration has no control over this substance and it is sold in head shops under such tradenames as "Bullet" and "Rush." (See FAKE COKE.)

The increase in drug abuse among adolescents must be due in part to the prevalence of head shops. They are, in fact, "learning centers" for inexperienced users and handy shopping centers for experienced ones. The existence of head shops is a continuation of the casual public attitude toward drug use.

Children who start out using marijuana, as most do, can go to a head shop to purchase a roach clip and come away with a knowledge of much harder drugs.

Head shops not only sell paraphernalia, they glamorize, condone and advocate the use of drugs. The head shop business is turning into a multi–million dollar industry. Some states have attempted to control the sale of drug paraphernalia, but their laws are usually ineffective. In response to the need for legislation, the Drug Enforcement Administration has drafted a Model Drug Paraphernalia Act. It will cover the control of all equipment, products and materials of any kind which are used, intended for use, or designated for use in planting, propagating, cultivating, growing, harvesting, manufacturing, compounding, converting, producing, processing, preparing, testing, analyzing, packaging, repackaging, storing, containing, concealing, injecting, ingesting, inhaling, or otherwise introducing into the body a controlled substance in violation of the Controlled Substances Act. The act will further amend the offenses and penalties section of the Controlled Substances Act to cover the possession of such drug paraphernalia. It has been successfully adopted by a number of municipalities and states.

heart   A muscular organ which rhythmically contracts and relaxes to pump the blood throughout the body. The heart is one of the body's most complex organs and it is susceptible to temporary and permanent damage from a variety of causes.

Heart disease does not necessarily result from drug abuse, although most toxic substances do affect heart action in some way. LSD and other hallucinogens can cause temporary tachycardia (increased heart rate) as well as occasional bradycardia (lowered heart rate). One of the most consistent physical effects of smoking marijuana is increased heartbeat, possibly caused by increased secretion of epinephrine, a hormone which stimulates the heart. Marijuana–induced tachycardia usually peaks about 15 minutes after the drug is smoked and subsides almost completely while psychological effects are still noted. The rate increase correlates directly to dosage and, with large doses of THC, the heartbeat can almost double. Pulse rate was once considered an effective gauge of how much marijuana a subject had smoked, but the theory has been discarded since the heartbeat is affected by so many other factors. Tolerance to the tachycardia will occur in chronic users. Very high doses of THC in sequence will change the tachycardia to a bradycardia due to tolerance development.

Inhalation of aerosols and volatile solvents may cause death from cardiac arrest. Trichlorethane and the fluorohydrocarbons, especially, exhibit strong toxic effects on the myocardium (heart muscle) and can produce cardiac arrhythmia and edema (fluid accumulation) in the heart and other organs. Necrosis, fatty degeneration of the heart, liver and adrenal glands, and myocarditis, inflammation of the heart muscle, have resulted from abuse of these drugs.

In the past AMYL NITRITE, a depressant inhalant, was often prescribed to relieve chest pain associated with heart problems such as angina pectoris. It increases the heart rate considerably by dilating the blood vessels and relaxing the smooth heart muscle. The inhalant enjoys widespread but decreasing recreational use, primarily to enhance and prolong sexual pleasure.

Heroin and other narcotics generally reduce heart rate, although vast fluctuations can occur during heroin withdrawal. Moreover, heroin addiction exposes the heart, as well as the liver, to diseases which are attributable to the method of administration rather than to the drug itself. Endocarditis, an infectious inflammation of the heart's inner lining and valves, usually occurs in addicts with some history of heart problems and is caused by staphylococcus and other anti-biotic–resistant bacteria and fungi. (Endocarditis that occurs in non–users is usually caused by a variety of streptococcus.) Antibiotics are used in the treatment of this disease, which is characterized by nodules on the edges of the heart valves. Scarring impairs valve function, blood clots can develop, and fatal congestive heart failure can result. The disease has a high mortality rate when its development follows drug injection.

Using unclean needles also makes heroin addicts susceptible to tetanus, which creates an imbalance in the autonomic nervous system and consequent cardiac instability. Disruption of heart rhythm regulation can lead to cardiac arrest.

Stimulants such as cocaine and amphetamines obviously increase heart rate and can expose users to the risk of heart disease. Amphetamines have the added effect of strengthening myocardial contraction. Cardiac arrhythmia occurs with these drugs in direct proportion to their overall toxicity, and cardiac arrest is a frequent result of their abuse.

Of the stimulants, nicotine is certainly the most widely publicized and effective substance in inducing heart disease and other circulatory damage. Including such conditions as coronary artery disease, arteriosclerosis, and hypertension, heart disease accounts for more than 50% of deaths related to smoking cigarettes.

Nicotine mimics acetylcholine, blocking the impulses that acetylcholine normally transmits, and affecting nerve synapses to produce greater excitability. These effects combine with nicotine's release of ephinephrine to overwork the heart—stimulating it without providing for the return of additional blood to the organ.

Epinephrine stimulated by nicotine also releases fatty acids into the blood, and one of the major risks of heavy smoking is the early development of coronary heart disease (CHD), a progression of arteriosclerosis consisting of an accumulation of fats in the lining of the large to medium–sized arteries to the heart. Coronary heart disease claims almost a million Americans each year, and smokers are twice as likely as non–smokers to die from it.

Studies have indicated that the risk of coronary heart disease in the non–smoking population can be lowered by moderate consumption of alcohol (up to two ounces a day). Alcohol increases levels of high density lipoproteins (HDL) which break up cholesterol deposits in the arteries. Heavy alcohol consumption, however, does not have this beneficial effect and instead increases the likelihood of sudden death from CHD and alcoholic myocarditis.

Alcoholics commonly suffer from hypertension (high blood pressure) but this condition cannot be attributed solely to alcohol use; like alcoholism itself, it frequently results from stress. Long–term chronic consumption of alcohol can cause alcoholic cardiomyopathy, a disease of the heart muscle associated with coronary artery disease, in which the organ appears large and flabby. Ethanol, or more precisely its metabolite, acetaldehyde, directly depresses myocardial function and damages mitochondria (as in the liver). Symptoms of cardiomyopathy include difficulty in breathing, swelling of the feet and ankles, fatigue, palpitations and chest pain. Heart failure can follow. Alcoholism and malnutrition combine to produce heart disease which involves thiamine deficiency.

Chronic alcoholism can also combine with previous heart trouble to produce irregular heartbeat. Because cardiac arrhythmias can also involve previously unaffected nonalcoholic individuals during binges of heavy drinking (with an especially high incidence during the Christmas season), it is frequently referred to as the "holiday heart syndrome." Abstinence eliminates the problem.

The combination of the heavy use of alcohol and other drugs—marijuana, for example—is especially dangerous because the cumulative effect can tax the organ past its capacity

Daniel & Dorothy Girdano, *Drugs—A Factual Account* (Reading, Ma.: Addison–Wesley Publishing Co., 1973).

Frederick G. Hofmann, *A Handbook on Drug and Alcohol Abuse, The Biomedical Aspects* (New York: Oxford University Press, 1975).

Ralph W. Richter, editor, *Medical Aspects of Drug Abuse* (Hagerstown, Md.: Harper & Row, 1975).

heavy drinker   One who drinks in excess of the normal limits of moderation as defined by his or her society.

hedonistic   A term meaning "pleasure–seeking" that is often used to describe the motivations of chronic drug users.

heliotrope   A plant of the genus *Heliotropium*. There are claims that when the flowers are brewed as a tea they can produce a tranquilizing effect.

hemochromatosis   A condition that involves excess deposits of iron in the body tissues which can cause extensive damage. The cause of this relatively uncommon disorder is not known though alcoholism is associated with many cases. It may be a form of CIRRHOSIS, and has been found to be prevalent among heavy and chronic users of wine that contains a large amount of iron.

henbane   *Hyoscyamus niger,* a fetid Old World herb. Its leaves yield an extract containing hyocyamine that has properties similar to belladona.

hepatitis   An inflammation of the liver that occurs frequently in alcoholics and in addicts who administer drugs with dirty syringes. Hepatitis B is the type found in drug addicts. (See also LIVER.)

hepatoma   A cellular cancer that affects the liver and is often associated with CIRRHOSIS. It is also known as hepatocarcinoma.

herbals   Certain plants were dried and used as medicinal agents before modern medicine emerged. The herbals are now enjoying renewed interest along with the movement toward natural foods. Some herbals have psychoactive effects while some are inert and can be used as teas. Potentially toxic herbals include poke root and ginseng preparations. Instances of lead and pyrolizidine poisoning have been reported.

heredity   The sum of qualities and potentialities that are genetically handed down through families.

Studies using natural and adopted children have been made to try to determine whether environment or genetics causes a predisposition to alcoholism. While the results have been inconclusive, it has been suggested that at least a tendency toward alcoholism might be inherited as it is a recognized fact that alcoholism is common in certain families. In addition, it has been shown that inherited traits may ward off alcoholism; possibly because of excessive production of acetaldehyde in the metabolic process (Orientals show a low incidence of alcoholism and a high level of acetaldehyde). Although heredity may play a role, it is generally agreed that other factors are also responsible for the development of alcoholism.

Few studies have been conducted to determine the genetic or heredity susceptibility to drugs other than alcohol. There is the possibility, however, that there may be an inherited difficulty in dealing with anxiety, depression and frustration that may lead to the abuse of drugs.

There are numerous drugs that pass through the placenta during pregnancy and reach the unborn child, including alcohol, THC, nicotine, heroin and morphine. These drugs are also believed to enter the mother's milk. Babies have been known to go through WITHDRAWAL SYMPTOMS at birth if the mother is a chronic user of a depressant drug. If a baby is breast-fed and the mother continues the use of a drug, withdrawal symptoms are warded off until the baby is weaned. Long-term effects on babies born with withdrawal symptoms are inconclusive, and there is an obvious need for further research in the field. There has been extensive controversy over the question of whether a child is "born addicted" or whether the long-term effects are a result of an undeveloped, immature central nervous system. (See also PREGNANCY.)

heroin   A narcotic, diacetylmorphine, derived from morphine, which it greatly resembles. Heroin is a central nervous system depressant which also relieves pain. It was developed in 1898 by the Bayer Company in Germany. Found to be more potent than morphine, its name comes from the German word *heroisch* (powerful, heroic). Originally the drug was considered a better analgesic than morphine, a more efficient cough suppressant and a non-addictive cure for morphine and opium withdrawal symptoms. It took some 12 years for the medical profession to realize that heroin was at least as addictive as morphine.

The Harrison Narcotic Act of 1914 was the first attempt to control the use of heroin medically. By 1924 its manufacture in the United States was prohibited and law enforcement agencies were made responsible for its control. Nevertheless, more than 20 years went by before all existing stocks on hand were surrendered. The dangers involved in heroin use became recognized world-wide, and by 1963 it was used medically in only five countries and manufactured in only three.

Meanwhile, heroin was steadily replacing opium and morphine on the street. An international black market with underground laboratories and well-organized smuggling operations grew rapidly. Two things made such operations fairly easy—the comparatively simple chemical equipment needed to convert morphine to heroin, and the reduced bulk of heroin compared to morphine.

Appearance: Pure heroin is a white, crystalline powder with a bitter taste. It is soluble in water. Until recent years, most of the heroin smuggled into the United States was supplied from Southeast Asian opium sources and was converted to heroin in clandestine laboratories in the area of Marseilles, France. After this supply was curtailed (see GOLDEN TRIANGLE), production of the drug increased in Mexico, which remained the major source for several years. Simpler, faster methods than those used in Marseilles resulted in impurities which gave the Mexican heroin a brown color.

Effects: Heroin depresses the central nervous system in a way similar to alcohol and barbiturates but, unlike those drugs, it also relieves pain. While abuse of alcohol and barbiturates can increase belligerent behavior by removing inhibitions, heroin acts to depress aggression as well as appetite and sexual drive. Other effects include constipation and suppression of the coughing reflex. Depending on the method of administration, heroin induces varying degrees of euphoria; orgasmic reactions often follow intravenous injection. After a "fix" a sense of well-being replaces feelings of depression or low

self–esteem and this is followed by sleep—
"going on the nod."

Administration: Addicts usually inject
("shoot up" or "mainline") heroin into a
vein. Although it can also be mixed with a
liquid and swallowed, sniffed like cocaine,
placed under the tongue, and even smoked—
as it was occasionally in Vietnam where it
was cheap, potent and plentiful—these
methods of administration are rarely used in
the U.S. This is because of the high cost of
the drug; addicts need a number of fixes a
day and want the maximum effect from their
supply. Also, heroin has a disagreeable taste
and the "rush" that addicts crave (an intense
feeling similar to orgasm) only follows intravenous injection.

The cautious first–time user who tries
swallowing or sniffing heroin usually soon
graduates to "skin popping" or "joy popping" (subcutaneous injection of heroin) but
the effects are comparatively mild and there
is no "rush." Some users continue at this
level, skin popping only sporadically and allegedly running less risk of addiction (although whether or not this is true remains in
doubt), but most go on to mainlining.

Before preparing the powder for injection
the user measures out what he thinks is his
usual dose. This can be difficult to estimate
because the heroin sold on the street has been
adulterated (diluted or "cut") many times as
it passes down the line from the large distributor to the street pusher. Since an epidemic
of malaria among addicts in the 1940s, QUI-
NINE has often been used to cut heroin. Quinine also enhances the "rush" effect and
gives heroin diluted with milk sugar a bitter
taste. Other adulterants include mannite (a
mild laxative) and milk sugar. Talcum powder is sometimes used as an adulterant and
can be extremely dangerous because it does
not dissolve in the bloodstream.

To prepare an injection the addict dilutes
the heroin powder in a little water, puts it
into a spoon or other device known as a
"cooker" and holds it over a match, candle,
cigarette lighter or other single flame until
the mixture has boiled for a few seconds.
After the liquid is filtered through a piece of
cotton to remove any solid impurities and
drawn up into a syringe or medicine dropper
attached to a hollow needle, it is ready for
injection.

If the user is skin popping, the needle is
pushed under the skin in any convenient place;
if mainlining, the usual area that is chosen is
the large vein inside the elbow. A tourniquet
is applied between the vein and the heart, the
needle is inserted and the syringe is pulled up
to draw blood (a step called "verifying" or
"registering") to make sure the needle is in
a vein and not in muscle tissue or flesh. The
bulb or syringe is then pushed down to inject
the heroin and the rush follows immediately.
Some users employ the process of BOOTING
to prolong the initial effects. When heroin is
booted, a small amount is injected and then
blood is withdrawn back into the syringe and
the process is repeated.

Dangers of heroin use: Abcesses at the
site of the injection are common and the preferred vein may inflame after repeated use.
Veins in the thigh, wrist or foot may then be
used. Addicts who have run out of usable
veins may resort to skin popping and end up
covered with sores. One of the great dangers
in mainlining is the chance of hitting an artery instead of a vein. The result is extreme
pain at best, and permanent necrosis and
scarring of the arm or leg at worst. Infection
from unsterile needles is an ever–present
danger. Along with abcesses, serum hepatitis, tetanus, and endocarditis (infection of
the heart lining) can also occur. While numerous studies have indicated that heroin is
not physiologically harmful, and does not
cause brain deterioration, it is characteristic
of addicts to neglect their health. Because
the drug suppresses hunger, malnutrition is

common and chronic bronchitis often develops as a result of suppression of the cough reflex. Addicts are also prone to accidents and violent death, living as they often do in contact with the underworld that controls the distribution of heroin. Many must become small–time pushers themselves to earn their own supply.

The greatest danger of heroin use is death from what the media calls an overdose. Actually, the heroin sold on the street has been adulterated so much the addict is unlikely to get a large enough amount to suppress respiration. Most deaths are due to what medical examiners now call acute reactions. These include hypersensitivity with pulmonary edema, infections, complications associated with the adulterants used and the combination of heroin with alcohol or barbiturates (see SYNDROME X). The death rate is high among young people under 35. Only a small percentage of addicts in the U.S. are over 40.

Heroin and pregnancy: Women addicts run a high risk of complications during pregnancy and childbirth. The most common medical problems are anemia, heart disease, hepatitis and pneumonia. Children born to addicted mothers have a significantly higher mortality rate, are smaller than average and often show signs of acute infection. Some experts believe they are also "born addicted" because they develop varying degrees of withdrawal symptoms within a short time after birth.

Tolerance: Tolerance to heroin builds rapidly and stronger doses and more frequent shots are needed to produce the effects craved. In an attempt to duplicate the intensity of earlier rushes some addicts inject "speedballs" (heroin and amphetamines or cocaine), increasing the danger of acute reactions and death. Unlike barbiturates, a very high tolerance to heroin can build up but there is always a lethal dosage. Tolerance to

heroin carries over to other opiates (all drugs derived from opium) as well as to opioids (synthetic drugs which resemble opium alkaloids and their derivatives).

Dependence: Both psychological and physical dependence develop rapidly with regular use of heroin. In psychological dependence there is an uncontrollable craving for the drug's effects. In physical dependence the body comes to rely on the drug to avoid withdrawal sickness.

Withdrawal symptoms: Although withdrawal symptoms from heroin are neither as severe nor as dangerous as those associated with depressants, especially barbiturates, they are bad enough. Their severity depends on several factors—how long an addiction has lasted, how frequently a fix is needed, the general state of health, and whether withdrawal is forced or voluntary. The first symptoms are usually noticed just before the time for the next regular shot. They include restless sleep, gooseflesh (from quitting "cold turkey"), tremors, yawning, irritability, joint and muscle pains, abdominal cramps, chills alternating with profuse sweating, runny nose, nausea, vomiting, diarrhea, urinary incontinence, shortness of breath, and muscle spasms ("kicking the habit"). Reactions usually peak in a few days and linger for a week or more. Fluid loss coupled with a failure to eat or drink can cause dehydration, extensive loss of weight, and destruction of fatty acids (ketosis). All this can lead to extreme debilitation, possible heart arrhythmia and death. Although physical withdrawal symptoms subside in a week or so, psychological craving can continue for months and even years—a fact which makes treatment difficult and which causes many addicts to resume their habits. A protracted physical withdrawal syndrome has been observed in which for years an addict reacts differently to an injection of heroin than a non–addict.

Treatment: At present a lasting cure is

problematic. Addicts who undergo forcible withdrawal in prison head straight for a fix after release. An addict who wants to get off or stay off heroin voluntarily can join a therapeutic community–living program such as SYNANON. In a rehabilitation center addicts help each other through group therapy, mutual reinforcement, companionship and social pressure. There are also similar movements such as Phoenix House and Odyssey House where addicts can replace their drug habit with a dependence on the "movement." The cure rate, however, is low and estimated at only 10 percent of all who enter therapeutic communities. Chemotherapy, the use of narcotic blocking drugs such as METHADONE, shows some promise. Methadone maintenance has helped a number of addicts to break the heroin habit, hold down jobs and live normally with their families. However, although less harmful, it is in itself another addictive drug and the goal for most should be eventual abstinence.

Who uses heroin?: There are now an estimated 400–750,000 heroin users in America. Although once concentrated in metropolitan areas, heroin use has spread to all levels of society from the inner city ghettos to the prosperous suburbs. Narcotics have become a problem on college campuses and in rural as well as city high schools. No class, race, educational level or community is free from the problems of heroin abuse. The major, most visible social evils and criminal activities, however, are found in large cities. A heroin habit is expensive: in one city it was estimated to average $10,000 a year. For the addict who must support his habit through theft this means stealing some $50,000 worth of goods because they can be fenced for only one–fifth their value. Heroin addicts are not apt to commit violent crimes (barbiturate users have the highest rate) but many have been found to have criminal records before they became dependent on drugs.

Traffic and Control: Heroin is listed in Schedule I of the Controlled Substances Act of 1970 as a drug most susceptible to abuse. It is completely illicit in the U.S. and it is not considered to have any medical value. Its manufacture, importation and use are illegal but in spite of strenuous control efforts a black market flourishes. When the manufacture and smuggling of heroin from Southeast Asia through Marseilles, the well–known FRENCH CONNECTION, was curtailed many operations shifted to Mexico. Most of the heroin supplying the U.S. market today comes from Southwest Asia (see GOLDEN CRESCENT). It has enjoyed great success because it is more potent and less expensive than heroin from Southeast Asia.

Smuggling by land and by sea is very difficult to control. When enforcement efforts are increased in one border area or seaport, drug smugglers quickly switch to another. The profits of the illicit drug trade are so great that the risk of being caught is disregarded and others are always waiting to take the place of those arrested. To make things more difficult, world–wide organized crime is deeply involved in heroin manufacture, smuggling and distribution as well as in prostitution and in the sort of crimes which many users must commit to support their habits.

Synonyms: H, big H, horse, Harry, hairy, junk, joy powder, Mexican brown or mud, smack, white stuff, thing.

Richard R. Lingeman, *Drugs from A to Z* (New York: McGraw–Hill Book Company, 1974), pp. 101–112.

Jack Margolis, *Complete Book of Recreational Drugs* (Los Angeles: Price/Stern/Sloan Publishers, Inc., 1978), pp. 227–231.

"Facts About Opiates" (Toronto, Canada: Addiction Research Foundation, 1980).

Edward M Brecher, ed., *Licit and Illicit Drugs* (Boston: Little, Brown and Company, 1972).

Sidney Cohen, *The Substance Abuse Problems* (New York: The Haworth Press, 1981).

History of Heroin

1874   Heroin is isolated from morphine.

1898   Bayer Company of Germany produces heroin commercially and it is found to be more potent than morphine.

1900   Heroin is recognized as being addictive though it was originally thought to be a cure for opium and morphine addiction. U.S. authorities estimate ¼ to 1 million users.

1914   Harrison Narcotics Act taxes manufacture, importation and distribution of heroin.

1924   Manufacture is prohibited in the U.S. and heroin becomes available on the black market.

1930s   Abuse becomes widespread and the French Connection becomes main supplier of U.S. market until broken up in 1973.

1965   Drs. Dole and Nyswander present methadone maintenance program to treat heroin addiction.

1970   Controlled Substances Act classifies heroin as a Schedule I drug.

1980s   Government authorities estimate 400-750,000 users in U.S. Southwest Asia becomes the major supplier.

---

hexane   A major volatile solvent that is found in plastic cement. (See INHALANTS.)

hexobarbital   A short–acting BARBITURATE. Its rapid onset and short duration of action makes it undesirable for purposes of abuse. It is sold under the trade name Sombulex.

high   Being under the influence of a drug, particularly marijuana. The term usually refers to a state of pleasurable intoxication and drug euphoria. A "high" associated with alcohol is generally expressed by uninhibited behavior which borders on or lapses into the irresponsible. It is an ironic effect of the sedative nature of the drug that the "high" phase actually involves sedation of those areas of the brain that would normally guard against abnormal behavior by producing inhibitions. The high induced by such stimulants as amphetamines or cocaine is actually the opposite of a high produced by alcohol.

high blood pressure   Also referred to as HYPERTENSION. A number of studies have linked high blood pressure to heavy alcohol consumption.

hippie   A hedonist whose life centers on meditation and drug–taking. During the mid–1960s a hippie subculture developed in the HAIGHT–ASHBURY section of San Francisco and in New York City on the Lower East Side. The hippies rejected many of the values held by society, existed on as little money as possible, and were nonagressive. They were characterized by their long hair, beads and shabby clothing. The term is becoming obsolete.

histamine   A compound found in human tissue and highly concentrated in the skin, lungs and stomach. It is responsible for the dilation and increased permeability of blood vessels and plays a major role in allergic reactions. It is also a potent stimulator of gastric acid secretion. Release of histamine occurs very quickly after an intravenous injection of heroin, morphine or codeine and can cause intense itching, sometimes over the entire body. Histamine can also cause a reddening of the eyes and a fall in blood pressure. The latter can result in dizziness and sometimes shock.

holiday heart syndrome   An irregularity or disturbance in the heartbeat (arrhythmia) which can occur after a period of heavy alcohol consumption. (See also HEART.)

holistic medicine   A medical approach that deals with a patient's whole complex of needs rather than just treating a diseased or malfunctioning part of the body. The latter Western approach is known as allopathy. Along with traditional bio–medical techniques, holistic medicine employs exercise plans, diet regimes, methods of self–healing, and suggests different less stressful ways of living. Frequently several teams of health care workers are involved in a patient's treatment.

homicide   See CRIME.

homosexuals   Studies have shown there is a higher incidence of alcoholism among homosexuals than among the general population. Conservative estimates report that one out of every four homosexuals is an alcoholic as compared to one out of ten in the general population.

Few studies have been made of other drug abuse but with the recent increase in dual addiction and polydrug use, it is probably safe to assume that because of their social structure there is also a higher incidence of other drug abuse among homosexuals. The homosexual community has a social structure that encourages drinking; a great deal of time may be spent at bars and parties where alcohol and drugs are available. This exposure may produce a gradual increase in alcohol and drug tolerance. Although a homosexual may not drink excessively at first and may only experiment with drugs, the long–term result of this life–style can be alcoholism or drug dependency. The homosexual alcoholic in his or her mid–30s has typically been drinking in bars for at least 10 years. According to one estimate, a homosexual frequents bars an average of 19 times a month and drinks six drinks per visit.

The stigma that is still attached to homosexuality (many homosexuals perceive themselves as being outside society) may be a contributing factor in alcoholism and drug abuse. Homosexuals who have difficulty dealing with their sexuality may turn to alcohol as a way of coping; and ego defenses used to protect themselves against a hostile society may block their awareness of an increasing dependency on drugs. In addition, there is the "coming out" process, whereby a person publicly acknowledges his or her homosexuality. As this public acknowledgment usually takes place in an environment where alcohol is prevalent, a pattern of drinking may develop as part of the homosexual identity.

Marian Sandmaier reports in her book, *The Invisible Alcoholics,* that lesbians are more likely to have a problem with alcohol than homosexual men, probably because lesbians suffer from two stigmas: that of being homosexual and the additional stigma attached to WOMEN who drink. A study found that 35% of lesbians had problems related to alcohol compared with 28% of homosexual men and only 5% of heterosexual women.

Treatment centers for alcoholism are not generally geared to the specific problems of homosexuals; some even have a negative attitude toward them and refuse to treat them. Consequently the success rate for homosexuals in existing programs is lower than that of the general population. This may be due in part to the fact that many treatment programs emphasize the role of an alcoholic's family (spouse and children) in the recovery program. Homosexual families are non–traditional and relationships are usually divided into three categories: relationships with "original" family members, parents and siblings; relationships with an "extended family," close homosexual friends with whom holidays and anniversaries and other social events are celebrated, and who represent an important source of identity; and third, the intimate on–going relationship with another homosexual, in which the pair perceive themselves as a "couple" and develop a commitment similar to that of any married couple. Relationships in this last category can often lead to alcoholism or alcohol–related problems because of the special stress factors inherent in gay relationships: there are more equality and power issues involved in a homosexual relationship than in a heterosexual one because of the absence of traditional gender–based roles. In addition, a homosexual relationship can be more easily dissolved because of the absence of legal norms.

Until treatment centers can identify with these specific homosexual family structures and orient their programs accordingly, the success rate for alcoholic homosexuals has little chance of rising. The National Association of Gay Alcoholism is currently publishing a newsletter and is working to improve treatment for alcoholic clients. The Homophile Alcohol Treatment Service (HATS) in Boston, which is funded in part by the Massachusetts Division of Alcoholism, also helps homosexuals with alcohol problems. In urban areas there are Alcoholics Anonymous groups for homosexuals.

Whether alcoholism or alcohol–related problems among homosexuals are a result of oppression, of opposition from a hostile public, or because alcohol is an important part of the homosexual's social life, homosexuals are a large and important minority group that warrants far more research than is presently being done.

Although alcohol abuse is the main problem among homosexuals, in recent years there has been an increase in the use and abuse of AMYL NITRITE, particularly in gay baths and discos. (See also AIDS.)

hormone   A body chemical secreted into the bloodstream by the endocrine glands, and which brings about specific effects in tissues throughout the body.

hormones, male sex   See SEX.

hot lines   Telephone numbers that can be called for information and help. They are often toll–free and generally operate on a 24–hour basis. Hotlines cover a wide range of problems—from battered women, runaways and child abuse to mental health and drug problems. Some are very specific, such as the cocaine hotline and the number for Alcoholics Anonymous.

Hughes Act   The act that established the National Institute on Alcohol Abuse and Alcoholism in 1970. This federal legislation was named after its sponsor, Senator Harold Hughes.

Hycodan® (Endo)   A narcotic antitussive for cough relief that contains hydrocodone bitartrate (a CODEINE derivative) and homatropine methylbromide. It has a potential for abuse and can produce drug dependence. When used with alcohol or other central nervous system depressants it can have an additive effect. Overdosage can result in depressed respiration, somnolence and muscle flaccidity; with extreme overdosage cardiac arrest and death may occur. It is supplied in white scored tablets and as a cherry–flavored syrup.

Hycomine® (Endo)   A narcotic antitussive for cough relief. It contains hydrocodone bitartrate (a CODEINE derivative) and phenylpropanolamine for nasal congestion. It may be habit–forming and has the potential

for abuse. Hycomine is supplied as an orange fruit-flavored syrup. Hycomine–Pediatric
is a green fruit–flavored syrup.

hydrocodone   A synthetic CODEINE derivative that is usually used as an antitussive.
It is a Schedule II drug. (See HYCODAN.)

hydromorphone   A semisynthetic MOR-
PHINE derivative. Used as an analgesic, its
potency exceeds that of morphine. (See
DILAUDID.)

hyoscine, hyoscyamine   See SCOPOLA-
MINE.

hyperactive   A condition of excessive or
pathological activity, often seen in young
children. Stimulant drugs are sometimes used
in the treatment of children with Minimal
Brain Dysfunction (MBD). Many children
diagnosed as suffering from MBD are also
hyperactive; their hyperactivity is characterized by constantly moving, handling, touch-
ing, and otherwise drawing attention (usually critical) to themselves. It seems paradoxical that stimulants can be helpful in a
condition where hyperactivity is present, but
studies have shown that the use of stimulants
can decrease aggressive behavior and hyperactivity and improve concentration and attention. This use of stimulants is controversial, however, and some authorities suggest
that hyperactivity may be due to situational
or personality factors, and that stimulants
may aggravate the condition they were prescribed to alleviate. It has also been suggested that use of stimulants may condition
children to psychotropic drug use in later
years, but this has not been proven.

hyperglycemia   Unusually high blood
sugar level.

hypertension   High blood pressure. This
condition has been associated with excessive
consumption of alcohol. PCP, cocaine and
amphetamines produce temporary hypertension.

hypnosis   In recent years hypnosis has
gained popularity as a way of controlling
habits, particularly among smokers. Originally identified with the work of Anton Mes-
mer in the 1770s, hypnosis gained a certain
respectability in 1843 when James Braid
published a book entitled *Neurypnology* which
served to remove the taint of "occultism"
from the procedure. Hypnosis has been
questioned right up to the present, however.
Today it is recognized as a process, not a
therapy, but one that can be successfully utilized in combination with therapy.

Hypnosis has been far more successful in
helping people stop smoking than it has in
dealing with alcoholism or abuse of other
drugs. The reason probably is that to be effective hypnosis must be based on a coherent
theory and directed toward that end; to date
there is no unified consistent theory of alcoholism or other drug abuse. In some cases,
though, if the underlying problem is found to
be a straighforward question of self–esteem,
hypnotic treatment will be more successful.

When a person is in a hypnotic state he or
she has enhanced receptivity; and the unconscious state accepts suggestions. If used cor-
rectly, hypnosis can be an integral part of the
therapeutic technique to end dependency on
a particular drug; but alone, it will not affect
a long–lasting cure until there is a consistent
and coherent theory of alcoholism or other
drug abuse to deal with.

The recent popularity of hypnosis has led
to an increase in untrained and incompetent
practitioners entering the field, which has
caused the American Society of Clinical
Hypnosis and the International Society of
Hypnosis to take a strong stand against un-

skilled hypnotists. Lacking training, they are unaware of the importance of trance states and there can be untoward and possibly dangerous consequences.

(Hypnosis also refers to sleep, and drugs that produce sleep are called HYPNOTICS.)

hypnotic   A drug used to induce sleep. Hypnotics slow down the action of the central nervous sytem. This group of drugs includes BARBITURATES and nonbarbiturates.

hypodermic administration   See ADMINISTRATION.

hypoglycemia   Low blood sugar level. This condition is occasionally seen in alcoholics.

hypotension   Abnormally low blood pressure. Hypotension may be caused by drugs, especially narcotics, sedatives or diuretics.

I

iatrogenic addiction   Addiction to a drug that has resulted from the drug being prescribed by a physician for medical purposes.

ibogaine   A psychedelic alkaloid found in the roots, stems and leaves of *Tabernanthe Iboga,* and also in the plants *Peschiera lundii, Stemmademia donnellsmithi, S. galleottiama* and *Conopharyngia durissma* which are native to Africa, Asia and South America. It has hallucinogenic effects similar to those of LSD and it is also a STIMULANT. The alkaloid was isolated in 1901 and synthe-

sized in 1966. Iboga extracts, or ibogaine, are still sold in Europe in tonics and stimulants. Used in Africa by hunters stalking game, iboga has the effect of allowing the user to remain motionless for long periods of time while remaining conscious and mentally alert. Indian tribes in South America use iboga in a rite of passage into adulthood and it is known as the Ordeal Bean.

illusions   Distorted or mistaken perceptions that differ from hallucinations and delusions because they always involve the distortion of external stimulus patterns. Illusions may be of various sorts and include distortions of space, perspective and movement. For a person suffering from illusions, a crack in a wall may, for example, be seen as a crawling snake.

impairment   A term used to describe both short and long–term damage to an individual caused by the use of drugs. A drug may interfere with an individual's ability to function in society, for instance. Signs of such social dysfunction or impairment may be skipping meals; not attending school or work; difficulty in sleeping, walking or talking; and general confusion.

inability to abstain   A characteristic of JELLINEK'S fourth category of alcoholism, the term is used to describe someone who although unable to abstain from drinking for even a day, can control the amount consumed on any given occasion.

India   Although no comprehensive survey has been taken to assess the magnitude of drug abuse in India, research studies sponsored by the Ministry of Social Welfare in selected cities showed alcohol and tobacco to be the most commonly abused drugs. Although the prevalence rate of drugs such as cannabis, LSD, heroin and opium was very small, it should be noted that cannabis, in various potent forms, is often used in religious ceremonies. While there has been an increase in the use of GHANGA (a form of cannabis that is midway in potency between charas and bhang) among college students in recent years, the drug has been mostly used for experimental purposes. Normally drug abuse in India is not concerned with altering consciousness or "getting high"; rather it is a way of relieving social injustices, tensions, harsh poverty or epidemic illness.

Charas, a potent form of cannabis, has been forbidden since the mid–1940s. There is heavy smuggling of the drug from Tibet, though, and most of the supplies pass through India before being channeled into other countries. An increase in trade has prompted the Indian government to consider stronger penalties for smuggling.

Although there have been partially successful attempts to abolish the caste system in India, alcoholism and drug abuse are still conditioned by the system which is based on religion and affluence. There are a number of individual patterns even within the various religions. The Islamic religion forbids drinking but some Moslems drink; Sikhism forbids smoking but some Sikhs smoke; Christianity permits the use of alcohol but some Christians abstain. The Brahmins, the highest caste among Hindus, are not allowed alcohol but are permitted to use ghanga. Thus there is no single pattern of substance use and abuse.

India claims that alcohol is the most commonly abused drug, but the term "abuse" has a much wider connotation in India than in other countries and includes not only addiction but also occasional and experimental use of alcohol. By most Western standards "experimental" and "occasional" is more *use* than abuse. Compared with other nations, India, actually has a low rate of alcohol abuse—somewhere in the range of 0.2–1.9% of the total population. But when

you consider the lack of money and facilities available for treatment, these figures represent an enormous burden.

Thus far the Indian government is focusing a substantial portion of its study of drug and alcohol problems on the student population. This group is more readily available to the centers conducting the research, and is easier to communicate with than the rest of the population. There is also a higher incidence of drug use among college students than among other groups.

As of the late 1970s there were no centers in the country devoted exclusively to the treatment of drug and alcohol abuse. Although there are limited inpatient facilities in mental and psychiatric departments of general hospitals, the government tends to feel that "it is not desirable to promote specific and separate treatment facilities for drug addicts." In outpatient programs the principal method of treatment emphasizes the use of antagonistic drugs such as Antabuse.

inebriate   An alcoholic.

inebriety   ALCOHOLISM or excess drinking.

infancy   See PREGNANCY and ORAL FIXATION.

infection   Infection from unsterile needles is a serious danger to addicts who inject drugs. Two of the most common diseases associated with unclean needles are HEPATITIS and TETANUS. Hepatitis is associated with intravenous injection and tetanus with subcutaneous injection (SKIN POPPING). Thrombophlebitis and bloodstream infections from contaminated injections are also a hazard. (See also ADMINISTRATION and LIVER.)

inhalants   Inhaling substances for their euphoric and intoxicating effects has had a long history of use and abuse. Thousands of years ago people inhaled the vapors from burning spices and herbs, particularly in religious ceremonies. Today people use commercial inhalants which are usually broken down into two categories: anesthetic gases and volatile hydrocarbons. Inhalants are absorbed through the lungs and their effects have a rapid onset but are usually of short duration.

Anesthetics: The anesthetics NITROUS OXIDE, ETHER and CHLOROFORM were used recreationally long before they were used medically. Discovered in the 1700s, they were most often abused by students and physicians and "inhalant parties" were popular during the 19th century. Although some abuse of gaseous and vaporous anesthetics, which produce effects similar to alcohol intoxication, still exists today, the trend now is toward the use of volatile hydrocarbons and organic solvents.

Volatile hydrocarbons and organic solvents: Volatile hydrocarbons, used commercially as aerosols and solvents, are compounds of distilled petroleum and natural gas and include gasoline, kerosene, benzene and other related chemicals. Varnish, varnish removers, paint thinners and lacquers, lighter fluid, nail polish remover, cleaning solutions, spot removers, glues and cements and various aerosols are common household products containing organic solvents. Toluence, acetone, naphtha, cyclohexane, carbon tetrachloride and various alcohols are some of the active chemicals found in these products.

Absorbed by the lungs, vapors rapidly enter the bloodstream and are then distributed to the brain and liver. Because most solvents are fat soluble they are quickly absorbed into the central nervous system and consequently depress such body functions as heartbeat and respiration. In fatty tissue, accumulation occurs less rapidly. The kidneys metabolize and excrete some solvents; others are eliminated unaltered, primarily through the lungs.

When the lungs are the route of elimination the solvent odor will linger on the breath for several hours.

After the quick onset of effects, the duration can usually be measured in minutes; maximum duration is probably an hour depending on the substance and the dosage. Among the effects generally felt are excitement, the lowering of inhibitions, restlessness, uncoordination, confusion and disorientation, and—after prolonged inhalation—delirium and coma. The effects are similar to alcohol intoxication and intoxication from other sedatives, though some inhalants are reported to produce psychedelic–like effects. In industrial settings, where chemicals are inhaled for prolonged periods in unventilated areas, they are toxic. Prolonged exposure can result in nausea, vomiting, muscular weakness, fatigue and weight loss. There can also be extensive damage to the kidneys, liver, bone marrow and brain. Most people who inhale substances for their giddy and intoxicating effects stop long before these more serious symptoms appear.

In moderate doses inhalants can produce sedation, changes in perception, impaired judgment, fright and panic—symptoms which in some cases have resulted in accidental deaths. Some inhalants seem to be capable of sensitizing the heart to adrenaline, a substance which is present in the body and is manufactured in greater quantities in times of stress. This has been thought to be a cause of cardiac arrhythmia fatalities in some cases. In larger doses inhalants produce sleep, unconsciousness and even seizures. Long–term effects of inhaling are usually reversible after drug use is stopped. Permanent brain, liver or kidney impairment is rare if the abuse is temporary. Chromosome damage among inhalant abusers is still under study by researchers and the effects of blood abnormalities are still not proven.

Inhalants are often referred to as "deliriants," drugs capable of producing illusions, hallucinations and mental disturbances. While these effects are possible, they usually only occur in cases of overdose.

Dependence: Physical and psychological dependence have occurred in cases of long–term abuse but solvents are not considered as dangerous as other DEPRESSANTS, such as alcohol and barbiturates. Tolerance can develop and a user will need a larger dose in order to get the same effect. There have also been reports of withdrawal symptoms among solvent abusers, such as hallucinations, chills, abdominal cramps and delirium tremens. Studies have shown that a cross–tolerance can develop between solvents and other central nervous system depressants, such as alcohol. In addition there is a SYNERGISTIC or additive effect when alcohol or barbiturates are taken with certain solvents.

Patterns of Abuse: Recreational use of inhalants is usually seen in young teenagers (particularly boys) between the ages of 13 and 15, probably because they have access to many common household products that contain organic solvents and do not have access to the more conventional drugs. Hostility, lack of affection and peer pressure are among the reasons that are said to contribute to abuse by teenagers. The use of inhalants by prisoners in institutions and people in economically deprived communities has also been reported probably because common household products are the only substances readily available. Alcoholics who are trying to forestall withdrawal symptoms are also known to inhale solvents when alcohol is not available.

TOBACCO and MARIJUANA, as well as various other substances which are inhaled through smoke and absorbed through the lungs are classified as inhalants. Cocaine is also often referred to as an inhalant although it is sniffed and actually absorbed through the membranes of the nostrils.

AMYL NITRITE, a depressant inhalant which dilates the blood vessels and is used particularly to intensify and prolong sexual orgasm, is also often classified as an inhalant although it, too, is absorbed through the membranes of the nostrils.

In the 1960s glue–sniffing became a nationwide concern as numerous deaths were reported. A campaign was mounted against it and received mass media coverage. Studies reported that most deaths (approximately six out of nine) were actually the result of asphyxiation because the person (usually a child) placed a plastic bag over his head to intensify the effects of the fumes. It has been suggested that the nationwide attention given to the campaign may have actually alerted potential users to the substance and contributed to the extensive abuse.

Inhalants are absorbed through the lungs, one of the most rapid routes to obtaining a "high." Various methods are employed, including putting the substance on a piece of cloth and then inhaling the fumes; spraying or placing the substance in a paper bag and then inhaling; and, in the case of pressurized gases, filling a balloon then waiting for the vapor to warm before inhaling.

Local and state governments now prohibit minors from purchasing certain substances, particularly plastic model glues. The abuse of organic solvents will most likely continue, however, because of the large variety of household products on the market which contain them.

input–output model for treatment   A method of matching alcoholic clients with the most suitable treatment center for successful results. It was proposed by the authors of the RAND REPORT. "Input" is divided into client and treatment inputs. The first lists client characteristics, such as symptoms, drinking history, social background and physical characteristics, that might be relevant in determing the best type of treatment. The second lists the type and amount of treatment available at a particular center, such as the techniques used, and the characteristics of the therapists and the facility. The success of the treatment (the "output") depends on the appropriateness of the treatment chosen.

insomnia   A disturbance of the biologic rhythm of waking and sleeping, insomnia is characterized by insufficient or poor sleep, and fatigue during waking hours. Common complaints of insomniacs include difficulty falling asleep and frequent awakenings during the night. A detailed study of a person's insomnia is generally not made because sleeping pills can usually provide a simple and effective cure. Although true insomnia does exist, there can be numerous other causes such as depression, misinformation about sleep requirements, and a preoccupation about getting enough sleep. Certain drugs, such as amphetamines, can also cause insomnia. Alcohol can cause sleeplessness in some individuals and relaxation and sleep in others.

instability and crisis etiological theory
A sociocultural theory that suggests that social factors which produce heavy stress may cause the onset of alcoholism. In other words, turning to alcohol to alleviate stress may begin a cycle in which a stressful event leads to heavy drinking which, in turn, causes more stress and more drinking. This theory may also apply to the use of other sedative drugs.

insurance   Although insurance companies paid out large sums of money during the first half of the 20th century to cover complications and secondary manifestations of alcoholism, the disorder of alcoholism itself went undiagnosed and untreated. The Kemper Insurance Companies and Wausau became the first, in 1964, to provide coverage

for the treatment of alcoholism, and other companies began to follow suit. Early coverage was generally restricted to inpatient care and it wasn't until the mid–1970s that it began to be extended to some outpatient facilities. Kemper was again the leader in providing group health coverage for outpatient treatment in qualifying nonhospital alcoholism centers. By 1979, 24 states had enacted legislation concerning the coverage of alcoholism; some mandated coverage, others required coverage to be available as an option. Insurance coverage for the treatment of other substance abuse was still ignored, however, and it wasn't until very recently that it was recognized as an area where coverage was needed. Treatment for those addicted to heroin, cocaine, etc., is still often limited to EMPLOYEE ASSISTANCE PROGRAMS set up by an individual company, and these programs, in turn, are often limited to large corporations that can afford to finance them.

On October 1, 1983, Medicare, which covers approximately 29.4 million eligible Americans, implemented a new hospital reimbursement system that affects a large number of alcohol and drug abuse treatment centers. Under the new system, referred to as *prospective payment,* hospitals are reimbursed with fixed payments, determined in advance, rather than the previous cost–based payment method. The Health Care Financing Administration (HCFA) has announced that alcohol or drug abuse treatment services provided at psychiatric facilities will be temporarily exempt from the new system *if* they meet HCFA criteria (a key criterion is that the unit be under the direction of a psychiatrist). The preset rates of the new system are based on an extensive list of Diagnosis Related Groups (DRGs) which cover most illnesses. The HCFA established 470 DRGs which are based on specific diagnosis, patient age and sex, treatment procedure and clinical and statistical analysis of all cases treated. The system was designed to curb the rapid growth in Medicare costs in recent years but according to authorities in the field of substance abuse treatment, it will most likely negate any advances in treatment achieved in the past. For example, the National Association of Alcoholism Treatment Programs estimates that the average length of stay in a hospital, including detoxification, is 28.5 days. According to the new system, Medicare payments are based on an average 11.3 day stay. They also reflect the cost of living and differences in hospital wages in different parts of the country.

The DRG–based payment plan will be watched very closely by private insurance carriers and also by self–insuring employers to see if it works, particularly in the area of costs. It is possible that the new system could set a trend that will become the norm in the future. If this does occur, most drug treatment authorities concur that it will be a major setback in recent research breakthroughs. The new system does not allow for continuing care and neglects the fact that different modes of approach and treatment are required by different patients. Authorities contend that the treatment of alcoholism cannot be restricted to an 11–day regimen, and suggest that the patient's family will be the ultimate victim as it will be left to pay additional treatment bills.

The limit on detoxification coverage, either through the new Medicare system or through private insurance carriers, does not reflect the recent upsurge in DUAL ADDICTION which requires longer detoxification. In addition, few companies cover treatment for family members of a drug–dependent person even though they are often involved in the problem.

Perhaps one of the reasons why there has been little motivation to develop an insurance plan with broad coverage that extends into the area of substance abuse, is that afflu-

ent people often pay for drug abuse treatment without health insurance coverage and often receive their treatment in expensive settings. Treatment coverage is generally not available to disadvantaged members of minority groups because many of them do not belong to a group insurance plan and cannot afford an individual policy.

The National Institute on Alcohol Abuse and Alcoholism estimates that the cost of treatment per year, per client, is $13,730 for hospital alcoholism treatment (the new Medicare system will reimburse approximately $2,300); $20,780 for hospital detoxification; $4,730 for an intermediate long–term alcoholism treatment service; and $740 for an outpatient treatment program. Although alternative programs (halfway houses, residential programs, etc.) are less expensive, they have not generally been included in insurance coverage and most are not covered by the new Medicare system. Because recent research data seems to indicate that treatment of a drug user will decrease subsequent health care costs, it would seem there is a need for a movement by insurance carriers to encourage their clients to cover treatment programs and prevent the progression of drug use and its costly effects.

intemperance   Excessive or habitual drinking.

International Commission for the Prevention of Alcoholism and Drug Dependence (ICPA)   Founded in 1952, ICPA is a nonsectarian, nonpolitical organization of the United Nations operated exclusively for scientific and educational purposes. It seeks to reveal the impact of alcohol and other drug dependencies upon the economic, political, social and religious life of nations, and to point up effective preventive actions. The commission is made up of 250 prominent men and women from around the world. The number of invited representatives is based on the population of a country.

intervention   In the treatment of drug abuse, intervention strategy is the therapist's direction of or influence on a client's actions.

interview, structured   An interview with a client or subject that follows a set form, usually for purposes of systematic data collection. No deviation from the series of questions is permitted.

interview, unstructured   An interview format that uses the responses of the client or subject as a stimulus for subsequent inquiries. This method of questioning exploits unusual answers and attempts to obtain in depth data on pertinent issues.

Ionamin® (Pennwalt)   A central nervous system stimulant that contains phentermine resin and is used as an anorectic for weight control. It is chemically and pharmacologically related to AMPHETAMINES and consequently has a significant potential for abuse. Overdosage can result in rapid respiration, tremors, confusion and hallucinations. It is supplied in 15 mg yellow and gray capsules, and 30 mg yellow capsules.

Ipecac® (Lilly)   A syrup used as an emetic to induce vomiting in cases of poisoning. It contains 7 gr of ipecac per 100 ml. If it is absorbed instead of vomited it can exert a cardiotoxic effect.

Iran   Opium abuse has long been widespread in Iran but until very recently it was used in a different form from the one known in the United States. In Iran opium is eaten or smoked. The goals of the abusers also differ. Iranians do not seek opium's euphoric, mind–altering effects; they use it mainly to

deaden the realities of life among the poor. Use is particularly widespread in rural areas among poor farmers. Opium is also used extensively among the sick and aged to numb pain.

In 1972 it was estimated that there were 110,000 registered and 200,000 unregistered opium addicts. Since 1980 the use of heroin has become widespread in Iran, as it has in other Asian countries (see GOLDEN CRESCENT), and there are now an estimated 300–500,000 heroin addicts in a population of 40 million.

Large amounts of cannabis which is either cultivated in Iran or imported from neighboring countries, are also used, usually in the form of hashish and ghanga. The hashish is more potent than most types of marijuana used in the U.S.

In the past, Iran responded favorably to requests from other countries to cut back on the amount of opium it produced and exported. While Iran was ruled by the Shah, constructive steps were taken; in 1955 he imposed a ban on domestic opium production although he later permitted some legal production to meet the requirements of registered addicts. In 1969 the cultivation of the opium poppy was made a government monopoly under very stringent laws that imposed harsh fines and prison sentences for possession, trafficking, importing and exporting of opium and hashish.

As the Shah's hold on Iran weakened, law and order began to break down; the ban on cultivation began to be ignored and there was a major increase in illicit export. In 1979 when the Shah and his government were overthrown by the Ayatollah Khomeini regime, the government structure that had held production and trafficking in check over the years collapsed. Police and military forces who had enforced the narcotics laws were diverted from their primary tasks and became involved in internal security. In addition, many of those who had staffed law enforcement units became political outcasts and were considered enemies of the people. Since 1979 Iran has become a major country in the GOLDEN CRESCENT, the primary source of heroin smuggled into Europe and on to the United States. The political chaos in Iran has diverted government attention to other priorities and trafficking has become much easier. In addition to Iran's role as a major source and transit country, it has also become a significant producer of heroin and morphine base in clandestine laboratories.

If the current turmoil in Southwest Asian countries continues it can be expected that traffickers will continue to exploit the situation and the flow of heroin will probably increase.

Ireland   Ireland lies just outside the mainstream of drug trafficking in Europe, but there has been an upward trend in drug abuse during the last few years. It has been suggested that the increase is due to the relatively recent industrialization of Ireland; others theorize that it is due to recent restrictive government measures concerning drug abuse and a rebellion among the people who feel their rights are now being impinged. Still others attribute the increase to the country's political unrest.

Government recognition of the problem led to the Misuse of Drugs Act of 1977, a law which strictly defined controlled substances but which is more flexible than previous legislation. Under the law, heavier penalties were to be enforced on serious offenses, while penalties on minor offenses were to be less severe. In cases where drug dealing or possession is suspected, the 1977 law supercedes normal provisions which protect individuals from warrantless search and seizure.

Although the Irish are striving for more effective methods to control drug abuse they have not yet found any satisfactory solutions. Treatment programs and facilities are available only around Dublin; in other areas drug addiction is usually treated by local psychiatric services. In Dublin itself there is just one treatment facility. While it provides 24–hour service seven days a week, its detoxification unit contains only nine beds and is run mainly for suicide cases. Patients are usually discharged within 24 hours and are sent on to an outpatient facility on Usher's Island. This latter facility provides daily counseling, occupational therapy and group therapy and deals mainly with adolescents who have behavioral disorders related to drug abuse.

For those patients who have made a determined effort to overcome addiction, there is a therapeutic community in the town of Coolemine, near Dublin. Therapy involves social rehabilitation through self–help.

The abuse of alcohol in Ireland far exceeds the abuse of other drugs. The Irish spend 12% of their income on alcoholic beverages, a higher percentage than any other country. This is probably due to the high excise tax on alcohol which the government treasury is heavily dependent on as a source of revenue. To many individuals, the thought of Ireland is likely to conjure up images of heavy drinking, boisterous pubs and alcohol–related problems. However, by international standards, alcohol consumption in Ireland is quite low; when adjusted by population figures it is beneath that of the U.S. It should be noted that there is a high percentage of nondrinkers among the Irish: in 1974 it was 43% of the population over the age of 15, although this percentage has been declining annually at a rate of 2.9%. Consequently, the average consumption of alcohol (in 1974, 9.9 quarts of absolute alcohol for every person aged 15 and over, as compared to 11.1 quarts in the U.S. and 27.3 in France) is maintained by heavier consumption on the part of the drinking population.

The high percentage of abstainers in Ireland is possibly due to the number of temperance movements. These movements were very common in the 19th century, and one in particular had disastrous results. In the 1840s, a vigorous crusade led by a Catholic priest resulted in thousands pledging never to drink. There was a physician in Draperstown, Northern Ireland, however, who had been experimenting with the use of ether and the news quickly spread that it was a pleasant substitute for alcohol. Not only was it cheap, because unlike alcohol it was not subject to tax, the effects were quick and even when used several times a day there were no hangover effects. In fact, the effects wore off so quickly that a person exhibiting signs of drunkenness was usually sober even before he reached a police station. The sniffing of ether in Draperstown and in other parts of Ireland became epidemic for some time and it wasn't until the 1920s that ether abuse finally died out.

Although beer has long been the traditional drink in Ireland, the consumption of wine and distilled spirits has increased in recent years. The relatively high cost of alcoholic beverages does not seem to deter those who drink and evidence suggests that the expenditure for alcohol rises at least in proportion to income.

Admissions to mental hospitals for the treatment of alcoholism increased by over 300% from 1965 to 1977, and the upper socioeconomic group has one of the highest hospital admission rates. The average hospital stay, however, is much shorter for this group than for the average unskilled worker.

isocarboxazid   See MONOAMINE OXIDASE (MAO) INHIBITORS.

isopropyl alcohol   A major component of rubbing alcohol that has solvent properties similar to ethanol and is poisonous if taken internally. It has replaced ethanol for many uses because it is less expensive.

Italy   Aside from alcohol, abuse of drugs in Italy is a relatively new occurrence. Probably because it is less expensive than other drugs, hashish is the most commonly abused drug, but in urban areas there has also been a recent trend toward the abuse of heroin, cocaine and other "hard drugs." The use of heroin is thought to have risen 600% since 1976 and may well become the country's most abused drug. Because of its geographic location, Italy has been an important transit country. Heavy trafficking and processing of heroin in the late 1950s led to the establishment of a Rome branch office of the U.S. Bureau of Narcotics and Dangerous Drugs. The office was moved to Paris, France, in 1969 when it was believed that activity had shifted to that area. The FRENCH CONNECTION, active from the 1930s to the 1970s involved Italian underground criminals: raids of clandestine heroin laboratories in Italy during 1980 suggest that either the French Connection is not really dead or it has been replaced by a Franco–Italian Connection. The source of opium found in Italy is Southwest Asia (see GOLDEN CRESCENT), and trafficking continues to increase in the early 1980s.

Although cocaine is not widely abused in Italy, there has been a recent increase and seizures of cocaine were numerous in 1981. The pattern of entry was usually from Peru through Paris, Zurich or Frankfurt. Most seizures were made at non–airport locations and the cocaine was generally smuggled in by Italians.

Until new legislation was passed in 1973 to alter the definition, drug addiction was not considered a disease in Italy but was instead considered a criminal act. The new laws provide for harsher penalties for traffickers and pushers and allow addicts to be treated as "sick individuals."

Treatment programs in Italy during the

early 1970s generally centered on those addicted to hashish and marijuana, although doctors are obligated to report persons using narcotics. In 1979 general health care was nationalized in Italy; medical care is virtually free but because of the scarcity of bed space people are generally detoxified, or dried out, then released. The exception to this occurs with heroin addicts. Because of the recent increase in heroin abuse and because addicts are now considered "sick," there are numerous specialized services available.

There have been no national surveys concerning alcohol abuse in the last 30 years. Alcohol is not considered a problem in Italy and the consumption of wine in particular is viewed as a social event that centers around meals. Although Italy is one of the top wine producing countries in the world, there has been a shift in per capita wine consumption over the past 15 years. In 1968 per capita consumption was 116 litres; in 1979 per capita consumption had decreased to 90.1 litres. On the other hand, there has been an increase in the consumption of both beer and distilled spirits. The decreased consumption of wine has not hurt the Italian wine industry. Exportation of wine is increasing and wine that was previously shipped to France to be mixed with French wine is now simply exported directly to other countries. This situation has triggered a French–Italian wine war which continues to escalate.

Because drinking in Italy is traditionally associated with wine, and wine consumption is generally associated with meals and is an integral part of family life, public drunkenness is not a common occurrence. Moreover, alcohol control laws do not regulate wine or beer because they are not considered alcoholic beverages, a reflection of the traditional wine culture of the country. The government of Italy does not recognize alcohol abuse as a major health care concern and since 1979, when health care was nationalized, alcohol abuse has become a "forgotten problem" and the only treatment usually found is in private facilities.

While no recent surveys have been conducted on alcohol abuse, and research into social attitudes is lacking, there is a bill pending in the Italian Parliament to restrict advertising for distilled spirits. There is also an attempt to form a permanent national commission on alcohol problems which would collect data and suggest reforms. Because alcohol consumption is so closely tied to the family and home, the history and background of this aspect of Italian culture will have to be extensively explored before contemporary problems of alcohol abuse can be dealt with.

IV   Intravenous (see ADMINISTRATION).

J

Jamaica   The cultivation and use of *ganja*, as marijuana is called in Jamaica, has been going on for over 100 years and is thought to have been introduced by indentured laborers from India. In the past it was generally smoked only by isolated social groups but in recent years use has spread to all ages and segments of society; an estimated 60–70% of the island's population now ingests ganja in one form or another. Although the Jamaican government has made attempts to control usage (ganga has been illegal since 1913), the drug is such big business that most law enforcers turn their backs on incidents of cultivation, use and possession. It has been suggested that marijuana is the basis of the Jamaican economy and the United States government claims that 10% of the U.S. marijuana market comes from Jamaica. The usual route is through South Florida, by both plane and boat.

Ganja is particularly important to the RASTAFARIANS and their way of life. Reggae music, popularized by the Rastafarians, is known worldwide and many of the lyrics condone and encourage the use of ganja. Popular Rastafarian musicians, including the late Bob Marley, are idols of young people in the U.S. and throughout Europe who are influenced by the songs praising the "mystical herb."

Members of Jamaica's medical profession are more than aware of the health hazards involved in the widespread use of ganja, although they are often criticized as having a "middle–class bias." Dr. John Hall, consultant physician with the Jamaica Ministry of Health, has been conducting research on the effects of marijuana for the last 11 years. Among the clinical observations that he has made is the fact that the seasonal upsurges in stomach hemorrhages tend to occur during the twice–yearly marijuana harvests, and the fact that the whites of the eyes often turn brown among heavy users of marijuana. Neither of these two phenomena have appeared in published research and Dr. Hall is continuing studies in both areas.

The use of ganja is more widespread among men than women, although both women and children are known to consume marijuana in a beverage called "green tea." Common conditions among ganja users are impotence, low blood sugar and a bronchitis–type of cough. Apathy and a tendency to retreat from reality are also noted among heavy users. The extensive poverty in Jamaica is certainly a reason for the use of marijuana as an escape from problems, but it causes a vicious circle when users become apathetic and unproductive and lose all power to overcome economic conditions.

As in other countries throughout the world, Jamaica also has an alcoholism problem. Jamaican rum, known the world over, is in-expensive and readily available. The consumption of rum by all socioeconomic classes is a major problem.

Japan   Prior to 1945 there were no substantial drug abuse problems in Japan although some cocaine and opium addicts did exist. After World War II, however, serious problems arose; they can be divided into three separate periods. Immediately following the war, during Japan's reconstruction period, stimulants were in great demand particularly among students, night laborers and entertainers. Though the abuse of stimulants began in the major cities it soon spread and was prevalent throughout the country. The government enacted the Stimulants Control Law (1951) and amended its Mental Health Law to provide for compulsory hospitalization of those addicted to stimulants. The increased law enforcement, treatment of addicts, and intensive public campaigns seemed to have conquered the problem by the late 1950s.

No sooner was the stimulant problem seemingly brought under control than widespread heroin abuse appeared on the scene. While there had been heroin abuse since World War II, it suddenly increased to the point where in 1961 it was estimated that there were some 40,000 addicts. Government countermeasures included strengthening penalties for offenders, and the compulsory hospitalization of addicts. After 1964 there was a sharp decrease in the amount of heroin abuse and for several years the country entered a period of declining drug problems.

In the 1970s stimulant abuse again surfaced and rapidly spread throughout the country. The government amended the Stimulants Control Law and increased the penalties for violation to the same level as those for heroin offenses. It also strengthened control over stimulant precursors. As a result, there was a 30% reduction in 1974 but it was only temporary. At the present time stimulant abuse is considered the most serious drug problem in Japan. Approximately 20,000 users were arrested in 1980 and increases seem to run at 20–30% annually. The actual number of abusers is estimated to be 10 times the number known to authorities. The 30–39 age group is the most affected (38%); 31% are in the 20–29 age group; and 10% are under 19 years old. The latter group has shown a large increase in abuse over the past few years. Methamphetamine is the stimulant most abused, and is usually administered by injection. There is negligible illicit domestic manufacture and little is diverted from licit channels. The drug is usually smuggled from Korea and Taiwan. Street prices run from $600 to $800 U.S. dollars per gram of pure substance. Public health and social problems have resulted from the widespread stimulant abuse. An individual's economic and social life is seriously hampered by his psychological dependence on the drug. In addition, "amphetamine psychosis"—or the occurrence of hallucinations and illusions—has been responsible for a marked increase in traffic accidents, arson and murder. The large profits from illicit

Narcotics and Heroin Violations, 1963–81

Year	Total*	Heroin	Percent
1963	2,571	1,883	7.32
1964	792	375	47.3
1965	1,090	296	27.2
1966	974	33	3.4
1967	658	72	10.9
1968	361	27	7.5
1969	239	41	17.1
1970	245	15	6.1
1971	229	44	19.1
1972	341	206	60.4
1973	429	323	75.3
1974	393	264	67.2
1975	232	134	57.8
1976	165	113	68.5
1977	125	83	66.4
1978	102	65	63.7
1979	103	20	19.4
1980	158	35	22.2
1981	98	23	23.5

*Total means the number of violators of Narcotic Control Law.

Drug Seizures in Japan 1970-81

Year	Opium (gms.)	Heroin (gms)	Morphine (gms)	Cannabis (gms)	LSD (tab.)	Stimulants (gms)
1970	4,988	2,141	1	39,316	325	5,850
1971	1,072	472	25	75,421	531	28,806
1972	5,862	588	33	84,629	4,291	30,305
1973	2,208	6,306	240	69,996	16,023	36,287
1974	915	2,976	73	87,916	2,522	25,217
1975	2,712	2,375	343	67,995	1,024	35,971
1976	233	4,918	21	155,196	207	34,184
1977	495	5,362	0.2	125,445	434.5	68,411
1978	803	982	—	92,197	255	102,765
1979	38	12	—	174,477	327	128,692
1980	354	489	2	92,536	5,400	156,125
1981	70	2,849	—	82,903	1,755	142,097

Source: *A Brief Account of Drug Abuse and Counter-Measures in Japan, 1981.* Japan Ministry of Health and Welfare.

sales have also brought about an increase in organized crime.

. Marijuana is second to amphetamines in substance abuse today. The 20–29 age group in particular has shown a slow but constant increase in abuse. Heroin offenses in 1980 reached a very low level. As for opium, it has never constituted a problem in Japan; most offenses involve ignorance of the law

when poppies are grown for ornamental purposes. Under the Opium Law of 1954 the cultivation of the opium poppy is only permitted under license, and the government monopolizes its import, export, and domestic purchase.

The Japanese government's measures to reduce drug abuse include a nationwide eradication campaign, the establishment of a

Drug Control Law Violations in Japan, 1954-1981

Law	Narcotic Control Law		Opium Law		Cannabis Control Law		Stimulants Control Law	
Year	Number of cases	Number of persons	Number of cases	Number of persons	Number of cases	Number of persons	Number of cases	Number of persons
1954	1,527	2,092	25	30	16	17	53,221	55,664
1955	1,280	1,753	157	181	42	52	30,670	32,140
1956	1,060	1,575	128	140	27	33	4,876	5,047
1957	1,013	1,365	144	173	25	29	787	781
1958	1,616	2,073	63	76	7	13	268	271
1959	1,394	1,714	137	147	28	30	332	372
1960	1,667	1,987	310	315	9	10	426	476
1961	2,023	2,442	190	199	22	24	459	477
1962	1,773	2,176	203	208	34	34	530	546
1963	2,135	2,571	402	417	144	147	1,061	971
1964	707	792	419	425	158	164	969	908
1965	1,035	1,090	890	902	255	259	885	736
1966	899	974	917	920	157	158	838	722
1967	592	638	702	705	301	298	867	710
1968	298	361	1,136	1,148	392	410	1,088	791
1969	210	239	377	377	426	413	915	735
1970	212	245	230	230	707	733	2,453	1,682
1971	256	229	207	202	831	717	4,431	2,634
1972	354	341	253	251	853	726	7,702	4,777
1973	455	429	310	287	799	761	14,260	8,510
1974	436	393	176	171	781	720	9,771	6,119
1975	268	232	158	140	971	909	13,590	8,422
1976	195	165	184	185	1,064	960	17,929	10,919
1977	201	125	191	191	1,225	1,096	24,022	14,741
1978	136	102	140	142	1,771	1,253	30,287	18,027
1979	147	103	217	217	1,571	1,314	31,991	18,552
1980	241	158	269	264	1,745	1,433	34,808	20,200
1981	144	98	261	262	1,596	1,346	36,855	22,331

Source: *A Brief Account of Drug Abuse and Counter-Measures in Japan, 1981.* Japan Ministry of Health and Welfare.

council to check the dependence–producing properties of new drugs, and harsher penalties for abusers. On an international level, Japan cooperates with the United Nations in the field of drug abuse.

Social consumption of alcoholic beverages is widely accepted and deeply ingrained in Japan. This attitude has led to a pattern of infrequent but heavy consumption on special occasions. In a recent survey 52% of the Japanese polled considered alcohol a part of their lives, while 35% considered abstinence harmful to social life.

Sake, a fermented rice wine, is the preferred beverage in Japan. There is some actual encouragement of drunkenness during festive celebrations and a favored gift to hosts at social functions is distilled spirits. A general trend toward westernization since World War II and wider advertisement of alcoholic beverages seems to have resulted in increased levels of drinking, particularly among women and youths. Although habitual heavy drinking is limited to 4% of the male population and 1.6% of the female population, a survey in 1976 reported that 85% of the male population drinks and 52% of the female population. The rate of drinking was heaviest among males between 40 and 49 years old. According to definitions established by the Japanese government, 2.5% of the total population of the country may be considered alcoholics. In 1977 the national rate of hospitalization for a primary diagnosis related to alcohol abuse was 12.8 per 100,000 population. The rate of mortality from liver cirrhosis was 13.8 (male deaths were three times that of female deaths); and 3.6% of the hospital beds in the country were occupied because of alcoholism or alcohol related diseases. Alcohol was also involved in 12% of all traffic fatalities in 1977. The economic cost of alcohol abuse, including premature death, absenteeism and medical care is calculated to be 260 billion yen (about $1.3 billion) annually.

Government controls on alcohol abuse include a stiff penalty for public drunkenness and a permissible blood alcohol level for drivers of 0.25 grams of ethanol per 1,000 grams of blood (about one drink). There are, as yet, no school programs for the prevention of alcoholism, and no limitation on the advertising of alcoholic beverages. There is, however, a government funded organization called the Liaison Conference for Alcoholic Problems which coordinates its prevention and treatment programs with private organizations such as the All Nippon Sobriety Society (Japan's version of Alcoholics Anonymous).

Jellinek, E.M. (1890–1963)   The founder of the Center of Alcohol Studies and Summer School of Alcohol Studies, formerly at Yale University and now centered at Rutgers University. Jellinek was also a cofounder of the National Council on Alcoholism and was consultant on alcoholism for the World Health Organization. He was also the author of *The Disease Concept of Alcoholism.* In this influential study Jellinek distinguished between five categories of alcoholism which he referred to as Alpha, Beta, Delta, Epsilon and Gamma.

1. *Alpha Alcoholism:* Sometimes known as problem drinking, it represents a continual purely psychological dependence or reliance upon alcohol's effects to relieve emotional or bodily pain. It can develop into Gamma alcoholism but often continues in the same state for years with no signs of progression. The damage it causes is usually limited to disturbances in the person's family or social relationships and does not lead to loss of control. There are no withdrawal effects.

2. *Beta Alcoholism:* Possibly as a result of poor nutritional habits or of the customs of certain social groups, the person who suffers from this kind of alcoholism eventually develops medical complications such as cirrhosis or alcoholic polyneuropathy. Beta al-

coholism is not associated with physical or psychological dependence and withdrawal symptoms do not appear but the condition can develop into Gamma alcoholism.

3. *Gamma Alcoholism:* This type of alcoholism causes the most damage to an individual's health and to his interpersonal relationships. Recognized by Alcoholics Anonymous, it is apparently the dominant form of alcoholism in the United States. It is characterized by acquired increased tissue tolerance; adaptive cell metabolism; physical dependence (craving and withdrawal symptoms); and loss of control. In Gamma alcoholism psychological dependence progresses to physical dependence.

4. *Delta Alcoholism:* The predominant form of alcoholism in France and other countries where there is significant wine consumption, Delta alcoholism is characterized by an acquired tolerance to alcohol. Unlike Gamma alcoholism which is characterized by loss of control, Delta alcoholism involves the inability to abstain. The person can control his or her intake but cannot stop drinking for even a few days; his consumption, although heavy, is steady, not "explosive."

5. *Epsilon Alcoholism:* The term refers to periodic alcoholism. Less is known about this category than the other four.

K

---

kava A beverage made from the roots of the shrub, *Piper methysticum,* which produces a mild marijuana–like high. It also has a sedative action and if enough is consumed will produce sleep. The roots are also sometimes chewed.

kerosene See INHALANTS.

Ketaject® (Bristol) A nonbarbiturate rapid–acting general anesthetic that is normally used for short surgical procedures; with additional doses, however, it can be used for longer operations. It contains ketamine hydrochloride, which is related to phencyclidine, and has the potential for abuse. Ketaject is supplied in vials for injection. (See KETAMINE HYDROCHLORIDE.)

Ketalar® (Parke–Davis) Contains ketamine hydrochloride and is the same as KETAJECT. See KETAMINE HYDROCHLORIDE for abuse potential.

ketamine hydrochloride A nonbarbiturate rapid–acting general anesthetic that is normally used for short surgical procedures. Discovered in 1961, it was frequently used during the Vietnam War. Manufactured as KETAJECT and KETALAR it is supplied in vials for injection. It is an abused drug but not in its liquid form since injection only produces a rapid onset of sleep. Drug abusers evaporate the liquid by heating it and reducing it to a fine white powder. It is then sprinkled on marijuana or tobacco and smoked, or it is snorted. The crystalline powder is called "green" and has both depressant and psychedelic effects similiar to those of phencyclidine. It relieves tension and anxiety, is purported to be a sexual stimulant, and intensifies sounds and colors. Large doses produce delusions and hallucinations. When taken with alcohol or other central nervous system depressants the drug can have an additive effect.

khat An East African plant, *Catha edulis,* whose leaves and buds are chewed or brewed as a beverage. It is said to produce stimulant effects similar to but milder than those induced by amphetamines, and psychological dependence can develop.

Korsakoff's psychosis   A disease (syndrome) that usually only affects people who have been drinking heavily and steadily for many years, although it has also been found in nonalcoholics who suffer from extreme nutritional deficiencies. Identified in 1897 by the Russian psychiatrist Sergei Korsakoff (1854–1900), who founded the Moscow school of psychiatry, the disease is characterized by memory failure, confusion, disorientation, and emotional apathy. The person is often unaware of his or her condition and usually remains quite cheerful. The disease, usually preceded by WERNICKE'S ENCEPHALOPATHY, is generally irreversible.

L

LAAM (levo–alpha–acetylmethadol) A narcotic analgesic agonist. LAAM is an opioid that has been tried as an alternative to METHADONE. Unlike methadone which must be taken daily, LAAM is taken only three times a week, and appears to provide a sustained level effect.

lacquer thinner   Sometimes inhaled for its intoxicating effects, lacquer thinner usually contains the liquid hydrocarbon TOLUENE.

lactose   See MILK SUGAR.

La Guardia Report   In 1938 New York City Mayor, Fiorella La Guardia, commissioned a study on marijuana use. The report suggested that marijuana might have valuable therapeutic applications and found no evidence that its use might lead to the use of opiates. The report has since been succeeded by more contemporary studies, but when it was published in 1944 as *The Marijuana Problem in the City of New York, by the Mayor's Committee on Marijuana* it was a landmark study and is still cited today, especially by those who favor the legalization of marijuana.

laudanum   Originally any of various opium preparations, it is now a tincture (alcoholic extract) of opium. Laudanum was first compounded by Paracelsus in the 16th century. Before it was discovered to be addictive, it was used extensively in the 19th century to treat various illnesses.

L–Dopa (Levodopa)   A miscellaneous drug not easily classified that is currently used in the treatment of Parkinson's disease. It has been used experimentally, without particular success, as a possible counteragent to the acute effects of alcohol intoxication and alcoholism.

legal aspects of drug use   The legal foundation for the government's strategy for reducing drug consumption is the CONTROLLED SUBSTANCES ACT of 1970. The most common and well–known control mechanism is the criminal penalty for trafficking. Trafficking is defined as the unauthorized manufacture, distribution or possession of a drug with intent to distribute. Criminal penalties are based on the drug "Schedules" listed in the act.

For narcotics in Schedules I and II, a first offense is punishable by up to 15 years in prison and up to a $25,000 fine. For trafficking in a Schedule I or II non–narcotic drug, or any Schedule III drug, the penalty is up to five years in prison and up to a $15,000 fine (with the exception of phencyclidine and certain related drugs, for which a penalty is provided of not more than 10 years imprisonment and a $25,000 fine). Trafficking in a

Schedule IV drug is punishable by a maximum of three years in jail and up to a $10,000 fine. Trafficking in a Schedule V drug is a misdemeanor punishable by up to one year in prison and up to a $5,000 fine. Second and subsequent offenses are punishable by twice the penalty imposed for the first offense. The Controlled Substances Act carefully distinguishes between trafficking offenses (those who supply illicit drugs to abusers) and use offenses (those possessing drugs solely for personal use). Possession for one's own use of any controlled substance in any Schedule is always a misdemeanor on the first offense, and is punishable by one year in jail and up to a $5,000 fine. A first offender under the age of 21 may receive up to one year probation and thereafter motion court for expungement of all records. When compared to some countries, particularly Turkey where not only the penalties but the jails themselves have a reputation for harshness, the U.S. is considered lenient. (See Appendix III, Tables 2 and 3.)

The National Organization for the Reform of Marijuana Laws (NORML) is the most active group attempting to decriminalize the use of marijuana and remove the country's estimated 30 million marijuana users from the criminal justice system. In recent years eleven states have changed their laws and no longer treat possession of a small quantity of marijuana for personal use by adults as a criminal offense: Alaska, California, Colorado, Maine, Minnesota, Mississippi, Nebraska, New York, North Carolina, Ohio and Oregon now provide written citations for offenses and charge small fines. This procedure replaces the system of arrest, prosecution and jail sentences. In Alaska there are no state laws prohibiting the private possession and cultivation of marijuana for personal use by adults. As a result of follow–up surveys in these states NORML cites substantial monetary savings to the criminal justice system, public approval of the new laws,

only a slight increase in the number of first–time marijuana users, and a decline in frequency of use. The move toward decriminalization appears to have halted recently as research uncovers a number of adverse consequences of marijuana use.

As of November 1982, 33 states had enacted legislation authorizing programs of legal access to THC for victims of cancer and glaucoma. In addition, three state supreme courts, Washington, Illinois and Michigan, have held marijuana penalties unconstitutional on the grounds that they deny equal protection because marijuana was classified with far more dangerous drugs, including narcotics.

In June 1982, a committee appointed by the National Academy of Sciences released a detailed report that endorsed marijuana decriminalization. The report concluded, however, that marijuana is not a single drug but a complex preparation containing many biologically active chemicals, and recommended that comprehensive studies of the affects on the health of the American public be undertaken. Both the president of the academy and the director of the National Institute of Drug Abuse rejected the committee's recommendation to eliminate criminal penalties.

The only legally grown marijuana in the United States is found on a federal government farm in Faulkner County, Mississippi. It is operated by scientists from the Research Institute of Pharmaceutical Sciences of the University of Mississippi. A 5.6 acre farm with more than 100 varieties of cannabis plants, it has been under contract to the National Institute on Drug Abuse (NIDA) since 1968. The drug is grown under carefully controlled conditions strictly for research and therapeutic purposes, and is sent through NIDA to approved researchers. The farm has a sophisticated analysis laboratory located nearby. Here the crude plant material is extracted and filtered off to yield a resin extract that is then dissolved in ethanol. Various levels of the cannabinoids in each specimen are pinpointed; some are then isolated and synthesized. All crude plant material is carefully labeled as to seed origin, plant sex, and dates of planting and harvest, so that uniform study results can be obtained.

legal high   A term for substances that can alter the mind and produce a HIGH and are readily available without a prescription. For example, NUTMEG, DILL, MOUTHWASHES with a high alcohol content, CLEANING FLUIDS, airplane GLUE, etc.

Lemmon   The manufacturer of QUAA-LUDE. The company produced this drug with their name stamped on the tablet. A Lemmon 714 was the 300 mg size. On the street these came to be known as "Lemmons" or "714s." Quaaludes were widely adulterated with substances other than methaqualone. This drug has been withdrawn from the pharmaceutical market by the manufacturer because of its widespread misuse.

lesbian drug users   See HOMOSEXUALS.

lethal dose   The dosage of a drug that results in death. There are so many factors involved, however, including the amount taken, the purity of the drug, what it was taken in combination with, the physical state of the person taking it, and so on, that it is impossible to say what actually constitutes a "lethal" dose. Depending on the conditions, it could be an extremely small amount.

lettuce   There are claims that both wild lettuce and head lettuce sold in supermarkets can produce marijuana–like effects when dried and smoked. This is extremely doubtful, however, and any effects that are felt are probably a result of the person hyperventilating while smoking.

levallorphan   A narcotic antagonist used to lessen respiratory depression caused by the use of narcotics. (See LORFAN.)

Levo–Dromoran® (Roche)   A synthetic NARCOTIC that contains levorphanol tartrate and acts as a highly potent analgesic for moderate to severe pain. It may be habit–forming and has an addictive potential similar to morphine. It is supplied in ampules, vials, and 2 mg white, scored tablets.

levorphanol   An OPIOID NARCOTIC ANAL-GESIC similar to but more potent than morphine. Levorphanol tartrate is applied in many of the same ways as other opioids, including relief of moderate to severe pain in cases of renal or biliary colic, myocardial infarction and pain associated with cancer. It also supplements nitrous oxide in pre– and post–operative anesthesia. The effects of levorphanol peak in 60–90 minutes and last four to eight hours. It is prescribed in quantities of 2–3 mg to be taken orally or subcutaneously; a dose that is equivalent to 10 mg of morphine.

Levorphanol achieves the same analgesic effects as morphine, but side effects typical of morphine, such as nausea, constipation, and vomiting, occur less frequently. The drug can cause respiratory depression, and use of narcotic antagonists may be called for to counteract it.

Although tolerance and dependence do occur, levorphanol is not subject to great abuse.

Available from Roche in 2 mg tablets, as well as in ampules and vials for injection, it is marketed as LEVO–DROMORAN and is a Schedule II drug under the Controlled Substances Act.

Librax® (Roche)   A minor TRANQUILIZER that combines Librium (chlordiazepoxide hydrochloride) and Quarzan (clidinium bromide, an anticholinergic drug), both developments of Roche research. Psychological dependence can occur if the recommended dosage is exceeded. When taken with alcohol or other central nervous system depressants it can have an additive effect. Overdosage can result in diminished reflexes, somnolence, confusion and coma. Librax is supplied in green capsules containing 5 mg Librium and 2.5 mg Quarzan.

Libritabs® (Roche)   A sedative–tranquilizer that contains chlordiazepoxide, a BENZODIAZEPINE derivative. Both psychological and physical dependence can occur if the recommended dosage is exceeded. When taken with alcohol or other central nervous system depressants it can have an additive effect. Overdosage can result in diminished reflexes, somnolence, confusion and coma. It is supplied in 5, 10 and 25 mg green tablets.

Librium® (Roche)   One of the most widely prescribed sedative–tranquilizers. It contains chlordiazepoxide hydrochloride (a BENZODIAZEPINE derivative) and is used to reduce both simple and severe forms of tension, anxiety and fear. It is also used in the treatment of alcoholism. Chemically and pharmacologically it is similar to diazepam and oxazepam. Physical and psychological dependence can occur if the recommended dosage is exceeded and it has a significant potential for abuse. As is the case with other central nervous system drugs, use with alcohol or other CNS depressants can produce an additive effect. Overdosage can result in diminished reflexes, somnolence, confusion and coma. Librium is supplied in ampules for injection, and in capsule form: 5 mg green and yellow; 10 mg green and black; 25 mg green and white.

lidocaine   A synthetic local anesthetic that has a relatively weak effect on the central nervous system and consequently has little potential for abuse.

lighter fluids   See INHALANTS.

lipid soluble   A substance, such as THC, that is soluble in fats and fatty tissues. Lipid solubility is usually associated with insolubility in water.

liquid hashish   Hashish is made only from the resin of the plant *Cannabis sativa;* liquid hashish is made from plant material which is ground or chopped up. It is turned into liquid form by distillation. Considerably more potent in liquid form, as little as one drop can produce a HIGH. It is smoked (a very small amount is put on a cigarette) and it can be ingested orally, but because of its potency it has to be used in cooking or put into wine. When it is smoked, the smoker can regulate the degree of his high by spacing out the intake. (See also HASHISH.)

liquor   A term generally used to refer to spirits, rather than beer or wine, but it may cover any alcoholic beverage. During its early English usage the word referred to any mixed liquid, or to any measured solution of a solid in liquid. During the 17th century the term became specifically associated with alcoholic beverages.

liver   The liver is located in the upper right hand side of the abdomen and is partially protected by the lower rib cage. Weighing about three pounds in adults, it is the largest and most metabolically complex organ in the human body. Its functions include circulation, metabolism, excretion, immunology and detoxification. Seventy–five per cent of the blood carried to the liver comes from the intestinal tract; the liver is, therefore, the first to receive digested material.

Alcohol abuse has directly harmful effects on the liver. Ninety percent of the alcohol a person consumes must be oxidized, or detoxified, in the liver and both alcohol and acetaldehyde (a metabolic product of alcohol) can scar the liver and break down its tissues. This damage affects all parts of the body since the liver cannot then convert vitamins and foods into forms usable by the other organs and tissues, or perform its many other functions.

There are several distinct types of *alcoholic liver disease* that can result from heavy drinking. In its mild form, it is characterized by an accumulation of fat in the liver and is the most common liver disease found in hospitalized alcoholics. Alcoholic hepatitis is a more serious form of the disease. It involves inflammation of the liver and cell death and can be accompanied by fever, jaundice and an abnormal accumulation of fluid in the abdominal cavity. *Alcoholic hepatitis* has a mortality rate of 10% or more. The most serious form of alcoholic liver disease is cirrhosis which is characterized by scarring of the liver with fibrous tissue and breakdown of the liver structure. This disease is irreversible although it is not always fatal.

One does not have to be an alcoholic to fall victim to an alcoholic liver disease— heavy social drinking can also result in damage to the liver. Nor will an adequate diet protect a heavy drinker from liver injury, as many people belive, though malnutrition may certainly contribute to liver damage. The liver can repair itself to a remarkable degree, however, and with the exception of cirrhosis, most liver diseases can be corrected to some extent through proper diet (high protein, high vitamin content) and rest—provided the individual stops drinking.

Acute hepatitis is the most common medical complication that results from injecting drugs such as heroin or methedrine. Narcotics themselves seem to have little direct affect on the liver; hepatitis is transmitted through the use of contaminated needles. In one study, 76% of addicts with a history of hepatitis had their first episode within 24 months of starting to use a needle; 50% within the first year. Some 30% of addicts who get hepatitis have recurring bouts of the disease. The first symptoms of hepatitis are nausea, vomiting, jaundice and pain in the upper right side of the body. In New York City, the fatality rate for hepatitis in hospitalized addicts is estimated to be 1–2%.

Liver dysfunction has been reported in adolescents who have abused inhalants, particularly cleaning fluid preparations. Abuse of glue, the most popular inhalant among young abusers, does not seem to affect the liver.

In studies of the effects of cannabis on the liver, no laboratory evidence was found of liver dysfunction in heavy smokers, with the exception of individuals who used cannabis in conjunction with alcohol.

The use of LSD and other psychedelic drugs does not seem to result in liver damage. In the case of cocaine, studies have shown that from 10% to 20% of the cocaine administered was excreted unchanged in the urine and that "the liver can detoxify one minimal lethal dose of cocaine in an hour" (Richter).

Ralph W. Richter, ed., *Medical Aspects of Drug Abuse* (Harper & Row, 1975), p. 61.

lobelia   There have been claims that smoking the dried leaves of the plant, *Lobelia inflata,* can produce a marijuana–like effect. It does not have a significant potential for abuse because of extremely unpleasant side effects, such as nausea and vomiting.

Lomotil® (Searle & Co.)   An antidiarrheic. A synthetic drug containing diphenoxylate hydrochloride and atropine sulfate, it is chemically related to the narcotic MEPERI-DINE. Because of its similarity to meperidine it has addiction potential and the prescribed dosage should be strictly adhered to. Overdosage can result in severe or even fatal respiratory depression. It is supplied in white tablets and in liquid form.

Iophophorine   An alkaloid contained in PEYOTE.

Lorfan® (Roche)   A NARCOTIC ANTAGO-NIST that contains levallorphan tartrate. It is used in cases of deliberate and accidental opioid overdose for the treatment of respiratory depression. If used in the absence of a narcotic it can *cause* respiratory depression, or if the respiratory depression has been caused by a barbiturate or other non–narcotic agent, it can increase the depression.

Lotusate® (Winthrop)   A short–acting BARBITURATE that contains talbutal and is used as a hypnotic sedative. It can produce dependence and has a high potential for abuse.

LSD   (d–lysergic acid diethylamide, lysergide, LSD–25) A semisynthetic drug derived from the alkaloid lysergic acid which is found in ergot, a parasitic fungus or "rust" that grows on rye and other grains.

LSD was originally synthesized in 1938 by two Swiss chemists. Five years later in the spring of 1943 one of its co–discoverers, Dr. Albert Hofmann, inadvertently ingested some of the drug. He experienced restlessness and dizziness followed by a mild delirium in which he experienced "fantastic visions of extraordinary vividness accompanied by a kaleidoscopic play of intense colouration." To make certain that LSD was the source of these visions Hofmann took another dose, 25 mg, which today is considered to be two and a half times the normal

dose for a major trip. He again experienced intense visual changes and also synesthesia, or the merging of senses: "sounds were transposed into visual sensations so that from each tone or noise a comparable coloured picture was evoked changing in form and colour kaleidoscopically."

After 1943, LSD was "a drug in search of a use" (Edward M. Brecher in *Licit & Illicit Drugs*, p. 349). The United States Army tested it for use as a brainwashing agent and as a way of making prisoners talk more readily, and it was stockpiled by the armed forces for possible use in disabling an enemy. Psychiatrists, believing that its effects mimicked a psychotic state, used LSD on themselves and on staff members of mental hospitals in order to better understand mental illness. LSD came into widespread use as an adjunct to psychotherapy in the late 1940s and early 1950s in the U.S., England and Europe. It was used on chronically withdrawn, seriously ill mental patients and had initially promising results. Longer term and more careful follow–up studies were not as favorable, but the ultimate scientific proof of its effectiveness in psychotherapy has not been established.

Until the 1960s self–administration of LSD was mostly restricted to a small number of intellectuals. In *The Doors of Perception* (1954), Aldous Huxley's favorable reports of his experiences with MESCALINE, another hallucinogen whose effects are similar to those of LSD, encouraged others to explore the possibilites of mystical visions and the potential for increased creativity. The illicit use of LSD on a broad national scale began in the U.S. around 1962. Prior to this time, almost all the LSD available in the U.S. and Canada was produced by Sandoz Laboratories. New Food and Drug Administration (FDA) laws and restrictions on LSD and other investigational drugs was followed by an *increase* in the availability and use of

LSD. This was helped by Dr. Timothy Leary, an instructor at Harvard University, who left Harvard in 1963 under a cloud of scandal because of his activities involving LSD. He became a media figure overnight and used his newfound fame to propagandize ("turn on, tune in and drop out") for LSD on a national and international scale.

LSD is commonly prepared as a tartrate salt which is soluble in water. When pure it is a white odorless crystalline material, but street preparations are generally mixed with colored substances. LSD may be manufactured in capsule, tablet, or liquid form. It is always taken orally but it has been injected in clinical situations. LSD is one of the most potent drugs known to man: dosages are measured in micrograms—millionths of a gram—and 25–150 micrograms constitute a dose. Because such small amounts are required, LSD is often impregnated on sugar cubes, blotter paper or small gelatin squares. In relation to other psychedelic drugs, LSD is considered to be 200 times as potent as psilocybin and 5,000 times as potent as mescaline (according to Richard R. Lingeman in *Drugs from A to Z*, p. 132).

When taken orally the effects of LSD are usually felt within an hour. They can last from six to 12 hours and usually peak after three to five hours. LSD can be considered "the king of psychedelics" because it produces the most intense effects of "mind–expansion" with little or no adverse physical side effects. The subjective experiences that LSD induces can be spectacular. Sensory perceptions are altered and intensified so that colors appear brighter and sounds become magnified or are perceived as patterns; there is a merging of senses (synesthesia) so that sounds become swirling patterns of vivid color; perceptions of time and space are distorted so that seconds may seem like an eternity and objects become fluid and shifting. The user may experience himself as being both within and without himself, or as merged with an object or another person. Hallucinations, visions, religious revelations and personality insights have all been reported. The majority of users have both pleasant and unpleasant reactions to the drug, but for those whose overall reaction has been positive, the unpleasant side effects are seen as transitory and valuable in terms of self–knowledge.

As the use of LSD became more widespread in the 1960s, the incidence of "bad trips" also increased. One of the main reasons was because LSD was now available to everyone—including schizophrenics and schizoid personalities who are the most likely to experience adverse effects. On a totally "bad trip," the user may feel that he no longer has control of the psychological effects experienced and may want to end the drug state immediately. The most common reaction to a bad trip is one of acute anxiety or panic, often accompanied by a fear of insanity. Confusion, depression and paranoia may also result.

One widely publicized adverse effect of LSD is the FLASHBACK—a reexperiencing of the effects of the drug weeks or even months after taking it. There are a few theories that seek to explain flashbacks, but none of them are conclusive: one is that flashbacks are induced by stress, fatigue or the use of other drugs. Flashbacks seem to occur most frequently in people who have used LSD repeatedly.

The size of a lethal dose of LSD is not known and so far there are no well–documented reports of human deaths attributable to the action of LSD. In 1967 it was reported that the drug caused damage to white–blood–cell chromosomes in test tubes; however, subsequent studies produced mixed results and to date there has not been any conclusive evidence of its deleterious effects on the chromosomes. Also, it has not been proven that brain damage or other permanent psychological or physical change is caused by LSD.

Use of LSD appears to be related to an increased risk of spontaneous abortion among pregnant women. It may also be linked to a higher than normal incidence of congenital abnormalities in newborns. However, as chronic users of LSD are also likely to be users of other drugs, it is difficult to establish what effects are due to each particular drug.

Use of LSD peaked in the late 1960s and, after a steady decline, seemed to have stabilized in the 1970s. In the early 1980s there appears to be increasing interest in LSD, but little hard evidence that there is much increase in the actual use of the drug. In a nationwide comparison of drug trends among high school students in 1975–1980, the Institute for Social Research found that 9.3% of high school seniors used hallucinogenic drugs at some time in 1980 compared to a rate of 11.2% in 1975.

Early typical users of LSD were generally creative–type personalities, college students and hippies. Regular users in the late 1970s and the 1980s are not confined to these groups, though; in one comparative study of regular users of LSD, occupations included plumbers, longshoremen, janitors and tractor mechanics.

Classification: LSD is classified as a HALLUCINOGEN, a Schedule I drug under the CONTROLLED SUBSTANCES ACT.

Effects: The effects of LSD depend on the quality of the drug and, largely, on the psychological and emotional state of the user and the setting in which the drug is taken. Effects can also vary in an individual, so that one experience may be pleasant and the next unpleasant.

Physiological effects: LSD is quickly distributed to the brain and throughout the body. It acts on the central and autonomic nervous systems. All traces of LSD are gone from the brain after 20 minutes although its effects last for many more hours. It is metabolized in the liver and kidneys and excreted in the feces.

There is no evidence that even long–term, high dosage use of LSD results in any permanent damage to the body or brain. However, like all other drugs, it should not be taken by people who are unstable or those with psychotic tendencies.

Physiological effects are associated almost entirely with the central and autonomic nervous systems. They include increased blood pressure, a rise in body temperature, dilated pupils, and a rapid heartbeat. Occasionally trembling, nausea, loss of interest in food, chills and flushing occur. Body motor skills may be impaired.

Psychological effects: Organic hallucinogenic drugs producing LSD–like effects have been used by people throughout the world, especially in North and South America, for thousands of years in religious ceremonies because of the mystical experience they offer, purportedly bringing the user closer to God and nature. They are called ''mind–expanding'' drugs because that is what they do—break down the barriers which keep an individual locked into his ''normal'' perception of the world, and free his mind to other ways of perceiving the universe. Users have reported experiences ranging from hallucinations, visions, synesthesia, great euphoria and feelings of well–being and ''oneness'' with the world, to anxiety, panic, fear, depression and despair. Prolonged anxiety and psychotic reactions following the use of LSD have occurred. Reactions to the drug are very much related to the expectations of the user, which may account for many of the ''bad trips'' which happened after nationwide warnings against LSD in 1962.

Addictive aspects: Physical DEPENDENCE does not develop with LSD.

Tolerance: If used daily, tolerance to the

effects of LSD can develop rapidly but it will disappear after a few days abstinence. Because the very nature of the drug limits its use (few individuals, if any, would take LSD on a daily basis), tolerance is not generally an issue.

Sources: "Basement chemists" have been readily able to obtain the materials for synthesis of LSD and it is fairly easily made. Supply has equalled demand.

Traffic and control: In 1978 the U.S. Drug Enforcement Administration seized 386,543 doses of LSD; in the first quarter of 1979, the DEA seized over 800,000 doses. While this enormous increase may be due to an increase in use, figures on one–year use by seniors in high school compiled nationally by the Institute for Social Research do not show such a pattern.

Synonyms: acid, the beast, blotter acid, blue cheer, California sunshine, chocolate chips, the cube, dots, the ghost, the hawk, pellets, sacrament, windowpane.

LSM   Lysergic acid morpholide, a chemical substance related to LSD.

Luminal® (Winthrop)   A hypnotic sedative and long–acting BARBITURATE that contains phenobarbital. It is often used to control seizures. Physical dependence can occur

---

History of LSD

1938	Drs. Albert Hofmann and W. A. Stoll, chemists at Sandoz Laboratories (Basel, Switzerland) discover d-lysergic acid diethylamide while experimenting with ergot fungus.
1943	Dr. Hofmann accidentally absorbs a synthesized compound in the lysergic acid series and experiences "fantastic visions." He later deliberately self-administers LSD and again experiences visions.
1949-1954	LSD widely studied for use in the treatment of mental disorders, epilepsy and alcoholism.
1956-1960	Early recreational use of LSD by the medical and psychiatric community and their friends.
1962	Drs. Timothy Leary and Richard Alpert of the Harvard Center for Research in Human Personality treat inmates at the Massachusetts Correctional Institute.
	Thalidomide scare focuses attention on LSD. As fears arise, laws banning LSD appear.
1963	Government investigates Leary and Alpert who then leave Harvard under a cloud of scandal with much national publicity.
	Black market in high quality LSD begins. Adulterated, contaminated or improperly manufactured LSD appears.
1965	New York is the first state to pass legislation against possession, use and sale.
1967	LSD is reported to damage white-blood-cell chromosomes in test tubes.
1968	Incidents of "bad trips" and flashbacks increase across the nation. Use of LSD peaks in the late 1960s.
1970s-1980s	Use steadily declines and stabilizes in the 1970s. Early 1980s show an increasing interest in LSD but little evidence of actual increase in use.

as the drug can be habit–forming and tolerance will develop. A Schedule III drug, it is supplied in sugar–coated 16 and 32 mg oval tablets and in ampules for injection.

lungs   The two conical, saclike organs where respiration, or the exchange of gases between blood and the external atmosphere, takes place. Cartilaged passageways of smooth muscle, called bronchi, conduct air to smaller bronchioles which terminate in alveoli. It is in the alveoli, tiny membranous air sacs filled with vast networks of blood vessels and capillaries, that the absorption of oxygen and the emission of carbon dioxide occur. The sympathetic and parasympathetic nerve fibers regulate respiration through their respective effects on the blood vessels and bronchi of the lungs.

Although DEPRESSANT drugs do not seem to inflict direct damage to the lungs, their effect on the medulla, the brain's respiratory center, explains the danger of death by respiratory failure which may result from the abuse of these drugs. High doses of barbiturates, volatile solvents, tranquilizers and alcohol can cause oxygen deficiency and difficulty in breathing which can result in apnea—temporary suspension of breathing—and death by suffocation. Many alcoholics are also smokers and a correlation between alcohol abuse and respiratory disorders, such as bronchitis and emphysema, has been established through association with heavy smoking.

STIMULANTS such as amphetamines, cocaine, caffeine and nicotine, increase respiratory rate and depth, causing labored breathing. In the case of an overdose, however, their effects during the depressive phase can cause death from respiratory failure. The long–term effects on the lungs from smoking cocaine freebase are unknown.

Abuse of the addictive stimulant nicotine, through smoking, definitely leads to serious lung damage, though this is attributable to the particulate and gaseous contents of tobacco smoke rather than to the action of nicotine. Tars and other particles in the smoke damage the lungs in several ways. By trapping air they cause alveolar ruptures, scarring and inflammation. The decreased suface area of the lungs severely inhibits exchange of gases and causes emphysema victims to suffer from very labored breathing, which can make them barrel–chested. Twenty thousand American smokers die from emphysema each year.

Furthermore, the hydrocarbons in cigarette tar contain carcinogens and co–carcinogens which promote the development of cancerous cells in the lungs and other parts of the body. Cancerous cells eventually replace functioning respiratory cells. Lung cancer, which is the second major cause of deaths from smoking (after coronary heart disease), claims approximately 84,000 Americans annually.

Cigarette smokers risk even further damage to the lungs from such gases as ammonia, formaldehyde, acetaldehyde and hydrogen cyanide, which are contained in cigarette smoke and irritate and eventually kill the mucus–producing and ciliary cells lining the respiratory tract. This destruction of the respiratory system's protective mechanisms sharply increases the smoker's susceptibility to bronchial inflammation (bronchitis) and other infectious diseases.

Heroin abuse increases the likelihood of pulmonary infections such as abcesses and pneumonia, not because of the drug itself but because of the unsanitary conditions under which heroin is often administered—through unsterilized or shared needles. Usually attributable to staphylococcus, such diseases are common among addicts. In addition, "street" heroin is often contaminated or adulterated with binding agents, such as talc or cellulose, which can lodge in the small vessels of the lungs and cause fibrosis and thrombosis.

Heroin itself can depress respiration and decrease the volume and diffusing capacity of the lungs. Pulmonary hypertension and even cardiopulmonary collapse can follow the reduction of lung function. Narcotic overdose can involve abnormally fast or slow breathing, congestion and edema. This last condition manifests as froth which fills the bronchial tree, comes out through the nose and mouth, and can cause death by suffocation. Autopsies of overdose victims have revealed fluid–filled lungs weighing five and six times the normal weight.

In general, psychedelic drugs produce no characteristic adverse effects on the lungs or on respiration. There have been reported cases of LSD precipitating asthma but it is not known if the individuals involved suffered from asthma before taking the drug, in which case the asthma may have been the result of a panic reaction to the LSD.

The effects of marijuana smoking on the lungs have not yet been satisfactorily established. No causal relationship has been established between marijuana use and emphysema or lung cancer. In fact, until early in this century marijuana was used in the United States to treat a variety of illnesses, including asthma. Like tobacco, marijuana contains tars which may conceivably produce deleterious effects but since the rate at which most marijuana joints are smoked does not even approach the number of cigarettes smoked by a tobacco addict, the risk of lung damage seems to be minimal. On the other hand, cancer–causing chemicals in marijuana smoke are present in amounts 50–70% higher than in old–fashioned, high tar cigarettes. Furthermore, the marijuana smoker deliberately inhales and holds the smoke in his lungs as long as possible, placing the irritants and carcinogens in long and direct contact with lung tissue. As people continue to use marijuana over the years that it takes to develop a symptomatic lung cancer, we may see primary malignancies on the lungs due to cannabis. Chronic heavy daily use can significantly impair lung function. Excessive smoking of hashish and other forms of potent marijuana have produced bronchial irritation, asthma and chronic catarrhal laryngitis.

M

mace   The dried arillode of the nutmeg seed. It is mixed with hot water to form a beverage which has psychedelic properties.

macromerine   An alkaloid found in the cactus DONA ANA. It has psychedelic properties similar to, but far less potent than, mescaline which is found in the peyote cactus.

macronodular cirrhosis   A contemporary classification of a type of cirrhosis that is similar to POSTNECROTIC CIRRHOSIS which follows liver inflammation or hepatitis. (See also LIVER.)

Madagascar periwinkle   *Catharanthus roseus*. The leaves of the plant produce stimulant and hallucinogenic effects when smoked but can cause extremely severe adverse reactions.

magic mushrooms   PSILOCYBIN. See also MUSHROOMS, SACRED.

mainline, mainlining   Injecting heroin into a vein, particularly the main arterial vein of the arm. (See ADMINISTRATION.)

maintenance therapy   See METHADONE.

major tranquilizer Tranquilizers are generally classified as either minor or major. The major tranquilizers, such as phenothiazene, are usually used only in psychiatric hospitals for the control of seriously disturbed patients in acute and chronic psychotic states. Though they can produce adverse reactions there is little likelihood of physical or psychological dependence developing. Minor tranquilizers, such as meprobamate (Equinal® and Miltown®) and benzodiazepines (Librium® and Valium®), rather than major tranquilizers, are usually sought after by drug abusers.

malaria The disease was once suffered by a significant number of narcotic addicts, but is now almost eradicated in the United States. An epidemic of malaria, spread by contaminated needles, occurred in New York City in 1939. QUININE then became a popular dilutant of heroin on the East Coast. Although it supresses malarial symptoms, it is not the reason why very few cases of heroin-related malaria are seen. Instead, the malarial plasmodium has been eradicated in North America, and the causative agent would have to be introduced into the country from abroad.

Mallory–Weiss syndrome Lacerations of the esophagus due to frequent vomiting and morning retching. It is a condition found in some alcoholics but is not limited to them. The syndrome can lead to massive hemorrhage and surgery is usually necessary to stop the bleeding.

mandrake *Mandragora officinarum.* An herb that grows in southern Europe and northern Africa. It contains anticholinergic belladonna alkaloids and can cause severe adverse reactions.

Mandrax® A British brand of methaqualone, a non-barbiturate sedative hypnotic. It has a significant potential for abuse. Tolerance can develop and physical and psychological dependence can occur.

MAO inhibitors See MONOAMINE OXIDASE (MAO) INHIBITORS.

marijuana The dried flowering tops, leaves, and stems of the Indian hemp plant *Cannabis sativa,* which contain the psychoactive substance TETRAHYDROCANNABINOL (THC) and are usually smoked in cigarettes ("joints") or pipes. Marijuana is a tall, leafy weed which grows best in hot dry climates like Central Asia, where it probably originated, but also grows wild in most parts of the world. An herbaceous annual with palm–like leaves, it has a hollow six–sided base which is about two inches in diameter at maturity. The plant grows four to eight feet high.

Probably the oldest cultivated nonfood plant, the hemp plant has been a valuable source of products for man's commercial, medical, religious and recreational use for thousands of years. Its cultivation in the eastern hemisphere, both for its fibers and its psychoactive substance, has been widely chronicled. The earliest known written reference occurs in a Chinese pharmacological treatise dating from 2737 B.C. and attributed to the Emperor Shen Nung who, according to tradition, was the first to teach his people the medicinal value of cannabis. In India the first known reference to marijuana is found in the *Atharva Veda* which probably dates back to the second millenium B.C. There are references to marijuana on cuneiform tablets from Asia Minor dating back to 650 B.C., and some believe there are references to the drug in the Bible, in Homer, Herodotus, Pliny, Dioscorides, *The Arabian Nights,* and Marco Polo's writings. It is not known exactly when cannabis was introduced to Western Europe but it must have been very early; an urn found near Berlin, Germany, containing marijuana leaves and seeds is believed to date back to 500 B.C. Marijuana was also in early use in all parts of Africa.

The first record of marijuana in the New World dates from 1545 A.D. when the Spaniards introduced it to Chile, although it has been suggested that African slaves who used marijuana as an intoxicant and as a medicine brought it to Brazil earlier in the 16th century. It is not known if the Pilgrims brought marijuana to Plymouth but the plant was introduced to Virginia in 1611 and cultivated for its fiber. It was brought to New England in 1629 and until the end of the Civil War it was a major crop in North America and played an important role in colonial economic policy. In 1765 George Washington was growing hemp at Mount Vernon, presumably for its fiber though some say Washington was interested in the medicinal and intoxicating qualities of his plants.

Raised for thousands of years as a source of fiber, the hemp plant has also been used in medicine for centuries. The *United States Pharmacopeia* listed it as a recognized medicine in 1850 under the name *Extractum Cannabis* (extract of hemp) and it appeared in the list until 1942. During the latter half of the 19th century, American doctors used cannabis in the treatment of pain, convulsive disorders, hysteria, asthma, rheumatism and labor pains. Cannabis preparations were on the shelves of every pharmacy and were widely prescribed until medical use of the plant was prohibited in 1937.

Marijuana was also used recreationally during the last half of the 19th century and became quite popular in the early part of the 20th century. In 1856, *Putnam's Magazine* published an account of hashish–eating by a 16–year–old Poughkeepsie, N.Y., resident named Fitz Hugh Ludlow who had read and been influenced by De Quincey's *Confessions of an English Opium Eater*. Ludlow continued to experiment with hashish and marijuana extracts over the next few years and published an expanded account of his

experiences in *The Hasheesh Eater*. Marijuana "tea pads," resembling opium dens, were established in New York about 1920. They were tolerated in much the same way that speakeasies were tolerated and by the 1930s there were an estimated 500 of them in New York City alone. During the 1920s New Orleans was a center of marijuana use as black musicians made it part of the jazz scene. Prohibition and the unrestrained life–styles of the Roaring Twenties contributed to the spread of marijuana use, and until it began to be linked to the crime wave which swept the country during the 1930s (a link that was magnified by the sensational reports of yellow journalism) it was largely considered innocuous.

The belief that the nationwide upsurge of depraved criminal behavior was closely linked to the growing use of marijuana was particularly encouraged by Harry Anslinger, commissioner of the Federal Bureau of Narcotics. He conducted a personal campaign (felt by some individuals to be primarily an effort to gain political power) against the "killer weed" which resulted in state legislation banning marijuana. It also resulted in the passage of the 1937 Marijuana Tax Act which, while it did not actually ban marijuana on a federal level, outlawed the nonmedical, untaxed possession or sale of the drug. Anslinger's campaign was based on the contention that marijuana was "criminogenic," that is, it directly caused criminal behavior. In 1939 New York Mayor Fiorello LA GUARDIA appointed a committee to study the use of marijuana, particularly in New York City. The committee cleared the drug of the criminogenic charge and further testified to its relative harmlessness. The committee's report was not published until 1944, however, when stereotypes fostered by Anslinger, and such propaganda films as *Reefer Madness,* were already strongly imbedded in the consciousness of the American people who were too preoccupied with World War II to pay it much attention anyway. During the 1955 Senate committee hearing Anslinger testified that marijuana use inevitably led to heroin addiction—an apparently false allegation that stuck in the public mind.

Despite the lurid stories of sexually depraved and criminal behavior which resulted from smoking marijuana, cannabis use continued to spread. Encouraged by the "Beat Generation," represented by such authors as Jack Kerouac, during the 1950s marijuana found a broad new audience: the American middle class and intelligentsia. In the 1960s it gained even more widespread popularity on college and high school campuses, becoming almost a symbol of American youth and the generation gap that separated young people from their parents.

During the 1970s and 1980s marijuana use has spread to all strata of American society and to all age groups. The increase in its popularity has brought with it a growing lobby for its legalization, which recent legislation does not reflect. The Controlled Substances Act of 1970 deems marijuana a Schedule I drug ("no known medical use"), and makes possession of it a misdemeanor. The sale, transfer, and intent to sell marijuana are felonies. A 1972 presidential commission suggested that the government focus on controlling traffic of the drug rather than on prosecuting recreational users of it. President Nixon rejected the recommendation.

After caffeine, nicotine and alcohol, marijuana is the fourth most popular abused substance in the world. Despite its illegal status in the United States, there are an estimated 16 million regular users (according to *Marijuana Under the Microscope*, a reprint from the Drug Enforcement Administration magazine, Vol. 7, No. 1, March 1980, p. 9), and the number of users increased each year until 1978. Since that time the two most reliable surveys, the high school senior survey and the household survey (performed by the Alcohol, Drug Abuse and Mental Health Ad-

ministration of the U.S. Department of Health and Human Services), have shown significant drops in marijuana use. For example, in 1977 nearly 17% of all 12 to 17–year olds reported past–month use of marijuana; this figure dropped to 11.5% during the month prior to the 1982 survey. Similarly, in the 1979 survey, 35.4% of all young adults (aged 18–25) reported past–month use (an all time high), but by 1982 this figure had dropped to 27.4%. This decrease in use is attributed to a change in attitude among young people. In 1978, 35% felt that regular marijuana use was associated with great risk; by 1982, this figure had risen to 60%. In many states, the law remains unchanged while actual enforcement policies testify to a diminishing concern among police officers with recreational users of marijuana.

Classification: Marijuana is classified as a HALLUCINOGEN, a Schedule I drug under the Controlled Substances Act of 1970.

Activity: The active principal in *Cannabis sativa* is delta–9–tetrahydrocannabinol (THC) which was first synthesized in 1966 at Hebrew University, Israel. It is most concentrated in the resin but is distributed throughout the plant, except in the root and seeds. Absorbed slowly and incompletely by the stomach, THC is much more effective when smoked and absorbed by the lungs. It is distributed to all the organs and almost completely metabolized in the liver. It is LIPID SOLUBLE, and deposits form in fatty tissues. It crosses the placental barrier and is excreted in the urine and feces. THC is insoluble in water and destroyed by heat. Its half life, the time required to eliminate half of the dose from the body, is 28–56 hours.

Dosage: It is impossible to say how much marijuana constitutes an effective dose since different varieties contain different concentrations of THC. The THC content can vary from 1% to 5% and more. Jamaican and South American marijuana contains the most THC while domestically cultivated marijuana contains about 1%. When smoked, THC's effects manifest in a few minutes, peak in 10–30 minutes and last two to three hours (depending on the potency). About 50% of the THC content of a marijuana cigarette is lost in burning and in the sidestream smoke; the rest is available for absorption if the ROACH is consumed. If a joint contains 1000 mg of 1% THC, it would have 10 mg of the active ingredient and about 5 mg would be available for absorption. Since the brain only receives its share by weight, approximately 0.05 mg of THC would arrive in the brain during the first few minutes.

After eating THC, effects materialize in 30–60 minutes, peak in two to three hours, and last three to five hours. THC is only one–half to one–third as effective when eaten as it is when smoked.

A lethal dose has never been established since no deaths directly related to the action of marijuana have been reported. Research with mice indicates that for a human weighing approximately 154 pounds a lethal dose of marijuana containing 1% THC would be 15 pounds smoked or 30 pounds eaten—all at once.

Effects: The effects of marijuana are highly subjective and are affected by a number of variables such as the quality of the drug, the dosage, the experience and expectations of the user and his environment. In very high doses, THC can produce hypnotic and psychedelic effects, including time and space distortions, enhanced sensory perceptions, euphoria and free–flowing thoughts. Adverse psychological reactions such as anxiety and paranoia can occur, usually in novice users. Some researchers have cited an apparent "amotivational syndrome" which occurs with regular marijuana use, especially among the younger age groups. They claim that some chronic smokers became lethargic and lose their ambition and interest in everything except smoking marijuana. It has been counterproposed, however, that a person who is

predisposed to this kind of life–style might simply find reinforcement of his views and desires in the sedative effect of marijuana. What is remarkable is that those daily users who stop marijuana use, come out of their apathy and loss of drive after a month or two of abstinence.

The most common physiological effects reported with moderate use are dryness of the mouth and throat, an increase in pulse rate and heart action (tachycardia), increase in appetite (especially for sweets), red eyes, slight impairment of reflexes and psychomotor coordinated tasks such as driving, and sometimes nausea due to dizziness or anxiety. These symptoms are transitory and disappear after a few hours except for impaired driving skills which can last up to 10 hours.

During 1982 three major reports reviewed research findings to date. They are the reports of the Institute of Medicine (IOM), the World Health Organization (WHO) and the National Institute on Drug Abuse (NIDA). Their general conclusions were similar and are briefly reported here. The NIDA study makes the following points: adolescents are beginning to smoke marijuana at an earlier age; marijuana is being used intensively by adolescents of both sexes; and the marijuana now available is five to 10 times more potent than it was a half dozen years ago. These facts are all unprecedented in history, especially in a demanding, highly industrialized society. Adolescence is a vulnerable period when coping mechanisims are learned and psychological maturation should be taking place. Instead, the report states, too many youngsters are intoxicated on marijuana during a good part of their waking hours. The IOM conclusion is worth quoting: "What little we know now about the effects of marijuana on human health—and all we have reason to suspect—justifies serious national concern." The WHO summary states that "intermittent use of low potency cannabis is not generally associated with obvious symptoms of toxicity. Daily or more frequent use, especially of the highly potent preparations, may produce a chronic intoxication that may take several weeks to clear after drug use is discontinued.''

A recent Canadian study on the effects of marijuana on the fetus has found a link between marijuana smoking and temporary exaggerated tremors, vision problems, and startle reflexes among the babies of mothers smoking five or more marijuana cigarettes per week during pregnancy. Other recent studies have found evidence of a fetal cannabis syndrome that resembles the fetal alcohol syndrome in many respects. (See PREGNANCY.)

Marijuana and Alcohol: People who smoke marijuana are also apt to drink alcohol. According to findings of the National Commission on Marijuana and Drug Abuse, alcohol and tobacco are the two substances most commonly used by regular marijuana smokers. When alcohol is taken with marijuana there is greater impairment of motor and mental skills than with either drug alone (see SYNERGY). Among the young (under 21) there

---

History of Marijuana

c.2737 B.C.	**Reference to marijuana in Chinese pharmacology treatise.**
c.2000 B.C.	**Reference to marijuana found in India.**
c.500 B.C.– 1500 A.D.	**500 B.C. urn containing marijuana found near Berlin, Germany.**
	Cloth made from hemp in Europe.
1545	**Hemp plant introduced to Chile.**
1611	**Hemp is cultivated by early colonists in Virginia.**
1850	**U.S. Pharmacopeia lists marijuana as a recognized medicine.**
1856	**Putnam's Magazine publishes an account of Fitz Hugh Ludlow's marijuana-eating experiences.**
c.1875	**"Hasheesh houses" modeled after opium dens begin to appear.**
1920s– 1930s	**Commerce in marijuana for recreational use begins to increase during Prohibition.**
	"Tea pads" spring up in major cities.
	Marijuana linked to crime-wave of the 1930s.
1937	**Marijuana Tax Act outlaws nonmedical, untaxed possession or sale.**
1939	**La Guardia Report in NYC clears the drug of being criminogenic and attests to its relative harmlessness.**
1950s– 1960s	**Recreational use grows in the 1950s and becomes widespread in the 1960s on college and high school campuses.**
1970	**Controlled Substances Act lists marijuana as a Schedule I drug, and makes possession a misdemeanor; sale, transfer and intent to sell are felonies.**
1970s– 1980s	**Use spreads to all segments of society and increases each year until 1978-79. In 1979 35.4% of young adults (aged 18-25) report use in past month; in 1982 27.4% report past month use.**

seems to be a growing trend toward the combined use of alcohol and marijuana.

Addictive aspects: The use of marijuana does not produce physical dependence but psychological dependence on the euphoric and sedative effects can result after long–term chronic use. Abstinence may result in feelings of irritability, nervousness or insomnia but these pass quickly.

Tolerance: Studies have shown that moderate and infrequent use of marijuana does not produce tolerance. Most experts agree, however, that heavy daily use produces tolerance to the tachycardia. "Reverse tolerance" has been suggested, a syndrome characterized by the user needing progressively smaller doses to achieve a HIGH. This phenomenon has been attributed to the theory that smoking marijuana is a learned behavior, in the sense that with use the smoker learns how to smoke more efficiently and to recognize the effects of the drug more quickly.

Sources: In 1980, 75% of the U.S. marijuana market was supplied by Colombia; Mexico supplied 8% (a decrease in recent years); Jamaica supplied 10%, and 7% was grown domestically. Domestic cultivation is centered in seven primary states: California (where it is estimated that marijuana is the state's largest cash crop worth over $1 billion annually), Hawaii, Oregon, Arkansas, Missouri, Kentucky and Florida.

mazindol   A stimulant drug whose activity is similar to that of the amphetamines. Some patients notice mild sedation from it. It is found in the anorectic SANOREX.

MDA   (3, 4–methylenedioxyamphetamine) A semisynthetic drug produced by modifying the major psychoactive components of nutmeg and mace. It can also be produced from safrole, the oil of sassafras. The drug was first synthesized in 1910.

The effects of MDA combine some of the properties of MESCALINE and AMPHETAMINES. Physical effects with low doses include pupil dilation, increased blood pressure and pulse rate; with high doses, there may be an increase in body temperature, profuse sweating and muscular rigidity. A sense of physical well–being with heightened tactile sensations may occur with low doses, while high doses may produce illusions and hallucinations. Subjective reports emphasize warm loving feelings (it has been called "the love drug" and "speed for lovers") and the desire for close communication and increased reflectiveness. This drug seems to induce age regression and has been used in psychotherapy as a way of helping a patient to relive specific childhood experiences. While this phenomena happens with other hallucinogenic drugs, it occurs so regularly with MDA that it seems to be inherent in the pharmacology of the drug itself. MDA can be highly toxic—even fatal—in various dosages depending on the individual's sensitivity to it.

The average dose of MDA is from 50 to 150 mg. The effects begin to be felt about 30 to 60 minutes after ingestion and they last about eight hours. Mental and physical exhaustion may follow the use of MDA.

Although insufficient research has been carried out, it appears that tolerance to MDA does not develop. No physical or psychological dependence has been conclusively demonstrated.

Mebaral® (Breon)   A long–acting BARBITURATE that contains mephobarbital. It is used as a sedative hypnotic particularly in the treatment of epilepsy, its anticonvulsive action being much stronger than its hypnotic effect. Physical and psychological dependence can occur and when used with alcohol or other central nervous system depressants it can have an additive effect. Overdosage can result in respiratory depression; severe overdosage can result in coma and death. It is supplied in white scored tablets of 32, 50, 100 and 200 mg.

Mediatric® (Ayerst)   A stimulant that contains estrogen, androgen, nutritional supplements and a mild antidepressant, and is used in the case of aging patients. Tolerance and psychological dependence can occur but it has little potential for abuse. It is supplied in red tablets, dark blue capsules, and in liquid form.

Melfiat® (Reed–Provident)   An anorectic drug containing phendimetrazine tartrate that is used for weight control. Its activity is similar to that of the AMPHETAMINES. Tolerance can develop within a few weeks and psychological dependence and social disability can occur. As with other anorectics it has a high potential for abuse. Overdosage can result in restlessness, tremors, rapid respiration, confusion and hallucinations. The drug is supplied in round orange 35 mg tablets, and in 70 mg tablets that are white with speckles of red.

Mellaril® (Sandoz)   A major TRANQUILIZER that contains thioridazine and is used for acute or chronic psychoses. When taken with alcohol or other central nervous system depressants it can have an additive effect. It is supplied in 10, 15, 25, 50, 100, 150 and 200 mg tablets, and as a concentrate containing 30 mg per ml and 100 mg per ml.

memory   Memory is defined as the power or process of reproducing or recalling what has been learned in the past and retained. In this literal sense, what is remembered can be given a more or less sharply defined position in time and space.

Neither the mechanisms of memory itself, nor those of memory loss induced by drugs or other factors, are well understood at present, but both continue to be the subject of much scientific study. The memory process includes short–term and long–term storage and retrieval facilities which appear to be centered in the brain's limbic system. Electrical stimulation of this area has enabled some patients to recall long–forgotten events and other information.

Information storage seems related to such chemical structures as proteins and nucleic acids. Pituitary hormones may also contribute to the memory process. Information appears to be filed chronologically and by sense; that is, there is a separate memory "file" for vision, hearing, taste, and so on.

Symptoms of memory loss, regardless of the cause, include inability to concentrate, absent–mindedness, poor sequence retention and general temporal confusion. A number of recreational drugs interfere, probably chemically, with the transfer of information from short–term to long–term memory, preventing users from storing and remembering information received while intoxicated. Scientists have been studying a theory known as "state dependency": it postulates that information received under intoxication can be recalled only when that state is reproduced, but so far findings have been inconsistent. Storage blockage is known to occur with the use of alcohol, marijuana, heroin and other depressants. Furthermore, information that is stored during drug intoxication may be distorted and therefore disturb the reasoning process.

Heavy drinkers commonly suffer "alcoholic haze," a reversible memory disturbance which correlates to the amount of alcohol ingested. After about 10 years of chronic alcoholism this condition can progress to more severe memory failure which abstinence may correct to some degree. Such irreversible memory disturbance is especially likely when organic brain damage develops. In KORSAKOFF'S PSYCHOSIS, patients experience extreme difficulty in retrieving information from long–term memory although immediate recall is not affected.

The majority of chronic alcoholics frequently suffer lapses of memory called "blackouts" in which they lose all recollection of entire blocks of time during which they were ostensibly conscious. This too is attributed to severe impairment of information storage facilities and can happen to anyone—not just alcoholics—when very large quantities of alcohol are ingested quickly. Risk of blackout is increased by fatigue and by the combination of alcohol and other sedative drugs.

Myriad studies on the effect of marijuana on memory processes have yielded a variety of results. Some have shown that only immediate recall is affected during intoxication and that this is due to the user's inability to concentrate. Other reports state that the transfer of information from short–term to long–term memory is impaired while the user is high but that there are no long–term effects. Marijuana's suppression of nucleic acid synthesis may be responsible for this effect, which is significant in light of the large numbers of students of both high school and college age who smoke marijuana during school hours. If memory storage is impaired, information received while the person is high will not be remembered and clearly learning cannot take place at the student's full capacity. However, marijuana smoking is a learned behavior in a number of ways and many users have reported being able to overcome the drug's effects on memory storage by concentrating harder on the material at hand.

Use of hallucinogens like LSD has precipitated a well–known phenomenon of memory disturbance known as FLASHBACK, in which the user's drug experience is so vivid and impressive that it becomes firmly implanted in the memory and can be re–experienced long afterward. No satisfactory explanation for flashbacks has been developed. The perceptual distortion which results from taking psychedelic drugs has also included temporal confusion in which the user projects a memory into his present situation.

Hardin & Helen Jones, *Sensual Drugs* (New York: Cambridge University Press, 1977).

Elizabeth Loftus, *Memory* (Reading, MA: Addison–Wesley Publishing Company, 1980).

Robert O'Brien and Morris Chafetz, *The Encyclopedia of Alcoholism* (New York: Facts on File Publications, 1982).

Menrium® (Roche)   A minor TRANQUILIZER that contains chlordiazepoxide and esterified estrogens and is usually used for the treatment of menopausal syndrome. It can produce dependency and it can have an additive effect when taken with alcohol or other central nervous system depressants. Overdosage can result in diminished reflexes, somnolence, confusion and coma. Menrium 5–2 is supplied in green tablets; Menrium 5–4 in dark green tablets; and Menrium 10–4 in purple tablets.

meperidine   A NARCOTIC ANALGESIC, meperidine hydrochloride is best known by the brand name DEMEROL. It is an OPIOID, a synthetic opiate, similar pharmacologically but not structurally to morphine, and is one–tenth as potent. Eislab & Schaumann introduced the drug, also known as penthidine, to the medical profession in 1939, proclaiming its usefulness in reducing spasms of the smooth muscles of the stomach and small intestine. The discovery of its analgesic properties some time afterward produced a wave of excitement among doctors, who believed the drug had morphine's effects without being addictive. This supposition was subsequently proven false.

Appearance: Meperidine hydrochloride appears as a fine white crystalline powder. It is odorless, soluble in water and alcohol, and slightly soluble in ether. Its melting point is between 186–189 degrees fahrenheit.

Activity: Rapidly absorbed and metabolized in the liver, meperidine brings relief in 15 minutes when taken orally and in 10 minutes when administered hypodermically. Its effects peak in one hour and last two to four hours which is briefer than morphine's effects. The drug's half–life is three to four hours. Meperidine crosses the placental barrier and appears in mother's milk.

Dosage: For pain relief, meperidine is administered orally, intramuscularly or subcutaneously every three to four hours in doses of 50–200 mg. The lethal dose has not yet been determined; 1200 mg have been fatal and 2000 mg have been survived. Cases of extreme tolerance have been recorded in which the addict's daily habit reached 3000–4000 mg. Intravenous administration should be slow and in diluted solution to accommodate the higher potency of the drug through that route.

Effects: Meperidine relieves moderate to severe pain and produces a euphoric effect less intense than that of morphine. It is a respiratory depressant and has proved fatal when administered to patients suffering asthmatic attacks. In therapeutic doses meperidine causes the side effects usually associated with narcotic drugs, such as dizziness, nausea and sweating. Larger doses can cause tremors, twitches and seizures.

Tolerance: Tolerance to meperidine's sedative effects develops more quickly than tolerance to its analgesic action. The drug's short duration necessitates repeated administration to maintain euphoria and this accounts in part for the not uncommon development of meperidine dependence. Special care should be exercised with patients receiving other narcotic–analgesic and sedative hypnotic drugs. Symptoms of addiction include extreme drowsiness, respiratory depression and cold clammy skin. Abusive doses can result in circulatory collapse, cardiac arrest and death. Withdrawal symptoms are less severe than those associated with morphine and are of relatively short duration.

Usage: Used medically for the short–term relief of moderate to severe pain, meperidine often serves, in combination with other drugs, as a pre–operative analgesic, particularly in obstetrics. After morphine, meperidine is the second most widely used analgesic for severe pain.

Recreational use of and addiction to meperidine occurs most frequently, though not exclusively, among members of the medical profession to whom the drug is most readily available.

Availability: Winthrop manufactures meperidine hydrochloride in white tablet form under the brand name Demerol. The drug is also available in syrups and injectable form.

mephobarbital   A long–acting BARBITURATE that exerts a strong sedative and anticonvulsive action but has a relatively mild hypnotic effect. Onset of action is from 30 to 60 minutes; duration is from 10 to 16 hours. It is manufactured as MEBARAL and appears in tablet form. It is converted in the liver to PHENOBARBITAL but is less effective as a sedative than phenobarbital. Mephobarbital is used in the treatment of epilepsy, anxiety, tension and apprehension.

meprobamate   A sedative hypnotic and minor TRANQUILIZER, first marketed under the name MILTOWN in tribute to the New Jersey town where it was developed in the early 1950s. Meprobamate was heralded as a unique drug which relieved anxiety without producing undue sedation. It enjoyed instant popularity and liberal prescriptions were given to patients suffering from anxiety and tension. As early as 1956 reports of addiction appeared, encouraging caution in its prescription but curbing its use only slightly. In the late 1960s over a million pounds of meprobamate were manufactured and distributed.

Meprobamate is a bitter white powder,

slightly soluble in water and freely soluble in alcohol. Readily absorbed in the gastrointestinal tract and rapidly distributed throughout the body, meprobamate is metabolized by the liver and excreted by the kidneys. It crosses the placental barrier and appears in mother's milk. Cases of congenital malformation associated with meprobamate use by pregnant women have been reported.

The drug depresses the central nervous system, with effects peaking in two hours. It has a half–life of four to ten hours. Usual oral doses range from 1200–1600 mg daily, divided into three or four doses. A dose of 800 mg taken at one time may cause sleep and daily doses above 2400 mg are not recommended. Overdose can cause respiratory depression, coma and death. No lethal dose has been established, however, although 20,000–40,000 mg have been survived.

Less potent than the minor tranquilizers derived from benzodiazepines (Librium, Valium), meprobamate is used for muscle relaxation and sedation. It is prescribed for the short–term relief of symptoms of anxiety. Large doses can result in euphoria and intoxication similar to that induced by BARBITURATES, including such symptoms as slurred speech and loss of coordination and muscular control.

Adverse reactions include drowsiness, dizziness, headache, visual impairment, nausea, vomiting, rash, prickly or burning sensations and diarrhea.

Tolerance, along with physical and psychological dependence can develop with meprobamate use. Withdrawal symptoms include tremors, insomnia, gastrointestinal distress, convulsions and hallucinations, as well as the recurrence, in magnified degree, of the symptoms of anxiety which lead to the use of the drug.

Meprobamate exhibits cross–tolerance to barbiturates and is potentiated by other central nervous system depressants. Accidental deaths have occurred from combinations of meprobamate and other depressants and it has been used in suicide attempts—usually unsuccessfully.

Meprospan® (Wallace)   A nonbarbiturate minor TRANQUILIZER that contains MEPROBAMATE. It is used for the relief of tension and anxiety and as a muscle relaxant. Tolerance can develop and physical and psychological dependence can occur. When taken with alcohol or other central nervous system depressants it can have an additive effect. Overdosage can result in drowsiness, stupor, coma and respiratory collapse. It is supplied as Meprospan 200, yellow–topped capsules; and as Meprospan 400, blue–topped capsules.

mescal   A beverage made from plants of the genus *Agave* (maguey, pulque) which grow in the southwestern United States. It has an intoxicating effect. Also a slang term for PEYOTE.

mescaline   The principal alkaloid in the peyote cactus, *Lophophora williamsii,* found in northern Mexico and Texas.

Mescaline was one of the first hallucinogens to be chemically isolated. Arthur Heffter (1860–1925), a German chemist and professor of pharmacology, was studying peyote and individually tested four alkaloids that were isolated from the cactus. On November 23, 1897, Heffter took 150 mg of mescaline hydrochloride and reported: "2:00 p.m. Violet and green spots appear on the paper during readings. When the eyes are kept shut the following visual images occur . . . carpet patterns, ribbed vaulting, etc. . . . . Later on landscapes, halls, architectural scenes (e.g. pillars decorated with flowers) also appear. The images can be observed until about 5:30 p.m. Nausea and dizziness are at times very distressing. . . . In the evening well–being and appetite are undisturbed and there is no sign of sleeplessness.''

The chemical structure of mescaline was determined in 1918. Mescaline attracted widespread intellectual interest in the early part of the century by such people as Havelock Ellis, Weir Mitchell and Aldous Huxley, but today it is rarely available illicitly.

Mescaline is usually taken orally but it can be inhaled by smoking ground peyote buttons or, more rarely, it can be injected. It is considerably less potent than LSD. Average doses range from 300 to 500 mg. Of the alleged mescaline samples analysed at the Addiction Research Foundation in Toronto, Canada, nearly 90% were not mescaline; usually they contained either PCP or PCP combined with LSD.

Mescaline offers the user the opportunity to achieve a hallucinogenic state without undergoing all of the preliminary emetic effects of peyote, and to achieve it more rapidly. The hallucinatory effects of peyote and mescaline are reported to be fairly similar to the effects of LSD.

Classification: Mescaline is classified as a HALLUCINOGEN, a Schedule I drug under the CONTROLLED SUBSTANCES ACT. It is in the same chemical group of drugs as TMA and MDA and is chemically related to adrenaline.

Effects: Common mental effects include euphoria, heightened sensory perception, a dream–like state, sometimes with hallucinations or synesthesia, and difficulty in thinking. At low doses the effects appear within one to three hours and last for four to 12 hours or more. Physical effects include dilation of the pupils, an increase in body temperature, some muscular relaxation and sometimes vomiting. At higher doses mescaline may also induce fever, headache, low blood pressure and depressed heart and respiratory activity.

Addictive aspects: No physical dependence on the effects of mescaline develops regardless of the frequency of usage.

Tolerance: Tolerance to mescaline develops but evidence regarding its nature and magnitude is scarce. Mescaline is rarely taken on the kind of regular basis which would allow tolerance to develop. When tolerance is observed, CROSS–TOLERANCE to LSD can be demonstrated.

Sources: Mescaline can be made synthetically or from peyote cactus. The heads or "buttons" of the cactus are dried and then sliced, chopped, or ground and sometimes put in capsules. The demand for mescaline is small and there is little on the market.

Jan G. Bruhn, "Three Men and a Drug: Peyote Research in the 1890s," *The Cactus and Succulent Journal of Great Britain,* vol. 30, no. 2, 1977, pp. 27–30.

"Facts About Hallucinogens," pamphlet, Toronto, Canada: Addiction Research Foundation, 1980.

Frederick G. Hofmann, *A Handbook on Drug and Alcohol Abuse* (New York: Oxford University Press, 1975), pp. 169–171.

Jerome Jaffe, Rovert Petersen, and Ray Hodgson, *Addictions: Issues and Answers* (New York: Harper and Row Publishers, 1980), pp. 61–61.

metabolism   The process by which the body uses food, water and oxygen to sustain itself. The process begins with absorption of a substance, such as food or a drug, into the body system and continues until the substance is excreted. There are two metabolic processes: assimilation and dissimilation. Assimilation is the chemical change that turns the introduced substance into the complex substances of which the body is built. Dissimilation involves the breaking down process involved in tissue building. See individual drug categories for specific metabolic patterns.

methadone   An OPIOID. A synthetic NARCOTIC ANALGESIC, methadone was first introduced during World War II when it was developed by German chemists (the brand name DOLOPHINE is a tribute to Adolph Hitler). Though structurally dissimilar to morphine, it shares its effects. Methadone is best known for its application in the controversial Methadone Maintenance program which some experts believe has been our most useful tool in the treatment and rehabilitation of heroin addicts.

Appearance and Activity: Methadone is an odorless white crystalline powder which is soluble in water, alcohol and chloroform and insoluble in ether. The body absorbs and responds to the substance in much the same way as it does to morphine (see MORPHINE for details).

Dosage: As an antitussive, methadone is prescribed in 1–2 mg doses to be taken every four to six hours. For pain relief, 2.5–20 mg are prescribed hypodermically or orally every 3–4 hours. Doses in the Methadone Maintenance program range from 20–120 mg orally and effects last from 24–48 hours, whereas the average addict's dose of heroin lasts only four to six hours.

Effects: The effects of methadone resemble those of morphine and heroin in most respects. The drug produces the same euphoria and drowsiness but does not slow the respiration as much as heroin. Most importantly, it produces cross–tolerance to that drug, thereby blocking its effects. It is this quality that makes the drug so valuable in heroin addiction therapy. It also reduces the craving for opiates. Methadone is as likely as heroin to produce dependence but while withdrawal symptoms are more prolonged, they are less severe than those associated with heroin. Symptoms include pain in the bones, sweating and diarrhea.

Usage: Methadone is used to relieve chronic pain of moderate to severe intensity. Methadone is also useful as an antitussive and as a detoxicant for patients withdrawing from heroin and morphine. The drug's primary use today is in the Methadone Mainte-

nance program aimed at helping heroin addicts overcome their addiction and accompanying destructive life–style. The program includes weaning the addict away from heroin and providing him with the counseling and training needed to rejoin society in a constructive capacity. The program has been applied at numerous rehabilitation centers all over the United States and abroad and its philosophy and results have been the subject of longstanding debate and disagreement.

There are two types of programs: the original high–dose model developed in the early 1960s by Drs. Vincent Dole and Marie Nyswander, and the low–dose model. Both models use the oral administration method; the dose is generally in liquid form and dissolved in fruit drinks. In the high–dose model, the treatment begins by increasing the patient's tolerance until he can accommodate a daily dosage of between 50 and 120 milligrams. The low–dose model stabilizes the patient on 30 milligrams or less a day.

On each visit to a clinic the patient leaves a urine sample which is tested for signs of morphine (heroin is excreted as morphine) and other drugs. Although methadone blocks heroin's effects, some patients continue to use heroin, at least in the initial stages of treatment. Abuse of cocaine, alcohol and barbiturates has been well documented among methadone patients. Once he has demonstrated responsibility and commitment to rehabilitation, the patient is allowed to take home a one– and later a three–day supply of "juice."

Detoxification is effected by gradually reducing the methadone content of the mixture. Some patients, however, find their psychological dependence more difficult to overcome than their physical addiction. Many either revert to their heroin habit or require indefinite methadone treatment. Opponents of the program focus their arguments on the fact that it replaces one addiction with another and that it is doubtful that the patient will ever withdraw from methadone.

The distinct advantages methadone treatment holds over other rehabilitation efforts (abstinence and social therapy, for example), include the drug's cross–tolerance to heroin, which blocks the effects of heroin even if the patient continues to use it. Methadone also allows the addict to experience a similar but longer lasting "high" than heroin and decreases his craving for the drug. The oral administration of methadone is especially important because it breaks the ritual of injecting and eliminates infection. Finally, and maybe most significantly, methadone can be obtained legally. The heroin addict can satisfy his dependence without reverting to criminal activities and, at the same time, work under a controlled program to free himself of his addiction.

Statistics on the success of the Methadone Maintenance program differ and it remains a controversial issue. New problems have arisen as a result of the program: large quantities of legal methadone are diverted to the illicit drug market each year, for example, and in 1973 there were more methadone–related deaths than heroin–related ones in New York City. On the other hand, the treatment developed by Drs. Dole and Nyswander has certainly enabled large numbers of heroin addicts to reshape their lives and to rejoin society, free of their crippling addictions. Methadone maintenance seems to be the most effective way yet of accomplishing that goal.

Commercial Availability: Methadone is manufactured in tablets, syrups and injectable forms. Brand names include DOLOPHINE (also known as dollies), METHADONE HYDROCHLORIDE DISKETTES, and Methanex.

Methadone and Alcohol: Investigations have shown a considerable amount of crossover between the use of alcohol and heroin.

Alcoholism among heroin addicts is frequent. Studies have suggested that alcohol is the drug most frequently abused before the initial use of heroin, and that addiction has already occurred. When heroin is not available, heroin addicts will most often use alcohol as a substitute to relieve their withdrawal symptoms. The figures on the prevalence of alcoholism among methadone–maintained addicts vary from 5% to 40%. These rates can be misleading, however, because they are no greater and may even be less than the rates of alcoholism for similar socioeconomic populations of nonaddicts.

Alcoholism among methadone–maintained addicts not only interferes with the rehabilitation process, it also causes dangerous side effects. Because a majority of heroin addicts have had an episode of viral hepatitis, the consumption of large amounts of alcohol may aggravate a pre–existing liver condition and progress rapidly to CIRRHOSIS. In addition there is the increased danger of a synergistic effect between the depressant properties of alcohol and methadone. Mortality rates for methadone patients who are also alcoholics are much higher than for those who are not alcoholics.

Alcoholism plays a disruptive role in the rehabilitation process of heroin addicts. A patient suffering from alcoholism is likely to become aggressive and refuse to follow rules which often leads to the termination of his methadone therapy. Premature discharge from a program can also occur because the alcohol interferes with proper detoxification from heroin. After detoxification from heroin and withdrawal from methadone, alcoholism is not necessarily alleviated, and because of the complexities of CROSS–ADDICTION alcoholism can be the single most important obstacle which prevents a heroin–addicted individual from functioning in society. Because many alcoholism programs will not accept methadone–maintained patients, methadone treatment programs should be oriented toward dealing with alcoholism.

Methadone Hydrochloride Diskettes®

(Lilly)   A synthetic narcotic analgesic whose activity is similar to that of morphine. It is used for detoxification and maintenance treatment in cases of narcotic addiction. It is a long–acting depressant and, when doses are given daily, its effects last 24–48 hours. Tolerance can develop and physical and psychological dependency can occur. The drug has a high potential for abuse. Overdosage can result in respiratory depression; circulatory collapse, cardiac arrest and death can occur. It is suppled in 40 mg pillow–shaped, peach colored tablets. It is a Schedule II drug under the CONTROLLED SUBSTANCES ACT.

methamphetamine   A synthetic amphetamine used as an anorectic. (See DESOXYN and AMPHETAMINES.)

methanol   Methanol (also known as methyl alcohol or wood alcohol) is a colorless flammable liquid that can be mixed with water in all proportions. It is a poison and, because it oxidizes slower than ethyl alcohol, the formaldehyde produced may cause blindness even in small doses. When used as a denaturant for ethanol it makes the latter unfit for drinking. Methanol is also called wood alcohol because at one time it was primarily produced as a by–product of wood distillation. Today methanol is produced synthetically and is generally used as a solvent or antifreeze. People have died from unknowingly drinking wood alcohol in bootleg whiskey or moonshine. Others have died after knowingly consuming it in the absence of their usual alcoholic beverages. Initially it has intoxicating effects.

methaqualone   (2–Methyl–3–(2–methylphenyl)=4(3H)quinazolinone)   First synthesized in 1951 in India as an antimalarial drug, methaqualone was introduced to the American medical market in the mid–1960s for the treatment of insomnia and anxiety and was believed to have none of the abuse potential of short–acting barbiturates. Because it was alleged to be safe and non–addictive it became quite popular with individuals looking for a new safe high. Since that time, however, many instances of addiction and some cases of overdose have been reported and its abuse potential has been documented in scientific research.

Intoxication from methaqualone is similar to intoxication from barbiturates and alcohol. The risks are the same: death by overdose, accidents due to confusion and impaired motor coordination. Coma has been known to occur following 2.4 grams of methaqualone; 8 to 20 grams have produced severe toxicity and death. Like barbiturates, methaqualone has a SYNERGISTIC effect when used with alcohol and other central nervous system depressants. Overdose can result in delirium, restlessness, excessive tension and muscle spasms leading to convulsions. An addict should not discontinue the drug abruptly and to avoid the risk of convulsions during withdrawal, a patient should be detoxified in a hospital.

As more doctors have become aware of the abuse and addictive potential of methaqualone, their willingness to prescribe it has declined. This has resulted in a large traffic in illicitly produced tablets. The most commonly produced imitations are of the brands Quaalude and Mequin, both of which, before they were withdrawn from the market, contained 300 mg of methaqualone. The imitations may contain between 10 and 150 mg of methaqualone, between 20 and 300 mg of diazepam (Valium), or combinations of other substances. The level of diazepam found in just one tablet may at times be enough to render the user unconscious. Other imitations may be so weak that a small handful of pills are needed in order to get high—a danger if someone accustomed to a weak form unknowingly obtains an identical–looking but much more potent form.

The heaviest concentration of users of illicit methaqualone is between high school age and the mid–30s.

Appearance: Methaqualone is a white crystalline powder with little or no odor and a bitter taste. It is stable in light and air, and soluble in alcohol and ether. It is slightly soluble in water.

Classification: Methaqualone is a non–barbiturate sedative hypnotic. LEMMON, the last manufacturer of methaqualone under the brand names Quaalude and Mequin, removed the drug from the market in the early 1980s because of its widespread abuse.

Effects: Methaqualone is readily absorbed from the gastrointestinal tract. It is transported in the plasma and is distributed in the body fat, the liver and the brain tissue. Relatively low doses (75 mg four times a day) produce sedation; larger doses (150–300 mg) lead to sleep. With hypnotic (sleep–inducing) doses there may be transient "pins and needles" sensations prior to sleep. Excessive dreaming and sleepwalking sometimes occur. Hangover is frequent. Side effects can include nausea, vomiting, stomach discomfort, sweating, hives, rapid heart beat and lack of appetite.

Users who take the drug for pleasure typically resist its sedative effects in order to achieve a dissociative high similar to that induced by barbiturates. They generally take larger doses, 600–900 mg, or more if TOLERANCE has developed. Users experience a pleasant sense of well–being, an increased pain threshold, loss of muscle coordination and a prickling of the fingers, lips and tongue. The "high" is reputed to enhance sexual performance; there is little evidence of this, however, and it is more likely that, like alcohol, the drug acts on the central cortex of the brain to release normal inhibitions.

Addictive aspects: Psychological dependence has occurred with methaqualone. Physical dependence also develops producing distinctive WITHDRAWAL symptoms similar to those occurring with barbiturate dependence: headaches, severe cramps, convulsions and tremors. Symptoms of withdrawal also include irritability and sleeplessness followed by mania and delirium tremens. Some authorities believe that the potential for methaqualone addiction and abuse are as serious as those of barbiturates and heroin.

Tolerance: Tolerance to the drug's euphoric effects develops at a more rapid rate than tolerance to its respiratory depressant effects, increasing the danger of overdose.

Sources: Legitimate supplies are now unavailable in the United States. There is a strong black market of lookalike capsules or tablets which may or may not contain actual methaqualone. A large amount of illicit methaqualone arrives in the U.S. from Colombia.

metharbital   A long–acting BARBITURATE with anti–convulsant properties similar to those of MEPHOBARBITAL and PHENOBARBITAL. Metharbital is a derivative of BARBITAL, to which it is converted in the liver. Milder and less toxic than phenobarbital, it is manufactured as GEMONIL. It is used in the treatment of grand mal, petit mal, myoclonic and mixed types of seizures.

methyl alcohol   See METHANOL.

methyldihydromorphinone   An analgesic. A semisynthetic MORPHINE derivative, used mainly in the treatment of cancer, it is a Schedule II drug and is more potent than morphine. It is also known as Metopon.

methylmorphine   See CODEINE.

methylphenidate   A central nervous system stimulant with action somewhat like that of the AMPHETAMINES. It is used in the treatment of narcolepsy and also in the treatment of hyperkinetic children. (See RITALIN.)

methyphenobarbital   A long–acting barbiturate with an onset time of up to one hour and duration of action up to 16 hours. It is also known as MEPHOBARBITAL. (See BARBITURATES and MEBARAL.)

methyprylon   A central nervous system depressant and hypnotic used in the treatment of insomnia. Its action is similar to that of the BARBITURATES but it is chemically unrelated. (See NOLUDAR.)

metopon   See METHYLDIHYDROMORPHINONE.

Mexico   Since 1970 there have been several investigations aimed at estimating the prevalence of drug use in Mexico. The surveys reported that inhalants were the most commonly abused substances, followed by amphetamines, cannabis and tranquilizers. Use of heroin, LSD and cocaine was reported by only a small percentage of the population in Mexico City and the northern region of the country. The surveys were conducted in hospitals and treatment centers, in the general population through household surveys, among students and the imprisoned population, and among other high risk groups. Although the surveys indicate certain problem areas, the government acknowledges that they are far from comprehensive and that the actual number of abusers is unknown.

In a 1980 survey carried out in a representative sample of the school population (14–18 year olds) of Mexico City and its metropolitan area, 12.3% of the students reported some pattern of abuse. This figure was further broken down to: 10.7% light users; 1.1% moderate users; and .5% heavy users. The percentage of heavy users increased to 5.6% when alcohol and tobacco were included. When compared to a 1976

survey, the frequency of regular use did not show a significant increase. There was an increase, however, in the percentage who had "ever used" a drug. A recent study carried out in Mexico City among younger children (11–14 years old) reported that 27% had used inhalants.

The kinds of drugs that are abused vary greatly among different groups and according to geographical areas. It should be noted that most surveys were carried out in metropolitan areas and not in the numerous rural communities. Use of non–medical drugs was most common among the male population under 25 years of age; the abuse of medically used drugs was more common among the female population of the same age.

Nearly all health institutions in the country provide some sort of service for drug abusers. There are also small pilot programs in which new approaches to the treatment of high risk groups are tried and evaluated— particular attention has been given to those who use inhalants. Centros de Integración Juvenil, a civil association and one of the biggest organizations specializing in treatment facilities, has received government funding. Since 1970 the association has established 32 centers in 28 cities. Before 1981 every young person who asked for treatment was accepted; after 1981 the admission policy had to be modified because of the number of applicants and now only the most severe cases are accepted.

For thousands of years Mexicans used "native" hallucinogens in religious rites; peyote and sacred mushrooms were the most common. In recent years the use of these substances has dwindled but a kind of occultism centered around these hallucinogens has sprung up in other countries—largely influenced by the writings of Carlos Casteneda— and generated a movement of those who want to experience Mexico's wondrous drugs. Consequently the Mexican government has to contend with trafficking in "occult" drugs, as well as the current exoteric drugs of abuse.

Because of its border situation, Mexico has also long been a center for other kinds of drug trafficking. Until the late 1970s Mexico was the primary source for the marijuana market in the United States. This dubious distinction has since been bestowed on Colombia. From 1977 to 1978 Mexico's share of the U.S. marijuana market dropped from 40% to 18%; from 1978 to 1980 it declined to 8%. Significant traffic in diverted amphetamine powder and other illicit drugs from Europe to the U.S. via Mexico has been well documented, along with trafficking in illicit methaqualone. The majority of these drugs now pass through Colombia because of concerted efforts by both the U.S. and Mexican governments.

In past years Mexico was also involved in heroin trafficking. When the FRENCH CONNECTION fell apart, Mexico became a main supplier of heroin to the U.S. During the mid–1970s it was estimated that 60% of the heroin consumed in the U.S. was of Mexican origin. Mexican "brown" heroin was at that time assayed at about 17% heroin—a high percentage when compared with the other heroin available which assayed at about 2–3%. Mexico had a corner on the market for only a short time, though, and has since been replaced by the GOLDEN CRESCENT.

Mexican poppy cultivation dates back to World War II. Shipments from Europe were all but cut off due to the war and the New York Mafia began to finance Mexican production. After the war France again took over and poppy cultivation in Mexico declined until its brief comeback in the mid–1970s. Opium fields are still cultivated today in rural areas but only an insignificant amount of the drug is exported.

In 1969 the United States and Mexico signed an agreement calling for joint action against drug trafficking. Called "Operation Cooperation," it resulted in the confiscation of many tons of drugs, particularly marijuana, and the arrest of many smugglers. In addition the Mexican government has made numerous changes in its National Health Code and many chemicals are now subject to strict control.

Penalties for drug use and possession have also undergone changes. There is no bail or bond now for individuals charged with a narcotics crime: they must stand trial and, if convicted, there is no parole or suspended sentence. Long pre–trial imprisonment can be expected in Mexico because the courts are backed up with pending cases.

micronodular cirrhosis   A contemporary classification for a kind of cirrhosis that is similar to PORTAL CIRRHOSIS, the most common cirrhosis found among alcoholics. (See CIRRHOSIS.)

milieu therapy   A socioenvironmental therapy that is an essential part of inpatient treatment. In this therapy the behavior and attitudes of the staff and the activities prescribed for a patient are determined by the patient's interpersonal and emotional needs. This interaction between patient and staff includes learning how to interact with others without letting anger turn to violence; learning to talk to people about things other than drugs; and learning to ask for help when it is needed.

military   See AMERICAN MILITARY.

milk sugar   Lactose crystals that are used to dilute heroin. It resembles heroin in appearance.

Milpath® (Wallace)   A minor tranquilizer that contains MEPROBAMATE and tridihexethyl chloride. It is used to treat peptic ulcers and colon disorders particularly when they are accompanied by anxiety and tension. Milpath has the potential for abuse and both physical and psychological dependence can occur. When taken with alcohol or other central nervous system depressants it can have an additive effect. It is supplied as Milpath–400, yellow scored tablets containing 400 mg of meprobamate; and Milpath–200, yellow coated tablets containing 200 mg of meprobamate.

Milprem® (Wallace)   A minor tranquilizer that contains MEPROBAMATE and conjugated estrogens. It is generally used in the treatment of menopausal syndrome. Milprem has a potential for abuse and both physical and psychological dependence can occur. When taken with alcohol or other central nervous system depressants it can have an additive effect. It is supplied as Milprem–400, dark pink coated tablets containing 400 mg of meprobamate; and Milprem–200, light pink coated tablets containing 200 mg of meprobamate.

Miltown® (Wallace)   A widely used minor tranquilizer that contains MEPROBAMATE and is used for the relief of tension and anxiety. It has a significant potential for abuse, and both physical and psychological dependence can occur. When taken with alcohol or other central nervous system depressants it can have an additive effect. Overdosage can result in drowsiness, stupor, respiratory collapse, coma, shock and death. It is supplied as Miltown in 400 mg white scored tablets, and 200 mg white sugar–coated tablets; and as Miltown 600, white capsule–shaped tablets containing 600 mg of meprobamate.

Miltrate® (Wallace)   A minor tranquilizer that contains MEPROBAMATE (for tension and anxiety) and pentaerythritol tetranitrate (to relax smooth muscle). It is used for the relief of pain associated with coronary artery disease. Miltrate has the potential for abuse and both physical and psychological dependence can occur. When taken with alcohol or other central nervous system depressants it can

have an additive effect. It is supplied as Miltrate–10, white tablets containing 10 mg of pentaerythritol tetranitrate; and Miltrate–20, orange tablets containing 20 mg of pentaerythritol tetranitrate. Each variety contains 200 mg of meprobamate.

minerals   See NUTRITION.

minor tranquilizer   Tranquilizers are generally classified as major and minor. Major tranquilizers, such as phenothiazenes, are usually only used for psychoses. Minor tranquilizers, the type most sought after by drug abusers, are used in the treatment of anxiety and tension. They include meprobamate (EQUANIL and MILTOWN) and chlordiazepoxide (LIBRIUM). (See also TRANQUILIZERS.)

mixed addiction   See POLYDRUG USE.

mixed cirrhosis   A combination of macronodular and micronodular cirrhosis. (See CIRRHOSIS.)

mixing drinks   Changing alcoholic beverages in the course of a drinking session. Though commonly thought to cause or intensify a hangover, the fact is the alcohol content and concentration of the drinks are actually to blame. Mixing drinks can, however, be a factor in how rapidly a person becomes intoxicated. If, for example, beer is taken first and then followed by whiskey, the beer slows the absorption of the whiskey and its effects are somewhat delayed. If whiskey is taken first and then beer, the result is more rapid intoxication because the beer reinforces the concentrated rush of the whiskey to the bloodstream.

MMDA   A derivative of the alkaloid myristicin found in nutmeg. It has psychedelic properties and purportedly intensifies present experiences, as opposed to MDA which intensifies experiences in the user's past. It is the same as MDA except that its chemical formula includes a 3–methoxy group.

moderate drinking   Occasional drinking or a regular habit of drinking small amounts of alcohol; a level and frequency of drinking consistent with the pattern in the community and resulting in no pathological behavior or consequences.

monoamine oxidase (MAO) inhibitors
Central nervous system stimulants that are used in the treatment of moderate to severe depressive states. The main types are isocarboxazid (Marplan), phenelzine (Nardil) and tranylcypromine (Parnate). They are extremely potent and adverse reactions are frequent and can be severe. When used in combination with many other types of drugs—depressants, stimulants, narcotics—such an intense additive effect can be produced that death may result. The same is true when MAO inhibitors are taken with common foods that contain tyramine, such as cheese, herring, salami and chocolate. MAO inhibitors are considered extremely dangerous drugs and are usually only administered under close medical supervision.

moonshine   Potstill corn whiskey that is not aged to any extent and is usually made secretly. Like pure alcohol it has a clear color and raw taste. It is also called "white lightning," a name which is well merited. When the government first started imposing taxes on whiskey in the late 1700s, distillers began setting up stills in concealed places, usually working at night (hence the name moonshine). In parts of Tennessee, Kentucky, North Carolina and other areas of the rural South, moonshining is still carried on and in some areas moonshine is now legally available.

morning drinking   Sometimes engaged in to relieve the symptoms of a HANGOVER,

morning drinking is a warning sign that indicates the possibility of alcoholism.

morning glory seeds   The seeds of certain members of the bindweed family *Convolvulaceae*, which contain HALLUCINOGENIC substances similar to those found in LSD—principally lysergic acid amides, d–isolysergic acid amide, chanoclavine, and clymoclavine. All of these substances are also found in the fungus ergot, *Clavicips purpurea*, from which LSD was first synthesized. The active ingredients in morning glory seeds have about one–tenth the potency of LSD–25.

As with so many of the organic hallucinogens, morning glory seeds have long been used by native peoples of America in religious ceremonies and as healing agents. The Aztecs were the first to discover their hallucinogenic possibilities and the Aztec word *ololiuqui* is now used to refer to all varieties of the seeds. It is believed that the Aztecs used the word only when referring to the seeds of one species, *Rivea corymbosa*. *Tlitliltzen*, it is thought, was the Aztec name for morning glories of the genus *Ipomoea*.

Effects: As might be expected, the effects of morning glory seeds are somewhat like those of LSD. The user may experience perceptual disturbances, mood changes and even psychomimetic reactions. Physical effects are wide–ranging: nausea, vomiting, intense headache, drowsiness, diarrhea, chills, impaired vision, decreased blood pressure and even shock can result from their use. The onset of the experience is 20–45 minutes after ingestion and duration can be upwards of six hours. Cases of prolonged reactions or FLASHBACKS following ingestion of morning glory seeds have been reported.

Sources: Several seed varieties commonly planted in gardens are used, including Heavenly Blue, Pearly Gates, Blue Star, Flying Saucers and Wedding Bells, but those sold commercially are often covered with methyl mercury to prevent spoilage. Some may also be covered with vomit–inducers which have been applied to discourage psychotropic use. As a result, many users grow their own seeds.

The appearance of morning glory seeds on the illicit drug market is rare as LSD is readily available and preferred. When the seeds are used, they are first pulverized or ground and then soaked in water. The liquid is strained and drunk.

Traffic and control: No laws regulate the sale of morning glory seeds.

Synonyms: ololiuqui, bador, loquetico, tlitliltzen, bindweed, Heavenly Blue, Pearly Gates, Blue Star, Flying Saucers, Wedding Bells.

morning shot   For an alcoholic, the first drink of the day (see MORNING DRINKING). For an addict, it is the first narcotic shot of the day.

morphine   A NARCOTIC ANALGESIC, the principal alkaloid of OPIUM. The isolation of morphine around 1802 is usually attributed to Serturner, who named the drug for Morpheus, the god of sleep and dreams. The most potent medication known for pain relief, it remains the standard by which all other analgesics are judged. Complete synthesis of morphine was achieved in 1952.

Appearance: Morphine constitutes by weight about 10% of opium, the coagulated exudate of the poppy plant, *Papaver somniferum,* which also contains codeine and about twenty other alkaloids. Because pure morphine is only slightly soluble in water, morphine sulfate is the form most commonly used both medically and recreationally. It appears as odorless white crystals, or white crystalline powder, which loses water on exposure to air and darkens on exposure to light. Morphine sulfate is soluble in water, slightly soluble in alcohol and insoluble in chloroform and ether. Morphine hydrochloride is also occasionally used in injections.

Activity in the body: Readily but slowly absorbed from the gastrointestinal tract, morphine acts directly on the central nervous system, specifically affecting pain receptor neurons. After initial stimulation, the drug depresses the cerebral cortex and medullary centers.

Within 24 hours, 90% of the total excretion process is complete. Like other narcotics and depressant drugs, morphine crosses the placental barrier. Babies of addicted mothers usually exhibit withdrawal symptoms soon after birth.

Dosage: Recommended dosage for relief of moderate to severe pain is 10 mg/70 kg (approximately 154 pounds) bodyweight. When taken orally, morphine produces longer–lasting effects but it is only about one–tenth as potent as when it is injected intramuscularly. With subcutaneous injection, pain relief manifests in 20–60 minutes and lasts four or five hours. Intravenous administration brings almost immediate pain relief and effects peak within 20 minutes. Analgesia lasts a much shorter time when morphine is injected intravenously.

Toxic and lethal doses vary with individual tolerance; 120 mg taken orally and 30 mg injected intravenously have caused no toxic reactions in a non–addicted person, though less than 30 mg have caused death by respiratory depression on some occasions. Addicts have been known to take daily doses of up to 5000 mg because of tolerance.

Effects: Morphine is prized for its ability to relieve almost any kind of pain—particularly dull, continuous pain—along with the fear and anxiety associated with such suffering. In addition to analgesia, the drug produces drowsiness (and, in sufficient doses, sleep), euphoria, and impairs mental and physical performance. When given to people who are not experiencing pain, initial doses can produce dysphoria—heightened fear and anxiety—rather than euphoria. Vomiting after the first dose is common. Morphine increases the smooth muscle tone of the genitourinary and gastrointestinal tracts (causing constipation), depresses respiration, and decreases hunger and sometimes the sex drive (although in some people, especially women, it can enhance sexuality by disinhibition). It may also have the effect of delaying ejaculation in men. (It has been suggested that opium's popularity in 19th century India was largely due to that effect.) In women, morphine use can cause menstruation to become irregular; with daily use some women stop menstruating altogether. Studies indicate that narcotic use also decreases the likelihood of pregnancy.

Typical adverse effects include nausea, vomiting (which is not always experienced as unpleasant) and sweating. Yawning, lowered body temperature, flushing of the skin, a heavy feeling in the limbs and itchiness around the face and nose are also usually present, along with pupillary constriction and consequent dimming of vision. Soon after injecting morphine intravenously, users experience an orgasmic rush beginning in the upper abdomen and spreading to the rest of the body. This rush is perhaps the principal attraction of morphine and heroin.

In overdose, the effects described above are magnified. Respiratory depression can be severe enough to cause coma and death—respiratory failure (apnea) is in fact the principal danger of morphine abuse. The skin of overdose victims is cold, clammy and bluish, and the pupils are so constricted they become pinpoint. Skeletal muscles become flaccid. Overdose also frequently involves pulmonary congestion and edema. Until the patient can be admitted to emergency hospital care, he should be kept awake by walking, administering smelling salts and by stimulating the skin. NALOXONE (Narcan) is a specific antidote for morphine overdose. Given intravenously it will restore a comatose, barely breathing patient to consciousness within a minute or two.

Tolerance: Tolerance and severe psychological and physical dependence develop quickly with regular use of morphine. Psychological dependence, due probably primarily to the orgasmic–like feeling produced by the drug, develops before actual physical craving. Tolerance, however, develops only to morphine's depressant effects and not to other physical effects such as constriction of the pupils. Morphine exhibits CROSS–TOLERANCE and dependence to other narcotics, and its depressant effects are prolonged and intensified when used with other depressant drugs.

Up to a threshold of 500 mg a day, the severity and duration of WITHDRAWAL symptoms from morphine depends on the quantity of the drug regularly ingested. Usual symptoms include nausea, lacrimation, yawning and sweating alternating with chills. Withdrawal from morphine generally lasts 36–72 hours.

Usage: When morphine was introduced to the medical profession, it was hailed as a powerful analgesic effective in the relief of all kinds of pain and, falsely, as it turned out, as a cure for opium addiction. Opium, either in the form of laudanum (a hydroalcoholic tincture) or in a form suitable for smoking, was already a popular "remedy" for every imaginable ailment—and some imaginary ones. Morphine quickly replaced opium in many applications, though it did not cure opium addiction. In the 1850s, with the advent of the hypodermic syringe which made possible almost immediate relief from pain and anxiety, morphine proved especially valuable and doctors prescribed it liberally. Unfortunately, the new drug proved equally popular among recreational users, particularly in conjunction with the hypodermic needle. Morphine could be purchased at the local drugstore or through the mail in powder, tablet or liquid form. Hypodermic kits were also readily available. Compared to alcohol it was a "respectable" intoxicant and was heartily recommended by many of those who tried it. During the Civil War it served as a priceless surgical anesthetic and analgesic. Doctors distributed supplies of the drug, along with hypodermic syringes, to soldiers for use at home to ease the continuing pain of battle wounds. It was not until several decades after the war that doctors realized their mistake in assuming that injections of morphine carried no risk of addiction be-

---

History of Morphine

c.1803   **Serturner, German pharmacist, isolates morphine from opium.**

1825   **Morphine is first used in medicine as an analgesic and is thought to be a cure for opium addiction.**

1853   **Hypodermic needle is introduced and used to inject morphine.**

1866   **Morphine use during Civil War in U.S. creates an estimated 400,000 addicts.**

1870s   **Franco-Prussian War in Europe creates morhpine addicts.**

1874   **Heroin is isolated from morphine.**

1906-
1920   **Legislation regulates cultivation and distribution of opium, outlaws prescriptions of narcotics to addicts and imposes criminal penalties.**

1920s   **Heroin, because of its higher potency and illicit availability, becomes favored over morphine.**

1952   **Complete synthesis of morphine is achieved.**

1970   **Prescriptions containing morphine are classified as Schedules II and III drugs under the Controlled Substances Act.**

1980s   **Morphine rarely appears on the illicit market and addicts are generally members of the medical profession or hospital personnel.**

---

cause when administered this way the drug bypassed the digestive tract. Approximately 2% of the population (400,000 people) was estimated to be suffering from the "army disease"—opiate or morphine addiction. Many of the addicts were doctors.

Today opiate addicts prefer the more potent and shorter–acting heroin. Morphine rarely appears on the illicit market and most addicts nowadays are probably members of the medical profession or hospital personnel who have access to the drug. Morphine is generally used as a sulfate rather than in its pure form. Recreational users inject the drug, take it orally in capsules or liquid solution, heat and inhale it, or absorb it from rectal suppositories. It is also often taken in combination with stimulant drugs such as amphetamines or cocaine, in order to counteract the depression, weakness and dizziness it produces, as well as to increase the analgesic effect.

Current medical applications of morphine include severe pain, cough suppression, relief of diarrhea, and as a preanesthetic to relieve the fear and anxiety associated with surgery and to reduce the amount of anesthetic needed. It is not recommended for patients suffering from bronchial asthma or other respiratory depression.

Morphine is a Schedule II drug under the CONTROLLED SUBSTANCES ACT.

Synonyms: M., morph, dreamer, Miss Emma, M.S.

morpholinylethylmorphine   Another name for PHOLOCODINE, a semisynthetic morphine derivative.

Mothers Against Drunk Driving (MADD)   A community action group that seeks to change the legal system's casual response to drunk driving and the whole climate of acceptance and tolerance of the drunk driver. The group was organized in 1979 by a mother whose daughter was killed by a drunk driver. Based in California, the organization has recently gained nationwide attention: petitions instigated by MADD have been instrumental in the recent rise in the drinking age in many states. The organization is also aimed at helping those who have been victimized by drunk drivers.

mouth   The mouth is the entry into the digestive tract and any impairment to its functions, which include mastication, salivation, swallowing, tasting and speaking, will subsequently affect the functioning of the digestive system.

Of all the recreational drugs, alcohol and tobacco have the most directly harmful effects on the mouth. Alcohol alone has not been proved to be carcinogenic but it is believed to act as a "co–carcinogen" in conjunction with a substance that is carcinogenic, such as tobacco. Studies have shown that alcohol and cigarettes act synergistically (see SYNERGY) to increase the potential for cancer, especially in the mouth and throat. Most heavy drinkers are also heavy smokers and it is estimated that people who drink and smoke heavily run a risk of developing cancer which is 15 times greater than that of nondrinkers and nonsmokers. One theory states that the carcinogens in tobacco have easier access to the mucous membranes of the mouth if the cells are bathed in alcohol, with its solvent effects. Another theory suggests that alcohol and tobacco independently affect the mucous membrances. Tobacco may contribute to cancers of the roof of the mouth, of the nasopharynx (which connects with the nostrils), of the larynx and of the lungs. Pipe and cigar smoking increase the incidence of cancer of the lip and jaw. Alcohol plays more of a role in cancers of the floor of the mouth, the lower pharynx and the esophagus—areas where contact is most direct.

Few other drugs of abuse produce directly harmful effects on the mouth. Marijuana smoking often produces dryness in the mouth and throat, and many users of amphetamines and other stimulants have experienced teeth grinding, but these symptoms disappear quickly.

Many opiate users neglect oral and personal hygiene and this results in rampant tooth decay. However, a large segment of the population—particularly the poor—receives unsatisfactory dental care so it is difficult to establish if dental neglect is due to poverty or drug abuse.

mouthwash   Numerous mouthwashes contain high percentages of alcohol. Listerine, for example, has 26.9%, while most hard liquor (gin, vodka, whiskey) contains about 40% alcohol. While they do have a potential for abuse, the main concern posed by mouthwashes containing alcohol is that an alcoholic who legitimately uses one may develop a craving for more. In addition, an alcoholic who is abstinent may be started on a relapse by drinking mouthwash. Mouthwashes may also produce adverse reactions in people taking ANTABUSE. Other mouthwashes with a high alcohol content are: Cepacol, 14%; Scope, 18.5%; and Signal, 15.5%.

multihabituation   See POLYDRUG USE.

multimodality programs   A drug treatment program that uses a variety of treatment approaches.

muscarine   See FLY AGARIC.

muscimol   See FLY AGARIC.

muscles   The effects of drug abuse on the muscles range from a slight muscular weakness that allegedly follows marijuana use to the severe, permanent muscular damage that can result from alcohol and heroin abuse. The mechanisms of most of these disorders remain unclear although the symptoms are well known and frequently encountered.

Tranquilizers such as VALIUM (diazepam) act as muscle relaxants and are commonly used in the treatment of spastic disorders. Cumulative effects of abuse of such depressants (including barbiturates, alcohol, sedatives and narcotics) can cause muscular necrosis, or cell death. Alcohol abuse in particular has been recognized as a causative agent in the development of muscle disease. In their early stages, muscle diseases caused by alcohol can be reversed through abstinence.

Alcoholic myopathy is probably a direct effect of ethanol or acetaldehyde on the muscle cells. The subclinical form of alcoholic myopathy develops in as much as one–third of the alcoholic population and is indicated by abnormally high levels of the enzyme creatine phosphokinase, which is produced by muscle cells. Lactic acid levels also rise and victims may suffer muscle cramps and tenderness. If the patient does not stop drinking, his condition may worsen.

Sudden severe muscle cramps, pain or swelling of the arms and legs after heavy alcohol consumption are usually signs of acute alcohol myopathy, a localized, benign condition which also improves with abstinence. Myoglobinuria, a condition characterized by muscle fiber necrosis, fluid leakage and high enzyme levels may appear later. If undetected, it can progress and cause renal insufficiency and death.

Chronic alcoholic myopathy progresses slowly, often painlessly and without myoglobinuria, and involves weakness and atrophy of the limbs (usually the legs).

Wasting of the muscles also occurs with the abuse of AMPHETAMINES, accompanying and partially resulting from weight loss. Amphetamines and other stimulants increase skeletal muscle tension while relaxing smooth muscles of the bronchi and intestine. After several days of a speed run, the user experiences pain in the muscles and joints and distinct tremors. These involuntary movements, which have also been noted in connection with alcohol and sedative abuse, sometimes continue to trouble the individual after he or she has stopped using the drug.

Heroin's usual effect on the muscles is to induce spasms in the hollow organs. Muscle spasms are a well known recognizable symptom of withdrawal from narcotic drugs and can involve the facial muscles as well as entire limbs (hence the expression "kicking the habit"). Muscular rigidity is a usual condition in babies born of addicted mothers.

It is still unclear whether disorders related to heroin abuse constitute toxic or allergic reactions. Several disorders seem to be associated with adulterant agents used to dilute street heroin. Acute rhabdomyolysis, for example, manifests within a few hours after injection as skeletal muscular pain, tenderness, swelling and weakness in the extremities. In this condition, muscular fibers can undergo structural change with or without necrosis. Random or total necrosis can also occur, sometimes accompanied by edema and hemorrhage.

Years of subcutaneous or intramuscular heroin injection can also cause muscular fibrosis or abcesses as well as chronic infections. Permanent muscular contractions— "frozen" limbs or extremities—can result from muscular scarring.

Bacterial infection is a common complication of heroin use in unsanitary conditions. It strikes the muscles in the form of pyomyositis, which involves fever and swelling and tenderness of the limbs. Extensive areas of dead muscle have been found in some cases. Muscular rigidity and convulsions are frequently present during tetanus infections and can interfere with respiration.

Another muscular disorder associated with heroin addiction is the "crush syndrome," which afflicts overdose victims. It sometimes appears as massive swelling of the extremity which received the injection. Localized limb compression has been seen in individuals who lost consciousness.

Marijuana and hallucinogenic drugs have only a slight affect on the muscles. The muscular weakness previously mentioned in connection with marijuana smoking is not universally accepted as an effect of cannabis use, although the drug has been used medically as a muscle relaxant since the mid–19th century. Extremely high doses of cannabis may, however, cause involuntary jerking of the muscles and the lower extremities and sometimes other parts of the body.

LSD and other psychedelics generally constrict smooth muscles of the uterus, blood vessels and bronchioles. Skeletal muscles may show tremor and weakness but, again, these effects do not commonly result from the use of these drugs.

mushrooms, sacred   Several varieties of mushrooms with hallucinogenic properties have been used for centuries by Mexican Indians in religious rites and ceremonies. When eaten, the mushrooms affect mood and perception in a way similar to LSD and MESCALINE. They contain the active alkaloids PSILOCYBIN and PSILOCIN (psilocin changes to psilocybin in the body). In 1958 Dr. Albert Hofmann, who synthesized LSD, isolated psilocybin and later synthesized it. The psilocybin which is sold on the illicit market today is more often than not another chemical compound, such as LSD or PCP.

Another name for sacred mushrooms is teonanactl which means "flesh of the gods" or "god's flesh." The most common types of mushrooms are *Psilocybe mexicana, Conocybe siliginoides, Psilocybe aztecorum, Psilocybe zapotecorum, Psilocybe caerulescens* and *Stropharia cubensis.* Effects begin 20–30 minutes after ingestion and the duration can be from six to 12 hours. Peak effects are usually felt in one hour and include visions, often perceived from great heights. The mushrooms can be lethal in large doses.

Psilocybin, which is expensive to synthesize, is a Schedule I drug under the CONTROLLED SUBSTANCES ACT.

music and drugs   It has been suggested that currently popular music and currently popular drugs go hand–in–hand. This suggestion of a link between the two dates back to the 1880–1920 era, a time of widespread poverty when the great majority could only obtain inexpensive drugs, such as alcohol and tobacco, and an inexpensive form of entertainment—in this case "the blues" because it was basically piano music requiring only one performer.

Dixieland jazz which was popular during the blues era but came into its own after World War I, is associated with the use of alcohol and the limited use of cocaine (a habit brought home by World War I servicemen). The National Prohibition Act of 1919 which aimed at curtailing the use of alcohol, actually enhanced the desire for it and people would drink anything that even resembled it, such as wood alcohol.

From 1930 to 1942 the "swing era" was prominent and coincided with the repeal of Prohibition. The availability of alcohol and an atmosphere of permissiveness lead to a boom in legitimate dance halls and nightclubs. This was also a time when many Americans, musicians included, were called into service for World War II and newly developed "music and dance rooms" in many popular hotels were forced to close. Those who could afford it and who were not involved in the war effort attended private "jam sessions" and the small groups that evolved developed "bop" music. With the development of bop music, which was somewhat restless and angular compared to previous forms, came an increase in heroin abuse.

The interaction of music and drugs was further demonstrated in the decade from the late 1940s to the late 1950s when the soft, intimate sounds of the newly evolved "cool" music was enjoyed by a host of marijuana users who preferred quiet intoxication.

In the 1960s "electric" sounds became popular and there was an increase in the use of hallucinogens, and acid rock parties centered around the use of LSD. As the drug's popularity waned in the 1970s, the use of amphetamines, barbituates and other dangerous drugs took over.

Musicians and singers have long inhabited an environment that is conducive to drug abuse: along with the irregular pay, frequent traveling, contact with the criminal underworld in order to get bookings, and irregular working hours, there is the pressure and tension inherent in performing itself. Musicians are also apt to abuse drugs because of their desire to perceive "life" more deeply and come up with unusual visions which they can express through their music. The lyrics of songs often contain references to LSD, marijuana, alcohol and cocaine and the "good" feelings they can produce. Adolescents in particular are greatly influenced by popular singers and by song lyrics, sometimes even unconsciously. They often model their own life–styles on those of their idols'. (See also RASTAFARIANS.)

mydriasis   Dilation of the pupils of the eyes that occurs with intoxication from hallucinogens, scopolamine, atropine, cocaine and amphetamines. Mydriasis does not occur from the use of marijuana, barbituates or alcohol. (See also EYES..)

myoglobinuria   A syndrome characterized by severe muscle pain, along with weakness, tenderness and swelling. It can be accompanied by cardiac arrhythmias, respiratory failure and renal insufficiency (the latter possibly leading to death). Depressant drugs (barbiturates, alcohol, narcotics) have been known to be responsible for muscle necrosis resulting in myoglobinuria. There is

also a syndrome of myoglobinuria referred to as "heroin user's myoglobinuria" which is thought to be related to heroin adulterant mixtures.

myristicin   An alkaloid found in NUTMEG and thought to produce hallucinogenic effects.

N

N_2O See NITROUS OXIDE.

nail polish remover   A volatile hydrocarbon that is inhaled for its intoxicating effects. (See INHALANTS.)

nalbuphine   A synthetic narcotic agonist/antagonist analgesic chemically related to oxymorphone and naloxone. (See NUBAIN.)

Nalline® (Merck, Sharpe, & Dohme)   A narcotic antagonist which is no longer available. It contained nalorphine hydrochloride and was used in the treatment of morphine and opiate drug overdose to counter respiratory and central nervous system depression. (It did not counter respiratory depression caused by barbiturates or other drugs.) A small dose of Nalline could also be used to avoid full–blown withdrawal symptoms. The drug was used in the NALLINE TEST to ascertain whether or not an addict who had stopped using narcotics had resumed his habit.

Nalline test   A test which used the narcotic antagonist NALLINE, to determine if a paroled addict had returned to the use of drugs. If a narcotic was present in the person's system Nalline would reverse its effects and the pupils would dilate. The Nalline test has been replaced by the NARCAN TEST.

nalorphine   A semisynthetic morphine antagonist. (See NALLINE).

naloxone   A pure narcotic antagonist that is used to reverse the effects of overdose, particularly respiratory depression. It is effective only with opiate overdose and does not act on barbiturates. (See NARCAN.)

Naloxone Challenge Test   See NARCAN TEST.

naltrexone   A pure opiate narcotic antagonist that was developed in 1963. It does not produce opiate withdrawal symptoms with sudden discontinuation, and it is long–acting, effective orally, and relatively free of side effects.

nanogram   A billionth of a gram. Laboratory testing of abused drugs, such as THC, is often reported in nanograms per milliliter (a thousandth of a liter).

Narcan® (Endo)   A narcotic antagonist that contains naloxone hydrochloride. It is used to reverse depression effects caused by narcotics (natural and synthetic) and also to diagnose recent opiate use. Unlike other narcotic antagonists it does not produce respiratory depression; in the absence of narcotics it exhibits relatively little pharmacological activity. It will not reverse the effects of respiratory depression caused by non–opiate drugs.

Narcan test   Similar in procedure to the NALLINE TEST, this test is used to determine opiate dependence. Both tests rely upon the narcotic antagonistic properties of the drugs to induce visible symptoms of the presence of opiates, such as pupillary dilation.

narcotic   Narcotics are medically defined as central nervous system depressants with analgesic and sedative properties. Under United States laws, narcotics are considered to be addictive drugs that produce physical and psychological dependence and include opium and its derivatives, heroin, morphine and codeine. Also included are synthetic substances which can produce morphine–type addiction (Demerol, methadone, etc.). Under the Harrison Narcotics Act of 1914, the first U.S. law regulating narcotics, cocaine (which produces psychological but not well–defined physical dependence) was included in the classification but it has been removed under contemporary legislation. Cocaine is still classified as a narcotic in some states, as is marijuana, but many states have taken corrective action on these improper classifications. Both narcotics and non–narcotics are included under the CONTROLLED SUBSTANCES ACT.

Narcotic Addict Rehabilitation Act (NARA)   Enacted in 1966, this federal law established civil commitment of drug abusers to an in–hospital phase of treatment and an aftercare phase in their home communities. In addition, the act provided assistance and support to states and municipalities in developing facilities and treatment programs. Title I of the program covered narcotic addicts charged with certain federal offenses who desired to be committed for treatment in lieu of prosecution. Persons eligible under Title II of the act were addicts convicted of federal crimes who were committed by the court. Title III covered addicts who voluntarily wished to apply for commitment. The National Institute of Drug Abuse (NIDA) was responsible for patients under Title I and the Department of Justice was responsible for those covered under Titles II and III. NARA has been repealed and the federal hospitals at Lexington and Fort Worth have been closed.

narcotic antagonist   A drug that counteracts or blocks the effects of opiate narcotics. In sufficient doses, these drugs can block such physiological effects as the development of tolerance and physical dependency, and can reverse or prevent toxic effects. Some narcotic antagonists have been developed by chemically altering natural or synthetic opiate narcotics. In dependent persons who have not been detoxified, a low dose of an antagonist can also produce dilation of the pupils and this property has been employed for identifying persons who are physically dependent (see NALLINE TEST and NARCAN TEST). Among the best known antagonists are naloxone (NARCAN) and naltrexone.

Narcotics Anonymous (NA)   A self–help organization, founded in 1953, composed of individuals who meet regularly to stabilize and facilitate their recovery from drug addiction. Their rehabilitation involves a 12–step program similar to the one adopted by Alcoholics Anonymous. The organization also publishes informational pamphlets and a quarterly publication, *Voice of Narcotics Anonymous*.

Narcotics Education, Inc.   A private non–profit organization, founded in 1954, that conducts nationwide educational programs for the prevention of drug addiction and alcoholism. The group publishes two subscription publications, *Winner,* a magazine for children in grades three to six, and *Smoke Signals,* a monthly issue on topics related to tobacco. Pamphlets, books and filmstrips are also available for purchase or rental.

nasal septum   The dividing wall inside the nose between the nostrils. Individuals who snort cocaine heavily on a regular basis are inclined to suffer severe nasal problems, including erosions and perforation of the septum. (See COCAINE.)

National Association of State Alcohol and Drug Abuse Directors (NASADAD)   An organization, founded in 1978, that is composed solely of directors of state alcoholism agencies (SAAs) and single state agencies (SSAs) for drug abuse prevention. NASADAD's purpose is to represent and promote the interests of state agencies before Congress and federal agencies, with the aim of encouraging and developing comprehensive programs in each state. The organization is based on two predecessor organizations: the National Association of State Drug Program Coordinators, established in 1971, and the Council of State and Territorial Alcoholism Authorities, established in 1974.

National Clearinghouse for Drug Abuse Information (NCDAI)   A component of the Department of Health and Human Services, NCDAI was established in March 1970 to serve as the federal government's focal point for the collection and dissemination of drug abuse information. In this capacity, NCDAI collects, classifies, stores and disseminates scientific and general information on drug abuse and drug misuse; develops information resource materials; and maintains an inventory of over 300 publications that are distributed to the public without charge in response to phone or mail inquiries. The inventory includes publications targeted to various audiences (parents, educators, students, community program workers, for example). NCDAI also supports a nationwide Drug Abuse Communications Network (DRACON) of satellite information centers affiliated with federal, state and local government agencies, universities and training centers.

National Commission on Marijuana and Drug Abuse Appointed by President Nixon in 1971, the commission was comprised of nationally prominent citizens who undertook a two–year examination of drug use, misuse and abuse. They concluded that old ways of looking at things, and old definitions required a new set of terms and perspectives. The commission issued two reports (1972, 1973) that defined issues, provided data on drug–using behavior, assessed its social impact, and formulated a rationale toward a coherent social policy regarding illicit drugs. It also recommended the decriminalization of marijuana. President Nixon rejected the recommendation.

National Federation of Parents for Drug Free Youth (NFP) This national organization covers over 1,000 self–help parent groups throughout the United States that have banded together to deal with illicit drug use among their children. The NFP promotes, encourages and assists in the formation and strengthening of local parent groups.

National Institute on Alcohol Abuse and Alcoholism (NIAAA) A component institute of the Alcohol, Drug Abuse and Mental Health Administration (which it predates), NIAAA was established in 1971. Its mandate is similar to the NATIONAL INSTI-TUTE ON DRUG ABUSE (NIDA) and it is charged with providing "leadership, policies, and goals for the federal effort in the prevention, control, and treatment of alcohol abuse and alcoholism and the rehabilitation of affected individuals."

NIAAA has published four special reports to the U.S. Congress as part of its information program; the first in 1971, followed by others in 1974, 1978 and 1981. The reports focus on advances in knowledge in the field of alcoholism, effects on health, causes, and treatment methods. The findings are described in extensive detail.

Various research projects in the field are also funded by NIAAA; the most well–known is probably the controversial RAND REPORTS.

National Institute on Drug Abuse (NIDA) Established in 1972, NIDA is a component institute of the Alcohol, Drug Abuse and Mental Health Administration. Its mandate is similar to that of the NATIONAL INSTITUTE ON ALCOHOL ABUSE AND ALCO-HOLISM. NIDA is charged with providing "leadership, policies, and goals for the federal effort in the prevention, control, and treatment of narcotic addiction and drug abuse, and the rehabilitation of affected individuals." Although drug abuse services are now administered primarily at the state level under the new Alcohol, Drug Abuse and Mental Health block grant, NIDA continues to be responsible for providing national leadership in the critical areas of research, research training, data collection and analysis, information dissemination, and technical assistance and it is the lead agency responsible for federal efforts to reduce the demand for drugs.

National Organization for the Reform of Marijuana Laws (NORML) A volunteer citizen action group founded in 1970 to seek changes in U.S. laws regarding marijuana. NORML lobbies for legislative reform of laws, collects and disburses educational material, and provides speakers for interested groups in an effort to end criminal penalties for the possession, use and cultivation of marijuana. An organization of 25,000 members, NORML brought legal action against the Federal Drug Enforcement Administration to make marijuana legally available for medical uses, and was instrumental in the passage of legislation which now allows marijuana to be used as medicine in 33 states.

National Parents' Resource Institute for Drug Education, Inc. (PRIDE)
Based at Georgia State University, PRIDE is a non–profit organization which provides parents, educators, physicians, counselors and other concerned citizens with the most current research informaton on drug abuse. It also helps in the organization of parent groups, parent–school teams and community action groups.

National Prohibition Act   See VOL-STEAD ACT.

Native American Church   See PEYOTE.

Nembutal® (Abbott)   A BARBITURATE sedative that contains pentobarbital sodium. It is used as a sedative, a hypnotic and as preanesthetic medication. Nembutal may be habit–forming and has a high potential for abuse. Physical and psychological dependence can occur. Overdosage can result in circulatory collapse, respiratory depression, diminished reflexes and coma. It is supplied in several forms: Nembutal Granulet 100 mg tablets; Nembutal Sodium Capsules: 30 mg, yellow; 50 mg, orange and white; 100 mg yellow; Nembutal Elixir, 18.2 mg per ml teaspoon; and Nembutal Sodium Solution in ampules and vials for injection. Synonyms: nebbies, nemmies, nemish, nimby, nimbies, yellow bullets, yellow dolls, yellow jackets and yellows.

Netherlands, The   Heroin abuse is on the increase in the Netherlands, just as it is throughout Western Europe. In 1980 the estimated number of heroin addicts was between 10,000 and 12,000. In 1983 the number was estimated to be 15,000: with a population of 14 million this means about 0.1% of the population is affected. Roughly one–third of the heroin addicts belong to ethnic minority groups; Surinamese and Mollucans. Annual consumption of heroin in 1980

(based on an assumed average daily intake equivalent to 50 milligrams of pure heroin) was 182–219 kilograms. Because European addicts generally smoke heroin rather than inject it, consumption rates are somewhat higher than in the United States. As in the rest of the European market, nearly all the heroin originates in Southwest Asia.

The Netherlands has some of the most relaxed hashish legislation in Western Europe. At one time youth centers in Amsterdam permitted the open sale of the drug. There are no estimates of the number of cannabis users in the general Dutch population. However, the percentage of high school students using cannabis is estimated to be 4%.

There are 20 Consultation Bureaus dealing with drug abuse problems in the Nether-lands. They are centered in large and medium–size cities and towns. There are also numerous branches and consulting facilities in smaller areas. The bureaus are funded by grants from the government: 60% is paid by the Ministry of Welfare, Public Health and Culture and 40% by the Ministry of Justice since the bureaus also act as probation offices. In 1983 the consultation bureaus had an estimated 7,200 drug clients. Beside the bureaus, there are counseling centers and day treatment centers financed by local authorities. (The government contributes 90% of all local expenditures as long as the authorities meet certain conditions which conform to its grant scheme for Social Assistance and Services for Youth and Young Adults.) Several religious organizations, private psychiatrists and general practitioners also offer outpatient treatment to drug addicts.

Detoxification centers, addiction clinics and therapeutic communities (offering treatment to those addicted to various drugs including alcohol) help addicts on an inpatient basis. The Health Insurance Funds Act and the Exceptional Medical Expenses Compensation Act finance most of the inpatient treatment centers. Psychiatric and general hospitals also treat drug addicts and together they account for some 650 admissions per year.

Alcohol consumption is widely accepted by the Dutch: 93% of the male population drinks and 82% of the female population. Only 3% of the population recommends abstinence from alcoholic beverages. Two–thirds of the nation's annual consumption takes place in the home and an overwhelming majority approve of drinking by adolescents when they reach the legal age of 16. Although consumption is widespread, less than a quarter of the population drinks daily. Beer is the preferred alcoholic beverage by a vast majority of the country's drinkers.

In 1975 the number of hospital admissions for alcohol–related problems numbered 2,357, up from 1,724 in 1973. This increase prompted a governmental inquiry that was intended to lay the groundwork for the country's first official policy on alcohol. A problem of equal or greater concern is abuse of other drugs aggravated by alcohol. Until an official body is created to oversee the government's as yet undetermined policy, prevention and treatment efforts for alcohol–related problems remain in the hands of private agencies, particularly the National Commission on Alcoholism, a national temperance organization. Indications are that a number of programs are forthcoming from nationalized industries, law enforcement groups and medical associations.

New Zealand   Aside from alcohol and tobacco, which are the major health hazards in New Zealand, cannabis is the most abused drug and most of it is produced locally. LSD and the synthetic drug, bromo–DMA (which has effects similar to LSD), were popular during the 1970s but their use has been rapidly declining. Heroin abuse is also down; principally because the drug is in short supply and consequently costs $500–$700 a gram. The GOLDEN TRIANGLE is the traditional

source of heroin for New Zealand and indications point to a bumper crop in 1983 which may mean heroin will be more readily available in the future. Amphetamine and barbiturate use remain fairly widespread and have proved difficult to monitor. Deaths classified by the police as "drug–related" usually involved the use of these two drugs.

In 1977 the New Zealand government established a Caucus Committee to recommend legislative and administrative action to control the misuse of licit and illicit drugs. A 1978 act substantially increased the penalties for possession and dealing. The maximum penalty for dealing is now life imprisonment.

One of the government's most important though circumscribed powers is the use of listening devices. This power was introduced in 1979 and there is no doubt of its value in monitoring the activities of those thought to be dealing in drugs. In the year ending March 1982, for example, prosecutions resulted from nearly all warrants in force. If it had not been for the use of listening devices several of the biggest drug importers in New Zealand would not have been apprehended.

All members of the police force are now trained in drug identification and are expected to handle drug offenses in the course of their normal duties. Police units are also upgrading their intelligence network and new units are concentrating their efforts on stemming such national trends as the buildup of drug organizations, chemist shop burglaries, and criminal gangs. The government attributes the declining use of hard drugs to these concentrated efforts. The effort is not just concentrated on hard drugs in particular: from January through November 1982, 604.5 kilos of cannabis leaf material were seized.

Along with stepping up police action, the government is continuing its work in the education field and in the treatment and rehabilitation of addicts.

As in most other countries, alcohol remains the major drug of abuse. Among a population of just over three million, surveys estimate that there are some 50,000 "chronic alcoholics," and another 200,000 "excessive drinkers." Adolescents have easy access to alcohol and the pattern of consumption relates to this fact. Annual per capita consumption of absolute alcohol rose from 5.8 liters in 1965 to 8.4 liters in 1975. In 1977, 45% of fatal traffic accidents were attributed to alcohol; hospital admission rates because of alcoholism are also up. The social cost of alcoholism to the country is overwhelming and there is an acknowledged need for new clinics to deal with the problem. Existing efforts to control alcoholism are indirect and tend to target the potential problem rather than the existing one. Recent revisions of regulations concerning the sale and public consumption of alcohol, and stricter enforcement of legislation concerning drunk driving will not handle the problem without concerted educational measures.

NIAAA   See NATIONAL INSTITUTE OF ALCOHOL ABUSE AND ALCOHOLISM.

nicotine   ($C_{10}H_{14}N_2$)   Used for centuries by natives of the Americas, nicotine was first encountered by Europeans during the 16th century explorations of the New World. It was named in honor of Jean Nicot who claimed that it had great medicinal potential. Columbus noted that Indians "drank the smoke" from dried leaf rolls, not for medicinal purposes, but rather for the paradoxical stimulant–sedative effects it had on the mind and body. To date no therapeutic or healthful applications of nicotine have been found.

Nicotine is a potent oily alkaloid found in concentrations of 2–5% in the tobacco plant, *Nicotiana tabacum*. Native to South America, the plant is now cultivated in areas throughout the world. Pure nicotine is colorless and has a strong odor and acrid taste. It is highly poisonous and, when dissolved in water, has been used as a potent insecticide.

Volatized somewhat by heat, nicotine is inhaled as smoke from cigarettes, cigars and pipes. It is also ingested through chewing and snuffing tobacco. It is estimated that nearly 45 million Americans smoke tobacco, making it the most addictive drug in the United States.

Since colonial times nicotine has supported a large and prosperous tobacco industry. Despite its ill effects on people's health, it was consumed as fast as it could be supplied. One Bohemian observer in 1662 indicated that "the common people are so given up to the abuse that they imagine they cannot live without several pipes of tobacco a day—thus squandering in these necessitous times the pennies they need for their daily bread." The use of tobacco was prohibited by the Roman Catholic Church as early as the 17th century, and Russian czars were known to torture smokers. The Sultan of Constantinople imposed the death penalty for smoking in 1633, but "even the fear of death was of no avail with the passionate devotees of the habit."

Before the 20th century most nicotine was taken by chewing tobacco, smoking pipes and cigars, and inhaling snuff. In the early 1900s cigarettes became the most popular method of taking nicotine. This popularity came about for several reasons. First, public health warnings stated that chewing tobacco had been shown to cause tuberculosis. Unaware of the high risks of cigarette smoking—irreparable damage to the lungs, heart, blood and nervous system—people switched to smoking instead. Second, the cigarette industry began using automatic machinery for mass production which lowered the price of cigarettes. The industry also embarked on extensive advertising campaigns. Third, and probably the foremost reason for the public switch, was the fact that a new "milder" type of Virginia tobacco was used in cigarettes and it allowed for deeper inhalation.

As cigarette smoking increased in popularity so did the number of anti–smoking leagues and campaigns. Several states enacted cigarette prohibition and other states passed laws prohibiting the sale of cigarettes to young people. Despite the campaigns and regulations, however, the production of cigarettes increased from 4.2 billion (1900–1909) to 80 billion (1920–1929); by 1970 the figure had jumped to 583 billion.

In 1964 the first Surgeon General's report was issued. Entitled *Report of the Surgeon General''s Advisory Committee on Smoking and Health,* it received extensive media coverage and convinced many smokers of the risks they were taking. For a while cigarette sales dropped. President Johnson signed legislation, effective on January 1, 1966, requiring all cigarette packs and cartons to carry the statement: "Caution: Cigarette smoking may be hazardous to your health." In 1971 cigarette advertising was banned from radio and television. The ban resulted in increased print advertising and in 1977 the U.S. Department of Agriculture reported that cigarette companies had spent $779 million that year alone on promotion and advertising. The tobacco industry is one of the world's wealthiest enterprises.

There has been an increase in recent years in the manufacture of filter and low–tar low–nicotine cigarettes. Brands of cigarettes now on the market have tar and nicotine yields ranging from 1 mg to 20 mg. Although low–tar and nicotine cigarettes may be safer, there is no such thing as a "safe" cigarette. Because of the smaller amount of nicotine, however, people may become less dependent and eventually stop smoking altogether. Opponents of "safer" cigarettes argue that users will find them less satisfying and simply smoke more of them, which will make the health risks even greater.

Studies have shown that smokers are more likely to use other drugs, particularly alcohol and marijuana. This is especially disturbing in the light of teenage smoking statistics. A 1979 government survey showed there were 1.7 million teenage girls and 1.6 million teenage boys who smoked. It is thought that peer pressure, the "kick" of risk–taking, and parental use of cigarettes are the main reasons why teenagers begin smoking. School and government–funded anti–smoking programs are becoming increasingly popular and they have obviously had some success: during the period 1974–1979 the number of teenage smokers dropped from 15.6% to 11.7%.

Classification: Nicotine is both a transient STIMULANT and a SEDATIVE to the central nervous system and to both voluntary and involuntary muscle systems. It is physically and psychologically addictive and some studies indicate that it is even more addictive than heroin. The ingestion of nicotine results in a transient stimulation or "kick" because it causes a discharge of epinephrine from the adrenal cortex. This stimulates the central nervous system, as well as other endocrine glands which cause a sudden release of glycogen (a simple sugar). Stimulation is then followed by depression and fatigue, leading the abuser to seek more nicotine to restimulate the adrenals. Meanwhile, stress causes a rise in the acidity level of urine, thus enhancing the elimination rate of nicotine and the further need for more nicotine. Many people who try to break this vicious cycle and are not able to, become further depressed. Perhaps the most devastating social effect of nicotine is that it leaves its countless addicts feeling guilty and/or powerless.

Effects: Pure nicotine is highly poisonous, and only a drop or two (about 50 mg) on the tongue can kill a person within minutes. Ingesting a cigarette or cigar may well prove lethal or, at the least, produce serious physical and mental reactions. There are approximately 15–20 mg of nicotine in a typical cigarette (although some of the newer low–nicotine brands contain as little as 0.5) but usually less than 1 mg reaches the bloodstream. The amount can vary according to how frequenctly the smoker inhales, whether or not the cigarette is filtered, the type of filter, and so on. Nicotine taken in smoke takes only 60 seconds to reach the brain, but has a direct effect on the body for up to 30 minutes. For this reason, smokers who are dependent on nicotine—and virtually all regular smokers are—generally find that they need at least one cigarette every half hour. This can add up to about a pack and a half per day. It is difficult to discern the exact effects of nicotine since it is taken in combination with many other substances found in tobacco. Cigarette smoke is mainly comprised of a dozen gases (particularly carbon monoxide) and the particulate matter, nicotine and tar. The tar in a cigarette (approximately 15 mg, though as little as half this amount is found in low–tar brands) disposes the user to a high expectancy rate of lung cancer, emphysema and bronchial disorders. The carbon monoxide in the smoke increases the chances of being vulnerable to cardiovascular diseases. But in any case, nicotine plays a significant role in many serious diseases, most of which have high fatality rates. Bronchial and cardiovascular disorders are increased by the effects that nicotine has on bronchial and heart muscles, and the arteries. Chronic bronchitis and emphysema are particularly common diseases among smokers. Nine–tenths of those who suffer Buerger's disease are smokers: this affliction involves the progressive constriction of the vascular system, particularly in the legs. By impeding blood circulation, it eventually leads to arterial occlusions. These cause gangrenous conditions that often lead to amputation. For much the same reason, users of nicotine have at least a 70% greater chance of suffering from coronary and cerebral occlusions which manifest as heart attacks and strokes.

The risk of congestive heart failure is also increased by the effects of nicotine. Coronary and cerebral thromboses (blood clots in the blood vessels of the heart or brain) and emboli (dislodged particles which break off from a main clot and travel through the vascular system) are also precipitated indirectly by nicotine since the vasoconstriction increases the possibility of blood flow interference.

Bronchial and pulmonary dysfunction are caused partly by the displacement of oxygen by the carbon monoxide in cigarette smoke (especially in the case of emphysema), and by the irritant effect of the tars.

The most common and serious of all long–term effects of smoking is lung cancer, which proves to be fatal in over 90% of cases. Relatively rare in the early 1900s, today lung cancer is a leading cause of death from cancer. An average male smoker runs a 10–times greater risk of death from lung cancer than a nonsmoker: women smokers run a 5–times greater risk. The tar in a cigarette contains many constituents known to cause cancer in experimental animals. The hair–like cilia on the membranes of the lungs (which work to keep the lungs clean) can become damaged or paralyzed by the tar and when the cilia are not working properly the lungs become vulnerable to pneumonia and chronic obstructive pulmonary disease. Cancer of the esophagus, mouth, lips, and larynx are also associated with cigarette smoking.

Cigar and pipe smoking do not have as great an effect on health as cigarette smoking, probably because the smoke is not usually inhaled. Pipe and cigar smokers do run a greater risk of cancer of the oral cavity, however, and lip cancer has been related to pipe smoking.

Nicotine has many deleterious effects on pregnant women and lactating mothers. Women who smoke run two times the risk of having a stillborn infant. Most babies born of women smokers are smaller than normal and they are also frequently premature. Babies sometimes suffer overt signs of nicotine addiction and withdrawal, and are often afflicted with related mental and physical impairments. Miscarriages are much more likely among smokers, and congenital heart defects (those occurring at birth) are more likely if the father smokes. In addition, women who smoke generally have earlier menopause and, if they also take oral contraceptives, are much more prone to cardiovasular and cerebrovascular diseases; this is especially true for women over 30. Lactating mothers excrete nicotine directly through breast milk, and pregnant women transport it through their blood supply to the fetus.

Smoking among women increased dramatically during World War II when women began "doing men's work." It is now estimated that 30.5% of the adult women in the United States are smokers. While the number of male smokers has dropped sharply over the last 20 years there has been no similar decline for women. The number of teenage girls who smoke is larger than the number of teenage boys.

Besides the many serious long–term effects of nicotine, there are also less severe short–term ones. Sweating, vomiting, and throat irritation number among them, along with others that typically lead to more serious conditions over longer periods: increased heart rate and blood pressure, leading to myocardial dysfunctions and arteriosclerosis; a drop in skin temperature accompanied by increased respiration which may cause chronic hyperventilation; and dimness or blurring of vision culminating in blindness, a condition known as Tobacco Amblyopia.

Effects on Nonsmokers: Research studies indicate that the health of nonsmokers can be affected by the toxic substances, particularly carbon monoxide, that are released in the air around them by smokers. Nonsmokers are also subject to eye and nasal irritation, headache and cough from cigarette smoke. In some parts of the United States recent legislation and regulations now restrict smoking to certain areas or prohibit it altogether.

Addictive Aspects: Casual use of even small amounts of nicotine (three or four cigarettes, for example) can develop into a definite physical and psychological dependence on the drug in just a matter of days. The dependence increases until it reaches a fairly stable level at which the user stays for many years; often for the rest of his life. About 75% of smokers attempt to overcome their addiction but only one out of four under the age of 60 usually succeed. Interruption of nicotine use leads to a WITHDRAWAL syndrome, featuring irritability, weight gain, depression and preoccupation with the lack of smoking. It generally takes a full year to break the habit. Fatigue, dizziness, headache and shortness of breath are physical characteristics of withdrawal which usually subside rapidly. Because smoking is sometimes used as a tranquilizer during periods of stress, or as a pleasure–enhancer after meals, during coffee breaks and in such social situations as parties, the psychological difficulties involved in withdrawal (quitting) can be far worse than the physical difficulties.

To help people break their dependency on the drug, a number of nicotine "congeners" (chemically similar substances) have been developed to displace it. Lobeline is the most common of these. It is used in Nikoban, and marketed as an aid to breaking the habit but is thought by many to be little more than a placebo. Nicotine chewing gums and pills have also been employed in this way, but they usually give the user as much nicotine as he gets from smoking and hence have little effect on breaking the nicotine habit even if they do sometimes help break the smoking habit.

Smoking–withdrawal clinics and support groups have become particularly popular in the last 15 or 20 years, although the majority of people who stop smoking still tend to do it on their own without outside help. The National Clearinghouse for Smoking and Health reports that from 1966 to 1970 the number of ex–cigarette smokers in the adult population rose by 10 million; from 19 million in 1966 to 29 million in 1970. There has also been a slow but steady decline in the per capita consumption of cigarettes per day; 11.73 in 1967 to 10.86 in 1971.

Tolerance: The body rapidly develops tolerance to the short–term effects of nicotine, thus making it more likely that the habit will take hold. Increased and more frequent dosages taken in order to satisfy the craving for nicotine are also quickly adapted to.

NIDA   See NATIONAL INSTITUTE ON DRUG ABUSE.

niopo   Pods from the plant *Acacia niopo* which grows in Venezeula. They are ground up and used as a snuff which produces psychedelic effects.

nitrous oxide   (N_2O) A general anesthesia normally used in dentistry. It is also called nitrogen monoxide and has the common name "laughing gas." When supplemented with other agents it is used for surgical anesthesia. It has been abused for its eurphoric effects and mild hallucinations. Sustained inhalation of nitrous oxide without adequate oxygen can result in anoxia (arrested respiration) and death.

Noctec® (Squibb)   A sedative hypnotic that contains CHLORAL HYDRATE, and is used for nocturnal sedation and as a pre– and post–operative medication. It may be habit–forming and when taken with alcohol or other central nervous system depressants it can have an additive effect. It is supplied as Noctec Syrup, a flavored syrup containing 500 mg per ml teaspoon; and as Noctec Capsules in 250 mg and 500 mg red capsules.

Noludar® (Roche)   A sedative hypnotic that contains METHYPRYLON and is used for insomnia. Physical and psychological de-

pendence can occur and it has the potential for abuse. When taken with alcohol or other central nervous system depressants it can have an additive effect. Overdosage can result in somnolence, respiratory depression, confusion and coma. It is supplied in 300 mg amethyst and white capsules, and in 50 mg and 200 mg white tablets.

nonaddictive pathological drinker (nonaddictive alcoholic)   A person who handles and seeks relief from unconscious problems and discomfort by drinking excessively. The pathological drinker is usually impaired in some way by his drinking but does not manifest the loss of control or compulsion which is characteristic of alcohol addiction.

North Conway Institute (NCI)
Founded in 1951 by a group of concerned clergy and lay persons, the institute is an outgrowth of the Yale University School of Alcohol Studies. It is an interfaith, ecumenical, non–profit organization, governed by a board of church people, which works as a catalyst with religious and secular organizations in all areas of alcohol and drug problems. In addition to holding an annual seminar, NCI also serves as a resource center.

Norway   Although Norway has one of the most stringent approaches to alcohol consumption (and drunk driving) in the world, the government's attitude toward the abuse of other drugs has not changed in recent years even though there has been an increase in use. According to the government, existing programs will be continued and general preventive measures will be taken but no new treatment programs will be implemented. This is because the government looks upon the drug abuse problem as a symptom of personal, family and social problems.

Up to 1940, drug dependence was not considered a problem in Norway. During the

1940s there was an increase in the use of tranquilizers, particularly in the middle and older age groups. By 1965 use of drugs had spread to younger people and the favorite substance was usually marijuana or hashish. Abuse of tranquilizers continued and amphetamines began to make their appearance.

Illicit trade in drugs has, until recently, not been an issue in Norway. In addition, possession of narcotic drugs (with the exception of heroin) is legal. Distribution, possession and use of marijuana, hashish and LSD are unlawful. As of 1976, the government reported that there was no heroin problem in Norway, although methadone and some morphine–based drugs had gained popularity. Doctors were specifically warned not to prescribe methadone.

Addicts with complex and serious addiction problems receive treatment in mental health institutions. But because the government believes that drug dependency is not an illness but a symptom of personal or social problems, a generally accepted treatment model for drug dependency does not exist. Instead, the problem is approached from the standpoint of prevention. Along with educational programs, the government believes in implementing programs that help the youth of the country channel its energies and demands for acceptance in new directions.

Developments since 1975 have included the establishment of therapeutic communities modeled after Daytop and Phoenix House in the United States. As of 1983, regional contact groups have been set up in various counties which establish contact between country doctors, schools, social services, and the police and prison systems in an effort to coordinate information and help on drug abuse questions. Tighter pharmaceutical control has also been implemented and these recent controls may be an indication that dependency on drugs other than alcohol is being acknowledged as a specific problem in need of special attention.

Although there is very little information available concerning the specific nature of treatment for alcoholics, in 1980 the Norwegian government proposed over 30 measures to reduce alcohol consumption. While the level of consumption is substantially below that of other European countries, it has nonetheless been increasing each year. According to a 1979 report in *News of Norway*, the consumption level rose by approximately 156% between 1955 and 1979. This notable increase no doubt accounts for the stringent approach to alcoholism in the country. A driver with a blood alcohol concentration of 0.05% or more must serve a minimum of three weeks in prison, and if a person causes a motor vehicle accident while drunk there is no insurance compensation. In addition, there is a ban on advertising alcoholic beverages in the print media and a ban on wine–making in the home.

noscapine   An opium alkaloid that is non-addictive and is used as a cough suppressant in cough medicines. It is a Schedule IV drug under the Controlled Substances Act.

Nubain® (Endo)   A synthetic NARCOTIC agonist–antagonist analgesic which is chemically related to both OXYMORPHONE and NALOXONE. A potent analgesic, it is used for the relief of moderate to severe pain, as a pre–operative analgesia and as a supplement to surgical anesthesia. Nubain contains nalbuphine hydrochloride and caution should be used in prescribing it to a person with a history of narcotic abuse because psychological and physical dependence, along with tolerance, can develop. Nubain is supplied in ampules for injection. If it is administered intravenously onset of action occurs in two to three minutes; onset time is less than 15 minutes if administered intramuscularly or subcutaneously. Analgesic activity can range from three to six hours.

Numorphan® (Endo)   A potent analgesic that contains the opium derivative OXYMOR-PHONE and is similar to morphine in its effect. It may be habit–forming and physical dependence can occur. A Schedule II drug, it is supplied in suppositories, solution (for injection), and in 10 mg tablets.

nutmeg   The dried seed of *Myristica fragrans,* an evergreen tree indigenous to East India. MACE, its seed coat, has similar properties. Both are common cooking spices as well as HALLUCINOGENS. The two hallucinogenic substances in both nutmeg and mace are elemicin and myristicin which are closely related to MESCALINE and TMA.

Because of their unpleasant side effects, nutmeg and mace have limited popularity. They are used chiefly by prison inmates who have little access to other drugs and by teenagers as substitutes for illegal drugs.

In their powdered forms the substances may be brewed into a tea and then drunk or added to a hot beverage such as hot chocolate. Some users add them to orange juice or to mashed bananas.

A normal dose is one to two tablespoons, or about 10 grams. Occasionally these substances are snorted but they are poorly absorbed when used this way and can be irritating and mildly painful. They can also be obtained in an oil form which is nearly unpalatable.

Effects: Commonly, nutmeg and mace produce a euphoric or intoxicating effect not unlike a mescaline high, in conjunction with unpleasant physical effects such as nausea and dizziness. In high doses—over 20 grams—the substances can produce more intense effects, ranging from strong visual hallucinations to feelings of fear, anxiety and sometimes acute panic. Physical reactions intensify with higher doses: vomiting, rapid heartbeat, excessive thirst, bloodshot eyes, temporary constipation and difficulty in urinating are all typical. Physical reactions may

begin within 45 minutes after ingestion; psychological effects usually occur after one to two hours. The effects generally last two to four hours and then begin to subside, though the user may experience residual effects for up to 24 hours.

Sources: Nutmeg and mace are common grocery store items and are found on the spice shelves of most households and eating establishments.

Traffic and control: No laws regulate the sale of these substances.

nutrition   Nutritional deficiencies usually arise from the prolonged use of drugs. Drugs often decrease the appetite, change the sense of smell and taste, and alter metabolic processes which can result in hindered absorption and hastened excretion, and impair the use and storage of nutrients.

When an addict is in a drug–induced state he is often disinterested in food, and in the case of an alcoholic the individual will often prefer to devote his time and energy to drinking instead of eating. If funds are limited, an addict will generally use his money for drugs rather than food. The neglect of good eating habits is also a consequence of the disorganized life addicts lead and heroin addicts often experience large weight losses. Drugs do not contain vitamins, proteins or minerals so replacing food intake with drugs will obviously cause problems. Alcohol does contain calories but they are not the kind of calories that can be stored for later use, nor do they aid in building body tissue as carbohydrates, proteins and fats do.

The use of marijuana often brings on periods of increased appetite; the same is true of morphine early in the addictive process. The foods craved, however, are usually high in carbohydrates and low in nutrition ("junk" foods such as soda, candy and other sweets). These foods are often picked for their convenience and low cost.

Some drugs are actually taken to depress

the appetite. When taken in large doses, anorectics, particularly amphetamines, can lead to ketosis—the process in which a low carbohydrate diet causes the body's fat stores to be broken down for energy faster than they can be used by the body. Body protein can eventually waste away during prolonged and heavy amphetamine or cocaine use.

Barbiturate users experience a decrease in the absorption of thiamine and an increase in urinary ascorbic acid. Barbiturate and heroin users also have low serum B vitamin levels. A bad diet, especially insufficient consumption of leafy green vegetables, can cause low folate (folic acid) levels, further complicating their B–complex deficiencies. Heroin users frequently suffer from acute and chronic infections which can alter their nutritional needs. Hepatitis, a common occurrence among heroin users, can cause decreased appetite and nausea.

Some drugs, however, will increase appetite and result in weight gain. This is particularly true of phenothiazines, such as Thorazine®.

The drugs which have the least effect on nutrition are the benzodiazepines (tranquilizers such as Librium® and Valium®). Unlike other drugs they do not disturb metabolic functions.

Drug use, particularly alcohol, can also impair the digestion of food and the absorption of nutrients into the blood, thus causing malnutrition. Alcohol can also interfere with the activation of vitamins by the liver cells, which often results in deficiency diseases. Some theorists suggest that vitamin deficiencies play a role in the initial development of alcoholism but this theory has not been proven and most nutritional deficiencies appear as a result of alcoholism, not the cause. Alcohol is absorbed rapidly from an empty stomach and more slowly from a full stomach. Consequently, nutrition plays an important role in the rate that alcohol is absorbed.

The chronic drinker suffers from malabsorption of folate thiamin and B12. The diarrhea which alcoholics often suffer from causes a loss of fat and fat soluble vitamins, water, electrolytes and minerals. A damaged liver has difficulty in converting vitamins into their usable forms, and it cannot store vitamins well. The body needs increased amounts of vitamins and proteins to restore the damage that alcohol does to tissues and from bleeding. So the nutrient deficiencies of the alcoholic are multiple and severe with malnutrition compounding the effects of alcohol on almost every body system.

Nutrition also plays an important role in the treatment of alcoholism. High protein diets and massive amounts of B vitamins are prescribed, along with regularly scheduled meals, because the lowering of blood sugar at any time of day increases the desire for alcohol. Although good nutrition is not a cure for alcoholism, an alcoholic who is properly nourished may find it easier to abstain. The correction of nutritional problems is also an important part of rehabilitation in the case of other drugs.

nystagmus   Involuntary rapid eyeball movement. It is a common symptom of toxic reaction resulting from excessive drug use. (See also EYES.)

O

Obetrol® (Obetrol)   A single entity AMPHETAMINE that is used as an anorectic for weight control and in the treatment of narcolepsy and Minimal Brain Dysfunction. Tolerance can develop and as with other amphetamines, psychological dependence and social disability can occur. It has a significant potential for abuse, and when taken with alcohol or other central nervous system depressants it can have an additive effect. Overdosage can result in restlessness, tremors, rapid respiration, hallucinations and confusion. It is supplied in 10 mg blue and 20 mg pink tablets.

Odyssey Resources, Inc.   Founded in 1966 as a treatment center for adult drug addicts in New York City, Odyssey Houses are now located in other parts of the United States as well as in Australia and New Zealand. They are drug–free, therapeutic communities which are psychiatrically oriented and believe that personal growth can replace the need for drugs. Odyssey Houses now treat a wide range of patients: adolescents, alcoholics, female addicts with children, and child abuse victims. Odyssey claims a success rate of 98% of all residents who have graduated from their program. This success rate is based on follow–ups of up to five years. A recent study showed that 60% of all residents who had left against medical advice, but had spent at least four months in the program, have remained drug–free despite their failure to complete the program. A large number leave before the four month period. Odyssey Houses are staffed by 50% professional personnel and 50% trained ex–addicts.

ololiuqui   See MORNING GLORY SEEDS.

opiates   Opium alkaloids: heroin, codeine and morphine.

opioids   Synthetic drugs with characteristics similar to OPIATES.

opium   A narcotic which acts as a depressant on the central nervous system (CNS). Unlike other CNS depressants, however, such as barbiturates and alcohol, narcotics also relieve pain.

Opium is made by air drying the juice which has been extracted from the unripe seed pods of the oriental poppy *(Papaver somniferum)*. The resulting brownish gum is then formed into bricks or cakes which eventually harden.

There is evidence that opium has been used since prehistoric times. The opium poppy is thought to have originated in Asia Minor and was first used medicinally in Egypt. From there, its use spread to Greece. Arab traders carried it to India and China where it was used to control dysentery and for its euphoric and sedative effects. Opium use became so widespread in China and was considered so harmful that the Chinese government tried to control its importation, sale and use. This was opposed by the British because it interfered with their profitable trade in opium grown in India, and led to the Opium War (1839–42). The British won the war and as a result, opium cultivation and importation were legalized in China and Chinese emigrants carried the habit of opium smoking to the United States and elsewhere.

In the early 1500s, the physician Paracelsus made a tincture of opium (powdered opium dissolved in alcohol) he called laudanum; it was the first medicinal form of opium. In Europe laudanum was used to relieve pain and control dysentery, and as a cough suppressant and sedative. It became a standard drug until the end of the 19th century when its use began to decline. Several other opium mixtures were developed in the 1700s and 1800s but the most important was paregoric, a tincture of opium combined with camphor. Although considered an old–fashioned remedy today, it is still used to control diarrhea and is listed in Schedule III of the Controlled Substances Act. However, it is obtainable in some places without a prescription and heroin addicts often resort to it when they cannot get their usual "fix."

The danger of developing dependence on these staple opium remedies was not well understood, and by the end of the 19th century many people including famous poets and writers had become addicted. After doctors became aware of the problem, laws were passed making opium and its derivatives available only on prescription. The first of these was the 1914 Harrison Narcotics Act which placed opium under strict federal control. Other legislation followed, culminating in the Controlled Substances Act of 1970 which regulated all drugs likely to be abused. The drugs are listed under five schedules according to their abuse potential. Heroin is a Schedule I drug, and drugs containing narcotics such as opium are listed in Schedule II.

The chemical substance (alkaloid) in opium which causes its effects is morphine. Morphine was first extracted from opium in 1803 and because it was found to be a more effective drug, the medical use of opium began to decline. Except for a few prescription drugs, it is rarely used medically today. Only two of the alkaloids extracted from opium—morphine and the milder codeine—are still in clinical use.

When heroin, a derivative of morphine, was developed in 1898 it was heralded as a better pain killer than morphine and a highly effective cough suppressant. Considered to be nonaddictive, physicians used heroin to treat opium and morphine addicts until the drug's own—even worse—addictive effects were recognized. By that time addicts whose opium and morphine supplies had been cut off by stringent laws, and the underworld, had discovered the far greater potency of heroin. By the early 1900s heroin had replaced both opium and morphine on the street and the era of the "junkie" was born. Today the manufacture and use of heroin is completely illegal in the United States and it is considered to have no medical use.

Opium smoking, the most common form of abuse, is practiced mostly in China, Hong Kong and Southeast Asia. It was introduced into the United States by Chinese immigrants in the 19th century. More recently some American soldiers acquired the habit during the war in Vietnam. Illicit use of opium in the United States, however, is mostly confined to such opium–containing remedies as paregoric which is used intravenously—with disastrous results on the veins—by heroin addicts when they are cut off from their regular supplies. The use of opium per se is not a major drug problem in America—the main problems lie primarily with morphine and its derivative heroin.

Appearance: Raw opium comes in a solid mass of varying shape weighing from one–half to five pounds. It is processed in several ways.

Though now rarely used, granulated opium is a medically approved drug for treating diarrhea.

Powdered opium is more finely ground than the granulated variety. It is used in the manufacture of a few prescription drugs, notably PANTOPON and B & O SUPPRETTES.

Dissolved in water, filtered, then boiled down into a sticky paste the substance becomes the preparation used by opium smokers.

Dissolved in alcohol, the substance becomes the tincture of opium used in making laudanum and paregoric.

Broken down chemically into its alkaloids (chemical substances found in all plants), the substance yields morphine and codeine.

Effects: Used medically, opium dulls sensations of pain, controls diarrhea because it has a constipating action, suppresses coughing, induces drowsiness, alleviates anxiety, and gives a feeling of euphoria or well–being. It is the drug's euphoric effect which the opium abuser is seeking, as well as its ability to make him indifferent to hunger, sexual urges, tension and anxiety. Unlike barbiturates, alcohol and other drugs, narcotics do not trigger aggressive behavior. On the contrary, they usually make the user docile and dreamy.

There can also be unpleasant side effects with opium use such as nausea and vomiting, but the user is normally indifferent to these reactions because they are quickly followed by sedation and euphoria.

Tolerance: Opium tolerance develops as inexorably as tolerance to barbiturates and other CNS drugs. With regular use, dosage must be steadily increased to achieve the desired effects. As dosage increases dependence can develop.

Dependence: Long–term use of opium can cause both psychological and physical dependence. With psychological dependence, the user has a craving for the drug and feels life is not worth living without it. With physical dependence, the body grows to rely on the drug to take over some of its normal

---

History of Opium

5000 B.C.	**Opium is known in Mesopotamia and mentioned in Assyrian medical texts.**
1500 B.C.	**Used as an anesthetic by Egyptian physicians.**
c.7th century	**Opium poppy is brought to China via Middle East and India.**
1200	**Used in the Middle East as a medicine and an intoxicant.**
1541	**Paracelsus, Swiss alchemist, introduces laudanum and it becomes popular throughout Europe.**
1650	**Opium smoking becomes rampant in China.**
c.1803	**Morphine is isolated from opium and used medically in 1825.**
1839-1842	**Opium War between China and England.**
1866	**Use of opium and morphine during Civil War in U.S. creates estimated 400,000 addicts.**
1870s	**Sales of patent medicines containing opium proliferate in Europe and America.**
1875	**San Francisco passes first ordinance against opium dens.**
1909	**Legislation is passed making opium smoking a criminal offense.**
1914	**Harrison Narcotics Act taxes manufacture, importation and distribution of opium and products containing opium.**
1920s	**Opium dens operate in most U.S. ctities.**
1930s	**Opium abuse almost completely replaced by heroin.**
1931	**Agreement for Control of Opium Smoking in the Far East is signed at Bangkok.**
1942	**Opium Poppy Control Act prohibits cultivation except under license in U.S.**
1946	**Iran prohibits opium cultivation.**
1948	**World Health Organization becomes responsible for narcotics control. Only a few nations are allowed to cultivate opium for export.**
1970	**Controlled Substances Act classifies medicines containing opium as Schuedules II, III and V drugs.**
1971	**Turkey agrees to stop cultivation of opium poppies in 1972.**
1980s	**Opium itself not a major abuse problem in the U.S. In the Middle and Far East it is still smoked or eaten.**

functions. When the drug is stopped or sharply reduced, physical reactions of varying degrees of severity follow.

Withdrawal: When physical dependence has developed, opium users experience a number of withdrawal symptoms if the drug is suddenly stopped. These develop rapidly and reach their height in two or three days; they continue for a week or more before subsiding, although it may take as long as six months for some effects to wear off. There are occasional fatalities among deeply dependent users who are in poor health but opium withdrawal is much less dangerous to life than barbiturate withdrawal.

Since morphine is the alkaloid in opium which causes its effects, the symptoms of opium withdrawal are the same as those for morphine—anxiety, restlessness, yawning, tears, runny nose, nausea, diarrhea, cramps, general body aches, gooseflesh and dehydration.

Source: The opium poppy is grown in China, Southeast Asia, Mexico, Turkey and Lebanon. The amount of raw opium required by legitimate drug houses to manufacture morphine and other prescription drugs is only a fraction of the supply available. The rest makes its way into black market laboratories in Europe and elsewhere to produce illicit heroin and morphine.

Traffic and control: Raw opium is too bulky for profitable long–distance smuggling and does not present a major traffic and control problem in the U.S. Even morphine is in the form of a solid block before it is processed into a soluble salt. In North America the real problem is heroin. It has only half the bulk of morphine and control of smuggling is extremely difficult and requires international cooperation.

Synonyms: O, op, black pills, black stuff, gum, hop, tar.

oral administration   See ADMINISTRATION.

oral fixation   A psychoanalytic theory which is suggested by some to be the cause of alcoholism. The earliest stage of psychosexual development occurs during the time when an infant's only means of achieving security and release from tension is through stimulation of the oral cavity. According to the oral fixation theory, if an infant is deprived of a warm and loving relationship during this time, he will be traumatized and will continue to seek gratification of his primary emotional hunger. In other words he becomes fixated at the oral stage of development and his unconscious desire for warmth and nurturance cannot be satisfied in normal interpersonal relationships. An alcoholic seeks liquid nourishment as a way of generating sensations of warmth and satisfaction, much as an infant seeks to fill his emptiness through oral ingestion. Along with this need for gratification, there is the alcoholic's feelings of anger and rage at parents who failed him—a rage which he redirects through alcohol consumption.

organic disorder   A disorder which is the result of known or hypothesized pathological changes in the tissues, as opposed to a functional disorder which is a condition in which one or more of the normal activities of the organism cannot be properly performed, though there is no known pathological change in organic structure.

organic solvents   See VOLATILE HYDROCARBONS and INHALANTS.

organized crime   See CRIME, ORGANIZED.

outreach   The effort to reach out to a drug dependent person who does not voluntarily enter a treatment situation is called outreach. It may be made by street workers who are recovered addicts or by social workers visiting in storefront coffee houses where young people come to socialize.

overdose   The ingestion of a drug in an amount larger than the body's system can deal with. Whether accidental or deliberate, overdose is a great danger in the use and abuse of drugs.

A deliberate overdose of a drug, particularly a short–acting barbiturate such as amobarbital, secobarbital or pentobarbital, is a widely used method of suicide. Studies have shown that a high percentage of those who use this method are also alcoholics. Although the amount of a barbiturate required to produce a lethal dose can vary from person to person, it is usually in the range of 10–15 times a normal dose. Cardiovascular collapse precedes respiratory depression in a lethal dose and is followed by coma and death.

Accidental overdose can result from a variety of factors. In recent years the increase in polydrug use has been a leading factor in overdose cases, particularly the use of alcohol with other drugs. Because of the synergistic effect, even a small, normal dose of a drug can prove fatal when taken with alcohol. The combination of barbiturates and amphetamines, often taken by amphetamine dependent people to bring themselves down from a "wired up" state or to ward off withdrawal symptoms, can also prove fatal. In polydrug use a person can never be completely certain what his or her reaction will be to a combination of drugs, and overdoses are common.

An overdose of an amphetamine, which is a central nervous system stimulant, is characterized by hyperactivity, restlessness, tremulousness and mental confusion. In severe overdose the symptoms are delirium, cardiac arrhythmia and convulsions, followed by circulatory collapse and coma. The lethal dose of an amphetamine is not known but it is estimated to be 5–10 mg per kilo-

gram of body weight for a nontolerant person. Among some individuals, however, a much smaller dose can prove fatal, while a habitual user who has developed tolerance can consume a much larger dose. Tolerance to amphetamines builds quickly and the need for larger amounts is the primary factor in overdose.

Overdose of cocaine, also a central nervous system stimulant, can result in confusion, depression, headache and dizziness. During severe overdose there is circulatory collapse, respiratory failure and cardiac arrest. In cases of acute toxicity, death can occur in as little as two to three minutes or in as long as 30 minutes. Lethal doses vary according to the method of administration. Ingested cocaine is less toxic than cocaine that is injected; 120 mg taken intravenously is said to be a lethal dose but as little as 20 mg applied to mucous membranes can also be lethal in sensitive individuals.

Overdoses of barbiturates, which in normal doses act as central nervous system depressants, relieve tension and anxiety and produce drowsiness and sleep, are common. When the desired effect is not achieved by a normal dose, a user will often increase the dosage. Another cause of overdose is when a user takes repeated doses because he is in a state of mental confusion and cannot remember how many doses he has already taken. Symptoms of overdose include cold sweaty skin, a weak rapid pulse, breathing that is either slow or rapid and shallow, and coma. Treatment for barbiturate overdose by support of breathing and heart action is usually effective if the person is discovered in time.

Heroin overdose is characterized initially by lethargy and stupor, followed by a prolonged coma. Death from an overdose can be prevented by an injection of a narcotic antagonist. Deaths that are reported as heroin overdoses are generally inaccurate. Because death from heroin is a slow process, the sudden death of an addict is more likely to be caused by such complications as a combination of heroin and alcohol or a sensitivity to an adulterant. (See SYNDROME X.) Overdose patients admitted to hospitals often show signs of pulmonary edema, pneumonia, shallow breathing and coma. A lethal dose of heroin is related to a person's tolerance level and increases as tolerance increases. A lethal dose for a nonaddict has been variously estimated at between 120 and 500 milligrams. Addicts have been known to survive injections of 1800 milligrams. Overdoses have occurred when an addict's tolerance is low and also in cases when he has taken heroin that is unusually potent. Addicts can never be sure what percentage of the mixture they have purchased is pure heroin. Sometimes a dealer will give a buyer a "hot shot"—a deliberate overdose—if the latter is suspected of being an informer.

There is no known lethal dose of marijuana, although it can produce highly toxic reactions whether it is taken orally or injected. Prolonged heavy use can result in chronic bronchitis, asthma and pulmonary disorders. Large amounts of marijuana are not usually smoked at one time because heavy doses cause a user to become extremely sleepy.

An overdose of hallucinogens (LSD, mescaline, psilocybin, and so on) is not likely to be fatal. Large doses can produce unconsciousness, however. One of the great dangers associated with the use of hallucinogens is that they impair the user's judgment, and deaths have been reported to have occurred while a person was under the influence of such a drug. Temporary panic states can occur, and sometimes chronic psychoses occur that last for months.

Deaths have resulted from the use of inhalants but, as in the case of glue sniffing, the cause of death is most likely to be from suffocation because a plastic bag has been placed over the head to enhance the effects. In the case of solvents, a high dose can produce general sedative–anesthetic effects— drowsiness, stupor, respiratory depression and unconsciousness. In extremely heavy use death has been reported from inhibited breathing. The fluorocarbons in aerosols have been associated with deaths due to cardiac arrhythmia.

over–the–counter medications (OTC) OTC drugs are those that may be purchased without a prescription. Some of the estimated 350,000 OTC products (with annual sales of $5 billion) are subject to abuse, particularly those that contain analgesic, sedative or stimulant ingredients. Among the most abused are cough syrups, sleeping aids and appetite depressants (diet pills).

oxazepam   A BENZODIAZEPINE derivative that has a relatively slow onset of action but long–lasting effects. It is used to relieve tension, anxiety and muscle spasm; to produce sedation; and to prevent convulsions. (See SERAX.)

Oxford Group   A nondenominational, theologically conservative, evangelical group that attempted to recapture what its members referred to as "primitive Christianity." It was founded in 1908 by Frank Buchman. Bill Wilson, the founder of ALCOHOLICS ANONYMOUS, included a number of the Group's principles in the AA philosophy (self–survey, restitution, confession). Originally called the First Century Christian Fellowship, it became popularly known as the Oxford Group during the 1920s and 1930s because of Buchman's preaching among Oxford students.

oxycodone   A semisynthetic MORPHINE derivative, it is a narcotic usually used for sedation or as an analgesic. Its potency is similar to morphine. (See PERCOCET and PERCODAN.)

oxymorphone   A semisynthetic MOR-PHINE derivative whose analgesic potency is much higher than morphine. It is sold under the trade name Numorphan® (Endo).

P

Pakistan   Pakistan is faced with a twin problem in the area of drug abuse. Not only has the poppy, the source of opium, been cultivated since time immemorial, the cannabis plant grows wild in the northern areas of the country. In the face of small landholdings, the absence of employment opportunities, depleted soil and inadequate irrigation, it is not hard to understand the temptation to sell and gain an easy profit from these products. During the 1960s only a fraction of the total production of opium and cannabis was consumed within the country; the majority found its way into illicit foreign trade. It has been estimated that 50% of the heroin smuggled into the United States, and 85% of the heroin smuggled into Great Britain, was from Pakistan.

The government of Pakistan, aware of the complexity, magnitude and repercussions of drug abuse within the country as well as the serious implications of illicit exportation, set up a Pakistan Narcotics Control Board in 1973. In 1979 the Prohibition (Enforcement of Hadd) Ordinance was set into effect by the government: it imposed a complete ban on the production, processing, manufacture, sale and use of all intoxicating drugs. The ordinance introduced Islamic disciplines into the domain of drug abuse and the deeply re-

ligious bent of the people has helped to assure their determination to combat the drug problems.

Poppy cultivation in Pakistan was formerly divided into three diverse areas: (1) settled districts; (2) merged areas; and (3) tribal areas. In settled areas, poppy cultivation was under license of the government (licensed production is now forbidden by law); it was understood that the entire harvest would be turned over to the government and after processing would be issued by the government opium factory for scientific, medical and quasi–medical uses. In merged and tribal areas, cultivation was not governed by licensing and was largely administered according to tribal customs. Following the enactment of the Prohibition Ordinance, the government of Pakistan appealed to tribal elders to respect the drug and alcohol law according to Islamic injunctions against the use of intoxicants. Most of the tribal leaders responded and the 800 tons of opium produced in 1978–79 was reduced to 100 tons in 1979–80, and further reduced in 1980–81 to 85 tons.

The withdrawal of poppy cultivation has imposed an enormous socio–economic hardship, particularly in neglected areas of the country. One of the major problems facing the Pakistan government today is to find a viable alternative crop that will produce a sufficient economic return. Approximately $45 million of the U.S. Aid Program package has been designated to help in the development of rural areas. The Buner Project, a development already implemented in Thailand, is currently underway. These projects include road–building, providing water supplies for villages and crops, supplying farm credit, land leveling and terracing, and improving livestock health and production.

In a country where it is reported that between 450,000 and 800,000 people abuse various types of drugs, it is not enough to ban the cultivation of poppies. The Pakistan

Total of Major Narcotic Drugs Seized in Pakistan by Drug Law Enforcement Agencies		
Drug	**Quantity Seized**	**Quantity Seized**
	(1973–79)	(1980–81)
Heroin	28 Kgs.	93,575 Kgs.
Morphine	146 Kgs.	1,168. Kgs.
		233 Ampules
		672 Injections
		4,501 Tablets
Mandrax (Methaqualone)		1,530,362 Tablets
Other Opiates		45,075 Tablets
Opium	48,611 Kgs.	11,647 Kgs.
Cannabis	171,507 Kgs.	72,951. Kgs.

Source: Pakistan Narcotics Control Board.

Narcotics Control Board, in cooperation with the United Nations, is also involved in a detoxification and after–care program for drug abusers and addicts. It is a slow and costly process, however: in 1979 only seven detoxification and rehabilitation centers were in operation. The government's program for the future calls for another 12 centers and 20 specialized hospitals. Between March 1979 and June 1981, the centers claim to have detoxified 6,000 addicts. A lack of properly trained and organized narcotic law enforcement agents has led the government to establish a forensic laboratory for chemical analysis and testing. In 1980 the Pakistan government negotiated a contract with the Federal Republic of Germany to conduct a survey on the exact extent of drug abuse in the country, covering patterns of abuse, age, sex, availability, income group, and so on.

Although the amount of narcotic drugs seized during the years 1980–81 (see chart) is extremely impressive, the crux of Pakistan's problem is still one of substituting a profitable crop in place of the poppy.

panaddiction   See POLYDRUG USE.

pancreas   A small glandular organ located below and behind the stomach and connected to the small intestine at the duodenum. The pancreas secretes insulin and glucagon—hormones which regulate the blood's glucose level—and enzymes necessary for the digestion of proteins, carbohydrates and fats. A failure to produce sufficient insulin results in diabetes mellitus.

Most drugs have little direct effect on the pancreas whether taken in therapeutic or abusive doses. Alcohol, however, appears to stimulate pancreatic secretion while prompting spasms which obstruct pancreatic duct outflow. The pressure on the pancreatic ducts causes tissues in the organ to swell, and the resulting condition is pancreatitis.

Malnutrition may also be partly responsible for pancreatitis which can occur after bouts of heavy drinking but more frequently develops after years of excessive alcohol consumption. Chronic alcoholics show a particularly high incidence of both acute and chronic pancreatitis. It does not develop in all alcoholics, however; cirrhotic patients are more than twice as likely to develop pancreatitis than those without cirrhosis.

Symptoms of pancreatitis include severe abdominal pain, nausea, vomiting, abdominal bleeding, digestive distress and diabetes mellitus, in varying degrees of severity. Abstinence from alcohol and a low–fat diet can relieve the acute state of the disease, which is evidenced by abnormally high concentrations of serum amylase. Pancreatitis can sometimes produce striking mental changes due to electrolyte disruptions in the suffering individual. More severe cases can involve pancreatic necrosis, hemorrhage and scarring.

Chronic relapsing pancreatitis is relatively common among alcoholics, who are also more likely than the rest of the population to develop carcinoma of the pancreas.

Pantopon® (Roche)   A narcotic analgesic that contains hydrochlorides of OPIUM alkaloids. It is used in place of morphine for the relief of severe pain. In addition to the action of morphine, it exhibits the action of codeine and the other alkaloids present in opium. It can be habit–forming and dependency can occur. Pantopon has a high potential for abuse. It is supplied in 1 ml ampules for injections; each ml contains 20 mg hydrochlorides of opium alkaloids.

papaverine   An alkaloid of opium in the benzylisoquinoline class that has no central nervous system or analgesic effect. It is usually used as a cough suppressant and in the treatment of cardiovascular disease. Dependency does not develop, and because it does not produce euphoric effects it is not an abused drug.

Papaver somniferum   The oriental opium poppy plant from which opium and its derivatives are produced.

para–alcoholic   A person who has a close relationship with an alcoholic (a parent, spouse, or employer, for example), and be-

cause of the relationship is also an indirect victim of the disease and its effects. A para–alcoholic (or co–alcoholic) also needs counseling in many cases and will often find that his or her needs have been vicariously served by the relationship in some way. There is often an attempt by para–alcoholics to assign blame, particularly in the case of wives who feel at fault because of their husbands' drinking. Denial of a person's drinking problem may also be a fault of para–alcoholics. Denial only delays the treatment which should begin immediately. Problems for a para–alcoholic can also continue after a person stops drinking. During the time an alcoholic is drinking his or her spouse will often take control of the household; when the drinking stops the alcoholic is no longer dependent, and the para–alcoholic may feel unnecessary, unneeded, and unappreciated. AL–ANON is an organization which was founded to help the friends and relatives of alcoholics in these types of situations.

parahexyl   A synthetic cannabinoid resembling THC. (See PYRAHEXYL.)

paraldehyde   A synthetic non–barbiturate sedative hypnotic. Discovered in 1829, it was first used medically in 1881 and was long considered one of the safest hypnotics. It enjoyed widespread use. Paraldehyde is now thought to be potentially dangerous, however, and has been largely replaced by barbiturates and benzodiazepines.

Appearance and Activity in the Body: Paraldehyde appears as a colorless inflammable liquid with a strong bitter taste and odor. Taken orally or by injection, it is rapidly absorbed by the body and metabolized in the liver. Up to 28% of the substance is exhaled which gives the breath a characteristic pungent odor. Paraldehyde crosses the placental barrier, and large doses can depress neonatal respiration.

A problem encountered with paraldehyde

relates to the substance's quick absorption of oxygen. When exposed to air, it oxidizes to strong acetic acid and loses a great deal of its effectiveness. Since the products of decomposition can be very dangerous, sometimes causing death, strict guidelines for the storage of paraldehyde must be observed. It is stored in amounts no greater than 30 mg and at temperatures no higher than 25 degrees centigrade. It must be discarded if not used within 24 hours after opening.

Dosage: Paraldehyde is administered in doses ranging between 5–30 mg. As little as 12 mg has proved fatal to patients with liver disease, and over 100 mg have been survived.

Effects: Although paraldehyde acts much more quickly than chloral hydrate, barbiturates, alcohol and other depressants, its effects are very similar, including intoxication and diminished reflexes. Hypnotic doses induce sleep in as little as 10 minutes and the drug's effects last from four to eight hours. Respiration is not significantly depressed nor is circulation affected. Oral administration causes burning of the mucous membranes, and intramuscular injection causes severe permanent injury if the injection is close to the sciatic nerve. Intravenous administation is both difficult and dangerous: difficult because paraldehyde reacts with plastic syringes, and dangerous because the minimal injectable anesthetic dosage and the lethal dosage are extremely close.

Cross–tolerance to other depressants develops with the use of paraldehyde. Dependence can also occur, especially in the case of alcoholics who receive the drug in withdrawal treatment. Abusive doses can cause stomach bleeding, blood dysfunctions and, in some cases, a deep coma similar to ether anesthesia. Symptoms of WITHDRAWAL from paraldehyde parallel those that occur with alcohol withdrawal.

Usage: Paraldehyde is used most commonly in connection with withdrawal treatments for alcoholics, particularly those suffering from delirium tremens. It is also used to treat insomnia, convulsions and tetanus, and as an obstetric anesthetic and analgesic.

Despite its addictive qualities, paraldehyde is not commonly abused, probably because of its bitter taste, unpleasant and identifiable odor, and its burning effect on the mucous membranes.

Availability: Paraldehyde is available as a liquid to be administered orally with juice, as rectal suppositories, in olive oil or cottonseed oil enemas and in injectable form. It is a Schedule IV drug under the CONTROLLED SUBSTANCES ACT.

paranoia   In this case, a drug user's constant fear of arrest which leads him to take obsessive and extensive steps to avoid being caught buying or possessing drugs. Unlike the imaginary paranoia of a psychotic, a drug user's paranoia may have a basis in fact.

Paranoid states do occur with the use of amphetamines, cocaine, phencyclidine and hallucinogens. The user has delusional thoughts that he is being persecuted, or that he is all–powerful (megalomaniacal). Alcoholic paranoia is supposed to involve a quality of pathological jealousy.

paraquat   A herbicide which has recently been used by the Drug Enforcement Administration (DEA) to eradicate marijuana crops on federal land areas in the United States. The U.S. government has also been encouraging the spraying of paraquat in South American countries.

In July 1979, the United Nations Narcotics Laboratory issued the following statement about paraquat: ". . . the toxic properties of paraquat are such that the handling of the concentrate requires care. Although fibrosis of the lung can result from the ingestion of paraquat, there is no known instance of this occurring in humans following the ingestion of paraquat. Furthermore, residues of sprayed formulations on cannabis would not be sufficient to cause toxic effects to the marijuana user.''

Opponents of paraquat use include the National Organization for Reform of Marijuana Laws, the Sierra Club, Friends of the Earth, the National Coalition Against the Misuse of Pesticides and several citizen action groups, who argue that the spraying poses a serious health threat to the estimated 30 million marijuana smokers in the U.S. The government claims that it is not paraquat that is the issue, but rather marijuana. They further claim that farmers use an estimated four million pounds of paraquat annually over an estimated 10.7 million acres for the control of weeds among crops. A suit brought against the DEA by the above mentioned groups resulted in a court order on September 13, 1983, temporarily restraining paraquat spraying because the DEA had not assessed the environmental impact before beginning the operation. The day after the court ruling, the Reagan Administration announced that spraying would be suspended for the rest of the 1983 growing season.

paregoric   A narcotic that acts as a central nervous system (CNS) depressant. Paregoric is an opium tincture (powdered opium dissolved in alcohol) combined with camphor and has an alcohol content equivalent to 90 proof whiskey. It has been used medically since its first appearance in the early 1700s. Although considered an old–fashioned remedy today, it is still medically accepted and used principally to treat diarrhea.

In the 19th century the danger of addiction to opium–containing medicines was not well understood and abuse of paregoric and laudanum (an earlier tincture of opium) was common. Countless people, including a number of famous poets and writers, developed at least psychological dependence on them.

Well into the 20th century mothers gave paregoric to their babies not only to control infant diarrhea but also to quiet their crying and put them to sleep. There is no way of estimating the harm this practice caused before the Narcotics Act of 1914 placed opium and its products under federal control, making them available only on prescription. Paregoric is a Schedule III drug under the CONTROLLED SUBSTANCES ACT of 1970.

Today paregoric is in demand by heroin addicts when heroin is not available. Paregoric is a liquid and most addicts drink it, requiring about a quart a day to get the effects they need. Others inject it intravenously after processing it to remove the camphor and alcohol. At one time, addicts sometimes added the antihistamine tripelennamine to paregoric and the mixture was referred to as "Blue Velvet." Because the intravenous injection of Blue Velvet resulted in plugged veins and sometimes death its popularity quickly waned.

Tolerance and physcial dependence can develop with heavy use over a long period of time. If it does, stopping suddenly or sharply reducing the accustomed dosage can bring on the same symptoms as those that follow opium withdrawal.

Richard R. Lingeman, *Drugs from A to Z* (New York: McGraw–Hill Book Company, 1974), p. 203.

Jack Margolis, *Recreational Drugs* (Price/ Stern/Sloan Publishers, Inc., 1978), pp. 311–312.

parenteral   The injection of a substance, either intravenously, intramuscularly or subcutaneously, as opposed to oral ingestion.

Parest® (Parke–Davis)   A rapid–acting sedative hypnotic that contained METHAQUALONE hydrochloride and was used for sedation and sleep. It was taken off the market because of widespread abuse.

parica   A psychedelic snuff used by the Yekwana Indians in Venezuela. It is made from the bark of the virola tree.

passion flower   *Passiflora incarnata*. The leaves and stems of this plant contain a small amount of the alkaloid harmine. There are claims that they produce mild psychedelic effects when they are smoked or brewed in a tea.

passive inhalation   Small amounts of smoke enter the lungs of non–smokers when they are in the presence of marijuana or tobacco smokers. This amount is minute even in closed unventilated places. It is practically impossible to become "high" from passive inhalation of marijuana. Any "contact high" is the result of psychological identification with the smoker rather than THC intoxication.

Pathibamate® (Lederle)   A minor tranquilizer that contains tridihexethyl chloride and MEPROBAMATE. It is used in the treatment of peptic ulcers and colon disorders, particularly when they are accompanied by tension and anxiety. It has the potential for abuse and physical and psychological dependence can occur. When taken with alcohol or other central nervous system depressants it can have an additive effect. Overdosage can result in stupor, coma and respiratory collapse. It is supplied as Pathibamate–400, yellow scored tablets containing 400 mg of meprobamate; and Pathibamate–200, yellow coated tablets containing 200 mg of meprobamate.

pathological drinker   A problem drinker or alcoholic. A person who handles unconscious problems or discomforts by excessive drinking.

pathological intoxication   A radical change in a person's behavior which usually takes the form of aggressive explosive rage, and follows the ingestion of a small amount of alcohol that is insufficient to produce intoxication. Deep sleep ends the episode and there is no memory of the outburst. This condition, which is fairly rare, is thought to be due to hypersensitivity to alcohol. Pathological intoxication also occurs after head injuries or in cases of severe liver disease.

PCP   Phencyclidine hydrochloride. (Chemical name: 1–(1–phenylcyclohexyl) piperdine.)

PCP was first developed in 1959 as one of a new class of anesthetic agents, known as dissociative anesthetics because they detach or dissociate patients from all bodily sensations so that no pain is felt during surgery. It was found that patients often became agitated, delusional and irrational while recovering from the anesthetic effects of PCP, however, so use was discontinued. It was used in veterinary medicine until the late 1970s when it was replaced by an equally effective anesthetic with fewer side effects.

PCP is a white crystalline powder which is readily soluble in water or alcohol. It has a distinctive bitter "chemical" taste. PCP can be mixed easily with dyes and turns up on the illicit drug market in a variety of tablets, capsules and colored powders. It is normally used in one of three ways: it is snorted, smoked, or eaten. It can also be injected but it is not often used this way. When smoked it is most often mixed with another substance such as mint leaves, parsley, tobacco or marijuana.

PCP is easily manufactured and is in plentiful supply wherever there is a demand. It is also commonly found as an adulterant—or complete misrepresentation—in mescaline, psilocybin and LSD. Less frequently it is found as a substitute for cocaine and heroin or as an adulterant in these drugs. It is often difficult to know if PCP is a component of a drug, and it is sold by at least 100 different street names.

PCP was first introduced in the latter part of the 1960s as a street drug and quickly gained a reputation as a chemical that could cause bad reactions and wasn't worth the risk. It was then used to dilute or replace other drugs that were more expensive or more difficult to synthesize.

In the 1960s, PCP was commonly sold as THC, a synthetic marijuana which is costly to manufacture and is never available. As ersatz THC, the drug spread nationwide and increasingly users began wanting PCP itself. The use of PCP among young adults in the United States jumped from 9.5% in 1976 to 14% in 1977. In the psychiatric wards at Metropolitan State Hospital in Norwalk, California, approximately 30% of all admissions have PCP in their blood. Many of these users declared PCP to be their primary drug of choice. Its use appears to be decreasing, however, and by 1982 this figure was down to 10.5% (according to the U.S. Department of Health and Human Services, *National Survey on Drug Abuse: Main Findings 1982*).

PCP is unusual in that it appears to have a higher percentage of undesirable reactions than any other commonly used psychoactive drug. In spite of its many bizarre and unpleasant effects it has enough desirable qualities to make it in demand. Dr. Ronald Siegel, a Los Angeles psychologist, tested and interviewed 310 adult users and all agreed that on every occasion there were unpleasant negative aspects to the PCP experience. The positive effects described by Dr. Siegel's users included heightened sensitivity to outside stimuli, dissociation, elevation in mood, inebriation and relaxation. Only one in 12 reported experiencing euphoria.

Voluntary patients at Metropolitan State hospital with a history of PCP abuse without current major behavioral, mental or physical disorders reported experiencing the following effects sometime during PCP abuse:

80% reported organicity: forgetfulness, difficulty in concentrating, thinking clearly and understanding, etc.;
75% reported behavior dyscontrol: physical violence, aggression and agitation;
74% reported estrangement: feelings of derealization and depersonalization;
60% reported paranoia: transient suspiciousness;
55% reported altered mood states: elation to depression;
41% reported hallucinations: tactile, visual or auditory;
20% reported suicidal impulses.

PCP is a DEPRESSANT and interactions with other CENTRAL NERVOUS SYSTEM depressants such as ALCOHOL and TRANQUILIZERS can lead to coma or accidental overdose. Use of PCP among adolescents may interfere with hormones related to normal growth and development as well as with the learning process. According to the University of Michigan's Institute for Social Research, as of 1980 9.6% of high school seniors had used PCP at some time, 4.4% in the previous year. The incidence of male users is about two–thirds larger than female users. Typically, PCP users are young single males of all ethnic backgrounds.

Classification: PCP is a hallucinogen with neurologic and autonomic activity, originally developed as an anesthetic. It is difficult to classify accurately as different doses produce different effects: they may resemble the actions of a stimulant, analgesic, anesthetic or HALLUCINOGEN. PCP is really in a class by itself—the Student Organization for the Study of Hallucinogens has called it a ''delusionogen.''

Effects: At low to moderate doses physiological effects include a slight increase in breathing rate and a more pronounced rise in blood pressure and pulse rate. Respiration becomes shallow, and flushing and profuse sweating frequently occur. Generalized numbness of the extremities and muscular incoordination may also develop. At high doses there is a drop in blood pressure, pulse rate and respiration. This may be accompanied by nausea, vomiting, blurred vision, nystagmus (flicking of the eyes), drooling, loss of balance and dizziness. Large amounts of the drug can cause convulsions and coma; several deaths have been associated with PCP use.

Psychological effects with small doses include distinct changes in body awareness, similar to those associated with alcohol intoxication. Effects of higher doses mimic certain primary symptoms of schizophrenia such as delusions, mental turmoil and a sensation of distance from one's environment. Illusions and hallucinations, usually of hearing, occasionally of vision, have also been reported following administration of large amounts of the drug. Bizarre behavior of many types sometimes occurs in response to them. Speech is often blocked and to the outsider it may also appear meaningless. Paranoid thinking is common. Users may react with frightening violence in response to imagined threats. Because PCP has anesthetic action, touch and pain sensations are dulled and the user may severely injure himself without knowing it. He may be difficult to control in a hospital situation.

Addictive aspects: The popularity of PCP indicates some degree of psychological dependence. Physical dependence and WITHDRAWAL in humans has not been observed.

Tolerance: In two studies published in 1978 tolerance was reported, making increased doses of PCP necessary to produce the same effects. The degree of tolerance developed is still unknown.

Sources: PCP is difficult to control by law because it is easily and inexpensively synthesized. The starting chemicals are in widespread industrial use; very simple equipment is needed; and no special skill is required. The drug is manufactured only in illicit laboratories within the U.S. and efforts to control

the precursors have been only partly successful.

Synonyms: angel dust, horse tranquilizer, animal tranquilizer, tic, dust, crystal, superweed, rocket fuel, street drug, peace pill, Shermans.

PDR   The PHYSICIANS' DESK REFERENCE. Also called the BOOK or the BIBLE.

peer pressure   Perhaps the most vulnerable individual to confront the growing social acceptance of drug use in the United States is the adolescent. Peer pressure, the *desire* and *need* to belong to a certain group and to *show* that one belongs, has long been acknowledged as a reason for adolescent drug use and abuse.

In 1979 there were 10,000 emergency room visits related to the use of marijuana and they primarily involved adolescents. PCP accounted for 14,000 emergency room visits and 260 deaths. In 1978 a nationwide survey conducted for the National Institute on Alcohol Abuse and Alcoholism reported 87% of senior high school students had tried alcohol at least once and over 20% drank at least once a week.

Peers may pressure adolescents to try a drug at a stage when their sense of individual identity is still undeveloped and the need to be accepted is very strong. Adolescents may also use drugs with peers in order to relax and be comfortable as much as from the pressure to conform to the dictates of the group. Because of peer pressure, children are also likely to adopt the group's attitude toward drugs.

pemoline   A central nervous system stimulant that is most commonly used in the treatment of Minimal Brain Dysfunction. Because it has an activity similar to that of AMPHETAMINES dependency can occur. (See CYLERT.)

pentazocine   A potent ANALGESIC and mild NARCOTIC ANTAGONIST that was first synthesized in 1961 by Sterling–Winthrop. Pentazocine resembles codeine and morphine in most of its properties. It is used for the relief of moderate to severe pain and as a supplement to anesthetics. When given to a patient who has previously received a narcotic, it may act as a narcotic antagonist and withdrawal symptoms are experienced. The drug is best known by the brand name TALWIN and Talwin NX (Winthrop) and is one of the 100 most prescribed drugs.

Appearance and Activity: Pentazocine is a white crystalline substance soluble in acidic aqueous solution. It is extensively metabolized in the body, with only 13% appearing in the urine.

Dosage and Effects: Talwin is prescribed orally in doses of 30–50 mg every three or four hours. In intravenous administration, 30 mg is equivalent to 10 mg of morphine but the duration of effects may be less than morphine. Pentazocine's analgesic effects materialize more quickly than morphine's, in as little as 15–30 minutes with oral administration and in two to three minutes with intravenous administration. They include euphoria and the usual range of narcotic effects. Like DARVON, the drug can cause hallucinations, disorientation and confusion.

Usage: Talwin's abuse is related to its medical use and is partially a result of overprescription. It is abused on the street in a combination of Talwin and pyribenzamine ("T's and blues"), often intravenously. It is a Schedule IV drug under the Controlled Substances Act. The tablets have recently been reformulated to contain NALOXONE and they are now sold as Talwin NX to make intravenous use undesirable because of the possible onset of withdrawal symptoms. Death due to Talwin overdose is known. (These deaths may have been due to the talcum powder contained in commercially available tablets.)

pentobarbital   A short–acting barbiturate that is used as a sedative hypnotic. In the depressant category, it is one of the most sought after drugs by abusers. It is sold under the trade name NEMBUTAL. (See also BARBITURATES.)

Pentothal® (Abbott)   A short–acting central nervous system depressant that contains thiopental sodium. It is used intravenously to induce hypnosis and as an anesthesia for brief procedures. It is also used in the control of convulsive states and for narcoanalysis in psychiatric disorders. Overdosage can result in respiratory depression and paralysis. This Schedule III drug should only be administered by a trained anesthetist.

peptides, endogenous   See ENDORPHINS.

Percocet–5® (Endo)   A semisynthetic narcotic analgesic that is used for mild to moderate pain and for sedation. It contains 5 mg of oxycodone hydrochloride and 325 mg acetaminophen. It can produce morphine–type drug dependency and has a potential for abuse. When taken with alcohol or other central nervous system depressants it can have an additive effect. It is supplied in white scored tablets.

Percodan® (Endo)   A semisynthetic narcotic analgesic that contains oxycodone hydrochloride and oxycodone terephthalate, along with aspirin, caffeine and phenacetin. Its activity is similar to morphine and it is usually used for analgesia and sedation. It may be habit–forming and has a significant potential for abuse. Tolerance, along with physical and psychological dependence can develop. When used with alcohol or other central nervous system depressants it can have an additive effect. Overdosage can result in respiratory depression, muscle flaccidity, somnolence and coma; severe overdosage can result in circulatory collapse, cardiac arrest and death. It is supplied as Percodan: yellow scored tablets containing 4.50 mg of oxycodone hydrochloride and 0.38 mg of oxycodone terephthalate; and Percodan–Demi, pink scored tablets containing half the above amounts.

periodic alcoholism   Also known as Epsilon alcoholism as defined by JELLINEK, it is characterized by sporadic bouts of excessive drinking which are followed by intervals of moderate drinking or abstinence.

peripheral neuritis   See ALCOHOLIC POLYNEUROPATHY.

personality trait theories   In this case, personality trait theories seek to explain the reasons for the addictive personality. These theories concentrate on determining a specific set of characteristics that would be associated with the development of drug abuse. Although studies have not identified a particular set of personality traits that distinguish drug users from other groups, the following traits were most often observed: low thresholds for frustration, ambiguity and dissonance; high levels of hopelessness, anxiety and helplessness; negative self–image; and feelings of isolation and depression. It should be noted that it is often difficult to determine if these traits preceded drug use or were a consequence of it.

Peru   For more than 2,000 years Peruvians have grown and chewed coca. Today the government permits and licenses substantial cultivation of coca for traditional domestic use as well as for pharmaceutical purposes. Despite government controls, however, coca cultivation has expanded to an estimated 50,000 metric tons; only 12–14,000 tons are used licitly. About half of the cocaine consumed in the United States is provided by Peru; most of it is processed and distributed by Colombia. Peru has a weak economy and cocaine trafficking provides several hundred million dollars. It is the principal and often only income for thousands of farmers—an income that is many times the daily wage for growing other crops. Coca is an attractive crop for farmers because it is a deep–rooted plant with a life span of about 30 years. In addition, it can be harvested three to six times a year and grown in poor soil unsuitable for other crops.

The smoking of coca paste is of particular concern to the Peruvian government. In this semi–refined state, coca contains harmful impurities such as cement, large amounts of coca alkaloids and kerosene, and inhaling it into the lungs can be extremely dangerous. Recent reports show an increase in smoking coca paste among high school youths.

In 1980 the government doubled its resource commitment to curbing production in excess of that used for licit purposes. In a cooperative effort with the U.S., 1,500 acres of coca were eradicated in 1980 and 57 laboratories were destroyed. In 1981 a five–year eradication and enforcement project was initiated by the Bureau of International Narcotics Matters (INM) concurrently with a five–year plan by the Agency for International Development (AID) to diversify agricultural development. By mid–1982 about 5% of coca cultivation had been abandoned and other cultivations were not being fully harvested.

pethidine   A generic name for MEPERIDINE.

peyote   A spineless cactus, *Lophophora williamsii*, native to central and northern Mexico whose top crown, or button, is a hallucinogenic drug. The button is dried, then ingested by holding it in the mouth until it is soft and then swallowing it whole. Generally it takes three to four buttons to achieve a "trip."

Peyote was first used by the Aztecs and then by other Mexican Indians to enhance awareness in religious ceremonies. It is a very nauseating drug and vomiting is considered a part of the purgation by Indian peyotists. Peyote purportedly produces a deep insight into reality, along with highly complex sensory experiences. The richly colored "kaleidoscope" type of hallucination is one of its most sought–after effects by abusers.

In the 1800s the use of peyote spread northward to the American Indians and "peyote cults" began to spring up. As total abstinence from alcohol was required in peyote cults, and this was a time when alcohol use was becoming epidemic among the Indians, many tribes encouraged the use of peyote. Indian leaders who were striving to maintain peace with the white men also encouraged the use of peyote among their tribes because those using it were less hostile to the white men.

An attempt, particularly by missionaries, to have peyote outlawed by the various western states, gained some success but many state legislatures which enacted such laws eventually repealed them to permit ritual use in religious services.

During the 1950s and early 1960s it was a simple matter to purchase peyote buttons; mail order companies advertised them in numerous publications. The drug's availability led to widespread abuse, particularly among college students. LSD also became popular during the 1960s and the government's attitude and the public hostility toward its use influenced the attitude toward peyote. Investigations were conducted into the possible dangerous effects of peyote.

In 1969, the federal government granted the Native American Church of North America the legal right to consume peyote in their religious services. The church claims some 250,000 members in the U.S. and Canada. The principal supporters of this move were anthropologists and psychiatrists. They sug-

gested that there is something to be learned from the long use of peyote among Indians. Their ability to take a potentially dangerous drug and to use it well, warranted continued study. When peyote is taken, the Indians use safeguards far greater than those employed by some LSD users. Peyote services are held at strictly defined times; no one is allowed to leave a meeting so consequently a hallucinating person is not allowed to wander off by himself; and customarily there are meetings the following morning until well after the time it has taken for the drug's effects to wear off.

Peyote is currently the only hallucinogen whose use is sanctioned by the United States government, but only for those who are members of the Native Church of North America.

pharmaceuticals   Pills, capsules, liquids, medicinal suppositories, lotions and other preparations that have a medical use.

pharmacogenic orgasm   The pleasurable sensation (see RUSH) felt by a HEROIN addict after intravenous injection. (See also ADMINISTRATION.)

pharmacokinetics   A study, made over a period of time, of a drug's action and movement through the body. The processes studied include the dynamics of absorption, distribution and excretion.

pharmacological etiology   Drug addiction as a result of the medical administration of drugs can, and has, been a cause of drug abuse. Although this was probably one of the main causes of addiction during the 19th century, it is not as prevalent in the modern world. The majority of physicians are now quite aware of the addictive qualities of drugs, although some are still inclined to prescribe them freely simply because it is easier to cover symptoms than take the time to treat, if possible, the causes of an illness. On the other hand, some patients have been known to complain that physicians are overcautious in the prescription of drugs; a complaint that is most common in patients who are recovering from surgery and are in extreme pain. No extensive studies have been made to determine the effects of medical narcotic use for short periods of time (several days to a couple of weeks), to discover the extent of withdrawal symptoms (if any) when a drug is stopped, or to find out if patients develop a craving or substitute another drug for the one that has been withdrawn. It is known, however, that after a week of full doses of a narcotic, tolerance and some degree of withdrawal may be seen. With sedative hypnotics, the process may take a few weeks and with the minor tranquilizers, it can take months.

phenacetin   A central nervous system depressant and synthetic analgesic used for the relief of minor pain (headache and neuralgia) and also to reduce fever. In prescription drugs it is generally combined with other drugs such as butalbital and codeine. Phenacetin in large amounts can cause kidney damage.

Phenaphen with Codeine® (Robbins)

A narcotic analgesic that contains codeine phosphate and acetaminophen. No. 2 and No. 3 are used for mild to moderate pain; No. 4 is used for moderate to severe pain. Tolerance, along with psychological and physical dependence can develop. It has a significant potential for abuse, and when taken with alcohol or other central nervous system depressants it can have an additive effect. Overdosage can result in respiratory depression, somnolence, muscle flaccidity and coma. It is supplied as Phenaphen with Codeine No. 2, containing 15 mg codeine in black and yellow capsules; No. 3 containing 30 mg in black and green capsules; and No. 4 containing 60 mg in green and white capsules. It is also available as Phenaphen without codeine, containing 325 mg acetaminophen (Tylenol).

phenazocine   A synthetic narcotic analgesic, derived from OPIUM, that is used for acute and chronic pain. Classified as a Schedule II drug, it has a potency that exceeds morphine.

phencyclidine (PCP)   An anesthetic which was once used for childbirth but is no longer available licitly. (See PCP.)

phendimetrazine tartrate   A central nervous system stimulant whose activity is similar to that of the AMPHETAMINES. It is used as an anorectic for weight control and has a significant potential for abuse. Tolerance can develop within a few weeks. Phendimetrazine tartrate is found in many marketed anorectics.

phenelzine   See MONOAMINE OXIDASE (MAO) INHIBITORS.

phenmetrazine   A central nervous system stimulant that is used as an anorectic for weight control. Its activity is similar to that of the AMPHETAMINES and it has a significant potential for abuse. (See also PRELUDIN.)

phenobarbital   A long–acting BARBITURATE with an onset time of up to one hour and a duration of action up to 16 hours. It is used as a sedative hypnotic and anticonvulsant. (See also LUMINAL.)

phentermine   A central nervous system stimulant whose activity is similar to that of the AMPHETAMINES. It is used as an anorectic for weight control and has a significant potential for abuse. (See also IONAMIN.)

phenylpropanolamine   A synthetic drug that effects the autonomic nervous system. Used as a mucous membrane decongestant and as a treatment for allergic conditions, it is found in over–the–counter preparations for colds and weight control.

phenytoin   A central nervous system depressant that is used mainly as an anticonvulsant in the treatment of epilepsy. Its highly selective action effects only motor centers and it has little or no hypnotic or sedative action. The use and dosage of phenytoin should be carefully monitored because of numerous severe side effects. It is marketed as Dilantin.

pholcodine   An OPIATE derivative that is used as a cough suppressant in England and France.

Phrenilin® (Carnrick)   An analgesic that is used for head pain associated with tension and upper respiratory infection. It contains 15 mg of the BARBITURATE sodium butabarbital, 325 mg of acetaminophen and 40 mg of caffeine. Because it contains a barbiturate, it may be habit–forming. It is supplied in pale violet tablets.

Physicians' Desk Reference (PDR)

An annual volume listing commercial drug preparations. It is also referred to as "the Book" and "the Bible," and drug users refer to it for pill identification and drug descriptions. A PDR for non–prescription drugs is also available.

physiological models of etiology   One of the three major categories of theories about the cause of alcoholism. As alcohol is a sedative drug it is possible that this theory can be expanded to include the use of all sedative drugs.

Theories belonging to this group postulate that individuals are predisposed to develop alcohol problems because of an organic defect and underlying biological malfunction.

To date, however, there is only limited genetic evidence about the role that physiology plays in alcoholism.

Physiological theories include those dealing with the endocrine system and nutritional needs of the body. Because one cause alone may not account for alcoholism or the abuse of other sedative drugs, physiological etiological theories are generally considered in conjunction with psychological and sociocultural theories. (See also GENETOTROPIC ETIOLOGICAL THEORIES and ENDOCRINE ETIOLOGICAL THEORIES.)

physostigmine   An acid derivative of an alkaloid extracted from the seeds of the calabar bean. It is used to reverse toxic effects on the central nervous system (hallucinations, delirium, disorientation, etc.) caused by drugs which have produced anticholinergic poisoning. (See also ANTILIRIUM.)

Pil–Anon Family Program

A self–help support organization founded in 1978 and sponsored by PILLS ANONYMOUS, for the families of chemically dependent people. It is based on the 12–step program of Alcoholics Anonymous.

Pills Anonymous World Service (PA)

A self–help, self–supporting group with a 12–step program based on that of Alcoholics Anonymous. The only requirement for membership is a desire to stop taking pills and/or other mood altering chemicals. Founded in 1975, the group also sponsors PIL–ANON FAMILY PROGRAM for the families of those who are chemically dependent.

piloerection   The involuntary bristling or erection of hair (gooseflesh) which is an objective diagnostic sign of opioid withdrawal and therefore opioid dependency.

pinpoint pupils   See EYES.

piptadenia   A hallucinogenic snuff used by Indians in Venezuela and Colombia. It is made from the seeds of shrubs in the mimosa family (*Leguminosae*).

pituri   *Duboisia hopwoodii*, a plant that grows in Australia and whose leaves are chewed by Aborigines for a stimulating effect. After the initial stimulation, it can cause severe adverse effects.

Placidyl® (Abbott)   A sedative hypnotic that contains ethchlorvynol and is used for insomnia. It has the potential for abuse and when taken with alcohol or other central nervous system depressants can have an additive effect. Overdosage can result in severe respiratory depression and deep coma. It is supplied in capsule form: 100 mg round red; 200 mg round red; 500 mg oblong red; and 750 mg oblong green.

Plegine® (Ayerst)   A brand of phendimetrazine tartrate that is used as an anorectic for weight control. Chemically and pharmacologically it is similar to the AMPHETAMINES; thus it has a high potential for abuse and can cause psychological dependence and social dysfunction. Overdosage can result in restlessness, confusion, hallucinations and coma. It is supplied in yellow scored tablets of 35 mg.

Plexonal® (Sandoz)   A BARBITURATE sedative that is used for anxiety, tension and insomnia. It contains barbital sodium, butalbital sodium, phenobarbital sodium, scopolamine and dihydroergotamine. Tolerance can develop along with physical and psychological dependence and it has a significant potential for abuse. Overdosage can result in shallow respiration, coma and possibly death. It is supplied in white sugar–coated triangular tablets.

PMB 200 & PMB 400® (Ayerst)   A minor tranquilizer that contains Premarini (conjugated estrogens) and MEPROBAMATE. It is usually used for menopausal syndrome when accompanied by tension and anxiety. It has a potential for abuse and can produce physical and psychological dependence. When overdosage occurs, sleep ensues rapidly and blood pressure, pulse and respiratory rates are reduced to basal levels. PMB–200, supplied in green tablets, contains 200 mg of meprobamate; PMB–400, supplied in pink tablets, contains 400 mg of meprobamate.

polydrug use   The use of two or more drugs simultaneously. This may be done for a variety of reasons: to enhance or POTENTIATE one drug's effects; to neutralize or counteract undesirable effects of one of the drugs; or to achieve a less expensive HIGH by combining an inexpensive drug with a small amount of an expensive one. The practice of polydrug use is becoming more and more popular and single drug users now tend to be in the minority. There are an infinite number of combinations; probably the most popular is marijuana and alcohol. Other favorites are barbiturates and alcohol, methaqualone and alcohol, barbiturates and amphetamines, analgesics with tranquilizers or sedatives, and more recently, sleeping pills and codeine. Heroin users will supplement their habit with barbiturates if the only heroin they can obtain is highly diluted. The practice of polydrug use is also known as multihabituation.

polystyrene cement   Model airplane glue, sniffed for its intoxicating effects.

Pondimin® (Robins)   An anorectic that is used for weight control. It is a brand of fenfluramine hydrochloride. Unlike other anorectics that have an amphetamine activity, Pondimin produces more central nervous system depression than stimulation. When taken with alcohol or other CNS depressants it can have an additive effect. It has a significant potential for abuse and psychological dependence can occur. Overdosage can result in agitation, confusion, hyperventilation and pupil dilation. It is supplied in orange scored tablets of 20 mg.

portal cirrhosis   Named for the portal vein which transports blood from the stomach, intestines and spleen to the liver, it is the most prominent type of cirrhosis and the one most frequently found among alcoholics. It is also known as Laennec's, nutritional or alcoholic cirrhosis.

postintoxicated state   A general term used to refer to the agitated state immediately following a drinking bout. It has no specific meaning and is sometimes used to refer to a HANGOVER or to the symptoms attributed to WITHDRAWAL.

postnecrotic cirrhosis   A form of CIRRHOSIS that follows hepatitis or other liver inflammations and is sometimes found in alcoholics.

potentiation   The ability of one drug to increase the activity of another drug which is taken simultaneously. The overall effect is greater than the total effects of each drug taken alone. Also called supradditive. (See also ADDITIVE and SYNERGY.)

Pre–Sate® (Warner/Chilcott)   An anorectic that contains 65 mg chlorphentermine hydrochloride and is used for weight control. Its activity is similar to that of the amphetamines and consequently it has the potential for abuse. Dependency can occur. Overdosage can result in restlessness, aggressiveness, hallucinations and panic, and can progress to convulsions and coma. It is supplied in blue tablets.

pregnancy   When a woman is pregnant, her health and nutrition are crucial not only to her own well–being but also to the developing baby's. Almost everything that a pregnant woman ingests passes directly from her bloodstream through the placenta to the fetus. Since there is no chemical known to science which has proved to be entirely harmless during all phases of pregnancy, most doctors today advise women not to take *any* drug during pregnancy unless there is a specific need for it, and then only under the strictest medical supervision, in the amounts and at the times specified by the physician. This restriction on drug intake applies not only to medically prescribed drugs but also to recreational drugs and even to over–the–counter, self–prescribed remedies such as aspirin.

There is evidence that women who are heroin addicts suffer a high incidence of complications during pregnancy, including toxemia, abruptio placentae, retained placenta, postpartum hemorrhage, premature births by weight, breech deliveries and high neonatal morbidity and mortality (George Blinick, Robert C. Wallach, and Eulogio Jerez, "Pregnancy and Menstrual Function in Narcotics Addicts Treated with Methadone," *American Journal of Obstetrics and Gynecology*, Dec. 15, 1969). These complications, however, are also associated with poverty, malnutrition and a lack of prenatal care—conditions which affect many women addicts in the United States. Although babies born to heroin–addicted women do not seem to suffer a higher risk of congenital abnormalities, they often display withdrawal symptoms soon after birth including tremors, irritability, a shrill cry, restlessness and watery stools. These symptoms may be accompanied by vomiting, fever, twitching, yawning and sneezing. The severity of the symptoms seem to be in direct proportion to the amount of heroin consumed on a daily basis by the mother. Babies born to mothers who are addicted to methadone, barbiturates, tranquilizers, and amphetamines can also experience withdrawal.

Heroin addiction in pregnant women can also present other hazards to infants. One hospital study of 22 addicted women showed a low birth weight in 56.5% of their infants (compared to 13.7% for the hospital as a whole), and a mortality rate at the time of birth of 17.4% compared with 2.2% for infants of nonaddicted mothers. The deaths were not attributed directly to the infants' withdrawal symptoms, but were associated with problems due to their low birth weight, poor nutrition and lack of prenatal care.

Studies have shown that cigarette smoking during pregnancy is hazardous to the unborn baby. Babies born to women who smoke have a two to three times greater chance of being born premature than babies of non-smoking mothers and they are on the average 150–240 grams lighter (C.M. Fletcher and Daniel Horn, *Smoking and Health,* World Health Organization publication, 1970). In addition, babies of mothers who smoke during pregacy are twice as likely to be aborted, to be stillborn, or to die soon after birth.

During the 1960s and 1970s there was much publicity linking the use of LSD to birth defects and chromosome damage. While studies have not ruled out the possibility, there has been no conclusive evidence that the use of LSD by either the mother or father increases such risks. However, a study reported evidence that the incidence of spontaneous abortion (miscarriage) *is* higher among women who use LSD.

Dr. Peter A. Fried, professor of psychology at Carleton University in Ottawa, Canada, conducted the first extensive research on the effects of marijuana on the human fetus. In a study (1978–1983) of more than 700 expectant mothers, Dr. Fried found evidence of a link between marijuana smoking and exaggerated tremors, vision problems and startle reflexes among their babies. Although

there was no increase in stillbirths or the risk of miscarriage, babies of mothers who smoked marijuana were born a few weeks sooner. THC in marijuana does cross the placental barrier and enters the fetus's system where it has an effect on the central nervous system. Babies of mothers who smoked five or more marijuana cigarettes per week "consistently display many more tremors in their arms, legs, and lower jaw than do infants of non–users," according to Dr. Fried. He also reported a tendency of the babies to display more startle reflexes in the absence of obvious external causes. In addition, in a test given three days after birth, Dr. Fried found that the babies showed abnormal responses in reacting or habituating to a light which was shone on them, which suggests "subtle alterations in the nervous system." All of these symptoms disappeared within a month; however, Dr. Fried's study will follow the children until they enter school to establish whether or not they display any subtle long–term manifestations of their early symptoms.

There is evidence that heavy prolonged alcohol consumption during pregnancy can be dangerous to the fetus. When a pregnant woman drinks, the alcohol passes through the placenta and reaches the bloodstream of the fetus in about the same concentrations as in the mother. Since the fetus lacks the mature metabolism and elimination capabilities of an adult, alcohol is more toxic to its system. The most severe damage to a developing fetus caused by heavy drinking is known as FETAL ALCOHOL SYNDROME which is characterized by growth deficiences, physical malformations and mental retardation. A safe limit of alcohol consumption during pregnancy has not been established. Some experts and organizations such as the NATIONAL INSTITUTE ON ALCOHOL ABUSE AND ALCOHOLISM recommend complete abstinence during pregnancy, arguing that since the effects of even small amounts of alcohol are unknown, the wisest course is to abstain completely. Others point out that millions of moderate social drinkers (whose alcohol intake is three ounces or less a day of ABSOLUTE ALCOHOL) have perfectly healthy babies. These experts and organizations prefer not to frighten patients whose custom may be to have a drink or two in the evening, but rather to counsel them on the potential dangers of drinking during pregnancy. Rather than strictly prohibiting their patients from drinking, they suggest instead that moderation is the wisest choice.

Another aspect to be considered in relation to the use of drugs during pregnancy concerns the administration of analgesics and anesthetics to women in labor and during childbirth itself. These drugs, which are intended to make birth easier for the mother and to help in emergency situations, all directly affect the fetus. These medical drugs in combination with whatever recreational or self–prescribed drugs a woman may be using can have a synergistic effect which can stupefy the infant throughout the first days of his life. Furthermore, many drugs which were once common obstetrical medications have recently been discovered to be unsafe. For these reasons more and more women are choosing natural childbirth.

In order to ensure the healthy and natural development of a child, safeguard the health of the mother during and after pregnancy and enhance the birth experience, the consensus of opinion is that pregnant women should abstain from all unnecessary medication and should indulge only minimally in alcohol consumption.

Preludin® (Bohringer Ingelheim)   An anorectic that is used for weight control. A brand of phenmetrazine hydrochloride, its activity is similar to that of AMPHETAMINES and tolerance can develop within a few weeks. It has a high potential for abuse and psychological dependence and social dysfunction can occur. Overdosage can result in rapid respiration, confusion and hallucinations. It is supplied in 25 mg square white tablets; 50 mg round white tablets; and 75 mg round pink tablets.

prisoners and drug use   According to a 1979 survey of inmates in state correctional facilities, almost one–third of 213,000 prisoners surveyed were under the influence of an illegal drug when they committed the crimes for which they were incarcerated. More than half had taken drugs during the month prior to the crime. While more than three–fourths of the prisoners had used drugs at some time during their lives, only one–fourth had ever been in a drug treatment program. Inmates were asked about their experiences with eight specific substances: heroin, methadone (outside of a treatment program), cocaine, marijuana or hashish, amphetamines, barbiturates, LSD and PCP. In an effort to minimize attempts by inmates to cite drugs as the reason for their crimes, no attempt was made to determine how much of each drug had been used on any one occasion or the extent to which the user was affected by it. The extent of drug use reported was, if anything, understated. Although complete confidentiality was promised, one would expect that an inmate would be more likely to deny past drug use than to report a use that did not exist.

Marijuana was by far the most commonly used drug; three–fourths had used it at some time in their lives, roughly the same proportion that had used any illegal drug. Almost all inmates who had used only one drug, therefore, had used marijuana and almost all inmates who had used other drugs had also used marijuana. Authorities in the drug field have found that this is a characteristic of the general population as well: the total number of drug users is only slightly larger than the total number of marijuana users. With the exception of marijuana (and methadone which was used by only 9% of the inmates), the other six drugs had each been used by a third of the prisoners.

Inmates were about twice as likely to have used drugs as the public at large. Nevertheless the proportion who had used only marijuana was the same for both groups—one–fifth. Consequently people who had used only marijuana accounted for half of all the drug users in the general population but only one–fourth of all the inmate users. For all other drugs, use by the general population was substantially below that of the inmates. The greatest difference was for heroin: it was used by only 2% of the general population but by one–third of the inmates. Recent drug use (defined as occurring the month before the survey) for the general population was also substantially lower than for inmates.

It was also found that male inmates were somewhat more likely than female inmates to have used some form of drugs and to have used them recently. The differences were not large and disappeared entirely for cocaine. Heroin use, as well as recent heroin use, was somewhat more frequent among the women.

A common complaint of female inmates was that they were being over–tranquilized while in prison. At the first sign of restlessness, prison doctors were apt to prescribe a tranquilizing medication and sometimes did so without performing a comprehensive medical examination. Dr. Nancy Shaw, a medical sociologist with the University of California, states that in 1978 about 10.5% of female inmates and 3.6% of male inmates in state prisons were on psychotropic medication, with higher rates in short–term facilities. Although the U.S. Bureau of Prisons announced a plan to reduce dependency, a follow–up study (1982) found that although the overall use of medication among female inmates had dropped, women still had consistently high rates of dependency.

Drug use varied little among racial and ethnic groups. It was found, however, that American Indians were less likely than other racial groups to have used heroin, and blacks were less likely than whites to have ever used cocaine. Hispanics were substantially more likely than others to have used heroin and to have used it recently.

When drug use was applied to age groups, it was found that illicit use peaked among those age 18–25; declined moderately for those age 26–34; and dropped off sharply among those 35 years and older. Heroin use was greatest for those age 26–34. Education and marital status are strongly related to age, and patterns of drug use reflect this. Drug use was found to be highest among the never married and lowest among the widowed—typically older—inmates. Inmates who had not graduated from high school clustered among the youngest inmates and the oldest, and their drug use patterns were a combination of those for both groups.

Statistics concerning income were considered suspect: 12% of the inmates volunteered that they had income from illegal sources. Although marijuana use appeared totally unrelated to income, the same was not true of cocaine use. Those who had no income and those who had high incomes were equally likely to have used heroin, but those with high incomes were most likely to have ever used it or to have used it during the year before their crimes and these inmates were the ones to report illegal income. Use of more than one drug was also higher for persons with illegal incomes.

As expected, those imprisoned for crimes involving drugs were more likely than other inmates to have used drugs; nine–tenths had lifetime drug use and three–fourths had used drugs recently. They were also twice as likely as other inmates to have used heroin and to have used it recently. Approximately three–fifths of these inmates were in prison for trafficking rather than for possession or use. And, although marijuana is by far the most commonly used drug, less than 1% of the inmate population was serving time for marijuana use or possession.

It was also found that the more convictions inmates had, the more likely they were to have taken drugs during the month prior to their offense. The likelihood of having used more than one drug was also related to the number of prior convictions.

The more frequently the inmates used drugs, the more likely it was that they had been in a treatment program. Slightly more than one–fourth of the 213,000 inmates surveyed who had used drugs at some time in their lives had been in a program. A higher enrollment rate, about one–third, was found among recent drug users. The rate rose to two–fifths for inmates who said they were under the influence of drugs at the time they committed their offense. Because of the highly addictive nature of the substance, heroin users were the most likely to have been in a treatment program.

Murderers, rapists and violators of public order were found to be the least likely to have been under the influence of a drug (except alcohol) at the time of the offense. Drug offenders and burglars were the most likely.

For those drinking prior to the offense, rapists and assaulters were the most likely and forgers and larcenists the least likely. In comparison to other drug use, a third of the inmates drank daily during the year before the offense and two–thirds of them drank very heavily. At the time of the offense, three–fifths of those under the influence of drugs had also been drinking, including two–fifths (12% of all inmates) who have been drinking very heavily.

Being imprisoned does not necessarily mean the end of a drug habit. It is almost commonplace for drugs to be smuggled into prisons. They have been known to be supplied by prison guards—a system that has been linked to organized crime operations. Drugs are also received through the mail in postcards that have been slit and resealed, for example, and delivered in clothing that has been saturated with a drug. If illegal drugs are not available, inmates have been known to inhale common cleaning fluids for their intoxicating effects, and to sniff cooking spices such as nutmeg and mace.

problem drinker   A problem drinker is one who experiences personal, social, vocational and/or health problems whenever he or she drinks. Problem drinkers are almost always HEAVY DRINKERS but there are exceptions. Often the distinction between problem drinking and alcoholism is a matter of degree or depends on whether tolerance is present and withdrawal symptoms appear when the drinking is stopped.

procaine   A local anesthetic (Novocain®) whose action prevents the initiation and transmission of nerve impulses. It has a rapid onset of action (two to five minutes) and its duration is one to one and a half hours depending on the type of block, the concentration and the individual patient. Procaine has been found as a dilutant in cocaine. Procaine, sometimes in combination with cortisone, has also been used in sports events to allow a participant who is in pain to continue in a contest.

progression   The risk of moving from experimental or occasional drug use to regular social/recreational use and on to dysfunctional use. It has been suggested that the use of "soft" drugs, such as marijuana, may lead to the use of "hard" drugs, such as heroin. The progresson risk is also found in the manner of administration of a drug; when applied to heroin it can be the escalation from intramuscular or subcutaneous injection to mainlining (intravenous use).

Prolixin® (Squibb)   A major tranquilizer that contains fluphenazine hydrochloride and is generally used for psychotic disorders.

Prolixin is not an abused drug. It is supplied in 1 mg pink tablets; 2.5 mg yellow tablets; 5 mg green tablets; and 10 mg coral tablets. It is also available in an orange–colored and flavored elixir.

proof   An official measurement, usually made with an alcoholometer or hydrometer, of the amount of absolute alcohol in a distilled spirit. The American system of proof measurement is based upon the percentage of absolute alcohol in the liquor at 60 degrees F. The proof measurement is double the percentage of alcohol: 100 proof = 50% alcohol. The British system is based upon a comparison of equal volumes of liquor and water at 51 degrees F.

propoxyphene   A SYNTHETIC ANALGE-SIC. Propoxyphene hydrochloride was first synthesized in 1953 by Pohland and Sullivan. It was first marketed in 1957 as DAR-VON by Lilly & Co., who claimed that the new drug was as effective as codeine but did not share its side effects or addictive nature. Propoxyphene is in fact very similar to codeine and methadone, except that it lacks an antitussive effect. Nearly 20 million prescriptions for Darvon are written annually, making it one of America's most widely used narcotics.

Appearance and Activity: Propoxyphene hydrochloride is an odorless bitter–tasting white crystalline solid, soluble in water and slightly soluble in alcohol. It also occurs as propoxyphene napsylate which is not water soluble. The effects of the drug peak in two to two and a half hours. This drug has not been determined safe for use during pregnancy.

Dosage: Propoxyphene is prescribed in 32–65 mg doses to be taken three or four times daily: 90–120 mg is equivalent to 60 mg of codeine, and 100 mg of the napsylate form is equivalent to 65 mg of the hydrochloride form. The drug is not prescribed for children. Intravenous administration is not recommended either—it is very irritating and results in damage to the veins and soft tissue.

Effect: Darvon and other forms of propoxyphene produce the drowsiness and euphoria typically associated with morphine and codeine, as well as pain relief. The drug acts as a CNS depressant and has side effects such as dizziness, headache and nausea. It brings on withdrawal symptoms when given to addicts of heroin and other opiates. Overdoses can cause gastrointestinal distress, convulsions, respiratory depression, circulatory collapse and even coma and psychosis. In cases of overdose, a narcotic antagonist such as NALOXONE should be administered. Tolerance and physical and psychological dependence can develop.

Usage: Propoxyphene is used medically to relieve mild to moderate pain and occasionally for withdrawal treatment for morphine and heroin addiction. Recreational use does occur but very large doses (over 500 mg) are required to achieve and maintain a "high" and hallucinations may also occur. Such high levels of ingestion are dangerous and can result in side effects. Overdosage can result in convulsions, depressed respiration, coma and death. The medical profession agrees that Darvon is overprescribed and therefore somewhat abused.

Availability: Propoxyphene hydrochloride is commercially available as Darvon, football–shaped capsules colored light pink, red and gray, or red and pink (Darvon is known on the street as "pinks" or "red and grays"). The drug is also available in combination with aspirin and other drugs, in capsule or tablet form. DOLENE is another brand name, while Darvon–N and such variations refer to the napsylate form.

Propoxyphene is a Schedule IV drug under the Controlled Substances Act.

propoxyphene napsylate   See PROPOX-YPHENE HYDROCHLORIDE. The substance differs from propoxyphene hydrochloride in that it allows more stable liquid dosage forms and tablet formations. It is also longer acting than the hydrochloride.

prostitution   Many women, particularly street addicts, obtain money for drugs through prostitution; some work on their own, and others are involved in ORGANIZED CRIME. There is, consequently, a high incidence of venereal disease among women addicts involved in prostitution. An addict who supports her habit in this way is also apt to become more deeply addicted: it provides an escape from a dismal life.

Although the likelihood of pregnancy is reduced for a heroin addict, it is possible, and the effects of addiction are passed on to the child. (See also PREGNANCY.)

protopine   A crystalline alkaloid found in small quantities in opium and some papaveraceous plants.

psilocybin   The active hallucinogenic ingredient of the mushroon *Psilocybe mexicana* and some of the other psilocybe and conocybe species. Ritual use of psilocybin among Mexican and Central Amercian cultures is known to date back to at least 1500 B.C.

Some tribes of Indians in Mexico have used certain mushrooms with hallucinogenic properties in their religious ceremonies for centuries. These mushrooms, specimens of the genera *Conocybe Stropharia,* and *Psilocybe* were considered to be sacred and were named *teonanacatl,* or flesh of the gods.

In 1958 Albert Hofmann, a Swiss chemist, isolated psilocybin and its congener, psilocin, from *Psilocybe mexicana.* Psilocybin is the only naturally occurring hallucinogen identified thus far that contains phosphorus.

In pure form psilocybin is a white crystalline material, but it may also be distributed in crude mushroom preparations, in intact dried mushrooms, or as a capsule containing a powdered material of any color. It is usually taken orally but may also be injected. Doses generally vary from 4 mg to 5 mg, although 20–60 mg is not unusual. The potency of psilocybin lies somewhere between that of mescaline and LSD and the effects are reported to be much like those of LSD.

Classification: Psilocybin is a hallucinogen. It shows cross–tolerance to LSD and mescaline.

Effects: When taken orally psilocybin is one of the most rapid–acting hallucinogens: initial effects may be felt 10 to 15 minutes after ingestion. Reactions often reach maximum intensity after about 90 minutes and do not begin to subside until two to three hours later. The effects of psilocybin usually last five to six hours in all but doses larger than 8 mg probably prolong their duration. Physiological effects include increased pulse rate, respiratory rate and body temperature, dilated pupils and elevation of systolic blood pressure. Larger doses, 13 mg or more, can produce dizziness, lightheadedness, abdominal discomfort, numbness of tongue, lips or mouth, nausea, anxiety and shivering. Psychological effects with small doses may include mental and physical relaxation, detachment from surroundings and sometimes coexisting feelings of anxiety or elation. With larger doses individuals may experience difficulty in thinking and concentrating, visual distortions and other changes in perception.

Addictive aspects: Physical DEPENDENCE on psilocybin has not been reported.

Tolerance: Tolerance to psilocybin does develop, and there is a CROSS–TOLERANCE to the effects of LSD and MESCALINE.

Sources: It is difficult to estimate how much psilocybin is available to users. Some may be extracted from mushrooms for street sale, and some may be synthesized. Some users grow their own mushrooms. Psilocybin can be bought as a liquid or powder or as whole mushrooms. Much of what is sold as psilocybin is actually PCP and, sometimes, LSD.

Synonyms: sacred mushroom.

psychedelic   See HALLUCINOGEN.

psychoactive   Drugs that alter thinking, perception, emotions or consciousness are termed psychoactive. They are sought after by drug abusers.

psychodrama   Acting out a problem. A form of drug rehabilitation generally used in group therapy to heighten a person's awareness of his problem, it is thought to provide more immediacy than simple discussion. Under the direction of a therapist, a member of the group portrays himself while another member takes on the role of the person associated with the problem—spouse, parent, employer or whoever. Sometimes role-reversal is also used; the member takes on the role of the person he believes is associated with his problem.

psychological dependence   A broad general term which refers to a craving or compulsion to continue the use of a drug because it gives a feeling of well–being and satisfaction. The term HABITUATION is frequently used interchangably with the term psychological dependence; the syndrome is also known as behavioral, psychic or emotional dependence.

In chronic drug use psychological dependence is considered more serious and more difficult to deal with than physical dependence. Psychological dependence can vary in intensity from a mild preference for a drug to a strong craving for it. The World Health Organization defines psychic dependence as "a feeling of satisfaction and a psychic drive that requires periodic or continuous administration of a drug to produce a desired effect or to avoid discomfort." An individual can be psychologically dependent on a drug and not physically dependent and the reverse is also true.

psychological models of etiology   Along with sociocultural and physiological theories, this is one of the three major categories of theories on the cause of alcoholism. As alcohol is a sedative drug, it is possible that psychological etiological theories can also be applied to other sedative drugs.

The theories are based on the assumption that some element in the personality structure leads to the development of alcoholism. Although studies have failed to come up with specific personality traits that differentiate alcoholics from other people, there is evidence that once a pattern is established alcoholics have certain traits in common: a low tolerance to stress; insecurity; depression; negative self–image; and dependency. It is not clear whether these traits are a result of alcoholism or precede alcoholism because most studies have been conducted on alcoholics. (See also ORAL FIXATION and BEHAVIORAL LEARNING THEORIES.)

psychosis   A mental state characterized by defective or lost contact with reality. In toxic psychosis, acute or chronic psychotic–like behavior results from impairment of brain cell function; symptoms can include extreme confusion, hallucinations, disorientation, depression and aggressive behavior. Schizophrenic and manic depressive psychosis are examples of what has been called functional psychoses.

psychostimulant   See STIMULANT.

psychotogenic   Drugs that produce hallucinations and delirium when taken in large doses. In smaller doses they produce euphoric effects.

psychotomimetic   Drugs that produce hallucinations and alter perception; many of the effects resemble forms of psychosis. Psychotomimetic drugs are usually stimulants and psychedelics.

psychotropic   The term is used interchangeably with PSYCHOACTIVE and is applied to mind–altering drugs.

Public Affairs Committee   A nonprofit educational organization founded in 1935. Its purpose is to "develop a new technique to educate the American public on vital economic and social problems and to issue concise and interesting pamphlets dealing with such problems." The committee offers an extensive variety of pamphlets dealing with substance abuse and its consequences.

public drunkenness   The most visible kind of alcoholic, a public inebriate has symbolic significance for all alcoholics. The English Parliament in 1606 considered public intoxication a legal matter and this approach was brought to America. In 1980 the number of arrests for public drunkenness numbered more than 1.1 million. In 1971 the Uniform Alcoholism and Intoxification Treatment Act was established to decriminalize alcoholism and intoxication and to approach them from a health standpoint. The act states that "alcoholics and intoxicated persons may not be subjected to criminal prosecution because of their consumption of alcoholic beverages but rather should be afforded a continuum of treatment in order that they may lead normal lives as productive members of society." The act has helped to destigmatize alcoholism and to reduce the number of alcoholics who are incarcerated, but it has not brought chronic public inebriates into treatment voluntarily or kept them in treatment. In addi-

tion, treatment programs often write off public inebriates as unlikely to recover.

Puerto Rico   From 1966 to 1972 heroin was the major drug of abuse in Puerto Rico. From 1972 to the present, there has been a significant increase in polydrug use and a preference for marijuana; heroin use has shown a noticeable reduction.

Heroin use in Puerto Rico closely follows the pattern set by Puerto Ricans living in the United States. In 1976 there were an estimated 125,000 opiate addicts in New York City and one–third were Puerto Rican (Puerto Ricans at that time comprised 12% of the metropolitan area population). The high proportion of Puerto Rican addicts in New York is thought to be due to the unfavorable conditions in which they live, often in poor slum areas, along with the cultural differences and the physical separation from parents and other relatives. Although there have been mass migrations to the U.S. in the past, a recent trend seems to be a return to Puerto Rico, perhaps as a result of dissatisfaction with being an ethnic minority in a country where they are citizens.

In the past 15 years drug addiction has become a social problem of epidemic proportions in Puerto Rico, a result of both economic and sociocultural factors. The unemployment rate has been steadily increasing since 1970, particularly among young males. Education is closely tied to the unemployment rate, and although 50% of the work force has completed 12 years of schooling, the highest rate of unemployment persists among those who dropped out of school between grades 6 and 12. In 1978 the per capita income was $2,678; while this was high compared to most Latin American countries, it still left 60% of the island's families living below the federal poverty level. The life–style of the island's inhabitants has also changed drastically, particularly since Puerto Rico became a U.S. territory (1898) and its inhabitants became citizens (1917). There have been rapid changes in industrial development, occupation patterns (women are joining the work force), and social structures.

The Department of Drug Addiction Services (DAS), created in 1973, has the responsibility for reducing alcohol and drug dependence and addiction. According to the DAS, heroin use among its clients declined from 63% in 1975–76 to a current 45%. Marijuana use rose from 19% to 46% in the same time period. Arrests and interventions for drug–related incidents, reported by the Criminal Investigation Bureau of the Police of Puerto Rico, reflect the same pattern. Polydrug use has also increased. Among young clients, 88% admitted use of marijuana and inhalants. The popularity of cocaine has increased in the past few years and, in polydrug use, cocaine is becoming the secondary drug of abuse. Only in a small number of cases is it the primary drug of abuse.

While drug abuse trends in Puerto Rico generally follow the trends on the mainland, there is one exception: the use of inhalants. The popularity of inhalants as an intoxicating drug waned in the U.S. quite a number of years ago, but in Puerto Rico they are still extensively used particularly by young people.

Authorities in Puerto Rico acknowledge a shortage of treatment centers, particularly centers to deal with young people using minor drugs such as marijuana. They tend to agree that a major problem on the island is the fact that marijuana is classified with heroin under the Controlled Substances Act and most treatment centers are now designed for heroin addicts. There are plans for future treatment centers to help young people, women and the elderly, particularly detoxification centers, hotlines, and therapeutic communities. Puerto Rico is well aware of its drug problem and its lack of treatment fa-

cilities, and plans to emphasize a community approach to treatment and prevention education. This approach has also been directed toward the alcohol problem on the island.

The consumption of alcoholic beverages is a deeply ingrained tradition in Puerto Rico and is increasingly becoming more of a problem. Undoubtedly, the same economic and sociocultural factors that are thought to account for the abuse of other drugs are the root cause. In 1978, 18.6% of the per capita income was spent on alcohol, the most popular beverage being the locally produced rum which is known and highly prized throughout the world.

Statistics show that "heavy drinkers" (three out of every 10 drinkers fall into this category) tend to be males between the ages of 20 and 49, and the age at which this group begins drinking grows younger all the time. From 1979–80, 92% of all arrests for drunkenness were for drunk driving and the rate of deaths per 100,000 miles traveled by car was twice that of the U.S.

pyrahexyl   A semisynthetic derivative of cannabis which has similar effects.

pyribenzamine   An antihistamine (also called PBZ and manufactured by Geigy). Its generic name is tripelenamine. There was a short–lived fad of injecting "Blue Velvet," a mixture of pulverized pyribenzamine tablets and boiled paregoric. There were numerous deaths from plugged veins, thought to have been a result of the talc used as a filler in the tablets. Recently, pyribenzamine has been combined with Talwin as "Ts and blues," the "blues" referring to the color of the scored 50 mg tablets.

Q

Quaalude® (Lemmon)   A non–barbiturate sedative hypnotic that contained methaqualone. The Lemmon Company removed the drug from the market in the early 1980s because of its widespread abuse. It was prescribed for daytime sedation and to produce sleep, and was once thought to be nonaddictive. It was supplied as Quaalude–150, white scored tablets containing 150 mg methaqualone; and Quaalude–300, 300 mg white scored tablets. The most common illicit methaqualone produced today resembles the original Quaaludes. It is a Schedule II drug under the Controlled Substances Act. (See also METHAQUALONE.)

Quibron Plus® (Mead Johnson)   A bronchodilator that contains theophylline, guaifenesin, ephedrine and butabarbital, and is usually used in the treatment of bronchial asthma, bronchitis and emphysema. It may be habit–forming. It is supplied in yellow capsules and as an elixir.

quinine   A bitter crystalline alkaloid derived from the bark of the cinchona tree that is used as an antipyretic, antimalarial medicine. After an outbreak of malaria among heroin addicts in New York City in the 1930s, quinine became a popular dilutant of heroin. In the amounts found in street heroin, quinine cannot cure malaria but when the solution is dissolved for injection the quinine may kill the malaria parasite. Quinine is also added because it is thought to enhance the "rush" felt after injection, and because it has a bitter taste. Heroin is often diluted with milk sugar (lactose) which masks its bitter taste, so quinine is added to provide the bitterness in case an addict wishes to taste–test the heroin before buying it to ensure its po-

tency. Some addict deaths labeled "heroin overdose" are thought to be due to sensitivity to intravenous quinine.

R

radioimmunoassay (RIA)   A technique used for urine testing to detect the presence of drugs in the body.

Rand Report   In 1971 the National Institute on Alcohol Abuse and Alcoholism (NIAAA) sponsored and subsidized the Rand Corporation, an independent nonprofit research organization, to prepare an analysis of NIAAA's comprehensive alcoholism treatment program. In June 1976, the Rand Corporation published its findings in a report entitled *Alcoholism and Treatment*.

The highly controversial report contained the following conclusions and considerations:

Treatment: A slightly higher rate of remission was reported for clients who underwent treatment than for those who had a single contact with a treatment center (the terms "single contact" and "untreated" were used synonymously in the report). As the amount of treatment increased, there were slight additional advantages.

Remission Rates: Treated clients, 70% (results varied little from one treatment program to another); untreated clients with Alcoholics Anonymous attention, nearly 70%; untreated clients (natural remission), 50%. Throughout the report the term "remission" was used to include both abstention and "normal drinking." Normal drinking was used to cover consumption in moderate quantities where no serious signs of impairment were present.

Relapse rates: The report stated that "relapse rates for normal drinkers are no higher than those for long–term abstainers." The study further suggested "the possibility that for some alcoholics moderate drinking is not necessarily a prelude to full relapse."

Other conclusions of the report: No pattern was found to suggest that one program was better for a client than another. The study did conclude, however, that "recovery from alcohol dependency may depend on mechanisms quite unrelated to the factors that led to excessive drinking in the first place."

Future considerations of the report: If future research were to confirm the initial conclusions of the survey, total abstinence would not be the only goal of treatment. Research would be needed to determine which alcoholics could return to normal drinking. And if the study's theory that the results of most programs are uniform was corroborated, in regard to a client's drinking and other behavior patterns, then less expensive methods of treatment could be used.

Throughout the report, the authors pointed out the limitations of their sample: that conclusions about behavior were not based on controlled experimental data, just observation; that the time frame of the study was limited and the size of the sample was small; and that future behavior would not necessarily conform to the survey data. These limitations noted by the authors were seized upon by critics. They claimed that the report was actually harmful and deluded alcoholics into believing they could actually resume drinking without disastrous results. Critics suggested that the samples were not randomly selected and that a large portion of interviewing was done over the phone by people with only limited training. They also questioned whether all the clients in the survey were actually alcoholics. They noted, too, the time period involved (18 months after a client entered treatment) and said that previous studies over substantially longer periods had rejected the conclusions given in the report.

Rand Report II. A second report, published in January 1980, under the title *The Course of Alcoholism: Four Years After Treatment,* was a continuation of the previous study. Although not a "retraction," the second report modified many of the conclusions in the original. The authors suggested that the issues were more complex than originally suggested and characterized the second report as another phase of continued study.

Also sponsored by NIAAA, the second study was a follow–up on the sample clients involved in the first study. The report confirmed the earlier finding that some alcoholics are able to return to social drinking. For most alcoholics, however, they found that total abstinence seemed to be the surest method of maintaining remission.

The Rand Report II concluded that for younger unmarried alcoholics (under 40 years old), who were often under social pressure to drink, attempts at abstinence might be more stressful than non–problem social drinking. For older married alcoholics who remained abstinent there was less likelihood of relapse.

The report found that 46% of the 900 men studied were in remission, with 28% abstaining and 18% drinking socially. The study showed that alcoholics who entered treatment programs were highly unstable in their ability to refrain indefinitely from problem drinking, with many relapsing several times during the four years and entering various treatment programs from time to time. The highest rate of long–term abstinence was found among men who regularly attended AA; although it was shown that they were just as likely to have relapses as those who did not attend. The worst prognosis was for short–term abstainers (less than six months); they had a much higher rate of relapse and many more alcohol–related deaths.

The authors of this four–year study, the most comprehensive and extensive to date (at a cost of half a million dollars), do not recommend a particular treatment approach nor do they recommend that an alcoholic resume drinking. What the report does is to raise questions about the nature and treatment of alcoholism. Less controversial in its findings, the second report received less criticism and press coverage than the first.

Rastafarians   In 1930, when Ras Tafari was crowned Emperor of Ethiopia and took the name Haile Selassie, the first Rastafarians appeared in Jamaica and looked to Selassie as their messiah. Their objective was— and still is—to revitalize and promote their African heritage.

The Rasta God is called Jah and some orthodox followers grow dreadlocks (long unaltered locks formed by washing the hair and allowing it to dry without combing) as a symbol of their devotion. The Rastafarians believe the smoking of GANJA (the Jamaican word for marijuana, taken from the Hindu) is one of their strongest shared experiences and look on ganja as a divine herb important to their spiritual, mental and physical health. Most probably marijuana was introduced to Jamaica by indentured laborers from India in the mid–1800s and there are estimates that between 60% and 70% of the island's population now ingests ganja in one form or another. The "herb" (as it is often referred to) has been illegal to use, possess and sell since 1913 but the police are usually nonchalant about enforcing the law and the ganja trade has been unofficially tolerated. Recently, however, the Jamaican government has felt the trade was slipping out of control and called in the U.S. Drug Enforcement Administration for assistance.

The Rastafari smoke ganja in "spliffs," five–inch cone–shaped rolls made from paper or cornhusks. It is also brewed in a green tea and this is the form usually used by women and children. Ganja tea is a major folk remedy often used for rheumatism, sleeping difficulties and especially male impotence. It is also used as an external tonic for wounds, infections and allergies. Kali (the Hindu black goddess of strength) is the most potent grade of ganja.

Reggae music, a basic rock–steady sound with a two–beat riff that swells and hypnotizes, brought the Rastafari to worldwide attention in the late 1960s and was especially popularized by Bob Marley. The lyrics of many reggae songs reflect the near–worship of the "mystical herb," as the Rastas refer to it. (See also JAMAICA.)

Rauwolfia serpentina   A DEPRESSANT obtained from the dried root of a small climbing shrub of the *apocynaceae* family, which is native to India and known in English as SNAKEROOT. Indians have used it for 2,500 years in powdered form as a tranquilizer for such conditions as snakebite, hypertension, insomnia and insanity. It is the source of the drug RESERPINE.

Activity: Rauwolfia serpentina is rapidly absorbed from the gastrointestinal tract, widely distributed throughout the body, and excreted slowly in the urine and feces. It depresses the central nervous system at the hypothalamic level, suppressing the sympathetic branch of the autonomic system. Rauwolfia serpentina crosses the placental barrier and also appears in breast milk.

Dosage: The recommended dose for hypertension is 0.5–3.0 mg, and the dosage suggested for emotional disorders is 0.1–2.0 mg.

Effects: Rauwolfia serpentina is an antihypertensive drug which calms symptoms of anxiety such as headache and palpitations without analgesia. It lowers the blood pressure, slows the pulse, causes pupil constriction, and increases gastrointestinal secretion (and should therefore be used cautiously in patients with peptic ulcers and ulcerative colitis). Unlike the minor tranquilizers, Rauwolfia serpentina does not potentiate other CNS depressants, nor does its use lead to tolerance or physical or psychological dependence.

Side effects reported in conjunction with the use of Rauwolfia serpentina include infrequent paradoxical excitation, increased respiratory secretions, gastrointestinal hypersecretion, nasal congestion, nausea, vomiting, diarrhea, drowsiness, depression, rash, impotence, and anorexia in babies of women treated with the drug.

Usage: The Indians who first ground up the Rauwolfia serpentina root and used it to treat hypertension and insanity applied the substance wisely. It is still used in the treatment of mild hypertension and, with additional drugs, for more severe hypertension as well as more agitated psychotic states such as schizophrenia. It should not be used in patients who are suffering from or prone to depression; it induces a depression which has been known to be severe enough to result in suicide, particularly after withdrawal from the drug.

Availability: Rauwolfia serpentina is manufactured as tablets under the name of the root and Raudixin and Harmonyl. It is also available in tablets mixed with thiazides and potassium chloride.

reassurance   A simple therapeutic method of decreasing a client's anxieties or fears by assuring him that his reactions are excessive or his fears groundless. Reassurance is given with sincerity and certainty along with positive, realistic evidence of the needlessness for the anxiety that is being experienced.

receptor sites   Sites within the body where chemical substances interact to produce pharmacological actions. Receptors recognize a substance by its chemical configura-

tion and electrical charge, distinguish it from others, and transmit the signal indicating the presence of the substance which brings about pharmacological action in the target tissue. Opiate receptor sites have been identified in the brain, intestines and spinal cord. Endogenous opioid peptides, or ENDORPHINS, were discovered in 1975 and the discovery of others has followed. Very little is known, however, about where and how the endorphins are produced, and what their exact role is in modulating pain and mood.

recovery   A term often used in the treatment of alcoholism which has no clear definition. It may be applied to a stable remission of symptoms over a period of time. In the case of Alcoholics Anonymous, however, it means complete *abstinence* for a long period. The term does not usually apply to social or psychological factors but to the absence of alcoholic drinking behavior.

recreational drug use   The U.S. Commission on Marijuana and Drug Abuse defined recreational/social drug use as that which occurs in social settings among friends or acquaintances who wish to share a pleasurable experience. Unlike EXPERIMENTAL DRUG USE recreational and social use tends to have more of a pattern but is considerably more varied in terms of frequency, duration and intensity. Regardless of the duration of use, it tends not to escalate in either intensity or frequency.

rectal administration   See ADMINISTRATION.

red eye   See EYES.

rehabilitation   The techniques used to help drug users give up the drug (or drugs) to which they are addicted, and make them feel that they can be useful and respected among their families, friends and community. After detoxification, some sort of rehabilitation is generally needed as follow–up treatment because even though a person is now *physically* free of dependence, his behavior patterns and needs may not have changed. Detoxification usually occurs in a hospital but only a small number of hospitals have rehabilitation centers. Rehabilitation centers are more apt to be private and are often situated in rural areas with pleasant surroundings. In the case of alcoholism, whether or not a rehabilitation center is part of the plan, nearly all modes of treatment emphasize membership in Alcoholics Anonymous. (See also HALFWAY HOUSES, GROUP THERAPY, and EMPLOYEE ASSISTANCE PROGRAMS.)

reinforcement, positive and negative
Positive reinforcement is a process by which a response to a stimulus is strengthened usually by rewarding the response. Negative reinforcement is the reverse process; a response to a specific stimulus is punished. When a response has been frequently rewarded or punished so that it becomes regularly elicited or avoided, the organism has been conditioned. During classical conditioning the stimulus may be paired with a second stimulus, and it will evoke a similar response.

relapse   The return to the use of a drug and the revision of old habits following a seemingly satisfactory adjustment. Relapse may be related to, or attributable to, the availability of the drug, mixing with friends who are still addicted to the drug, returning to an old environment, or for reasons of physiology or personality. Although relapse may be because of depression or frustration, it also occurs because of overconfidence. When a patient has made progress in treatment he often feels ready to handle difficult situations which he may not be ready for.

relaxation training   Any number of techniques that are used to achieve muscle relaxation. Anxiety states may persist because the client is unaware that his muscles are in a state of chronic tension. A feedback loop exists between tensed muscles and psychological tensions. If muscle tension can be relaxed by biofeedback, self–hypnosis or progressive muscle relaxation exercises, it is difficult to feel anxious. Even when drugs are required for anxiety reduction, relaxation training improves the effect of the anti–anxiety drugs.

Release   Based in England, with headquarters in London, Release is a national 24–hour welfare and advice agency which specializes in urgent problems, particularly in the area of drugs and criminal law. Staffed by both professionals and volunteers, Release provides counseling, advice, education and information on drug use and abuse.

REM (Rapid Eye Movement)   One of the various stages of sleep, and the stage in which a person dreams. All the orders of the sleep cycle are biologically essential, and when deprived of REM a person may become hostile, irritable and anxious. Barbiturates and other sedatives suppress REM, and alcohol, at some consumption levels, also reduces REM sleep.

remission   According to *Webster's Second International Dictionary,* remission is defined as "a temporary and incomplete subsidence of the force or violence of a disease or of pain." Since it is extremely difficult to say when someone is completely recovered from a drug abuse problem, the term "remission" is often used instead of the word "recovery."

In the case of alcohol, both abstainers and CONTROLLED DRINKING alcoholics are considered to be in remission. Alcoholics Anonymous believes that remission is a state of complete abstinence. On the other hand, the RAND REPORT expands the definition to cover an alcoholic who is able to maintain a course of "normal" drinking—a daily consumption of less than 3 ounces of ABSOLUTE ALCO-HOL—with no tremors or other serious symptoms related to drinking. Other alcohol specialists consider that such an amount of alcohol is excessive, especially if consumed within a short period of time.

Repan® (Everett)   A sedative and analgesic that contains 50 mg of butalbital (an intermediate–acting BARBITURATE), caffeine, phenacetin and acetaminophen. It is used for the relief of pain associated with nervous tension. Because it contains a barbiturate it may be habit–forming and dependence can occur. It is supplied in yellow tablets.

reserpine   A DEPRESSANT and TRANQUIL-IZER. Reserpine is an alkaloid of RAUWOLFIA SERPENTINA and can also be synthesized. In the last 20 years, it and other Rauwolfia derivatives have been significant in the treatment of patients suffering from psychotic disorders.

Appearance and Activity in the Body: Reserpine is an odorless white, off–white or yellowish crystalline powder. It is insoluble in water, slightly soluble in alcohol and freely soluble in acetic acid.

Rapidly absorbed in the gastrointestinal tract and widely distributed throughout the body, reserpine crosses the placental barrier, appears in breast milk and is excreted in the urine and feces.

Dosage: Recommended dosages of reserpine range from 0.1–1.0 mg, with 0.5 mg daily suggested for hypertension. Administered intravenously, effects begin to manifest in one hour and last six to eight hours. The onset of effects with intramuscular injection is slower, but they can last 10–12 hours.

Effects: Reserpine's effects resemble those of Rauwolfia serpentina. The drug alleviates anxiety and tension without causing disequilibrium or loss of motor control. It lowers blood pressure. Reserpine does not have anticonvulsant or antihistaminic properties. Tolerance and dependence do not develop. The drug can induce depression, and its cardiovascular and central nervous system depressant effects continue after use of the drug has stopped.

Usage: Like Rauwolfia serpentina, reserpine is used to relieve rapid heartbeat, symptoms of anxiety, tension and hypertension, and agitated psychotic states such as schizophrenia. It has a low abuse potential and is not available on the black market.

Availability: Reserpine is manufactured as tablets under the names Diutensen®, Diupres®, Hydropres®, Regroton® and Reserpine®, and in injectable form under the name Serpasil®.

resin   The oily substance secreted by the CANNABIS plant. It contains TETRAHYDRO-CANNABINOL and other cannabis derivatives.

reverse tolerance   A condition in which the response to a certain dose of a drug increases with repeated use. In marijuana use, consistent users sometimes claim to require lesser amounts to achieve the desired effect. Some experts attribute this to more efficient smoking and earlier identification of the symptoms of marijuana intoxication than to tolerance.

rhinophyma   A skin condition of the nose characterized by swelling, redness and, often, broken capillaries. It is also called whiskey nose and is sometimes caused by excessive drinking over a prolonged period. (See also GROG BLOSSOM and ACNE ROSACEA.)

Ritalin® (CIBA)   A central nervous system stimulant that contains methylphenidate hydrochloride. It is used in the treatment of narcolepsy, Minimal Brain Dysfunction, and to treat patients showing withdrawn senile behavior. Tolerance can develop and it has a potential for abuse. Physical and psychological dependence can occur. Overdosage can result in agitation, tremors, convulsions and hallucinations. It is supplied in 5 mg pale yellow tablets; 10 mg pale green tablets; and 20 mg peach–colored tablets.

RNA   Ribonucleic acid. RNA is a protein found in the chromosomes of all living cells and is one of the two main types of nucleic acid (the other is DNA). RNA plays an important part in the storage and replication of hereditary information and in protein synthesis.

Robitussin A–C® (Robins)   An expectorant and cough suppressant that contains 100 mg of guaifenesin and 10 mg codeine phosphate. It may be habit–forming. It is supplied as an amber–colored elixir with 3.5% alcolhol.

rock groups   See MUSIC AND DRUGS.

rubbing alcohol   A poisonous nondrinkable solution made with isopropyl alcohol rather than ethyl alcohol or ethanol. It is used externally for medicinal purposes.

rum fits   Convulsive seizures of the grand mal type in which the patient loses consciousness. They are associated with withdrawal from alcohol and appear to develop in a minority of alcoholics. Rum fits often appear in clusters, and can start as early as 12 hours after abstinence. They may be associated with DELIRIUM TREMENS, the last stage of withdrawal.

S

sacred mushrooms   See MUSHROOMS, SACRED.

Salvia divinorum   A plant belonging to the mint family. Its leaves are chewed or brewed into a tea for their hallucinogenic effects.

Sanorex® (Sandoz)   An anorectic that contains mazindol and is used for weight control. Its activity is similar to that of the AMPHETAMINES and tolerance can develop within a few weeks. It has a significant potential for abuse and psychological dependence can occur. Overdosage can result in restlessness, tremors and rapid respiration. It is supplied in 1 mg elliptical white tablets, and in 2 mg round white scored tablets.

San Pedro cactus   *Trichocereus pachanoi.* A native of Peru and Ecuador, the stem of the plant is peeled and eaten or brewed into a beverage for its psychedelic effects.

Sansert® (Sandoz)   A sympatholytic antagonist to epinephrine and similar drugs. Used for the prevention or reduction of intense, frequent vascular headaches, it causes vasodilation and increases the tone of alimentary tract muscles and other smooth muscle tissue. It contains 2 mg of methysergide maleate. Chemically related to LSD, in large amounts it can produce similar effects and therefore may have the potential for abuse. It is supplied in bright yellow tablets.

sassafras   *Sassafras officinal albidum.* Though there are claims that it has psychedelic properties, the plant contains the toxic ether, safrole.

S.B.P. Plus® (Lemmon)   A sedative hypnotic that contains three BARBITURATES—50 mg sodium secobarbital, 30 mg sodium butabarbital, and 15 mg phenobarbital—along with 2.5 mg homatropine methylbromide. It is used to induce sleep. Tolerance can develop and both physical and psychological dependence can occur. The drug has a potential for abuse. It is supplied in orange scored tablets.

scheduled drugs   See CONTROLLED SUBSTANCES ACT.

schizophrenia   A mental disorder characterized by withdrawal from reality. It involves emotions, drive, behavior and thinking. Several drugs subject to abuse, such as alcohol, amphetamines and hallucinogens, can produce schizophrenic–like symptoms in an individual which can last up to a week. In the case of LSD these symptoms can continue for several years in isolated instances.

scopolamine   A belladonna alkaloid. It is a nonbarbiturate sedative hypnotic that has been used as a "truth serum." Large doses can produce hallucinations and are accompanied by adverse toxic reactions. It appears as scopolamine hydrobromide in several non–prescription sedatives such as Sominex.

Scotch broom   *Cytisus scoparius,* a toxic plant containing CYTISINE.

Seconal® (Lilly)   A sedative hypnotic that contains secobarbital sodium, a short–acting BARBITURATE. It is used for insomnia and for pre–operative sedation. It may be habit–forming and when taken with alcohol or other central nervous system depressants can have an additive effect. Both physical and psychological dependence can occur and

it has the potential for abuse. Overdosage can result in respiratory depression, depression of reflexes, lowered body temperature and coma. It is supplied as Seconal Sodium in 30 mg, 50 mg and 100 mg orange–red capsules. It is also supplied as an elixir, in suppositories, and in ampules and hyporets for injection.

Sedapap® (Mayrand)   A sedative hypnotic that contains 648 mg of acetaminophen and 16 mg butabarbital (a short–acting BARBITURATE). It is generally used as an analgesic for arthritic and rheumatic conditions and for tension headache. It may be habit–forming and can produce dependence.

sedative   A drug that relaxes and calms. (See TRANQUILIZERS.)

sedative hypnotic   A drug that relaxes, calms and also induces sleep depending on the dose. These drugs depress the central nervous system and can be either barbiturates or nonbarbiturates.

sedativism   Addiction to a sedative drug. The word is also used to describe excessive use of sedatives, or dual or multiple dependence on sedatives.

Sed–Tens Ty–Med® (Lemmon)   A sedative hypnotic that contains 50 mg of amobarbital (an intermediate–acting BARBITURATE) and 7.5 mg homatropine methylbromide. It is used for spasm–tension, nausea and vomiting during pregnancy and for motion sickness. It may be habit–forming and has a significant potential for abuse. Physical and psychological dependence can occur. It is supplied in oblong tablets that are white with pink specks.

seizures   See CONVULSIONS and GRAND MAL CONVULSIONS.

self–help groups   See TREATMENT, RE-
HABILITATION, ALCOHOLICS ANONYMOUS,
NARCOTICS ANONYMOUS and HALFWAY
HOUSES.

sensitivity   A general term which may refer to an allergy or to a hypersensitivity to alcohol or a drug. It is sometimes used as an
explanation of why an individual may be
prone to alcoholism.

Serax® (Wyeth)   A central nervous system depressant that contains the BENZODI-
AZEPINE oxazepam and is used as a tranquilizer for anxiety and tension. Tolerance can
develop and prolonged use can result in
physical and psychological dependence. When
taken with alcohol or other CNS depressants
it can have an additive effect. It is supplied
in 10 mg pink and white capsules; 15 mg red
and white capsules; 30 mg maroon and white
capsules; and 15 mg yellow tablets.

serotonin   A neurohormone, like adren-
alin and acetylcholine, that acts as a transmitter and relays messages in the brain. There
are numerous theories about the relationship
of serotonin and LSD; LSD seems to either
inhibit the action of serotonin or compete
with it. One theory suggests that when serotonin is blocked, subconscious material takes
over a person's consciousness and alters perception. Another theory suggests that when
LSD inhibits serotonin's orderly manner of
transmitting messages, the brain is overcome
with so many messages that it cannot handle
them. A third theory postulates that LSD
monopolizes the monoamine oxidase enzymes which would otherwise be acting on
serotonin to produce metabolites. Without
normal metabolism there is a possibility that
BUFOTENINE might develop as a byproduct,
and bufotenine itself might produce the hallucinations. All of these theories, especially
the latter, are still experimental and have yet

to be proved, and the function of serotonin
itself is still not completely understood.

Sernyl®   An anesthetic and analgesic containing PHENCYCLIDINE that was used in veterinary medicine.

sex   Aphrodisiacs have traditionally been
defined as substances which increase sexual
drive and pleasure, and the search for effective aphrodisiacs has been going on since
time immemorial. Folklore is full of references to foods, herbs, drinks, love potions
and medications which are reputed to stimulate the sexual appetite. A modern redefini-
tion of aphrodisiacs, however, takes into account the subjective pleasure experienced,
not just changes in sex drive. Within this
context, a number of drugs are believed to be
aphrodisiacs. With a few exceptions, they do
not directly affect the genitourinary tract but
act on the brain in such a way as to relieve
the user of social and sexual inhibitions,
making him more apt to express sexual feelings. Research on the effects of such drugs
has been limited by small numbers of sample
subjects, lack of control groups, reliance on
drug–dependent subjects who are in treatment, and an under–representation of women.
It is also difficult to give an accurate account
of the specific effects that drugs have on sexual behavior and response because they vary
from person to person and from time to time
in the same individual, depending on the
dose, the expectations and desires of the user
and the setting in which the drugs are used.

While small doses of alcohol depress the
cerebral cortex and provoke uninhibited behavior, larger doses and chronic use adversely affect neural control and coordination and inhibit sexual performance. Hormonal
changes due to large amounts of alcohol include increased breakdown and reduced synthesis of testosterone, the male sex hormone
which influences the development of mascu-

line secondary sex characteristics, and the lack of which makes sustained penile erection difficult. Alcohol may also stimulate the production of leutinizing hormones which increase sexual drive, leaving the male user in the frustrating position of being sexually stimulated though unable to perform. Male alcoholics sometimes suffer from testicular atrophy and impotence while female alcoholics may experience menstrual irregularity and even amenorrhea (absence of menses).

Low doses of barbiturates and other sedative hypnotics affect the higher cortical functioning of the brain: this reduces anxiety about sexual matters, allowing some individuals to express themselves more freely. Many people are extremely sensitive to even low doses of these drugs, however, and experience a decrease in sexual drive, excitement and orgasm. As with most other substances, high doses and chronic use interfere with sexual pleasure.

The use of STIMULANT drugs, especially amphetamines and cocaine, seems to increase sexual drive at low doses. In addition to enhancing sensory perception and heightening emotional response, this type of drug impedes the venous drainage of erectile tissue and thus prolongs sexual stimulation. (Cocaine is often applied directly to the genitals and prolongs intercourse, partly through anesthetization.) However, at higher doses they decrease sensation, causing delay or failure to ejaculate in men and failure to achieve orgasm in women. Some consistent abusers of stimulant drugs report disinterest and distaste for sexual activity, especially those who administer amphetamines or cocaine intravenously.

According to a 1982 research project conducted at the Haight–Ashbury Free Medical Clinic, a significant number of men and women who had suffered some sexual dysfunction prior to using heroin reported an improvement in sexual functioning when they first began to use the drug. The women reported an increase in relaxation and a lessening of inhibitions, and the men reported delayed ejaculation. Long–term use of heroin has a negative effect on sexual functioning, though, decreasing sexual drive and generally impairing performance. Menstrual irregularity, frigidity and reduced fertility are relatively common among female heroin addicts, while males commonly experience impotence due to decreased testosterone production. These problems occur not only with the use of heroin but also with other opiate drugs, but they usually rectify themselves after withdrawal from the drug.

The effect of hallucinogens on sexuality is inconsistent. Some users are completely disinterested in sex, consumed instead by more profound perceptions, while for others the pleasure of the sexual act is enhanced and heightened in intensity. Erotic feelings may remain on a mental level, with strong spiritual/mystical overtones, rather than on a physical level.

Marijuana and other cannabis drugs relax the part of the brain which records and stores social inhibitions. It can also enhance sensory awareness, stimulating sexual pleasure. The psychological effects of marijuana are not uniform, however, and the drug produces no direct physical reaction which stimulates sexual desire or performance. Like alcohol, large doses of cannabis affect the pituitary gland which may lower the testosterone level and can cause temporary impotence in men. In women it can reduce the production of follicle–stimulating and leutinizing hormones, temporarily reducing sexual drive.

One substance that has been used as an aphrodisiac for centuries is YOHIMBE, a crystalline alkaloid derivative isolated from the bark of the yohimbe tree, found in central Africa. While some researchers recognize this substance as an aphrodisiac, others believe that any increase in sexual powers is probably due to suggestion. Stimulant effects occur with high doses—which can also be highly toxic.

Two other substances which reputedly act as aphrodisiacs are methaqualone (Quaalude), and amyl nitrite, or "poppers." Although frequently used as sex drugs, neither directly affects sexual functioning. Methaqualone dilates the capillaries just below the surface of the skin, producing a tingling sensation which could, depending on the setting and the individual, enhance sexual enjoyment. Amyl nitrite is sold as an "incense" in HEAD SHOPS under a variety of brand names, such as Rush and Locker Room. A vasodilator, it produces a brief high and is alleged to subjectively prolong orgasm. Its relaxation of the anal sphincter also helps to explain its popularity among the gay population.

The research that has been done seems to substantiate the idea that when drugs are used infrequently and at low doses, they can increase the sex drive and enhance sexual pleasure. But pleasure and performance diminish when individuals move from low to high doses and from infrequent to chronic use.

sinsemilla   The potent flowering top (with leaves removed) of the seedless and unpollinated female marijuana plant. The THC content of unpollinated plants is increased when the plant does not devote a large part of its chemical energy to making seeds. To grow sinsemilla, it is necessary to identify and separate female plants before they begin pollination, and to harvest the plants at the peak of their pollen–luring secretions. It is a difficult process, but sinsemilla is highly prized because the THC content can be four to six times that of ordinary marijuana.

Shiva   See SIVA.

Siva   A Hindu god who is credited with bringing cannabis to the world.

SK–Bamate® (Smith, Kline, & French)
A central nervous system depressant that contains MEPROBAMATE and is used as a tranquilizer for states of anxiety and tension and to produce sleep. Physical and psychological dependence can occur and it has a significant potential for abuse. Overdosage can result in stupor, coma and respiratory collapse. It is supplied in 200 and 400 mg white tablets.

SK–65® (Smith, Kline & French)   An analgesic containing 65 mg of PROPOXYPHENE hydrochloride, along with aspirin, phenacetin and caffeine, that is used for mild to moderate pain. Pharmacologically, it is similar to narcotics but does not compare in potency. Psychological and physical dependence can occur, and it has a potential for abuse. When taken with alcohol or other central nervous system depressants it can have an additive effect. Overdosage can result in respiratory depression, extreme somnolence progressing to coma and circulatory collapse. It is supplied in gray and white capsules.

skid row   A hangout for alcoholics and vagrants. Also a term for a convalescent ward in a narcotics hospital. The term originated in Seattle, Washington, when the city's first sawmill was constructed in 1852. The set of tracks over which logs were hauled were called skids and the road was soon called Skid Row. As the area became dilapidated the term took on the meaning it has today.

skinning, skin popping   Subcutaneous injection of a narcotic. This type of injection provides a slower onset of the effects of the drug. Intravenous injection (MAINLINING) results in immediate onset of effects. Addicts usually begin by sniffing a drug, move on to skin popping, and then to mainlining. Abcess formation and, rarely, tetanus are complications of subcutaneous use. (See also AD-MINISTRATION.)

smoking   See NICOTINE.

smuggling   It has been estimated that over 90% of the illicit drugs consumed in the United States are produced in foreign countries. Supplies originate in diverse areas but basically they come from Latin America, Southeast Asia and Southwest Asia.

Shipment into the U.S. is accomplished in a variety of ways. Large–scale professional smugglers use commercial planes and ships for trafficking, but they also tend to use small private aircraft. A private plane is often used on a one–time only basis, to avoid detection, and landings are made at makeshift airfields in rural areas. Small boats are also used extensively for trafficking; often they are disguised as charter fishing craft. Drug trafficking networks are not always this sophisticated, however. Often they employ amateur couriers who are relatively safe from arrest. The couriers are well paid and use every conceivable way of concealing drugs, either on their person or among their possessions. Drugs have been found in suitcases with hollow bottoms; in toy dolls and animals; pressed thin and placed in books. Other innovative smugglers have been known to hide drugs in body cavities; soak their clothes in a drug solution; or swallow small pouches of a drug and later excrete them.

Most illicit drugs are smuggled into the U.S. by way of New York City, Florida and California. The Drug Enforcement Administration is responsible for developing interdiction intelligence and participation in cooperative efforts with the U.S. Customs Service, the U.S. Coast Guard, and the U.S. Border Patrol (part of the Immigration and Naturalization Service), which provide the principal anti–smuggling operations at ports of entry and along land and water borders. These co-operative efforts are having an effect. The South Florida Task Force, for example, which was established in 1982, seems to have reduced the flow into this key trans–shipment point. Although smugglers appear to have diversified their traffic lanes into Texas, the Carolinas and the Northeast, the Task Force has at least kept them off balance and similar task forces are now being established in these new areas as well.

In 1980 an estimated four metric tons of heroin were smuggled into the U.S.; about 60% was refined from opium cultivated in Southwest Asia, 25% from Mexico and the balance from Southeast Asia. Approximately 44 metric tons of cocaine, the top illicit income producer, were smuggled into America in 1980, nearly all of it from South America, particularly Colombia. The traffic in marijuana, which also generates tremendous profits (an estimated $24 billion), is also principally a Colombian operation (75%). The rest comes from Jamaica (10%) and from Mexico (8%); the balance is home–grown domestic. There has also been an extensive increase in the amount of other dangerous drugs brought into the U.S. illegally—such as amphetamines, barbiturates and methaqualone—which have been diverted from legitimate sources or manufactured in highly sophisticated clandestine laboratories many of which are in Europe. A large quantity of these drugs are channeled through Colombia. In 1980 the Drug Enforcement Administration began to take note of large seizures of methaqualone tablets (loads of 1,000 or more pounds) which were arriving surreptitiously in the Southeast U.S. The seizures were often the result of citizen complaints about mysterious aircraft landing on rural roads. The nature of these seizures suggest that authorities are probably only seeing the tip of the iceberg in drug smuggling.

snakeroot   See RAUWOLFIA SERPENTINA.

sniff, sniffing   To inhale a drug through the nostrils. Also referred to as SNORTING. (See also ADMINISTRATION.)

snort, snorting   To inhale a drug through the nostrils. Also a term for COCAINE and HEROIN. (See also ADMINISTRATION.)

sober   A term used for a person who is not under the influence of alcohol or other psychotropic drugs. It is also used to describe an alcoholic who is no longer drinking. To be considered ''legally sober'' a person must have a blood alcohol concentration (BAC) of 0.05% or less. Such a person is not, however, as sober as one who has had nothing to drink.

sober up, sobering up   To become detoxified after drinking. Other than kidney dialysis there is no known way of speeding up the detoxification process. A 150–pound person will usually take an hour to metabolize ¾ of an ounce of absolute alcohol.

social class   There are different attitudes toward drug abuse among the various social classes in the United States. For example, it has been found that as education and income rise, there is also a rise in the frequency of drinking and in the number of drinkers. Upper–class groups generally have a more permissive attitude toward drinking and do not regard it as a moral problem. This attitude is taken less often by lower socioeconomic groups which generally contain a greater number of abstainers. Drinking patterns also differ among social classes: upper–class groups do more drinking in cocktail party settings and lower–class groups are more apt to drink in pub atmospheres. There is less of a difference in drinking patterns between men and women in upper social classes and they also appear less often in alcoholism statistics than men and women of lower–class

groups. Often this is because their style of drinking is less visible and they are usually protected by people close to them who help to hide their alcoholism. In lower social classes individuals who drink in public places are more visible and therefore more likely to encounter trouble with the police. In the treatment of alcoholism, it has been shown that those in lower social classes drop out of therapy more often than those in the middle and upper classes.

Although the trend is now changing, the abuse of cocaine was originally found only among members of the upper socioeconomic group, a fact probably attributable to the high cost of the drug. For years cocaine was thought of as a status symbol.

There are generally more heroin addicts among lower–class groups centered in the slums of metropolitan areas. This high incidence of abuse is attributed to the easy availability of narcotics ''on the street,'' to feelings of defeat and helplessness in individuals living in these areas and to their need to belong to a group. Many heroin addicts simply drift into the habit because of their need for companionship with others who share their feelings. Social class factors are also responsible for the relapse of rehabilitated addicts who return to their old neighborhoods. The goal of therapeutic communities such as SYNANON is to move ex–addicts into drug–free settings.

Amphetamine use does not seem to be centralized in any particular socioeconomic group. Amphetamines have been used by housewives (often as anorectics); by students studying for exams; by truck drivers who need to stay awake on long trips; and by athletes who wish to excel.

Inhalants are sometimes called the ''scrubwoman's high'' because of reports of cleaning women becoming high from the use of cleaning solvents. Although there may be some truth to this, the use of inhalants has spread to all social classes. Certainly glue sniffing among children has not been confined to those of a particular social class, although chronic inhalant abuse is found most often among Mexican American and American Indian youngsters.

Barbiturate use is generally found in middle– and upper–class individuals, particularly women. Anxiety, depression and insomnia were problems that were often simply accepted in past years. Today they may cause some people to rush to the doctor for treatment. Instead of trying to help a patient face and handle the problems that cause anxiety, many physicians will simply prescribe a barbiturate or a benzodiazepine as a sedative hypnotic.

LSD and other hallucinogens first became popular among college students and can thus be linked to middle and upper social classes. As they became readily available on the illicit market, their use spread to all social classes. This phenomenon is not limited to hallucinogens but is seen in the increased use of many other drugs.

Marijuana, one of the most (if not the most) abused drug in the United States, is certainly not restricted to a particular social class; whether because of its availability or its relatively inexpensive cost, its use is widespread. Marijuana use seems to be as prevalent among the teenage children of blue–collar workers as it is among college–educated adults in their 30s—it has been said that marijuana is "the opiate of the masses."

The reported high incidence of drug use among minority populations is sometimes the result of socioeconomics and sometimes not. Because black Americans and Hispanics often fall into the lower socioeconomic groups, social class certainly has a bearing on their drug use. In the case of homosexuals, it is not a matter of education and money: the abuse is more related to the life–style of the group. Drug use among the elderly is not necessarily based on econom-

ics but is certainly rooted in their feelings of loneliness and uselessness to society.

social drinking   The term usually refers to moderate drinking on social occasions. It is also used to refer to drinking in a way that is acceptable to a certain cultural group.

sociocultural etiological theories   One of the three major groups of theories on the cause of alcoholism; the other two being theories based on physiological and psychological causes. Alcohol is a sedative and it is certainly possible that all three groups of theories can also be applied to the use and abuse of other sedative drugs.

Sociocultural etiological theories focus on relationships between various factors in society. For example, different cultures set different standards for what is considered the appropriate use of alcohol; cultural support for the consumption of alcohol is high in France but among Jews, Moslems and Mormons there is a cultural proscription against the use or abuse of alcohol. This same pattern is true of countries that have a long tradition of opiate use (Iran, Pakistan) and countries with a long history of coca use (Peru, Bolivia), whereas the abuse of both cocaine (derived from coca) and opium are frowned upon in the United States.

Cultural stress factors may also contribute to the abuse of sedative drugs, such as crises generated by external events; social instability; family patterns of drug use, and so on. Traumatic events seem to lead to heavy consumption, particularly among women.

Although sociocultural theories are receiving wide support as the cause of alcoholism and drug use, they are generally considered in conjunction with the two other etiological theories—physiological and psychological—since no one theory alone seems to completely explain the causes.

sodium butabarbital   An inter-mediate–acting BARBITURATE usually used to produce sedation and sleep.

Solfoton® (Poythress)   A sedative hyp-notic that contains 16 mg of the long–acting BARBITURATE phenobarbital. It is used for sedation and to produce sleep. Both physical and psychological dependence can occur and it has the potential for abuse. Overdosage can result in respiratory depression and coma. It is supplied in pale green uncoated tablets; light pink sugar–coated tablets; and yellow and brown capsules.

solitary drinking   One of the signs of a drinking problem is when a person drinks alone. Excessive drinking is characteristic of solitary drinkers who, because there are no social activities to divert them, often drink continuously. They often choose to be alone as a way of escaping from their problems and the combination of seclusion, drinking and their initial problems leads to a vicious circle which feeds on itself. Those who take a drink alone after work, or a drink before bed, or who have a beer or two while doing chores are usually not considered to be solitary drinkers.

solvents   See VOLATILE HYDROCARBONS and INHALANTS.

Sominex®   An over–the–counter (OTC) sleep aid that can be potentially harmful be-cause it contains SCOPOLAMINE. Some of the significant side effects of scopolamine are blurred vision, confusion, delirium and heart effects. Scopolamine is generally used to dry up secretions and there is no evidence that the amount in Sominex can be an aid to sleep. In 1975 the Food and Drug Adminis-tration recommended that scopolamine be removed from sleep aids but thus far no ac-tion has been taken.

South Africa   Dagga (cannabis) has long been used in South Africa, particularly among the Bantu people. The South African mine workers often use dagga as an energizer dur-ing their work day. With the exception of al-cohol, the abuse of other drugs was practi-cally unknown until the late 1960s when it appeared that the age of narcotics—and stimulants and depressants—had arrived.

In 1969 the government appointed a com-mittee of inquiry to investigate the extent of drug use. It was found that there was in-creasing experimentation among young peo-ple, and in 1971 the Substances and Rehabil-itation Centres Act was passed. It provided penalties for drug dealing, and use of or pos-session of dangerous drugs. It also estab-lished a National Advisory Board on Reha-bilitation Matters which was instructed to plan and coordinate measures to combat drug use and provide treatment for those persons dependent on drugs. The act also provided for the establishment of both government and private rehabilitation centers and their inspection. Any drug–dependent person who voluntarily desires treatment may apply for admission to a center but the 1971 act also provided for compulsory treatment in cases where a magistrate decided it was necessary. The provisions of the act apply not only to the abuse of dangerous drugs but also to al-cohol abuse which has long been recognized as a problem in South Africa.

Along with the establishment of treatment centers, the government is also establishing national drug education programs. Voluntary welfare organizations are also working on the drug problem. The most active organiza-tion is the South African National Council on Alcoholism and Drug Dependence (SAN-CAD).

Spanish broom   *Spartium junceum,* a toxic plant containing CYTISINE.

Special Action Office for Drug Abuse Prevention (SAODAP)   An agency established by the Office of the Presidency in 1972 to review and evaluate the functions and policies of all government agencies involved in the area of drug abuse, and to establish policies and provide direction necessary to properly coordinate government efforts. It is no longer in existence.

spirits   A term commonly used to refer to the alcoholic essence of a fermented substance. It is also a synonym for alcoholic beverages, as distinguished from the many varieties of chemical alcohols and denatured ethanols which are nondrinkable.

sports and drugs   The use of drugs by competing athletes dates back a hundred years or more; then the popular drugs to use for increased performance were alcohol and caffeine. Today the use of drugs by athletes is far more widespread and while any number of drugs are used, the most popular are amphetamines, steroids and cocaine. Drug use is not limited to professional athletes: it has also been found on both the college and high school levels.

The reasons for drug use vary. In some sports they are taken to diminish pain or fatigue and to increase strength and endurance; in other sports they are taken to provide greater concentration, intensify aggressiveness and the desire to achieve, or to reduce tension and anxiety. Steroids are taken by athletes in order to gain weight and increase body mass.

There has been a recent campaign among athletic organizations, particularly the professional football leagues and the International Olympic Committee, to eliminate the use of drugs. Olympic contestants are aware that they will be tested for evidence of drugs during the Games; in professional football the testing is usually sporadic and players are never sure when they will be tested. The use of drugs by football players was prohibited in 1972. Up to that time it had been common practice for team doctors and trainers to hand out amphetamines and a 1970 survey had shown that 60% of National Football League players took the drugs on a regular basis. Although heavy drug use was violently denied by football officials, a survey taken a year after use was prohibited suggested that many players were continuing to take amphetamines and turning to illicit sources when they were unable to obtain them legally. The testing controversy continues today with many players protesting the practice as an "invasion of privacy."

Amphetamine use by athletes was first reported in the 1940s. They were used by top athletes primarily in endurance sports such as cycling, track, swimming and football. Amphetamines increase respiratory flow, the metabolic rate and cardiac output. They also increase alertness and intensify aggressiveness. In moderate to large doses, they also have an analgesic effect. This ability to relieve pain and increase drive and strength makes amphetamines extremely sought after by athletes involved in contact sports. There are adverse reactions to the use of amphetamines, however: irritability, restlessness, insomnia and impotence, not to mention the possibility of dependence. Amphetamine deaths have also occurred in sports, usually as a result of the drug's cardiovascular effect in combination with heat and overexertion.

The International Olympic Committee defines "doping" as using substances alien to the body in abnormal amounts or by abnormal methods with the aim of taking unfair advantage during competition. If such a substance is used to treat an illness, the fact must be reported. Testing for drugs in Olympic competitions has become mandatory and during the IX Pan American Games held in Caracas, Venezuela, in August 1983, tests proved positive in a number of cases. The presence of steroids was found in eight weightlifters, one an American, and they were stripped of their medals. When this was revealed, 12 U.S. track athletes left the games to return home. The reason for their departure and withdrawal from the Games was not given and it is unsure at this time if it was a protest move or fear of involvement. All competitors were aware they would be tested but the equipment used was so sophisticated and advanced that for the first time it was possible to detect the use of steroids up to a year previously.

The aim of an athlete who takes steroids is muscle hypertrophy. Steroids increase body mass because they improve nitrogen utilization and increase the appetite, though some authorities suggest that fluid retention rather than weight gain actually occurs. Steroids can have adverse reactions on liver function, can diminish libido and cause testicular atrophy along with hypertension. Steroids are generally taken during training periods and not just before a competition.

Testing at the Pan American Games was conducted by a highly advanced laboratory in East Germany (which also has the approval of the Olympics Committee) and involved a two–step procedure. First a urine sample was taken immediately after a competitor had taken part in an event. If the test was positive, the athlete's national Olympic Committee was notified and a second sample was taken in the presence of a committee member. If this test also proved positive, the Pan American Committee was notified and then had to decide on a course of action. The U.S. Olympic Committee has endorsed the testing and has announced that it will cooperate with the testing procedure in the future.

Narcotics are rarely used by athletes unless there is a need to perform in spite of

pain, and consequently they are not a major problem in sports. Alcohol, tranquilizers and other sedatives are sometimes abused, on the other hand, because they have a calming effect on tension, anxiety and tremors. When they are employed it is usually with a certain amount of caution so that oversedation is avoided.

In a June 1982 *Sports Illustrated* article, former Miami Dolphin, New Orleans Saint and San Diego Charger, Don Reese, described in graphic detail the course of his growing dependence on cocaine during his career with the National Football League. Stating that cocaine "controls and corrupts" professional football, Reese told the painful story of how he acquired an expensive habit and how it involved daily freebasing with other players and memory blackouts during games. Cocaine is readily available to NFL players, he said, not only from dealers who sometimes attend practices but also from respected veteran players.

Typical reactions to Reese's confession included accusations that he must be mentally unbalanced to have fallen prey to such a habit and that, accordingly, his allegations must be dismissed. Nevertheless, insiders' reports reveal that as many as 60% of pro football players may regularly snort and freebase cocaine. Coaches and players consistently deny the existence of any drug problem yet continue to oppose urine tests to detect the presence of drugs. The result, as Reese points out, is that "what you see on the tube Sunday afternoon is a lie. When players are messed up, the game is messed up. The outcome of games is dishonest when playing ability is impaired."

Enormous profits are generated by sports events in the United States. While sports fans encourage and demand victory and condone aggressiveness from athletes, it is not difficult to understand why competitors use drugs to achieve what the public wants. Nor is it hard to see why owners, trainers and officials in the various sports want to please the public. Until competitors and management are educated to the dangers of drug use, it will probably continue and grow worse.

spouse abuse   Drug abuse and family violence are clearly connected, particularly violence involving drinking. Although it is a significant problem in the United States, family violence is often ignored, perhaps because of an unwillingness on the part of society to interfere in private lives.

While women are more often seriously injured because of their physical disadvantage, men or women may be the aggressor in cases of spouse abuse. It is estimated that there are some 1.7 million such assaults a year. The FBI's *Uniform Crime Report* indicates that 25% of all murders are committed within families and of these half are spouse killings. Women are just as likely to kill their spouses as men, and they often cite abuse as the motivation.

In what often becomes a vicious circle, spouse abuse is related to child abuse (see CHILDREN OF DRUG DEPENDENT INDIVIDUALS). A man may beat his wife, for example, and she may, in turn, take out her anger and resentment on the children. In addition, a husband or wife who abuses his or her spouse may also abuse the children.

Violent behavior between spouses is often the result of a breakdown of inhibitions because of drug use. Drug use can also be an *excuse* for violence instead of the cause. Violence and drug use may be connected in several ways: a person may take drugs to avoid hitting a person or, in some instances, may hit someone instead of taking a drug. Drug use and family violence can also be part of a cycle that repeats itself from generation to generation: children from abusive families learn coping patterns (the use of drugs and then violence to resolve problems and reassert control) from the same individuals who teach them to love. In this way,

loving and hitting become linked in their minds.

American society in general tolerates a high level of violence and perhaps because of this acceptance victims often hide the fact that they have been abused. A fear of reprisal or lack of understanding by the community is particularly common among women. Feelings of helplessness and despair, along with guilt that she may have failed in a marriage, may lead a wife to feel that she has gotten what she deserves. Women are also likely to remain in an abusive situation because of the fear of divorce and its social and economic impact.

It has been suggested that abused wives have a masochistic streak that keeps them with abusive husbands. Opponents of this theory claim that violence is a result of a build–up of tension and that following a violent episode there is an ensuing period of remorse and apology which rekindles hope in the wife that her husband will revert to previous loving ways.

Initial violence between spouses can lead to more violence. If the abused spouse does not seek help it is taken as a sign of acquiescence and generally leads to more violence.

It has only been recently that women have tended to report spouse abuse to the police. In the last few years alternative help has also been made available to abused women through various women's centers and "hotlines" for battered wives. Men are much less likely than women to report abuse for reasons of pride. It has been estimated that 280,000 men are beaten by their wives each year. Although the number is small compared to the estimated six million abused wives, it is nevertheless significant.

Violence can also occur in more subtle forms; a drug user can emotionally neglect or psychologically abuse his or her family to such an extent that it causes severe damage. The results of emotional or mental abuse can be as destructive as physical abuse.

Alcohol is acknowledged to be the major drug leading to spouse abuse in the U.S. According to one estimate, 80% of all cases of family violence include drinking—either before, during or after the incident (Jerry Flanzer, *The Vicious Circle of Alcoholism and Family Violence*, Alcoholism 1, No. 3, Jan./ Feb. 1981, pp. 30–32). Both moderate and problem drinkers are more frequently involved in incidences of violence than light drinkers. Treatment programs designed to help victims of battering are frequently not capable of addressing alcohol problems. In addition, alcohol counselors themselves do not always know about the mechanics of family violence. As the two problems are closely linked, it is obviously important for programs to consider both aspects during treatment.

spree   A drinking bout, particularly one of prolonged excessive drinking and usually associated with alcoholism.

Stadol® (Bristol)   A narcotic agonist–antagonist that contains butorphanol tartrate. It is a potent analgesic, equivalent to morphine, and is used for moderate to severe pain. It has a potential for abuse and dependency can develop. Because of its antagonist properties it should not be given to patients with a physical dependence on narcotics and it is not recommended for those who have a history of drug abuse. Adverse reactions to Stadol include sedation, nausea and sweating. Overdosage can result in respiratory depression. It is supplied in vials for intravenous and intramuscular injection. Onset of effects when administered intravenously is within 10 minutes and duration of effects is three to four hours.

stall   A stall is the inability to provide a urine specimen on demand. It may be a deliberate withholding of a voided specimen to avoid detection of a drug in the urine. Some people may have difficulty in voiding while being observed. Others may require fluids and the passage of time before being able to pass a sample of urine. When a person is unable to provide a urine sample even after fluids and the passage of time, a stall is considered a positive urine (that is, containing drugs) in many programs.

Statobex® (Lemmon)   An anorectic that contains phendimetrazine tartrate and is used for weight control. Tolerance can develop within a few weeks and because it is chemically and pharmacologically related to the AMPHETAMINES it has the potential for abuse. Psychological dependence and social dysfunction can occur. Overdosage can result in restlessness, tremors, rapid respiration and a confused hallucinogenic state. It is supplied as Statobex, oblong green tablets of 35 mg; and Statobex–D, 70 mg tablets that are white with green specks, and 70 mg capsules that are green and white.

status epilepticus   Convulsive seizures which follow each other with no intervening periods of consciousness. They can result from rapid withdrawal from anticonvulsant or depressant drugs, or they may be spontaneous. Status epilepticus is also possible during withdrawal from amphetamines and cocaine. In the case of grand mal status epilepticus the seizures may persist for hours or even days and can be fatal.

stereotypy   Persistent and often mechanical repetition of senseless words or acts. It is characteristic of schizophrenics and is often seen in amphetamine, phencyclidine and cocaine abusers and alcoholics.

steroids   See SPORTS AND DRUGS.

stimulants   Drugs that stimulate the central nervous system and increase the activity of the brain or spinal cord. They produce greater energy, increase alertness and produce a feeling of euphoria. Amphetamines, antiobesity agents and cocaine are highly abused stimulants. Caffeine and nicotine are also classified as stimulants but have a lesser effect on the body.

stomach The stomach is the hollow muscular organ located between the esophagus and the upper small intestine (duodenum). Its functions include storing and diluting ingested food, secreting gastric juices containing enzymes and other substances important to digestion and nutrition, and contracting to further hasten the breakdown of food through agitation.

Depressant drugs depress the entire metabolic and digestive process. The abuse of alcohol compounds this general disruption by directly damaging the stomach because it increases hydrochloric acid secretion. Factors such as stress and malnutrition often accompany alcoholism and can also contribute to its deleterious effects.

Some 20–25% of ingested alcohol is absorbed in the stomach, and the rest in the duodenum. The rate at which the stomach empties its contents (motility) is extremely important in alcohol absorption and effect. A patient who has had part of his stomach removed becomes intoxicated very quickly on small amounts of alcohol because of quick absorption by the duodenum. Conversely, the presence of food can slow alcohol absorption in the stomach and thus diminish the drug's effect.

Small doses (dilutions of up to 10% alcohol) actually aid digestion, stimulating salivation and gastric secretion and increasing motility. Large doses anesthetize the stomach, irritate the organ's lining and affect the brain to reduce appetite. High concentrations of alcohol can also cause spasms of the pylorus, the opening between the stomach and the duodenum, which may manifest as retching. Alcohol also delays motility, which

causes acid to accumulate and results in hyperacidity.

Acute and chronic gastritis, inflammation of the stomach and its mucous membrane, frequently develops as a result of heavy drinking and is commonly evidenced by nausea, vomiting, diarrhea and belching. Acute gastritis can subside after a few weeks' abstinence but more severe cases are persistent. Membrane erosion, possibly culminating in ulceration, can occur with long–term alcohol abuse. The alcoholic also risks stomach hemorrhage, particularly when alcohol and a drug such as aspirin are combined. Hemorrhage is especially dangerous in the presence of alcoholic gastritis and peptic ulcer since malnutrition may impair coagulation.

Stimulants resemble alcohol in their effect on the stomach. Abuse of this kind of drug increases gastric acid secretion which, in turn, increases the risk of ulcers. Some individuals are so sensitive to caffeine that even relatively small amounts of coffee can make them nauseous and induce vomiting.

Narcotic drugs generally slow digestion by reducing gastric secretion and decreasing motility. Heroin can induce spasms in the stomach's smooth muscle; in fact, addicts often exhibit increased muscular tone in the smooth muscle of the stomach, duodenum and intestines. Heroin addicts are also susceptible to viral infections such as tetanus, which often involves gastrointestinal bleeding. Hypermotility, gastrointestinal cramps, nausea, vomiting and anorexia are symptoms of opiate withdrawal.

Synthetic derivatives of belladonna, stramonium (Jimson weed), and henbane—anticholinergics employed for centuries as poisons and as major components of witches' brews—have been used to reduce gastric secretion and peristalsis in the treatment of gastritis and peptic ulcer. Psychedelic drugs do not seem to share this effect; instead they sometimes cause nausea and vomiting.

Cannabis derivatives are being used medically to control the nausea, vomiting and an-orexia associated with chemotherapy. A few reports of inflammation of the stomach after long–term heavy use of strong cannabis preparations have emerged from Eastern countries, but it is not known if this is due to the cannabis use or to diet or other factors. There is little evidence that marijuana or other cannabis products have any direct effects on the stomach.

Esteban Mezey, "Effects of Alcohol on the Gastrointestinal System," *Practice of Medicine,* Vol. VII, Ch. 36 (Hagerstown, Md: Harper & Row, 1970).

Frederick G. Hofmann, *A Handbook on Drug and Alcohol Abuse* (New York: Oxford University Press, 1977).

Sidney Cohen, *The Substance Abuse Problems* (New York: Haworth Press, 1981).

Ralph W. Richter, ed., *Medical Aspects of Drug Abuse* (New York: Harper & Row, Publishers, Inc., 1975).

stramonium   An alkaloid found in the DATURA plant. It has deliriant effects similar to BELLADONNA, which belongs to the same plant family.

strychnine   An extremely dangerous and toxic central nervous system stimulant that affects the spinal cord first and the cerebrum last. Though rarely used today, it can increase muscle tone in gastrointestinal stasis, debility and paralysis. Its value has been questioned because of the narrow margin between its therapeutic and toxic action.

subculture, drug   An alternative life–style that centers around knowledge of drugs, use of drugs and obtainability of drugs. Members of a drug subculture share norms of behavior that are disapproved by the general culture, which gives them a certain respect and admiration in the eyes of adherents.

Sublimaze® (Janssen)   A narcotic analgesic that contains 0.05 mg fentanyl and whose activity is similar to that of MORPHINE and meperidine. It is used as a pre– and post–operative sedation supplement. A potent analgesic, it has a high potential for abuse and dependency can occur. It is supplied in 2 ml and 5 ml ampules for injection.

substance abuse   A general term used to describe the abuse of drugs.

succinylcholine   A central nervous system depressant that acts as a skeletal muscle relaxant during surgery.

suicide   The intentional taking of one's own life, suicide is generally a result of a depressive state. But there are "accidental" as well as intentional suicides, and these may result from a synergistic effect when depressant drugs are taken together. Because the combination of drugs results in confusion, an individual may take additional doses of a drug without concern for or memory of previous doses.

Taking a barbiturate overdose is a common manner of attempting suicide, particularly among women. Barbiturates are most often prescribed for insomnia, and depression and insomnia often go hand–in–hand. In a non–tolerant person a small amount can constitute a lethal dose, consequently even when doctors are careful not to prescribe more than two week's supply at one time, it is no guarantee against suicide attempts. Accidental deaths from barbiturates combined with alcohol (both sedative drugs) are even more common than planned suicides using just barbiturates.

The benzodiazepine derivatives, which are prescribed as tranquilizers, are very often used in suicide attempts. Valium, a minor tranquilizer, is one of the most widely prescribed drugs. The lethal dose of Valium alone is not known, and individuals ingesting 200 times the average dose have survived. Successful suicides involving Valium are usually a result of its being combined with another depressant.

Attempted or achieved suicides from amphetamines and hallucinogens are generally not the result of an overdosage of a particular drug, but are due to a psychotic state induced by taking the drug in the first place. When an individual's controls are reduced and a paranoid reaction sets in, he or she may impulsively attempt suicide. Accidental suicides have occurred when a person under the effects of a hallucinogen, particularly LSD, imagined that he could stop traffic or fly through the air.

Women are known to have a higher *attempted* suicide rate than men (they are also acknowledged, as a group, to experience depression more often) but men have a higher *completed* suicide rate. Among alcoholic women the number of attempted suicides far exceeds the number among the general female population, and completed suicides among female alcoholics is 23 times that of the general population.

Studies have shown that alcoholics are at a particularly high risk of attempting suicide, and those who commit suicide have attempted to kill themselves more often than nonalcoholics who commit suicide. Studies have also shown that between 15% and 64% of those who attempt suicide and up to 80% of successful suicides were drinking at the time of the event. Combining alcohol with other drugs is probably responsible for a large number of suicides and accidental deaths.

Because depression is usually the cause of suicide, individuals undergoing post-withdrawal depression symptoms from phencyclidine, amphetamines or cocaine are watched very closely.

supra–additive   An interaction of drugs (synergistic or potentiating) in which the effect of two drugs in combination is greater than it would be if the effects were ADDITIVE.

Surital® (Parke–Davis)   A rapid, ultra-short–acting barbiturate containing thiamylal sodium that is used as an intravenous anesthetic. It may be habit–forming but the rapid onset and brief duration of action make it undesirable for purposes of abuse.

susceptibility   During times of stress some individuals exhibit a strong tendency to turn to drugs; such people, who cannot cope in any other way, are said to be susceptible to drugs. It is a vague term, however, that does little to clarify or explain drug addiction.

Sweden   As in most European countries, alcohol is the most widely abused substance in Sweden. There are some 300,000 to 400,000 alcoholics in a population of around eight million. According to Thomas Nordegren of the nation's Committee on Health Education, an average of 16 people die each day as a direct result of their addiction. In comparison, Sweden has 50,000 regular users of cannabis, and 15,000 "mainliners" who inject narcotic drugs (especially heroin) directly into the bloodstream. Opium, morphine, cocaine, amphetamines, tranquilizers and solvents are also abuse problems in Sweden.

The Swedish Council for Information on Alcohol and Other Drugs published statistics in 1977 showing that out of 35 selected countries Sweden is 29th in terms of consumption of "absolute alcohol." The average consumption per capita (for those aged 15 and above) was 5.8 litres, slightly greater than the amount consumed in neighboring Norway (4.4 litres), but considerably less than the amounts consumed in Denmark (8.9 litres) and the United States (8.7 litres). Since alcoholism is by far the greatest drug abuse problem in Sweden, one can see why the country has taken some effective measures to cope with it.

Since the 19th century Sweden's strong voluntary temperance movement has received a good deal of government assistance and approval. Some 400 temperance societies were in existence before the beginning of the 20th century. Between 1922 and 1955 the government operated a passbook rationing system to hold down the alcohol consumption rate. During that time men over 25 years of age were entitled to purchase up to three litres of spirits per month, while women of the same age could obtain the same amount over a three–month period. Rationing was enforced by the adoption in 1922 of the Bratt system under which a state–owned company, Vin–Spritcentralen, was given control of all alcohol sales. This plan was adopted immediately after an all–out prohibition scheme was vetoed.

Parliament abandoned the rationing system in 1955 and transferred the burden of restricting alcohol use to the National Tax Board. Taxes were imposed according to the alcohol content of a beverage. (Today taxes on alcoholic beverages account for about 7% of the state income tax.) The state–controlled company, Systembolaget, was given a monopoly on the retailing of alcoholic beverages, while Vin–Spritcentralen became responsible for the importation and wholesale trade.

By the 1960s other drug abuse problems had arisen. The intravenous injection of central nervous system stimulants and opiates, the smoking of marijuana and hashish, the sniffing of solvents (mostly by young teenagers) and the abuse of amphetamines and tranquilizers (which had hit the market in the 1930s) were all prevalent. Parliament formed a tough plan of action in 1968 to cope with both alcohol and drug abuse. Police and customs units were beefed up to keep drugs not only off the streets but out of the country. Stricter penal laws were instituted and since

Swedes are generally not producers of drugs, but rather buyers, dealers and couriers, much of the new control efforts were aimed at limiting imports from drug–producing countries in Asia, Europe and North Africa. Toward this end, the government vowed to take an increasingly active role in international efforts to stem drug smuggling. For example, it participated in the activities of the agency known as the Single Convention of Narcotic Drugs, established in 1961.

In 1978 the Swedish Parliament adopted a new strategy in the fight against alcohol and drug abuse. Legislation was enacted that relates alcohol and drug problems to their social context rather than treats them simply as crimes. Since then the primary task of the government has been to educate the public about the dangers of drug abuse and to help addicts get treatment to overcome their dependency disorders.

In order to gain an overview of the problem and educate the public, the government has several agencies that provide its central Crime Prevention Council with statistics on alcohol and drug abuse. The National Board of Education, for instance, reports on drug abuse among sixth to ninth graders and high school sophomores; the National Defense Research Institute obtains similar information for 18 year olds; and the Stockholm police even check for needle marks on people taken into custody. These statistics are helpful because they help target certain segments of the population for special attention. For example, it has been shown that nearly three–fifths of all incarcerated criminals are drug and alcohol abusers.

Treatment has become a major element in Sweden's crackdown. Before 1978 public drunkenness was treated as a crime and offenders were arrested. Since that time, however, it has been seen as a small part of a larger social and sometimes medical problem. Now if offenders are taken into custody, they are dealt with leniently and usually turned over to proper counselors rather than jailors. The government has taken the view that drug addicts and alcoholics "often are people whose narcotics abuse is a consequence and an expression, among other things, of their psychological and social difficulties and perhaps it is an unconscious attempt to alleviate these or modify them." (Drug Addicts Care Committee, quoted from *Facts on Narcotics and Narcotics Abuse).*

The addict's "escape into abuse" is thought to result from Sweden's increasing industrialization and its accompanying ills: unemployment and the extreme pressure to increase productivity and efficiency. Because government statistics show that drug abusers are likely to attend school irregularly and eventually turn to criminal activities, Parliament has vowed to help alleviate the problem at its source. Offenders thought by police to pose a threat to themselves or others may be taken into immediate custody and given compulsory treatment and counseling on an intensive and/or long–term basis. Although forced into such programs, the long–range goal is for addicts to take voluntary control over their own recovery and well–being. As noted in the introduction to Sweden's Care of Alcoholics and Drug Abusers Act of 1982: "The possibility to inflict treatment on a person without his consent must never lead to the consequences that society takes over the individual's responsibility for his own life."

Sweden has also tightened up its laws against "pushers" or dealers. Criminal acts are classified as misdemeanors, offenses and felonies, in ascending order of seriousness. Narcotics felons are considered among the most serious offenders in Sweden's justice system and may be sentenced to a minimum of 10 years in prison. Drunk driving is taken very seriously: convicted offenders whose blood tests show an alcohol concentration of 1.5 promille or more may be incarcerated for 12 months. Wiretapping is now legal when it is necessary to track down drug dealers, and

there are stringent controls over the importation and sale of the hypodermic syringes and needles used by "mainliners."

The Fact Sheets on Sweden on "Alcohol and Drug Abuse" (1982) notes that the great majority of the 10,000 to 15,000 heavy drug abusers in the nation live in the large urban areas; but while the problem has leveled off in the cities it appears to be rising in outlying districts. Sweden offers considerable help to people who want to kick their abuse problems. The nation's mental hospitals contain 20 outpatient wards and an additional 200 beds in drug addiction wards, and they have specially trained addiction–care teams, as do many prison wards. There are some 30 boarding institutes with over 300 beds for addicts, and many private homes also provide beds and care. Once abusers are almost ready to re–enter society, they may go to "halfway homes." Here they associate almost exclusively with addicts and ex–addicts and have peer support in learning how to get back in touch with the "straight" world.

"Alcohol Policy in Sweden" (Stockholm 1982, 2nd rev. ed.) Swedish Council for Information on Alcohol and Other Drugs.

"Fact Sheets on Sweden" (The Swedish Institute, Stockholm: September, 1982)

"Care of Alcoholics and Drug Abusers (Certain Cases) Act" (Departementens Reprocentral, Stockholm: 1982). Prepared by the Ministry of Social Affairs, International Secretariat.

Thomas Nordegren, "Alcohol and Alcoholism in Sweden," part of *Social Change in Sweden* series, no. 23 (Swedish Consulate General, New York: 1981). Prepared for the Swedish Information Service.

Thomas Nordegren, "Narcotics Abuse and Care of Drug Addicts in Sweden: Problems and Development Tendencies," part of *Social Change in Sweden* series, no. 21, 1980.

Report 81: *On the Alcohol and Drug Situa-*

tion in Sweden (Swedish Council for Information on Alcohol and Other Drugs, Stockholm: 1981).

"Facts on Narcotics and Narcotics Abuse" (Liberforlag, Stockholm: 1979). Arranged by the Narcotics Group of the Crime Prevention Council of the National Swedish Board of Health and Welfare, Committee on Health Education.

sympathomimetic amines   Drugs that act on the autonomic nervous system which controls involuntary muscles. Sympathomimetic drugs are used in the treatment of a number of conditions, including bronchial asthma, glaucoma, respiratory failure, mucous membrane congestion and shock. Some of these drugs also act systemically as stimulants of the central nervous system and they are the ones most sought after by drug abusers.

symptomatic alcoholism   Alcoholism that is secondary to another medical problem, such as psychoneurosis, psychosis or mental deficiency.

symptomatic drinking   Controlled excessive drinking which is used as a method of handling tensions and unconscious problems. Also, drinking that is a symptom of some mental disorder other than alcoholism.

Synalgos® (Ives)   An analgesic that contains drocode, promethazine hydrochloride, aspirin, caffeine and phenacetin. It is used for the relief of moderate to moderately severe pain in situations when a mild sedative is also needed. It may be habit–forming and has the potential for abuse. Tolerance, along with physical and psychological dependence, can occur. When taken with alcohol or other central nervous system depressants it can have an additive effect. It is supplied as Synalgos (without drocode) in maroon and white capsules; and as Synalgos–DC (with 16 mg drocode) in blue and white capsules.

Synanon   Founded in 1958 by Charles E. Dederich, the Synanon Church operates communities in which drug addicts, alcoholics and other character–disordered people can learn a better way to live. The first of its kind, Synanon has served as a model for numerous other therapeutic communities in the United States and abroad. Synanon communities are located on two rural properties, one in central California and the other in Houston, Texas. Anyone with a problem of drug or alcohol addiction, delinquency or criminal behavior, or other character disorder is eligible for admission. There is no set entrance fee but individuals who can afford to contribute to their care are expected to do so. The Synanon Church also acquires and distributes food to charitable organizations, and has established the Synanon College, a California–approved vocational college offering a wide variety of classes.

Syndrome X   In *Licit & Illicit Drugs* (Little, Brown and Company, 1972) Edward M. Brecher and the editors of Consumer Reports used the term Syndrome X to describe the high incidence of deaths reportedly due to *heroin overdose*. Before 1943, few—if any—deaths among addicts were attributed to heroin overdose. During the 1950s, however, nearly 50% of such deaths were attributed to this cause, and by 1970, when some 800 addicts in New York City died, the figure had risen to 80%. According to Mr. Brecher, it is unlikely that these deaths were due to heroin overdose for several reasons. First, it is known that even enormous overdoses of heroin are not likely to kill. Second, most deaths attributed to heroin overdose occurred very suddenly; in true cases of heroin overdose the initial symptoms are stupor and lethargy, generally followed by coma—a process that can take up to twelve hours. Death can be forestalled effectively by administering a narcotic antagonist, such as NALOXONE. And, third, says Brecher, most addicts whose deaths are reportedly due to overdose are individuals who have developed a tolerance to the drug so that even an extremely large dose of heroin would not cause their deaths.

If a person is known to be addicted to a particular drug and is suddenly found dead, the natural suspicion and assumption is that the drug caused the death. If a heroin addict dies with the syringe still in his arm, or witnesses report that just minutes before he died he was injecting heroin, the obvious conclusion is death by overdose. Such evidence would be circumstantial, though. According to Brecher "a conscientious search of the United States medical literature throughout recent decades has failed to turn up a single scientific paper reporting that heroin overdose . . . is in fact a cause of death among American heroin addicts."

A 1966 study by Dr. Milton Helpern, Chief Medical Examiner for New York City, found that massive pulmonary edema (flooding of the lungs with fluid) was a conspicuous condition in alleged overdose deaths, and that these deaths occurred very suddenly. It is these two characteristics that have been labeled Syndrome X. Dr. Michael M. Baden, an associate of Dr. Helpern, suggested that the majority of deaths are due to "an acute reaction to the intravenous injection of the heroin–quinine–sugar mixture" and to classify them as heroin overdose is a misnomer. There were also other factors suggesting that the deaths were not due to heroin overdose: most of the victims were long–term addicts, a fact which rules out the possibility that they had not developed tolerance; in some cases a number of addicts used the same heroin and only one died; there was an absence of high heroin concentration in tissue surrounding the point of injection and no evidence of heroin overdose in the urine of victims; and there was no evidence that the heroin was

any "purer" than the addicts were accustomed to.

Author Edward Brecher suggests several possible causes for Syndrome X deaths. Clearly, heroin itself could not be the cause since the high incidence of deaths among addicts is a recent phenomenon and heroin has been used for a long time. The first Syndrome X deaths occurred in the early 1940s when quinine was first added to heroin after an outbreak of malaria hit New York City addicts. More deaths occurred in the 1950s when addicts began taking central nervous system depressants, especially barbiturates and alcohol. Previously, addicts had generally refrained from alcohol use but after World War II when heroin was in short supply many turned to alcohol as a substitute. A 1967 New York study involving the deaths of 588 addicts, found alcohol present in 43% of the cases. At the Haight–Ashbury Medical Clinic, 37% of the addicts attending used barbiturates when withdrawal symptoms began; 24% used alcohol for the same reason.

In 1970 two noted entertainers died of what was reported as "heroin overdose." The musician Jimi Hendrix was known to use both barbiturates and alcohol, and the singer Janis Joplin was known to be a heavy drinker. She had, in fact, been drinking heavily with friends the night she injected herself with heroin and died.

Great Britain has also studied the question of heroin overdose. The presence of quinine was all but ruled out since quinine is not used to "cut" heroin in Great Britain. However, although inconclusive, the British studies appear to confirm the alcohol–barbiturate–heroin theory.

Despite the accumulated evidence that there must be a cause other than heroin overdose for these deaths, research in the area is minimal and the classification remains.

synergistic effect See SYNERGY.

synergy   When two or more drugs are taken together, the combined action increases the normal effect of each drug. The condition is also referred to as POTENTIATION or an ADDITIVE EFFECT. Because of this phenomenon, an amount of a drug that might normally be safe can have a devastating effect if taken with a drug that acts synergistically with it.

For example, a small amount of alcohol combined with a very small dose of a barbiturate can have a much greater effect than alcohol or a barbiturate taken alone. The synergistic process begins in the liver, which metabolizes ingested material. When two drugs are taken together the enzyme system that processes them is overwhelmed because it does not have the capacity to metabolize both at the same time. In the case of alcohol and a barbiturate drug, which compete for the same enzymes, alcohol is always processed first. The barbiturate meanwhile accumulates in the blood where it has an exaggerated effect on the body and the mind. This delayed metabolization of the barbiturate can result in a tripling or quadrupling of its potency when it enters the central nervous system.

The Third Special Report to the U.S. Congress on Alcohol and Health defined an interaction between alcohol or other central nervous system depressants, and a drug as "any alteration in the pharmacologic properties of either due to the presence of the other." The report classified three different types by interactions:

> (1) Antagonistic, in which the effects of one or both drugs are blocked or reduced;
> (2) Additive, in which the effect is the sum of the effects of each;
> (3) Supra–additive (synergistic or potentiating), in which the effect of the two drugs in combination is greater than it would be if the effects were additive.

The supra–additive effect is the most dangerous because it can at times prove fatal. Although not quite as dangerous, the antagonistic effect can be hazardous when the therapeutic effects of one drug are reduced by the presence of the other.

Drugs also have a half–life: this is the amount of time it takes for the body to remove half of the drug from the system. For drugs with a half–life of 24 hours or more, such as Valium, half of the first dose may still be in the body when the next is taken. After several days the buildup can be fairly large, and when alcohol or another central nervous system depressant is taken the result can be devastating.

synhexyl   See PYRAHEXYL.

synesthesia   The crossover of sensory effects. This phenomenon is most common during hallucinogenic use; colors may be smelled, sounds may be seen. Seeing stars after a blow on the head is a form of non–drug synesthesia.

synthetic marijuana   THC. In the 1960s the term was erroneously used for PCP.

synthetic narcotics   Narcotics that are produced entirely within a laboratory, as opposed to pharmaceutical products which are derived directly or indirectly from narcotics of natural origin. The two most widely used synthetic narcotics are meperidine and methadone. Synthetic narcotics resemble morphine in their action and sometimes have greater analgesic potency. Consequently tolerance and dependence can develop with their use and they are all susceptible to abuse.

T

talbutal   An intermediate–acting BARBI-TURATE usually used to produce sedation and sleep.

tachycardia   An increase in heart rate. (See HEART.)

Talwin® (Winthrop)   A potent analgesic that contains pentazocine and is equivalent in effect to CODEINE. It is an agonist–antagonist and is used for the relief of moderate to severe pain and as a preanesthetic. It has a high potential for abuse and both physical and psychological dependence can occur. In large doses Talwin can cause acute central nervous system manifestations of hallucinations and disorientation. Its formulation has been changed by the addition of NALOXONE (Narcan) so that when abusers attempt to inject it intravenously, uncomfortable symptoms due to the strong narcotic antagonist will appear in an opiate–dependent person. It is supplied as Talwin Compound in white capsules: Talwin Hydrochloride in peach–colored scored tablets; and Talwin Lactate in vials and ampules for injection.

Taractan® (Roche)   A major tranquilizer that contains chlorprothixene and is used for the management of manifestations of psychotic disorders. It has little potential for abuse or dependency. Overdosage can result in respiratory depression, hypotension and convulsions. It is supplied as a fruit–flavored elixir; in ampules for injection; and in 10 mg, 25 mg, 50 mg and 100 mg tablets.

TASC   See TREATMENT ALTERNATIVES TO STREET CRIMES.

TCA   Tricyclic ANTIDEPRESSANT, the major category of antidepressants.

Tedral® (Parke–Davis)   A bronchodilator containing theophylline, ephedrine hydrochloride and the sedative PHENOBARBITAL. It is used for bronchial asthma and other bronchospastic disorders. Because of the presence of the barbiturate phenobarbital, which is added to counteract the stimulant ephedrine, it may be habit–forming. It is supplied as Tedral Elixir: red cherry–flavored elixir with 15% alcohol; Tedral: uncoated white scored tablets; Tedral SA: double–layered uncoated coral and white tablets which contain butabarbital instead of phenobarbital; Tedral Expectorant: white tablets; and Tedral Suspension: yellow licorice–flavored suspension.

telepathine   HARMINE.

temperance   In the early 1800s the word temperance, usually synonymous with moderation, took on the meaning of *abstinence* in reference to alcohol. A group of Litchfield, Connecticut, residents formed the first temperance organization in 1789 when they pledged total abstinence. In 1826 a national organization, the American Temperance Society, was formed. Churches supported the movement, particularly Methodist and Presbyterian churches, and by the 1830s temperance societies across the country numbered over 1,000, gaining most of their strength in rural areas. Leaders of the movement used moral attacks as a method to persuade people to join their cause. After the Civil War the movement became even more popular and in 1872 the Catholic Church formed the Total Abstention Union. In 1874 the Woman's Christian Temperance Union, which is still active, was formed. In the early 1900s the movement concentrated on legislative measures, which led to PROHIBITION in 1920.

temposil   A compound calcium carbamide which produces an ANTABUSE effect. It is used in the treatment of alcoholics participating in recovery programs. Effects last only 12 to 24 hours whereas the effects of Antabuse can extend four to five days before the danger of a reaction passes. It has not been approved for use in the United States but is administered in treatment programs in Canada and Japan.

Tenuate® (Merrell–Dow)   An anorectic that contains diethylpropion hydrochloride and is used for weight control. Tolerance can develop and because it is chemically and pharmacologically similar to the AMPHETAMINES it can produce psychological dependence. It has a high potential for abuse. Overdosage can result in restlessness, rapid respiration, confusion and hallucinations. It is supplied as Tenuate in light blue 25 mg tablets; and as Tenuate Dospan, 75 mg white capsule–shaped tablets.

Tepanil® (Riker)   An anorectic that contains diethylpropion hydrochloride and is used for weight control. Tolerance can develop and because it is chemically and pharmacologically similar to AMPHETAMINES it can produce psychological dependence and social dysfunction. It has a high potential for abuse. Overdosage can result in restlessness, rapid respiration, confusion and hallucinations. It is suppled as Tepanil in 25 mg white tablets; and as Tepanil Ten–tab, 75 mg white tablets.

terpin hydrate   A turpentine derivative and non–narcotic antitussive found in Terpin Hydrate & Codeine Elixir® (McKesson), Tussagesic Tablets and Suspension® (Dorsey), and Tussaminic Tablets® (Dorsey).

tetanus   An acute infectious disease, commonly known as ''lockjaw,'' which is caused by the bacillus *Clostridium tetani* found in the soil and in animal feces. It is usually transmitted through open wounds directly into the bloodstream, often by contaminated nails, knives or hypodermic needles. Tetanus is painful because of muscle spasms and can be fatal. Among addicts who regularly inject drugs the chances of contracting the disease are well above average and the prognosis for recovery is less than average because of the frequency of injection, carelessness about the sterility of instruments and the general poor health of the user.

tetrahydrocannabinol   (delta–9–tetrahydrocannabinol)   A hallucinogen which is the active principle in CANNABIS. Also referred to as THC, it is found in the resin of the hemp plant. It was first produced synthetically in 1966.

Thai sticks   Potent, seedless marijuana (see SINSEMILLA) that is grown in Thailand and Vietnam and is packaged and tied in bundles that resemble sticks.

THC   See TETRAHYDROCANNABINOL.

thebaine   A principal alkaloid of OPIUM, thebaine was isolated in 1835, three years after the isolation of codeine. Because of its toxicity, thebaine itself has no medical use. Its conversion products, however, include the narcotic antagonists NALOXONE and NALTREXONE. Some codeine is made from thebaine. A series of other compounds which have analgesic properties many times that of morphine are also conversion products of thebaine but their toxicity in humans limits their use to veterinary medicine.

therapeutic index   The rates between an average effective dose of a drug and the LD50—the lethal dose for 50% of the population.

therapeutic communities See HALF-WAY HOUSE and TREATMENT.

Thorazine® (Smith, Kline & French) A major tranquilizer and a brand of chlorprom-azine, a phenothiazine derivative. It is used in the treatment of severe tension and anxi-ety, psychotic states and as a pre–operative medication. It is not known to cause depend-ence but abrupt withdrawal can produce nau-sea, vomiting, restlessness and insomnia. Overdosage can result in respiratory depres-sion and when taken with alcohol or other central nervous system depressants it can have an additive effect. It is supplied in tab-lets, capsules, suppositories, as a concen-trate, and in vials and ampules for injection.

TM Transcendental meditation. TM is a popular form of meditation used by drug–using individuals and others. When successfully practiced, it produces a disso-ciative state, or out–of–the–body experi-ence. It has been claimed that TM decreases or abolishes drug abuse.

TMA (3, 4, 5–Trimethoxyphenyl–B–amino-propane) A little–known synthetic HALLU-CINOGEN derived from MESCALINE. It is more potent than mescaline but less potent than LSD–25. TMA–2 and TMA–6 are also hal-lucinogenic substances.

tobacco See NICOTINE.

tolerance A state of acquired resistance to the effects of a drug. Tolerance develops after the repeated use of certain drugs. When it occurs a person must increase the dosage to obtain the original effects. (See also ADDICTION.)

toluene A liquid aromatic hydrocarbon that is used chiefly as a solvent and is found in numerous common household products. It

has an intoxicating effect when inhaled. (See INHALANTS.)

tooth grinding Tooth grinding (brux-ism) is relatively common among the general population during sleep. When it occurs dur-ing waking hours it can be an indication of chronic amphetamine or cocaine use.

topical administration See ADMINIS-TRATION.

toxic Poisonous. Toxicity refers to the quality of being poisonous, and toxicology is the science that deals with poisons and their effects.

toxic psychosis See PSYCHOSIS.

trafficking Drug trafficking is probably the most serious law enforcement problem in the United States. The top illicit income pro-ducer is cocaine—it generated an estimated $29 billion in retail sales in 1980. Marijuana came close with an estimated $24 billion in sales, while sales of heroin generated over $8 billion. Other dangerous drugs, including amphetamines, methamphetamines, barbitu-rates, methaqualone and the hallucinogens produced an estimated $17 billion in U.S. retail sales.

Unlike heroin use which is relatively lo-calized in large urban areas, the use of co-caine has been spreading throughout the en-tire U.S. No longer restricted to the wealthy and famous, cocaine use is rising at an alarming rate among the nation's youth. In 1980 between 40 and 48 metric tons of co-caine hydrochloride were imported into the U.S., an increase of more than 40% over the previous year. Availability is a major factor in the rise of cocaine abuse and, unfortu-nately, supplies are abundant. Coca cultiva-tion is well established in COLOMBIA, PERU and BOLIVIA. Colombia now processes and distributes up to 70% of the cocaine entering the U.S. and is responsible for 50% of the world's supply. It also furnishes 75% of the marijuana and 80% of the illicit methaqualone consumed in the U.S. Illicit drugs from Colombia usually enter through South Florida. The government has made an attempt to reduce trafficking from South American countries through control of coca production but it is faced with many obstacles when trying to negotiate with these countries. Frequent changes in South American governments, local populations which are heavily dependent on coca sales for their principal income, and indifference to U.S. interests are just some of them.

In 1980 approximately 60% of the heroin imported into this country was refined from opium cultivated in Southwest Asia (see GOLDEN CRESCENT); 25% was from Mexico; and the balance was from Southeast Asia (see GOLDEN TRIANGLE). The figure for Mexico shows a sharp drop: just four years earlier it supplied over two–thirds of the U.S. market. To a large extent the reduction is due to the Mexican government's aggressive eradication campaign against the opium poppy. The major importation center for heroin in the U.S. is New York City but recently Detroit has also becme a major distribution center.

Although Mexico is still a source of marijuana, its overall share of the U.S. market is rapidly declining—from 18% in 1978 to 8% in 1980. Colombia suppled 75% of the marijuana imported into the U.S. in 1980; Jamaica supplied 10%; and domestic cultivation represented 7%. Domestic cultivation is centered in seven primary states: California (where it is estimated that marijuana is the state's largest cash crop, worth over $1 billion annually), Hawaii, Oregon, Arkansas, Missouri, Kentucky and Florida.

Other illicit drugs, such as amphetamines and barbiturates, come from several sources. Colombia is responsible for about 80% of

these drugs, particularly methaqualone. The balance comes from Europe and is often diverted through Mexico.

(See also SMUGGLING, GOLDEN CRESCENT, GOLDEN TRIANGLE, FRENCH CONNECTION and individual countries.)

Trancopal® (Breon)   A nonhypnotic antianxiety drug. It is a brand of chlormezanone and is used to improve the emotional state of a patient by quieting him without impairing his clarity of consciousness. It is supplied in 100 mg peach caplets and 200 mg green caplets.

tranquilizers   A group of depressant drugs that act selectively on the brain and spinal cord (central nervous system). They are similar to barbiturates in many ways, especially in their sedative (calming) effect, but in normal doses they do not induce sleep or cause drowsiness.

Classification: Tranquilizers are divided into two classes—major and minor. The major tranquilizers, also called neuroleptics, are haloperidol and chlorpromazine. They are used to treat serious mental illness. Since patients experience no euphoria and show little or no tendency to develop tolerance or dependence even during long–term therapy, neuroleptics present few if any abuse or addiction problems and are rarely used non–medically.

Minor tranquilizers, which include meprobamate (MILTOWN), chlordiazepoxide (LIBRIUM) and diazepam (VALIUM), are another story. They can produce happy carefree feelings (euphoria) and are frequently misused—not only for their own effects but as a way of offsetting the effects of alcohol, amphetamines and other drugs.

Appearance: Tranquilizers are manufactured as tablets and capsules in a variety of sizes, shapes and colors, and as liquids for injection.

Origin: RESERPINE is an extract from a

species of snakeroot plant named RAUWOL- FIA SERPENTINA. The plant has been used for hundreds of years in India as a sedative and in the treatment of a variety of ailments. It was first introduced into the United States in the early 1950s as a help in reducing high blood pressure, but it was quickly observed that the drug affected a patient's moods and behavior. Tense, excited people calmed down, and disturbed, anxious people relaxed and stopped worrying. Soon hospitals were trying the drug on alcoholics and psychotic patients but it is only infrequently used at this time.

CHLORPROMAZINE is a synthetic drug which was developed in France in 1950 and introduced into the United States in 1954 for use in anesthesia. The drug helps control certain reflexes during surgery and reduces post–operative vomiting, nausea and pain. Psychiatrists began to use it on psychotic patients with increasing success. It works by decreasing dopamine transmission to brain centers controlling emotionality.

MEPROBAMATE, another synthetic drug, produced little effect on patients in mental hospitals but psychiatrists found it more effective than other sedatives in calming the tensions and anxieties of psychoneurotic office patients. Early reports claimed that the new drug was harmless as well as effective, and physicians soon began to use it to treat otherwise normal patients who complained of tension and "nerves." Under the trade names of Miltown (after the town in New Jersey where it was developed) and Equanil, the use of meprobamate spread rapidly.

Drug houses quickly began to develop other tranquilizers, the best known of which are Librium and Valium—both benzodiazepine derivatives. Americans bought more than a billion capsules of Librium in one year at a cost of $120 million. The same year, $500 million was spent for three billion tablets of Valium, now one of the best–selling drugs in North America.

Effects: Unlike major tranquilizers, minor tranquilizers such as Miltown, Librium and Valium have a definite potential for abuse. In general, their effects are similar to those of barbiturates but they have a slower onset and a longer duration, and produce less euphoria and less danger of overdose. In normal doses they relieve tension, fear and anxiety. Unlike barbiturates, they do not generally cause hypnosis, drowsiness or loss of alertness; there are exceptions, however, if they are taken in larger than necessary doses. Because of their action in calming nerves and relaxing muscles, they are used medically in treating pre–surgical patients, epileptic convulsions, neuromuscular conditions such as cerebral palsy, and psychosomatic cardiovascular disorders.

Early reports of complete harmlessness have been disproved. Doses larger than those which are medically recommended can cause physical and psychological dependence and tolerance. Heavy doses can cause slurred speech, loss of muscular control and paradoxical excitement. Tranquilizers have been used in a number of suicide attempts but fatalities are rare when the drug is used alone. Successful suicides are generally the result of a synergistic effect between the tranquilizer and another drug such as alcohol.

Interaction with other drugs: Combining tranquilizers with alcohol or other depressant drugs is dangerous. Each drug increases the effect of the other so that the combined effect is more powerful than the effect of either alone. Heroin addicts in methadone programs sometimes use tranquilizers to enhance the effect of the heroin substitute, while amphetamine users turn to tranquilizers to neutralize the intense stimulation of these drugs.

Tolerance: As with barbiturates, tolerance can develop with regular prolonged use and increased doses may be needed to produce the original tranquilizing effects.

Dependence: Long–term heavy use of tranquilizers can result in the same psychological and physical dependence seen with barbiturate and alcohol abuse, although the degree of psychological dependence may be less. When compared to the large number of people who use tranquilizers, physical dependence is quite infrequent.

Research on the use of tranquilizers during pregnancy indicates that they may result in certain congenital defects, especially if they are used during the first three months. If the mother has habitually used meprobamate, her baby may show withdrawal symptoms after birth such as respiratory distress, feeding difficulties, disturbed sleep patterns, fever and excessive crying.

Withdrawal symptoms: Symptoms similar to those following barbiturate or alcohol withdrawal occur if the use of tranquilizers is stopped abruptly or sharply decreased. Although less severe in intensity, they include cramps, convulsions, nausea and vomiting, sweating and tremors. Symptoms can last as long as a week to 10 days because tranquilizers are eliminated slowly.

Sources and control: Tranquilizers are legally available only on prescription. Major tranquilizers, which include Serpasil (reserpine) and Thorazine (chlorpromazine), among others, are unscheduled drugs. Since euphoria does not follow their use, there is little or no demand for them on the black market.

Minor tranquilizers, such as Miltown, Librium and Valium lessen tension, anxiety and agitation and are in demand. They are in Schedule IV of the Controlled Substances Act. Some diversion of these into illicit channels has been reported but prescriptions for them are usually obtained with comparative ease so that there has been little incentive for an active black market trade.

Richard R. Lingeman, *Drugs from A to Z* (New York: McGraw–Hill Book Company, 1974), pp. 27–28, 129–130, 159–160, 249–250.

Jack S. Margolis, *Complete Book of Recreational Drugs* (Los Angeles, California: Cliff House Books, 1978), pp. 133–135, 245, 264–266, 373–374.

Samuel L. Levine, *Narcotics and Drug Abuse* (Cincinnati, Ohio: The W.H. Anderson Company, 1974), pp 2.42.–2.43.

Tranxene® (Abbott)   A sedative hypnotic that contains chlorazepate dipotassium, a BENZODIAZEPINE, and is used for the treatment of anxiety and for physical illnesses in which anxiety is manifested. When taken with alcohol or other central nervous system depressants it can have an additive effect. Overdosage can result in varying degrees of central nervous system depression from slight sedation to coma. It is supplied as Tranxene: 3.75 mg gray and white capsules; 7.5 mg gray and maroon capsules; and 15 mg all gray capsules; Tranxene–SD: 22.5 mg tan tablets; and Tranxene–SD Half Strength: 11.25 mg blue tablets.

tranylcypromine   See MONOAMINE OXIDASE (MAO) INHIBITORS. Its trade name is Parnate.

treatment   Treatment for drug abuse falls into various categories, including drug–free or maintenance; residential or ambulatory; medical or non–medical; selective or non–selective; voluntary or involuntary. Treatment programs also offer virtually any combination of these methods.

Maintenance programs include ANTABUSE and METHADONE. ALCOHOLICS ANONYMOUS is a drug–free program aimed at abstinence. Drug–free therapeutic communities, such as HALFWAY HOUSES, include Synanon and numerous others. Involuntary treatment includes both medical and court authorizations that do not require the patient's consent. An addict may be compelled to start treatment, continue it, or both. Ambulatory treatment involves programs in which a patient visits a treatment facility as an outpatient at periodic intervals. DETOXIFICATION programs often handle only physical dependency and psychological dependency remains.

Psychological dependency is generally believed to be more difficult to manage than physical dependency, and for this reason treatment programs employ a variety of methods. Detoxification is usually, but not invariably, done in a hospital or other medically oriented facility. Upon discharge a continuing program of treatment should be implemented or the incidence of RELAPSE will be high. Not all treatment programs will work for all patients. Upon detoxification some patients will benefit greatly from a program such as Alcoholics Anonymous; others will benefit more from individual or GROUP THERAPY. Still others will need the encouragement of the kind of drug–free supportive atmosphere provided by a therapeutic community. The particular drug of abuse involved will also have a bearing on the treatment method selected. Heroin addicts are often influenced by their environment, for example, and a therapeutic community will remove them from the pressures of returning to an area and life–style that encourage heroin abuse. Alcoholics, on the other hand, will generally gravitate toward either an AA program or group therapy.

Often treatment programs are centered around the patient who has abused the drug and fail to consider his family. Because families are involved in drug problems—physically, mentally and economically—it is hoped that all methods of treatment will soon include those who are directly involved with the patient.

Treatment Alternatives to Street Crimes (TASC)

A federally funded pilot treatment program through which, if local law enforcement authorities approve, a drug dependent person who has been arrested may enter treatment as a condition of release.

When the person's case comes to trial, the court then assesses his cooperation and success in the treatment program and determines if he should remain in treatment as an alternative to prosecution and possible incarceration. TASC treatment units are linked to community programs and use various approaches.

tremor   A shaking or trembling usually from weakness or disease; also a feeling of uncertainty or insecurity. Certain stimulants and hallucinogens induce tremors. (See also DELIRIUM TREMENS.)

trichloroethylene   A hydrocarbon and volatile solvent that is an ingredient in various cleaning fluids and is sometimes inhaled for its intoxicating effects. (See also INHALANTS.)

triclofos sodium   A depressant and sedative hypnotic generally used in the treatment of insomnia. It is a chloral derivative which converts to chloral hydrate in the body but lacks its bitter taste and smell. It is also less potent.

The drug reaches its peak level in one hour and has a half life of 11 hours. It may be habit–forming and dependency can develop. (See TRICLOS.)

Triclos® (Merrell–Dow)   A hypnotic agent that contains TRICLOFOS SODIUM. It is a chloral derivative generally used in the treatment of insomnia. It may be habit–forming and dependency can develop. It is supplied in 750 mg capsule–shaped orange tablets.

Trimstat® (Laser)   An anorectic that contains phendimetrazine and is used for weight control. Tolerance can develop and because its activity is similar to that of AMPHETAMINES it has a significant potential for abuse. it is supplied in 35 mg tan tablets.

Trimtabs® (Mayrand)   An anorectic that contains phendimetrazine tartrate and is used for weight control. Tolerance can develop and because its activity is similar to AMPHETAMINES it has a significant potential for abuse. It is supplied in 35 mg tablets.

Tuinal® (Lilly)   A sedative hypnotic that contains 150 mg each of the short– to intermediate–acting BARBITURATES secobarbital sodium and amobarbital sodium. A Schedule II drug, it is used for insomnia and as a pre–operative medication. Tolerance can develop and both physical and psychological dependence can occur. It has a high potential for abuse and when taken with alcohol or other central nervous system depressants it can have an additive or potentiating effect. Overdosage can result in respiratory depression, lowered body temperature and coma. It is supplied in 50 mg, 100 mg and 300 mg capsules with a blue body and orange cap. Synonyms: tooies, tuies, rainbows, red and blues.

Turkey   The use of drugs in Turkey, particularly opium and marijuana (hashish), has long been a tradition. It has been customary for so long, in fact, that there is no particular stigma attached to the use and abuse of these drugs. Although Turkey has always been a heavy producer and consumer of opium, the use of heroin is rare. Opium is generally smoked or is used as opium gum (the final raw product) often for strictly medicinal purposes.

In 1923 the new republic, under the leadership of Ataturk (Mustafa Kemal), sought to modernize the nation and programs were initiated to end many of the old customs including the use of opium and hashish. Little was actually accomplished and at the end of World War II the abuse of opium had not only increased but there was also an increase in the smuggling of illicit drugs. Stringent legislation was passed in 1953 to deter domestic use and illegal trade, but the government was aware that it would take time to become effective; there had been considerable opposition to legislation that would change long–established customs and dramatically affect the economy and welfare of the country. In 1971 further legislation was passed that banned opium production and, despite attempts for its repeal, the law is still in effect. The economic hardships caused by the 1971 legislation have led to compensation programs but it is an enormous undertaking because most of the former poppy farms must be rehabilitated and the social and economic structure of whole provinces must be reorganized.

There are very tough penalties in Turkey for the importation, exportation or manufacture of drugs without a license. In the case of morphine, cocaine, heroin or hashish, the penalty can be life imprisonment and Turkish jails have a considerable reputation for extreme harshness and very uncomfortable conditions.

Despite the 1971 ban on the cultivation of the poppy, there is still active involvement in the illicit market. Turkey has become a transit country, particularly for opium cultivated in Iran and Pakistan (see GOLDEN CRESCENT). During the days of the FRENCH CONNECTION, Turkey was a major producer of opium for the illicit market. The 1971 ban, which only allows opium production for scientific and medicinal markets, has led to an increase in trafficking of illicit opium, and Turkish nationals play an important role in both the refining and trafficking of imported opiates particularly through the Federal Republic of Germany. The U.S. Embassy, in an effort to assist the Turkish government's already vigorous narcotics laws, initiated a Protocol on Narcotics Cooperation which is designed to offer flexible and speedy commodity and training assistance to Turkish law enforcement officials.

Tussanil® (Misemer)   A decongestant and antitussive that contains several ingredients, including the codeine derivative dihydrocodeinone bitartrate. It may be habit–forming and both physical and psychological dependence can occur. It is supplied as a syrup.

Tussionex® (Pennwalt)   An antitussive that contains resin complexes of hydrocodone and phenyltoloxamine. It may be habit–forming. Overdosage can result in respiratory depression and convulsions. It is supplied as golden colored Tussionex Suspension; light brown tablets; and green and white capsules.

Twenty–first Amendment   The amendment which repealed the Eighteenth Amendment and ended PROHIBITION. It became part of the Constitution on December 5, 1933.

tybamate   A minor TRANQUILIZER that is similar structurally and pharmacologically to meprobamate, but is possibly more effective as a muscle relaxant. Tybamate resembles MEPROBAMATE in its effects, use and abuse.

Appearance and activity in the body: Tybamate is a white crystalline powder which is soluble in alcohol and slightly soluble in water.

Absorbed rapidly in the gastrointestinal tract and distributed evenly in the body, tybamate is metabolized in the liver and excreted by the kidneys. It acts on the thalmus and limbic systems of the brain, stablilizing the emotional circuits, but does not affect the cerebral cortex. The substance, which has a half–life of three hours, crosses the placental barrier and appears in mother's milk.

Dosage: Tybamate is prescribed in oral doses of 20–35 mg per kilogram of body weight, in three or four daily doses for children aged 6–12; and in doses of 250–500 mg three or four times daily for adults. No more than 3 gm (3000 mg) should be administered per day.

Effects: Like meprobamate, tybamate eliminates the symptoms of tension and anxiety associated with emotional stress. Mild adverse reactions such as drowsiness and confusion can usually be controlled by adjusting the dose. Other unpleasant side effects which have been reported include rash, nausea, anorexia and seizures.

Tolerance and physical and psychological dependence can occur, along with withdrawal symptoms. Barbiturates and tybamate display cross–tolerance to each other, and tybamate is potentiated by alcohol and other depressants. Overdosage can result in stupor and death.

Usage: Tybamate's medical application includes the treatment of tension, anxiety and insomnia resulting from psychoneurosis. It has a potential for abuse. (See TYBATRAN.)

Tybatran® (Robins)   A minor tranquilizer that contains TYBAMATE and whose activity is similar to meprobamate. Tolerance can develop and both physical and psychological dependence can occur. It is supplied in 125 mg, 250 mg and 350 mg green capsules.

Tylenol with Codeine® (McNeil)   An analgesic that contains acetaminophen and codeine phosphate. It is used for acute or chronic pain and to control cough. It may be habit–forming. Tolerance can develop, along with physical and psychological dependence. Overdosage can result in cardiorespiratory depression, circulatory collapse and coma. It is supplied in white tablets containing 7.5 mg, 15 mg, 30 mg and 60 mg of codeine.

U

under the influence of alcohol   The term, when used generally, refers to being affected by alcohol and exhibiting a disturbance of function or behavior because of it. In some parts of the U.S. the condition is legally defined in terms of specific concentrations of alcohol in the blood.

United Kingdom   Alcohol is acknowledged to be the most abused drug in the United Kingdom and has been for many years: in the late 19th century the government actively intervened to try to shift the drinking pattern from gin to beer. Although the abuse of other drugs is not nearly as serious as it is in the United States, it became a cause for concern in the 1920s and the government began to take preventive steps.

Drug addiction in the United Kingdom is treated as a medical rather than a criminal problem. A Ministry of Health committee in 1926 recommended that narcotic addicts (often people who had become addicted as a result of treatment for an illness) should receive narcotic prescriptions in the hope that they would gradually withdraw from the use of the drug. By 1960 the number of addicts had risen sharply and government committees undertook further studies. They reaffirmed the 1926 recommendations and established guidelines for what is now referred to as the "clinical system" or the "British system." A network of regular treatment centers was set up on both an inpatient and outpatient basis, and extremely controlled procedures were established for the prescribing of heroin, methadone and cocaine to addicts. The number of drug–prescribing doctors was also restricted and controlled, and the recording and registering of addicts was made compulsory.

In 1967 the Dangerous Drugs Act was passed. Along with providing detention powers for illegal possession, use and sale of "notifiable" drugs, it also provides for a doctor's license to be revoked if he or she overprescribes. The extent of an addict's habit has been a controversy in the clinical system. Addicts will obviously try to convince a doctor that they have a strong, heavy habit in order to obtain larger doses. However, doctors are rationed as to the amount they may prescribe and urine tests are frequently employed to ascertain the actual extent of an addict's habit. Once the existence of a habit has been ascertained, those addicted to notifiable drugs are registered with the government and prescriptions are filed with a pharmacy. The addict has to go to the pharmacy on a *daily* basis to collect his dose.

In 1971 the Misuse of Drugs Act was passed and came into full force in 1973. It modernized previous legislation and classified drugs according to the security required to prevent abuse and the penalties for illegal possession and sale. It also listed notifiable drugs as the following: heroin, methadone, cocaine, dextromoramide, diamorphine, dipipanone, hydrocodone, hydromorphone, levorphanol, morphine, opium, oxycodone, pethidine, piritramide and phenazocine.

The Misuse of Drugs Act also divided drugs into three categories according to their harmfulness. Maximum penalties for the chief types of offenses are related to the category of drugs involved. Class "A" drugs are the above mentioned notifiable drugs along with LSD; class "B" drugs include cannabis, cannabis plants, resin and liquid, amphetamines, dextroamphetamine, levamphetamine and methylamphetamine; class "C" drugs include methaqualone and other miscellaneous drugs.

Nearly 4,400 addicts were recorded as receiving notifiable drugs in the treatment of their addiction as of the end of 1982; nearly three times the number recorded at the end of

1972. The large increase of over 500 addicts (14%) between 1981 and 1982 followed a larger increase of about 1,000 (35%) between 1980 and 1981. Heroin addicts (those addicted solely to heroin or to heroin and other drugs) accounted for 76% of the new addicts in 1982, as compared to about 60% in 1973–78. From 1980–82 the second most frequent drug of addiction was dipipanone, for which the number of new addicts increased substantially from 20 in 1973 to over 300 in 1982. The number of new methadone addicts has remained fairly stable. The other most frequent drugs of addiction reported for new addicts were cocaine, dextromoramide, morphine and pethidine. Among former addicts, heroin was the most frequent drug of addiction, followed by methadone and dipipanone. As of December 31, 1982, the number of narcotic drug addicts recorded as receiving notifiable drugs in treatment of their addiction is broken down as follows: methadone, 3,117; dipipanone, 927; heroin, 126; other drugs (alone or in combination), 201.

The use of cannabis in the United Kingdom is not to be overlooked. Indeed, there were more seizures of cannabis and more persons found guilty of, or cautioned for, drug offenses related to cannabis than any other drug in 1982. Whereas the abuse of narcotics and other dangerous drugs is centered in the London area, cannabis use is far more widespread. This is a pattern that is found in countries throughout the world and is related to the availability and low cost of the drug. In the United Kingdom, as elsewhere, more attention is generally given to the abuse of "hard" drugs. There were about 10,700 seizures of cannabis *resin* in 1982, about 1,800 more than in 1981 and higher than in earlier years. However, in terms of potency the quality of the seizures was less. The number of cannabis *herbal* seizures was about the same as the numbers in 1980 and 1981 but was much higher than in earlier years. The number of cannabis *plants* was

lower in 1982 than in 1980–81 but higher than in earlier years. Overall seizures of *all* controlled drugs during 1982 was about 11% more than in 1981 and twice the number in 1974 which was the first full year of operation of the Misuse of Drugs Act.

The average age of *new* addicts increased between 1973 and 1979 but did not change greatly in the period 1979–82; about 20% of new addicts were aged 30 and over in 1982 as compared to 10% in 1973. The number of new addicts aged under 20 in 1982 was particularly high, nearly double that of 1980, possibly indicating a trend. The average age of *former* addicts increased between 1973 and 1981, with about 40% being aged 30 and over. Some 70% of known addicts at the end of 1982 were males, a similar proportion to the previous four years. In the first half of the 1970s, the corresponding proportion was about 75%.

The clinical system of drug treatment in the United Kingdom has been a controversial issue since it was first established. Opponents of the system look on it as a "drugs–for–free" program and contend that it encourages drug use. This position is held by some drug treatment authorities in the United Kingdom and also by some authorities elsewhere in the world. Those who promote the system credit it with preventing the development of a black market, limiting narcotic use, reducing drug–related crime, and enabling addicts to lead more useful lives. It has been suggested that the United States adopt the system but the usual medical and governmental response is a "wait and see" attitude; although viewed as an interesting solution to the drug problem it seems that long–term positive results will have to be forthcoming before it is adopted in the U.S.

As in other countries around the world, alcohol and tobacco consumption is increasing in the United Kingdom. A "pub society" has evolved in this century and drinking in public places has become the primary form of entertainment. Since the government intervened to shift the drinking pattern from gin to beer in the late 19th century, beer has remained the most popular alcoholic beverage. Per capita consumption of beer rose 3.9% between 1972 and 1978—the fourth highest per capita increase among Western European countries. In addition, the income spent on beer (4.5% of household expenses) represented the highest proportion of any Western European nation. In 1980 the average consumption per adult was: distilled spirits, 6 pints; wine, 15 pints; and beer, 270 pints. Economic factors are responsible for some of the increase in alcohol abuse: although the cost of alcoholic beverages has risen, they have not risen as fast as other items in the economy.

The government estimates that 700,000 people suffer from alcohol–related problems. This estimate is broken down geographically because drinking patterns vary considerably within the United Kingdom. In Scotland and Northern Ireland there is a far higher incidence of alcohol abuse than in England and Wales. Taking into account the impact of alcoholism on family and friends, the Department of Health and Social Services estimates that in England and Wales one in 25 persons is affected by the abuse of alcohol; the figure is one in 10 in Scotland and Northern Ireland. The economic cost of alcohol abuse, including labor loss, health services, police and prison costs, were estimated to be $1.44 billion in 1979.

Government measures have attempted to reverse, or at least slow down, drinking trends. Legislative measures include public education, promotion of stricter laws for alcohol–related offenses, and revision of taxing and licensing laws affecting alcohol consumption. Some of these measures have met strong public opposition: the public opposes prohibitive taxes on alcoholic beverages, and the liquor industry resists efforts to restrain a trade that employs 700,000 people and exports $1.63 billion worth of goods.

The treatment of both drug and alcohol–related problems in the United Kingdom is handled mostly by volunteer organizations. Organizations dealing with alcohol–related problems are generally assisted by the Department of Health and Social Security along with substantial grants from the liquor industry. Rehabilitation programs for other drug–related problems are handled both through the Disabled Person's Resettlement Service of the Department of Employment, and by volunteer organizations that run special hostels for addicts who have completed treatment in a hospital. Both the Phoenix House in London and the Alpha House in Portsmouth are rehabilitation hostels modeled after the Phoenix House in New York City.

United States   Drugs were in use in America long before Europeans came to the country. Early explorers found the Indians "drinking the smoke" of burning tobacco and took the habit home with them to Europe. Early colonists were skilled at distilling grain into alcoholic beverages and the rum trade flourished in New England early on. Although recognized as a stimulant, cocaine did not enjoy popularity in the U.S. until the late 1800s when it became an ingredient not only in many elixirs but in the original recipe for the popular soft drink Coca–Cola. (It was removed from the beverage in 1906 when the Pure Food and Drug Law was passed.) Cannabis was widely grown by Virginia colonists as a source of hemp, and in the 19th century large hemp plantations were found throughout the south. Cultivation of marijuana actually continued into the 1930s and it is estimated that at that time the commercial crop covered 10,000 acres. Although principally grown for hemp, marijuana was used medicinally and recreationally during the 18th and 19th centuries, but on a minute scale compared to today.

The use of opium was rampant during the

19th century; it was an ingredient in numerous patent medicines and was sold legally and at extremely low prices. Although most opium was imported, opium poppies were also cultivated in the U.S. The dangers of opium addiction were recognized but not acted upon until 1895 when San Francisco banned the smoking of opium and the opium dens that had proliferated in the city and which were supposedly a result of the influx of Chinese immigrants. Similar ordinances followed soon after in other cities, but nothing was done about the opium in patent medicines for many years. An often undisclosed aspect of the Civil War is the number of morphine addicts it produced. Soldiers were not only treated with morphine on the battlefields but were also sent home with a syringe and a supply of the drug. At that time morphine was not thought to be addictive if it was injected into the bloodstream and bypassed the stomach. The result of this belief was hundreds of thousands of addicts. The popularity of heroin over morphine developed in the early part of the 20th century when it was discovered that heroin was a more potent drug; it was also the drug being smuggled into the country at the time and addicts are always at the mercy of the availability factor.

The abuse of alcohol, a problem from America's early beginnings and one that continues today, was dealt with harshly in 1919 when Prohibition was enacted. Repeal came in 1933 when it was obvious that the government move was a failure.

During the 1940s and 1950s the abuse of other substances began to be a major concern. The use of newly developed drugs became widespread before their addictive qualities were acknowledged or made known. "Minor tranquilizers" were widely prescribed by doctors as a way of dealing with symptoms rather than treating them, and amphetamines were in widespread use as an "energizer." These patterns not only continue today, they are greatly magnified. Co-caine, previously not used to any great extent, is now a leading drug of abuse. When it first gained popularity it was considered a drug of the affluent because of its high cost, but despite that fact its use has now spread to many segments of the population. Heroin use has retained its popularity since the early 1900s but the number of heroin dependent people has remained fairly stable since the mid–1970s.

Aside from alcohol, tobacco and caffeine, the major drug of abuse today is marijuana. It has been estimated that 30 million people in the U.S. have used marijuana, though the actual number of users, whether regular or occasional, is impossible to pinpoint as sources of marijuana include not only imports from other countries but the vast amounts that are grown domestically. The U.S. government estimates that 7% of the marijuana used in America today is domestically cultivated; however, the number of people who grow a few dozen plants in the backyard for personal use, with no thought of selling or trafficking, could increase this estimate substantially.

Of major concern in the U.S. today is the early age at which drug users begin to experiment. The casualness which many parents have shown to the taking of drugs has extended to young people. A drug is often no further away than the family medicine cabinet. Drug use even seems to be condoned by the general public; a fact substantiated by the number of HEAD SHOPS that have sprung up around the country. They not only sell such items as water pipes for smoking marijuana, but books on how to cultivate your own marijuana, and pamphlets that describe how to convert cocaine into freebase for smoking.

Polydrug use has been on the increase in recent years and often with disastrous results. The SYNERGISTIC effects of certain drugs can be fatal. Alcohol, which remains one of the principal drugs of abuse in the U.S., is most often involved as a primary or secondary drug in polydrug use, and there are many users who take an "upper" in the morning and a "downer" at night.

The northeastern region of the U.S., an area that extends from Delaware to Maine, has more drug abusers than any other part of the country. An estimated 40% of the heroin addicts in the U.S. live in this region (the majority in New York City), and cocaine use is on the increase. Although for many years South Florida has been the hub of illicit drug trafficking, there has been a recent trend toward unloading drugs along the New England coastline. This may be due to the fact that there has been increased surveillance by enforcement authorities in Florida, but it may also be a result of the high concentration of organized crime in the northeast and the desire by smugglers to move their products as quickly as possible to a densely populated area where the demand is known. Despite this recent trend, Florida and the southeastern region of the country is still a prime importation area simply because of its geographical relation to Central and South America. The drugs most widely abused in the southeast include marijuana, cocaine and methaqualone.

The midwest, an area that previously served as a "customer" for drugs imported through the northeast, Florida or the West Coast, has recently developed its own distribution center: Chicago. Known for many years as the transportation capital of the U.S. (aircraft, trucking and train transportation) Chicago's central geographical location is now being exploited by drug traffickers.

In the south central U.S. there are several trafficking problems. Air smugglers have long been operating between the region and South America, with much of the air traffic using secondary roads and private airstrips. Because of the increased enforcement in South Florida, smugglers are now turning to the Texas Gulf coast for shipment by boat. The main problem in this area, however, is the flow of drugs from Mexico into Texas by land. The primary drugs of abuse in the south central region are marijuana and cocaine, followed by methamphetamine and heroin.

The western region of the U.S., which encompasses the area from Alaska to the southern California coast, faces three distinct drug abuse problems: it is a source area, an importation point, and a major distribution center. Marijuana is the major cash crop in California. The area is convenient for smuggling not only because of its deepwater ports and rugged shoreline but also because of Los Angeles' international airport. Geographically, California is an obvious point of entry for both southeast Asian and Mexican heroin. The state has also been prominent in the production of LSD, PCP and other dangerous drugs, many of which first gained their popularity in California.

The U.S. has the dubious distinction of being the world's "trend setter" for drug abuse. This has been substantiated by the abuse patterns for LSD, which was popular during the 1960s, and for the use of inhalants, which was also short lived (although it still continues on a small scale). As abuse of these substances became popular in the U.S., within a matter of months or a few short years their use also became popular in other countries. For more detailed figures on the number of addicts, the sources of a drug, and the various treatment and prevention methods involved, see individual drug entries. For information on how drug abuse has affected the U.S. economy, see BUSINESS and ACCIDENTS.

urine screen   If a person has used a drug, either the drug itself or its metabolite will be present in the urine. Although other body fluids can be used to screen for the presence of drugs (blood, sweat, saliva, body tissue), urine testing has become the preferred procedure because specimens can be easily obtained with minimal facilities and by an unskilled technician. The process is also painless, relatively inexpensive and it can provide highly reliable results. Urine testing for drugs first came into general use as a part of methadone maintenance treatment programs. It is now routinely performed as a part of military, sports, business and penal drug screening programs as well as in drug abuse treatment programs.

The most widely used urine tests currently performed to detect the presence of drugs are: gas CHROMATOGRAPHY (GC), RADIOIM-MOASSAY (RIA), gas chromatography mass spectometry (GC–MS) and enzyme multiplied immunoassay technique (EMIT). Two characteristics are basic to all the various urine tests—their sensitivity and their specifity. The sensitivity of a test is determined by the smallest concentration of a drug or metabolite that can be detected. The specifity of a test refers to the degree to which it can discriminate between closely related drugs, metabolites or naturally occurring substances.

The usual substances tested on a urine screen are THC (as acid metabolites) heroin (as morphine), amphetamines, cocaine, barbiturates and phencyclidine, though other compounds can also be detected. Methods for detecting LSD in urine are presently restricted to research laboratories.

The first over–the–counter urinalysis kit was marketed in early 1984 by Checkpoint Laboratories of Virginia. The kits are sold in drugstores and urine specimens are mailed to Checkpoint which screens for traces of marijuana, cocaine and other drugs.

V

Valium® (Roche)   A minor TRANQUIL-IZER and sedative hypnotic that contains diazepam, a BENZODIAZEPINE derivative. It is used in the treatment of tension and anxiety and for alcohol withdrawal. Tolerance can develop along with physical and psychological dependence. One of the most widely prescribed drugs in the United States, it has a significant potential for abuse and when taken with alcohol or other central nervous system depressants it can have an additive effect. It is supplied in 2 mg white tablets; 5 mg yellow tablets; and 10 mg blue tablets.

Valmid® (Dista)   A mild sedative hypnotic that contains ethinamate and is used when deep hypnosis is not needed. Tolerance can develop along with dependency. When taken with alcohol or other central nervous system depressants it can have an additive effect. Overdosage can result in respiratory depression. It is supplied in 500 mg capsules with a light blue opaque body and blue opaque cap.

vaporous anesthetics   Liquid anesthetics that are readily vaporizable at relatively low temperatures. The two vaporous anesthetics which are sometimes abused as INHALANTS are CHLOROFORM and ETHER.

Veronal®   A long–acting BARBITURATE that contained BARBITAL. First manufactured in 1903, Veronal was the first barbiturate used in medicine but is no longer available.

vinbarbital   A short– to intermediate–acting BARBITURATE.

vinho de jurumena   A hallucinogenic beverage made from the seeds of *Mimosa* *hostilis,* a plant native to Brazil. It contains an organic form of DMT, the plant's active principle.

violence   See CRIME, ORGANIZED CRIME, CHILDREN OF DRUG DEPENDENT INDIVIDUALS, and SPOUSE ABUSE.

virola   A tree belonging to the *Myristicaceae* family. The bark is made into a psychedelic snuff by the Yekwana Indians in Venezuala.

vitamins   See NUTRITION.

volatile solvents   See INHALANTS.

Volstead Act   The popular name for the National Prohibition Act of 1920 which enforced the EIGHTEENTH AMENDMENT. Representative Andrew Volstead of Minnesota was its sponsor. The act provided for the enforcement of wartime prohibition, banned intoxicating beverages and contained provisions for the industrial use of alcohol.

Voranil® (USV Pharmaceutical)   An anorectic that contains clortermine and is used for weight control. Tolerance can develop and because its activity is similar to that of AMPHETAMINES both physical and psychological dependence can occur. It has a significant potential for abuse. Overdosage can result in restlessness, tremors, confusion and hallucinations. It is supplied in 50 mg pale yellow tablets.

W

water of life   The term is applied to any of several distilled spirits. Originally, it was used in reference to a legendary elixir, probably not alcoholic, that would confer perpetual youth or immortality. Ponce de Leon, the Spanish explorer who discovered Florida, probably best exemplified the quest for such an elixir in his search for the Fountain of Youth. As early as Roman times, the term was associated with particularly strong drink that would produce a temporary feeling of blissful immortality. The Latin term was *aqua vitae* which was later anglicized to whiskey.

Webb–Canyon Law   In 1913, after a veto by President William Howard Taft, Congress passed this law which prohibited the shipment of liquor into dry areas. The law was designed to allow dry states to exercise sovereignty over alcohol–related affairs within their borders, and gave each state the right to make its own laws concerning shipments of liquor by mail order.

weight loss and control   See ANORECTICS.

Wernicke's encephalopathy   A disease of the BRAIN and CENTRAL NERVOUS SYSTEM which is related to thiamine deficiency and afflicts alcoholics after a number of years of heavy drinking. Victims commonly suffer a marked memory disturbance, including delirium, tremors, visual impairment and inability to maintain balance, as well as an increased risk of heart failure. Because of the amnesia, patients are likely to confabulate, that is, fill in the memory gaps with a contrived story rather than admit they cannot remember. It is common to call the syndrome the Wernicke–Korsakoff syndrome because both syndromes have common characteristics and etiology. If detected and treated early enough, Wernicke's encephalopathy may be reversed. (See also KORSAKOFF'S PSYCHOSIS.)

WHO   See WORLD HEALTH ORGANIZATION.

wild cucumber   *Exhinocystis lobata*. A vine native to the United States and a member of the melon family. There are claims that the seeds of the fruits can produce psychedelic effects.

wild fennel   *Foeniculum vulgare*. Though there are claims that it can produce psychedelic effects, the plant is poisonous and can cause severe adverse reactions.

wino   An alcoholic who drinks only wine. Also a person who consumes a large amount of wine because it can be obtained inexpensively and he wants to get the most alcohol for his money. Other alcoholic beverages are consumed when they are available.

withdrawal   A series of symptoms that appear when a drug on which the user is physically dependent is abruptly stopped or severely reduced. Withdrawal occurs most consistently in cases of addiction to central nervous system depressants or narcotics. The syndrome consists of symptoms which are broadly opposite to the drugs' usual effects—a kind of "rebound" effect.

The intensity and duration of withdrawal symptoms depends on individual susceptibility, properties of the particular drug and the degree of addiction. Generally speaking, shorter–acting substances, such as heroin, produce more rapidly developing, shorter and more severe withdrawal symptoms than longer–lasting, more slowly eliminated drugs such as methadone.

Alcohol: The precise mechanism of withdrawal from ALCOHOL, a CNS depressant, is not completely understood, although the syndrome is well–documented. The release from the burden of CNS depression over a sustained period of time results in CNS overactivity. This explains many of the symptoms and signs that are evoked. It is unclear how quickly dependence on alcohol develops and therefore exactly what symptoms constitute the first manifestations of withdrawal. The HANGOVER commonly experienced after a bout of heavy drinking and the slight tremulousness that can persist after several days' intoxication may be early withdrawal symptoms, but the more traumatic symptoms present themselves only after a drinker has consumed 400–500 ml (500 ml = 1 pint) of alcohol daily for about a month and a half. Abstinence after this level of consumption produces a three–stage withdrawal syndrome. The first stage appears within a few hours and generally includes tremulousness, weakness, sweating, nausea and vomiting, loss of appetite and abdominal cramps. The patient may suffer a cardiac dysrhythmia and pseudohallucinations. If dependency is mild, only some of the above symptoms may appear briefly. This stage is sometimes called the impending DTs (DELIRIUM TREMENS.) In cases of more severe withdrawal, this first anxious shaky stage may be followed by a period of convulsive seizures, usually on the second or third day after abstinence. These RUM FITS, which occur in only a minority of cases, require medical intervention because they can develop into STATUS EPILEPTICUS.

The third stage of withdrawal, most dramatic and terrifying to the victim, consists of delirium tremens (the DTs), a period of intense auditory, visual and tactile hallucinations which can last three or four days. During this time the patient suffers severe agitation and disorientation, sleeps very little, and experiences fever and profuse sweating that may cause serious dehydration. His behavior usually becomes very aggressive and even self–destructive. Death from hyperthermia, peripheral vascular collapse, or self–inflicted injury can occur during this stage of withdrawal: there is a 10% mortality rate for alcoholics suffering untreated delirium tremens.

Abrupt withdrawal from alcohol, rather than gradual detoxification, usually lasts 5–7 days and results in complete recovery from physical dependence, although certainly not from psychological dependence. In rare cases, and due to uncertain causes, patients have remained in chronic psychotic states resembling schizophrenia. Gradual detoxification is much safer than abrupt cessation, and convulsions can be avoided by the substitution of a drug that is cross–dependent with alcohol such as Librium or the early administration of an anticonvulsant, such as Dilantin, in large doses.

Barbiturates, tranquilizers and other sedative hypnotics: The addictive nature of barbiturates came to the attention of German chemists soon after the development of these drugs in the early 1900s, but the withdrawal syndrome was less consistent and more puzzling than the one already known to occur with narcotics. Abrupt cessation of a regular intake of even large doses of sedative hypnotic drugs did not *always* precipitate withdrawal symptoms, so evidence supporting the risk of addiction to these depressants seemed inconclusive. The difference, in fact, between depressants and narcotics is that dependence to depressants develops only above a certain threshold of daily intake; even large amounts below this threshold will not always cause physical addiction and, therefore, withdrawal.

How quickly such dependence develops is still unclear, but the withdrawal syndrome brought about by abstinence or the sharp reduction of intake closely resembles that occurring in alcoholics. Withdrawal symptoms from depressants may occur within a few hours after the drug is stopped and are char-

acterized by physical weakness, anxiety, nausea and vomiting, dizziness and sleeplessness. Hallucinations, delirium, delusions and convulsions may occur as long as three days to a week following withdrawal and may last for many days. Withdrawal from the minor tranquilizers is similar except that it may take longer to develop. The onset of withdrawal from tranquilizers with long half–lives is delayed but the withdrawal persists longer. Not all symptoms that emerge following cessation of tranquilizer use are withdrawal phenomena. Some represent emergent anxiety that was repressed by the medication.

Heroin and other narcotics: The duration and intensity of withdrawal symptoms from heroin and other narcotics is directly related to the quality of the drug, and the quantity and frequency of use. Because of limited finances and the poor quality of street drugs today, few addicts use more than 500 mg of morphine (125–150 mg of heroin) a day. Most addicts can afford to support only a relatively mild physical dependence and so are spared the most severe forms of opiate withdrawal.

If an addict who uses low regular intermittent doses does not receive his regular fix at the expected time (usually every six to twelve hours), symptoms resembling the flu are likely to occur: nausea, uneasiness, yawning, sweating alternating with chills, various aches and pains, tears and runny nose. Unless counteracted by a dose of heroin or a cross–tolerant drug such as methadone, these symptoms gradually intensify and broaden to include a range of symptoms showing central nervous system excitation: pupillary dilation, increased heart rate and blood pressure, twitching, spasms, gooseflesh, diarrhea, insomnia or a "yen" sleep, and spontaneous orgasm. Cardiovascular collapse is a risk. Withdrawal from a heavy chronic narcotic habit can be extremely severe and painful.

Heroin withdrawal generally peaks in 26–27

hours and is usually completed within a week. Certain effects, such as increased blood pressure and heart rate, can persist during a period of "protracted abstinence" of up to six months.

Because narcotics readily cross the placental barrier, babies born of female addicts share their mothers' physical dependence and almost always exhibit withdrawal symptoms soon after birth.

As previously mentioned, withdrawal from methadone is more prolonged but less severe than heroin withdrawal, since methadone is a longer acting, more slowly eliminated drug. If administered during heroin withdrawal, methadone can ease the intensity of the experience. Conversely, the administration of a group of drugs known as narcotic antagonists, of which NALORPHINE is an example, can precipitate the withdrawal process (and increase its unpleasantness).

Amphetamines and other stimulants: Stimulant drugs, such as amphetamines and caffeine, are generally considered to be more psychologically than physically addictive. Nevertheless, sudden abstinence from amphetamines, cocaine and even coffee does produce withdrawal symptoms in most people: headache, stomach cramps, lethargy, chronic fatigue and often severe emotional depression. Furthermore, abnormal EEG patterns which have been recorded under these circumstances have stabilized after administration of the drug in question.

Hallucinogens and cannabis: Neither hallucinogens nor cannabis are physically addictive; abstinence or abrupt cessation of intake from them will not produce distinct withdrawal symptoms.

women   In the late nineteenth and early twentieth centuries, when the use of patent medicines containing opiates and alcohol resulted in large numbers of addicts throughout American society, three times as many women as men developed such addictions. The typi-

cal addict was a middle–aged, middle– to upper–class housewife. Today women of all ages, classes and ethnic groups are heavily involved in drug use and abuse—perhaps less visibly than men, but in alarming and increasing numbers. Women currently account for 60% of all drug–related emergency room visits. Women exhibit particular patterns of substance abuse attributable, in part, to problems peculiar to their sex. Their drug–taking behavior also exposes them to dangers which do not affect men, such as those imposed on the fetus during PREGNANCY.

During this century and especially during the past few decades, women's consumption of alcohol and other drugs, as well as our awareness of it, has increased markedly as a result of social changes which have caused and allowed women to indulge more freely in mind–altering substances and to be more open about their use of drugs. There was a particularly noticeable increase in drug use during World War II when a large number of women joined the work force. Social changes experienced in recent years have increased the pressures which women face daily. Bored housewives have been likely candidates for alcohol and drug abuse for some time, but now many women regardless of their life–style turn to drugs to help them cope with increasing responsibilities, loneliness, inferiority feelings and conflicts about their sex role. Women's liberation has often had the effect of placing more demands and restrictions on women than they feel capable of managing alone.

The stress felt by today's working women is a contributing factor to the increase in alcohol and drug use. Women often feel they must work harder than their male counterparts to prove that they are competent. Many women also feel conflict about moving away from the traditional roles of wife and mother. In addition, working women who are divorced or separated often have financial difficulties and the responsibilities of child care; loneliness is also a frequent problem. Employed women are almost as likely to have drinking problems as unemployed women, whereas employed men are only about half as likely to have problems as unemployed men. When compared on a marital basis, the highest rate of alcohol–related problems is among divorced and separated women; single women are next, and married women and widows have the lowest rates.

Alcoholism is a particularly severe problem among female homosexuals. In 1970 a study found that 35% of all lesbians had severe drinking problems as compared with 28% of homosexual men and only 5% of heterosexual women. Women in minority groups, particularly black women, face oppression because of both their race and sex. Unemployment rates for black women are higher than those for either white women or black men and they are far more likely to head families subsisting below the official poverty level.

The tobacco and alcoholic beverage industries have recognized this growing market and many companies aim their advertising at women—not without results. Currently 30.5% of all women smoke cigarettes regularly, and while the number of male smokers has dropped sharply over the last 20 years, there has been no similar decline for women. In 1979 a government survey showed that 1.7 million teenage girls smoke as compared to 1.6 million boys. Statistics also indicate that men are twice as successful as women in their efforts to quit smoking.

The estimated number of women alcoholics in the United States is five million. Alcoholics Anonymous reports that one in three of its members is a woman and that in recent years more and more teenage girls with drinking problems have been attending meetings. Women are not only more susceptible than men to the transitory effects of alcoholic intoxication, because of their lower

weight, but they are also more vulnerable to cirrhosis of the liver.

Women with alcohol problems are more likely to use prescribed drugs, particularly tranquilizers, and it is harder to break a dual addiction than an addiction to alcohol alone. A 1977 survey of AA members showed that 29% of the women (but only 15% of the men) were addicted to drugs other than alcohol. Of new members 30 years and younger, 55% of the women were cross–addicted compared to 36% of the men.

There are an estimated two million female prescription–drug addicts in the United States. Women are prescribed tranquilizers more than twice as often as men and consume 71% of all antidepressant medications and 80% of all legal amphetamines (often in the form of diet pills). In 1980, 26 million Valium prescriptions were written for women.

Numerous explanations for these high percentages have been postulated. Twice as many women as men suffer from depression and such depression may be the result of the restricted and self–denying roles women often feel they must play. Some 67% of female problem drinkers correlate their drinking bouts with the days of the month when they are premenstrual, a time when many women experience emotional debility and depression. But the high rate of prescriptions for antidepressants seems also to be related to the fact that women are more likely than men to *express* their feelings and seek treatment from a physician. In general women see doctors more often than men and just by the fact of exposure are more likely to receive prescriptions. Doctors are also more inclined to pacify women with drugs, as they often do with the ELDERLY. In the case of alcohol–related problems, doctors may prescribe pills for the symptoms instead of confronting the alcoholism.

Society's reaction to women's alcohol and other drug abuse has traditionally been more condemnatory than toward men's equally destructive habits. Although today women's drinking is taken for granted, female drunkenness is still frowned upon. Similarly, while the wives of alcoholics typically endure their husbands' problems and try to help them get treatment, men are more likely to leave their alcoholic wives in disgust. Consequently, women have been more likely to indulge their addictions in secret and not to seek treatment. Until recently treatment programs specifically oriented toward helping women have been rare, but newer programs incorporating women's groups are proving successful. (See also DEPRESSION.)

wood alcohol   See METHANOL.

World Health Organization (WHO) A specialized agency of the United Nations. WHO has the primary reponsibility for international health matters and public health. Created in 1948, WHO has the benefit of 160 countries that exchange knowledge and experience with the aim of attaining a level of health that permits nations to lead socially and economically productive lives.

wormwood   See ABSINTHE.

X

xylene   A volatile solvent. Although the vapors of this aromatic hydrocarbon are extremely irritating to the nasal membranes, it has some potential for INHALANT abuse.

Y

yerba mate   A tea brewed from the leaves of *Ilex paraguariensis,* an evergreen shrub native to Paraguay and Brazil. It contains the stimulant CAFFEINE.

yohimbe   *Corynanthe yohimbe,* a tree native to West Africa whose bark and roots are purported to be an aphrodisiac. It does produce hallucinations and mild euphoria but is also toxic in large doses.

youths   The adolescent is perhaps the most vulnerable individual confronting the growing social acceptance of drug use in the United States. In 1980 there were 10,000 emergency room visits related to marijuana and they primarily involved adolescents. The 1981 nationwide government survey shows that one out of 14 high school seniors smoke marijuana daily, and in some communities adolescents who have not tried marijuana may be in the minority.

In the report published by the National Institute on Drug Abuse, *Highlights from Students Drug Use in America: 1975–1981,* key findings indicate that the use of many illicit drugs has declined or is declining from the peak levels of the 1970s. Despite these improvements, illicit drug use is still extremely prevalent among high school age youths and abuse figures are probably the highest to be found in any industrialized nation in the world. The report shows a continuing decline in cigarette smoking by students; the number of seniors smoking a half pack a day has declined from 19.4% in 1977 to 13.5% in 1981. This decline is attributed to a steady increase in young people's concern with health, and to a shift in peer attitudes regarding the acceptability of smoking. Despite this decline, however, nicotine and alcohol remain the two most abused drugs.

Marijuana smoking has shown a similar decline in daily (or nearly daily) use, from 11% of all seniors in 1978 to 7% in 1981. Although marked, this decline still means that one out of 14 seniors uses marijuana on a daily or near–daily basis. As with cigarette smoking, this decline has been attributed to a continuing concern with health issues and possibly to a decrease in peer acceptance (see PEER PRESSURE). Marijuana use at all levels is also declining: annual use dropped from 51% in 1979 to 46% in 1981. Also, students do not get as high, or stay high as long, as users did a few years ago—a pattern that suggests some moderation in behavior.

The use of PCP, which is often sprinkled on marijuana or parsley and smoked (although it can be snorted or swallowed), also shows a significant drop—from 7.0% in 1979 to 3.2% in 1981. This sharp fall–off could well be explained by PCP's reputation as a particularly dangerous drug. Another drug that shows a sharp decline in use is AMYL NITRITE, commonly known to students as "poppers" and "snappers." The number of seniors using this drug dropped from 6.5% in 1979 to 3.7% in 1981. The abuse of tranquilizers has shown a more gradual decline; over the four years spanned by the report, use has fallen from 11% to 8%. The use of inhalants has also dropped over the years. Despite an epidemic of GLUE SNIFFING in the 1960s, only 0.1% of high school seniors reported using inhalants on a daily basis. This figure may not be representative of all adolescents, however, because inhalants are generally used by those in their early teens.

The use of amphetamines, on the other hand, showed a significant increase, particularly from 1980 to 1981. In 1981, 32% of all high school seniors indicated having tried amphetamines without medical supervision; 16% said they had used amphetamines in the last month. Heroin, barbiturate, and LSD

use remained quite steady in 1981 (although this followed an earlier period of decline), but both the degree and duration of the highs experienced by users dropped. The use of cocaine in 1980 and 1981 also remained fairly steady. (From 1976 to 1979 the proportion of high school seniors using cocaine had doubled from 6% to 12%.) The statistics show an increase of only four–tenths of one percent for the nation as a whole. There are, however, large regional differences in the use of the drug; cocaine use has fallen in the south and north central areas of the U.S. and continues to rise in the northeast and west. Methaqualone use has also been on the rise; up from 8% in 1978 to 11% in 1981.

All levels of alcohol use, from daily use to occasional binge drinking, remained unchanged in the period from 1975 to 1981. Alcohol is the most widely used drug among teenagers and according to a 1978 survey conducted by the National Institute on Alcohol Abuse and Alcoholism, 87% of senior high school students reported that they had tried alcohol at least once; over 20% reported drinking at least once a week. The 1981 survey reported 6.0% of high school seniors used alcohol on a daily basis and 71% reported drinking during the month prior to the survey. Although state laws prohibit the sale or serving of alcoholic beverages to minors, surveys show that most teenagers drink, and that they begin to do so at age 13 or 14. While drinking can be a form of rebelliousness, for many teenagers it is normal adaptive behavior. Many teenagers look upon drinking as a mature, adult form of behavior and they try to emulate it. Both parental attitudes and peer pressure influence youthful drinking, but most studies show that children of parents who drink usually drink too, and children of parents who abstain are also likely to abstain.

Causes of Drug Abuse: The use of drugs is increasing among younger children. This is particularly disturbing because studies have

High school senior drug use: 1975–1981
Used in last year

Class of	75	76	77	78	79	80	81
Marijuana	40%	45%	48%	50%	51%	49%	46%
Inhalants	NA	3	4	4	5	5	4
Amyl & Butyl Nitrites	NA	NA	NA	NA	7	6	4
Hallucinogens	11	9	9	10	10	9	9
LSD	7	6	6	6	7	7	7
PCP	NA	NA	NA	NA	7	4	3
Cocaine	6	6	7	9	12	12	12
Heroin	*	*	*	*	*	*	*
Other Opiates	6	6	6	6	6	6	6
Stimulants	16	16	16	17	18	21	26
Sedatives	12	11	11	10	10	10	11
Barbiturates	11	10	9	8	8	7	7
Methaqualone	5	5	5	5	6	7	8
Tranquilizers	11	10	11	10	10	9	8
Alcohol	85	86	87	88	88	88	87
Cigarettes	NA	NA	NA	NA	NA	NA	NA

NA indicates data not available.
* indicates less than 1.0%

Terms:
Ever used: Used one or more times.
Daily users: Used 20 or more times in the month before survey.
Used in past month: Used at least once in the 30 days prior to survey.
Used in last year: Used in the 12 months prior to survey.

Source: *Student Drug Use in America: 1975–1981*, National Insitute on Drug Abuse.

Note: Separate questions about the use of PCP (angel dust) and amyl and butyl nitrites (poppers) were not asked until 1979.

shown that the younger a person begins to experiment with drugs, the more likely he is to progress to heavier use and stronger drugs. There are any number of theories as to why a child first experiments with drugs: questions of status, peer pressure, pleasure, thrills, boredom, stimulation, sophistication, difficulty coping with problems, and so on. Whatever the reasons, they have much to do with adolescence in general; a time when a child is developing physically and emotionally and is caught up in an identity crisis

High school senior drug use: 1975–1981
Used in past month

Class of	75	76	77	78	79	80	81
Marijuana	27%	32%	35%	37%	37%	34%	32%
Inhalants	NA	1	1	2	2	1	2
Amyl & Butyl Nitrites	NA	NA	NA	NA	2	2	1
Hallucinogens	5	3	4	4	4	4	4
LSD	2	2	2	2	2	2	3
PCP	NA	NA	NA	NA	2	1	1
Cocaine	2	2	3	4	6	5	6
Heroin	*	*	*	*	*	*	*
Other Opiates	2	2	3	2	2	2	2
Stimulants	9	8	8	9	10	12	16
Sedatives	5	5	5	4	4	5	5
Barbiturates	5	4	4	3	3	3	3
Methaqualone	2	2	2	2	2	3	3
Tranquilizers	4	4	5	3	4	3	3
Alcohol	68	68	71	72	72	72	71
Cigarettes	37	39	38	37	34	31	29

When an adolescent has difficulty meeting society's demands and has his own internal demands to face as well, the result can be extreme anxiety and a feeling of powerlessness. The need to relieve these tensions can result in drug experimentation and give the adolescent a temporary high feeling and an exaggerated sense of competence and power. Instant gratification and the feeling of euphoria can dampen the fear of developing independence and decision–making. However, because every adolescent is a unique individual with his or her own physical and psychological problems, there can be no one definitive cause of drug use.

The 1975–1981 NIDA report suggests some factors that can contribute to drug abuse:

1. The use of illicit drugs generally begins when an individual associates with a friend or acquaintance who is a drug user. This association is followed by an opportunity to use the drug and actual use itself.

2. Continuing contact with people who use drugs will lead to an individual's experimentation. Most people do not try an illicit drug at the very first opportunity.

3. There is more likely to be drug abuse among adolescents whose mothers smoke cigarettes and/or drink moderately than among those whose mothers abstain.

4. If an older sibling uses alcohol and/or illicit drugs, there is a tendency for use and for the use of the specific drug that the older sibling uses.

5. The following factors do not appear to be related to a child's drug use: the fact that the father may use drugs, the family's socioeconomic status, the mother's current em-

High school senior drug use: 1975–1981
Daily users

Class of	75	76	77	78	79	80	81
Marijuana	6%	8%	9%	10.7%	10.3%	9.1%	7%
Inhalants	NA	0.0	0.0	0.1	0.0	0.1	0.1
Amyl & Butyl Nitrites	NA	NA	NA	NA	11	11	10
Hallucinogens	0.1	0.1	0.1	0.1	0.1	0.1	0.1
LSD	0.0	0.0	0.0	0.0	0.0	0.0	0.1
PCP	NA	NA	NA	NA	0.1	0.1	0.1
Cocaine	0.1	0.1	0.1	0.1	0.2	0.2	0.3
Heroin	0.1	0.0	0.0	0.0	0.0	0.0	0.0
Other Opiates	0.1	0.1	0.2	0.1	0.0	0.1	0.1
Stimulants	0.5	0.4	0.5	0.5	0.6	0.7	1.2
Sedatives	0.3	0.2	0.2	0.2	0.1	0.2	0.2
Barbiturates	0.1	0.1	0.2	0.1	0.0	0.1	0.1
Methaqualone	0.0	0.0	0.0	0.0	0.0	0.1	0.1
Tranquilizers	0.1	0.2	0.3	0.1	0.1	0.1	0.1
Alcohol	5.7	5.6	6.1	5.7	6.9	6.0	6.0
Cigarettes	26.9	28.8	28.8	27.5	25.4	21.3	20.3

ployment status, or the mother's marital status.

6. The presence of children seems to be an influence on drug use in parents in the 26–34 age group. Over 60% of married people with no children have tried marijuana and 24% are current users; by comparison, 40% of married people with children have tried marijuana but only 10% are current users.

Prevention and Treatment: While the treatment of drug dependence is extremely important, the greatest hope for combating the problem lies in preventing drug use from starting in the first place, or interfering with its use during the early experimentation stage. There are four prevention strategies:

1. *Information.* This includes providing accurate and objective information about all types of drugs and their effects on the body.

2. *Intervention.* This includes providing assistance and support to adolescents during critical periods of their life through counseling, the use of hotlines, etc.

3. *Education.* This includes clarifying values and improving problem–solving skills within a structured setting. Group discussions and role playing are common techniques in helping young people improve their ability to cope and make decisions.

4. *Alternatives.* This includes promoting confidence and self–reliance through new, challenging experiences in school, and providing positive alternatives to drug–taking behavior. Such alternatives include restoration projects, volunteer services in the community, and helping such causes as environment preservation.

Along with numerous federal and state

High school senior drug use: 1975–1981
Ever used

Class of	75	76	77	78	79	80	81
Marijuana	47%	53%	56%	59%	60%	60%	60%
Inhalants	NA	10	11	12	13	12	12
Amyl & Butyl Nitrites	NA	NA	NA	NA	11	11	10
Hallucinogens	16	15	14	14	14	13	13
LSD	11	11	10	10	10	9	10
PCP	NA	NA	NA	NA	13	10	8
Cocaine	9	10	11	13	15	16	17
Heroin	2	2	2	2	1	1	1
Other Opiates	9	10	10	10	10	10	10
Stimulants	22	23	23	23	24	26	32
Sedatives	18	18	17	16	15	15	16
Barbiturates	17	16	16	14	12	11	11
Methaqualone	8	8	9	8	8	10	11
Tranquilizers	17	17	18	17	16	15	15
Alcohol	90	92	93	93	93	93	93
Cigarettes	74	75	76	75	74	71	71

funded programs designed to educate America's youth about the dangers of drug and alcohol abuse, the 1970s brought about a rash of newly formed parent and community organizations: FAMILIES IN ACTION (FIA); DO IT NOW FOUNDATION (DIN); etc. Parents and friends of youthful drug abusers, along with community and church leaders now seem to realize that drug education cannot be restricted to school programs. Young people also need to experience care and concern from other outlets. There are Drug Abuse Prevention Coordinators in every state, usually located with the Department of Mental Health or the Department of Health, and groups interested in organizing prevention programs are urged by the government to contact these coordinators.

Probably one of the driving forces behind the organization of parent groups stems from the feeling of helplessness parents feel when they realize their child has been experimenting with drugs. Many parents have no idea what actions to take, what questions to ask, and where to turn for help. One of the biggest conflicts parents face is the moment of truth when they actually find drugs in a child's possession. Do they talk it out? Do they simply seize and destroy? Do they institute punishments? Do they stop a child from seeing his friends? Because of the unpredictable nature of drug use among adolescents, where there are no patterns and use can simply come and go because of fads and pressures, parents are often at a loss for guidelines in handling the problem. Unfortunately, there are also parents who are simply unwilling to look at or deal with the problem; many feel

self–guilt, anger and embarrassment and refuse to cooperate. This unwillingness works
at cross–purposes with professionals who are
trying to cope with the problem. There are
other parents who simply want to turn the
problem over to a counselor and expect him
to deal with the issue without any cooperation on their part.

Professional counselors, particularly those
working with school guidance programs, are
deluged with cases and are simply too busy
to cope effectively. Not only are drug problems a demand on their time, they often have
no clear policy to follow and their expectations are often unrealistic. They also feel under pressure because they realize they cannot
"do it alone" and many parents expect them
to. Misclassification of drug use can also be
a problem among counselors. Due to the demands on their time, many counselors often
treat all drug use as "dependency" and do
not really address the causes. In addition,
there seems to be a tendency among elementary school teachers to ignore drug use altogether and wait for high school teachers and
counselors to take over the problem because
they have had more training in dealing with
the issue. Passing the buck, however, simply
means that elementary school children become forgotten in the shuffle and lack objective information which could help them as
they advance in school.

In the last ten years numerous organizations have been formed to combat use and
abuse of drugs, probably as a result of a rise
in awareness about the risks to health. Helping those who are becoming addicted to alcohol has been of particular importance.
Throughout the country high school groups
are being organized to help their classmates.
Telephone numbers are available at all times
for teenagers who have had too much to
drink. They call a "hot line," manned by
their peers, and someone is sent to drive
them home. As these groups are fairly new,
there has been no evaluation of their effectiveness thus far, but the trend is encouraging.

APPENDICES

Appendix 1 Street Language

Appendix 2 Slang Synonyms for Drugs

Appendix 3 Tables

Appendix 4 Sources of Information

Appendix 1

Street Language

A

Slang Terms

A-bomb   Marijuana and heroin mixed together and smoked.

A–head   A heavy amphetamine user.

Acapulco gold   An especially potent high-quality marijuana grown near Acapulco, Mexico.

ace   An obsolete term for a marijuana cigarette.

acid   A slang term for LSD-25; from d-lysergic acid diethylamide tartrate.

acid freak   A person who exhibits bizarre behavior induced by the use of LSD.

acid head   A person who is a habitual heavy user of LSD.

acid rock   A type of rock 'n' roll music using electronic sound which is associated with the use of hallucinogens, particularly LSD. It originated in San Francisco in the 1960s.

acid test   Parties held in the 1960s at which LSD was served. Guests dressed in bizarre clothing and listened to acid rock music to enhance the effects of the drug.

action   A term that refers to the sales activity of drugs; ''there's great action in this area.''

a la canona   To undergo heroin withdrawal without the aid of medication.

amies   AMYL NITRITE.

AMT   AMPHETAMINES.

amys   AMYL NITRITE.

angel dust   PHENCYCLIDINE. In powder form, it is mixed with another hallucinogen, usually marijuana, and smoked, snorted or taken orally.

angel off   The arrest of a drug pusher's customers either to obtain information on the pusher's activities or to try to put him out of business.

angel trumpet or **angel's trumpet**
DATURA.

animal trank   PHENCYCLIDINE.

anywhere   A slang term for having drugs in one's possession.

Areca nut   ARECOLINE.

army disease   MORPHINE addiction. A Civil War term born from the frequent and indiscriminate use of morphine at that time which caused the addiction of an estimated 400,000 soldiers. (See AMERICAN MILITARY.)

artillery   Apparatus needed for the injection of a drug.

aurora borealis   A slang term for THC, (tetrahydrocannabinol), the active principle in marijuana. Most THC sold illicitly is not THC but more often phencyclidine (PCP).

B

baby   MARIJUANA. It is also a term for a person who uses heroin on an irregular basis.

back up   The act of withdrawing blood back into the syringe after injecting part of a shot of heroin. It is done to prolong the initial sensation and effects of the drug.

backwards   The use of tranquilizers to reverse the effects of LSD. The term is also used in reference to someone who renews a drug habit.

bad   A term for drugs that are considered very good and very potent.

bad seed   PEYOTE.

bad trip   A frightening reaction after the use of a hallucinogenic drug, particularly LSD, which can cause a temporary or chronic psychosis.

bador   Aztec term for MORNING GLORY SEEDS.

bag   A measurement of heroin or marijuana. A bag of heroin usually contains about 5 grains of diluted heroin (1–5% pure). A bag of marijuana usually contains ⅐–⅕ oz. The term is also applied to a person who is using one drug exclusively: "He's in an LSD bag."

bagman   The person who handles the money in a drug transaction.

bale   A pound of marijuana.

balloons   Drugs are sometimes packaged for sale in balloons: if a sale is interrupted by police the balloon can be swallowed and later excreted. This method of concealing drugs is also used in smuggling.

bam   AMPHETAMINE.

Bambu   A brand of cigarette papers used to roll marijuana cigarettes.

bang   A narcotics injection, or the act of injecting a narcotic.

bangers   DEPRESSANTS.

bank bandit pills   BARBITURATES.

banker   A person who puts up the capital for a drug–buying trip (particularly in the case of marijuana).

bar   A solid block of marijuana. The drug is mixed with honey or sugar water to hold it together in this way.

barbs   BARBITURATES.

base   Cocaine FREEBASE.

basing   Using cocaine FREEBASE.

B–bomb   A Benzedrine inhaler. The wad

inside, heavily impregnated with Benzedrine, was taken out and soaked in water. The Benzedrine extracted by this process was equal to approximately 25 tablets. The inhalers were removed from the market in 1949 because of this widespread abuse.

B.C.   A slang term for birth control pills.

beans   AMPHETAMINES, MESCALINE.

beast, the   LSD.

beat   Counterfeit drug. Also a term applied to cheating a person out of money.

bee   The amount of marijuana it would take to fill a penny matchbook.

behind acid   Using LSD.

belly habit   To satisfy a drug habit by taking a drug orally (particularly methadone).

belt   The initial effect felt after taking a drug.

belted   Being in a state of drug euphoria.

bender   Being on a drug spree. Used particularly in the case of alcohol, as in "on a bender."

bennies   BENZEDRINE.

bent   Being in a state of drug euphoria, particularly from the use of hallucinogens.

benz   BENZEDRINE.

bernice   COCAINE.

bernies   COCAINE.

betel nut   See ARECOLINE.

bhang   The Indian word for MARIJUANA. It is also the name of a tea made from marijuana that is drunk in India.

Bible, the   The *Physicians' Desk Reference,* an annual volume listing commercial drug preparations. Drug users refer to it for pill identification and drug descriptions.

big bags   Five and ten dollar bags of HEROIN.

big C   COCAINE.

big chief, the   MESCALINE.

big con   A minor confidence game, as compared to a LONG CON.

big D, the   LSD.

big H   HEROIN.

big man, the   The person who supplies a PUSHER with drugs.

big supplier   The person who supplies a PUSHER with drugs.

bing   Prison. The term is also used to refer to a drug injection.

bit   Period of time served in prison. Also a person's favorite drug that he or she uses exclusively.

biz   Apparatus needed for the injection of a drug.

black beauties   BIPHETAMINES.

black drink   A tea containing caffeine which is made from leaves of the YAUPON plant.

black gunion   MARIJUANA that is highly

potent, black in color and has a gummy consistency. The word *gunion* may come from the word *gungeon* (an especially potent variety of marijuana from Jamaica or Africa), and may be a variation of the Jamaican word *ganga*; most of the marijuana that came into the United States during the 1940s was imported from Jamaica.

black mollies   BIPHETAMINES.

black pills   OPIUM in pellet form.

black Russian   HASHISH.

black stuff   OPIUM.

blackbirds   BIPHETAMINES.

blanco   Spanish word for HEROIN.

blast   To smoke MARIJUANA.

blast party   A party at which MARIJUANA is smoked.

blind munchies   The strong desire for food (sweets in particular) that is felt while under the influence of MARIJUANA.

block   MORPHINE in the shape of a cube and usually sold by the ounce.

blockbusters   BARBITURATES.

blond hash   HASHISH that is lighter in color and less potent than other varieties of hashish.

blow   The sniffing of HEROIN or the smoking of MARIJUANA. The term is also applied when a vein is missed during a heroin injection and some of the drug is wasted. Also, a slang word for COCAINE.

blow a fill   To smoke OPIUM.

blow a stick   To smoke MARIJUANA.

blow your mind   To feel the effects of HALLUCINOGENS. Also, to lose touch with reality and not have mental control.

blow–your–mind–roulette   A dangerous party game played with a variety of pills—uppers, downers, and so on—which are mixed together in a container and drawn out at random. The drawer does not know what he or she has taken until the effects are felt.

blue acid   LSD. The term comes from the color of LSD when it is seen in large amounts.

blue angels   AMYTAL Sodium.

blue bullets   AMYTAL Sodium.

blue cheer   LSD.

blue devils   AMYTAL Sodium.

blue dolls   AMYTAL Sodium.

blue heavens   AMYTAL Sodium.

blue mist   LSD.

blue morning glory seeds   MORNING GLORY SEEDS sold under the trade name Heavenly Blues.

blue tips   AMYTAL Sodium.

blue velvet   A mixture of elixir terpin hydrate, codeine and tripelenamine.

bluebirds   AMYTAL Sodium.

blues   AMYTAL Sodium. Also NUMORPHAN.

body drugs   Narcotics which depress the

conscious state as opposed to hallucinogens and psychedelics which stimulate the mind.

bogart   It is customary practice to pass a MARIJUANA cigarette around a group. To keep it to oneself is to bogart.

bogue   Initial withdrawal symptoms from a drug.

bolsa   Spanish term for HEROIN packaged in a bag.

bomb   A large–size MARIJUANA cigarette. Also high quality HEROIN which has had very little dilution.

bombed out   Feeling the effects of a drug.

bomber   A large–size MARIJUANA cigarette.

bombita   COCAINE and AMPHETAMINES in a solution so that they can be injected.

bong   A water pipe used to smoke Marijuana or tobacco. The smoke bubbles through the water and eliminates some of the harshness.

bonita   Lactose crystals (milk sugar), often used to dilute HEROIN. (See CUTTING.)

boogie   A drug–buying expedition.

book, the   The PHYSICIANS' DESK REFERENCE. Also called the Bible.

boost   To shoplift: a common way for an addict to obtain money to support a habit.

boot and shoot   A person who shoplifts and steals to support a drug habit.

booze fighter   A person who is determined to "fight" a BOOZE habit. The term

implies an ongoing, and therefore unsuccessful, battle characterized by a continuous stream of good intentions and broken resolutions.

booze hound   A person who consumes excessive amounts of BOOZE and whose life is greatly influenced by, and even dedicated to, its consumption.

boss   High potency drugs, meaning the best or the strongest.

B.O.T.   Balance of time. The sentence a parole violator must serve to fulfill the original sentence.

bouncing powder   COCAINE.

boxed   Feeling the high effects of, or being under the influence of, a drug.

boy   HEROIN.

brain ticklers   AMPHETAMINES. Also BARBITURATES.

brick   A pressed block of marijuana, opium or morphine. In the case of marijuana, it weighs one pound.

brick, throw a big   The impulsive desire to do something violent or commit a crime.

bring down   To cause someone to lose the exhilarated feelings induced by a drug.

broccoli   MARIJUANA.

brody   To feign sickness in front of a doctor in order to gain a prescription for a drug.

brother   HEROIN.

brown   HEROIN; particularly heroin from Mexico.

brown dots   LSD.

brown mixture   OPIUM.

brown rock   HEROIN.

brown stuff   OPIUM.

brown sugar   HEROIN.

brownies   AMPHETAMINES.

bum bend   A frightening reaction after taking LSD, one which could cause temporary or chronic psychosis.

bum kicks   Being anxious, worried or depressed about something.

bum trip   See BUMMER.

bumblebees   AMPHETAMINES.

bummer   A frightening reaction after taking a drug. A bum (or bad) trip.

bundle   HEROIN packaged (bundled) together in $5.00 bags by a wholesaler for selling to the pusher who, in turn, sells them individually to addicts.

bunk habit   Getting the effects of opium by inhaling the fumes when others are smoking without smoking oneself.

burese   COCAINE.

burn   Cheating or being cheated in drug deals.

burn artist   A person who uses the BURN technique.

burn out, burned out   The term has three separate meanings: (1) It refers to a chronic drug dependent person who is so weary of the "hassle" of obtaining drugs (like heroin) that he discontinues usage. (2) Heavy marijuana smokers, particularly young people, will become dull and apathetic and withdraw from their usual activities; they are called "burnouts" by their peers. (3) Some workers in the "helping professions," such as drug rehabilitation, social work and so on, become discouraged and leave their professions after years of trying to work with difficult patients. The usage has now spread to other professions.

burned   One who has been cheated in a drug deal.

burning   To smoke MARIJUANA.

bush   MARIJUANA.

businessman's lunchtime high   DMT, the effects of which last only 30 minutes to an hour.

bust   A police raid. The term "busted" refers to being arrested.

button, the   PEYOTE.

buy   The purchase of a drug.

buzz   Feeling the effects of a drug, particularly MARIJUANA, without unpleasant hallucinations.

buzz, rolling   To continue feeling the pleasant BUZZ effects of a drug.

C

C   COCAINE.

caapi   AYAHUASCA.

caballo   HEROIN (Spanish for horse).

cabeza de angel   A shrub, *Calliandra anomala,* which is dried and used by the Aztec Indians as a snuff.

ca–ca   Counterfeit HEROIN.

cactus   PEYOTE, MESCALINE.

California sunshine   LSD.

came down   To lose the effects of a drug, or to experience WITHDRAWAL symptoms.

can   A measurement of drugs, particularly marijuana, which is sometimes sold in 1 oz tobacco cans.

Canadian black   MARIJUANA grown in Canada.

canceled stick   A cigarette containing MARIJUANA.

C and H   A mixture of COCAINE and HEROIN.

C and M   A mixture of COCAINE and MORPHINE.

candy   Drugs.

candy man   A person who sells drugs.

canned sativa   HASHISH.

canned stuff   OPIUM that has been packaged.

carry, carrying   Having drugs on one's person.

cartwheels   AMPHETAMINES.

cassina   YAUPON.

cat   HEROIN.

CB   DORIDEN.

cent   In drug language a cent refers to a dollar; a nickel refers to $5; a dime refers to $10.

chalk   AMPHETAMINE tablets that crumble easily.

change   A prison sentence of short duration.

changes   Interruptions in an addict's drug habit because drugs are not available at the time he wants them and his routine is changed.

channel   A vein used for injecting HEROIN. Also a term that refers to a source of drugs.

charge   The first onset of a drug's effects. The term also applies to an injection of drugs, and to a marijuana cigarette.

charged   The sleepy, drowsy effects felt from an overdose of a depressant.

Charles   COCAINE.

Charlie   One dollar.

chaser   Water, beer or any mild liquid which is taken after a drink of strong liquor to provide a contrast in sensations.

chasing the bag   Being addicted to HEROIN. The term bag refers to a packet of the drug.

chasing the dragon   Inhaling the fumes of HEROIN which has been mixed with BARBITURATE powder amd melted over a flame.

chicalote   *Argemone mexicana,* also called the prickly poppy. There are claims that it produces a marijuana–like effect when smoked.

chicharra   Puerto Rican slang for a mixture of tobacco and MARIJUANA.

chick   HEROIN.

chicken powder   AMPHETAMINES.

chick shit habit   The occasional use of drugs.

chill   To refuse to sell drugs to a person.

chillum   A clay pipe for smoking GHANJA.

Chinese cure   Mixing opium with a tonic and gradually increasing the amount of the tonic in order to break an opium habit.

Chinese red   HEROIN, particularly brown heroin from Mexico.

Chinese (China) white   HEROIN that is pure white and very potent.

chip   To use drugs on an irregular basis in order to avoid addiction.

chipping, chippying   Using drugs irregularly and infrequently. See CHIP.

chiva   HEROIN.

chlorals   CHLORAL HYDRATE.

chocolate chips   LSD.

chota   Puerto Rican slang for a police informer, especially one who informs about drugs.

Christmas trees   DEXAMYL.

chuck habit   The strong desire for food experienced by a detoxified HEROIN addict.

chug–a–lug   To consume an alcoholic beverage, particularly beer, without pausing to breathe between swallows. The practice is common among teenagers and college students who hold chug–a–lug contests. These contests can be extremely dangerous because aside from producing rapid intoxication, the practice can result in coma or death—especially when hard liquor is being consumed.

chur   GANJA is often shaped into cakes. "Chur" is a term for the loose particles of ganja which fall off the cakes.

ciba   DORIDEN.

clean   Not using or possessing drugs. The term also applies to marijuana that has had the seeds and twigs removed.

cleaned up   To stop using drugs, or to go through a detoxification program.

coast   To experience the drowsy, somnolent effects of HEROIN.

cohoba   Hallucinogenic snuff. See PIPTADENIA.

coke   COCAINE.

coke bugs   Some cocaine users experience the hallucination that bugs are crawling under the skin. This can lead to excessive scratching and ulcerations.

Coke County   A name facetiously given to Marin County, north of San Francisco. It is the home of many affluent families, some of whom work in "Silicon Valley," south of San Francisco where a concentration of high technology industries are located. It is rumored that cocaine is a popular social drug in Coke Country.

coke head   A heavy user of COCAINE.

cold An abbreviation of the term COLD TURKEY.

cold bust Opposite of HOT BUST: the discovery that, by coincidence, an arrested person has drugs in his or her possession.

cold shot A drug deal that has gone wrong.

cold turkey The act of being taken off a drug suddenly and completely, without any preparation. Also the act of quitting a drug without the benefit of medication.

collar An arrest, or the act of arresting. Also applied to the injection of a drug, the term is used for a band which is placed on the tip of an eyedropper where it connects to a needle, ensuring a snug fit.

Colombian A potent variety of MARIJUANA grown in Colombia.

come (coming) down Returning to a normal state after the effects of a drug have worn off. For heroin addicts this state signals the beginning of withdrawal symptoms.

connect To purchase drugs, or to locate a drug dealer.

connection A person's source, or contact, for purchasing drugs.

connection dough The money used to purchase drugs from a connection.

contact A person's source, or drug dealer, for purchasing drugs.

contact habit To experience the effects of drugs vicariously when one is not addicted. The term has been applied to drug dealers.

contact high Feeling the effects of a drug—feeling high—without using it. For example, being around others who are using a drug and having their mood communicate to you.

contact lens LSD.

cook Heating heroin powder with water until it dissolves and is ready for injection.

cook up The act of cooking.

cooker The container used to cook HEROIN and water; often a bottle cap or spoon.

cool A person with carefully controlled emotions. Also one who is considered to be trustworthy.

cop The act of purchasing a drug.

cop man A drug dealer (pusher).

cop sickness Feeling withdrawal symptoms.

cope Functioning, with near–normal behavior, while under the effects of a drug.

copilot A person who stays with an LSD user in order to care for him but who is not under the influence of the drug himself.

copilots DEXEDRINE.

corrine COCAINE.

cotton HEROIN that has been mixed with water and cooked, is drawn through a small piece of cotton to filter out impurities on its way into the hypodermic.

cotton habit Using drugs irregularly to avoid addiction.

cotton shooter An addict who injects the residue left in the COTTON.

count   The amount (weight or volume) of drugs involved in a purchase.

courage pills   BARBITURATES.

cracking shorts   Burglarizing cars to support a drug habit.

crank   AMPHETAMINES.

crank bugs   An hallucination that bugs are crawling under one's skin after the heavy use of AMPHETAMINES.

crap   HEROIN that is highly diluted or of low quality.

crash   Suddenly falling asleep after the heavy use of stimulants, or to return to a normal state when the effects of a drug have worn off. (See COME DOWN.)

crater   A hole in an addict's flesh (at the site of a vein) caused by repeated injections in the same spot.

creep   An addict who begs for drugs, or who does small tasks in return for drugs, instead of purchasing them himself.

crib   A person's home, particularly a place where an addict injects drugs.

croaker   A doctor who illegally prescribes drugs for an addict.

crossroads   AMPHETAMINES.

crutch   An object (a pin, tweezers, etc.) used to hold a MARIJUANA cigarette when it has been smoked so far down that it cannot be held with the fingers.

crystal   AMPHETAMINES that are soluble for injection. They are so called because they are supplied in the form of white crystals (Methedrine, Desoxyn, etc.).

crystal palace   A place where people gather to use AMPHETAMINES.

cube, the   A sugar cube that has been impregnated with a dose of LSD. Also a slang term for MORPHINE.

cupcakes   LSD.

cura   HEROIN (Spanish for cure).

cure   The length of time a person voluntarily stays in a U.S. Public Health Narcotics Hospital.

cut ounces   To further dilute HEROIN. (See CUT.)

cyc   CYCLAZOCINE.

D

---

dabbling   The irregular use of drugs.

dagga   South African CANNABIS.

deal, dealing   To sell drugs, particularly NARCOTICS.

dealer   A person who sells drugs, particularly narcotics.

dealer's band   Drug dealers often fasten packets of HEROIN to their wrists with rubber bands in such a way that they can be flipped and sent flying in a hurry when police are seen.

death cap, death cup   MUSCIMOL.

debauch   A drinking spree or bout that usually includes excessive sexual activity.

deck   A folded paper containing HEROIN.

deck up   The act of filling DECKS with heroin.

deeda   LSD.

deprivation roll   Using any drug that is available in order to get high.

destroying angels   MUSCIMOL.

dexies   DEXEDRINE, DEXAMYL.

dillies   DILAUDID.

dime   In drug language a dime refers to $10; a cent refers to $1; a nickel refers to $5.

dip and dab   The irregular, occasional use of heroin.

dirty   Having drugs in one's possession (opposite of CLEAN). Also a term that refers to marijuana that still contains seeds, stems and twigs.

discon   An abbreviation for disorderly conduct.

djamba   Brazilian word for cannabis.

djoma   African word for cannabis.

do   To use a drug.

do rights   Someone who is a first–time patient at the U.S. Public Health Service (narcotics) Hospital at Lexington, Kentucky, and who is considered to have a good chance of being cured.

do up   To prepare a vein for an injection of heroin by tying something around the arm to distend the vein.

DOA   PHENCYCLIDINE (from "dead on arrival").

doctor   A person from whom one can purchase liquor, usually at a very high price, at a time when bars and liquor stores are closed. The term is also used as a verb when more alcohol is added to someone's drink, usually without his or her knowledge.

dogie   HEROIN.

dollar   In drug language a dollar is $100; a dime is $10.

dollies   DOLOPHINE.

dolls   AMPHETAMINES, BARBITURATES.

domestic   MARIJUANA which is grown in the U.S.

donana   DONA ANA.

doobie   MARIJUANA.

doojee   HEROIN.

dope   Narcotic drugs.

dope fiend   A person who uses dope.

dope run   A trip made for the purpose of buying drugs.

double cross   AMPHETAMINES.

down, downer, downie   An amphetamine user often takes a tranquilizer to reverse the stimulant effects of amphetamine when it becomes too intense. Also a slang term for any depressant.

down trip   To be worried, depressed or troubled.

drag   A panic reaction to a hallucinogenic drug.

dragged   An hysterical panic reaction to smoking marijuana.

dream   COCAINE.

dreamer   MORPHINE.

dried out   Detoxified from a drug.

drinker   One who consumes alcohol. The term is also used to refer to a drunk or alcoholic.

dripper   A medicine DROPPER which can be used for injecting heroin when a needle is attached to the tip.

drop   To take (swallow) a pill.

drop it   The act of concealing a drug.

druggies   People who frequently experiment with a wide variety of drugs, particularly college students.

dry   A prohibitionist who is against drinking, and against the sale of liquor. In the case of an alcoholic, it means abstinence and is the opposite of WET.

dry high   MARIJUANA.

dry up   To stop the use of drugs.

duby   MARIJUANA.

duji   HEROIN.

dust   COCAINE. Also ANGEL DUST.

duster   Tobacco and heroin mixed in a cigarette.

dusting   Mixing heroin with marijuana in a cigarette.

dynamite   A particularly potent drug, especially heroin or marijuana. The term also refers to a mixture of cocaine and heroin.

dyno   HEROIN that is highly potent and only slightly diluted.

E

eater   A person who only takes drugs orally.

eighth, an   A measurement of heroin (approximately ⅛ of an ounce).

electric   A substance containing a psychedelic drug. (See ELECTRIC KOOL–ADE.)

Electric Kool–Ade   A punch mixture containing the psychedelic drug LSD–25.

elephant   PHENCYCLIDINE.

embalao   A Puerto Rican term for a person with a severe addiction; one who is unable to function socially and is physically debilitated.

embroidery   The scars on an addict's veins caused by injecting heroin.

esrar   A Turkish term for mixing cannabis with tobacco in order to conceal the cannabis.

eye opener   For an alcoholic, his first drink of the day; for an addict, his first narcotics shot of the day.

eye openers   AMPHETAMINES.

F

f–40   SECONAL.

factory   A secret place where drugs are diluted, packaged, or otherwise prepared for sale.

fake a blast   To pretend to be under the effects of a drug.

fatty   A fat, thick marijuana cigarette.

feds   Members of a federal agency, particularly federal narcotics.

feeling the habit (or monkey) coming on   The beginning of withdrawal symptoms.

fiend   One who uses drugs in an excessive and uncontrolled way.

finger   Putting drugs in a condom then hiding it in the rectum or else swallowing and later excreting it. This is done in cases of pending arrest or for smuggling purposes.

fingers   Sticks of hashish that resemble the shape of a finger.

firing the ack–ack gun   Putting heroin on the tip of a cigarette and smoking it. It is a practice popular in China.

first line   MORPHINE.

fish   A new patient in a narcotics hospital.

fit   The apparatus for injecting heroin.

five cent paper   A paper filled with heroin that is sold for $5 and usually contains about 5 grains of diluted heroin.

five dollar bag   The same as a five cent paper but the heroin is packaged in a glassine envelope.

fix   The injecting of heroin or the heroin itself.

flake   COCAINE.

flaky   A person who is addicted to cocaine.

flash   The first euphoric effects of a drug.

flashing   A term applied to sniffing glue.

flea powder   Heroin of an inferior quality.

flip out   A panic reaction to a drug in which the user loses contact with reality. The term is also used for rapturous delight that is experienced in a state of trance.

floating   Being under the effects of a drug.

Florida snow   See FAKE COKE.

flow   To enter a relaxed state and allow a drug's effects to take over.

flowers   The buds on the top of the female marijuana plant where resin is exuded.

fluff   Filtering cocaine and heroin through a nylon stocking during the process of CUTTING. Fluffing it can make it appear to be twice the size.

flunky   One who takes foolish risks to obtain drugs or the money for drugs.

flush   The initial euphoric effects felt after an injection of heroin.

fly   COCAINE.

flying   Being HIGH on a drug.

Flying Saucers   A trade name for MORN-ING GLORY SEEDS.

fold up   To stop selling drugs or to stop taking drugs.

food of the gods   PSILOCYBIN.

footballs   DILAUDID.

forwards   AMPHETAMINES.

fours   TYLENOL with codeine.

freak   A person who prefers a particular drug, as in "LSD freak." Also, to experience hallucinations that are particularly grotesque or beautiful, or to have a panic reaction to a drug or situation.

freak out   A bad, panicky reaction to a drug; or simply to take a drug.

freak up   To purposely act in a bizarre manner.

freeze   Refusing to sell drugs to a person.

Frisco speedball   Heroin, cocaine and LSD mixed together.

front   An advance payment for drugs.

fruit salad   A game, usually played by teenagers, in which one pill is swallowed from each bottle in a medicine cabinet.

full moon   A large piece of PEYOTE, usually the entire top of the cactus.

fuzz   Police.

G

gammon   One microgram.

ganga, ganja   Extremely potent marijuana grown in Jamaica.

gangster   MARIJUANA.

gangster pills   BARBITURATES.

gaping   Yawning, which is a withdrawal symptom.

garbage   Heroin of a poor, inferior quality.

garbage head   A person who will use any drug available to get high.

G.B.   BARBITURATE. An abbreviation of goofball.

gee head   A person addicted to paregoric.

geeze   To inject heroin.

geronimo   A mixture of barbiturates and alcohol.

get down   To take a heroin injection.

get off   To experience the effects of a drug. Also, to take a heroin injection.

get on   To begin taking drugs.

get one's yen off   To satisfy a craving, particularly for drugs.

get the habit off   To relieve the beginnings of withdrawal symptoms by taking a drug.

getting on   To feel the effects of marijuana.

ghanja   An Indian form of cannabis, midway in potency between CHARAS and marijuana.

Ghost, the   LSD.

giggle weed   MARIJUANA.

gimmicks   The apparatus for injecting drugs.

girl   COCAINE.

globetrotter   A person who searches out the best grade of heroin he can get in an area.

glow   To feel the euphoric effects of a drug.

goblet of jam   DAWAMESK.

God's flesh   PSILOCYBIN.

God's medicine   MORPHINE.

going down   A situation when all is going well.

going high   Being in a state of a continuing HIGH.

gold   MARIJUANA. An abbreviation of Acapulco gold.

gold dust   COCAINE.

gold duster   A person who uses cocaine.

golden leaf   ACAPULCO GOLD (marijuana).

goods   Drugs, particularly narcotics.

good sick   The nausea and vomiting which

an addict sometimes experiences after an injection of heroin.

good stuff   HEROIN that is not heavily diluted.

goofball   BARBITURATES and AMPHETAMINES.

goofers   BARBITURATES and AMPHETAMINES.

goofing   Feeling the effects of barbiturates or amphetamines.

gorilla pills   TUINAL.

grass   MARIJUANA.

grass brownies   Brownies that contain marijuana.

gravy   A mixture of heroin and an addict's blood which, as a result of BOOTING, can clog a syringe. The mixture is heated, then after the blood dissolves it is injected.

greasy junky   An addict who obtains drugs by doing favors and begging rather than by buying them.

green   A cheap inferior grade of MARIJUANA that is grown in Mexico. It is also called Mexican green. Also, a slang term for KETAMINE HYDROCHLORIDE.

green dragons   BARBITURATES.

grefa   MARIJUANA.

greta   MARIJUANA.

grifa   MARIJUANA.

griffo   MARIJUANA.

grog blossom   A purple or reddish coloring of the nose often associated with excessive drinking over an extended period of time. (From GROG.)

groovers   Young teenagers who take drugs for excitement and thrills.

grooving   To feel the effects of a drug.

groovy   Feeling HIGH.

ground control   COPILOT.

ground man   COPILOT.

grower   A person who grows marijuana but does not get involved in its distribution or smuggling.

guide   An experienced LSD user who stands by, or acts as a guide to someone taking the drug for the first time in case he or she has a panic reaction.

gun   The needle used for injecting heroin.

gunja   MARIJUANA.

gungeon   MARIJUANA that is grown in Jamaica and is particularly potent.

guru   GUIDE.

gutter   A vein used for injecting heroin, particularly in the area inside the elbow.

H

H   HEROIN.

half   An abbreviation for HALF LOAD.

half load   Drug pushers purchase heroin

from wholesalers in half loads: 15 packages banded together.

hang tough   To undergo withdrawal symptoms, after stopping the use of narcotics, without giving in to the need for the drug.

happy hour   A designated time set by a public establishment (restaurant, bar, lounge), usually limited to an hour or two in the late afternoon, when drinks are often served at a reduced price.

hara, la   Puerto Rican term for police.

harry   HEROIN.

hash   HASHISH.

Hashbury, the   HAIGHT–ASHBURY.

hash oil   LIQUID HASHISH.

hassle, hassling   To have difficulties obtaining drugs, or any situation that is worrisome.

hawk, the   LSD.

hay   MARIJUANA.

haze   LSD.

head   A person who favors a particular drug, as in pot head.

head drugs   Drugs that affect the mind, such as hallucinogens, as opposed to narcotics.

hearts   AMPHETAMINES.

heat, the   Police.

heaven, heaven dust   COCAINE.

Heavenly Blue   A trade name for MORN-ING GLORY SEEDS.

heavy drugs, heavy stuff   HARD NAR-COTICS.

heeled   To have drugs in one's posses-sion.

hemp   MARIJUANA.

henry   HEROIN.

her   COCAINE.

herb   MARIJUANA.

him   HEROIN.

hit   Γo take a drug, particularly heroin.

hocus   MORPHINE.

hog   PHENCYCLIDINE.

hold, holding   To be in possession of drugs, either for one's own use or for the purpose of selling.

homegrown   MARIJUANA. The domestic variety grown in the United States.

hookah   BONG.

hooked   Addicted to a drug.

hop   OPIUM.

hop dog, hop head   A person addicted to opium.

horn   SNIFF.

horror drugs   Drugs containing the bel-ladonna alkaloids ATROPINE, SCOPOLAMINE and HYOSCYAMINE.

horse   HEROIN.

hot bust   Opposite of COLD BUST. A po-lice arrest made when drugs are expected to be found because of an informant's tip–off.

hot shot   An injection of what the addict believes to be heroin but which is actually a substitute, such as the poison strychnine.

hubbly bubbly   BONG.

huffer   A person who inhales deliriants

huilca   YOPO.

hustler, hustling   A person who engages in criminal activities to earn money for drugs.

hype   A hoax.

I

---

ice cream habit   Using drugs infre-quently and irregularly.

idiot pills   BARBITURATES.

in action   A pusher is ''in action'' when he has drugs for sale.

in paper   To smuggle drugs in a postcard which has been specially slit to contain them.

in transit   To be under the effects of LSD.

Indian hay   MARIJUANA.

Indian hemp   MARIJUANA.

intanfu   African name for CANNABIS.

intsaga   African name for CANNABIS.

iron cure   To go through the process of withdrawal when there is no possibility of obtaining drugs.

J

---

jab   To inject heroin.

jack, jacking   Stealing.

jackroller   A thief who usually steals from drunks. It is a SKID ROW term.

jag   To be under the effects of a drug for an extended period of time.

jam   COCAINE.

jammed up   A person who has taken an overdose.

jane   MARIJUANA.

jay, jay smoke   MARIJUANA.

jelly beans   AMPHETAMINES.

jerk off   BOOTING.

jimson weed   DATURA.

joint   A MARIJUANA cigarette.

jones   A term for a drug habit, particularly a heroin habit.

joy juice   CHLORAL HYDRATE.

joypop   To inject heroin infrequently. Someone who joypops is not addicted.

juanita   Mexican term for MARIJUANA.

juice   ALCOHOL.

juice head   A person who is a heavy consumer of alcohol.

jungle drug   AYAHUASCA.

junk   Drugs, particularly heroin.

junkie   A heroin addict.

K

---

kat   KHAT.

katzenjammers   DELIRIUM TREMENS.

key   A kilogram.

ki   KEY.

kick, kicking   To break a drug addiction, as in "kicking the habit."

kickback   To KICK a habit and then return to it.

kick cold turkey   To KICK a drug habit and go through the withdrawal process without the help of medication.

kicks   Thrills.

kick sticks   MARIJUANA cigarettes.

kick the habit   To break a drug addiction.

kief, kif   African name for CANNABIS.

killer drugs   Drugs of high potency that are considered good.

killer weed   High potency MARIJUANA, or marijuana that is mixed with PHENCYCLI-DINE.

kilo   A kilogram.

kilo connection   A high–level heroin distributor who purchases the substance from an importer, then cuts it once before selling it in kilos to the OUNCE MAN who further dilutes it.

kilter   MARIJUANA.

King Kong   A severe heroin habit that is extremely costly.

King Kong pills   BARBITURATES.

kit   The apparatus for injecting heroin.

knockout drops   A mixture of alcohol and CHLORAL HYDRATE that produces an additive effect; the person soon loses consciousness.

K.Y.   The United States Public Health Service (narcotics) Hospital in Lexington, Kentucky.

L

lady, lady snow   COCAINE.

lame   A person who doesn't use drugs.

laughing gas   NITROUS OXIDE.

layout   The apparatus for injecting heroin.

lay up   To purchase a large store of drugs, then just lie around using them without the HASSLE of having to continuously go out to purchase more.

L.B.   One pound.

leapers   AMPHETAMINES.

Lebanese   HASHISH from Lebanon.

lemon, lemonade   Highly diluted heroin, or a substitute substance sold as heroin.

Lexington   The United States Public Health Service (narcotics) Hospital in Lexington, Kentucky.

lid   A measurement of weight used for marijuana. Ranging from ¾ to 1 ounce, it is enough for approximately 40 marijuana cigarettes.

lid poppers   AMPHETAMINES.

life, the   A general term for all the characteristics surrounding an addict's life–style, including his environment, the lingo he speaks, his attitude toward crime and work, his sleeping and eating patterns, and so on.

lightning   AMPHETAMINES.

light stuff   The opposite of HARD DRUGS, the term covers nonopiate drugs.

light up   To smoke MARIJUANA.

line   The large, arterial vein in the arm. The term is an abbreviation of MAINLINE.

load   A measurement of heroin; approximately 25–30 envelopes or packets banded together.

loaded   To be heavily intoxicated, whether from alcohol or any other drug.

loads   A combination of Doriden (gluteth-imide), a sleeping pill, and Codeine #4 (a combination of 60 mg of codeine with aspirin or Tylenol). A load usually consists of one 400 mg Doriden tablet and two Codeine #4s. Sometimes two or three loads are swallowed together. Loads are used as substitutes for the diluted heroin sold on the street. The practice originated in Southern California and spread to a few cities in other parts of the country.

loco   MARIJUANA.

long con   A confidence game that has required extensive planning.

love drug   QUAALUDES, MDA.

ludes   QUAALUDES.

M

macon   West African word for CANNABIS.

maconha   Brazilian word for CANNABIS.

made, make   The act of purchasing a drug.

mahjueme   HASHISH in concentrated form.

majoon, majoun, ma'jun   Indian words for CANNABIS.

make it   To experience the effects of a heroin injection.

making a croaker for a reader   To feign sickness or bribe a doctor in order to gain a prescription for a drug.

man, the   The term can refer to the police or to a high–level drug dealer.

M and C   A mixture of four parts MOR-PHINE and one part COCAINE.

M and M's   SECONAL.

mandrakes   MANDRAX.

manicure   To remove the twigs and sticks from marijuana.

manita   Milk sugar used to dilute heroin.

marshmallow reds   BARBITURATES.

mary   MORPHINE.

mary ann, mary jane, mary warner, mary weaver   MARIJUANA.

mash allah   OPIUM.

matchbox   A measurement of marijuana. It is about ⅕ of an ounce and will make approximately six to eight cigarettes.

medical hype   To become addicted to a drug because of medical treatment.

meet   A meeting between a pusher and purchaser.

mellow yellow   LSD.

merc, merck, merk   High–quality drugs. The term probably originated from the name of the drug manufacturer Merck, Sharp & Dohme.

mesc   MESCALINE.

meth   METHAMPHETAMINE, METHEDRINE.

meth freak   A heavy user of methedrine.

Mexican brown   MARIJUANA grown in Mexico that has a higher resin content than MEXICAN GREEN. Also a slang term for brown HEROIN.

Mexican green   MARIJUANA grown in Mexico that is less potent than Mexican brown. It is one of the commonest types of marijuana used in the U.S.

Mexican locoweed   MARIJUANA.

Mexican mint   DIVINER'S SAGE.

Mexican mud   HEROIN.

Mexican mushrooms   See MUSHROOMS, SACRED.

Mexican quaaludes   Illicit QUAALUDES imported from Mexico.

Mexican reds   Illicit SECONAL imported from Mexico.

Mickey, Mickey Finn   A mixture of alcohol and chloral hydrate which can render a person unconscious in a very short time.

microdots   Drops of LSD supplied on blotter paper. They appear as very faint beige dots which darken to a brownish color when exposed to light.

Mighty Joe Young   A severe heroin habit that is extremely costly.

mike   One MICRODOT of LSD.

mini–bennies   BENZEDRINE.

mini–whites   AMPHETAMINES.

Miss Emma   MORPHINE.

M.J.   MARIJUANA. An abbreviation of mary jane.

mojo   Hard drugs such as heroin and morphine.

monkey, monkey on (my) back   A person's drug dependence or habit.

moon   PEYOTE. The term also refers to a block of HASHISH.

moota, mooters, mootie   MARIJUANA.

morf   MORPHINE.

morph, morpho, morphy   MORPHINE.

mota   MARIJUANA.

mother   MARIJUANA. Also a term for a drug dealer.

move   To deal in marijuana.

mu   MARIJUANA.

mud   MORPHINE.

muta, mutah   MARIJUANA.

N

nail   The needle, usually attached to an eye dropper, which is used for injecting heroin.

narc, narco   A police narcotics officer; also the U.S. Public Health Service (narcotics) Hospital in Lexington, Kentucky.

narghile   A Turkish water pipe. (See BONG.)

nark   NARC.

natch, on the   From the word natural, it refers to a person's life–style when he is not taking drugs.

natch trips   To take "natural" substances, such as lettuce, nutmeg or mace in an effort to achieve a HIGH.

nebbie   NEMBUTAL.

needle freak   An addict who is not particular about what drug he injects but gets his thrills simply from the act of injecting.

needle habit   Some addicts, often referred to as "needle freaks," are not particular about what drug they inject but get their thrills simply from the act of injecting. See ADMINISTRATION.

needle park   Sherman Square at Broadway and Amsterdam Avenue, in New York City. It was once a congregating place for addicts.

negative   See BAD TRIP.

nemish, nemmies   NEMBUTAL.

nickel   In street language it refers to $5, just as a dime refers to $10.

nickel bag   A package, usually of marijuana or heroin, which is worth $5.

nimbies, nimby   NEMBUTAL.

Nixon   Narcotic drugs that are not very potent.

nod, nodding   To feel the initial effects of a heroin injection—pleasurable drowsiness and peacefulness—probably so called because the head nods forward.

nose candy   COCAINE.

nuggets   AMPHETAMINES.

number two sale, the   A police term for a second narcotics conviction.

O

O.D.   Overdose.

O.D.ing   Showing signs of having overdosed.

off   Experiencing the intoxicating effects of a drug.

off artist   A person who steals to pay for a drug habit.

oil   HASHISH oil.

on   To use drugs: "He is on heroin," for example.

one and one   To sniff with both nostrils; applies particularly to the use of cocaine.

on the needle   Addicted to heroin.

op   OPIUM.

Orange County   QUAALUDES. So called because the area code for Orange County, California, is 714—the same as the code number on 300 mg Quaaludes.

orange mushrooms   LSD.

oranges   AMPHETAMINES.

ounce man   The person in between the KILO CONNECTION and the PUSHER in the heroin distribution process. Heroin is diluted (or cut) once by the kilo connection; the ounce man cuts it again before selling it to the pusher.

outfit   The apparatus for injecting heroin.

overcharged   A semicoma state which can occur when too much of a drug is taken.

overjolt   OVERDOSE.

over the hump, go   To feel the full euphoric effect of a drug.

Owsley   LSD. The name is taken from that of an illicit manufacturer during the 1960s.

O.Z., oz   One ounce.

P

---

packed up   HIGH.

pad   A person's residence. At one time the term was reserved only for a room in which drugs were used.

Pall Mall and paregoric   Cigarettes (any brand) which have been soaked in paregoric.

Panama Gold, Panama Red   Alternative names for MARIJUANA grown in Panama which is considered to be high quality.

panatella   A large, fat marijuana cigarette usually made from marijuana grown in Central or South America.

panic   Anxiety resulting from an addict's shortage of drugs or his inability to buy them.

panic man   A person suffering from PANIC.

papers   Folded pieces of paper, or packages containing narcotics, particularly heroin.

paper acid   LSD.

paracki   PARALDEHYDE.

paradise   COCAINE.

paraphernalia   The equipment needed to inject heroin.

partying   To share a supply of heroin with others.

pass   The act of taking possession of a drug once it has been paid for.

peace, peace pill   PHENCYCLIDINE.

peaches   BENZEDRINE.

peaking   The period during an LSD trip when the most intense effects are experienced.

peanuts   BARBITURATES.

pearls   AMYL NITRITE.

pellets   LSD.

people, the   KILO CONNECTION.

pep pills   AMPHETAMINES.

per   A prescription.

peter   CHLORAL HYDRATE.

peyote buttons   The button–like growths on the peyote cactus.

peyotl   PEYOTE.

P.G.   PAREGORIC.

phennies, phenos   PHENOBARBITAL.

picked up   To have recently smoked MARIJUANA.

piece   A measurement of diluted heroin. There are approximately 15 pieces in 1.1 pounds, each piece containing about 30 teaspoons which are further diluted by the pusher.

pill   AMPHETAMINES and BARBITURATES.

pill head   A person who frequently uses amphetamines and barbiturates.

pin   A MARIJUANA cigarette.

pinhead   A thin MARIJUANA cigarette.

pink ladies   BARBITURATES.

pinks   SECONAL.

pinned   Constricted eye pupils, characteristic of heroin addicts.

pipe   A vein, particularly a large vein, used for injecting heroin.

pit   The main vein used for injecting heroin.

place   The setting for an LSD trip.

plant   A cache of drugs. Also a police practice that involves placing drugs in a suspected addict's residence, then arresting him for possession.

plastic hippie   A person who occasionally acts like a hippie but who is not dedicated to the hippie life–style.

pod   MARIJUANA.

point   A needle used for injecting heroin.

poison   COCAINE or HEROIN.

poison people   Addicts who use COCAINE or HEROIN.

poke   To inhale a MARIJUANA cigarette.

pop, popping   To take a pill. Also a term for the subcutaneous injection of heroin.

popped   To be arrested by the police.

poppers   AMYL NITRITE in small glass vials which are broken and inhaled.

positive   Feeling the effects of a stimulant.

pot   MARIJUANA.

pot head   A heavy user of MARIJUANA.

potlikker   A beverage made by brewing marijuana stems, twigs and seeds.

pound   Five dollars.

powder   HEROIN.

P.R.   PANAMA RED (marijuana).

primo   High quality drugs.

psychos   Drugs that produce psychedelic effects.

puff, puffing   Smoking OPIUM.

pure   Heroin that is undiluted or only slightly diluted.

purple hearts   LUMINAL. DRINAMYL.

push, pushing   From PUSHER, to sell drugs at the street level.

pusher   A dealer who sells drugs directly to an addict; he is one step below the wholesaler in the drug distribution system.

put in writing or paper   A method of smuggling drugs by putting them in a split postcard, or in the case of a liquid drug, to saturate a piece of paper.

put somebody on   To introduce someone to marijuana.

Q

Q's   QUAALUDES.

q'at   KHAT.

quacks, quads, quas   QUAALUDES.

quarter   In drug language, $25.

quarter bag   Twenty–five dollars' worth of marijuana.

quarter moon   HASHISH.

quill   A matchbook which is rolled or folded and used to hold a drug while it is being sniffed.

R

raggae   See RASTAFARIANS.

ragweed   Poor quality MARIJUANA with a low level of potency.

rainbows   TUINAL.

rainy–day woman   A MARIJUANA cigarette.

rap, rapping   Talking, particularly in addicts' jargon.

rat   A police informer.

rat root   ASARONE.

R.D.   SECONAL.

reader   A narcotics prescription obtained by bribery or by feigning an illness.

red   PANAMA RED (marijuana).

red and blues   TUINAL.

red birds, red bullets, red devils, red dolls, red lillies, reds   SECONAL (from the color).

red chicken   Chinese heroin.

red dirt marijuana   Marijuana that grows wild.

red rock   Chinese heroin.

reefer   MARIJUANA.

rig   Apparatus for injecting heroin.

righteous   A good quality drug with high potency.

righteous bush   MARIJUANA.

ripped   To be highly intoxicated by a drug.

rippers   AMPHETAMINES.

roach   A MARIJUANA cigarette when it has burned down too far to be held with the fingers (at which point it looks like a cockroach).

roach clip   An instrument (pin, tweezers, etc.) used to hold a ROACH.

roach holder   See ROACH CLIP.

roach pick   See ROACH CLIP.

rock   COCAINE, HEROIN.

roll   The intoxicating effect of a HIGH.

root   A MARIJUANA cigarette.

rope   MARIJUANA.

roses   BENZEDRINE.

royal blue   LSD.

run   A period of heavy use of a particular drug, or a period of addiction.

rush   The initial euphoric effects felt after a heroin or amphetamine injection.

S

sacrament   LSD.

salt shot   An injection of a saline solution; a home remedy for a heroin addict who is unconscious from an overdose.

sassfras   A MARIJUANA cigarette made from low potency marijuana grown in the United States.

satch   Paper that has been saturated with a drug for smuggling purposes.

sativa   MARIJUANA.

scag   HEROIN.

scars   Scars from the frequent injection of narcotics. They appear as black and blue spots and are caused by collapsed veins.

scene   The social pattern of drug use; as in "the drug scene around here is very open."

schmack   Originally applied to heroin and cocaine, the term has now been extended to include all drugs.

schmeck   Yiddish term for heroin that is sniffed.

schmecker   A heavy user of SCHMECK (heroin).

schoolboy   CODEINE. COCAINE.

scoop   To sniff heroin or cocaine using a folded matchbook. See QUILL.

score   To buy a drug.

scratch, scratching   A drug addict. The term probably comes from an addict's compulsion to scratch himself.

script   A prescription for a narcotic; an abbreviation of the word prescription.

scrubwoman's kick   To inhale the fumes of naphtha, an ingredient used in cleaning preparations which can produce a mild intoxicating high.

seccies, seccy   SECONAL.

seggy, seggies   SECONAL.

set   The emotional and mental state of a person before he takes a drug. Also a particular locality frequented by addicts and drug sellers.

setting   The conditions and circumstances surrounding an LSD user when he takes the drug. LSD users feel that for a successful "trip" it is necessary to be in a pleasant setting, and to be accompanied by a trusted COPILOT.

set up   See PLANT.

seventeen–fifty–one   The number of the New York State statute concerning the possession of drugs with intent to sell.

seventeen–forty–seven B   The number of the New York State statute concerning possession of barbiturates.

seven–fourteens   QUAALUDES.

shit   HEROIN.

shlook   To inhale a marijuana cigarette.

shooting gallery   A location where addicts inject heroin. Also, the withdrawal ward in a narcotics hospital.

shooting gravy   BOOTING.

shoot up   To inject a drug, particularly heroin.

short   A car.

short con   A minor confidence game; the opposite of LONG CON.

short count, short go   When a drug dealer (PUSHER) receives a lesser amount of a drug from a wholesaler than he has contracted for.

short piece   A measurement of a drug, particularly heroin, that has been highly diluted.

shove   See PUSH.

shroom   MUSHROOMS, SACRED.

sick   To experience the beginning of withdrawal symptoms.

sixteenth   A measurement of heroin; 1/16 of an ounce.

sizzle   To have drugs on one's person.

skid bag   A bag of heroin that is highly diluted.

skin   The paper used for making marijuana cigarettes.

skin shot   Injecting a drug subcutaneously.

sleepers, sleeping pills   BARBITURATES.

sleepwalker   A person addicted to heroin.

smack   HEROIN.

smashed   Being HIGH on a drug.

smoke   MARIJUANA, as in "he was using smoke."

snappers   AMYL NITRITE in glass vials.

snop   MARIJUANA.

snow   COCAINE.

snow lights   Flickering bright lights at the periphery of the visual fields that are seen after cocaine has been used are called snow lights. They are probably not hallucinations, but may represent the overstimulation of the optic tracts by cocaine.

soapers, soaps   SOPOR.

sobering pill   L–DOPA.

softballs   Drugs which fall into the

DEPRESSANT category (tranquilizers, sedatives, hypnotics, etc.)

soft drugs　Drugs which are non–narcotic (amphetamines, barbiturates, marijuana, etc.).

soles　HASHISH.

source, the　KILO CONNECTION.

spaced, spaced out　To be under the influence of a mind–altering drug such as LSD.

sparkle plenties　AMPHETAMINES.

speed　AMPHETAMINES, particularly METHEDRINE.

speedball　A mixture of heroin and cocaine, or heroin and amphetamine, which is injected.

speed freak　A heavy user of amphetamines.

spike　The needle used for injecting a drug.

splash　AMPHETAMINES.

spliff　A Jamaican term for a thick fat marijuana cigarette. (See RASTAFARIANS.)

split　To leave or break away from a person, a place, or a drug.

spoon　A measurement of heroin (1/16 of an ounce), or cocaine (1/4 of a teaspoon).

square　A regular tobacco cigarette. Also a term for a person who doesn't use drugs.

S.S.　An abbreviation for suspended sentence.

star dust　COCAINE.

stash　A cache of hidden drugs.

steamboat　To smoke a marijuana cigarette that has been inserted in a toilet paper roll. The person puts his mouth over one end of the roll and his hand over the other, and the smoke is trapped inside.

stepped on　Diluted.

stick　A MARIJUANA cigarette.

sticks　The waste (sticks, twigs) that is left after marijuana has been CLEANED.

stoned　Being HIGH on a drug.

stool　To cooperate with or give information to the police.

STP　DOM. (Probably from the brand name motor oil additive that promises increased power.)

straight　A person who doesn't use drugs, a SQUARE. Also a term for a regular cigarette.

straighten out　To prevent the beginnings of withdrawal symptoms by taking more drugs.

strawberry fields　LSD.

street, on the　To be a drug user.

strung, strung out　An addict's panic feeling when he is unable to obtain drugs. The term is also applied to a severe habit, or to an addict's physical appearance because of a severe habit.

stuff　A general term for all drugs.

stumblers　BARBITURATES.

sugar　LSD.

sugar weed　MARIJUANA that has been

soaked in a mixture of sugar and water—a process known as "curing." This is done to retain the resin, add bulk and increase the weight.

sunshine   LSD.

Supercaine   See FAKE COKE.

supergrass   PHENCYCLIDINE. In the 1960s it was also a brand name of catnip which was sold as marijuana.

sweet flag   ASARONE.

sweet lucy   MARIJUANA.

swingman   A low level drug dealer. PUSHER.

system, the   A term used to describe an addict's TOLERANCE.

T

tabs   LSD capsules or tablets.

take off   To begin feeling the effects of a drug.

take off artists   Addicts who obtain their money for drugs by robbing (see TAKEN OFF).

taken off   Robbed.

taking care of business   Obtaining money for drugs by robbing.

taking off   Robbing for drug money.

taking on a number   The act of smoking MARIJUANA.

tall   HIGH on a drug.

tank   A cell or jail where drunks are kept while they sober up (from "drunk tank"). The term is also used to refer to a drunk, and to the act of drinking as in "tank up on booze."

tapita   A Spanish word for "little cap." It refers to the small bottle cap addicts use to cook heroin.

tapping the bag   PUSHERS often take a small amount of heroin out of the bags they sell and so shortchange addicts. The practice is particularly common when the pusher is also an addict.

tar   Gum OPIUM.

taste   A small amount of a drug.

tea   MARIJUANA. Also a term used for psychedelics that are brewed and made into a beverage.

tea bag   To smoke MARIJUANA.

tea head   A heavy user of MARIJUANA.

tea pad   A place where MARIJUANA users gather to smoke.

tecata   HEROIN.

teetotal, teetotaler   Total abstinence from alcohol, or one who totally abstains. From "tee-total," a local British intensive for "total."

tens   AMPHETAMINES; tablets of 10 mg.

ten cent pistol   A bag of what an addict thinks is heroin but which actually contains a poisonous substance.

Texas tea   MARIJUANA.

thing   HEROIN.

third eye   A psychedelic effect experienced by LSD users. It is the feeling of having an inward look into the mind.

thirty–three–oh–five   A felony under New York State statutes: the possession of narcotics but in a smaller amount than would be presumed to be possessed for selling.

throwing rocks   To commit serious violent crimes in order to obtain money for drugs.

thrupence bag   A bag of MARIJUANA that sells for $2.50. Compare NICKEL and DIME.

thrusters   AMPHETAMINES.

thumb   A large fat MARIJUANA cigarette.

ticket, the   LSD.

tie   The tourniquet a heroin addict uses to distend a vein when injecting intravenously.

tie off, tie up   To use a TIE.

tight   A person who is intoxicated by alcohol, and more intensely than someone who is HIGH.

tighten up   To give drugs to a person.

tin   See CAN.

tingle   The initial effects felt after a heroin injection.

TJ   Tijuana, Mexico. The town has long been known as a place where drugs can be easily purchased.

toak, toke   To smoke a MARIJUANA cigarette. The term refers to both smoking the whole cigarette and just taking a puff.

toke pipes   Pipes used to smoke MARIJUANA.

toke up   To light a MARIJUANA cigarette.

tooies   TUINAL.

tools   Apparatus used for injecting heroin.

toot   To snort or sniff cocaine, as in "Let's have a toot." Also a slang name for cocaine, as in "Do you have any toot?" (See also FAKE COKE.)

tootsies   TUINAL.

topi   PEYOTE.

torn up   Feeling the effects of a drug.

torpedo   A mixture of alcohol and chloral hydrate.

torture chamber   A jail where it is impossible to obtain drugs.

tossed   A police search for drugs.

toss out   To feign an illness in order to obtain a prescription for drugs.

toy   A needle used to inject heroin.

tracked up   Covered by scars from the frequent injection of drugs.

tracks   Black and blue needle scars caused by the frequent injection of drugs. Collapsed veins are also referred to as tracks.

train arrived   The successful smuggling of drugs, particularly into a prison.

trap A place where a cache of drugs is hidden.

travel agent A dealer (pusher) who sells LSD.

trees TUINAL.

trey A bag of heroin costing $3.

trick An illegal way of obtaining money for drugs. Probably from the word used by prostitutes for performing sexual favors.

trip The act of taking a hallucinogen, particularly LSD; or the effects of its ingestion.

tripsville San Francisco, which was the site of extensive LSD use in the late 1960s.

truck drivers AMPHETAMINES.

Ts and blues (Ts and Bs) An injected combination of Talwin (pentazocine, a narcotic agonist–antagonist) and pyribenzamine (tripelenamine, an antihistamine). It is a popular substitute for weak heroin in a number of midwestern cities in the United States. The "T" refers to Talwin and the "blues" refers to the color of the pyribenzamine tablet. Apparently, the antihistamine enhances the action of the narcotic or diminishes some of its side effects.

tuies TUINAL.

turnabouts AMPHETAMINES.

turn on To take a drug, to encourage another to take a drug, or to feel the effects of a drug.

turned out To begin to use drugs.

turp TERPIN HYDRATE with CODEINE.

twenty–five LSD–25.

twist MARIJUANA.

twisted Feeling the effects of a drug. Also a term for feeling the initial effects of withdrawal.

tying up Using a tourniquet to distend a vein in preparation for an injection.

U

U.C. A federal narcotics undercover agent.

Ultracaine See FAKE COKE.

uncle A federal narcotics agent.

up To feel the effects of a stimulant drug, particularly AMPHETAMINES. Also a term for amphetamines themselves.

up and down the lines An expression that refers to the TRACKS or collapsed veins on an addict's arm.

upper, uppies, ups AMPHETAMINES.

uptight Feeling tense, anxious and sometimes hostile.

user A person who uses drugs.

using Using drugs.

V

vendedor Spanish word for a drug PUSHER.

violated   To be arrested for violation of parole.

vipe   MARIJUANA.

viper   A person who uses VIPE (marijuana).

vitamin Q   QUAALUDES.

volunteer   A person who commits himself for treatment at the U.S. Public Health Service (narcotics) Hospital in Lexington, Kentucky.

voyager   A person who is feeling the effects of LSD.

W

wagon, on the   A term which refers to a temporary period of abstinence from alcoholic beverages. It was probably first used by American soldiers during the 1800s and referred to the water wagon which was taken on extended trips. Presumably the soldiers had no access to liquor during these periods.

wake up   An addict's first injection of the day.

wake ups   AMPHETAMINES.

wallbangers   METHAQUALONE. The term is of British origin and is based on abuse of the English drug MANDRAX, which contains methaqualone.

waste   To use, as in "I wasted the marijuana."

wasted   To lose consciousness from drug intoxication.

water   AMPHETAMINES, particularly methamphetamine.

watering out   To go through withdrawal without the help of medication.

wedges   LSD.

weed   MARIJUANA.

weeding out   To smoke WEED (marijuana).

weed marijuana   MARIJUANA that grows wild and is not particularly potent.

weekend habit   The infrequent and irregular use of a drug, particularly just on weekends.

weekend warrior   A person who uses drugs infrequently and irregularly, particularly just on weekends.

weight   A measurement of drugs, especially diluted heroin. The term can also apply to a supply or large quantity of a drug.

whacked   A drug, especially heroin, that has been diluted.

wheat   MARIJUANA.

whiskey nose   See GROG BLOSSOM.

white crosses   AMPHETAMINES.

white lady   COCAINE. HEROIN.

white light   A sensation experienced by STP users.

white lightning   LSD. Also a term for unaged corn whiskey. (See MOONSHINE.)

whites   BENZEDRINE.

white stuff   HEROIN.

wig   A person's mind.

wig out   To "lose your mind (wig)," while using a hallucinogenic drug. A loss of mental control and a state of altered consciousness.

wild geronimo   A mixture of alcohol and barbiturates.

winder   An addict who volunteers for treatment at a narcotics hospital and can consequently leave at any time.

window pane   LSD.

wingding, throw a   A person who tries to obtain a narcotics prescription by faking withdrawal symptoms.

wings   A person's first experience MAINLINING heroin.

wiped out   Acute drug intoxication.

wired   A person who is feeling the high effects of AMPHETAMINES. The term also applies to a heroin addict.

working   A person who is trying to obtain money for drugs in an illegal manner.

works   The apparatus for injecting narcotics, particularly heroin.

wrap   An inconspicuous covering for a package when smuggling drugs.

Y

yage, yaje   AYAHUASCA.

yakee   A psychedelic snuff made from the bark of the VIROLA tree by the Yekwana Indians of Venezuela.

yaupon   A stimulant tea with mild alcoholic effects. Made from shrubs of the genus *Ilex*, it was popular among early settlers in the United States, particularly in the southeastern region. It is known to have unpleasant adverse reactions such as vomiting.

yellow   LSD.

yellow bullets, yellow dolls, yellow jackets, yellows   NEMBUTAL, which is supplied in 30 mg and 100 mg yellow capsules.

yen   A CRAVING.

yenning   To experience the beginning of withdrawal symptoms.

yerba   Spanish word for MARIJUANA

yopo   See PIPTADENIA.

Z

Zacatecas purple   A potent MARIJUANA grown in the central Mexican state of Zacatecas.

zap, zapped   To overpower or defeat a person with violence. Originally a science fiction term.

Zigzag   A brand of cigarette paper used to smoke MARIJUANA.

ZNA   A mixture of MSG (monosodium glutamate) and dill weed. When smoked it is purported to produce psychedelic effects but the oil of dill weed can produce severe adverse reactions.

zonked   Acutely intoxicated by a drug.

zunked   To have a strong addiction to narcotics.

Appendix 2

Slang Synonyms for Drugs

AMPHETAMINES

"A"
AMT
bam
beans
bennies
black beauties
black mollies
brain ticklers
brownies
bumblebees
cartwheels
chalk
chicken powder
crank
Christmas trees
crossroads
cross tops
crystal
dexies
diet pills
dolls
double cross
eye openers
fives
footballs
forwards
hearts
jam
jellybeans
leapers
lid poppers
lightning
meth
pep pills
purple hearts
rippers
sparkle plenties
sparklers
speed
splash
sweets
tens
thrusters
truck drivers
turnabouts
uppers
uppie
ups
wake–ups
water
white crosses

AMYL NITRITE

amies
amys
blue angels
bluebirds
blue bullets
blue devils
blue dolls
blue heavens
blues
blue tips
pearls
poppers
snappers

BARBITURATES

barbs
beans
black beauties
block busters
blue angels
brain ticklers
candy
courage pills
dolls
downers
downs
G.B.
goofballs
goofers
gorilla pills
green dragons
King Kong pills
nebbies
nimbies
phennies
phenos
pink ladies
purple hearts
rainbows
reds
seccy
seggie
sleepers
yellow bullets
yellow jackets
yellows

BENZEDRINE

bennies
benz
peaches
roses
whites

BIPHETAMINES
black beauties
blackbirds
black mollies

CHLORAL HYDRATE
chlorals
joy juice
knockout drops
mickey
Mickey Finn
peter

COCAINE
bernice
bernies
big C.
blow
bombita
bouncing powder
burese
"C"
charles
charlie
coke
corrine
dream
dust
flake
fly
girl
gold dust
heaven
heaven dust
her
ice
incentive
jay
joy powder
lady
lady snow
nose candy
nose powder
paradise
poison

powder
rock
schoolboy
snow
star dust
sugar
white
white lady
white powder
white stuff

DATURA
angel trumpet
jimson weed

DEXAMYL
Christmas trees
dexies

DEXEDRINE
copilots
dexies

DMT
businessman's lunchtime high

HASHISH
black hash
black Russian
blond hash
canned sativa
hash
Lebanese
mahjuema

HEROIN
big bag
big H
blanco
bomb
boy
brother
brown
brown rocks
brown sugar

caballo
cat
chick
Chinese red
Chinese white
chiva
crap
dogie
doojee
dope
duji
dust
eighth
flea powder
garbage
good stuff
"H"
hard stuff
harry
H-caps
henry
him
horse
hombre
jones
joy powder
junk
Mexican mud
mojo
muzzle
pack
poison
powder
pure
red chicken
red rock
rock
scag
schmeck
smack
stuff
tecata
thing
white boy
white junk
white stuff

LIQUOR
booze
brew
juice
spirits

LSD
acid
barrels
beast
Big D
blotter
blue acid
blue cheer
blue heaven
blue mist
brown dots
California sunshine
cap
chocolate chips
contact lens
cubes
cupcakes
"D"
deeda
domes
dots
electric Kool–Aid
flash
ghost
hawk
haze
"L"
lysergide
mellow yellows
microdots
orange cubes
paper acid
peace
pearly gates
pellets
pink owsley
purple haze
sacrament
strawberries

strawberry fields
sugar
sugar cubes
sunshine
tabs
ticket
twenty–five
wedges
white lightning
window pane
yellow

MARIJUANA
Acapulco gold
ace
African black
aunt mary
baby
bale
black gunion
bomb
boo
brick
broccoli
bush
Canadian black
charge
Colombian
doobie
dry high
fatty
fingers
flowers
gage
ganga
gauge
giggleweed
grass
green
grefa
greta
grifa
grillo
grunt
hay
hemp

herb
homegrown
Indian hay
Indian hemp
"J"
jane
jay smoke
joint
joy stick
juanita
kick sticks
kif
killer
killer weed
kilter
loco
mary
maryann
maryjane
mary warner
mary weaver
meserole, messerole
Mexican brown
Mexican green
Mexican locoweed
M.J.
mooca
moota
mooters
mootie
mota
mother
mu
muggles
muta
number
Panama gold
Panama red
panatella
pin
poke
pot
ragweed
rainy day woman
red dirt
reefer

roach
root
rope
sassfras
smoke
snop
stick
sweet lucy
tea
Texas tea
twist
weed
wheat
yerba
Zacatecas purple

MESCALINE
beans
big chief
buttons
cactus
cactus buttons
mesc
mescal
moon
topi

MORPHINE
big M
birdie powder
dreamer
emm
first line
God's medicine

gunk
hocus
''M''
mary
miss emma
miss morph
morph
moocah
morpho
morphy
white stuff

MUSCIMOL
death cap
death cups
destroying angels

NEMBUTAL
nebbies
nemmies
nemish
nimby
yellow bullets
yellow dolls
yellow jackets
yellows

OPIUM
black pills
black stuff
brown stuff
canned stuff
hop

mash Allah
O
op
tar

PEYOTE
bad seed
big chief
buttons
cactus
''P''
peyotl
topi

PHENCYCLIDINE
angel dust
animal trank
aurora borealis
DOA
dust
elephant
hog
PCP
peace
peace pill
rocket fuel
supergrass
tic tac

PSILOCYBIN/PSILOCIN
magic mushrooms
mushrooms
sacred mushrooms
shrooms

Appendix 3

Tables

Contents

DRUG CONTROL LAWS

Table 1 Key Acts, Committee Recommendations and Supreme Court Rulings on Drug Control 1903–1970

Table 2 Characteristics of Marijuana Laws, by Jurisdiction, as of January 1, 1982

Table 3 Characteristics of Marijuana Laws in States that have Decriminalized Possession of Marijuana, as of March 1982

DRUG TREATMENT UNITS

Table 4 Number, Total Funding, Budgeted Capacity, and Utilization Rate of Drug Abuse Treatment Units, by Jurisdiction, as of September 30, 1980

Table 5 Physical Environment of Units Providing Combined Alcoholism and Drug Abuse Treatment, as of September 30, 1980

Table 6 Physical Environments of Alcoholism Only and Combined Treatment Units, as of September 30, 1980

Table 7 Principal Population Served in Alcoholism Only and Combined Treatment Units, as of September 30, 1980

Table 8 Demographic Characteristics of Clients in Alcoholism Only and Combined Treatment Units, as of September 30, 1980

Table 9 Distribution of Clients in Treatment and Treatment Capacity by Type of Care in Alcoholism Only and Combined Treatment Units, as of September 30, 1980

Table 10 Distribution of Clients in Treatment and Treatment Capacity by Facility Location in Alcoholism Only and Combined Treatment Units, as of September 30, 1980

Table 11 Distribution of Full–Time and Part–Time Paid and Volunteer Staff by Staff Category for All Units Providing Alcoholism and Drug Abuse Treatment, as of September 30, 1980

DRUG USERS IN TREATMENT

Table 12 Drug Users Admitted to Federally–Funded Drug Abuse Treatment Programs, by Ethnicity, Sex, Age at Admission, and Primary Drug of Abuse at Admission, United States, 1980

Table 13 Drug Users Admitted to Federally–Funded Drug Abuse Treatment Programs, by Ethnicity, Sex, Age at Admission, and Number of Arrests Within 24 Months Prior to Admission, United States, 1980

Table 14 Drug Users Admitted to Federally–Funded Drug Abuse Treatment Programs, by Primary Drug of Abuse at Admission, and Sex, United States, 1976–79

Table 15 Drug Users Admitted to Federally–Funded Drug Abuse Treatment Programs, by Selected Characteristics, and Primary Drug of Abuse at Admission, United States, 1980

Table 16 Use of Other Drugs Among Current Drinkers and Those who are not Current Drinkers

PUBLIC ATTITUDES TOWARD ALCOHOL AND DRUGS

Table 17 High School Seniors' Perceptions of the Harmfulness of Drug Use, by Type of Drug and Frequency of Use, United States, 1975–80

Table 18 High School Seniors' Perceptions of Availability of Drugs, by Type of Drug, United States, 1975–80

Table 19 High School Seniors Favoring Prohibition of Drug Use, by Type of Drug and Place of Use, United States, 1975–80

Table 20 Respondents' Concerns About Public Issues, United States, Selected Years 1974–82

Table 21 Attitudes Toward the Most Important Problems Facing Public Schools in own Community, United States, 1980

Table 22 Attitudes Toward who Should Deal with Specified Student Behavioral Problems in Public Schools, United States, 1980

Table 23 Attitudes Toward Causes of Increasing Crime, United States, 1981

Table 24 Respondents Agreeing that Selected Substances are Addictive, by Type of Substance and Age Category, United States, Selected Years 1971–79

Table 25 Attitudes Toward the Legalization of Marijuana Use, by Demographic Characteristics, United States, 1973–80

Table 26 Attitudes Toward the Treatment of Possession of Small Amounts of Marijuana as a Criminal Offense, United States, 1980

Table 27 Attitudes Toward a Law Forbidding the Sale of Beer, Wine and Liquor, by Demographic Characteristics, United States, 1981

Table 28 Respondents Favoring Stricter Drunk Driving Laws and Mandatory Jail Sentences for First Offenders, by Region, United States, 1982

REPORTED PATTERNS OF DRUG USE

Table 29 Reported Alcohol Use and Most Recent Use Among High School Seniors, by Sex, Region, Population Density, and College Plans, United States, 1980

Table 30 Reported Drug Use within Last 12 Months Among High School Seniors, by Type of Drug, United States, 1975–80

Table 31 Reported Drug Use within Last 30 Days Among High School Seniors, by Type of Drug, United States, 1975–80

Table 32   Reported Marijuana, Hashish, Cocaine, and Heroin Use and Most Recent Use Among High School Seniors, by Sex, Region, Population Density, and College Plans, United States, 1980

Table 33   Reported Drug Use Among Adults, Young Adults, and Youth, by Type of Drug, United States, Selected Years, 1972–79

Table 34   Reported Drug Use Among Adults, Young Adults, and Youth, by Type of Drug and Use of Alcohol, United States, 1979

Table 35   Reported Marijuana Use and Use in Past Month, Among Adults by Demographic Characteristics, United States, 1976, 1977 and 1979

Table 36   Reported Marijuana Use and Use in Past Month, Among Young Adults by Demographic Characteristics, United States, 1976, 1977 and 1979

Table 37   Reported Marijuana Use and Use in Past Month, Among Youth, by Demographic Characteristics, United States, Selected Years, 1971–79

TRAFFICKING IN AND GROWTH OF COCAINE ABUSE

Table 38   Sources of Drugs

Table 39   Growth of Cocaine Abuse: Estimated Coca Production in Metric Tons

Table 40   Growth of Cocaine Abuse: Retail Price and Purity Index per Gram

Table 41   Growth of Cocaine Abuse: Estimate of Illicit Cocaine Entering United States in 1981 (in Tons)

Table 42   Growth of Cocaine Abuse: Cocaine Injuries, Deaths and Treatment Admissions

Table 43   Growth of Cocaine Abuse: Theoretical Maximum Cocaine Available from Coca Leaf Produced in Peru and Bolivia

Table 44   Cocaine Prices at Successive Stages of Trafficking, 1980

VIOLATIONS OF DRUG LAWS

Table 45   Federal Trafficking Penalties

Table 46   Regulatory Requirements

Table 47   Drug Thefts, by Type of Drug and Region, 1976–81

Table 48   Estimated Average Illegal Market Retail Drug Prices, by Type of Drug, United States, 1973–81

Table 49   Arrests for Drug Law Violations and Arrest Rate per 100,000 Population, by Type of Drug, United States, 1970–80

Table 50   Percent Distribution of Arrests for Drug Violations, by Type of Drug, Region, and Type of Offense, 1980

Table 51   Drug Seizures by the U.S. Customs Service, by Type, Amount, and Value of Drugs Seized, Fiscal Years 1975–81

Table 52   Drug Removals from the Domestic Market by the Drug Enforcement Administration, by Type of Drug, 1972–81

Table 53   Seizures and Arrests by the U.S. Coast Guard, by Type and Amount of Property Seized, 1973–81

MISCELLANEOUS

Table 54   Controlled Substances: Uses and Effects

Table 55   Approximate Equivalents

Table 1
Key Acts, Committee Recommendations and
Supreme Court Rulings on Drug Control 1903–1970

1. *American Pharmaceutical Association ad hoc Committee on the Acquirement of the Drug Habit (1903)*
   The committee recommended:
   1. Severe penalties for illegal drug sales.
   2. Strong state enforcement of laws.
   3. Elimination of *all* opium importation.
   4. Heroin prescriptions to be issued only by a physician and to be unrefillable.

2. *Pure Food and Drug Act (1906)*
   There was one noteworthy provision in this act:
   1. Patent medicines traded in interstate commerce required labeling of any narcotic content.

3. *Harrison Act (1914)*
   This act had several significant provisions:
   1. Records were to be kept of drugs received by addicts from physicians.
   2. Revenue stamps were required on packages containing more than the permitted amount of opiates, and records of transactions involving retail sales of opiates were to be kept. Severe penalties were imposed for violation of these provisions.
   3. Registration with Internal Revenue Collector of agents involved in opiate manufacture, sale, or transportation was to be made.

4. *Webb et al. v. United States (1919)*
   Supreme Court Ruling: Outlawed addiction maintenance.
   Behran v. United States (1922)
   Supreme Court Ruling: Outlawed *any* prescription of narcotics for addicts.

5. *Narcotic Drug Import and Export Act (1922)*
   By this act, severe penalties (fine of not more than $5,000 and ten years in prison) were instituted for a narcotics conviction.

6. *Linder v. United States 268 U.S. 5 (1925)*
   Supreme Court Ruling: Physician could prescribe narcotics in moderate dosage to relieve withdrawal symptoms.

7. *Uniform Narcotic Act (1932)*
   This act was designed to coordinate federal and local record keeping of drug transactions.

8. *Narcotics Drug Control Act (1956)*
   This act imposed severe penalties for drug–related offenses.

Offense	Penalty
Possession, 1st	2 to 10 years
Possession, 2nd	5 to 10 years (mandatory sentence)*
Selling, 1st	5 to 10 years (mandatory sentence)*
Possession, 3rd	10 to 40 years (mandatory sentence)*
Selling 2nd	10 to 40 years (mandatory sentence) or possibly death sentence if seller is over the age of 18 and if the sale is to a minor.

Table 1 (continued)
Key Acts, Committee Recommendations and
Supreme Court Rulings on Drug Control 1903–1970

9. *American Medical Association and American Bar Association Joint Committe on Narcotic Drugs (1958)*
   The Committee recommended experimental outpatient treatment for addicts; less provision for severe penalties.

10. *Robinson v. United States 370 U.S. 660 (1962)*
    Supreme Court Ruling: Addiction should not be punished by imprisonment, except in those cases where civil commitment for treatment is refused.

11. *Comprehensive Drug Abuse Prevention and Control Act (1970) (Controlled Substances Act)*
    1. Superseded all other federal narcotic laws.
    2. Bureau of Narcotics and Dangerous Drugs (BNDD) was given enforcement powers over drugs controlled by the act.
    3. Penalties based on drug classification, whether it is a first or subsequent offense, and type of involvement (that is, possession, sale, manufacture).
    4. Severe penalties for anyone convicted of sale of narcotics to a minor.
    5. Leniency for first offender.

*Mitigating circumstances cannot be taken into account by the court.

Source: Robert J. Wicks and Jerome J. Platt. *Drug Abuse: A Criminal Justice Primer* (Beverly Hills, California: Glencoe Press, 1977), pp. 108-109. Adapted. Reprinted by permission.

Table 2
Characteristics of Marijuana Laws, by Jurisdiction, as of January 1, 1982

Note: The data below were compiled from a review of federal and state marijuana statutes.

Jurisdiction	Amount	Possession — First offense Imprisonment (years)	Possession — First offense Fine (dollars)	Possession — Second offense Imprisonment (years)	Possession — Second offense Fine (dollars)	Cultivation Imprisonment (years)	Cultivation Fine (dollars)	Sale Imprisonment (years)	Sale Fine (dollars)
Alabama	Up to 2.2 pounds—personal use	0 to 1	$1,000	2 to 15	$25,000	2 to 15	$25,000	2 to 15	$25,000
	Up to 2.2 pounds—not for personal use	2 to 15	25,000	2 to 30	50,000	2 to 15	25,000	2 to 15	25,000
	2.2 to 2,000 pounds	3 to 15	25,000	3 to 30	50,000	3 to 15	25,000	3 to 15	25,000
	2,000 to 10,000 pounds	5 to 15	50,000	5 to 30	100,000	5 to 15	50,000	5 to 15	50,000
	More than 10,000 pounds	15	200,000	15 to 30	400,000	15	200,000	15	200,000
Alaska	Any amount, personal use, in home	Legal	Legal	Legal	Legal	Legal	Legal	X	X
	Any amount, personal use, not in public		0 to 100		0 to 100		0 to 100	X	X
	Up to 1 ounce, in public		0 to 100		0 to 100		0 to 100	NA	NA
	Smoking marihuana in public		0 to 1,000		0 to 1,000	X	X	X	X
	More than 1 ounce, personal use, in public		0 to 1,000		0 to 1,000	NA	NA	X	X
	Any amount, personal use in car, plane, or by person under 18 years		0 to 1,000		0 to 1,000		0 to 1,000	X	X
	More than 1 ounce, not for personal use	0 to 25	20,000	0 to life	25,000	0 to 25	20,000	0 to 25	25,000
Arizona	Any amount	1.5	0 to 150,000	1.5 to 3	0 to 150,000	1.5	0 to 150,000	7	0 to 150,000
Arkansas	Up to 1 ounce	0 to 1	1,000	0 to 5	10,000	2 to 10	10,000	2 to 10	10,000
	More than 1 ounce*	2 to 10	10,000	2 to 10	10,000	2 to 10	10,000	2 to 10	10,000
California	Up to 1 ounce		0 to 100		0 to 100	16 mos. to 3	0 to 100	2 to 4	
	More than 1 ounce	0 to 6 mos.	500	0 to 6 mos.	500			2 to 4	
Colorado	Up to 1 ounce, not in public		0 to 100		0 to 100	1 to 14	1,000	1 to 14	1,000
	Up to 1 ounce, in public	0 to 15 days	100	0 to 15 days	100	1 to 14	1,000	1 to 14	1,000
	More than 1 ounce	0 to 1	500	0 to 2	500 to 1,000	1 to 14	1,000	1 to 14	1,000
Connecticut	Up to 4 ounces	0 to 1	1,000	0 to 5	3,000	0 to 2	1,000	0 to 7	1,000
	More than 4 ounces	0 to 5	2,000	0 to 10	5,000	0 to 2	1,000	0 to 7	1,000
	More than 2.2 pounds	0 to 5	2,000	0 to 10	5,000	5 to 20		5 to 20	

		0 to 2	500	0 to 7	500	0 to 10	1,000 to 10,000	0 to 10	1,000 to 10,000
Delaware	Any amount	0 to 2	500	0 to 7	500	0 to 10	1,000 to 10,000	0 to 10	1,000 to 10,000
Florida	Up to 20 grams	0 to 1	1,000	0 to 1	1,000	0 to 5	5,000	0 to 5	5,000
	20 grams to 100 pounds	0 to 5	5,000	0 to 5	5,000	0 to 5	5,000	0 to 5	5,000
	100 to 2,000 pounds	3 to 30	25,000	3 to 30	25,000	3 to 30	25,000	3 to 30	25,000
	2,000 to 10,000 pounds	5 to 30	50,000	5 to 30	50,000	5 to 30	50,000	5 to 30	50,000
	More than 10,000 pounds	15 to 30	200,000	15 to 30	200,000	15 to 30	200,000	15 to 30	200,000
Georgia	Up to 1 ounce	0 to 1	1,000	1 to 10		1 to 10		1 to 10	
	1 ounce to 100 pounds	1 to 10		1 to 10		1 to 10		1 to 10	
	100 to 2,000 pounds	5 to 10	25,000	5 to 10	25,000	5 to 10	25,000	5 to 10	25,000
	2,000 to 10,000 pounds	7 to 10	50,000	7 to 10	50,000	7 to 10	50,000	7 to 10	50,000
	More than 10,000 pounds	15	200,000	15	200,000	15	200,000	15	200,000
Hawaii	Up to 1 ounce	0 to 30 days	500	0 to 30 days	500	0 to 30 days	500	0 to 30 days	500
	1 to 2 ounces	0 to 1	1,000	0 to 1	1,000	0 to 1	1,000	0 to 1	1,000
	2 ounces to 2.2 pounds	0 to 1	1,000	0 to 1	1,000	0 to 1	1,000	0 to 1	1,000
	More than 2.2 pounds	0 to 5	5,000	0 to 5	5,000	0 to 5	5,000	0 to 5	5,000
Idaho	Up to 3 ounces	0 to 1	1,000	0 to 2	2,000	0 to 5	15,000	0 to 5	15,000
	More than 3 ounces	0 to 5	10,000	0 to 10	20,000	0 to 5	15,000	0 to 5	15,000
Illinois	Up to 2.5 grams	0 to 30 days	500	0 to 30 days	500	0 to 6 mos.	500	0 to 6 mos.	500
	2.5 to 10 grams	0 to 6 mos.	500	0 to 6 mos.	500	0 to 1	1,000	0 to 1	1,000
	10 to 30 grams	0 to 1	1,000	0 to 3	10,000	1 to 3	10,000	1 to 3	10,000
	30 grams to 500 grams	1 to 3	10,000	2 to 5	10,000	2 to 5	10,000	2 to 5	10,000
	More than 500 grams	2 to 5	10,000	2 to 5	10,000	3 to 7	10,000	3 to 7	10,000
Indiana	Up to 30 grams	0 to 1	5,000	0 to 2	10,000	0 to 1	5,000	0 to 1	5,000
	More than 30 grams	0 to 2	10,000	0 to 2	10,000	0 to 2	10,000	0 to 2	10,000
Iowa	Any amount	0 to 6 mos.	1,000	0 to 18 mos.	3,000				
	Up to 1 ounce					0 to 6 mos.	1,000	0 to 6 mos.	1,000
	More than 1 ounce					0 to 5	1,000	0 to 5	1,000
Kansas	Any amount	0 to 1	2,500	1 to 10	5,000	0 to 1**	2,500**	1 to 20	10,000
Kentucky	Any amount	0 to 90 days	250	0 to 90 days	250	0 to 1	500	0 to 1	500
Louisiana	Up to 100 pounds	0 to 6 mos.	500	0 to 5	2,000	0 to 10	15,000	0 to 10	15,000
	100 pounds to 2,000 pounds	5 to 10	25,000	5 to 10	25,000	5 to 10	25,000	5 to 10	25,000
	2,000 to 10,000 pounds	10 to 15	50,000	10 to 15	50,000	10 to 15	50,000	10 to 15	50,000
	More than 10,000 pounds	15 to 20	200,000	15 to 20	200,000	15 to 20	200,000	15 to 20	200,000
Maine	Up to 1.5 ounces, personal use		0 to 200		0 to 200		0 to 200	X	X
	1.5 ounces to 2 pounds***					0 to 1	1,000	0 to 1	1,000
	2 to 1,000 pounds***					0 to 5	2,500	0 to 5	2,500
	More than 1,000 pounds***					0 to 10	10,000	0 to 10	10,000

Table 2 (continued)
Characteristics of Marijuana Laws, by Jurisdiction, as of January 1, 1982
Note: The data below were compiled from a review of federal and state marijuana statutes.

Jurisdiction	Amount	Possession — First offense Imprisonment (years)	Fine (dollars)	Possession — Second offense Imprisonment (years)	Fine (dollars)	Cultivation Imprisonment (years)	Fine (dollars)	Sale Imprisonment (years)	Fine (dollars)
Maryland	Any amount, personal use	0 to 1	1,000	0 to 2	2,000	0 to 1	1,000	X	X
	Any amount, not for personal use	0 to 5	15,000	0 to 10	30,000	0 to 5	15,000	0 to 5	15,000
	More than 100 pounds imported into the State	0 to 25	50,000	0 to 50	100,000	X	X	0 to 25	50,000
Massachusetts	Up to 50 pounds	‡‡	‡‡	0 to 6 mos.	500	0 to 2	5,000	1 to 2	5,000
	50 to 100 pounds	‡‡	‡‡	0 to 6 mos.	500	1 ‡‡	500 to 10,000	1 ‡‡	500 to 10,000
	100 to 2,000 pounds	‡‡	‡‡	0 to 6 mos.	500	3 ‡‡	2,500 to 50,000	3 ‡‡	2,500 to 25,000
	2,000 to 10,000 pounds	‡‡	‡‡	0 to 6 mos.	500	5 ‡‡	5,000 to 50,000	3 ‡‡	5,000 to 50,000
	More than 10,000 pounds	‡‡	‡‡	0 to 6 mos.	500	10 ‡‡	20,000 to 200,000	10 ‡‡	20,000 to 200,000
Michigan	Any amount	0 to 1	1,000	0 to 2	2,000	0 to 4	2,000	0 to 4	2,000
Minnesota	Up to 1.5 ounces		0 to 100	0 to 90 days	2,000	0 to 5	15,000	0 to 5	15,000
	More than 1.5 ounces	0 to 3	3,000	0 to 6	6,000	0 to 5	15,000	0 to 5	15,000
Mississippi	Up to 1 ounce, not in vehicle	0 to 90 days	100 to 250	5 to 60 days	250	0 to 10	15,000	0 to 20	30,000
	Up to 1 ounce, in vehicle		500	0 to 180 days	1,000	0 to 10	15,000	0 to 20	30,000
	1 ounce to 1 kilogram	0 to 3	3,000	0 to 6	6,000	0 to 10	15,000	1 to 20	30,000
	More than 1 kilogram	3 ‡‡	10,000	6 ‡‡	20,000	0 to 10	15,000	3 to 20	30,000
Missouri	Up to 35 grams	0 to 1	1,000	0 to 5	1,000	0 to 5	1,000	5 to life	
	More than 35 grams	0 to 5	1,000	0 to 5	1,000	0 to 5	1,000	5 to life	
Montana	Up to 60 grams	0 to 1	1,000	0 to 3	1,000	1 to life		1 to life	
	More than 60 grams	0 to 5		0 to 5		1 to life		1 to life	
Nebraska	Up to 1 ounce	0 to 7 days	100	0 to 5 days	200	0 to 5	10,000	0 to 20	10,000
	1 ounce to 1 pound		500	0 to 7 days	500	0 to 5	10,000	0 to 20	10,000
	More than 1 pound	0 to 5	10,000	0 to 5	10,000	0 to 5	10,000	0 to 20	10,000
New Hampshire	Up to 1 pound	0 to 1	1,000	0 to 7	2,000	0 to 15	2,000	0 to 15	2,000
	More than 1 pound	0 to 7	2,000	0 to 15	2,000	0 to 15	2,000	0 to 15	2,000

State	Amount								
New Jersey	Up to 25 grams	0 to 6 mos.	500	0 to 6 mos.	500	0 to 5	15,000	0 to 5	15,000
	More than 25 grams	0 to 5	15,000	0 to 5	15,000	0 to 5	15,000	0 to 5	15,000
New Mexico	Up to 1 ounce	0 to 15 days	50 to 100	0 to 1	100 to 1,000	9	0 to 10,000	0 to 18 mos.	0 to 5,000
	1 to 8 ounces	0 to 1	100 to 1,000	0 to 1	100 to 1,000	9	0 to 10,000	0 to 18 mos.	0 to 5,000
	8 ounces to 100 pounds	0 to 5	5,000	1 to 5	5,000	9	0 to 10,000	0 to 18 mos.	0 to 5,000
	More than 100 pounds	3	0 to 5,000	9	0 to 10,000	9	0 to 10,000	0 to 18 mos.	0 to 5,000
New York	Up to 25 grams, in private		1 to 100		0 to 200				
	25 grams to 2 ounces, or 2 ounces in public	0 to 3 mos.	500	0 to 3 mos.	500				
	2 ounces to 4 ounces	0 to 1	1,000	0 to 1	1,000	0 to 1	1,000	0 to 1	1,000
	4 to 8 ounces	0 to 1		0 to 1		0 to 1		0 to 4	
	8 ounces to 1 pound	0 to 4		0 to 4		0 to 4		0 to 7	
	1 to 10 pounds	0 to 7		0 to 7		0 to 7		0 to 15	
	More than 10 pounds	0 to 15		0 to 15		0 to 15		0 to 15	
N. Carolina	Up to 1 ounce		100		100		100		100
	1 ounce to 50 pounds	0 to 5	5,000	0 to 5	5,000	0 to 5	5,000	0 to 5	5,000
	50 to 100 pounds	0 to 5	5,000	0 to 5	5,000	0 to 5	5,000	0 to 5	5,000
	100 to 2,000 pounds	7	25,000	7	25,000	7	25,000	7	25,000
	2,000 to 10,000 pounds	14	50,000	14	50,000	14	50,000	14	50,000
	More than 10,000 pounds	35	200,000	35	200,000	35	200,000	35	200,000
North Dakota	Up to 0.5 ounce, not in vehicle	0 to 30 days	500	0 to 60 days	1,000	0 to 10	10,000	0 to 10	10,000
	0.5 ounce, or up to 1 ounce in vehicle	0 to 1	1,000	0 to 2	2,000	0 to 10	10,000	0 to 10	10,000
	More than 1 ounce	0 to 5	5,000	0 to 5	5,000	0 to 10	10,000	0 to 10	10,000
Ohio	Up to 100 grams		0 to 100		0 to 100	6 mos. to 5	2,500	6 mos. to 5	2,500
	100 grams to 200 grams	0 to 30 days	250	0 to 30 days	250	6 mos. to 5	2,500	6 mos. to 5	2,500
	200 to 600 grams	6 mos. to 5	2,500	1 to 10	5,000	1 to 10	5,000	1 to 10	5,000
	More than 600 grams	1 to 10	5,000	2 to 15	7,500	2 to 15	7,500	2 to 15	7,500
Oklahoma	Any amount	0 to 1		2 to 10	5,000	2 to 10	5,000	2 to 10	5,000
Oregon	Up to 1 ounce		0 to 100		0 to 100	0 to 10	2,500	0 to 10	2,500
	More than 1 ounce	0 to 10	2,500	0 to 10	2,500	0 to 10	2,500	0 to 10	2,500
Pennsylvania	Up to 30 grams	0 to 30 days	500	0 to 30 days	500	0 to 5	15,000	0 to 5	15,000
	More than 30 grams	0 to 1	5,000	0 to 3	25,000	0 to 5	25,000	0 to 5	25,000
Rhode Island	Any amount	0 to 1	500	0 to 2	1,000	0 to 30	50,000	0 to 30	50,000
S. Carolina	Up to 1 ounce	0 to 30 days	100 to 200	0 to 1	200 to 1,000	0 to 5	5,000	0 to 5	5,000
	More than 1 ounce		1,000	0 to 1	2,000	0 to 5	5,000	0 to 5	5,000
	10 to 100 pounds***					1 to 10	10,000	1 to 10	10,000
	100 to 2,000 pounds					5 to 25	25,000	5 to 25	25,000
	2,000 to 10,000 pounds					10 to 25	50,000	10 to 25	50,000

Table 2 (continued)
Characteristics of Marijuana Laws, by Jurisdiction, as of January 1, 1982
Note: The data below were compiled from a review of federal and state marijuana statutes.

Jurisdiction	Amount								
S. Dakota	Up to 1 ounce	0 to 30 days	100	0 to 30 days	100	0 to 30 days	100	0 to 1	1,000
	1 to 8 ounces	0 to 1	1,000	0 to 1	1,000	0 to 1	1,000	0 to 2	2,000
	8 ounces to 1 pound	0 to 1	1,000	0 to 1	1,000	0 to 1	1,000	0 to 5	5,000
	More than 1 pound	0 to 2	2,000	0 to 2	2,000	0 to 2	2,000	0 to 5	5,000
Tennessee	Up to 0.5 ounce	0 to 1	1,000	1 to 2	1,000	1 to 5	3,000	0 to 1	1,000
	More than 0.5 ounce	0 to 1	1,000	1 to 2	1,000	1 to 5	3,000	1 to 5	3,000
Texas	Up to 2 ounces	0 to 180 days	1,000	30 to 180 days	1,000	0 to 180 days	1,000	2 to 10	5,000
	2 to 4 ounces	0 to 1	2,000	90 days to 1	2,000	0 to 1	2,000	2 to 10	5,000
	4 ounces to 50 pounds	2 to 10	5,000	2 to 20	10,000	2 to 10	5,000	2 to 10	5,000
	More than 50 pounds	‡‡	500,000	‡‡	500,000	‡‡	500,000	‡‡	500,000
Utah	Any amount	0 to 6 mos.	299	0 to 1	1,000	0 to 5	5,000	0 to 5	5,000
Vermont	Up to 0.5 ounce	0 to 6 mos.	500	0 to 2	2,000	0 to 5	5,000	0 to 5	5,000
	0.5 to 2 ounces	0 to 3	3,000	0 to 3	3,000	0 to 5	5,000	0 to 5	5,000
	More than 2 ounces	0 to 5	5,000	0 to 5	5,000	0 to 5	5,000	0 to 5	5,000
Virginia	Up to 0.5 ounce	0 to 30 days	500	0 to 1	1,000	0 to 1	500	0 to 1	1,000
	0.5 to 5 pounds	0 to 30 days	500	0 to 1	1,000	0 to 1	500	0 to 10	1,000
	More than 5 pounds	0 to 30 days	500	0 to 1	1,000	5 to 30	1,000	5 to 30	1,000
Washington	Up to 40 grams	0 to 90 days	250	0 to 90 days	250	0 to 5	10,000	0 to 5	10,000
	More than 40 grams	0 to 5	10,000	0 to 5	10,000	0 to 5	10,000	0 to 5	10,000
W. Virginia	Any amount ‡‡‡	3 to 6 mos.	1,000	3 mos. to 1	2,000	1 to 5	15,000	1 to 5	15,000
Wisconsin	Any amount	0 to 30 days	500	0 to 30 days	500	0 to 5	15,000	0 to 5	15,000
Wyoming	Any amount	0 to 6 mos.	1,000	0 to 1	2,000	0 to 6 mos.	1,000	0 to 10	10,000
District of Columbia	Any amount	0 to 1	100 to 1,000	0 to 10	500 to 5,000	0 to 1	100 to 1,000	0 to 1	100 to 10,000
Federal	Any amount	0 to 1	5,000	0 to 2	10,000				
	Up to 1,000 pounds					0 to 5	15,000	0 to 5	15,000
	More than 1,000 pounds					0 to 15	125,000	0 to 15	125,000

* Presumed to be not for personal use.
** Second offense: 1 to 10 years and $5,000.
*** Presumed to be for sale.
‡ Probation.
‡‡ Mandatory.
‡‡‡ Up to life.
‡‡‡‡ For possession of less than 15 grams, the presumption is against intent to distribute. One can get a conditional discharge.

Source: Table provided to SOURCEBOOK staff by the National Organization for the Reform of Marijuana Laws.

Table 3

Characteristics of Marijuana Laws in States that have Decriminalized Possession of Marijuana, as of March 1982

State	Maximum fine imposed	Maximum amount possessed	Classification of offense	Effective date
Alaska	$100	Any amount in private for personal use or 1 ounce in public*	Civil	Sept. 2, 1975
California	$100	1 ounce	Misdemeanor—no permanent criminal record	Jan. 1, 1975
Colorado	$100	1 ounce	Class 2 petty offense—no criminal record	July 1, 1975
Maine	$200	Any amount** for personal use	Civil	March 1, 1976
Minnesota	$100	1½ ounces	Civil	Apr. 10, 1976
Mississippi	$250	1 ounce	Civil	July 1, 1977
Nebraska	$100	1 ounce	Civil	July 1, 1978
New York	$100	25 grams (approximately ⅞ ounce)	Violation—no criminal record	July 29, 1977
North Carolina	$100	1 ounce	Minor misdemeanor	July 1, 1977
Ohio	$100	100 grams (approximately 3½ ounces)	Minor misdemeanor—no criminal record	Nov. 22, 1975
Oregon	$100	1 ounce	Civil	Oct. 4, 1973

*The Supreme Court of Alaska ruled in 1975 that the constitutional right of privacy protects the possession of marijuana for personal use in the home by adults. This decision invalidates the $100 fine for simple possession in the home.

**There is a rebuttable presumption that possession of less than 1½ ounces is for personal use and possession of more than 1½ ounces indicates an intent to distribute.

Source: Table provided to SOURCEBOOK staff by the National Organization for the Reform of Marijuana Laws.

Table 4
Number, Total Funding, Budgeted Capacity, and Utilization Rate of Drug Abuse Treatment Units, by Jurisdiction, on September 30, 1980

Jurisdiction	Number of drug abuse treatment units	Total funding in thousands of dollars	Total budgeted treatment capacity	Utilization rate per 100 budgeted capacity
Total	**3,449**	**$486,583**	**207,946**	**87.3**
Alabama	40	3,676	1,310	95.2
Alaska	2	231	31	87.1
Arizona	65	6,598	3,380	61.4
Arkansas	42	1,444	769	97.5
California	372	71,910	27,789	86.3
Colorado	39	5,344	2,303	84.4
Connecticut	76	11,188	3,491	93.4
Delaware	11	1,168	420	92.1
Dist. of Columbia ...	27	7,142	2,735	94.0
Florida	93	18,706	7,497	83.2
Georgia	62	9,028	2,883	80.6
Hawaii	17	3,100	879	84.0
Idaho	9	385	222	70.3
Illinois	93	16,498	6,911	89.9
Indiana	60	5,455	2,425	76.3
Iowa	34	3,193	767	81.4
Kansas	32	2,465	852	74.5
Kentucky	110	2,506	1,961	77.9
Louisiana	54	4,252	2,701	81.0
Maine	11	1,294	491	98.8
Maryland	78	13,264	5,736	94.0
Massachusetts	121	13,053	5,077	83.9
Michigan	132	19,159	8,610	87.7
Minnesota	65	12,079	2,196	79.5
Mississippi	60	822	699	72.7
Missouri	51	5,514	2,493	68.6
Montana	13	798	395	100.3
Nebraska	20	1,495	636	89.5
Nevada	20	1,932	872	88.2
New Hampshire	20	1,341	390	94.1
New Jersey	90	21,897	7,988	104.2
New Mexico	36	3,133	1,618	86.1
New York	388	101,094	47,167	95.1
North Carolina	38	3,168	1,650	83.0
North Dakota	14	833	467	70.7
Ohio	130	16,507	8,427	84.2
Oklahoma	45	2,339	1,200	59.9

Table 4 (continued)
Number, Total Funding, Budgeted Capacity, and Utilization Rate of Drug
Abuse Treatment Units, by Jurisdiction, on September 30, 1980

Jurisdiction	Number of drug abuse treatment units	Total funding in thousands of dollars	Total budgeted treatment capacity	Utilization rate per 100 budgeted capacity
Oregon	31	2,981	1,222	88.2
Pennsylvania	177	21,478	8,646	85.4
Rhode Island	15	2,558	952	95.0
South Carolina	47	1,983	1,688	69.5
South Dakota	12	370	317	42.7
Tennessee	57	6,912	2,098	76.1
Texas	101	20,311	7,842	79.2
Utah	38	2,762	1,264	98.0
Vermont	19	793	358	79.3
Virginia	42	7,052	2,602	89.2
Washington	71	6,751	2,968	88.0
West Virginia	16	759	672	78.6
Wisconsin	121	8,996	3,288	56.4
Wyoming	17	546	355	32.4
Guam	2	240	26	61.5
Puerto Rico	110	7,727	8,171	91.2
Trust Territories:				
Pacific Islands	1	31	18	100.0
Virgin Islands	2	271	20	90.0

Note: These data were collected through the National Drug and Alcoholism Treatment Utilization Survey. Prior to 1979, the survey included only those facilities involved in the treatment of drug abuse; expansion of the survey to include alcholism treatment units reflects a joint effort between the National Institute on Drug Abuse (NIDA) and the National Institute on Alcohol Abuse and Alcholism (NIAAA). Other agencies that cooperated in the survey are the Food and Drug Administration, the Veterans Administration, and each of the state agencies responsible for drug abuse and alcoholism programs.

A total of 8,935 units reported to NDATUS; of these, 6,466 were classified as treatment units. A treatment unit is defined as a "facility having (1) a formal structured arrangement for drug abuse treatment using drug-specified personnel, (2) a designated portion of the facility (or resources) for treatment services, and (3) an allocated budget for such treatment services". Of the 6,466 treatment units, 2,000 provided only drug abuse treatment services, 3,017 provided only alcoholism treatment services, and 1,449 provided both drug abuse and alcoholism treatment. These data are from the 3,499 treatment units providing drug abuse treatment only or both drug abuse and alcoholism treatment.

"Budgeted capacity" is defined as the maximun number of clients a unit can treat. "Utilization rate" is the number of actual clients in treatment divided by the budgeted treatment capacity. "Total funding" includes all sources of funding for all units. The funding data are not based on audits and should be considered estimates.

Source: U.S. Department of Heath and Human Services, National Institute on Drug Abuse, *Final Report September 1980, Data from the National Drug and Alchoholism Treatment Utilization Survey (NDATUS),* Statistical Series F., No. 9 (Washington, D.C.: U.S. Government Printing Office, 1981), p. 18.

Table 5
Physical Environment of Units Providing Combined Alcholism
and Drug Abuse Treatment (as of September 30, 1980)

State	Community Mental Health Center* Number	Mental/ Psychiatric Hospital Number	General Hospital Including Veterans Administration Hospital Number	Other Specialized Hospital Number
Alabama	8	2	0	0
Alaska	1	0	0	0
Arizona	24	0	2	1
Arkansas	26	0	0	0
California	8	1	8	1
Colorado	5	1	0	0
Connecticut	1	2	1	2
Delaware	0	1	0	0
District of Columbia	2	0	0	0
Florida	6	1	0	0
Georgia	19	8	1	0
Hawaii	1	0	0	0
Idaho	0	0	0	0
Illinois	11	0	0	0
Indiana	33	1	3	0
Iowa	1	3	6	0
Kansas	9	2	2	0
Kentucky	87	0	1	2
Louisiana	13	1	5	0
Maine	6	0	0	0
Maryland	4	0	1	0
Massachusetts	0	0	2	0
Michigan	5	0	5	1
Minnesota	4	1	8	0
Mississippi	40	1	1	0
Missouri	13	3	1	0
Montana	0	0	0	0
Nebraska	1	0	0	0
Nevada	0	0	0	0
New Hampshire	7	1	0	0
New Jersey	1	0	1	0
New Mexico	9	0	0	0
New York	3	0	3	0
North Carolina	18	1	0	0
North Dakota	5	1	3	1
Ohio	7	1	4	0
Oklahoma	23	2	1	0

Table 5 (continued)
Physical Environment of Units Providing Combined Alcholism
and Drug Abuse Treatment (as of September 30, 1980)

State	Community Mental Health Center*	Mental/ Psychiatric Hospital	General Hospital Including Veterans Administration Hospital	Other Specialized Hospital
	Number	Number	Number	Number
Oregon	11	1	0	0
Pennsylvania	18	3	11	0
Puerto Rico	0	0	0	0
Rhode Island	1	0	0	0
South Carolina	5	1	0	0
South Dakota	4	0	1	1
Tennessee	32	6	3	0
Texas	14	3	3	0
Utah	13	1	2	0
Vermont	7	0	0	1
Virginia	9	1	0	0
Washington	5	0	0	0
West Virginia	14	1	0	0
Wisconsin	33	4	10	3
Wyoming	9	1	1	0
National Total	576	56	90	13
Number of States Included	52	52	52	52
Virgin Islands	0	0	0	0
Guam	1	0	0	0
American Samoa	0	0	0	0
T.T. Pacific Islands	0	0	0	0
N. Mariana Islands	—	—	—	—

Table 5 (continued)
Physical Environment of Units Providing Combined Alcholism
and Drug Abuse Treatment (as of September 30, 1980)

State	Correctional Facilities Number	Freestanding Facilities Number	Other Units Number	Total Units Number
Alabama	0	2	0	12
Alaska	0	0	0	1
Arizona	0	15	5	47
Arkansas	0	0	0	26
California	0	39	2	59
Colorado	3	6	3	18
Connecticut	8	11	0	25
Delaware	0	3	0	4
District of Columbia	0	3	0	5
Florida	0	9	1	17
Georgia	0	13	1	42
Hawaii	0	7	1	9
Idaho	0	3	6	9
Illinois	0	6	1	18
Indiana	6	9	1	53
Iowa	1	13	4	28
Kansas	2	11	1	27
Kentucky	1	8	0	99
Louisiana	0	17	7	43
Maine	0	0	0	6
Maryland	2	7	6	20
Massachusetts	0	6	0	8
Michigan	3	36	10	60
Minnesota	2	22	7	44
Mississippi	5	2	11	60
Missouri	1	12	2	32
Montana	3	4	1	8
Nebraska	0	1	0	2
Nevada	0	5	3	8
New Hampshire	0	1	1	10
New Jersey	0	3	0	5
New Mexico	0	1	2	12
New York	1	9	1	17
North Carolina	0	4	0	23
North Dakota	0	2	2	14
Ohio	0	11	5	28
Oklahoma	1	6	3	36
Oregon	0	3	0	15
Pennsylvania	2	76	7	117

Table 5 (continued)
Physical Environment of Units Providing Combined Alcholism and Drug Abuse Treatment (as of September 30, 1980)

State	Correctional Facilities Number	Freestanding Facilities Number	Other Units Number	Total Units Number
Puerto Rico	12	8	0	20
Rhode Island	1	2	0	4
South Carolina	0	28	8	42
South Dakota	0	3	2	11
Tennessee	0	5	3	49
Texas	2	15	1	38
Utah	0	10	1	27
Vermont	0	0	2	10
Virginia	1	10	3	24
Washington	3	6	0	14
West Virginia	0	0		15
Wisconsin	3	48	8	109
Wyoming	0	5	0	16
National Total	63	526	122	1,446
Number of States Included	52	52	52	52
Virgin Islands	0	2	0	2
Guam	0	1	0	2
American Samoa	0	0	0	0
T.T. Pacific Islands	0	1	0	1
N. Mariana Islands	—	—	—	—

*CMHCs are defined here as institutions operating under P.L. 94-63 or state or local legislation modeled on that act.

Notes:
 The last five island territories are not included in calculations of summary statistics.
 Dashes (—) indicate that data are not available.
 The sum or row amounts may not equal the total due to rounding.
 The data in the table are the number of combined alcoholism and drug abuse treatment units within each state that can be categorized by each of the physical environments listed. Units included in this table provide treatment for all substance–abuse clients, whether alcohol or drugs are involved. Data are taken from the 1980 National Drug and Alcohol Treatment Utilization Survey (NDATUS).

Source: State Alcohol Profile System (SAPIS), *National Status Report* (Rockville, Md., National Institute on Alcohol Abuse and Alcoholism [NIAAA], May 1981), pp. 58–61.

Table 6
Physical Environments of Alcoholism Only and Combined Treatment Units
National Drug and Alcoholism Treatment Utilization Survey (NDATUS)
September 30, 1980

Facility	ALCOHOLISM ONLY		COMBINED		TOTAL	
	Number	(%)	Number	(%)	Number	(%)
Community mental health center	390	12.9	577	39.9	967	21.7
Mental/psychiatric hospital	101	3.4	56	3.9	157	3.5
General hospital (including VA hospital)	362	12.0	88	6.1	450	10.1
Other specialized hospital	59	2.0	13	.9	72	1.6
Correctional facility	15	.5	63	4.4	78	1.8
Freestanding facility	1,762	58.4	529	36.5	2,291	51.3
Other	326	10.8	122	8.4	448	10.0
TOTAL	3,015	100.0	1,448	100.0	4,463	100.0

Source: National Institute on Alcohol Abuse and Alcoholism (NIAAA), *National Drug and Alcoholism Treatment Utilization Survey (NDATUS)* (Rockville, Md., June 1981), p. 21.

Table 7
Principal Population Served in Alcoholism Only
and Combined Treatment Units
National Drug and Alcoholism Treatment Utilization Survey (NDATUS)
September 30, 1980

Population	ALCOHOLISM ONLY		COMBINED		TOTAL	
	Number	(%)	Number	(%)	Number	(%)
Inner city	666	22.1	130	9.0	796	17.8
Other urban	1,069	35.4	475	32.8	1,544	34.6
Suburban	550	18.2	233	16.1	783	17.5
Rural	731	24.2	611	42.2	1,342	30.1
TOTAL	3,016	100.0	1,449	100.0	4,465	100.0

Source: NIAAA, *Drug and Alcoholism Treatment Survey,* p. 20.

Table 8
Demographic Characteristics of Clients in Alcoholism Only
and Combined Treatment Units
National Drug and Alcoholism Treatment Utilization Survey (NDATUS)
September 30, 1980

Client Characteristics	ALCOHOLISM ONLY		COMBINED		TOTAL	
	Number	(%)	Number	(%)	Number	(%)
Race/Ethnicity						
American Indian	10,135	4.6	2,096	2.9	12,231	4.2
Asian	598	.3	197	.3	795	.3
Black	34,277	15.6	9,289	13.0	43,566	15.0
Hispanic	29,712	13.5	2,656	3.7	32,268	11.1
White	144,654	65.9	57,009	80.0	201,663	69.4
TOTAL	219,376	100.0	71,247	100.0	290,623	100.0
Sex						
Male	169,891	78.5	52,492	73.8	222,383	77.3
Female	46,586	21.5	18,606	26.2	65,192	22.7
TOTAL	216,477	100.0	71,098	100.0	287,575	100.0
Age						
18 and under	10,173	4.8	5,178	7.3	15,351	5.4
19-20	12,768	6.0	6,017	8.5	18,785	6.6
21-44	118,435	55.6	41,149	58.2	159,584	56.2
45-59	56,412	26.5	14,354	20.3	70,766	24.9
60-64	10,652	5.0	2,727	3.9	13,379	4.7
65 and over	4,752	2.2	1,338	1.9	6,090	2.1
TOTAL	213,192	100.0	70,763	100.0	283,955	100.0

Source: NIAAA, *Drug Alcoholism Treatment Survey*, p. 14.

Table 9
Distribution of Clients in Treatment and Treatment Capacity
by Type of Care in Alcoholism Only and Combined Treatment Units
National Drug and Alcoholism Treatment Utilization Survey (NDATUS)
September 30, 1980

	CLIENTS IN TREATMENT					
	ALCOHOLISM ONLY		COMBINED		TOTAL	
Type of Care	Number	(%)	Number	(%)	Number	(%)
Detox medical model	5,787	2.5	1,563	2.1	7,350	2.4
Detox social setting	3,879	1.7	417	0.6	4,296	1.4
Rehab model	32,333	13.9	4,838	6.5	37,171	12.1
Custodial domiciliary model	3,958	1.7	757	1.0	4,715	1.5
Ambulatory medical detox	2,075	0.9	334	0.5	2,409	0.8
Limited care (including day care)	2,922	1.3	722	1.0	3,644	1.2
Outpatient services	182,328	78.2	65,429	88.4	247,747	80.6
TOTAL	233,272	100.0	74,060	100.0	307,332	100.0
	TREATMENT CAPACITY					
Detox medical model	8,611	3.1	2,297	2.6	10,908	3.0
Detox social setting	5,114	1.8	725	0.8	5,839	1.6
Rehab model	37,879	13.6	6,172	6.9	44,051	12.0
Custodial domiciliary model	5,354	1.9	992	1.1	6,346	1.7
Ambulatory medical detox	2,646	1.0	685	0.8	3,331	0.9
Limited care (including day care)	3,366	1.2	1,199	1.3	4,565	1.2
Outpatient services	215,682	77.4	77,499	86.5	293,181	79.6
TOTAL	278,652	100.0	89,569	100.0	368,221	100.0

Source: NIAAA, *Drug and Alcoholism Treatment Survey*, p. 9.

Table 10
Distribution of Clients in Treatment and Treatment Capacity
by Facility Location in Alcoholism Only and Combined Treatment Units
National Drug and Alcoholism Treatment Utilization Survey (NDATUS)
September 30, 1980

| | CLIENTS IN TREATMENT | | | | | |
| | ALCOHOLISM ONLY | | COMBINED | | TOTAL | |
Facility Location	Number	(%)	Number	(%)	Number	(%)
Hospital	31,865	13.7	5,157	7.0	37,013	12.0
Quarterway House	1,332	0.6	309	0.4	1,641	0.5
Halfway house/recovery home	17,353	7.4	1,613	2.2	18,966	6.2
Other residential facility	19,113	8.2	2,933	4.0	22,046	7.2
Outpatient facility	158,421	67.9	62,802	84.8	221,223	72.0
Correctional facility	5,197	2.2	1,246	1.7	6,443	2.1
TOTAL	233,272	100.0	74,060	100.0	307,332	100.0
	TREATMENT CAPACITY					
Hospital	38,556	13.8	6,819	7.6	45,375	12.3
Quarterway house	1,649	0.6	352	0.4	2,001	0.5
Halfway house/recovery home	20,904	7.5	2,075	2.3	22,979	6.2
Other residential facility	24,077	8.6	4,195	4.7	28,272	7.7
Outpatient facility	188,265	67.6	74,402	83.1	262,667	71.3
Correctional facility	5,201	1.9	1,726	1.9	6,927	1.9
TOTAL	278,652	100.0	89,569	100.0	368,221	100.0

Source: NIAAA, *Drug and Alcoholism Treatment Survey*, p. 12.

Table 11
Distribution of Full-Time and Part-Time Paid and Volunteer Staff by Staff Category for All Units Providing Alcoholism and Drug Abuse Treatment National Drug and Alcoholism Treatment Utilization Survey (NDATUS)
September 30, 1980

| | FULL-TIME EMPLOYEES | | | | PART-TIME EMPLOYEES | | | | | |
| | PAID | | VOLUNTEER | | PAID | | | VOLUNTEER | | |
Staff Category	Number	Percent	Number	Percent	Number	Number of Full-Time Equivalent* (FTE)	Percent Distribution of FTE	Number	Number of Full-Time Equivalent* (FTE)	Percent Distribution of FTE
Psychiatrists	92	0.7			604	119.5	6.4	22	2.2	0.7
Other physicians	91	0.7			410	81.0	4.3	28	3.7	1.1
Psychologists—doctoral level	158	1.2			353	76.1	4.1	18	1.3	0.4
Psychologists—master's level	420	3.2			300	75.2	4.0	20	3.4	1.0
Nurse practitioners or physician's assistants	46	0.4			26	8.8	0.5	2	0.1	0.1
Registered nurses	870	6.7	1	0.4	504	184.8	9.9	20	3.8	1.1
Licensed practical and vocational nurses	534	4.1	1	0.4	162	75.1	4.0	7	1.4	0.4
Social workers—MSW	677	5.2	2	0.9	371	100.7	5.4	19	3.3	1.0
Counselors—bachelor's level and above—counselling degree	2,346	18.1	2	0.9	595	195.2	10.5	212	30.3	9.2
Counselors—others	2,115	16.3	39	17.1	398	156.9	8.4	313	45.5	13.8
Vocational recreational therapists	193	1.5			101	30.8	1.7	56	25.8	7.8
Other direct-care staff	1,570	12.1	26	11.4	447	175.1	9.4	633	70.6	21.3
Total direct-care staff	9,112	70.3	71	31.1	4,271	1,279.8	68.5	1,350	191.9	58.0
Administration staff	1,949	15.0	12	5.3	903	237.6	12.7	58	10.4	3.1
Other support staff	1,780	13.7	60	26.3	991	294.9	15.8	346	57.1	17.3
Student trainees	123	0.9	85	37.3	153	55.2	3.0	277	71.3	21.6
TOTAL	12,964	100.0	228	100.0	6,318	1,867.6	100.0	2,031	330.8	100.0

Note: This table is based on the 1,449 units providing both alcoholism and drug abuse treatment that responded to NDATUS.
*Full-time equivalent is calculated in the following manner: number of hours worked per week
—————————————————
35 hours per week

Source: NIAAA, *Drug and Alcoholism Treatment Survey*, p. 67.

Table 12

Drug Users Admitted to Federally-Funded Drug Abuse Treatment Programs, by Ethnicity, Sex, Age at Admission, and Primary Drug of Abuse at Admission, United States, 1980

[Percent*]

| | Total admissions | | PRIMARY DRUG OF ABUSE AT ADMISSION | | | | | | | | | | | |
	Number	Percent	Heroin	Other Opiates	Mari-juana	Barbitu-rates	Amphet-amines	Alcohol	Cocaine	Other halluci-nogens	PCP	Tranquil-izers	Other sedatives	Other
Total	253,574	100.0	37.0	7.9	18.1	3.4	7.5	8.1	4.5	2.2	3.3	2.7	3.2	2.2
White male	104,591	100.0	21.3	9.8	23.1	4.4	9.1	12.4	5.2	3.4	2.8	2.8	4.0	1.7
Under 18 years	15,374	100.0	0.3	0.7	61.6	3.4	7.8	6.1	2.1	5.4	2.3	1.9	5.0	3.5
18 to 19 years	9,922	100.0	2.1	2.2	42.8	5.3	11.1	8.1	5.4	7.4	4.7	2.7	5.9	2.3
20 to 24 years	25,741	100.0	13.3	7.3	23.1	6.4	12.5	9.2	8.1	4.9	5.6	2.7	5.3	1.7
25 to 29 years	25,225	100.0	35.0	15.9	10.9	4.1	8.9	8.7	5.6	1.8	2.0	2.5	3.4	1.1
30 years and older ...	28,329	100.0	34.6	14.3	6.1	2.9	6.3	23.5	3.6	0.8	0.7	3.6	2.3	1.1
White female	45,519	100.0	21.7	11.5	20.0	5.2	12.3	6.1	3.9	2.5	2.1	6.9	5.9	1.9
Under 18 years	9,337	100.0	0.6	0.9	52.1	4.2	13.5	5.9	2.8	5.9	2.9	2.5	6.1	2.7
18 to 19 years	3,980	100.0	7.6	4.2	30.9	6.3	18.2	6.3	6.0	4.8	3.9	3.3	7.1	1.5
20 to 24 years	11,172	100.0	25.9	12.1	13.9	6.3	14.7	4.3	5.6	2.2	3.3	3.9	6.3	1.4
25 to 29 years	10,743	100.0	38.0	18.0	8.0	4.5	10.3	3.8	4.2	1.1	1.1	5.6	4.4	1.1
30 years and older ...	10,287	100.0	24.7	16.3	5.8	5.2	8.3	10.8	2.1	0.5	0.5	16.8	6.2	2.8
Black male	52,228	100.0	61.2	4.6	10.2	1.4	4.2	6.3	4.9	0.6	3.9	0.6	0.8	1.4
Under 18 years	2,564	100.0	0.5	0.6	71.1	2.4	2.8	4.1	4.8	1.2	3.8	1.2	4.8	2.7
18 to 19 years	1,759	100.0	7.0	1.6	49.1	2.8	4.5	5.2	9.4	2.6	11.3	1.7	3.5	1.3
20 to 24 years	7,938	100.0	36.3	5.1	17.0	2.8	7.7	5.5	8.4	1.7	11.4	1.2	1.0	2.0
25 to 29 years	15,809	100.0	70.2	5.1	4.4	1.3	4.4	3.6	4.9	0.6	3.4	0.4	0.4	1.4
30 years and older ...	24,158	100.0	73.8	4.8	2.5	0.8	2.9	8.6	3.4	0.2	1.2	0.4	0.4	1.0
Black female	17,431	100.0	63.2	5.9	9.5	2.0	3.9	2.9	3.8	0.4	4.4	1.4	1.3	1.4
Under 18 years	1,235	100.0	1.6	0.8	64.0	2.6	4.8	5.1	5.9	1.5	3.6	2.3	6.2	1.7
18 to 19 years	733	100.0	14.5	3.0	40.9	3.4	7.2	3.3	8.6	1.4	10.2	2.0	4.1	1.4
20 to 24 years	3,480	100.0	53.2	6.1	8.8	2.8	5.8	2.0	6.1	0.8	10.3	1.5	0.9	1.6
25 to 29 years	6,006	100.0	76.2	6.4	2.6	1.7	3.3	1.3	3.0	0.1	3.2	0.6	0.5	1.1
30 years and older ...	5,977	100.0	74.7	6.7	1.9	1.5	2.7	4.5	2.3	0.2	1.4	1.9	0.8	1.4

Table 12 (continued)

Drug Users Admitted to Federally-Funded Drug Abuse Treatment Programs, by Ethnicity, Sex, Age at Admission, and Primary Drug of Abuse at Admission, United States, 1980

[Percent*]

| | Total admissions | | PRIMARY DRUG OF ABUSE AT ADMISSION | | | | | | | | | | | |
	Number	Percent	Heroin	Other Opiates	Mari-juana	Barbitu-rates	Amphet-amines	Alcohol	Cocaine	Other halluci-nogens	PCP	Tranquil-izers	Other sedatives	Other
Hispanic male	23,803	100.0	60.2	2.6	15.6	1.5	2.4	2.4	2.5	0.9	4.7	0.6	1.0	5.5
Under 18 years	2,251	100.0	3.0	0.4	48.1	1.8	3.1	2.0	2.6	2.0	6.1	0.9	2.6	27.4
18 to 19 years	1,583	100.0	16.5	1.2	38.8	1.7	4.3	1.9	3.7	3.2	11.9	0.8	3.2	12.9
20 to 24 years	5,304	100.0	46.2	2.1	21.2	2.4	3.6	2.0	3.3	1.5	9.7	0.5	1.4	6.1
25 to 29 years	5,969	100.0	73.5	3.4	8.8	1.4	2.1	1.7	2.3	0.6	3.5	0.5	0.6	1.7
30 years and older ...	8,696	100.0	82.4	3.1	4.4	0.9	1.3	3.3	2.0	0.2	0.9	0.6	0.3	0.6
Hispanic female	5,590	100.0	56.6	3.8	13.0	2.3	3.7	1.4	2.7	1.2	6.3	2.2	2.0	4.8
Under 18 years	791	100.0	2.9	0.9	46.4	2.7	7.2	2.7	2.9	3.3	7.0	0.6	4.7	18.8
18 to 19 years	432	100.0	25.5	2.1	29.4	4.9	6.5	2.5	3.5	2.5	13.2	0.9	1.9	7.2
20 to 24 years	1,429	100.0	57.2	4.1	9.2	2.2	4.3	1.0	4.1	1.0	11.7	0.9	1.5	2.9
25 to 29 years	1,504	100.0	77.1	4.5	4.5	1.3	2.4	0.9	1.9	0.6	3.1	1.5	1.0	1.3
30 years and older ...	1,434	100.0	73.6	5.1	2.6	2.3	1.6	1.3	1.7	0.5	1.7	5.6	2.0	2.1
Other male	2,748	100.0	23.5	3.8	28.3	3.9	4.5	11.1	4.8	3.2	2.6	1.7	2.4	10.2
Other female	1,190	100.0	22.3	4.1	28.9	5.0	7.7	8.2	3.8	2.1	2.2	4.1	2.2	9.3

*Percents may not add to 100 because of rounding.

Note: This table is based on data that were reported to the Client Oriented Data Acquisition Process (CODAP), an information system operated by the National Institute on Drug Abuse (NIDA), that collects admission and discharge reports on each client admitted to federally-funded drug abuse treatment programs in the United States and each of its territories. The data are edited manually at the state and national levels and the internal consistency of information provided on individual forms is checked in computer edits. The number of cases for each table may vary because of missing values in different categories. Clients for whom no primary drug was reported and transfer admissions between CODAP clinics are not included in these data. The "primary drug of abuse at admission" is the drug type causing the most dysfunction at the time of admission to treatment. The subtotals of each category do not sum to the total due to the exclusion of cases with missing data on one or more of these attributes.

Source: U.S Department of Health and Human Services, National Institute of Drug Abuse, *Annual Data 1980, Data from the Client Oriented Acquisiton Process (CODAP)*, Statistical Series E, No. 21 (Washington, D.C.: U.S. Government Printing Office, 1981), p. 7. Adapted.

Table 13
Drug Users Admitted to Federally-Funded Drug Abuse Treatment Programs, by Ethnicity, Sex, Age at Admission, and Number of Arrests within 24 Months Prior to Admission, United States, 1980

Note: See *Note* Table 12.

[Percent*]

	TOTAL ADMISSIONS		NUMBER OF ARRESTS WITHIN 24 MONTHS PRIOR TO ADMISSION							
	Number	Percent	None	1	2	3	4	5	6 to 10	11 or more
Total	252,985	100.0	51.1	25.4	11.1	5.1	2.6	1.5	2.5	0.8
White male	104,422	100.0	43.8	27.6	13.3	6.2	3.2	1.8	3.0	1.1
Under 18 years	15,370	100.0	43.5	27.0	13.4	6.1	3.4	2.1	3.4	1.1
18 to 19 years	9,910	100.0	26.2	31.9	18.4	9.4	4.9	2.8	4.6	1.7
20 to 24 years	25,700	100.0	30.9	32.2	16.6	8.3	4.2	2.5	4.0	1.3
25 to 29 years	25,161	100.0	48.1	26.9	12.1	5.5	2.8	1.4	2.4	0.9
30 years and older	28,275	100.0	57.9	22.9	9.5	3.9	2.1	1.1	1.8	0.8
White female	45,469	100.0	67.0	19.0	6.9	2.9	1.5	0.9	1.4	0.4
Under 18 years	9,333	100.0	70.5	17.0	6.0	2.5	1.2	0.8	1.5	0.5
18 to 19 years	3,977	100.0	63.0	21.9	7.0	3.3	1.7	1.0	1.7	0.4
20 to 24 years	11,155	100.0	59.5	22.9	9.2	3.6	1.9	1.0	1.4	0.4
25 to 29 years	10,730	100.0	64.7	19.9	7.5	3.4	1.5	0.9	1.6	0.5
30 years and older	10,274	100.0	75.8	14.7	4.8	2.0	1.0	0.6	0.8	0.2
Black male	52,065	100.0	50.4	26.7	11.2	5.0	2.3	1.4	2.2	0.7
Under 18 years	2,560	100.0	42.6	28.0	13.7	7.1	3.3	2.3	2.2	0.7
18 to 19 years	1,748	100.0	34.2	31.6	16.0	6.5	3.9	3.1	4.1	0.7
20 to 24 years	7,914	100.0	35.4	32.5	15.5	7.3	3.3	1.9	3.2	0.9
25 to 29 years	15,754	100.0	49.4	26.9	11.9	5.1	2.4	1.4	2.2	0.7
30 years and older	24,089	100.0	58.0	24.2	8.8	3.9	1.7	1.1	1.8	0.6
Black female	17,369	100.0	61.7	21.3	8.6	3.4	1.6	1.1	1.7	0.6
Under 18 years	1,233	100.0	73.9	15.8	5.1	2.6	0.4	0.8	1.1	0.3
18 to 19 years	728	100.0	63.0	21.4	8.1	2.9	1.1	1.0	1.6	0.8
20 to 24 years	3,466	100.0	52.8	23.9	11.8	4.5	2.2	1.6	2.6	0.6
25 to 29 years	5,989	100.0	60.1	22.1	8.6	3.7	1.8	1.3	1.8	0.7
30 years and older	5,953	100.0	65.8	20.0	7.5	2.8	1.3	0.8	1.3	0.5
Hispanic male	23,788	100.0	46.1	28.8	11.3	5.5	3.0	1.7	2.9	0.8
Under 18 years	2,251	100.0	33.3	27.7	15.7	7.7	4.5	2.0	6.2	2.0
18 to 19 years	1,583	100.0	29.7	36.7	15.0	6.9	4.0	2.7	3.9	1.1
20 to 24 years	5,302	100.0	35.2	33.4	13.7	7.2	3.8	2.1	3.5	1.1
25 to 29 years	5,966	100.0	49.8	28.4	10.5	4.7	2.5	1.3	2.3	0.6
30 years and older	8,686	100.0	56.5	25.2	8.5	4.1	2.2	1.2	1.9	0.5

Table 13 (continued)
Drug Users Admitted to Federally-Funded Drug Abuse Treatment Programs, by Ethnicity, Sex, Age at Admission, and Number of Arrests within 24 Months Prior to Admission, United States, 1980

Note: See *Note* Table 12.

[Percent*]

	TOTAL ADMISSIONS		NUMBER OF ARRESTS WITHIN 24 MONTHS PRIOR TO ADMISSION							
	Number	Percent	None	1	2	3	4	5	6 to 10	11 or more
Hispanic female	5,586	100.0	56.8	21.6	9.4	4.3	2.1	1.3	2.0	0.6
Under 18 years	791	100.0	61.8	19.6	8.8	4.0	2.0	1.4	1.4	0.9
18 to 19 years	432	100.0	59.0	19.9	9.7	4.2	1.6	1.6	3.0	0.9
20 to 24 years	1,428	100.0	51.9	24.1	10.4	6.1	2.7	2.0	2.3	0.6
25 to 29 years	1,503	100.0	58.6	21.9	9.6	3.7	2.6	1.0	2.2	0.5
30 years and older	1,432	100.0	64.3	20.3	8.4	3.4	1.3	0.6	1.3	0.3
Other male	2,658	100.0	39.1	25.4	13.9	6.9	4.1	3.0	5.6	1.9
Other female	1,173	100.0	57.5	19.4	9.2	5.4	3.2	0.9	3.0	1.5

*Percents may not add to 100 because of rounding.

Source: U.S Department of Health and Human Services, National Institute of Drug Abuse, *Annual Data 1980, Data from the Client Oriented Acquisiton Process (CODAP),* Statistical Series E, No. 21 (Washington, D.C.: U.S. Government Printing Office, 1981), p. 7. Adapted.

Table 14

Drug Users Admitted to Federally-Funded Drug Abuse Treatment Programs, by Primary Drug of Abuse at Admission, and Sex, United States, 1976-79

[Percent*]

Primary drug of abuse at admission	MALE				FEMALE			
	1976	1977	1978	1979	1976	1977	1978	1979
Opiates	66.0	60.0	52.3	48.3	63.1	59.4	52.0	47.0
Nonprescription methadone	63.3	55.3	45.9	41.2	60.2	54.0	44.4	38.4
Other opiates	0.6	1.3	1.7	1.3	0.5	1.4	1.8	1.4
Other opiates	2.1	3.4	4.7	5.7	2.4	4.0	5.8	7.2
Marijuana	9.4	10.4	13.9	16.5	9.5	10.5	13.1	15.6
Barbiturates	4.3	4.6	4.2	3.6	6.0	5.9	5.6	4.7
Amphetamines	4.3	4.7	5.5	5.9	5.9	6.5	7.4	8.1
Other drug types	16.0	20.3	24.1	25.7	15.5	17.7	21.9	24.7
Alcohol	8.2	9.1	9.5	8.7	5.0	4.5	4.9	4.4
Cocaine	1.4	1.9	2.9	4.1	0.9	1.4	2.2	3.3
Hallucinogens**	2.5	3.9	5.5	6.5	2.5	3.4	4.8	5.8
Tranquilizers***	NA	1.4	1.9	2.0	NA	3.7	5.0	5.7
Other sedatives***	2.0	1.7	1.7	2.0	5.5	2.9	2.9	3.2
Inhalants	1.4	1.6	1.7	1.6	0.7	0.9	0.9	0.9
Over-the counter	0.1	0.2	0.2	0.2	0.3	0.4	0.5	0.5
Other	0.4	0.5	0.6	0.6	0.5	0.5	0.7	0.9
Total	100.0	100.0	100.0	100.0	100.0	100.0	100.0	100.0
Number of clients	(162,709)	(146,083)	(157,597)	(169,839)	(57,490)	(56,369)	(62,474)	(65,490)

*Percents may not add to 100 because of rounding.

**Includes PCP.

***"Tranquilizers" was added as separate drug category beginning in 1977; during 1976 tranquilizers were included in the category "other sedatives."

Source: U.S. Department of Health and Human Services, National Institute on Drug Abuse, *Women in Drug Abuse Treatment 1979, Topical Data from the Client Oriented Data Acquisition Process (CODAP)*, Statistical Series C., No. 1 (Washington, D.C., U.S. Government Printing Offices, 1980), p. 59.

Table 15
Drug Users Admitted to Federally-Funded Drug Abuse Treatment Programs, by Selected Characteristics, and Primary Drug of Abuse at Admission, United States, 1980

Note: See *Note* Table 12.

[Percent*]

	Total admissions	Heroin	Other Opiates	Marijuana	Barbiturates	Amphetamines	Alcohol	Cocaine	Other hallucinogens	PCP	Tranquilizers	Other sedatives	Other
							PRIMARY DRUG OF ABUSE AT ADMISSION						
Highest grade level completed:													
Grade 0 to 9	22.5	15.7	13.1	37.1	22.9	23.1	24.7	14.7	32.4	18.8	21.9	25.5	47.9
Grade 10 to 11	28.7	28.3	22.5	32.7	29.0	30.3	24.5	27.4	33.3	39.2	22.3	28.7	25.4
Grade 12	32.6	37.3	37.6	21.1	33.4	33.5	34.8	34.6	25.4	33.8	36.0	29.5	19.0
Grade 13 and over	16.2	18.6	26.8	9.1	14.6	13.1	16.0	23.3	8.9	8.2	19.8	16.4	7.7
Total	100.0	100.0	100.0	100.0	100.0	100.0	100.0	100.0	100.0	100.0	100.0	100.0	100.0
Number of clients	(252,920)	(93,436)	(19,921)	(45,801)	(8,644)	(18,956)	(20,551)	(11,334)	(5,489)	(8,275)	(6,951)	(7,993)	(5,569)
Employment status:													
Unemployed	69.7	71.3	68.8	67.6	74.5	70.0	66.2	62.8	75.0	70.5	68.6	67.9	80.1
Not seeking work	54.0	54.8	52.3	53.8	58.3	53.0	51.7	47.6	59.2	53.9	54.0	51.7	63.4
Seeking work	15.7	16.5	16.5	13.8	16.1	17.0	14.5	15.2	15.7	16.6	14.6	16.1	16.7
Employed	30.3	28.7	31.2	32.4	25.5	30.0	33.8	37.2	25.0	29.5	31.4	32.1	19.9
Part-time	6.6	4.2	5.4	11.4	6.2	7.4	5.7	7.1	8.8	6.2	7.9	7.4	6.4
Full-time	23.7	24.5	25.8	21.0	19.3	22.6	28.2	30.1	16.2	23.3	23.5	24.8	13.5
Total	100.0	100.0	100.0	100.0	100.0	100.0	100.0	100.0	100.0	100.0	100.0	100.0	100.0
Number of clients	(252,616)	(93,210)	(19,877)	(45,808)	(8,621)	(18,963)	(20,557)	(11,311)	(5,486)	(8,266)	(6,952)	(7,990)	(5,575)

Marital status:

Never married	59.0	49.0	42.2	83.1	65.3	62.2	44.0	64.1	82.3	75.6	43.5	66.5	71.9
Married	18.6	23.9	27.3	8.8	12.7	13.8	23.0	15.0	7.6	11.3	25.6	14.5	12.8
Widowed	1.2	1.5	1.7	0.2	1.1	0.7	2.1	0.7	0.4	0.6	2.6	1.0	1.5
Divorced	12.2	12.6	18.5	4.9	13.5	14.3	20.2	12.7	5.7	6.1	19.4	12.2	8.2
Separated	9.1	12.9	10.4	3.0	7.4	8.9	10.7	7.5	4.0	6.4	8.8	5.7	5.5
Total	100.0	100.0	100.0	100.0	100.0	100.0	100.0	100.0	100.0	100.0	100.0	100.0	100.0
Number of clients	(253,042)	(93,423)	(19,911)	(45,873)	(8,649)	(18,972)	(20,556)	(11,339)	(5,496)	(8,271)	(6,960)	(8,003)	(5,589)

Source of referral:

Voluntary	76.4	85.8	87.3	62.8	74.2	70.2	73.7	66.4	69.4	58.2	84.2	77.7	68.9
Self-referral	40.6	59.5	53.1	18.2	31.4	29.7	32.5	30.8	24.8	22.5	35.0	30.2	28.4
Hospital	4.0	2.4	5.3	2.1	6.7	5.3	10.4	3.3	4.7	3.6	7.2	5.8	3.8
Community services	13.5	10.8	13.6	13.4	16.7	16.3	15.4	14.0	16.5	13.8	20.7	17.7	16.2
Community mental health center	2.6	1.4	3.3	2.2	4.6	4.2	3.1	2.8	4.6	2.8	6.1	4.3	3.3
Community service agency/individual	10.9	9.4	10.4	11.2	12.1	12.1	12.3	11.2	11.9	11.0	14.6	13.4	12.9
Family/friend	11.9	10.7	11.2	14.8	12.9	11.8	9.6	11.7	13.8	12.3	13.8	13.2	11.8
Employer/school	3.4	0.4	0.8	10.6	2.7	3.8	2.9	2.3	4.7	2.5	3.0	3.9	5.0
Employer	0.5	0.3	0.5	0.6	0.4	0.6	1.4	0.7	0.2	0.7	0.8	0.4	0.5
School	2.8	0.2	0.3	10.0	2.3	3.3	1.6	1.5	4.5	1.8	2.2	3.5	4.5
Other voluntary	3.1	2.0	3.2	3.7	3.9	3.3	2.9	4.3	4.9	3.5	4.4	6.9	3.7
Non-voluntary	22.6	12.6	12.2	36.7	25.0	28.6	25.6	31.6	30.0	41.1	15.5	22.1	30.7
Treatment Alternatives to Street Crime (TASC)	2.5	1.4	2.2	3.2	3.0	3.5	3.1	4.4	3.6	1.9	2.1	5.0	3.1
Federal, state, and county probation	13.2	5.4	6.4	24.8	14.5	16.9	14.3	19.5	17.5	32.2	9.0	11.7	18.6
Federal, state, and county parole	3.8	4.5	1.9	3.5	4.1	4.8	3.2	4.5	4.4	3.4	1.9	2.1	3.5
Other non-voluntary	3.0	1.4	1.6	5.2	3.4	3.5	5.0	3.3	4.5	3.5	2.6	3.2	5.4
Other	1.1	1.6	0.5	0.6	0.8	1.2	0.7	1.9	0.6	0.8	0.2	0.2	0.4
Bureau of Prisons**	1.0	1.6	0.5	0.5	0.8	1.2	0.7	1.9	0.6	0.8	0.2	0.2	0.4
Veterans Administration Armed Services Medical Referral Office (ASMRO)	0.0	0.0	0.0	0.0	0.0	0.0	0.0	0.0	0.0	0.0	0.0	0.0	0.0***
Total	100.0	100.0	100.0	100.0	100.0	100.0	100.0	100.0	100.0	100.0	100.0	100.0	100.0
Number of clients	(252,834)	(93,532)	(19,897)	(45,798)	(8,640)	(18,938)	(20,455)	(11,324)	(5,475)	(8,259)	(6,951)	(7,999)	(5,566)

Table 15 (continued)
Drug Users Admitted to Federally-Funded Drug Abuse Treatment Programs, by Selected Characteristics, and Primary Drug of Abuse at Admission, United States, 1980

Note: See Note Table 12.

[Percent*]

Number of arrests within 24 months prior to admission:	Total admissions	Heroin	Other Opiates	Marijuana	Barbiturates	Amphetamines	Alcohol	Cocaine	Other hallucinogens	PCP	Tranquilizers	Other sedatives	Other
None	51.1	56.7	56.6	47.5	46.8	45.8	50.1	41.5	41.2	28.4	66.3	47.0	44.4
1	25.4	22.9	22.2	30.5	23.7	26.0	24.4	32.5	26.9	30.5	16.2	27.8	24.3
2	11.1	9.7	10.3	11.5	12.5	12.6	12.0	12.5	12.6	17.3	8.1	12.3	12.1
3	5.1	4.4	4.6	4.6	6.2	6.4	5.3	5.7	7.3	9.1	4.0	5.4	6.5
4	2.6	2.2	2.3	2.2	3.3	3.1	3.0	2.7	4.1	5.0	1.7	2.3	3.7
5	1.5	1.3	1.3	1.3	2.2	1.7	1.6	1.6	2.3	3.0	1.2	1.5	2.5
6 to 10	2.5	2.1	2.1	1.9	3.9	3.3	2.5	2.4	3.9	5.0	1.9	2.5	4.5
11 or more	0.8	0.6	0.6	0.6	1.3	1.2	1.1	1.0	1.6	1.6	0.7	0.6	1.9
Total	100.0	100.0	100.0	100.0	100.0	100.0	100.0	100.0	100.0	100.0	100.0	100.0	100.0
Number of clients	(252,985)	(93,362)	(19,923)	(45,863)	(8,639)	(18,981)	(20,595)	(11,307)	(5,494)	(8,271)	(6,954)	(8,006)	(5,590)

*Percents may not add to 100 because of rounding.

**Bureau of Prisons (BOP) includes BOP/NARA II, BOP-IPDDR, BOP study, BOP probationer, and other BOP (formerly DAP).

***The number of cases in this cell is zero.

Source: U.S Department of Health and Human Services, National Institute of Drug Abuse, *Annual Data 1980, Data from the Client Oriented Acquisiton Process (CODAP), Series E, No. 21* (Washington, D.C.: U.S. Government Printing Office, 1981), p. 8, 9. Adapted.

Table 16
Use of Other Drugs among Current Drinkers
and Those Who Are Not Current Drinkers*

Use of Other Drugs	PERCENTAGE OF YOUTH: AGES 12 to 17 YEARS		PERCENTAGE OF ADULTS: AGES 18+ YEARS	
	Current Drinkers	Not Current Drinkers	Current Drinkers	Not Current Drinkers
Size of sample (unweighted base)	**302**	**684**	**1622**	**968**
Nonmedical psychotherapeutic pill user				
Yes	18.8	6.5	18.9	9.4
No	81.2	93.5	81.1	90.6
Ever used marijuana				
Yes	44.3	11.8	31.4	6.9
No	55.7	88.2	68.6	93.1
Ever used other illicit drugs				
Yes	36.7	10.2	19.7	4.7
No	63.3	89.8	80.2	94.6

*Those who report drinking alcoholic beverages within the past month.

Source: H.I. Abelson and P.M. Fishburne, *Nonmedical Use of Psychoactive Substances* (Princeton, N.J.: Response Analysis Co., 1976), reprinted in Ernest P. Noble, ed., Third Special Report, p. 197

Table 17

High School Seniors' Perceptions of the Harmfulness of Drug Use, by Type of Drug and Frequency of Use, United States, 1975-80

Note: These data are from a series of nationwide surveys of high school seniors conducted by the Institute for Social Research for the National Institute on Drug Abuse from 1975 through 1980. The survey design is a multistage random sample of high school seniors in public and private schools. Depending on the survey year, from 66 to 80 percent of the schools initially invited to participate agreed to do so. Completed questionnaires were obtained from 77 to 83 percent of all sampled students in participating schools each year. All percentages reported are based on weighted cases; the N's that are shown in the tables refer to the number of unweighted cases. Alcohol and cigarette use are included in selected tables.

Question: "How much do you think people risk harming themselves (physically or in other ways), if they . . .?"

	Percent saying "great risk"[*]					
Type of drug and frequency of use	Class of 1975 (N=2,804)	Class of 1976 (N=3,225)	Class of 1977 (N=3,570)	Class of 1978 (N=3,770)	Class of 1979 (N=3,250)	Class of 1980 (N=3,234)
Try marijuana/hashish once or twice	15.1	11.4	9.5	8.1	9.4	10.0
Smoke marijuana/hashish occasionally	18.1	15.0	13.4	12.4	13.5	14.7
Smoke marijuana/hashish regularly	43.3	38.6	36.4	34.9	42.0	50.4
Try LSD once or twice	49.4	45.7	43.2	42.7	41.6	43.9
Take LSD regularly	81.4	80.8	79.1	81.1	82.4	83.0
Try cocaine once or twice	42.6	39.1	35.6	33.2	31.5	31.3
Take cocaine regularly	73.1	72.3	68.2	68.2	69.5	69.2
Try heroin once or twice	60.1	58.9	55.8	52.9	50.4	52.1
Take heroin occasionally	75.6	75.6	71.9	71.4	70.9	70.9
Take heroin regularly	87.2	88.6	86.1	86.6	87.5	86.2
Try an amphetamine once or twice	35.4	33.4	30.8	29.9	29.7	29.7
Take amphetamines regularly	69.0	67.3	66.6	67.1	69.9	69.1
Try a barbiturate once or twice	34.8	32.5	31.2	31.3	30.7	30.9
Take barbiturates regularly	69.1	67.7	68.6	68.4	71.6	72.2
Try one or two drinks of an alcoholic beverage (beer, wine, liquor)	5.3	4.8	4.1	3.4	4.1	3.8
Take one or two drinks nearly every day	21.5	21.2	18.5	19.6	22.6	20.3
Take four or five drinks nearly every day	63.5	61.0	62.9	63.1	66.2	65.7
Have five or more drinks once or twice each weekend	37.8	37.0	34.7	34.5	34.9	35.9
Smoke one or more packs of cigarettes per day	51.3	56.4	58.4	59.0	63.0	63.7

[*]Answer alternatives were: (1) no risk, (2) slight risk, (3) moderate risk, (4) great risk, and (5) can't say, drug unfamiliar.

Source: Lloyd D. Johnston, Jerald B. Bachman, and Patrick M. O'Malley, *Highlights from Student Drug Use in America, 1975-80,* U.S. Department of Health and Human Services, National Institute on Drug Abuse (Washington, D.C.: U.S. Government Printing Office, 1981), p. 79.

Table 18
High School Seniors' Perceptions of Availability of Drugs, by Type of Drug, United States, 1975-80

See *Note* Table 17.

Question: "How difficult do you think it would be for you to get each of the following types of drugs, if you wanted some?"

| Type of drug | Percent saying drug would be "fairly easy" or "very easy" for them to get* | | | | | |
	Class of 1975 (N=2,627)	Class of 1976 (N=3,163)	Class of 1977 (N=3,562)	Class of 1978 (N=3,598)	Class of 1979 (N=3,172)	Class of 1980 (N=3,240)
Marijuana/hashish	87.8	87.4	87.9	87.8	90.1	89.0
LSD	46.2	37.4	34.5	32.2	34.2	35.3
Some other psychedelic	47.8	35.7	33.8	33.8	34.6	35.0
Cocaine	37.0	34.0	33.0	37.8	45.5	47.9
Heroin	24.2	18.4	17.9	16.4	18.9	21.2
Some other narcotic (including methadone)	34.5	26.9	27.8	26.1	28.7	29.4
Amphetamines	67.8	61.8	58.1	58.5	59.5	61.3
Barbiturates	60.0	54.4	52.4	50.6	49.8	49.1
Tranquilizers	71.8	65.5	64.9	64.3	61.4	59.1

*Answer alternatives were: (1) probably impossible, (2) very difficult, (3) fairly difficult, (4) fairly easy, and (5) very easy.

Source: Lloyd D. Johnston, Jerald G. Bachman, and Patrick M. O'Malley, *Highlights from Student Drug Use in America, 1975-1980*, U.S. Department of Health and Human Services, National Institute on Drug Abuse (Washington, D.C.: U.S. Government Printing Office, 1981), p. 105.

Table 19
High School Seniors Favoring Prohibition of Drug Use,
by Type of Drug and Place of Use, United States, 1975-80

See *Note* Table 17.

Question: "Do you think that people (who are 18 or older)
should be prohibited from doing each of the following?"

	Percent saying "yes"*					
Type of drug and place of use	Class of 1975** (N=2,620)	Class of 1976 (N=3,265)	Class of 1977 (N=3,629)	Class of 1978 (N=3,783)	Class of 1979 (N=3,288)	Class of 1980 (N=3,224)
Smoking marijuana/hashish in private	32.8	27.5	26.8	25.4	28.0	28.9
Smoking marijuana/hashish in public places	63.1	59.1	58.7	59.5	61.8	66.1
Taking LSD in private	67.2	65.1	63.3	62.7	62.4	65.8
Taking LSD in public places	85.8	81.9	79.3	80.7	81.5	82.8
Taking heroin in private	76.3	72.4	69.2	68.8	68.5	70.3
Taking heroin in public places .	90.1	84.8	81.0	82.5	84.0	83.8
Taking amphetamines or barbiturates in private	57.2	53.5	52.8	52.2	53.4	54.1
Taking amphetamines or barbiturates in public places	79.6	76.1	73.7	75.8	77.3	76.1
Getting drunk in private	14.1	15.6	18.6	17.4	16.8	16.7
Getting drunk in public places ..	55.7	50.7	49.0	50.3	50.4	48.3
Smoking cigarettes in certain specified public places	NA	NA	42.0	42.2	43.1	42.8

*Answer alternatives were: (1) no, (2) not sure, and (3) yes.
**The 1975 survey question asked about people who are "20 or older."

Source: Lloyd D. Johnston, Jerald G. Bachman, and Patrick M. O'Malley, *Highlights from Student Drug Use in America, 1975-1980,* U.S. Department of Health and Human Services, National Institute on Drug Abuse (Washington, D.C.: U.S. Government Printing Office, 1981), p. 84.

Table 20
Respondents' concerns about public issues,
United States, selected years 1974-82

Question: "Here is a list of things people have told us they are
concerned about today. Would you read over that list
and then tell me which two or three you personally
are most concerned about today?"

[Percent*]

	1974	1975	1976	1977	1979	1981	1982
Inflation and high prices	56	58	44	48	63	56	53
Crime and lawlessness	30	34	40	40	31	35	37
Money enough to live right and pay the bills	25	30	26	28	33	31	29
The fuel and energy crisis	46	27	22	31	25	30	17
The way the courts are run	20	22	30	27	23	24	25
A recession and rising unemployment	15	33	20	19	20	24	34
Our relations with foreign countries	18	10	13	9	15	19	21
Wrongdoing by elected government officials	40	26	32	22	24	18	17
Getting into another war	7	11	10	8	9	18	16
Drug abuse	23	20	24	21	14	16	17
The way young people think and act	10	14	15	17	14	14	12
Pollution of air and water	12	11	11	13	10	10	7
Alcoholism	**	**	6	7	6	7	7

Note: The above data were collected by the Roper Organization. These surveys were conducted in January of the year noted.

*Percents add to more than 100 due to multiple responses.
**Concern was not listed.

Source: "Opinion Roundup," *Public Opinion 5* (February/March 1982), p. 33. Reprinted by permission.

Table 21
Attitudes Toward the Most Important Problems Facing
Public Schools in Own Community, United States, 1980

Question: "What do you think are the biggest problems
with which public schools in this community must deal?"

[Percent*]

Most important problems	Total	Adults with no children in school	Adults with children in public school	Adults with children in nonpublic school**
Lack of discipline	26	24	26	48
Use of dope/drugs	14	15	12	10
Poor curriculum/poor standards	11	11	10	10
Lack of proper financial support	10	9	11	9
Integration/busing	10	10	10	10
Large school/too many classes/overcrowding	7	6	8	5
Difficulty in getting good teachers	6	5	7	7
Parents' lack of interest	6	5	6	5
Teachers' lack of interest	6	4	7	8
Pupils' lack of interest/truancy	5	5	6	7
Crime/vandalism	4	5	3	5
Mismanagement of funds/programs	3	2	3	1

*Columns total to more than 100 percent because of multiple responses.
**Includes parents of students attending private and independent schools as well as parochial (nonpublic) schools.

Source: George H. Gallup, *The Gallup Opinion Index,* Report No. 180 (Princeton, N.J.: The Gallup Poll, August 1980), p. 4. Reprinted by permission.

Table 22
Attitudes Toward Who Should Deal with Specified Student
Behavioral Problems in Public Schools, United States, 1980

Question: "Here are some student behavior problems which may occur
in your school. In your opinion, who should deal with each kind of
problem—should it be the parents, the school or the courts?"

[Percent*]

Behavioral problem	Who should deal with the problem			
	Parents	School	Courts	Don't know
Truancy (skipping school)	72	45	9	2
Vandalism of school property	44	39	50	2
Bringing weapons to school	41	35	59	3
Fighting in school	42	75	10	3
Using alcohol or drugs in school	50	57	35	2
Striking a teacher	43	56	35	3
Stealing money or clothing from other students	48	58	30	3

*Rows total to more than 100 percent because of multiple responses.

Source: George H. Gallup, *The Gallup Opinion Index,* Report No. 180 (Princeton, N.J.: The Gallup Poll, August 1980), p. 9.

Table 23
Attitudes Toward Causes of Increasing Crime, United States, 1981

Note: The Gallup Organization conducted 1,030 telephone interviews across the nation between Jan. 16-23, 1981, for the *Newsweek* poll. The margin of error is plus or minus 3 percent.

Question: "What is most responsible for the increasing rate of crime?

[Percent*]

Causes	
Unemployment	37
Courts too lenient	20
Breakdown of family, society, values	19
Punishment not severe enough	13
Drugs	13
TV violence, movies	3

*Percents do not add up to 100 because of mutliple responses.

Source: "The Plague of Violent Crime," *Newsweek,* Mar. 23, 1981, p. 47. Copyright 1981 by Newsweek, Inc. All rights reserved. Reprinted by permission.

Table 24
Respondents Agreeing that Selected Substances are Addictive, by Type of Substance and Age Category, United States, Selected Years 1971-79

Note: These data are based on six nationwide sample surveys conducted by the Response Analysis Corporation for the National Commission on Marihuana and Drug Abuse (1971 and 1972 surveys) and for the National Institute on Drug Abuse (1974, 1976, 1977 and 1979 surveys). "Not sure" and "no answer" have been omitted in this table.

Question: ". . . which things are *addictive?* That is, anybody who uses it regularly becomes physically and psychologically dependent on it and can't get along without it."

[Percent*]

Type of substance	Adults (26 and older)					
	1971 (N=1,664)	1972 (N=1,613)	1974 (N=2,221)	1976 (N=1,708)	1977 (N=1,822)	1979 (N=3,015)
Heroin	91.0	86.9	89.3	86.1	85.8	90.7
Alcohol	73.4	74.2	77.6	84.6	86.8	86.9
Marijuana	69.1	63.7	72.6	65.9	63.6	72.2
Tobacco	70.8	66.8	71.5	80.0	83.1	83.5
Barbiturates	**	66.4	69.9	68.0	67.1	75.2
Tranquilizers	**	**	**	**	**	79.1
Amphetamines	**	60.7	62.3	59.7	57.1	69.6
LSD	**	**	**	**	**	73.1
Cocaine	**	73.5	77.2	74.0	71.8	80.7

Type of substance	Young adults (18 to 25)					
	1971 (N=741)	1972 (N=772)	1974 (N=849)	1976 (N=882)	1977 (N=1,500)	1979 (N=2,044)
Heroin	94.9	95.2	95.2	92.1	92.6	92.4
Alcohol	73.9	79.0	81.7	86.9	87.6	90.4
Marijuana	49.3	41.7	49.9	45.8	43.7	50.2
Tobacco	67.4	67.3	74.0	77.5	78.6	81.0
Barbiturates	**	75.3	80.5	73.2	73.7	77.4
Tranquilizers	**	**	**	**	**	79.6
Amphetamines	**	74.0	77.3	62.8	68.2	71.7
LSD	**	**	**	**	**	72.4
Cocaine	**	79.6	83.1	76.3	72.1	75.1

Table 24 (continued)

Type of substance	Youth (12 to 17)					
	1971 (N=781)	1972 (N=880)	1974 (N=952)	1976 (N=986)	1977 (N=1,272)	1979 (N=2,165)
Heroin	85.0	88.0	87.0	86.7	78.0	77.2
Alcohol	69.0	71.0	78.0	83.3	80.9	83.4
Marijuana	48.0	50.0	54.0	54.3	47.3	59.7
Tobacco	58.0	58.0	62.0	61.8	62.4	61.3
Barbiturates	**	72.0	70.0	59.3	49.0	48.1
Tranquilizers	**	**	**	**	**	57.6
Amphetamines	**	67.0	61.0	51.9	40.0	41.9
LSD	**	**	**	**	**	65.2
Cocaine	**	66.0	74.0	72.4	65.4	72.7

*Total may not sum to 100 percent because of multiple responses.
**Not asked this year.

Source: Patricia M. Fishburne, Herbert I. Abelson, and Ira Cisin, *National Survey on Drug Abuse: Main Findings 1979*. U.S. Department of Health and Human Services, National Institute on Drug Abuse (Washington, D.C.: U.S. Government Printing Office, 1980), pp. 166-168. Table adapted.

Table 25
Attitudes Toward the Legalization of Marijuana Use, by Demographic Characteristics, United States, 1973-80

[Percent]

Question: "Do you think the use of marijuana should be made legal or not?"

	1973			1975			1976			1978			1980		
	Should	Should not	Don't know	Should	Should not	Don't know	Should	Should not	Don't know	Should	Should not	Don't know	Should	Should not	Don't know
National	18	80	2	20	75	5	28	69	3	30	67	3	25	72	3
Sex:															
Male	22	75	3	25	69	6	32	64	4	34	63	3	30	67	3
Female	15	83	2	16	80	4	24	73	2	26	71	3	21	76	3
Race:															
White	18	80	2	20	75	4	27	70	3	29	68	3	25	72	3
Nonwhite	18	79	4	22	71	7	33	60	6	38	59	2	27	71	2
Education:															
College	32	66	3	35	59	6	40	56	4	42	55	3	35	61	4
High school	15	83	2	16	79	4	26	70	3	27	70	3	23	75	2
Grade school	6	94	1	5	89	6	11	89	3	13	84	3	8	88	4
Occupation:															
Professional & business	23	74	3	29	65	6	36	60	4	37	60	3	29	68	4
Clerical	15	83	2	20	76	5	26	72	2	27	71	2	23	75	2
Manual	17	81	1	16	79	5	25	71	3	28	68	4	23	74	3
Farmer	13	86	1	16	81	2	19	76	5	24	74	2	12	79	9
Income:															
$15,000 and over	25	72	2	25	71	5	33	64	3	30	67	2	27	70	3
$10,000 to $14,999	14	84	1	19	76	5	26	71	3	33	63	4	25	73	1
$7,000 to $9,999	21	78	1	25	71	4	30	65	5	28	69	3	27	72	2
$5,000 to $6,999	10	89	2	20	78	2	24	73	3	30	67	3	19	76	5
$3,000 to 4,999	16	82	2	13	82	5	28	70	3	26	71	3	15	80	5
Under $3,000	17	80	3	15	80	5	22	77	2	32	67	1	25	69	6

Age:															
18 to 20 years	42	56	2	34	56	10	57	39	4	51	48	2	45	52	4
21 to 29 years	38	60	2	40	54	6	49	48	4	49	49	2	42	56	3
30 to 49 years	14	84	2	18	79	3	25	72	3	29	69	2	27	71	2
50 years and older	9	89	2	9	86	5	16	81	4	16	80	4	13	84	4
Region:															
Northeast	22	74	4	26	70	4	32	64	4	33	62	5	27	70	3
Midwest	20	78	2	20	75	5	25	72	3	26	72	2	20	77	3
South	11	89	**	12	84	5	22	74	4	27	72	2	20	78	2
West	24	73	3	32	63	6	37	61	2	38	59	4	38	57	6
Religion:															
Protestant	14	84	2	15	81	4	22	74	3	24	74	2	20	77	3
Catholic	18	81	1	21	73	6	32	64	3	31	64	6	26	71	3
Jewish	33	67	0	48	48	4	37	63	0	62	38	0	28	62	9
None	52	43	5	53	43	4	54	39	7	64	33	2	60	36	4
Politics:															
Republican	11	87	2	12	86	2	20	78	2	19	80	2	18	80	2
Democrat	17	82	1	19	77	4	26	71	3	29	67	4	24	73	3
Independent	25	72	3	26	67	7	34	62	4	37	60	3	30	66	4

*Percents may not add to 100 because of rounding.

**One-half of 1 percent or less.

Source: Table constructed by SOURCEBOOK staff from data provided by the National Opinion Research Center; data were made available through the Roper Public Opinion Research Center.

Table 26
Attitudes Toward the Treatment of Possession of Small
Amounts of Marijuana as a Criminal Offense,
United States, 1980

Question: "Do you think the possession of small amounts of
marijuana should or should not be treated as a criminal offense?"

[Percent]

	Should be treated as a criminal offense	Should not be treated as a criminal offense	No opinion
National	43	52	6
Sex:			
Male	42	53	5
Female	44	51	5
Race:			
White	25	71	4
Nonwhite	24	65	11
Education:			
College	30	67	3
High school	45	50	5
Grade school	58	33	9
Occupation:			
Professional or business	39	59	2
Clerical and sales	37	55	8
Manual workers	40	56	4
Nonlabor force	55	39	6
Income:			
$25,000 and over	36	62	2
$20,000 to $24,999	44	54	2
$15,000 to $19,999	43	53	4
$10,000 to $14,999	42	53	5
$5,000 to $9,999	46	46	8
Under $5,000	47	44	9
Age:			
Total under 30 years	27	68	5
18 to 24 years	27	67	6
25 to 29 years	26	70	4
30 to 49 years	45	52	3
50 years and older	54	39	7
City size:			
1,000,000 and over	35	60	5
500,000 to 999,999	26	64	10
50,000 to 499,000	44	50	6
2,500 to 49,999	49	48	3
Under 2,500 rural	52	44	4

Table 26 (continued)

	Should be treated as a criminal offense	Should not be treated as a criminal offense	No opinion
Region:			
East	43	52	5
Midwest	40	54	6
South	51	45	4
West	33	60	7
Religion:			
Protestant	49	47	4
Catholic	39	55	6
Politics:			
Republican	49	46	5
Democrat	47	49	4
Independent	33	63	4

Source: George H. Gallup, *The Gallup Opinion Index,* Report No. 179 (Princeton, N.J.: The Gallup Poll, July 1980), p. 15. Reprinted by permission.

Table 27
Attitudes Toward a Law Forbidding the Sale of Beer, Wine and Liquor, by Demographic Characteristics, United States, 1981
Question: "Would you favor or oppose a law forbidding
the sale of all beer, wine and liquor throughout the nation?"

[Percent]

	Favor a law forbidding sale	Oppose a law forbidding sale	Not sure
National	17	80	3
Sex:			
Male	15	83	2
Female	19	77	4
Race:			
White	17	81	2
Nonwhite	20	74	6
Education:			
College	9	90	1
High school	18	79	3
Grade school	28	66	6
Occupation:			
Professional and business ..	12	86	2
Clerical and sales	17	80	3
Manual workers	21	76	3
Nonlabor force	18	80	2
Income:			
$25,000 and over	9	90	1
$20,000 to $24,999	13	85	2
$15,000 to $19,999	18	80	2
$10,000 to $14,999	19	79	2
$5,000 to $9,999	21	74	5
Under $5,000	33	57	10
Age:			
Total under 30 years	17	82	1
18 to 24 years	17	81	2
25 to 29 years	17	83	0
30 to 49 years	17	79	4
50 years and older	17	80	3
City size:			
1,000,000 and over	14	82	4
500,000 to 999,999	14	84	2
50,000 to 499,999	13	85	2
2,500 to 49,999	22	76	2
Under 2,500 rural	21	75	4

Table 27 (continued)

	Favor a law forbidding sale	Oppose a law forbidding sale	Not sure
Region:			
East	10	86	4
Midwest	17	82	1
South	25	71	4
West	17	81	2
Religion:			
Protestant	21	76	3
Catholic	11	85	4
Politics:			
Republican	18	79	3
Democrat	18	79	3
Independent	17	81	2

Source: George H. Gallup, *The Gallup Report,* Report No. 186 (Princeton, N.J.: The Gallup Poll, March, 1981), p. 36. Reprinted by permission.

Table 28
Respondents Favoring Stricter Drunk Driving
Laws and Mandatory Jail Sentences
for First Offenders, by Region, United States, 1982

Questions: "Do you think that there should or should not
be stricter laws regarding drinking and driving?"
"In some states, drunk drivers convicted of a
first offense are required to serve a mandatory two-day
jail sentence. Would you like to see such a law
in this state, or not?"

Region	Percent favoring stricter drunk driving laws	Percent favoring two-day jail sentence for first offense drunk drivers
National	89	77
East	92	76
Midwest	91	78
South	87	77
West	86	82

Source: George H. Gallup, *The Gallup Poll* (Princeton, N.J.: The Gallup Poll, April 22, 1982), pp. 1, 2. Reprinted by permission.

Table 29
Reported Alcohol Use and Most Recent Use Among High School Seniors, by Sex, Region, Population Density, and College Plans, United States, 1980

Note: These data are from a series of nationwide surveys of high school seniors conducted by the Institute for Social Reseach for the National Institute on Drug Abuse from 1975 through 1980. The survey design is a multistage random sample of high school seniors in public and private schools. Depending on the survey years, from 66 to 80 percent of the schools initially invited to participate agreed to do so. Completed questionnaires were obtained from 77 to 83 percent of all sampled students in participating schools each year. All percentages reported are based on weighted cases. The N's shown in the tables refer to the approximate number (i.e. rounded to the nearest hundred) of unweighted cases. These data were derived from the questions indicated below.

Question: "On how many occasions have you had alcoholic beverages to drink in your lifetime? On how many occasions have you had alcoholic beverages to drink during the last 12 months? On how many occasions have you had alcoholic beverages to drink during the last 30 days?"
[Percent]

			Most recent use		
	Never used	Ever used	Within last 30 days	Within last 12 months but not last 30 days	Not within last 12 months
All seniors (N = 15,900)	6.8	93.2	72.0	15.9	5.3
Sex:					
Male	5.5	94.5	77.4	12.2	4.9
Female	8.0	92.0	68.8	17.4	5.8
Region:					
Northeast	3.6	96.4	79.4	13.7	3.3
North Central	5.0	95.0	75.1	15.2	4.7
South	10.1	89.9	65.5	16.7	7.7
West	8.6	91.4	67.6	18.6	5.2
Population density:					
Large SMSA*	3.9	96.1	78.0	14.3	3.8
Other SMSA*	7.3	92.7	70.8	16.4	5.5
Non-SMSA*	8.5	91.5	69.0	16.4	6.1
College plans:					
None or under 4 years	6.5	93.5	73.5	14.7	5.3
Complete 4 years	6.9	93.1	70.8	16.9	5.4

*Large SMSAs include the 12 largest Standard Statistical Metropolitan Areas as of the 1970 census: New York, Los Angeles, Chicago, Philadelphia, Detroit, San Francisco, Washington, Boston, Pittsburgh, St. Louis, Baltimore, and Cleveland.

Other SMSAs include all other Standard Statistical Metropolitan Areas excluding the 12 above. Except in the New England States, an SMSA is a county or group of contiguous counties that contains at least one city of 50,000 inhabitants or more, or "twin cities" with a combined population of at least 50,000. In the New England States, SMSAs consist of towns and cities instead of counties.

Non-SMSAs include all areas not designated as Standard Metropolitan Statistical Areas. The population living outside SMSAs constitutes the nonmetropolitan population.

Source: Lloyd D. Johnston, Jerald G. Bachman, and Patrick M. O'Malley, *Highlights from Student Drug Use, 1975-1980.* U.S. Department of Health and Human Services, National Institute on Drug Abuse (Washington, D.C.: U.S. Government Printing Office, 1981), pp. 20, 22, 24. Table adapted.

Table 30
Reported Drug Use Within Last 12 Months
Among High School Seniors, by Type of Drug, United States, 1975-80

Note: See *Note* Table 29. Data for the categories "inhalants" and "hallucinogens" are underestimated because some users of amyl and butyl nitrites, and PCP fail to report in these drug categories. The 1979 and 1980 surveys address this issue by asking specific questions about amyl and butyl nitrites (inhalants) and PCP (a hallucinogen) on one survey alternate form, representing approximately one-fifth of the total yearly sample. These data were then used to adjust the 1979 and 1980 data for underreporting in these drug categories.

Question: "On how many occasions, if any, have you used . . . in the last 12 months?"

Type of drug	Percent who used in last 12 months					
	Class of 1975 (N=9,400)	Class of 1976 (N=15,400)	Class of 1977 (N=17,100)	Class of 1978 (N=17,800)	Class of 1979 (N=15,500)	Class of 1980 (N=15,900)
Marijuana/hashish	40.0	44.5	47.6	50.2	50.8	48.8
Inhalants	NA	3.0	3.7	4.1	5.4	4.6
Adjusted	NA	NA	NA	NA	9.2	7.8
Amyl and butyl nitrites	NA	NA	NA	NA	6.5	5.7
Hallucinogens	11.2	9.4	8.8	9.6	9.9	9.3
Adjusted	NA	NA	NA	NA	12.8	10.6
LSD	7.2	6.4	5.5	6.3	6.6	6.5
PCP	NA	NA	NA	NA	7.0	4.4
Cocaine	5.6	6.0	7.2	9.0	12.0	12.3
Heroin	1.0	0.8	0.8	0.8	0.5	0.5
Other opiates*	5.7	5.7	6.4	6.0	6.2	6.3
Stimulants*	16.2	15.8	16.3	17.1	18.3	20.8
Sedatives*	11.7	10.7	10.8	9.9	9.9	10.3
Barbiturates*	10.7	9.6	9.3	8.1	7.5	6.8
Methaqualone*	5.1	4.7	5.2	4.9	5.9	7.2
Tranquilizers*	10.6	10.3	10.8	9.9	9.6	8.7
Alcohol	84.8	85.7	87.0	87.7	88.1	87.9
Cigarettes	NA	NA	NA	NA	NA	NA

*Only drug use that was not under a doctor's order is included here.

Source: LLoyd D. Johnston, Jerald G. Bachman, and Patrick M. O'Malley, *Highlights from Student Drug Use in America, 1975-1980,* U.S. Department of Health and Human Services, National Institute on Drug Abuse (Washington, D.C.: U.S. Government Printing Office, 1981), p. 29.

Table 31
Reported Drug Use Within Last 30 days
Among High School Seniors, by Type of Drug, United States, 1975-80

Note: See *Note* Tables 29 and 30.

Question: "On how many occasions, if any, have you used . . . during the last 30 days?"

	Percent who used in last 30 days					
Type of drug	Class of 1975 (N = 9,400)	Class of 1976 (N = 15,400)	Class of 1977 (N = 17,100)	Class of 1978 (N = 17,800)	Class of 1979 (N = 15,500)	Class of 1980 (N = 15,900)
Marijuana/hashish	27.1	32.2	35.4	37.1	36.5	33.7
Inhalants	NA	0.9	1.3	1.5	1.7	1.4
Adjusted	NA	NA	NA	NA	3.1	2.7
Amyl and butyl nitrites	NA	NA	NA	NA	2.4	1.8
Hallucinogens	4.7	3.4	4.1	3.9	4.0	3.7
Adjusted	NA	NA	NA	NA	5.5	4.4
LSD	2.3	1.9	2.1	2.1	2.4	2.3
PCP	NA	NA	NA	NA	2.4	1.4
Cocaine	1.9	2.0	2.9	3.9	5.7	5.2
Heroin	0.4	0.2	0.3	0.3	0.2	0.2
Other opiates*	2.1	2.0	2.8	2.1	2.4	2.4
Stimulants*	8.5	7.7	8.8	8.7	9.9	12.1
Sedatives*	5.4	4.5	5.1	4.2	4.4	4.8
Barbiturates*	4.7	3.9	4.3	3.2	3.2	2.9
Methaqualone*	2.1	1.6	2.3	1.9	2.3	3.3
Tranquilizers*	4.1	4.0	4.6	3.4	3.7	3.1
Alcohol	68.2	68.3	71.2	72.1	71.8	72.0
Cigarettes	36.7	38.8	38.4	36.7	34.4	30.5

*Only drug use that was not under a doctor's order is included here.

Source: LLoyd D. Johnston, Jerald G. Bachman, and Patrick M. O'Malley, *Highlights from Student Drug Use in America, 1975-1980,* U.S. Department of Health and Human Services, National Institute on Drug Abuse (Washington, D.C.: U.S. Government Printing Office, 1981), p. 30.

Table 32
Reported Marijuana, Hashish, Cocaine, and Heroin Use
and Most Recent Use Among High School Seniors, by Sex, Region,
Population Density, and College Plans, United States, 1980.

Note: See *Note* Table 29.

Question: "On how many occasions, if any, have you had
(marijuana/hashish, cocaine, heroin) in your lifetime?
On how many occasions, if any, have you had (marijuana/hashish,
cocaine, heroin) in the last 12 months? On how many occasions, if any,
have you had (marijuana, hashish, cocaine, heroin) in the last 30 days?"

[Percent]

| | | | MARIJUANA/HASHISH | | |
| | | | Most recent use | | |
	Never used	**Ever used**	**Within last 30 days**	**Within last 12 months, but not last 30 days**	**Not within last 12 months**
All seniors (N = 15,900)	39.7	60.3	33.7	15.1	11.5
Sex:					
Male	35.6	64.4	37.8	15.6	11.0
Female	43.9	56.1	29.1	15.0	12.0
Region:					
Northeast	32.6	67.4	39.3	16.2	11.9
North Central	39.8	60.2	34.0	14.9	11.3
South	46.4	53.6	28.4	13.6	11.6
West	37.1	62.9	35.2	16.5	11.2
Population density:					
Large SMSA	32.1	67.9	39.6	16.7	11.6
Other SMSA	39.0	61.0	34.5	15.3	11.2
Non-SMSA	46.1	53.9	28.3	13.6	12.0
College plans:					
None or under 4 years	35.7	64.3	37.7	14.0	12.6
Complete 4 years	43.2	56.8	29.4	16.5	10.9

Table 32 (continued)
Reported Marijuana, Hashish, Cocaine, and Heroin Use
and Most Recent Use Among High School Seniors, by Sex, Region,
Population Density, and College Plans, United States, 1980.

Note: See *Note* Table 29.

Question: "On how many occasions, if any, have you had
(marijuana/hashish, cocaine, heroin) in your lifetime?
On how many occasions, if any, have you had (marijuana/hashish,
cocaine, heroin) in the last 12 months? On how many occasions, if any,
have you had (marijuana, hashish, cocaine, heroin) in the last 30 days?"

[Percent]

	COCAINE				
			Most recent use		
	Never used	Ever used	Within last 30 days	Within last 12 months, but not last 30 days	Not within last 12 months
All seniors (N = 15,900)	84.3	15.7	5.2	7.1	3.4
Sex:					
Male	81.6	18.4	6.0	8.8	3.6
Female	87.2	12.8	4.3	5.5	3.0
Region:					
Northeast	82.1	17.9	5.4	8.8	3.7
North Central	86.0	14.0	4.4	6.5	3.1
South	89.1	10.9	3.2	4.6	3.1
West	75.4	24.6	10.2	10.4	4.0
Population density:					
Large SMSA	77.5	22.5	7.6	11.1	3.8
Other SMSA	85.0	15.0	4.7	6.6	3.7
Non-SMSA	88.4	11.6	4.2	4.7	2.7
College plans:					
None or under 4 years	82.4	17.6	5.9	7.3	4.4
Complete 4 years	86.8	13.2	4.2	6.6	2.4

Table 32 (continued)

	Never used	**Ever used**	**Within last 30 days**	**Within last 12 months, but not last 30 days**	**Not within last 12 months**
			HEROIN		
			Most recent use		
All seniors (N = 15,900)	98.9	1.1	0.2	0.3	0.6
Sex:					
Male	98.7	1.3	0.3	0.3	0.7
Female	99.1	0.9	0.1	0.3	0.5
Region:					
Northeast	98.8	1.2	0.2	0.3	0.7
North Central	98.7	1.3	0.4	0.3	0.6
South	98.9	1.1	0.1	0.2	0.8
West	99.3	0.7	0.2	0.2	0.3
Population density:					
Large SMSA	99.2	0.8	0.3	0.0	0.5
Other SMSA	98.8	1.2	0.2	0.3	0.7
Non-SMSA	98.8	1.2	0.2	0.4	0.6
College plans:					
None or under 4 years	98.5	1.5	0.3	0.3	0.9
Complete 4 years	99.3	0.7	0.1	0.2	0.4

Source: Lloyd D. Johnston, Jerald G. Bachman, and Patrick M. O'Malley, *Highlights from Student Drug Use, 1975-1980,* U.S. Department of Health and Human Services, National Institute on Drug Abuse (Washington, D.C.: U.S. Government Printing Office, 1981), pp. 20, 22, 24. Table adapted.

Table 33
Reported Drug Use Among Adults, Young Adults, and Youth, by Type of Drug, United States, Selected Years 1972-79

Note: These data are based on six nationwide sample surveys conducted by the Response Analysis Corporation for the National Commission on Marihuana and Drug Abuse (1971 and 1972 surveys) and for the National Institute on Drug Abuse (1974, 1976, 1977 and 1979 surveys). The data in this table were derived from any positive response to the questions listed below. For the years prior to 1979 the data reported for marijuana refer only to marijuana use. For 1979, the data reported for marijuana refer to marijuana and/or hashish use.

Questions: "About how old were you when you first tried a cigarette?
Did you ever take (sedatives, tranquilizers, stimulants, analgesics)
just to see what it was like and how it would work;
just to enjoy the feeling they give you;
for some *other* nonmedical reason, and not because you needed it?
When was the most *recent* time that you used (marijuana or hashish,
inhalants, LSD or other hallucinogens, cocaine, heroin)?
When was the most *recent* time you had a drink?"

[Percent reporting ever used drug]

Type of drug	Adults (26 and older)				
	1972 (N=1,613)	1974 (N=2,221)	1976 (N=1,708)	1977 (N=1,822)	1979 (N=3,015)
Marijuana	7.4	9.9	12.9	15.3	19.6
Inhalants	*	1.2	1.9	1.8	3.9
Hallucinogens	*	1.3	1.6	2.6	4.5
Cocaine	1.6	0.9	1.6	2.6	4.3
Heroin	**	0.5	0.5	0.8	1.0
Stimulants***	3.0	3.0	5.6	4.7	5.8
Sedatives	2.0	2.0	2.4	2.8	3.5
Tranquilizers***	5.0	2.0	2.7	2.6	3.1
Analgesics	****	****	****	****	2.7
Alcohol	****	73.2	74.7	77.9	91.5
Cigarettes	****	65.4	64.5	67.0	83.0

Type of drug	Young Adults (18 to 25)				
	1972 (N=722)	1974 (N=849)	1976 (N=882)	1977 (N=1,500)	1979 (N=2,044)
Marijuana	47.9	52.7	52.9	59.9	68.2
Inhalants	*	9.2	9.0	11.2	16.5
Hallucinogens	*	16.6	17.3	19.8	25.1
Cocaine	9.1	12.7	13.4	19.1	27.5
Heroin	4.6	4.5	3.9	3.6	3.5
Stimulants(c)	12.0	17.0	16.6	21.2	18.2
Sedatives	10.0	15.0	11.9	18.4	17.0
Tranquilizers***	7.0	10.0	9.1	13.4	15.8
Analgesics	****	****	****	****	11.8
Alcohol	****	81.6	83.6	84.2	95.3
Cigarettes	****	68.8	70.1	67.6	82.8

Table 33 (continued)

Type of drug	Youth (12 to 17)				
	1972 (N=880)	1974 (N=952)	1976 (N=986)	1977 (N=1,272)	1979 (N=2,165)
Marijuana	14.0	23.0	22.4	28.0	30.9
Inhalants	6.4	8.5	8.1	9.0	9.8
Hallucinogens	4.8	6.0	5.1	4.6	7.1
Cocaine	1.5	3.6	3.4	4.0	5.4
Heroin	0.6	1.0	0.5	1.1	0.5
Stimulants***	4.0	5.0	4.4	5.2	3.4
Sedatives***	3.0	5.0	2.8	3.1	3.2
Tranquilizers***	3.0	3.0	3.3	3.8	4.1
Analgesics	****	****	****	****	3.2
Alcohol	****	54.0	53.6	52.6	70.3
Cigarettes	****	52.0	45.5	47.3	54.1

*Not tabulated in this year
**Less than 0.5 percent
***1977 estimates based on split samples: adults (N=897), young adults (N=750), youth (N=623).
****Not asked this year.

Source: Patricia M. Fishburne, Herbert I. Abelson, and Ira Cisin, *National Survey on Drug Abuse: Main Findings 1979,* U.S. Department of Health and Human Services, National Institute on Drug Abuse (Washington, D.C.: U.S. Government Printing Office, 1980), pp. 32-34. Table adapted.

Table 34
Reported Drug Use Among Adults, Young Adults, and Youth by Type of Drug and Use of Alcohol, United States, 1979

Note: See *Note* Table 33. These data were constructed by combining the questions below into the four categories shown in the table. The "current drinkers" category was derived from any positive response to the question about alcohol use.

**Questions: "When was the most *recent* time you had a drink?
Did you ever take (barbiturates and other sedatives, tranquilizers,
amphetamines and other stimulants, analgesics) just to see what
it was like and how it would work; just to enjoy the feeling they give you,
or for some *other* nonmedical reason, and not because you needed it?
When was the most *recent* time you used (marijuana or hashish,
LSD or other hallucinogens, cocaine, heroin)?"**

(Percent reporting ever used drug)

(26 and over)	Adults (18 to 25)		Young Adults (12 to 17)		Youth	
Type of drug	Current drinkers (N=1,806)	Not current drinkers (N=1,209)	Current drinkers (N=1,491)	Not current drinkers (N=553)	Current drinkers (N=829)	Not current drinkers (N=1,336)
Ever used psychotherapeutic pill for nonmedical reason*:						
Yes	12.4	4.2	35.3	11.2	16.5	1.8
No	87.6	95.8	64.7	88.8	83.5	98.2
Ever used marijuana and/or hashish:						
Yes	28.2	6.1	77.2	39.9	60.6	13.3
No	71.8	93.9	22.8	60.1	39.4	86.7
Ever used hallucinogens, cocaine, heroin:						
Yes	8.7	2.4	39.8	12.6	20.2	2.0
No	91.3	97.6	60.2	87.4	79.8	98.0

*Questions on the nonmedical use of prescription psychotherapeutic drugs were on an interview schedule that was administered to a random half of the households.

Source: Patricia M. Fishburne, Herbert I. Abelson, and Ira Cisin, *National Survey on Drug Abuse: Main Findings 1979*, U.S. Department of Health and Human Services, National Institute on Drug Abuse (Washington, D.C.: U.S. Government Printing Office, 1980), p. 97.

Table 35
Reported Marijuana Use and Use in Past Month, Among Adults by Demographic Characteristics, United States, 1976, 1977 and 1979

Note: See *Note* Table 33. The "ever used" column reports data on those who reported any past experience with drugs.

Question: "When was the most recent time you used marijuana, hashish?"

[Percent]

	Ever Used			Use in past month		
	1976	1977	1979	1976	1977	1979
All adults (26 and older)	12.9	15.3	19.6	3.5	3.3	6.0
Sex:						
Male	19	21	26	6	4	9
Female	7	10	14	2	2	3
Race:						
White	12	15	19	3	3	6
Nonwhite	17	20	26	6	4	8
Education:						
Not high school graduate	6	6	9	1	1	3
High school graduate	12	16	18	3	3	5
College	20	25	30	6	7	10
Not a graduate	16	26	27	5	9	9
Graduate	24	24	33	7	4	11
Region:						
Northeast	16	19	20	5	5	7
North Central	10	14	16	2	3	4
South	10	9	18	3	1	5
West	18	23	27	4	5	9
Population density:						
Large metropolitan	19	20	23	5	5	8
Small metropolitan	12	16	21	4	3	6
Nonmetropolitan	7	9	14	1	1	4
Rural	*	*	13	*	*	3
2,500 to 24,999	*	*	13	*	*	3
2,499 or less	*	*	13	*	*	3

*Not tabulated this year.

Source: Patricia M. Fishburne, Herbert I. Abelson, and Ira Cisin, *National Survey on Drug Abuse: Main Findings, 1979,* U.S. Department of Health and Human Services, National Institute on Drug Abuse (Washington, D.C.: U.S. Government Printing Office, 1980), pp. 52, 56. Table adapted.

Table 36
Reported Marijuana Use and Use in Past Month, Among Young Adults
by Demographic Characteristics, United States, 1976, 1977 and 1979

Note: See *Note* Table 33. The "ever used" column reports data on those who reported any past experience with drugs.

Question: "When was the most recent time you used marijuana, hashish?"

[Percent]

	Ever Used			Use in past month		
	1976	1977	1979	1976	1977	1979
All young adults (18 to 25)	52.9	59.9	68.2	25.0	27.4	35.4
Sex:						
Male	62	66	75	31	35	45
Female	44	55	61	19	20	26
Race:						
White	55	61	69	26	28	36
Nonwhite	48	55	62	22	24	34
Education:						
Not high school graduate	48	52		23	21	41
High school graduate	50	60	65	21	29	30
College	60	65	73	32	30	38
Not a graduate	57	66	74	33	32	40
Graduate	68	58	69	28	22	33
Now a full-time college student	62	63	64	32	31	37
Region:						
Northeast	60	66	71	26	34	40
North Central	54	61	72	27	29	38
South	42	50	61	18	17	30
West	64	67	71	35	33	36
Population density:						
Large metropolitan	59	63	73	29	31	39
Small metropolitan	59	64	68	28	29	36
Nonmetropolitan	38	48	61	16	18	30
Rural	*	*	60	*	*	28
2,500 to 24,999	*	*	68	*	*	37
2,499 or less	*	*	54	*	*	23

*Not tabulated this year.

Source: Patricia M. Fishburne, Herbert I. Abelson, and Ira Cisin, *National Survey on Drug Abuse: Main Findings, 1979,* U.S. Department of Health and Human Services, National Institute on Drug Abuse (Washington, D.C.: U.S. Government Printing Office, 1980), pp. 51, 55. Table adapted.

Table 37
Reported Marijuana Use and Use in Past Month, Among Youth, by Demographic Characteristics, United States, Selected Years 1971-79

Note: See *Note* Table 33. The "ever used" column reports data on those who reported any past experience with drugs.

Question: "When was the most *recent* time you used marijuana, hashish?"

[Percent]

	Ever Used					
	1971	**1972**	**1974**	**1976**	**1977**	**1979**
All youths (12 to 17)	14.0	14.0	23.0	22.4	28.0	30.9
Sex:						
Male	14	15	24	26	33	34
Female	14	13	21	19	23	28
Race:						
White	15	16	24	22	29	31
Nonwhite	12	5	17	22	25	31
Region:						
Northeast	16	16	26	21	35	34
North Central	13	14	21	26	29	34
South	7	8	17	16	19	24
West	26	24	30	30	35	36
Population density:						
Large metropolitan	15	19	27	25	36	36
Small metropolitan	15	18	22	24	28	28
Nonmetropolitan	13	7	18	18	18	27
Rural	*	*	*	*	*	27
2,500 to 24,999	*	*	*	*	*	28
2,499 or less	*	*	*	*	*	26

Table 37 (continued)
Reported Marijuana Use and Use in Past Month, Among Youth, by Demographic Characterlstlcs, United States, Selected Years 1971-79

Note: See *Note* Table 33. The "ever used" column reports data on those who reported any past experience with drugs.

Question: "When was the most *recent* time you used marijuana, hashish?"

[Percent]

	Use in past month					
	1971	1972	1974	1976	1977	1979
All youths (12 to 17)	6.0	7.0	12.0	12.3	16.6	16.7
Sex:						
Male	7	9	12	14	20	19
Female	5	6	11	11	13	14
Race:						
White	*	8	12	12	17	17
Nonwhite	*	2	9	11	14	15
Region:						
Northeast	9	7	14	13	22	20
North Central	5	7	11	16	20	19
South	2	4	6	7	8	12
West	11	14	19	17	22	16
Population density:						
Large metropolitan	9	*	14	18	22	20
Small metropolitan	7	*	11	11	17	14
Nonmetropolitan	3	*	10	8	10	15
Rural	*	*	*	*	*	14
2,500 to 24,999	*	*	*	*	*	17
2,499 or less	*	*	*	*	*	13

*Not tabulated this year.

Source: Patricia M. Fishburne, Herbert I. Abelson, and Ira Cisin, *National Survey on Drug Abuse: Main Findings, 1979,* U.S. Department of Health and Human Services, National Institute on Drug Abuse (Washington, D.C.: U.S. Government Printing Office, 1980), pp. 50, 54. Table adapted.

Table 38
Sources of Drugs

HEROIN IMPORTATION	
Burma, Thailand, Laos	15%
Pakistan, Iran, Afghanistan	60%
Mexico	25%

MARIJUANA IMPORTATION	
Colombia	75%
Jamaica	10%
Mexico	8%
Domestic	7%

COCAINE IMPORTATION	
South America	100%

Source: Drug Enforcement Administration, *Drug Enforcement Summer 1982* (Washington, D.C.: U.S. Department of Justice). Adapted.

Table 39
Growth of Cocaine Abuse:
Estimated Coca Production in Metric Tons

Major indicators have reflected a persistent, and at times marked, growth in abuse and availability of cocaine in the United States since 1976. Likewise, cocaine availability is increasing in all source countries in South America, which will ensure a steady supply to the United States and other consumer countries in the near future.

	1980	1981
Peru	50,000	50,000
Bolivia	52,500	55,000
Colombia	2,000	3,000

Source: Drug Enforcement Administration, *Drug Enforcement Fall 1982* (Washington, D.C.: U.S. Department of Justice).

Table 40
Growth of Cocaine Abuse:
Retail Price and Purity Index per Gram

Retail prices and purities showed little long-range change from 1977 to 1981. This becomes more apparent when inflation and the rise in the consumer price index during this period is taken into consideration:

Year	Price	Purity %
1977	$570-720	12.2
1978	$590-650	12.5
1979	$570-780	11.5
1980	$630-710	12.5
1981	$630-700	11.8

Source: Drug Enforcement Administration, *Drug Enforcement Fall 1982* (Washington, D.C.: U.S. Department of Justice).

Table 41
Growth of Cocaine Abuse:
Estimate of Illicit Cocaine Entering United States in 1981 (in Tons)

Estimated maximum illicit cocaine hydrochloride theoretically available for world use:	140-172
Less cocaine hydrochloride not converted because of inefficient production methods, crop loss, excessive cultivation, spoilage, loss in transit, pilferage, eradication, and seizure of prime materials:	90
Subtotal:	50-82
Less amount seized worldwide:	8
Subtotal:	42-74
Less cocaine hydrochloride exported to third countries (Europe, Canada and Latin America):	12
Range of cocaine hydrochloride estimated to enter the U.S. market:	30-62

Source: Drug Enforcement Administration, *Drug Enforcement Fall 1982* (Washington, D.C.: U.S. Department of Justice).

Table 42
Growth of Cocaine Abuse:
Cocaine Injuries, Deaths and
Treatment Admissions

Major indicators reflect continued widespread availability and abuse of cocaine in the United States. During the first half of 1981, national cocaine injuries averaged 837 per quarter. This represents a 50 percent increase over the 1979 quarterly average and an increase of more than 110 percent over 1977 figures:

National Cocaine Injuries
(Quarterly Average)

Year	Number of Injuries
1977	397
1978	479
1979	557
1980	808
1981	866

National Cocaine Deaths

Year	Number of Deaths
1979	58
1980	96
1981	96 (estimated 1981)

Treatment Admissions

Treatment admissions during the same period also show an increase for cocaine admissions as a primary drug of abuse. This figure rose in 1981 to 3,393 per quarter, from 946 per quarter in 1977, an increase of more than 350 percent.

Cocaine Federally Funded Drug Treatment
Admissions (Quarterly Average)

Year	Number of Admissions
1977	946
1978	1,361
1979	1,961
1980	2,620
1981	3,393 (Based on first half of CY 1981)

Regional Cocaine Injuries
(Quarterly Average)

Cocaine has manifested significant long-range increases in abuse and availability in all geographic areas of the country. This phenomenon suggests an appeal to a broader sociological segment of the U.S. population than is the case with most abused substances. The following table indicates how these increases were consistent throughout most of the nation during 1977-1981:

	1977	1978	1979	1980	1981
Northeast	234	286	277	468	479
Southeast	58	78	108	118	90
North Central	58	60	85	95	103
South Central	8	13	24	24	39
West	41	44	63	105	155

Source: Drug Enforcement Administration, *Drug Enforcement Fall 1982* (Washington, D.C.: U.S. Department of Justice).

Table 43
Growth of Cocaine Abuse:
Theoretical Maximum Cocaine Available
from Coca Leaf Produced in Peru and
Bolivia

PERU

1. Annual Production

50,000	hectares under cultivation
× 1,000	kilos per hectare

50,000,000	kilos of leaf

2. Accountable Stocks:

12,000,000	kilos for chewing
UNKNOWN	kilos exported worldwide
+ 2,000,000	domestic use accountable

14,000,000	kilos accountable

3. Potential Unaccountable Stocks:

50,000,000	kilos of leaf
− 14,000,000	kilos accountable

36,000,000	kilos potentially unaccountable

BOLIVIA

1. Annual Production:

35,000	hectares under cultivation
× 1,500	kilos per hectare

55,000,000	kilos of leaf (rounded)

2. Accountable Stocks:

15,530,000	kilos for chewing
2,000,000	kilos exported worldwide
+ UNKNOWN	

17,530,000	kilos annually accountable

3. Potential Unaccountable Stocks:

55,000,000	kilos of leaf
− 16,000,000	kilos accountable

39,000,000	kilos potentially unaccountable

4. Reduction to Cocaine Hydrochloride:

A. Coca leaf to Coca Paste (Reduction Factor = 200:1)

36,000,000 kilos of leaf = 180,000 kilos paste

39,000,000 kilos of leaf = 195,000 kilos paste

B. Paste to Cocaine Hydrochloride (Reduction Factor = 2.5:1)

180,000 kilos paste = 72,000 kilos of cocaine

195,000 kilos paste = 78,000 kilos of cocaine

72 metric tons + 78 metric tons = 150 metric tons of cocaine hydrochloride

150,000 metric tons + 6 metric tons from Colombia leaf = 156 metric tons of cocaine hydrochloride

5. Allowing 10 percent margin of error each way, the 156 metric tons theoretical maximum of cocaine hydrochloride available from coca leaf produced in Peru and Bolivia produces a range of 140 to 170 metric tons.

Source: Drug Enforcement Administration, *Drug Enforcement Fall 1982* (Washington, D.C.: U.S. Department of Justice).

Table 44
Cocaine Prices at Successive Stages
of Trafficking (1980)

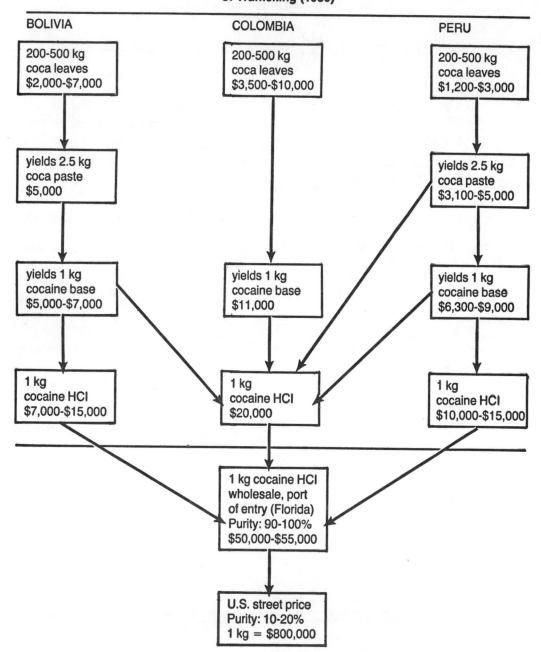

BOLIVIA

200-500 kg
coca leaves
$2,000-$7,000

yields 2.5 kg
coca paste
$5,000

yields 1 kg
cocaine base
$5,000-$7,000

1 kg
cocaine HCl
$7,000-$15,000

COLOMBIA

200-500 kg
coca leaves
$3,500-$10,000

yields 1 kg
cocaine base
$11,000

1 kg
cocaine HCl
$20,000

PERU

200-500 kg
coca leaves
$1,200-$3,000

yields 2.5 kg
coca paste
$3,100-$5,000

yields 1 kg
cocaine base
$6,300-$9,000

1 kg
cocaine HCl
$10,000-$15,000

1 kg cocaine HCl
wholesale, port
of entry (Florida)
Purity: 90-100%
$50,000-$55,000

U.S. street price
Purity: 10-20%
1 kg = $800,000

Note: All prices are in terms of undiluted product. Prevailing purities at distribution levels are indicated merely for convenience.

Source: Drug Enforcement Administration, *Drug Enforcement Fall 1982* (Washington, D.C.: U.S. Department of Justice).

Table 45
Federal Trafficking Penalties

CSA Schedule	Type of Drug	First Offence			Second Offence		
		Max. Imprison.	Max. Fine.	Min. Parole.	Max. Imprison.	Max. Fine.	Min. Parole.
I	Narcotic	15 yrs	$25,000	3 yrs	30 yrs	$50,000	6 yrs
	Non-narcotic	5 yrs	15,000	2 yrs	10 yrs	30,000	4 yrs
II	Narcotic	15 yrs	25,000	3 yrs	30 yrs	50,000	6 yrs
	Non-narcotic	5 yrs	15,000	2 yrs	10 yrs	30,000	4 yrs
III	Narcotic	5 yrs	15,000	2 yrs	10 yrs	30,000	4 yrs
	Non-narcotic	5 yrs	15,000	2 yrs	10 yrs	30,000	4 yrs
IV	Narcotic	3 yrs	10,000	1 yr	6 yrs	20,000	2 yrs
	Non-narcotic	3 yrs	10,000	1 yr	6 yrs	20,000	2 yrs
V	Narcotic	1 yr	5,000	0	2 yrs	10,000	0
	Non-narcotic	1 yr	5,000	0	2 yrs	10,000	0

For simple possession of any controlled substance: First offenders may receive up to one year, $5,000 fine, or both, and if under 21 may receive up to one-year probation and thereafter motion court for expungement of all records; second offenders may receive up to two years, $10,000 fine, or both.

Source: Drug Enforcement Administration, *Drug Enforcement Fall 1982* (Washington, D.C.: U.S. Department of Justice).

Table 46
Regulatory Requirements

Schedule	Registration	Recordkeeping	Distribution Restrictions	Dispensing Limits	Security	Manufacturing Quotas	Import/Export Narcotic/ Non-narcotic	Manfacturer/Distributor Reports to DEA Narcotic/Non-narcotic
I	required	separate	order forms	research use only	vault/safe	yes	permit/permit	yes/yes
II	required	separate	order forms	Rx: written, no refills	vault/safe	yes	permit/permit	yes/yes
III	required	readily retrievable	records required	Rx: written or oral with medical authorization, refills up to 5 in 6 months	secure storage area	NO but some drugs limited by Schedule II quotas	permit/declaration	yes/no
IV	required	readily retrievable	records required	Rx: written or oral with medical authorization, refills up to 5 in 6 months	secure storage area	NO but some drugs may be limited by Schedule I & II	permit/declaration	Manufacturer only/no
V	required	readily retrievable	records required	OTC (Rx drugs limited to M.D.'s order)	secure storage area	NO but some drugs limited by Schedule II	permit to import, declaration to export/declaration quotas	Manufacturer only/no

Source: Drug Enforcement Administration, *Drug Enforcement Fall 1982* (Washington, D.C.: U.S. Department of Justice).

Table 47
Drug thefts, by type of drug and region, 1976-81

Note: Registered handlers of controlled substances (pharmacies, practitioners, manufacturers and hospitals) are required, under the Controlled Substances Act, to report the theft of all controlled drugs to the Drug Enforcement Administration. This table includes drug thefts reported by these registered handlers.

The states included in the regions are as follows: Northeast—Connecticut, Delaware, Maine, Massachusetts, New Hampshire, New Jersey, New York, Pennsylvania, Rhode Island, Vermont; Southeast—Alabama, Arkansas, District of Columbia, Florida, Georgia, Louisiana, Maryland, Mississippi, North Carolina, South Carolina, Tennessee, Virginia; North Central—Illinois, Indiana, Iowa, Kansas, Kentucky, Michigan, Minnesota, Missouri, Nebraska, North Dakota, Ohio, South Dakota, West Virginia, Wisconsin; South Central—Arizona, Colorado, New Mexico, Oklahoma, Texas, Utah, Wyoming; West—Alaska, California, Hawaii, Idaho, Montana, Nevada, Oregon, Washington.

Drug theft data for 1981 are not available by geographic area.

(In thousands of dosage units)

Type of drug and region	1976	1977	1978	1979	1980	1981
Narcotics*	10,614	10,072	11,732	12,210	10,881	10,770
Northeast	3,891	2,572	3,222	2,587	1,463	NA
Southeast	2,147	2,400	2,708	2,988	2,711	NA
North Central	2,446	2,675	3,157	2,867	2,762	NA
South Central	791	979	1,025	1,497	1,498	NA
West	1,339	1,446	1,626	2,271	2,447	NA
Stimulants	12,315	9,596	11,636	11,268	5,555	6,639
Northeast	5,731	2,863	5,011	5,784	1,013	NA
Southeast	1,697	1,826	1,567	1,343	1,198	NA
North Central	2,942	1,980	2,592	1,814	1,489	NA
South Central	838	960	1,191	1,028	706	NA
West	1,107	1,967	1,275	1,299	1,149	NA
Depressants	43,512	24,601	23,349	21,436	18,755	22,363
Northeast	27,809	7,920	5,490	5,436	3,720	NA
Southeast	4,454	5,293	4,747	4,967	4,746	NA
North Central	6,515	5,658	7,537	5,635	5,368	NA
South Central	1,965	2,500	2,398	2,359	2,276	NA
West	2,769	3,230	3,177	3,039	2,645	NA
Total	66,441	44,269	46,717	44,914	35,191	39,773

*Includes methadone, cocaine and other narcotics.
Source: U.S. Department of Justice, Drug Enforcement Administration, *Drug Enforcement Statistical Report* (Washington, D.C.: U.S. Department of Justice, 1980), p. 39; and data provided by the U.S. Department of Justice, Drug Enforcement Administration. Table adapted.

Table 48
Estimated Average Illegal Market
Retail Drug Prices, by Type of Drug, United States, 1973-81

Note: The estimated average illegal market retail heroin price is calculated from a sample of evidence exhibits removed from the illicit market by the Drug Enforcement Administration. The sample is selected to include "only those exhibits which fall within a certain range of values representative of a retail level of the illicit market." Beginning in 1978, the estimated national average is derived from regional averages weighted for the "intensity of the narcotic problem." That is, through statistical procedures, a large number of transactions in one location are clustered to limit their influence on heroin price and purity statistics in the sample group.

Cocaine prices are derived from the Cocaine Retail Price Index, which is based upon evidence exhibits purchased by the Drug Enforcement Administration.

In 1979 and 1980, prices of dangerous drugs (marijuana, hashish, LSD, PCP, barbiturates and amphetamines) were based on reports for the last quarter of each year submitted by Drug Enforcement Administration's field offices in 24 large metropolitan areas. These prices are compiled through a newly-initiated collection method which reflects transaction data at the retail level. Comparison with prices of earlier years is not recommended by the *Sourcebook of Criminal Statistics 1979*, p.36 (Washington, D.C.: U.S. Department of Justice). Prices for 1981 reflect the average price reported for the first three quarters of the year.

The notation "d.u." means dosage unit.

Type of drug	1973	1974	1975	1976	1977	1978	1979	1980	1981
Heroin (gm)*	$1,150.00	$1,230.00	$1,150.00	$1,400.00	$1,590.00	$2,190.00	$2,290.00	$2,200.00	$2,340.00
Cocaine (gm)*	410.00	490.00	560.00	530.00	640.00	650.00	780.00	670.00	690.00
Marijuana (gm)	.63	.56	.65	.64	.69	.80	1.42	1.66	1.64
Hashish (gm)	9.66	9.85	8.38	10.20	8.67	9.64	5.37	2.61	3.82
LSD (d.u.)	1.56	1.66	1.73	1.91	2.06	2.18	3.18	3.23	3.58
PCP (d.u.)	NA	NA	NA	NA	NA	1.59	7.95	8.36	3.82
Methamphetamine (d.u.)	NA	NA	1.07	1.26	1.14	.93	NA	NA	NA
Barbiturates (d.u.)	.55	.75	.80	.83	.92	1.07	2.99	3.50	NA
Amphetamine (d.u.)	.45	.59	.63	.72	.74	.93	3.49	3.23	3.23
Methadone (d.u.)	4.48	3.45	5.17	4.62	3.49	3.79	NA	NA	NA

*Prices are per pure gram.

Source: U.S. Department of Justice, Drug Enforcement Administration, *Drug Enforcement Statistical Report, 1976.* pp. 33, 35; 1978, pp. 33, 35; 1979, pp. 35, 37; (Washington D.C.: U.S. Department of Justice); and data provided by the U.S. Department of Justice, Drug Enforcement Administration. Table adapted.

Table 49
Arrests for Drug Law Violations and Arrest Rate
per 100,000 Population, by Type of Drug, United States, 1970-80

Note: This information is compiled by the Drug Enforcement Administration in cooperation with the Federal Bureau of Investigation. State and local jurisdictions voluntarily submit arrest data to the FBI. The data in this table represent arrests made by state and local agencies acting alone, and arrests made by state and local agencies acting in collaboration with the Drug Enforcement Administration. This table excludes arrests made solely by the Drug Enforcement Administration. Because the number of police agencies reporting and the populations they represent vary from year to year, arrest rates are computed on the basis of the relevant population estimate for that year. As of 1977, drug law arrests are classified by sale or manufacture and possession.

Type of drug	1970	1971	1972	1973	1974	1975	1976	1977	1978	1979	1980
Total	346,412	400,606	431,608	484,242	454,948	508,189	500,540	569,293	596,940	519,377	580,900
Possession	NA	NA	NA	NA	NA	NA	NA	465,682	489,491	425,889	455,000
Sale or manufacture	NA	NA	NA	NA	NA	NA	NA	103,611	107,449	93,488	125,900
Heroin and cocaine, total	108,427	114,573	92,364	67,794	71,882	66,573	50,054	75,147	78,796	63,364	68,100
Possession	NA	NA	NA	NA	NA	NA	NA	52,375	56,709	44,147	45,900
Sale or manufacture	NA	NA	NA	NA	NA	NA	NA	22,772	22,087	19,217	22,200
Marijuana, total	157,271	183,878	239,111	323,958	315,734	351,667	360,388	405,336	423,231	363,565	405,600
Possession	NA	NA	NA	NA	NA	NA	NA	350,115	365,925	317,340	341,500
Sale or manufacture	NA	NA	NA	NA	NA	NA	NA	55,221	57,306	46,225	64,100
Dangerous drugs, total	80,714	102,155	100,133	92,490	67,332	89,949	90,098	88,810	94,913	92,448	107,200
Possession	NA	NA	NA	NA	NA	NA	NA	63,192	66,857	64,402	67,600
Sale or manufacture	NA	NA	NA	NA	NA	NA	NA	25,618	28,056	28,046	39,600
Arrest rate per 100,000 population	228.5	257.7	269.1	312.4	339.3	283.6	285.2	298.4	288.3	253.8	256.0

Source: U.S. Department of Justice Drug Enforcement Administration, *Drug Enforcement Statistical Report, 1975,* p. 24; *1979,* p. 23 (Washington, D.C.: U.S. Department of Justice); and data provided by the U.S. Department of Justice, Drug Enforcement Administration. Table adapted.

Table 50
Percent Distribution of Arrests for Drug Violations,
by Type of Drug, Region, and Type of Offense, 1980

Note: These data were compiled by the Federal Bureau of Investigation through the Uniform Crime Reporting Program. On a monthly basis, law enforcement agencies report the number of offenses that become known to them. In 1980, there were 533,010 arrests for drug law violations. Percents in the table are calculated separately for each region: the base for all percents for each region is the total number of arrests for drug law violations in the region. For a list of the states in each region, see Table 47.

[Percent]

Region and type of offense	Total*	Type of drug			
		Heroin or cocaine	Mari- juana	Synthetic narcotics	Other
Northeast	100.0	18.5	70.8	4.4	6.3
Sale or manufacture	22.0	7.3	11.4	1.2	2.1
Possession	78.0	11.2	59.4	3.2	4.2
North Central	100.0	8.0	73.8	3.5	14.7
Sale or manufacture	33.1	3.6	17.6	1.2	10.7
Possession	66.9	4.4	56.2	2.3	4.1
South	100.0	7.0	72.9	5.7	14.5
Sale or manufacture	20.4	2.2	9.9	1.7	6.6
Possession	79.6	4.7	62.9	4.0	7.9
West	100.0	17.1	59.6	1.1	22.1
Sale or manufacture	15.9	4.0	7.4	0.2	4.3
Possession	84.1	13.1	52.3	0.9	17.8
Total	100.0	12.1	69.2	3.8	14.9
Sale or manufacture	21.8	3.9	10.9	1.1	5.8
Possession	78.2	8.1	58.3	2.7	9.1

*Because of rounding, percents may not add to total.

Source: U.S. Department of Justice, Federal Bureau of Investigation, *Crime in the United States, 1980* (Washington, D.C.: U.S. Government Printing Office, 1981), p. 189.

Table 51
Drug Seizures by the U.S. Customs Service,
by Type, Amount, and Value of Drugs Seized, Fiscal Years 1975-81

Note: The data presented for 1975 and 1976 coincide with the former federal fiscal year, the period July 1 to June 30. The transition quarter refers to the period July 1, 1976 to Sept. 30, 1976. The federal fiscal year is now Oct. 1 to Sept. 30.

The drug value is computed using the Drug Enforcement Administration (DEA) retail value lists. The illegal market retail drug prices for heroin and cocaine are based on evidence exhibits purchased by DEA; other dangerous drug prices are derived from monthly availability reports submitted by DEA field offices.

(Dollar values in thousands)

Type of drug seized	1975*	1976*	Transition quarter	1977**	1978**	1979**	1980**	1981**
Heroin*								
Number of seizures	436	437	104	245	179	173	149	170
Quantity in pounds	114.8	367.7	45.3	277.7	188.6	122.5	268.7	234.1
Value	$39,367	$126,089	$15,534	$124,705	$86,823	$75,080	$166,150	$147,306
Cocaine:								
Number of seizures	1,011	1,167	330	1,025	846	1,259	1,307	1,372
Quantity in pounds	728.9	1,029.6	236.1	952.1	1,418.7	1,438.1	4,742.9	3,741.1
Value	$155,392	$219,561	$50,333	$246,167	$380,013	$424,383	$1,528,826	$1,126,645
Hashish:								
Number of seizures	4,003	5,162	1,343	6,323	4,919	4,379	3,979	2,689
Quantity in pounds	3,400.9	13,436.7	469.6	15,923.0	22,658.5	50,848.9	14,675.4	17,991.8
Value	$17,185	$67,896	$2,373	$75,332	$95,664	$198,056	$26,717	$29,003
Marijuana:								
Number of seizures	13,792	13,555	4,620	14,902	12,826	12,323	12,620	14,036
Quantity in pounds	466,510.3	759,359.9	115,334.4	1,625,772.7	4,616,883.7	3,583,555.5	2,361,141.5	5,109,792.5
Value	$143,685	$233,883	$35,523	$509,054	$1,426,617	$2,164,468	$1,661,535	$3,796,576

Table 51 (continued)
Drug Seizures by the U.S. Customs Service,
by Type, Amount, and Value of Drugs Seized, Fiscal Years 1975-81

Type of drug seized	1975*	1976*	Transition quarter	1977**	1978**	1979**	1980**	1981**
Opium:								
Number of seizures	46	72	18	50	51	41	33	52
Quantity in pounds	18.6	37.6	4.4	20.2	20.3	26.1	49.9	9.5
Value	NA	NA	NA	NA	NA	NA	NA	NA
Morphine:								
Number of seizures	7	15	1	15	6	21	15	75
Quantity in pounds	1.2	3.9	—	1.4	1.8	8.8	50.7	6.2
Value	NA	NA	NA	NA	NA	NA	NA	NA
Other drugs, barbiturates, and LSD:								
Number of seizures	2,606	2,581	836	2,105	2,911	3,130	3,495	3,877
Quantity in dosage units	11,625,507	21,418,652	2,114,245	7,813,721	7,683,298	15,912,218	43,000,416	38,947,804
Value	$9,649	$17,777	$1,755	$4,376	$7,837	$44,236	$148,351	$137,096
Total:								
Number of seizures	21,901	22,989	7,252	24,665	21,738	21,326	21,598	22,271
Value	$365,278	$665,207	$105,518	$959,634	$1,996,954	$2,906,224	$3,531,580	$5,236,630

*Value date were computed using retail values as of the fourth quarter of fiscal year 1976.

**Value data were computed using retail values as of the third quarter of the fiscal year.

***Heroin value was computed for 60 percent purity.

Source: U.S. Department of the Treasury, U.S. Customs Service, *Prologue '76* (Washington, D.C.: U.S. Department of the Treasury, 1976), p. 36; and U.S. Department of the Treasury, U.S. Customs Service, *Customs U.S.A.*, *1980*. p. 33; *1981*, p. 33 (Washington, D.C.: U.S. Department of the Treasury). Table adapted.

Table 52

Drug Removals from the Domestic Market

by the Drug Enforcement Administration, by Type of Drug, 1972-81

Note: The increase in opium removals for 1981 resulted from a major seizure in Georgia; increases in the amount of hallucinogens and stimulants removals were due to major laboratory seizures in Washington and Texas respectively. The notation "d.u." means dosage unit.

Type of drug	1972	1973	1974	1975	1976	1977	1978	1979	1980	1981
Opium (pounds)	14	4	14	20	11	79	27	4	NA	78
Heroin (pounds)	820	273	462	603	645	488	442	160	201	192
Cocaine (pounds)	295	315	465	447	512	399	1,009	1,139	2,590	3,151
Marijuana (pounds)	51,897	52,446	113,484	234,116	290,909	335,452	1,117,422	887,032	994,468	1,511,081
Hashish (pounds)	1,151	445	812	3,771	5,040	6,651	3,004	43,261	5,993	13,191
Hallucinogens (d.u.)	2,602,456	16,638,383	3,263,671	1,351,405	1,824,276	3,848,117	4,349,917	6,439,136	7,522,905	35,928,760
Depressants (d.u.)	663,542	892,681	793,131	385,404	907,029	867,960	311,044	5,671,379	8,337,806	6,596,005
Stimulants (d.u.)	9,159,747	6,007,345	16,009,317	6,242,105	4,975,021	5,917,767	2,901,948	7,711,628	6,434,742	46,870,772
Methadone (d.u.)	223,940	3,919	3,432	737	3,531	23	39	14,998	NA	2,562

Source: U.S. Department of Justice, Drug Enforcement Administration, *Drug Enforcement Statistical Report, 1976.* p. 3; *1978,* p. 3; *1979,* p. 3 (Washington, D.C.: U.S. Department of Justice); and data provided by the U.S. Department of Justice, Drug Enforcement Administration. Table adapted.

Table 53

Seizures and Arrests by the U.S. Coast Guard, by Type and Amount of Property Seized, 1973-81

	1973	1974	1975	1976	1977	1978	1979	1980	1981
Vessels seized	6	11	6	21	45	148	110	149	176
Vessels seized by other agencies with Coast Guard participation	1	4	2	13	20	30	25	19	20
Marijuana seized (pounds)	15,700	38,501	94,025	198,169	1,042,629	3,321,038	2,672,854	2,494,774	2,320,034
Marijuana seized by other agencies with Coast Guard participation (pounds)	4,600	4,976	653	149,405	169,518	326,826	353,450	243,127	576,026
Cocaine seized (pounds)	2.2	0	0	61.8	0	.01	.01	0	40.1
Cocaine seized by other agencies with Coast Guard participation (pounds)	0	0	0	4.4	0	.01	0	10.01	96.1
Hashish seized (pounds)	0	6,139	0	0	0	0	43,550	564	34,580
Hashish seized by other agencies with Coast Guard participation (pounds)	0	0	2,000	0	1,700	1,100	1	168	0
Hashish oil seized (gals.)	0	0	0	0	0	0	0	5	7
Thai sticks* seized (pounds)	0	0	0	10,185	17,130	0	0	12,623	0
Thai sticks* seized by other agencies with Coast Guard participation	0	0	0	0	0	5,550	251	0	0
Dangerous drugs seized (doses)	0	0	0	0	200	500,000	4,186,050	514,584	5,961,009
Arrests	15	58	28	184	306	904	572	719	776
Street value of contraband seized (millions)	$6.19	$37.39	$34.80	$146.28	$435.13	$1,345.04	$1,910.97	$1,967.26	$1,832.93

*A "Thai stick" is a Southeast Asian marijuana bud that is bound onto a short section of bamboo and that may be laced with opium, hashish or another narcotic in order to increase its potency. Definition provide by U.S. Coast Guard, General Law Enforcement Branch.

Source: Table provided by U.S. Coast Guard, General Law Enforcement Branch.

Table 54
Controlled Substances: Uses and Effects

	Drugs	Schedule	Trade or Other Names	Medical Uses
NARCOTICS	Opium	II, III, V	Dover's Powder, Paregoric, Parepectolin	Analgesic, antidiarrheal
	Morphine	II, III	Morphine, Pectoral Syrup	Analgesic, antitussive
	Codeine	II, III, V	Codeine, Empirin Compound with Codeine, Robitussin A,C	Analgesic, antitussive
	Heroin	I	Diacetylmorphine, Horse, Smack	Under investigation
	Hydromorphone		Dilaudid	Analgesic
	Meperidine (Pethidine)	II	Demerol, Pethadol	Analgesic
	Methadone		Dolophine, Methadone, Methadose	Analgesic, heroin substitute
	Other Narcotics	I, II, III, IV, V	LAAM, Leritine, Levo-Dromoran, Percodan, Tussionex, Fentanyl, Darvon, Talwin, Lomotil	Analgesic, anti-diarrheal, antitussive
DEPRESSANTS	Chloral Hydrate	IV	Noctec, Somnos	Hypnotic
	Barbiturates	II, III, IV	Amobarbital, Phenobarbital, Butisol, Phenoxbarbital, Seco-barbital, Tuinal	Anesthetic, anti-convulsant, sedative, hypnotic
	Glutethimide	III	Doriden	
	Methaqualone	II	Optimil, Parest, Quaaluke, Som-nafac, Sopor	Sedative, hypnotic
	Benzodiazepines	IV	Ativan, Azene, Clonopin, Dal-mane, Diazepam, Librium, Serax, Tranxene, Valium, Verstran	Anti-anxiety, anti-convulsant, sedative, hypnotic
	Other Depressants	III, IV	Equanil, Miltown, Noludar, Placidyl, Valmid	Anti-anxiety, sedative, hypnotic

Table 54 (continued)
Controlled Substances: Uses and Effects

	Drugs	Schedule	Trade or Other Names	Medical Uses
STIMULANTS	Cocaine	II	Coke, Flake, Snow	Local anesthetic
	Amphetamines	II, III	Biphetamine, Delcobese, Desoxyn, Dexedrine, Mediatric	Hyperkinesis,
	Phenmetrazine	II	Preludin	narcolepsy,
	Methylphenidate	II	Ritalin	weight control
	Other Stimulants	III, IV	Adipex, Bacarate, Cyclert, Did-rex, Ionamin, Plegine, Pre-Sate, Sanorex, Tenuate, Tepanil, Voranil	
HALLUCIN-OGENS	LSD	I	Acid, Microdot	
	Mescaline and Peyote	I	Mesc, Buttons, Cactus	None
	Amphetamine Variants	I	2.5 DMA, PMA, STP, MDA, MMDA, TMA, DOM, DOB	
	Phencyclidine	II	PCP, Angel Dust, Hog	Veterinary anesthetic
	Phencyclidine Analogs	I	PCE, PCP, TCP	
	Other Hallucinogens	I	Bufotenine, Ibogaine, DMT, DET, Psilocybin, Psilocyn	None
CANNABIS	Marijuana	I	Pot, Acapulco Gold, Grass, Reefer Sinsemilla, Thai Sticks	Under investigation
	Tetrahydrocannabinol	I	THC	Under investigation
	Hashish	I	Hash	None
	Hashish Oil	I	Hash Oil	None

Table 54 (continued)
Controlled Substances: Uses and Effects

	Drugs	Schedule	Physical Dependence	Psychological Dependence	Tol-erance	Duration of effect in hrs.
NARCOTICS	Opium	II, III, V	High	High	Yes	3 - 6
	Morphine	II, III	High	High	Yes	3 - 6
	Codeine	II, III, V	Moderate	Moderate	Yes	3 - 6
	Heroin	I	High	High	Yes	3 - 6
	Hydromorphone		High	High	Yes	3 - 6
	Meperidine (Pethidine)	II	High	High	Yes	3 - 6
	Methadone		High	High	Yes	12 - 24
	Other Narcotics	I, II, III, IV, V	High-Low	High-Low	Yes	Variable
DEPRESSANTS	Chloral Hydrate	IV	Moderate	Moderate	Possible	5 - 8
	Barbiturates	II, III, IV	High-Moderate	High-Moderate	Yes	1 - 16
	Glutethimide	III	High	High	Yes	4 - 8
	Methaqualone	II	High	High	Yes	4 - 8
	Benzodiazepines	IV	Low	Low	Yes	4 - 8
	Other Depressants	III, IV	Moderate	Moderate	Yes	4 - 8
STIMULANTS	Cocaine	II	Possible	High	Yes	2 - 4
	Amphetamines	II, III	Possible	High	Yes	2 - 4
	Phenmetrazine	II	Possible	High	Yes	2 - 4
	Methylphenidate	II	Possible	High	Yes	2 - 4
	Other Stimulants	III, IV	Possible	High	Yes	2 - 4

Table 54 (continued)
Controlled Substances: Uses and Effects

	Drugs	Schedule	Physical Dependence	Psychological Dependence	Tol-erance	Duration of effect in hrs.
HALLUCIN-OGENS	LSD	I	None	Degree unknown	Yes	8 - 12
	Mescaline and Peyote	I	Unknown	Degree unknown	Yes	8 - 12
	Amphetamine Variants	I	Unknown	Degree unknown	Yes	up to days
	Phencyclidine	II	Degree unknown	High	Yes	Variable
	Phencyclidine Analogs	I	Degree unknown	Degree unknown	Possible	Variable
	Other Hallucinogens	I	None	Degree unknown	Possible	Variable
CANNABIS	Marijuana	I	Degree unknown	Moderate	Yes	2 - 4
	Tetrahydrocannabinol	I	Degree unknown	Moderate	Yes	2 - 4
	Hashish	I	Degree unknown	Moderate	Yes	2 - 4
	Hashish Oil	I	Degree unknown			2 - 4

Table 54 (continued)
Controlled Substances: Uses and Effects

	Drugs	Schedule	Usual Methods of Administration	Possible Effects	Effects of Overdose	Withdrawal Syndrome
NARCOTICS	Opium	II, III, V	Oral, smoked	Euphoria drowsiness, respiratory depression, constricted pupils, nausea	Slow and shallow breathing, clammy skin, convulsions, coma, possible death	Watery eyes, runny nose, yawning, loss of appetite, irritability, tremors, panic, chills and sweating, cramps, nausea
	Morphine	II, III	Oral, injected smoked			
	Codeine	II, III, V	Oral, injected			
	Heroin	I	Injected, sniffed, smoked			
	Hydromorphone	II	Oral, injected			
	Meperidine (Pethidine)	II	Oral, injected			
	Methadone	II	Oral, injected			
	Other Narcotics	I, II, III, IV, V	Oral, injected			
DEPRESSANTS	Chloral Hydrate	IV	Oral	Slurred speech, disorientation, drunken behavior without odor of alcohol	Shallow respiration, cold and clammy skin, dilated pupils, weak and rapid pulse, coma, possible death	Anxiety, insomnia, tremors, delirium, convulsions, possible death
	Barbiturates	II, III, IV	Oral, injected			
	Glutethimide	III	Oral, injected			
	Methaqualone	II	Oral, injected			
	Benzodiazepines	IV	Oral, injected			
	Other Depressants	III, IV	Oral, injected			

Table 54 (continued)
Controlled Substances: Uses and Effects

	Drugs	Schedule	Usual Methods of Administration	Possible Effects	Effects of Overdose	Withdrawal Syndrome
STIMULANTS	Cocaine	II	Sniffed, injected	Increased alertness, excitation, euphoria, increased pulse rate and blood pressure, insomnia, loss of appetite	Agitation, increase in body temperature, hallucinations, convulsions, possible death	Apathy, long periods of sleep, irritability, depression, disorientation
	Amphetamines	II, III	Oral, injected			
	Phenmetrazine	II	Oral, injected			
	Methylphenidate	II	Oral, injected			
	Other Stimulants	III, IV	Oral			
HALLUCINOGENS	LSD	I	Oral	Illusions and hallucinations, poor perception of time and distance	Longer, more intense "trip" episodes, psychosis, possible death	Withdrawal syndrome not reported
	Mescaline and Peyote	I	Oral, injected			
	Amphetamine Variants	I	Oral, injected			
	Phencyclidine	II	Smoked, oral, injected			
	Phencyclidine Analogs	I				
	Other Hallucinogens	I	Oral, injected, smoked, sniffed			
CANNABIS	Marijuana	I	Smoked, oral	Euphoria, relaxed inhibitions, increased appetite, disoriented behavior	Fatigue, paranoia, possible psychosis	Insomnia, hyperactivity, and decreased appetite occasionally reported
	Tetrahydrocannabinol	I				
	Hashish	I				
	Hashish Oil	I				

Source: Drug Enforcement Administration, *Drug Enforcement Fall 1982* (Washington, D.C.: U.S. Department of Justice).

Table 55
Approximate Equivalents*

LIQUID

1000	milliliters or 1 liter	= 1 quart
500	milliliters or 0.5 liter	= 1 pint
250	milliliters or 0.25 liter	= ½ pint or 8 fluid ounces
30	milliliters	= 1 fluid ounce
15	milliliters	= 4 fluid drams or ½ fluid ounce
4	milliliters	= 1 fluid dram
1	milliliter	= 15 minims
0.6	milliliter	= 10 minims
0.2	milliliter	= 3 minims
0.06	milliliter	= 1 minim
0.3	milliliter	= ½ minim

WEIGHT

1	kilogram	= 2.2. pounds (avoirdupois)
30	grams	= 1 ounce
4	grams	= 1 dram
1	gram	= ¼ dram or 15 grains
0.75	gram	= 12 grains
0.6	gram	= 10 grains
0.5	gram	= 7½ grains
0.4	gram	= 6 grains
0.3	gram	= 5 grains
0.25	gram	= 4 grains
0.2	gram	= 3 grains
0.15	gram	= 2½ grains
0.12	gram	= 2 grains
0.1	gram	= 1½ grains
75	milligrams	= 1¼ grains
60	milligrams	= 1 grain
50	milligrams	= ¾ grain
30	milligrams	= ½ grain
25	milligrams	= ⅜ grain
20	milligrams	= ⅓ grain
15	milligrams	= ¼ grain
10	milligrams	= ⅛ grain
8	milligrams	= ⅛ grain
6	milligrams	= 1/10 grain
4	milligrams	= 1/15 grain
3	milligrams	= 1/20 grain
2	milligrams	= 1/30 grain
1.5	milligram	= 1/40 grain
1.0	milligram	= 1/60 grain
0.8	milligram	= 1/80 grain
0.6	milligram	= 1/100 grain
0.5	milligram	= 1/120 grain
0.4	milligram	= 1/150 grain
0.3	milligram	= 1/200 grain
0.25	milligram	= 1/250 grain
0.2	milligram	= 1/300 grain
0.15	millgram	= 1/400 grain
0.12	milligram	= 1/500 grain
0.1	milligram	= 1/600 grain
0.05	milligram	= 1/1200 grain

*From the United States Pharmacopeia, XVI.

Appendix 4

Sources of Information

This section contains selected major sources of information on alcohol and drug abuse, including some organizations which provide treatment. Further information on treatment programs is usually available from national or local government agencies. In addition it was not possible to provide information sources for every foreign country, since many countries failed to or chose not to supply such information despite repeated requests.

Contents

UNITED STATES

National Associations, Institutes, Organizations and Government Agencies

State and Territorial Agencies for Alcohol Abuse and Alcoholism, Drug Abuse Prevention, and Treatment Coordinators

CANADA

Provincial and Territorial Agencies

INTERNATIONAL AND FOREIGN AGENCIES AND ORGANIZATIONS

Specialized Agencies of the United Nations
Other International Organizations
Regional Intergovernmental Organizations
Non-governmental Organizations
Institutes in Different Countries or Areas

*MAJOR ENGLISH-LANGUAGE JOURNALS,
NEWSPAPERS AND PERIODICALS*

UNITED STATES

NATIONAL ASSOCIATIONS, INSTITUTES, ORGANIZATIONS AND GOVERNMENT AGENCIES

A.A. World Services, Inc.
Grand Central Station
New York, New York 10017

Al-Anon Family Group Headquarters
P. O. Box 182
Madison Square Station
New York, New York 10010

Alcohol and Drug Problems Association of
North America
1101 Fifteenth Street, N. W., #204
Washington, D. C. 10005

Alcoholics Anonymous
General Service Office
468 Park Avenue South
New York, New York 10016

Alcohol, Drug Abuse and Mental Health
Administration
Department of Health and Human Services
5600 Fishers Lane, Room 6C15
Rockville, Maryland 10857
Tel: (301) 443-4797

Alcohol-Narcotics Education Council, Inc.
of Virginia Churches
3202 West Cary Street
Richmond, Virginia 23221

American Association Against Addiction
1668 Bush Street
San Francisco, California 94109
Tel: (415) 775-0165

American Correction Association
4321 Hartwick Road
College Park, Maryland 20740

American Council on Alcohol Problems
119 Constitution Avenue, N. E.
Washington, D. C. 20002

American Council on Marijuana and Other
Psychoactive Drugs
6193 Executive Boulevard
Rockville, Maryland 20852

American Institute of Family Relations
5287 Sunset Boulevard
Los Angeles, California 90027

American Medical Association
Department of Health Education
535 N. Dearborn Street
Chicago, Illinois 60610

Americans for Democratic Action
Consumer Affairs Committee
3005 Audubon Terrace, N. W.
Washington, D. C. 20008

Association for Advancement of Health Education
1201 16th Street, N. W.
Washington, D. C. 20036

Association of Halfway House Alcoholism
Programs of North America
786 East 7th Street
St. Paul, Minnesota 55106

B'nai B'rith C.V.S.
1640 Rhode Island Avenue, N. W.
Washington, D. C. 20036

Center of Alcohol Studies
Rutgers, The State University of New Jersey
New Brunswick, New Jersey 08903

Center for Multicultural Awareness
2924 Columbia Pike
Arlington, Virginia 22204

Center for the Study of Drug Policy
530 Eighth Street, S. E.
Washington, D. C. 20003
Tel: (202) 547-3708

Center for the Study of Responsive Law
P. O. Box 19367
Washington, D. C. 20036

Commission for the Advancement of Public
  Interest Organization
1875 Connecticut Avenue, N. W.
Washington, D. C. 20009

Committee on Problems of Drug Dependence
4105 Dunnel Lane
Kensington, Maryland 20795

Committees of Correspondence
6 South Main Street
Topsfield, Massachusetts 01983
Tel: (617) 887-5008

Consumer Federation of America
1314 14th Street, N. W.
Washington, D. C. 20005

Do It Now Foundation
P. O. Box 5115
Phoenix, Arizona 85010
Tel: (602) 257-0797

Drug Enforcement Administration
1405 I Street, N. W.
Washington, D. C. 20537

Families in Action
3845 North Druid Hills Road
Decatur, Georgia 30333
Tel: (404) 325-5799

Families Anonymous
P. O. Box 344
Torrance, California 90501
Tel: (213) 775-3211

Family Life Publications
Box 427
Saluda, North Carolina 28773

Federal Trade Commission
Bureau of Consumer Protection
Division of Professional Service
6th Street & Pennsylvania Avenue, N. W.
Washington, D. C. 20580

Food and Drug Administration (FDA)
Consumer Inquiries HFI-10
5600 Fishers Lane
Rockville, Maryland 20857

Hazelden Foundation, Inc.
Box 11
Center City, Minnesota 55012

House Select Committee on Narcotics Abuse
  & Control
3287 House Office Building-Annex 2
2nd and D Streets, S. W.
Washington, D. C. 20515

Independent Community Consultants, Inc.
Design and Planning Assistance Center
120 Yale, S. E.
Albuquerque, New Mexico 87109

Institute on Pluralism and Group Identity
165 East 56th Street
New York, New York 10022

Mental Health Material Center
30 East 29th Street
New York, New York 10016

The Myrin Institute
521 Park Avenue
New York, New York 10021

Narcotic Educational Foundation of America
5055 Sunset Boulevard
Los Angeles, Calfornia 90027
Tel: (213) 663-5171

Narcotics Anonymous
Box 622
Sun Valley, California 93352

Narcotics Education
6830 Laurel Avenue, N. W.
Washington, D. C. 20012
Tel: (202) 723-4774

Narcotics Educational Foundation of America
5055 Sunset Boulevard
Los Angeles, California 90027

National Anti-Drug Coalition
304 West 58th Street, 5th Floor
New York, New York 10019
Tel: (212) 247-8820

National Association for City Drug and
Alcohol Coordination
House Officers Building, Suite 711
818 Harrison Avenue
Boston, Massachusetts 02118
Tel: (617) 424-4757

National Association on Drug Abuse
Problems
355 Lexington Avenue
New York, New York 10017
Tel: (212) 986-1170

National Association of State Alcohol and
Drug Abuse Directors
918 F Street, N. W., Suite 400
Washington, D. C. 20004
Tel: (202) 783-6868

National Center for Voluntary Action
1785 Massachusetts, N. W.
Washington, D. C. 20036

National Clearinghouse for Alcohol
Information
P.O. Box 2345
Rockville, Maryland 20852

National Clearinghouse for Drug Abuse
Information
Department of Health and Human Services
5600 Fishers Lane, Room 10A53
Rockville, Maryland 20857
Tel: (301) 443-6500

National Committee for the Prevention of
Alcoholism and Drug Dependency
6830 Laurel Street, N. W.
Washington, D. C. 20012

National Council on Alcoholism
733 Third Avenue
New York, New York 10017

National Council on Alcoholism, Inc.
1424 16th Street, N. W.
Washington, D. C. 20036

National Council on Crime and Delinquency
Continental Plaza
422 Hackensack Avenue
Hackensack, New Jersey 07601

National Family Council Against Drug Abuse
40 Westminister Drive
Pearl River, New York 10965
Tel: (914) 735-9250

National Federation of Parents for Drug-Free
Youth
9805 Dameron Drive
Silver Springs, Maryland 20902
Tel: (301) 593-9256

National Foundation—March of Dimes
Public Health Education Department
Box 2000
White Plains, New York 10602

National Institute on Alcohol Abuse and
Alcoholism
Department of Health and Human Services
P. O. Box 2345
5600 Fishers Lane
Rockville, Maryland 20857
Tel: (301) 468-2600

National Institute on Drug Abuse
Division of Research
Department of Health and Human Services
5600 Fishers Lane
Rockville, Maryland 20857

National Organization for the Reform of
Marijuana Laws (NORML)
2035 P Street, N. W., Suite 401
Washington, D. C. 20036

National Self-Help Clearinghouse
Graduate School and University Center—
CUNY
33 West 42nd Street
New York, New York 10036

New York City Affiliate, Inc.
National Council on Alcoholism
133 East 62nd Street
New York, New York 10021

North Conway Institute
14 Beacon Street
Boston, Massachusetts 02108

Odyssey Institute
656 Avenue of the Americas
New York, New York 10010
Tel: (212) 691-8510

Parent Resources and Information on Drug
  Education
Georgia State University
University Plaza
Atlanta, Georgia 30303
Tel: (404) 658-2548

Pharmaceutical Manufacturers Association
Consumer Services
115 15th Street, N. W.
Washington, D. C. 20005

Phoenix House Foundation
164 West 74th Street
New York, New York 10023
Tel: (212) 595-5810

Pil-Anon Family Program
P. O. Box 120
Gracie Square Station
New York, New York 10028
Tel: (212) 744-2020

Pills Anonymous
P. O. Box 473
Ansonia Station
New York, New York 10023
Tel: (212) 375-8872

Potsmokers Anonymous
316 East 3rd Street
New York, New York 10009
Tel: (212) 254-1777

The Proprietary Association
1700 Pennsylvania Avenue, N. W.
Washington, D. C. 20006

Public Affairs Pamphlets
381 Park Avenue South
New York, New York 10016

Public Citizen, Inc.
Health Research Group
2000 P Street, N. W.
Washington, D. C. 20036

Synanon Church
P. O. Box 786
6055 Marshall-Petaluma Road
Marshall, California 94940
Tel: (415) 663-8111

U.S. Department of Health and Human
  Services
Office of Education
Alcohol and Drug Education Program
400 Maryland Avenue, S. W.
Washington, D. C. 20202

Valium Anonymous
P. O. Box 404
Altoona, Iowa 50009
Tel: (515) 967-6781

Women for Sobriety
P. O. Box 618
Quakertown, Pennsylvania 18951
Tel. (215) 536-8026

STATE AND TERRITORIAL AGENCIES FOR ALCOHOL ABUSE AND ALCOHOLISM, DRUG ABUSE PREVENTION, AND TREATMENT COORDINATORS

Alabama
State Department of Mental Health
135 South Union Street
Montgomery, Alabama 36130
Tel: (205) 265-2301

Division of Alcoholism and Drug Abuse
Department of Mental Health
502 Washington Avenue
Montgomery, Alabama 36104
Tel: (205) 834-4350

Alaska

Department of Health and Social Services
Pouch H-05F
231 South Franklin
Juneau, Alaska 99811
Tel: (907) 586-3585

Arizona

Drug Abuse Section Bureau of Community
  Services
2500 East Van Buren Street
Phoenix, Arizona 85008
Tel: (602) 255-1239

Arkansas

Arkansas Office of Alcohol and Drug Abuse
  Prevention
1515 West 7th Street
Little Rock, Arkansas 72202
Tel: (501) 371-2604

California

Department of Alcohol and Drug Abuse
  Programs
111 Capitol Mall, Suite 450
Sacramento, California 95814
Tel: (916) 445-1940

Colorado

Alcohol and Drug Abuse Division
Department of Health
4210 East 11th Avenue
Denver, Colorado
Tel: (303) 320-1167

Connecticut

Alcohol and Drug Abuse Council
90 Washington Street
Hartford, Connecticut 06115
Tel: (203) 566-4145

Delaware

Bureau of Alcoholism and Drug Abuse
Department of Health and Social Services
1901 North du Pont Highway
New Castle, Delaware 19720
Tel: (302) 421-6101

District of Columbia

Department of Human Resources
Mental Health, Alcohol and Addiction
  Services Branch
421 8th Street, N. W.
Washington, D. C. 20004
Tel: (202) 724-5637

Florida

Alcoholic Rehabilitation Program
Department of Health and Rehabilitative
  Services
1323 Winewoon Boulevard
Tallahassee, Florida 32301
Tel: (904) 488-0900

Georgia

Alcohol and Drug Abuse Section
Department of Human Resources
618 Ponce de Leon Avenue, N. E.
Atlanta, Georgia 30308
Tel: (404) 894-4785

Metropolitan Atlanta Council on Alcohol and
  Drugs
2045 Peachtree Road, N. E., Suite 320
Atlanta, Georgia 30309

Hawaii

Department of Health
State Substance Abuse Agency
Alcohol and Drug Abuse Branch
1270 Queen Emma Street, Room 505
Honolulu, Hawaii 96813
Tel: (808) 548-7655

Idaho

Bureau of Substance Abuse
Department of Health and Welfare
450 West State Street, 4th Floor
Boise, Idaho 83720
Tel: (208) 334-4368

Illinois

Alcohol Division
Department of Mental Health and Develop-
  mental Disabilities
160 North LaSalle Street, Room 1500
Chicago, Illinois 60601
Tel: (312) 793-2907

Illinois Dangerous Drugs Commission
300 North State Street
Chicago, Illinois 60610

Indiana
Division of Addiction Services
Department of Mental health
5 Indiana Square
Indianapolis, Indiana 46204
Tel: (317) 232-7818

Iowa
Department of Substance Abuse
Insurance Exchange Building, Suite 202
505 5th Avenue
Des Moines, Iowa 50319
Tel: (515) 281-3641

Kansas
Alcoholism and Drug Abuse Section
Department of Social Rehabilitation Service
2700 West Sixth Street
Biddle Building
Topeka, Kansas 66606
Tel: (913) 296-3925

Kentucky
Alcohol and Drug Branch
Bureau of Health Services
Department of Human Resources
275 East Main Street
Frankfort, Kentucky 40621
Tel: (502) 564-7450

Louisiana
Office of Mental Health and Substances Abuse
Department of Health and Human Resources
655 North 5th Street
Baton Rouge, Louisiana 70829
Tel: (504) 342-2590

Maine
Office of Alcoholism and Drug Abuse
    Prevention
Department of Human Services
32 Winthrop Street
Augusta, Maine 04330
Tel: (207) 289-2781

Maryland
Department of Health and Mental Hygiene
201 West Preston Street
Baltimore, Maryland 21201
Tel: (301) 383-3959

Massachusetts
Massachusetts Division of Alcoholism
755 Boylston Street
Boston, Massachusetts
Tel: (617) 727-1960

Michigan
Office of Substance Abuse Services
Department of Public Health
3500 North Logan Street
Lansing, Michigan 48909
Tel: (317) 373-8600

Minnesota
Chemical Dependency Program Division
Department of Public Welfare
4th Floor Centennial Building
658 Cedar Street
St. Paul, Minnesota 55155
Tel: (612) 296-4610

Mississippi
Division of Alcohol and Drug Abuse
Department of Mental health
619 Robert E. Lee State Office Building
Jackson, Mississippi 32901
Tel: (601) 354-7031

Missouri
Division of Alcoholism and Drug Abuse
Department of Mental Health
2002 Missouri Boulevard
Jefferson City, Missouri 65102

Montana
Alcohol and Drug Abuse Division
Department of Institutions
1539 11th Avenue
Helena, Montana 59601
Tel: (406) 449-2827

Nebraska
Nebraska Commission on Drugs
P. O. Box 94726

Lincoln, Nebraska 68509
Tel: (402) 471-2591

Nebraska Department of Public Institutions
Nebraska Division of Alcoholism and Drug
    Abuse
801 West Van Dorn
Lincoln, Nebraska 68509
Tel: (402) 471-2851

Nevada
Bureau of Alcohol and Drug Abuse
Department of Human Resources
505 East King Street
Carson City, Nevada 89710
Tel: (702) 885-4790

New Hampshire
Office of Alcohol and Drug Abuse
    Prevention
Health and Welfare Building
Hazen Drive
Concord, New Hampshire 03301
Tel: (603) 271-4626, 4630

New Jersey
Alcohol, Narcotic and Drug Abuse
Department of Health
129 East Hanover Street
Trenton, New Jersey 08608
Tel: (609) 292-5760

New Mexico
Substance Abuse Bureau
Behavioral Health Service Division
Health and Environment Department
P. O. Box 968
Santa Fe, New Mexico 87503
Tel: (505) 827-5271

New York
New York Office of Alcoholism and
    Substance Abuse
Executive Park South
Box 8200
Albany, New York 12203
Tel: (518) 488-4270

Addiction Research and Treatment
    Corporation

22 Chapel Street
Brooklyn, New York 11201
Tel: (212) 834-5300

North Carolina
Alcohol and Drug Abuse Services
325 North Salisbury Street
Albemarle Building, Room 1100
Raleigh, North Carolina 27611
Tel: (919) 733-4670

North Dakota
Division of Alcoholism and Drug Abuse
State Department of Health
909 Basin Avenue
Bismarck, North Dakota 58505
Tel: (701) 224-2768

Ohio
State Methadone Authority
Ohio Department of Mental Health and Mental
    Retardation
65 South Front Street
Columbus, Ohio 43215

Division of Alcoholism
Ohio Department of Health
246 North High Street
Columbus, Ohio 43215
Tel: (614) 466-3425

Oklahoma
Division of Alcoholism and Drug Abuse
    Programs
Department of Mental Health
4545 North Lincoln Boulevard, Suite 100
P. O. Box 53277
Oklahoma City, Oklahoma 73152

Oregon
Program for Alcohol and Drug Problems
Oregon Mental Health Division
2575 Bittern Street, N. E.
Salem, Oregon 97310
Tel: (503) 378-2163

Pennsylvania
Governor's Council on Drug and Alcohol
    Abuse

2101 North Front Street
Harrisburg, Pennsylvania 17120
Tel: (717) 787-9857

Rhode Island
Division of Substance Abuse
General Hospital
Building 303
Rhode Island Medical Center
Cranston, Rhode Island 02920
Tel: (401) 464-2091

South Carolina
South Carolina Commission on Alcohol and
  Drug Abuse
3700 Forest Drive
Landmark East, Suite 300
Columbia, South Carolina 29204
Tel: (803) 758-2183

South Dakota
South Dakota Division of Alcoholism and
  Drug Abuse
Joe Foss Building
Pierre, South Dakota 57501
Tel: (605) 773-4806

Tennessee
Division of Alcohol and Drug Abuse
Tennessee Department of Mental Health
501 Union Building
Nashville, Tennessee 37219
Tel: (615) 741-1921

Texas
Texas Commission on Alcoholism
809 Sam Houston State Office Building
Austin, Texas 78701
Tel: (512) 475-2725

Utah
Division of Alcoholism and Drugs
150 West North Temple, Suite 350
P. O. Box 2500
Salt Lake City, Utah 84110
Tel: (801) 533-6532

Vermont
Alcohol and Drug Abuse Division
Department of Social and Rehabilitation
  Services

103 South Main Street
State Office Building
Waterbury, Vermont 05676
Tel: (802) 241-2170

Virginia
Division of Substance Abuse
Department of Mental Health and Mental
  Retardation
P. O. Box 1797
109 Governor Street
Richmond, Virginia 23214
Tel: (804) 786-5313

Washington
Bureau of Alcoholism and Substance Abuse
Department of Social and Health Services
Mailstop OB-44W
Olympia, Washington 98504
Tel: (206) 753-3073

West Virginia
Department of Health
Alcohoism and Drug Abuse Program
State Capitol
1800 Kanawha Boulevard East
Charleston, West Virginia 25305
Tel: (304) 348-3616

Wisconsin
State Bureau of Alcohol and Other Drug
  Abuse
One West Wilson Street, Room 523
Madison, Wisconsin 53702
Tel: (608) 266-3442

Wyoming
Alcohol and Alcohol Abuse Programs
Hathaway Building
Cheyenne, Wyoming 82002
Tel: (307) 777-7115

Puerto Rico
Department of Addiction Control Services
P. O. Box B-Y
Piedras Station
Puerto Rico 00928
Tel: (809) 764-5014

American Samoa
Mental Health Clinic

Government of American Samoa
Pago Pago, American Samoa 96799

Guam
Mental Health and Substance Abuse Agency
P. O. Box 20999
Guam, Guam 96921
Tel: (404) 477-9704

Trust Territories
Department of Health Services

Office of the High Commissioner
Saipan, Trust Territories 96950
Tel: (615) 741-1921

Virgin Islands
Division of Mental Health, Alcoholism and
    Drug Dependency
P. O. Box 520
Christiansted
St. Croix, Virgin Islands
Tel: (809) 773-1192, 774-4888

CANADA

PROVINCIAL AND TERRITORIAL AGENCIES

Alberta
Alberta Alcoholism and Drug Abuse
    Commission
10909 Jasper Avenue
Edmonton, Alberta T5J 3M9
Tel: (403) 427-4275

British Columbia
The Alcohol and Drug Commission of
    British Columbia
805 West Broadway, 8th Floor
Vancouver, British Columbia V5Y 1P9
Tel: (604) 731-9121

Manitoba
Alcoholism Foundation of Manitoba
1580 Dublin Avenue
Winnipeg, Manitoba R3E 0L4

Alcohol and Drug Programs Division of
    Inter-Regional Operations
Department of Health and Social
    Development
139 Tuxedo Boulevard, Building 21, Box 17
Winnipeg, Manitoba

New Brunswick
Alcoholism and Drug Dependency
    Commission
103 Church Street

P. O. Box 6000
Fredericton, New Brunswick E3B 5H1
Tel: (506) 453-2136

Alcoholism Program
Department of Health
P. O. Box 6000
348 King Street
Fredericton, New Brunswick

Newfoundland
Department of Health
Confederation Building
St. John's, Newfoundland A1C 5T7
Tel: (709) 737-2300

Alcohol and Drug Addiction Foundation of
    Newfoundland
3 Blackmarsh Road
St. John's, Newfoundland A1E 1S2
Tel: (709) 579-4041

Nova Scotia
Nova Scotia Commission on Drug
    Dependency
5668 South Street
Halifax, Nova Scotia B3J 1A6
Tel: (902) 424-4270

Ontario
Ministry of Health
9th Floor, Hepburn Block
Queen's Park

Toronto, Ontario M7A 1S2
Tel: (416) 965-5167

Alcoholism and Drug Addiction Foundation
33 Russell Street
Toronto, Ontario M5S 2S1

Drug Advisory Bureau
Department of National Health and Welfare
Tunney's Pasture
Ottawa, Ontario

Prince Edward Island
Addiction Foundation of Prince Edward
  Island
Box 37
Charlottetown, Prince Edward Island C1A
  7K2
Tel: (902) 892-4265

Quebec
Department of Social Affairs
Information Centre on Alcoholism and Other
  Addictions
1075 Chemin Ste. Foy
Quebec, P.Q. G1S 2M1
Tel: (418) 643-9621

Saskatchewan
Alcoholism Commission of Saskatchewan
3475 Albert Street
Regina, Saskatchewan S4S 6X6
Tel: (306) 565-4085

The Canadian Foundation of Alcohol and
  Drug Dependence
602 Main Street
Noosomin, Saskatchewan

Northwest Territories
Alcohol and Drug Program
Department of Social Services
Government of the Northwest Territories
Yellowknife, N. W. T. X1A 2L9
Tel: (403) 873-7155

Alcohol and Drug Coordinating Council
Box 1769
Yellowknife, N. W. T. X0E 1H0
Tel: (403) 873-7155

Yukon
Alcohol and Drug Services
Box 2703
Whitehorse, Y. T. Y1A 2C6
Tel: (403) 667-5777

INTERNATIONAL AND FOREIGN
AGENCIES AND ORGANIZATIONS

SPECIALIZED AGENCIES OF THE
UNITED NATIONS

International Labour Office (ILO)
4, rue de Morillon
CH-1218 Grand Saconnex, Switzerland

Pan American Health Organization
Regional Office of the WHO
525 Twenty-third Street, N. W.
Washington, D. C.

United Nations
Division of Narcotic Drugs (DND)

P. O. Box 500
A-1400 Vienna, Austria

United Nations Educational, Scientific and
  Cultural Organization (UNESCO)
7, place de Fontenoy
F-7500 Paris, France

United Nations Social Defence
Research Institute
Via Giulia 52
I-00186 Rome, Italy

World Health Organization (WHO)
Regional Office for the Western Pacific

P. O. Box 2932
12115 Manila, Philippines

World Health Organization (WHO)
Regional Office for Europe
Scherfigsvej, 8
DK-2100 Copenhagen, Denmark

World Health Organization (WHO)
20, avenue Appia
CH-1211 Geneva, Switzerland

OTHER INTERNATIONAL ORGANIZATIONS

Centre for Social Development and Humanitarian Affairs (CSDHA)
P. O. Box 500
A-1400 Vienna, Austria

Customs Cooperation Council
40, rue Washington
B-1050 Brussels, Belgium

International Commission for the Prevention of Alcoholism
6830 Laurel Street, N. W.
Washington, D. C. 20012

International Council of Volunteer Agencies
17, avenue de la Paix
CH-1202 Geneva, Switzerland

International Criminal Police Organization (ICPO/Interpol)
26, rue Armengaud
F-9200 Saint Cloud, France

International Federation of the Temperance Blue Cross Societies
52, rue de Florissant
CH-1206 Geneva, Switzerland

International Narcotics Control Board (INCB)
P. O. Box 500
A-1400 Vienna, Austria

International Council on Social Welfare
Berggasse None A-1090
Vienna, Austria

REGIONAL INTERGOVERNMENTAL ORGANIZATIONS

Pan-Arab Anti-Narcotics Bureau
Pan-Arab Organization for Social Defence Against Crime
P. O. Box 17225
Amman, Jordan

Pompidou Group
Council of Europe
Strasbourg, France

South American Agreement
Combate de los Pozos 2133
1245 Buenos Aires, Argentina

Colombo Plan Bureau
12 Melbourne Avenue
Colombo, Sri Lanka

NON-GOVERNMENTAL ORGANIZATIONS

International Council on Alcohol and Addictions
Case Postale 140
CH-1001 Lausanne, Switzerland

International Union for Child Welfare
1, rue de Varembi
CH-1211 Geneva, Switzerland

INSTITUTES IN DIFFERENT COUNTRIES OR AREAS

Argentine
Comision Nacional de Toxicomanias y Narcoticos
Ministerio de Bienestar Social de la Nacion
Defensa 120, piso 1
Buenos Aires, Argentina

Centro Nacional de Reeducacion Social
Combate de los Pozos 2133
Buenos Aires, Argentina

Australia
Alcohol and Drug Addicts Treatment Board

1st Floor, 3/161 Greenhill Road
Parkside, South Australia 5063

Alcohol and Drug Services
Mental Health Division
Health Commission of Victoria
Enterprise House
555 Collins Street
Melbourne, Victoria 3000
Australia

Australian Council of Social Services, Inc.
149 Castlereagh Street
Sydney, New South Wales 2000
Australia

Australian Foundation on Alcoholism and
   Drug Dependence
2nd Floor, T and G Building
London Circuit
Canberra City, A.C.T. 2601
Australia

Department of Health
Alcohol and Drug Dependence Service
"BIALA"
279 Roma Street
Brisbane, Queensland 4000
Australia

Department of Health
Drug Information Centre
Box 3944 V, G.P.O.
Sydney, New South Wales 2001
Australia

Department of Health Services
Public Buildings
Davey Street
Hobart, Tasmania 7000
Australia

National Drug Information Service
   Commonwealth
Department of Health
P.O. Box 100
Wooden, A.C.T. 2606
Australia

Western Australia Alcohol and Drug
   Authority

Greenchurch House
25 Richardson Street
West Perth, Western Australia 6005

Austria
Republik Oesterreich
Bundeministerium fuer Gesundheit und
   Umweltschutz
Stubenring 1
1010 Wein, Austria

Belgium
Comite National pour l'Etude et la
   Prevention de l'Alcoolisme et des Autres
   Toxicomanies
Ministere de Sante Publique
Cabinet du Ministre
Rue Joseph II 30
Brussels 1040, Belgium

Brazil
Instituto Oscar Freire
Caixa Postal 22215
Sao Paulo, Brazil

Bulgaria
Centre de nevroligie, psychiatrie et
   neurochirurgie
Secteur pour la lutte contre l'alcoholisme et
   les narcomanies
Sofia 62, Bulgaria

Colombia
Coordinador de la Oficina de Control y
   Prevencion del Alcoholismo y las Drogas
   Heroicas
Calle 13, No. 9-33
Oficina 605-606
Apartado Aereo 13891
Bogota, Colombia

Seccion de Control de Drogas
Laboratories y Farmacias del Servicio
   Seccional de Salud del Risaralda
Pereira, Colombia

Denmark
Commission on Drug Abuse in Youth
Sundhedsstyrelsen

Store Kongensgade 1
Copenhagen K, Denmark

Husset
Readhusstrade 13
1466 Copenhagen K, Denmark

Egypt
Ministry of Health
People's Assembly Street
Lazoglie
Cairo, Egypt

Finland
The Finnish Foundation for Alcohol Studies
Kalevankatu 12
SF-00100 Helsinki 10, Finland

France
Association Regionale Contre la
    Toxicomanie chez les Jeunes
39, boulevard Carnot
Toulouse, France

Centre DIDRO
9, rue Pauly
F-75014 Paris, France

Comite de Lutte contre l'Aggression de la
    Drogue et Aide aux Jeunes Drogues
31, rue Dieude
Marseilles, France

Club Social
"Drug Information"
4, rue Edith Cavell
Rennes, France

Haut Comite d'Etude et d'Information sur
    l'Alcoolisme
27, rue Oudinot
75700 Paris, France

Germany, East
Ministerium fuer Gesundheitswesen der
    DDR
Hauptabt. Int. Beziehg
GDR 1020 Berlin
Rathausstrasse
German Democratic Republic

Hygiene Museum
GDR 8010 Dresden
Julius—Fucik—Allee

German Democratic Republic

Germany, West
Deutsche Hauptstelle gegen die
    Suchtoefahren
Westring 2 4700
Hamm, West Germany

Hong Kong
Caritas Lok Heep Club
P. O. Box K2089
Kowloon, Hong Kong

The Society for the Aid and Rehabilitation
    of Drug Addicts
290-296 Tak Wah Building
Hennessy Road
Hong Kong

Hungary
Alkolizmus Elleni Orszagos Bizottsag
Budapest, V., Arany Janos v. 31
1051
Hungary

Egeszsegugyi Miniszterium
Budapest, V., Akademia v. 10
1055
Hungary

Iceland
Liquor Prevention Council
Eiriksgata 5
101 Reykjavik
Iceland

India
Indian Council on Medical Research
Ansari Nagar
P. O. Box 4508
New Delhi 110029
India

Iraq
Drug Combating Bureau Directorate
General of Police
Operation Branch
Baghdad, Iraq

Ireland
The Economic and Social Research Institute
4 Burlington Road

Dublin 4, Republic of Ireland

Eastern Health Board Day Centre
9 Usher's Island
Dublin S, Republic of Ireland

Public Relations Unit
Department of Health
Custom House
Room 36A
Dublin 1, Republic of Ireland

The Drug Treatment and Advisory Centre
Jervis Street Hospital
Dublin 1, Republic of Ireland

Israel
Department of Alcoholism Treatment
   Services
Ministry of Labour and Social Affairs
10 Yad Harutzim Street, Talpiot
P.O. Box 1260
Jerusalem 9100, Israel

Italy
Ministero della Sanita
D.G. Servizi Medicina Sociale
Viale della Civilta' Romana (EUR)
00144 Roma, Italy

Stampa Alternative
Casella Postale 741
Roma, Italy

Jamaica
The Permanent Secretary
Ministry of Health
10 Caledonia Avenue
Kingston 5, Jamaica W.I.

Japan
Mental Health Division
Public Health Bureau
Ministry of Health and Welfare
1-2-3 Kasumigaseki
Chiyoda-ku, Tokyo, Japan

Luxembourg
Centre de Sante Mentale
30, avenue Marie
Therese, Luxembourg

Service Multidisciplinaire de la Lutte contra
   la Toxicomanie
Ministere de la Sante Publique
1, rue Aug. Lumiere
Luxembourg

Malaysia
Central Narcotics Bureau
P. O. Box 85
Petaling Jaya, Selangor
Malaysia

Mexico
Centro Mexicano de Estudios en
   Farmacodependencia (CEMEF)
Insurgentes Sur 1991-B, piso 7
Mexico 20, D.F.

Censejo Nacional de Saud Mental
Secretaria de Salubridad y Asistencia
   Reforma y Lieja
Mexico 5, D.F.

Centros de Integracion Juvenil, A.C.
Jose Ma. Olloqui 48
Mexico 12, D.F.

Instituto Mexicano de Psiquiatria
Antiguo Camino a Xochimilco 101
Mexico 22, D.F.

Netherlands
Information and Education Department
Medisch Consultatie Bureau voor
   Alcoholisme
Jellinek Kliniek
Keizersgracht 674
Amsterdam, Holland

New Zealand
National Soceity on Alcoholism and Drug
   Dependence New Zealand (Inc.)
Box 1642
Wellington, New Zealand

Philippines
Dangerous Drugs Board
P. O. Box 3862
Manila, Philippines

The Narcotics Foundation of the Philippines
P. O. Box 3849
Manila, Philippines

Prevent and Rehabilitate Drug Abusers
PREDA Foundations, Inc.
Olongapo, Luzon, Philippines

Poland
Research Center on Alcoholism
Department of Information on Alcoholism
    and Drug Addiction
UL. Narbutta 54
02-541 Warsaw, Poland

Spoteczny Komitet Przeciwalkoholowy
(Committee to Fight Alcoholism)
Ul. Kopernika 36.40
00-328 Warsaw, Poland

South Africa
Department of Health, Welfare and Pensions
Private Bag X88
Pretoria 0001
Republic of South Africa

South African National Council on
    Alcoholism and Drug Dependence
Indian Branch
W.O. 1997 Indian Information Office
84 C.N.R. House
22 Cross Street
Durban, South Africa

Sweden
Centralforbundet for Alkohol
Karlavagen 117
Box 27302
10254 Stockholm, Sweden

Drug Dependence Bureau (SN4)
National Board of Health and Welfare
Stockholm, Sweden

Alkohol och Narkotika
Centralforbundet for Alkohol-och
    narkotikanpplysning
Fach 102 50
Stockholm, Sweden

Switzerland
Drop-In
Rheingasse 23
4058 Basel, Switzerland

Institut Suisse de Prevention de
    L'Alcoolisme et Autres Toxicomanies
Case Postale 1063
CH-1001 Lausanne, Switzerland

Institut Suisse de Prophylaxie de
    L'Alcoolisme
ISPA, Case Postale 203
1000 Lausanne 13, Switzerland

International Council on Alcohol and
    Addictions
Case Postale 140
1001 Lausanne, Switzerland

Office Federal de la Sante Publique
Coordination et Information en Matiere de
    Drogues
Bollwerk 27
CH-3001 Bern, Switzerland

Schweizerische Fachstelle fuer
    Alkoholprobleme
Avenue Ruchonnet 14
CH-1003 Lausanne, Switzerland

Thailand
Central Bureau of Narcotics
Parusakawan Palace
Bangkok, Thailand

United Kingdom
Alcoholics Anonymous
11 Redcliffe Gardens
London SW10, England

Association for the Prevention of Addiction
(APA)
32-33 Long Acre
London WC2, England

Drug Information Centre
Pharmacy Department
City Hospital
Huckmall Road
Nottingham, England

Government Advisory Committee on
    Alcoholism
Department of Health and Social Security
    Alexander Fleming House

Elephant and Castle
London SE1, England

Health Education Council
78 New Oxford Street
London WC1A 1AH, England

Institute of Psychiatry
Addiction Research Unit
DeCrespigny Park
London SE5, England

Institute for the Study of Drug Dependence
Kingsbury House
3 Blackburn Road
London NW6 1XA, England

Mental Health
c/o National Association for Mental Health
39 Queen Anne Street
London W1, England

Medical Council on Alcoholism
3 Grosvenor Crescent
London SW1, England

Narcotics Anonymous
37 Albert Square
London SW8, England

Release
1 Elgin Avenue
London W9, England

The Society for the Study of Addiction to
Alcohol and other Drugs

Tooting Bec Hospital
London SW17, England

Venezuela
Division de Higiene Mental
Ministerio de Sanidad
Edifico Sur, Picso 8
Centro Simon Bolivar
Caracas 1010, Venezuela

Comision contra el Uso Indebido de las
Drogas
Fiscalia General de la Republica
Despacho del Fiscal
General de la Republica
Ministerio Publico
Caracas, Venezuela

Yugoslavia
Institute for Study and Prevention of
Alcoholism and Drug Dependence
Clinical Hospital "Mladen Stojanovic"
Zagreb, Yugoslavia

Institute of Mental Health
Palmoticeva 37
Belgrade, Yugoslavia

Institute on Alcoholism and Drug
Dependence
Gornjacka 21
Belgrade, Yugoslavia

MAJOR ENGLISH-LANGUAGE JOURNALS, NEWSPAPERS AND PERIODICALS

Alcohol Health and Research World
P. O. Box 2345
Rockville, Maryland 20852

Alcoholism: The National Magazine
P. O. Box C19051
Queen Anne Station
Seattle, Washington 98109

The Alcoholism Report
744 National Press Building
Washington, D. C. 20045

American Journal of Drug and Alcohol Abuse
Marcel Dekker, Inc.
270 Madison Avenue
New York, New York 10016

American Journal of Epidemiology
Johns Hopkins University
School of Hygiene and Public Health
615 North Wolfe Street
Baltimore, Maryland 21205

*American Journal of Obstetrics and
    Gynecology*
C. V. Mosby Co.
11830 Westline Industrial Drive
St. Louis, Missouri 63141

*American Journal of Pharmacy and the
    Sciences Supporting Public Health*
Philadelphia College of Pharmacy and
    Science
43rd Street and Kingsessing Mall
Philadelphia, Pennsylvania 19104

American Journal of Psychiatry
American Psychiatric Association
1700 18th Street, N. W.
Washington, D. C. 20009

American Journal of Psychology
University of Illinois Press
Urbana, Illinois 61801

American Journal of Public Health
American Public Health Association
1015 18th Street, N. W.
Washington, D. C. 20036

American Journal of Sociology
University of Chicago Press
5801 South Ellis Avenue
Chicago, Illinois 60637

Annals of Internal Medicine
American College of Physicians
4200 Pine Street
Philadelphia, Pennsylvania 19104

*Annals of the New York Academy of
    Sciences*
The New York Academy of Sciences
2 East 63rd Street
New York, New York 10021

Archives of General Psychiatry
American Medical Association

535 North Dearborn Street
Chicago, Illinois 60610

British Journal of Addiction
Longman Group, Ltd.
Journals Division
43-45 Annandale Street
Edinburgh EH7 4AT, Scotland

British Journal on Alcohol and Alcoholism
3 Grosvenor Crescent
London SW1X 7EE, England

British Journal of Criminology
Sweet and Maxwell Stevens Journals
11 New Fetter Lane
London EC4 P4EE, England

British Journal of Psychiatry
Headley Bros. Ltd.
Ashford, Kent TN24 8HH, England

British Medical Journal
British Medical Association
B.M.A. House, Tavistock Square
London WC1, England

Canadian Medical Association Journal
Canadian Medical Association
Box 8650
Ottawa K1G 068, Ontario, Canada

Clinical Pharmacology and Therapeutics
C.V. Mosby Co.
11830 Westline Industrial Drive
St. Louis, Missouri 63141

Clinical Toxicology
Marcel Dekker Journals
270 Madison Avenue
New York, New York 10016

Contemporary Drug Problems
Federal Legal Publications, Inc.
95 Morton Street
New York, New York 10014

Crime and Delinquency
National Council on Crime and Delinquency
411 Continental Plaza
Hackensack, New Jersey 07601

Criminology
Sage Publications, Inc.
275 South Beverly Drive
Beverly Hills, California 90212

Digest of Alcoholism Theory and
*   Application (DATA)*
10700 Olson Memorial Highway
Minneapolis, Minnesota 55441

Diseases of the Nervous System
Physicians Postgraduate Press
Box 38293
Memphis, Tennessee 38138

Drug Abuse and Alcoholism Newsletter
Vista Hill Foundation
3420 Camino del Rio North, Suite 100
San Diego, California 92108

Drug and Alcohol Dependence
Elsevier Sequoia S.A.
Box 851
CH-1001 Lausanne 1, Switzerland

Drug Forum
Baywood Publishing Co., Inc.
120 Marine Street
Farmingdale, New York 11735

Federal Probation
Administrative Office of the U.S. Courts
Supreme Court Building
Washington, D. C. 20544

The Forum
1 Park Avenue
New York, New York 10016

The Grapevine
The Alcoholics Anonymous Grapevine, Inc.
468 Park Avenue South
New York, New York 10016

Human Pathology
Saunders Co.
West Washington Square
Philadelphia, Pennsylvania 19105

International Journal of the Addictions
Marcel Dekker Journals

270 Madison Avenue
New York, New York 10016

John Marshall Journal of Practice and
*   Procedure*
John Marshall Law School
315 South Plymouth Court
Chicago, Illinois 60604

The Journal
Addiction Research Foundation
33 Russell Street
Toronto, Ontario M5S 2S1, Canada

Journal of Abnormal Psychology
American Psychological Association
1200 17th Street, N. W.
Washington, D. C. 20036

Journal on Alcohol and Drug Education
1120 East Oakland
P. O. Box 10212
Lansing, Michigan 48901

Journal of Altered States of Consciousness
Baywood Publishing Co., Inc.
43 Central Drive
Farmingdale, New York 11735

Journal of the American Medical
*   Association*
535 North Dearborn Street
Chicago, Illinois 60610

European Journal of Clinical Pharmacology
Springer-Verlag
175 Fifth Avenue
New York, New York 10010

Journal of Clinical Psychology
Clinical Psychology Publishing Co., Inc.
4 Conant Square
Brandon, Vermont 05733

Journal of Consulting and Clinical
*   Psychology*
American Psychological Association
1200 17th Street, N. W.
Washington, D. C. 20036

Journal of Criminal Law and Criminology

Williams and Wilkins Co.
428 East Preston Street
Baltimore, Maryland 21202

Journal of Drug Education
Baywood Publishing Co., Inc.
120 Marine Street
Farmingdale, New York 11735

Journal of Drug Issues
Box 4021
Tallahassee, Florida 32303

Journal of Forensic Sciences
American Society for Testing and Material
1916 Race Street
Philadelphia, Pennsylvania 19103

Journal of General Psychology
Journal Press
2 Commercial Street
Provincetown, Massachusetts 02657

Journal of Health and Social Behavior
American Sociological Association
1722 North Street, N. W.
Washington, D. C. 20036

Journal of Nervous and Mental Diseases
Williams and Wilkins Co.
428 East Preston Street
Baltimore, Maryland 21202

Journal of Personality
Duke University Press
6697 College Station
Durham, North Carolina 27708

*Journal of Personality and Social
   Psychology*
American Psychological Association
1200 17th Street, N. W.
Washington, D. C. 20036

Journal of Pharmacy and Pharmacology
Pharmaceutical Society of Great Britain
1 Lambeth High Street
London SE1 7JN, England

*Journal of Pharmacology and Experimental
   Therapeutics*
Williams and Wilkins Co.

428 East Preston Street
Baltimore, Maryland 21202

Journal Psychology
Journal Press
2 Commercial Street
Provincetown, Massachusetts 02657

Journal of Social Psychology
Journal Press
2 Commercial Street
Provincetown, Massachusetts 02657

Journal of Studies on Alcohol
Rutgers Center of Alcohol Studies
Publications Division
New Brunswick, New Jersey 08903

New England Journal of Medicine
Massachusetts Medical Society
10 Shattuck Street
Boston, Massachusetts 02115

New York State Journal of Medicine
Medical Society of the State of New York
420 Lakeville Road
Lake Success, New York 11040

Psychiatry
William Alanson White Psychiatric
   Foundation, Inc.
1610 New Hampshire Avenue, N. W.
Washington, D. C. 20009

Psychological Reports
Box 9229
Missoula, Montana 59801

Psychology
Box 6495, Station C
Savannah, Georgia 31405

Psychopharmacology
Springer-Verlag
174 Fifth Avenue
New York, New York 10010

Social Problems
Society for the Study of Social Problems
114 Rockwell Hall
State University College
Buffalo, New York 14222

Sociological Quarterly
Midwest Sociological Society
Department of Sociology
Southern Illinois University
Carbondale, Illinois 62901

U.S. Journal of Drug and Alcohol
  Dependence
2119-A Hollywood Boulevard
Hollywood, Florida 33020

BIBLIOGRAPHY

Aafen, Brent. *Marijuana*. Center City, Minn.: Hazelden Foundation, 1980.

Abel, Ernest L. *Marijuana: The First Twelve Thousand Years*. New York: Plenum Publishing Corp., 1980.

Abramson, H. A., ed. *The Use of LSD in Psychotherapy and Alcoholism*. Indianapolis: Bobbs-Merrill Co. Inc., 1967.

Acherman, Robert J. *Children of Alcoholics*. Hollywood, Fla.: Health Communications, 1978.

Ackoff, R. L.; Gupta, S.; and Minas, J. S. *Scientific Method: Optimizing Applied Research Decisions*. New York: John Wiley and Sons, 1969.

Addiction Research Foundation. *Alcohol, Drugs and Traffic Safety*. Toronto, 1976.

————. *The Forgotten Children*. Toronto, 1969.

————. *R.I.D.E.—A Driving–While–Impaired Countermeasure Program*. Toronto, 1979.

Akins, Carl, and Beschner, George. *Ethnography: A Research Tool for Policymakers in the Drug and Alcohol Fields*. Rockville, Md.: National Institute on Drug Abuse, 1980.

Alcoholics Anonymous World Services. *Alcoholics Anonymous*. New York, 1965.

————. *Alcoholics Anonymous Comes of Age: A Brief History of A.A.* New York, 1957.

————. *Twelve Steps and Twelve Traditions*. New York, 1952.

Alexander, M. *The Sexual Paradise of LSD*. North Hollywood, Calif.: Brandon House, 1967.

Alexander, Tom. *The Drug Takers*. New York: Time Inc., 1965.

Allen, Lloyd V., Jr. *Drug Abuse: What Can We Do?* Ventura, Calif.: Regal Press, 1981.

Alpert, R., and Cohen, S. *LSD*. New York: New American Library, 1967.

American Medical Association. "Dependence on Cannabis (Marijuana)." *Journal of the American Medical Association,* 201:368-371, 1967.

————. *Manual on Alcoholism*. Chicago, 1977.

————. "Marijuana and Society." *Journal of the American Medical Association,* 204:1181-1182, 1968.

American Pharmaceutical Association. *Handbook of Nonprescription Drugs*. Sixth edition. Washington, D.C., 1979.

Anders, Rebecca. *A Look at Drug Abuse*. Minneapolis: Lerner Publications, Co., 1977.

Anderson, J. R., and Bower, G. H. *Human Associative Memory*. Washington, D.C.: Winston and Sons, 1973.

Andrews, G., and Vinkenoog, S., eds. *The Book of Grass: An Anthology of Indian Hemp*. New York: Grove Press, 1967.

Andrews, George, and Solomon, David, eds. *The Coca Leaf and Cocaine Papers*. New York: Harcourt, Brace, Jovanovich, 1975.

Angmann and Associates. *Health Insurance Coverage of Alcoholism Benefits: Results of a National Survey and Implications for California*. San Francisco: California State Senate Committee on Health and Welfare, n.d.

Anon. "Cocaine Smuggled in Water Skis." *Washington Post*. August 26, 1974.

Anon. "Cocaine: Middle Class High." *Time Magazine,* July 6, 1981.

Anon. *Legal Highs, A Concise Encyclopedia of Legal Herbs and Chemicals with Psychoactive Properties*. New York: High Times Press, 1973.

Anon. "Private Violence: Child Abuse, Wife Beating, Rape." *Time Magazine,* September 5, 1983.

Anon. "The Cocaine Scene." *Newsweek Magazine,* May 30, 1977.

Ansbacher, H., and Ansbacher, R. *The Individual Psychology of Alfred Adler*. New York: Basic Books, 1946.

Armor, David J.; Polich, J. Michael; and Stambul, Harriet B. *Alcoholism and Treatment*. New York: John Wiley and Sons, 1978.

Arndt, J. R., and Blockstein, W. L. *Problems in Drug Abuse*. Madison, Wis.: University of Wisconsin, 1970.

Ashbrook, Debra L., and Solley, Linda C. *Women & Heroin Abuse: A Survey of Sexism in Drug Abuse Administration*. Palo Alto, Calif.: R & E Research Associates, 1979.

Ashley, R. *Cocaine: Its History, Uses and Effects*. New York: St. Martin's Press, 1975.

Asimov, I. *The Human Brain: Its Capacities and Functions*. Boston: Houghton Mifflin, 1964.

Augsburger, David. *So What? Everybody's Doing It!* Chicago: Moody Press, 1969.

Australian Foundation on Alcoholism and Drug Dependence. *National Alcohol and Drug Dependence Multidisciplinary Institute, August 27 to September 1, 1978*. Canberra, 1978.

Ausubel, David P. *Drug Addiction: Physiological, Psychological and Sociological Aspects*. New York: Random House, 1958.

————. *What Every Well–Informed Person Should Know About Drug Addiction*. Chicago: Nelson-Hall Publishers, 1980.

Avogaro, P.; Sirtori, C. R.; and Tremoli, E. *Metabolic Effects of Alcohol*. New York: Elsevier, 1979.

Bacon, M., and Jones, M. B. *Teen–age Drinking*. New York: Crowell, 1968.

Bacon, Selden D. *Understanding Alcoholism*. Philadelphia: American Academy of Political and Social Science, 1958.

Bahr, Howard M. *Skid Row: An Introduction to Disaffiliation*. New York: Oxford University Press, 1973.

Bailey, C. B.; Ginter, D. J.; and Woodlock, B. K. *Handbook for Alcoholism Counselors*. Cleveland: Alcoholism Services of Cleveland, 1978.

Bandura, Albert. *Principles of Behavior Modification*. New York: Holt, Rinehart and Winston, 1969.

Barber, Bernard. *Drugs and Society*. Beverly Hills, Calif.: Russell Sage, 1967.

Barnes, G. M.; Abel, E. L.; and Ernst, C. A. S. *Alcohol and the Elderly: A Comprehensive Bibliography*. Westport, Conn.: Greenwood Press, 1980.

Barnes, T., and Price, S. *Interaction of Alcohol and Other Drugs—Supplement*. Toronto: Addiction Research Foundation, 1973.

Barr, H. L., and Cohen, A. *The Problem–Drinking Drug Addict*. Washington, D.C.: National Institute on Drug Abuse, 1979.

Bauman, Carl E. *Predicting Adolescent Drug Use*. New York: Praeger Publishers, 1980.

Beauchamp, Dan E. *Beyond Alcoholism: Alcohol and Public Health Policy*. Philadelphia: Temple University Press, 1980.

Becker, Howard S. *Outsiders: Studies in the Sociology of Deviance*. San Francisco: Jossey-Bass, 1969.

Beckman, Harry. *Dilemmas in Drug Therapy*. Philadelphia: W. B. Saunders Co., 1967.

———— . *Pharmacology: the Nature, Action and Use of Drugs*. Philadelphia: W. B. Saunders Co., 1961.

Begleiter, H. *Biological Effects of Alcohol*. New York: Plenun Publishing Corp., 1980.

Bejerot, Nils. *Addiction and Society*. Springfield, Ill.: Charles C. Thomas, 1970.

Bell, Judith, and Billington, D. Rex. *Annotated Bibliography of Health Education Research Completed in Britain from 1948–1978*. Edinburgh: Scottish Health Education Unit, 1980.

Bemko, Jane. *Substance Abuse Book Review Index 1980*. Toronto: Addiction Research Foundation, 1981.

Benjamin, Fred. B. *Alcohol, Drugs, and Traffic Safety: Where Do We Go from Here?* Springfield, Ill.: Charles C. Thomas, 1980.

Bennett, James C., and Demos, George D. *Drug Abuse and What We Can Do About It*. Springfield, Ill.: Charles C. Thomas, 1979.

Benson, W. M., and Schiele, B. C. *Tranquilizing and Anti–depressive Drugs*. Springfield, Ill.: Charles C. Thomas, 1962.

Bergin, A. E., and Strupp, H. H. *Changing Frontiers in the Science of Psychotherapy*. Chicago: Aldine Atherton, 1972.

Berkow, Robert, ed. *The Merck Manual of Diagnosis and Therapy*. Rahway, N.J.: Merck Sharp and Dohme Research Laboratories, 1977.

Berman, A. *Analysis of Drugs of Abuse*. Philadelphia: Heyden and Son, Inc., 1977.

Bermandt, Gordon, et al. *Psychology and the Law*. Lexington, Mass.: Lexington Books, 1976.

Birdwood, George. *The Willing Victim*. New York: International Publications Service, 1969.

Birnbaum, Isabel M., and Parker, Elizabeth S. *Alcohol and Human Memory*. Hillsdale, N.J.: Lawrence Erlbaum Associates, 1977; dist. John Wiley and Sons.

Bishop, M. G. *The Discovery of Love: A Psychedelic Experience with LSD-25*. New York: Dodd, Mead & Co., 1963.

Blachly, Paul H., ed. *Drug Data and Debate*. Springfield, Ill.: Charles C. Thomas, 1973.

Black, P., ed. *Drugs and the Brain*. Baltimore: Johns Hopkins Press, 1969.

Blakeslee, Alton. *What You Should Know about Drugs and Narcotics*. New York: Associated Press, 1969.

Blane, H. T. *The Personality of the Alcoholic: Guises of Dependency*. New York: Harper and Row, 1968.

———— . and Chafetz, M. E. *Youth, Alcohol, and Social Policy*. New York: Plenum Publishing Corp., 1979.

Blocker, Jack S., Jr. *Alcohol, Reform and Society: The Liquor Issue in Social Context*. Westport, Conn.: Greenwood Press, 1979.

Blombert, R. D.; Preusser, D. F.; Hale, A.; and Ulmer, R. G. *A Comparison of Alcohol Involvement in Pedestrians and Pedestrian Casualties*. Springfield, Va.: National Technical Information Service, 1979.

Bloomquist, Edward R. *Marijuana, the Second Trip*. Beverly Hills, Calif.: Glencoe Press, 1971.

Blum, R. H. *The Dream Sellers*. San Francisco: Jossey-Bass, 1972.

———— . and Associates. *The Utopiates: Uses and Users of LSD*. New York: Atherton Press, 1964.

———— . et al. *Society and Drugs*. San Francisco: Jossey-Bass, 1969.

———— . et al. *Students and Drugs: Drugs II*. San Francisco: Jossey-Bass, 1969.

Blume, Sheila B. *Fetal Alcohol Syndrome: Task Force Report to the Governor*. Albany: New

York State Division oɪ Alcoholism and Alcohol Abuse, 1979.

Bonnie, Richard J, and Whitebread, Charles H. *Marihuana Conviction: A History of Marihuana Prohibition in the United States*. Charlottesville, Va.: University Press of Virginia, 1974.

――――. *Marijuana Use and Criminal Sanctions: Essays on the Theory and Practice of Law Reform*. Charlottesville, Va.: Michie/Bobbs-Merrill Law Publishing, 1980.

Bourne, Peter G. *Methadone: Benefits and Shortcomings*. Washington, D.C.: Drug Abuse Council, 1975.

――――. ed. *Acute Drug Abuse Emergencies: A Treatment Manual*. New York: Academic Press, 1976.

――――. ed. *Addiction*. New York: Academic Press, 1974.

Bowen, Haskell, and Landin, Les. *About Drugs*. Belmont, Calif.: Pitman Publishers, 1971.

Bowker, Lee H. *Drug Use Among American Women, Old & Young: Sexual Oppression & Other Themes*. Palo Alto, Calif.: R & E Research Associates, 1977.

Braden, William. *The Private Sea: LSD and the Search for God*. Chicago: Quadrangle Books, 1967.

Braude, M. C., and Szara, S., eds. *Pharmacology of Marijuana*. New York: Raven Press, 1976.

Brecher, Edward M. and the Editors of Consumer Reports. *Licit & Illicit Drugs*. Boston: Little, Brown and Company, 1972.

Brill, L., and Liberman, L. *Authority and Addiction*. Boston: Little, Brown and Company, 1969.

――――. and Winick, Charles. *The Yearbook of Substance Use and Abuse*. Vol. II. New York: Human Sciences Press, 1980.

――――. et al. *The Treatment of Substance Abusers*. New York: Free Press, 1981.

Brisolara, Ashton. *The Alcoholic Employee: A Handbook of Useful Guidelines*. New York: Human Sciences Press, 1979.

British Royal College of Psychiatrists. *Alcohol and Alcoholism*. Report of a Special Committee of the Royal College of Psychiatrists. London: Tavistock Publications, 1979.

Brody, Jane. *Jane Brody's Nutrition Book*. New York: W. W. Norton & Company, Inc., 1981.

Bronetto, J. *Alcohol Price, Alcohol Consumption and Death by Liver Cirrhosis*. Toronto: Addiction Research Foundation, 1960-63.

Brook, Robert, and Whitehead, Paul. *Drug-free Therapeutic Community*. New York: Human Sciences Press, 1980.

Brown, B. B. *New Mind, New Body*. New York: Harper & Row, 1974.

Bugenthal, J. F. *The Search for Authenticity*. New York: Holt, Rinehart & Winston, 1965.

Bullington, Bruce. *Heroin Use in the Barrio*. Lexington, Mass.: Lexington Books, 1977.

Burack, Richard, and Fox, Fred J. *The Handbook of Prescription Drugs*. New York: Ballantine Books, 1975.

Bureau of Narcotics and Dangerous Drugs. *Glossary of Terms in the Drug Culture*. Washington, D.C.: U.S. Department of Justice, 1970.

Burger, Alfred E. *Drugs Affecting the Central Nervous System*. New York: Marcel Dekker Inc., 1968.

Burns, John. *Answer to Addiction*. Blauvelt, N.Y.: Multimedia Publishing Corp., 1980.

Burroughs, William. *Naked Lunch*. New York: Grove Press, 1966.

Burt, Marvin R. *Drug Abuse: Its Natural History and the Effectiveness of Current Treatments*. Cambridge, Mass.: Schenkman Publishing Co. Inc., 1979.

Bush, Patricia J. *Drugs, Alcohol & Sex*. New York: Richard Marek, 1980.

Busse, S., et al. *Disulfiram in the Treatment of Alcoholism: An Annotated Bibliography*. Toronto: Addiction Research Foundation, 1978.

Butters, Nelson, and Cermak, Laird S. *Alcoholic Korsakoff's Syndrome: An Information–Processing Approach to Amnesia*. New York: Academic Press, 1980.

Buys, Donna, and Saltman, Jules. *The Unseen Alcoholics—The Elderly*. Pamphlet No. 602. New York: Public Affairs Pamphlets, 1982.

Byck, Robert, ed. *Cocaine Papers by Sigmund Freud*. New York: Stonehill Publishing Co., 1972.

Byrd, P. D., ed. *Medical Readings on Drug Abuse*. Reading, Mass.: Addison-Wesley, 1970.

Cahalan, Donald; Cisin, I. H.; and Crossley, H. M. *American Drinking Practices*. New Haven: College and University Press, 1969.

_____ . *American Drinking Practices: A National Survey of Behavior and Attitudes*. Monograph No. 6. New Brunswick, N.J.: Rutgers Center of Alcohol Studies, 1969.

_____ . *Implications of American Drinking Practices and Attitudes for Prevention and Treatment of Alcoholism*. Berkeley: Social Research Group, School of Public Health, University of California, n.d.

Cahn, S. *The Treatment of Alcoholics: An Evaluation Study*. New York: Oxford University Press, 1970.

Caldwell, William V. *LSD Psychotherapy*. New York: Grove Press, 1968.

Callaway, E., et al. *Neuropsychological Studies of Alcohol: Final Report*. Springfield, Va.: National Information Service, 1978.

Canada Commission of Inquiry into the Non-medical Use of Drugs (The Le Dain Commission). *Cannabis, A Report of the Commission* . . . Ottawa: Information Canada, 1972.

_____ . *Final Report of the Commission* . . . Ottawa: Information Canada, 1973.

_____ . *Interim Report of the Commission* . . . Ottawa: Information Canada, 1970.

_____ . *Treatment, A Report of the Commission* . . . Ottawa: Information Canada, 1972.

Candlin, A. H. S. *Psychochemical Warfare*. New Rochelle, N.Y.: Arlington House, 1973.

Caplovitz, David. *The Working Addict*. White Plains, N.Y.: M. E. Sharpe, 1976.

Carey, J. T. *The College Drug Scene*. Englewood Cliffs, N.J.: Prentice-Hall, 1963.

Carney, Richard E., ed. *Risk–Taking Behavior: Concepts, Methods, and Applications to Smoking and Drug Abuse*. Springfield, Ill.: Charles C. Thomas, 1971.

Carone, Pasquale A., and Kreinsky, Leonard W. *Drug Abuse in Industry*. Springfield, Ill.: Charles C. Thomas, 1973.

_____ . et al. *Addictive Disorder Update: Alcoholism, Drug Abuse, Gambling*. New York: Human Sciences Press, 1981.

Carriel, D. *So Fair a House: The Story of Synanon*. Englewood Cliffs, N.J.: Prentice-Hall, 1963.

Cashman, John. *The LSD Story*. Greenwich, Conn.: Fawcett Publications, 1966.

Castenada, C. *Journey to Ixthlan: The Lessons of Don Juan*. New York: Simon and Schuster, 1972.

Chafetz, M. E. *Liquor: The Servant of Man*. Boston: Little, Brown and Company, 1965.

_____ . *Why Drinking Can Be Good for You*. New York: Stein and Day, 1976.

_____ ., and Demone, H. W. *Alcoholism and Society*. New York: Oxford University Press, 1962.

_____ . Blane, Howard T.; and Hill, Marjorie J. *Frontiers of Alcoholism*. New York: Science House, 1970.

Chambers, Carl D., and Brill, Leon, eds. *Methadone Experiences and Issues*. New York: Human Sciences Press, 1973.

――――. and Heckman, Richard D. *Employee Drug Abuse: A Manager's Guide for Action*. Boston: CBI Publishing Co. Inc., 1972.

Chapin, W. *Wasted: The Story of My Son's Drug Addiction*. New York; McGraw-Hill, 1972.

Chasen, Dave. *The Gourmet Cokebook, A Complete Guide to Cocaine*. New York: White Mountain Press, 1972.

Chein, I., et al. *The Road to H*. New York: Basic Books, 1964.

Chesler, Phyllis. *Women and Madness*. New York: Doubleday, 1972.

Chopra, G. S., and Chopra, I. C. *Drug Addiction with Special Reference to India*. New York: International Publications Service, 1965.

Clark, P. M. S., and Kricka, L. J. *Medical Consequences of Alcohol Abuse*. New York: Halsted Press, and John Wiley and Sons, 1980.

Clarke, Frank H., ed. *How Modern Medicines Are Developed*. Mount Kisco, N.Y.: Futura Publications, 1977.

Clarke, Robert C. *Marijuana Botany*. Berkeley, Calif.: And/Or Press, 1981.

Clouet, D. H., ed. *Narcotic Drugs: Biochemical Pharmacology*. New York: Plenum Publishing Corp., 1971.

Cohen, Charles P., et al. *Psychotherapy and Drug Addiction: Diagnosis and Treatment*. New York: Irvington Publishers, Inc., 1974.

Cohen, Sidney, ed. *Drug Abuse and Alcoholism*. New York: The Haworth Press, 1981.

――――. *The Beyond Within: The LSD Story*. New York: Atheneum, 1967.

――――. *The Drug Dilemma*. New York: McGraw-Hill, 1975.

――――. *The Substance Abuse Problems*. New York: The Haworth Press, 1981.

Coleman, James S. *The Adolescent Society*. New York: Free Press, 1961.

Coleman, Richard. *Is Your Prescription Killing You?* Port Washington, N.Y.: Ashley Books, Inc., 1981.

Coles, Robert. *The Grass Pipe*. Boston: Little, Brown and Company, 1969.

Collins, James J., Jr. *Drinking and Crime: Perspectives on the Relationships between Alcohol Consumption and Criminal Behavior*. New York: Guilford Publications, 1981.

Committee on Mental Health Services. *Drug Misuse: A Psychiatric View of a Modern Dilemma*. Volume VII. Report No. 80. Pamphlet. New York: Group for the Advancement of Psychiatry, June 1971.

Connell, P. H. *Amphetamine Psychosis*. London: Chapman and Hall, 1958.

Coombs, Robert, et al., eds. *Socialization in Drug Abuse*. Cambridge, Mass.: Schenkman Co. Inc., 1976.

Cooper, M. L.; Schawar, T. G.; and Smith, L. S. *Alcohol, Drugs and Road Traffic*. Cape Town: Juta and Co., 1979.

Corsini, Raymond J. *Current Psychotherapies*. 2nd ed. Itasca, Ill.: F. E. Peacock Publishers, 1979.

Cowan, Ronald, and Roth, Rodney. "The Turned On Generation: Where Will They Turn To?" *Journal of Drug Education*, 2 (1):39-47, 1972.

Cox, Ann E. *Training Guidelines and Workbook for the Behavioral Management of Intoxicated and Disruptive Clients*. Toronto: Addiction Research Foundation, 1981.

Craig, Robert, and Baker, Stewart. *Drug Dependent Patients*. Springfield, Ill.: Charles C. Thomas, 1981.

Crenshaw, Mary. *The End of the Rainbow*. New York: Macmillan, 1981.

Crohn, Leslie P. *Self–Awareness, Drug Abuse and Drug Control*. New York: McGraw-Hill, 1981.

Crowley, Aleister. *Cocaine*. Reprint of the 1918 edition. San Francisco: Level Press, 1973.

———. *The Diary of a Drug Fiend*. New York: Lancer Books, 1972.

Cull, J. G., and Hardy, R. E. *Types of Drug Abusers and Their Abuse*. Springfield, Ill.: Charles C. Thomas, 1974.

Cutler, R., and Storm, T. *Drinking Practices in Three British Columbia Cities II. Student Survey*. Vancouver: Alcoholism Foundation of British Columbia, 1973.

Dahlstrom, W. G., and Welsch, G. S. *An MMPI Handbook: A Guide to Use in Clinical Practice and Research*. Minneapolis: University of Minnesota Press, 1965.

David, Kenneth, and Cowley, James. *Pastoral Care in Schools and Colleges*. London: Edward Arnold, n.d.

Dawkins, Marvin P. *Alcohol and the Black Community: Exploratory Studies of Selected Issues*. Saratoga, Calif.: Century Twenty-One, 1980.

De Leon, George, ed. *Phoenix House: Studies in a Therapeutic Community*. New York: Irvington Publishers Inc., 1974.

De Long, J. V. "The Methadone Habit." *New York Times Magazine*. March 16, 1975.

De Quincey, T. *Confessions of an English Opium Eater*. Reprint. New York: Three Sirens Press, 1932.

DeRopp, Robert S. *Drugs and the Mind*. New York: Grove Press, 1961.

———. *The Master Game*. New York: Delta Books, 1968.

Department of Health and Human Services. *The Alcohol, Drug Abuse, and Mental Health National Data Book*. Rockville, Md., 1980.

———. *National Survey on Drug Abuse: Main Findings 1982*. Rockville, Md., 1983.

Department of Health, Education, and Welfare. *Smoking and Health: A Report of the Surgeon General*. Washington, D.C.: Government Printing Office, 1979.

Diehm, A. P.; Seaborn, R. F.; and Wilson, G. C. *Alcohol in Australia: Problems and Programmes*. New York: McGraw-Hill, 1978.

Do It Now Foundation. *Alcohol, Drugs, and Safety*. Phoenix, 1975.

Dominick, John. *The Drug Bust*. New York: The Light Co., 1970.

Domino, E. F., ed. *PCP (Phencyclidine): Historical and Current Perspectives*. Ann Arbor, Mich.: NPP Books.

Drake, Bill. *The Cultivator's Handbook of Marijuana*. Berkeley, Calif.: Book People, 1970.

Drake, William Daniel, Jr. *The Connoisseur's Handbook of Marijuana*. San Francisco: Straight Arrow Books, 1971.

Drug Abuse Council. *The Facts About Drug Abuse*. New York: Free Press, 1980.

Drug Enforcement Administration. *Drugs of Abuse*. Vol. 6, No. 2 (Reprinted from Drug Enforcement). Washington, D.C., July, 1979.

———. *Drug Enforcement*. Vol. 6. No. 3. Washington, D.C. October, 1979.

———. *Marijuana*. Vol. 7, No. 1. Washington, D.C. March, 1980.

———. *Drug Enforcement*. Vol. 8, No. 1. Washington, D.C. Summer, 1981.

———. *Drug Enforcement*. Vol. 9, No. 1. Washington, D.C. Summer, 1982.

———. *Drug Enforcement*. Vol. 9, No. 2. Washington, D.C. Fall, 1982

———. *Drug Enforcement*. Vol. 10, No. 1. Washington, D.C. Spring, 1983.

Du-Torr, B. M. *Drugs, Rituals, and Altered States of Consciousness*. Rotterdam: A. A. Balkema, 1977.

Dubos, Rene. *Man Adapting*. New Haven, Conn.: Yale University Press, 1965.

Duncan, T. L. *Understanding and Helping the Narcotic Addict*. New York: Prentice-Hall, 1965.

Dunlap, James. *Exploring Inner Space: Personal Experiences under LSD-25*. New York: Harcourt, Brace, Jovanovich, 1961.

Dunnell, Karen, and Cartwright, Ann. *Medicine Takers, Prescribers and Hoarders*. London: Routledge and Kegan Paul, 1972.

Durkheim, Emile. *Suicide*. New York: Free Press, 1962.

Dusek, Dorothy, and Girdano, Daniel. *Drugs: A Factual Account*. Reading, Mass.: Addison-Wesley Publishing Co., 1980.

Duster, T. *The Legislation of Morality: Law, Drugs, and Moral Judgment*. New York: Free Press, 1970

Ebin, David, ed. *The Drug Experience*. New York: Grove Press, 1961.

Edwards, Griffith, et al. *Drugs and Drug Dependence*. Lexington, Mass.: Lexington Books, 1976.

Eells, Kenneth. *Pot: Medical and Psychological Aspects of Marihuana*. Pasadena, Calif.: California Institute of Technology, 1968.

Efron, D. H., ed. *Psychotomimetic Drugs*. New York: Raven Press, 1969.

Einstein, Stanley. *Beyond Drugs*. Elmsford, N.Y.: Pergamon Press, 1974.

––––––– . ed. *The Community's Response to Drug Use*. Elmsford, N.Y.: Pergamon Press, 1980.

––––––– . *Drugs in Relation to the Drug User*. Elmsford, N.Y.: Pergamon Press, 1980.

––––––– . *Use and Misuse of Drugs*. Belmont, Calif.: Wadsworth Publishing Co., 1970.

Eldridge, William Butler. *Narcotics and the Law*. New York: New York University Press, 1962.

Elgin, Kathleen, and Osterritter, John F. *The Ups and Downs of Drugs*. New York: Alfred A. Knopf, 1972.

Ellinwood, E. H., and Cohen, S. *Current Concepts on Amphetamine Abuse*. Washington, D.C.: Government Printing Office, 1972.

Ellis, Albert. *Reason and Emotion in Psychotherapy*. New York: Lyle Stuart, 1962.

Endore, G. *Synanon*. Garden City, N.Y.: Doubleday, 1967.

Engel, Madeline, H. *The Drug Scene: A Sociological Perspective*. Rochelle Park, N.J.: Hayden Book Co., Inc., 1974.

Englemann, Larry. *Intemperance: The Lost War against Liquor*. New York: Free Press, 1979.

Engs, Ruth C. *Responsible Drug and Alcohol Use*. New York: Macmillan, 1979.

Epstein, Samuel, and Lederberg, Joshua, eds. *Drugs of Abuse: Their Genetic and Other Chronic Nonpsychiatric Hazards*. Cambridge, Mass.: The MIT Press, 1971.

Eriksson, K.; Sinclair, J. D.; and Kiianmaa, K. *Animal Models of Alcohol Research*. New York: Academic Press, 1980.

Etons, Ursula. *Angel Dusted: A Family's Nightmare*. New York: Macmillan, 1981.

Faber, Stuart J., et al. *Angel Dust: What Everyone Should Know About PCP*. Los Angeles: Lega Books, 1979.

Falco, Mathea. *Methaqualone: A Study of Drug Control*. Washington, D.C.: Drug Abuse Council, 1975.

Farrere, Claude. *Black Opium*. San Francisco: And/Or Press, 1974.

Feit, Marvin D. *Management and Administration of Drug and Alcohol Programs*. Springfield, Ill.: Charles C. Thomas, 1979.

Fenichel, Otto. *The Psychoanalytic Theory of Neurosis*. New York: W. W. Norton and Co., 1945.

Fiddle, S. *Portraits from a Shooting Gallery*. New York: Harper and Row, 1967.

Fisher, Richard B., and Christie, George A. *A Dictionary of Drugs: The Medicines You Use*. New York: Schocken Books, 1976.

Follmann, Joseph F., Jr. *Helping the Troubled Employee*. New York: Amacom, 1978.

Ford Foundation. *Dealing with Drug Abuse*. New York: Praeger Publishers, 1972.

Forney, Thomas, and Hughes, Frances. *Combined Effects of Alcohol and Other Drugs*. Springfield, Ill.: Charles C. Thomas, 1968.

Fort, Joel. *The Addicted Society: Pleasure–Seeking and Punishment Revisited*. New York: Grove Press, 1981.

_____ . *The Pleasure Seekers: The Drug Crisis, Youth and Society*. New York: Grove Press, 1970.

Fox, Ruth. *The Alcoholic Spouse*. New York: National Council on Alcoholism, 1956.

Frank, Jerome D. *Persuasion and Healing*. Baltimore, Md.: Johns Hopkins Press, 1961.

Frank, Mel, and Rosenthal, Ed. *Marijuana Grower's Guide*. San Francisco: And/Or Press, 1974.

Frazier, J. *Marijuana Farmers: Hemp Cults and Cultures*. Indian Mill, W.V.: Solar Age Press, 1973.

Freedman, M., and Kaplan, H. I. *Comprehensive Textbook of Psychiatry*. Baltimore: Williams and Wilkins, 1967.

Freidson, Eliot. *Profession of Medicine*. New York: Dodd, Mead, 1970.

French, Scott. *The Complete Guide to the Street Drug Game*. Secaucus, N.J.: Lyle Stuart, Inc., 1980.

Freund, E. Edith. *Drugs! Why?* New York: Carlton Press, 1980.

Fuqua, Paul. *Drug Abuse: Investigation and Control*. New York: McGraw-Hill, 1977.

Gage, Freddie. *Everything You Always Wanted to Know About Dope*. Houston: Pulpit Productions, 1971.

Galanter, Marc. *Alcohol and Drug Abuse in Medical Education*. Rockville, Md.: National Institute on Drug Abuse, 1980.

Gannon, Frank. *Drugs: What They Are, How They Look, What They Do*. New York: Warner Books, 1972.

Garattini, S.; Mussini, E.; and Randall, L. O. *The Benzodiazepines*. New York: Raven Press, 1973.

Geller, Allen, and Boas, Maxwell. *The Drug Beat: A Complete Survey of the History, Distribution, Uses and Abuses of Marijuana, LSD and the Amphetamines*. Chicago: Contemporary Books, 1969.

Gibbins, Robert J., et al. *Research Advances in Alcohol and Drug Problems, Vol. 1*. New York: John Wiley and Sons, 1974.

_____ . et al. *Research Advances in Alcohol and Drug Problems, Vol. 2*. New York: John Wiley and Sons, 1975.

_____ . et al. *Research Advances in Alcohol and Drug Problems, Vol. 3*. New York: John Wiley and Sons, 1976.

Gillette, Paul J., ed. *The U.S. Government's Directory of Prescription Drugs and Over–the–Counter Drugs*. New York: Award Books, 1971.

Girdano, Dorothy Dusek, and Girdano, Daniel. *Drugs—A Factual Account*. Reading, Mass.: Addison-Wesley Publishing Company, 1973.

Glasser, William. *The Identity Society*. New York: Harper and Row, 1975.

Glatt, M. M. *Drug Scene in Great Britain*. Baltimore: Williams and Wilkins, 1968.

Goldstein, Paul J. *Prostitution and Drugs*. Lexington, Mass.: Lexington Books, 1979.

Goode, Erich. *Drugs in American Society*. New York: Alfred A. Knopf, 1972.

—————. *The Drug Phenomena: Social Aspects of Drug Taking*. Indianapolis: Bobbs-Merrill Co. Inc., 1973.

—————. ed. *Marihuana*. New York: Atherton Press, 1969.

Goodman, Donald. *Is Alcoholism Hereditary?* Oxford, New York and London: Oxford University Press, 1976.

Goodman, L. S., and Gilman, A. Z., eds. *The Pharmacological Basis of Therapeutics*. New York: Macmillan, 1975.

Goodman, William. *Only Dopes Use Drugs*. Grand Rapids, Mich.: Baker Book House, 1979.

Goodwin, Donald W., and Erickson, Carlton K. *Alcoholism and Affective Disorders: Clinical, Genetic, and Biochemical Studies*. New York: SP Medical and Scientific Books, 1979.

Gordon, Barbara. *I'm Dancing As Fast As I Can*. New York: Bantam Books, 1980.

Goshen, Charles E. *Drinks, Drugs and Do-Gooders*. New York: Free Press, 1973.

Gottheil, Edward A., et al. *Matching Patient Needs and Treatment Methods in Alcoholism and Drug Abuse*. Springfield, Ill.: Charles C. Thomas, 1981.

—————. and Alterman, Arthur I. *Addiction Research and Treatment: Converging Trends*. London: Pergamon Publishing Co., 1979.

—————. McLellan, A. Thomas; and Druley, Keith A. *Substance Abuse and Psychiatric Illness: Proceedings of the Second Annual Coatsville–Jefferson Conference on Addiction, 1978*. New York: Pergamon Press, 1980.

Gottlieb, A. *The Pleasures of Cocaine*. San Francisco: And/Or Press, 1976.

Gould, Leroy, et al. *Connections: Notes from the Heroin World*. New Haven, Conn.: Yale University Press, 1974.

Graedon, Joe. *The People's Pharmacy*. New York: Avon Books, 1977.

—————. *The People's Pharmacy–Two*. New York: Avon Books, 1980.

Grassroots: A Comprehensive Alcohol and Drug Information Service. Hollywood, Calif.: The U.S. Journal, 1981-83.

Gray, Nancy. *Chemical Use and Abuse and the Female Reproductive System*. Phoenix: Do It Now Foundation, 1976.

Greer, Germaine. *The Female Eunuch*. New York: McGraw-Hill, 1971.

Griffin, J. P., and D'Arcy, P. F. *A Manual of Adverse Drug Interactions*. Chicago: Year Book Medical Publications, Inc., 1980.

Grifith, J. Winter. *Drug Information for Patients*. Philadelphia: W. B. Saunders, 1978.

Grinspoon, Lester. *Marijuana Reconsidered*. Cambridge, Mass.: Harvard University Press, 1971.

—————. and Bakalar, J. B. *Cocaine: A Drug and Its Social Evolution*. New York: Basic Books, 1976.

—————. and Hedblom, Peter. *The Speed Culture: Amphetamine Use and Abuse in America*. Cambridge, Mass.: Harvard University Press, 1975.

Groves, W. E.; Rossi, P. H.; and Grafstein, D. *Study of Life Styles and Campus Communities: Preliminary Report*. Baltimore: Johns Hopkins University, 1970.

Grupp, Stanley. *Marijuana*. Columbus, Ohio: Charles E. Merrill Publishing Co., 1971.

Guthrie, D. *A History of Medicine*. London: Nelson and Sons, 1945.

Haberman, Paul W., and Baden, Michael M. *Alcohol, Other Drugs and Violent Death*. New York: Oxford University Press, 1978.

Halper, Sibyl Cline. *The Heroin Trade: From Poppies to Peoria*. Washington, D.C.: Drug Abuse Council, 1977.

Hardy, Richard E., and Cull, John G. *Drug Dependence and Rehabilitation Approaches.* Springfield, Ill.: Charles C. Thomas, 1973.

──── . and Cull, John G., eds. *Drug Language and Lore.* Springfield, Ill.: Charles C. Thomas, 1975.

Harms, E. *Drug Addiction in Youth.* Elmsford, N.Y.: Pergamon Press, 1965.

Hayes, Bill, and Hoffer, William. *Midnight Express.* New York: Popular Library, Inc., 1978.

Heath, Dwight B., and Cooper, A. M. *Alcohol Use and World Cultures: A Comprehensive Bibliography of Anthropological Sources.* Toronto: Addiction Research Foundation, 1981.

Heffern, Richard. *Secrets of the Mind–Altering Plants of Mexico.* New York: Pyramid Books, 1975.

Helmer, John. *Drugs and Minority Oppression.* New York: The Continuum Publishing Corp., 1975.

Hendin, Herbert. *Age of Sensation.* New York: McGraw-Hill, 1977.

High Times Magazine Editors. *The High Times Encyclopedia of Recreational Drugs.* New York: Stonehill Publishing Co., 1978.

Hill, N., ed. *Marijuana: Teenage Killer.* New York: Popular Library, 1971.

Hoffer, A., and Osmond, H. *The Hallucinogens.* New York: Academic Press, 1967.

Hofmann, Frederick G. *A Handbook on Drug and Alcohol Abuse: The Biomedical Aspects.* New York: Oxford University Press, 1975.

Hogins, Burl, and Bryant, Gerald, Jr. *Drugs and Dissent.* New York: Macmillan, 1970.

Hollander, C., ed. *Background Papers on Student Drug Involvement.* Washington, D.C.: U.S. National Student Association, 1967.

Hollister, L. E. *Chemical Psychosis: LSD and Related Drugs.* Springfield, Ill.: Charles C. Thomas, 1967.

Houser, Norman W. *Drugs: Facts on Their Use and Abuse.* New York: Lothrop, Lee & Shepard Books, a division of William Morrow & Co. Inc., 1969.

Huelke, D. F., and David, R. A. *Pedestrian Fatalities.* Ann Arbor: Highway Safety Research Institute, University of Michigan, 1969.

Hunt, W. A., ed. *Learning Mechanisms in Smoking.* Chicago: Aldine Press, 1970.

Huxley, Aldous. *The Doors of Perception.* New York: Harper & Row, 1954.

Hyde, Margaret O. *Mind Drugs.* New York: McGraw-Hill, 1974.

Ianni, F. A. *Black Mafia: Ethnic Succession in Organized Crime.* New York: Simon and Schuster, 1974.

Idestrom, Carl-Magnus, ed. *Alcohol and Brain Research.* Copenhagen: Munksgaard, 1980.

Inciardi, James A., ed. *The Drugs–Crime Connection.* Beverly Hills, Calif.: Sage Publications, Inc., 1981.

Indian Hemp Drugs Commission. *Report of the . . . Commission, 1893–94.* Reprinted as *Marijuana: The Report of the . . . Commission, 1893–94.* Introduction and Glossary by John Kaplan. Silver Springs, Md.: Jefferson, 1969.

Institute of Medicine, Division of Health Promotion and Disease Prevention. *Alcoholism, Alcohol Abuse and Related Problems: Opportunities for Research.* Washington, D.C.: Academy Press, 1980.

Isabell, Harris. "Clinical Research on Addiction in the United States." In *Narcotic Drug Addiction Problems,* edited by Robert B. Livingston. Bethesda, Md.: National Institute of Mental Health, 1958.

Iverson, S., and Iversen, L. *Behavioral Pharmacology.* New York: Oxford University Press, 1975.

Jacobson, Richard, and Zinberg, Norman E. *The Social Basis of Drug Abuse Prevention.* Washington, D.C.: Drug Abuse Council, 1975.

Jaffe, Jerome, et al. *Addictions: Issues and Answers*. New York: Harper & Row, 1979.

James, John D., et al. *A Guide to Drug Interaction*. New York: McGraw-Hill, 1978.

Jeffee, Saul. *Narcotics—An American Plan*. New York: Paul S. Eriksson, Inc., 1972.

Jellinek, E. M. *Government Programs on Alcoholism: A Review of the Activities in Some Foreign Countries*. Ottawa: Department of National Health and Welfare, 1963.

————. *The Alcoholism Complex*. New York: Christopher D. Smithers Foundation, 1960.

————. *The Disease Concept of Alcoholism*. New Haven, Conn.: Hillhouse Press, 1960.

Jessor, Richard, et al. *Society, Personality, and Deviant Behavior*. New York: Holt, Rinehart and Winston, 1968.

Johnson, B. D. *Marihuana Users and Drug Subcultures*. New York: John Wiley and Sons, 1973.

Joint Commission on Accreditation of Hospitals. *Consolidated Standards for Child, Adolescent, and Adult Psychiatric Alcoholism and Drug Abuse Programs*. Chicago, 1979.

Joint Committee of the American Bar Association and the American Medical Association on Narcotic Drugs. *Drug Addiction: Crime or Disease?* Introduction by Alfred R. Lindesmith. Bloomington, Ind.: Indiana University Press, 1971.

Jones, E. *The Life and Work of Sigmund Freud*. Vol. 1. New York: Basic Books, 1961.

Jones, Hardin, and Jones, Helen. *Sensual Drugs*. New York: Cambridge University Press, 1979.

Jones, Kenneth L., et al. *Drugs and Alcohol*. New York: Harper and Row, 1978.

Josephson, Eric, and Carroll, Eleanor E., eds. *Drug Use: Epidemiological and Sociological Approaches*. New York: John Wiley and Sons, 1974.

Judson, H. F. *Heroin Addiction in Britain: What Americans Can Learn from the English Experience*. New York: Harcourt, Brace, Jovanovitch, 1974.

Julien, Robert M. *A Primer of Drug Action*. San Francisco: W. H. Freeman and Co., 1981.

Kalant, Harold, and Kalant, Oriana Josseau. *Drugs, Society and Personal Choice*. Don Mills, Ontario: General Publishing, 1971.

Kalant, Oriana Josseau. *Alcohol and Drug Problems in Women*. Vol. 5. New York: Plenum Publishing Corp., 1980.

Kalant, P. J. *The Amphetamines: Toxicity and Addiction*. Toronto: University of Toronto Press, 1966.

Kalent, L. *Mushrooms, Molds, and Miracles*. New York: John Day, 1965.

Kaplan, John. *Marijuana: The New Prohibition*. New York: World Press, 1970.

————. *The Hardest Drug: Heroin and Public Policy*. Chicago: University of Chicago Press, 1983.

Kaplan, Eugene H., and Wieder, Herbert. *Drugs Don't Take People, People Take Drugs*. Secaucus, N.J.: Lyle Stuart, 1974.

Kastl, Albert J., and Kastl, Lena. *Journey Back: Escaping the Drug Trap*. Chicago: Nelson-Hall Publishers, 1975.

Kaufman, Edward, and Kaufman, Pauline N. *Family Therapy of Drug and Alcohol Abuse*. New York: Gardner Press, 1979.

Kavaler, L. *The Amphetamines*. Springfield, Ill.: Charles C. Thomas, 1966.

Keller, Mark; McCormick, Mairi; and Efron, Vera. *A Dictionary of Words About Alcohol*. New Brunswick, N.J.: Rutgers Center of Alcohol Studies, 1982.

Keniston, Kenneth. *Youth and Dissent: The Rise of a New Opposition*. New York: Harcourt, Brace, Jovanovich, 1971.

Kerlinger, Frederick N. *Foundations of Behavioral Research*. New York: Holt, Rinehart and Winston, 1964.

Keup, Wolfram, ed. *Drug Abuse: Current Concepts and Research.* Springfield, Ill.: Charles C. Thomas, 1972.

Kiloh, L. G., and Bell, D. S., eds. *Alcoholism and Drug Dependency.* London: Butterworth, 1969.

King, Rufus. *The Drug Hang–up: America's Fifty Year Folly.* Springfield, Ill.: Charles C. Thomas, 1974.

Kissin, Benjamin, and Begleiter, Henri, eds. *The Biology of Alcoholism, Vol. 1, Biochemistry.* New York: Plenum Press, 1972.

——— . and Begleiter, Henri, eds. *The Biology of Alcoholism, Vol. 2, Physiology and Behavior.* New York: Plenum Press, 1972.

——— . and Begleiter, Henri, eds. *The Biology of Alcoholism, Vol. 3, Clinical Pathology.* New York: Plenum Press, 1974.

——— . and Begleiter, Henri, eds. *The Biology of Alcoholism, Vol. 4, Social Aspects of Alcoholism.* New York: Plenum Press, 1976.

——— . and Begleiter, Henri, eds. *The Biology of Alcoholism, Vol. 5, Treatment and Rehabilitation of the Chronic Alcoholic.* New York: Plenum Press, 1977.

Kleps, Arthur J. *The Boo Hoo Bible.* New Mexico: Toad Books, 1971.

Kline, Nathan S.; Alexander, Stuart F.; and Chamberlain, Ampero. *Psychotropic Drugs: A Manual for Emergency Management of Overdosage.* Oradell, N.J.: Medical Economics Company, 1974.

Kluver, H. *Mescal and Mechanics of Hallucination.* Chicago: University of Chicago Press, 1966.

Knapp Commission. *The Knapp Commission Report on Police Corruption.* New York: G. Braziller, 1973.

Kolb, Lawrence. *Drug Addiction: A Medical Problem.* Springfield, Ill.: Charles C. Thomas, 1962.

Krasnegor, N. A. *Behavioral Analysis and Treatment of Substance Abuse.* Washington, D.C.: National Institute on Drug Abuse, 1979.

Kron, Yves J. *Mainline to Nowhere: The Making of a Heroin Addict.* New York: Pantheon, 1965.

Kropp, Paul. *Dope Deal.* St. Paul, Minn.: EMC Corp., 1981.

Krusich, Walter S. *Drugs: It Can't Happen to Me!* Denver, Col.: Accent Books, 1979.

Laing, R. D. *The Divided Self.* Harmondsworth, England: Penguin, 1965.

Lall, Bernard, and Lall, Geeta. *Marijuana—Friend or Foe?* Washington, D.C.: Review and Herald Publishing Association, 1979.

Larkin, E. J. *The Treatment of Alcoholism: Theory, Practice, and Evaluation.* Ontario: Addiction Research Foundation, 1974.

Laurie, Peter. *Drugs: Medical, Psychological and Social Facts.* Harmondsworth, England: Penguin, 1967.

Leary, T.; Metzner, R.; and Alpert, R. *The Psychedelic Experience.* New Hyde Park, N.Y.: University Books, 1964.

Leary, Timothy. *High Priest.* Cleveland, N.Y.: World Publishing Company, 1968.

Lee, David. *Cocaine Consumer's Handbook.* Berkeley, Calif.: And/Or Press, 1976.

Leech, K., and Jordan, Brenda. *Drugs for Young People: Their Use and Misuse.* Elmsford, N.Y.: Pergamon Press, 1968.

Leech, Kenneth. *Youthquake: The Growth of a Counter Culture Through Two Decades.* Totowa, N.J.: Littlefield, Adams and Co., 1977.

Leiberman, M. A., and Borman, L. D. *Self–Help Groups for Coping with Crises: Origins, Members, Processes. and Impact.* San Francisco: Jossev-Bass 1979

Leonard, Henry L., et al. *Mystification and Drug Misuse*. San Francisco: Jossey-Bass, 1971.

Lewin, Louis. *Phantastica: Narcotic and Stimulating Drugs*. Trans. by P. H. A. Wirth. London: Routledge & Kegan Paul, 1964.

Lewis, Arthur J., ed. *Modern Drug Encyclopedia and Therapeutic Index: A Compendium*. New York: Yorke Medical Books, 1981.

Lewis, B. *The Sexual Power of Marijuana: An Intimate Report on 208 Adult Middle–Class Users*. New York: Wyden, 1970.

Li, T. K.; Schenker, S.; and Lumeng, L. *Alcohol and Nutrition: Proceedings of a Workshop, September 26–27, 1977, Indianapolis, Indiana*. Washington, D.C.: Government Printing Office, 1979.

Lieberman, Florence, et al. *Before Addiction: How to Help Youth*. New York: Human Sciences Press, 1973.

Linder, Ronald L. *PCP: The Devil's Dust*. Belmont, Calif.: Wadsworth Publishing Co., 1981.

Lindesmith, A. R. *Addiction and Opiates*. Chicago: Aldine Publishing Co., 1965.

––––––– . *The Addict and the Law*. New York: Random House, 1965.

Lingeman, Richard R. *Drugs from A to Z*. New York: McGraw-Hill, 1974.

Linkletter, Art, and Gallup, George. *My Child on Drugs? Youth and the Drug Culture*. Cincinnati, Ohio: Standard Publishing Co., 1981.

Liska, Ken. *Drugs and the Human Body*. New York: Macmillan, 1981.

Lockhart, D. L. *The Swinging Door: An Evaluation of Services to and Needs of Street People in Downtown Salinas*. Salinas, Calif.: Sun Street Centers, Community Alcoholism Programs, 1979.

Loftus, Elizabeth. *Memory*. Reading, Mass.: Addison-Wesley Publishing Company, 1980.

Long, James W. *The Essential Guide to Prescription Drugs: What You Need to Know for Safe Drug Use*. New York: Harper and Row, 1980.

Lotter, J. M. *Social Problems in the RSA*. Pretoria: Institute for Sociological, Demographic and Criminological Research, South African Human Sciences Research Council, 1979.

Louria, D. B. *Overcoming Drugs*. New York: McGraw-Hill, 1971.

––––––– . *The Drug Scene*. New York: McGraw-Hill, 1968.

––––––– . *Nightmare Drugs*. New York: Simon & Schuster, 1966.

Lowinson, Joyce H., and Ruiz, Pedro. *Substance Abuse: Clinical Problems and Perspectives*. Easton, Md.: Williams and Wilkins Co., 1981.

MacLennan, Anne. *Women: Their Use of Alcohol and Other Legal Drugs*. Toronto: Addiction Research Foundation, 1976.

MacLeod, Anne. *Growing Up in America*. Rockville, Md.: National Institute on Drug Abuse, 1978.

Madden, J. S. *Guide to Alcohol and Drug Dependence*. Bristol, England: J. Wright and Sons, 1979.

––––––– . Walker, Robin; and Kenyon, W. H. *Aspects of Alcohol and Drug Dependence*. Kent, England: Pitman Medical Limited, 1980.

Madison, Arnold. *Drugs and You*. New York: Pocket Books, 1972.

Majchrowicz, Edward, and Noble, Ernest P. *Biochemistry and Pharmacology of Ethanol*. 2 vols. New York and London: Plenum Publishing Corp., 1979.

Malcolm X. *Autobiography*. New York: Grove Press, 1965.

Malcolm, A. I. *The Craving for the High*. New York: Simon & Schuster, 1975.

Malcolm, Andrew I. *The Pursuit of Intoxication*. New York: Pocket Books, 1971.

Malzberg, Benjamin. *The Alcoholic Psychosis*. New Haven: Yale Center of Alcohol Studies, 1960.

Mann, George A. *Recovery of Reality: Overcoming Chemical Dependency*. New York: Harper and Row, 1979.

Mann, Marty. *New Primer on Alcoholism*. New York: Holt, Rinehart and Winston, 1963.

────── . *Primer on Alcoholism*. New York: Holt, Rinehart and Winston, 1958.

Manning, Peter K. *The Narc's Game: Organizational and Informational Limits on Drug Law Reinforcement*. Cambridge, Mass.: The MIT Press, 1980.

Margolis, Jack S. *Complete Book of Recreational Drugs*. Los Angeles: Price/Stern/Sloan, 1978.

────── . and Clorfene, Richard. *A Child's Garden of Grass*. Los Angeles: Cliff House Books, a division of Price/Stern/Sloan, 1976.

Marin, P., and Cohen, A. Y. *Understanding Drug Use*. New York: Harper and Row, 1971.

Markham, J. M. "What's All This Talk of Heroin Maintenance?" *New York Times Magazine*, July 2, 1972.

Marr, John S. *The Good Drug and the Bad Drug*. New York: M. Evans and Company, Inc., 1970.

Marriott, Alice, and Rachlin, Carol K. *Peyote*. New York: New American Library, 1972.

Maslow, Abraham H. *Religions, Values, and Peak Experiences*. New York: The Viking Press, 1970.

Mason, David, and Dyller, Fran. *Pharmaceutical Dictionary & Reference for Prescription Drugs*. New York: Playboy Paperback, 1982.

Masters, W. R., and Houston, J. *The Varieties of Psychedelic Experience*. New York: Dell Publishing, 1966.

Maurer, David W., and Vogel, Victor H. *Narcotics and Narcotic Addiction*. Springfield, Ill.: Charles C. Thomas, 1973.

McClelland, David C. *The Achieving Society*. Princeton: Van Nostrand, 1961.

────── . Davis, William N.; Kalin, Rudolf; and Wanner, Eric. *The Drinking Man*. New York: Free Press, 1972.

McCord, William, and McCord, Joan. *Origins of Alcoholism*. Stanford, Calif.: Stanford University Press, 1960.

McCoy, A. M. *The Politics of Heroin in Southeast Asia*. New York: Harper and Row, 1972.

McLennan, Ross J. *Booze, Bucks, Bamboozle and You!* Oklahoma City: Sane Press, 1978.

Mechoulam, R., ed. *Marijuana: Chemistry, Pharmacology, Metabolism, and Clinical Effects*. New York: Academic Press, 1973.

Mello, Nancy K. *Advances in Substance Abuse: Behavioral and Biological Research*. Greenwich, Conn.: JAI Press, 1980.

Meltzoff, Julian, and Kornreich, Melvin. *Research in Psychotherapy*. New York: Atherton Press, 1970.

Mendelson, Wallace B. *The Use and Misuse of Sleeping Pills: A Clinical Guide to Treatment*. New York: Plenum Publishing Corp., 1980.

Menditto, Joseph. *Drugs of Addiction and Non–Addiction: Their Use and Abuse*. Troy, N.Y.: Whitson Publishing Co., 1970.

Messick, Hank. *Of Grass and Snow*. Englewood Cliffs, N.J.; Prentice-Hall, 1979.

Meyer, N. *The Seven Per Cent Solution*. New York: Ballantine Books, 1976.

Miller, L. L., ed. Marijuana: *Effects on Human Behavior*. New York: Academic Press, 1974.

Miller, William R. *The Addictive Behaviors: Treatment of Alcoholism, Drug Abuse, Smoking and Obesity*. Elmsford, N.Y.: Pergamon Press, 1980.

Mishara, Brian L., and Kastenbaum, Robert. *Alcohol and Old Age*. *New York:* Grune and Stratton, 1980.

Mitchell, Alexander. *Drugs—The Parents' Dilemma*. Westport, Conn.: Technomic Publishing Co. Inc., 1972.

Modell, Walter. *Drugs in Current Use and New Drugs*. New York: Springer Publishing Co., 1981.

Moller, Richard. *Marijuana: Your Legal Rights*. Reading, Mass.: Addison-Wesley Publishing Co., 1981.

Moore, Mark H. *Buy and Bust*. Lexington, Mass.: Lexington Books, 1977.

Morgan, H. Wayne, ed. *Yesterday's Addicts: American Society and Drug Abuse*. Norman, Okla.: University of Oklahoma Press, 1980.

——— . *Drugs in America: A Social History 1800–1980*. Syracuse, New York: Syracuse University Press, 1981.

Mortimer, W. Golden. *History of Coca, The Divine Plant of the Incas*. San Francisco: And/Or Press, 1974.

Moskowitz, Herbert, ed. *Drugs and Driving*. Elmsford, N.Y.: Pergamon Press, 1976.

Musto, D. *The American Disease: Origins of Narcotic Control*. New Haven: Yale University Press, 1973.

Musto, D. F. "A Study of Cocaine: Sherlock Holmes and Sigmund Freud." *Journal of American Medical Association*, 1968, 204(1):27-32.

Myer, R. E., and Mirin, S. M., eds. *The Heroin Stimulus: Implications for a Theory of Addiction*. New York: Plenum Publishing Corp., 1979.

Nahas, G. G. *Marihuana: Deceptive Weed*. New York: Raven Press, 1973.

National Anti-Drug Coalition. *What Every Parent Should Know About Drugs*. New York: New Benjamin Franklin House, 1981.

National Clergy Conference on Alcoholism. *The Blue Book, Vol XXXI. Proceedings of the 31st National Clergy Conference on Alcoholism, Omaha, Nebraska, May 22–26, 1979*, n.d.

National Commission on Marihuana and Drug Abuse. *Drug Use in America: Problem in Perspective*. 4 vols. Washington, D.C.: Government Printing Office, 1973.

National Council on Alcoholism. *The Rights of Alcoholics and Their Families*. New York, 1976.

National Institute of Mental Health. *Peanuts and Tea: A Selected Glossary of Terms Used by Drug Addicts*. Lexington, Ky.: the Institute, 1972.

National Institute on Alcohol Abuse and Alcoholism. *Alcohol and Health*. First Special Report to the U.S. Congress from the Secretary of Health, Education and Welfare. Washington, D.C.: Government Printing Office, 1971.

——— . *Alcohol and Health: New Knowledge*. Second Special Report to the U.S. Congress from the Secretary of Health, Education and Welfare. Washington, D.C.: Government Printing Office, 1978.

——— . *Alcohol and Health*. Third Special Report to the U.S. Congress from the Secretary of Health, Education and Welfare. Washington, D.C.: Government Printing Office, 1978.

National Institute on Drug Abuse. *Research Monograph Series:* Willette, Robert, ed. *Narcotic Antagonists: The Search for Long–acting Preparations;* Williams, Jay R. *Effects of Labeling the "Drug Abuser": An Inquiry;* Willette, Robert, ed. *Drugs and Driving;* Blaine, Jack D., and Julius, Demetrios A., eds. *Psychodynamics of Drug Dependence;* Petersen, Robert C., and Stillman, Richard C., eds. *Cocaine: 1977;* Sharp, Charles Wm., and Brehm, Mary Lee, eds. *Review of Inhalants: Euphoria to Dysfunction;* Rittenhouse, Joan Dunne, ed. *The Epidemiology of Heroin and other Narcotics;* Jarvik, Murray E., et al., eds. *Research on Smok-*

ing Behavior; Petersen, Robert C., ed. *The International Challenge of Drug Abuse;* Petersen, Robert C., and Stillman, Richard C., eds. *Phencyclidine (PCP) Abuse: An Appraisal;* Gottschalk, Louis A., et al. *Drug Abuse Deaths in Nine Cities: A Survey Report;* Petersen, Robert C. *Marijuana Research Findings: 1980.* Washington, D.C.: Government Printing Office.

Nellis, Muriel. *The Female Fix.* New York: Penguin, 1981.

Nicholi, Armand M., Jr. *The Harvard Guide to Modern Psychiatry.* Cambridge, Mass.: Harvard University Press, 1979.

Non-Medical Use of Drugs Directorate. *Core Knowledge in the Drug Field.* Edited by Lorne A. Phillips, G. Rosee Ramsey, Leonard Blumenthal, and Patrick Crawshaw. Ottawa, Canada: National Health and Welfare, 1978.

Norback, Judith. *The Alcohol and Drug Abuse Yearbook/Directory 1979–80.* New York: Van Nostrand Reinhold Co., 1979.

Nowlis, Helen. *Drugs on the College Campus.* New York: Anchor Books, 1969.

————. *Drugs Demystified.* Paris: UNESCO, 1980.

Null, Gary, and Null, Steven. *How to Get Rid of the Poisons in Your Body.* New York: Arco Publishing Co., 1977.

O'Brien, Robert, and Chafetz, Morris. *The Encyclopedia of Alcoholism.* New York: Facts on File, 1982.

O'Donnell, John A., and Ball, John C., eds. *Narcotic Addiction.* New York: Harper and Row, 1966.

Olive, G. *Drug–Action Modification—Comparative Pharmacology.* Oxford, England: Pergamon Publishing Corp., 1979.

Osol, Arthur, and Pratt, Robertson, eds. *The United States Dispensatory.* Philadelpha: J. B. Lippincott Company, 1973.

Patterson, H. Robert, et al. *Falconer's Current Drug Handbook: 1980–1982.* Philadelphia: W. B. Saunders Co., 1980.

Patterson, H. Robert; Gustafson, Edward A.; and Sheridan, Eleanor. *Current Drug Handbook 1982–1984.* Philadelphia: W. B. Saunders Co., 1982.

Pattison, E. Mansell, and Kaufman, eds. *Encyclopedic Handbook of Alcoholism.* New York: Gardner Press, Inc., 1982.

————. Sobell, Mark B.; and Sobell, Linda Carter. *Emerging Concepts of Alcohol Dependence.* New York: Springer, 1977.

Pearl, Raymond. *Alcohol and Longevity.* New York: Alfred A. Knopf, 1926.

Peele, Stanton. *Love and Addiction.* New York: Signet, 1976.

————. *The Addiction Experience.* Center City, Minn.: Hazelden Foundation, 1980.

Perry, Samuel W. *The Simon and Schuster Pocket Encyclopedia of Prescription and Nonprescription Drugs.* New York: Simon and Schuster, 1982.

Peterson, David M., et al. *Drugs and the Elderly: Social and Pharmacological Issues.* Springfield, Ill.: Charles Thomas, 1979.

Phillips, Joel L., and Wynne, Ronald D. *Cocaine: The Mystique and the Reality.* New York: Avon Books, 1980.

Phillipson, R. V. *Modern Trends in Drug Dependence and Alcoholism.* Woburn, Mass.: Butterworth Publications, Inc. 1970.

Physicians' Desk Reference, 36th edition. Oradell, N.J.: Medical Economics Company, 1982.

Pittman, David Joshua. *World Health Organization Committee of Experts in Alcoholism.* New York: Harper and Row, 1967.

_____ . and Gordon, C. W. *Revolving Door. A Study of the Chronic Police Case Inebriate.* Glencoe, Ill.: Free Press, 1958.

Polacsek, E., et al. *Interaction of Alcohol and Other Drugs.* Toronto: Addiction Research Foundation, 1972.

Polich, J. Michael, and Armor, David J. *The Course of Alcoholism: Four Years after Treatment.* Santa Monica: Rand Corp., 1980.

Pope, Harrison, Jr. *Voices from the Drug Culture.* Boston: Beacon Press, 1971.

Popham, R. E., ed. *Alcohol and Alcoholism.* Toronto: University of Toronto Press, 1970.

Powell, David J. *Clinical Supervision, Skills for Substance Abuse Counselors: Manual.* New York: Human Sciences Press, 1980.

Pradhan, S. N., and Dutta, S. N. *Drug Abuse: Clinical and Basic Aspects.* St. Louis, Mo.: Mosby, 1977.

Pratt, Arthur. *How To Help and Understand the Alcoholic or Drug Addict.* Louisville: Love Street Books, 1980.

Prattenberg, J. F. X. Carroll, and Bolognese, C. *Treating Mixed Psychiatric–Drug Addicted and Alcoholic Patients.* Eagleville, Pa.: Eagleville Hospital and Rehabilitation Center, 1979.

Puharich, A. *The Sacred Mushroom.* Garden City, N.Y.: Doubleday, 1959.

Rachman, S., and Teasdale, J. *Aversion Therapy and Behavior Disorders.* London: Routledge and Kegan Paul, 1969.

Rankin, J. G., ed. *Alcohol, Drugs and Brain Damage.* Toronto: Alcoholism and Drug Addiction Research Foundation of Ontario, 1975.

Richard, J.; Whitehead III, Bonnie and Charles. *The Marihuana Convictions: A History of Marihuana Prohibition in the United States.* Charlottesville: University of Virginia Press, 1974.

Richter, Derek. *Addiction and Brain Damage.* Baltimore: University Park Press, 1980.

Richter, Ralph W., ed. *Medical Aspects of Drug Abuse.* Hagerstown, Md.: Harper and Row, 1975.

Riesman, David. *The Lonely Crowd.* New Haven, Conn.: Yale University Press, 1950.

Robins, L. N. *The Vietnam Drug User Returns.* U.S. Executive Office of the President, Special Action Office for Drug Abuse Prevention. Special Action Office Monograph, Series A, No. 2. Washington, D.C.: Government Printing Office, 1974.

Rock, Paul, ed. *Drugs and Politics.* New Brunswick, N.J.: Transaction Books, 1977.

Rodman, Morton J., and Dipalma, Joseph R. *More Readings in Drug Therapy.* Oradell, N.J.: Medical Economics Company, 1972.

Roe, Daphne. *Alcohol and the Diet.* Westport, Conn.: AVI Press, 1981.

Roffman, R. A., and Sapil, E. "Marijuana in Vietnam." *Technical Report for the Surgeon–General.* Department of the Army, 1969.

Roffman, Roger. *Marijuana as Medicine.* Austin, Tex.: Madrona Press Inc., 1981.

Rorabaugh, W. J. *The Alcoholic Republic: An American Tradition.* New York: Oxford University Press, 1979.

Roseman, Bernard. *LSD: The Age of Mind.* Hollywood, Calif.: Wilshire Book Co., 1966.

_____ . *The Peyote Story.* Hollywood, Calif.: Wilshire Book Co., 1966.

Rosenbaum, Max. *Drug Abuse and Drug Addiction.* New York: Gordon and Breach, Science Publishers, Inc., 1973.

Rosenthal, M. S. *Drugs, Parents, and Children.* Boston: Houghton Mifflin, 1972.

Rosevear, John. *Pot, A Handbook of Marijuana.* New Hyde Park, N.Y.: University Books, 1967.

Rossi, Peter H.; Freeman, Howard E.; and Wright, Sonia R. *Evaluation: A Systematic Approach.* Beverly Hills: Sage Publications, 1979.

Rubenstein, Morton K. *A Doctor's Guide to Non–Prescription Drugs*. New York: Signet, 1977.

Russel G. K. *Marihuana Today: A Compilation of Medical Findings for the Layman*. Elmsford, N.Y.: Pergamon Press, 1979.

Russo, J., ed. *Amphetamine Abuse*. Springfield, Ill.: Charles C. Thomas, 1968.

Rutman, L., ed. *Drugs: Use and Abuse*. Winnipeg: University of Winnipeg Press, 1969.

Sabbag, R.*Snowblind:A Brief Career in the Cocaine Trade*. New York: Avon Books, 1978.

Saltman, Jules. *Marijuana and Your Child*. New York: Grosset and Dunlap, 1970

Sanders, Ed. *Coming Down*. New York: The United International Copyright Representatives, Ltd., 1966.

Satinder, Paul K. *Drug Use: Criminal, Sick or Cultural?* Rosalyn Heights, N.Y.: Libra Books, 1980.

Schecter, A. et al, eds. *Drug Abuse: Modern Trends, Issues and Perspectives*. New York: Marcel Dekker, Inc., 1978.

_____ . ed. *Drug Dependence and Alcoholism, Vol. 1, Biomedical Issues*. New York: Plenum Publishing Corp., 1980.

_____ . ed. *Drug Dependence and Alcoholism, Vol. 2, Social and Behavioral Issues*. New York: Plenum Press, 1980.

Scher, Jordan M. *Drug Abuse in Industry: Growing Corporate Dilemma*. Springfield, Ill.: Charles C. Thomas, 1981.

Scherer, Roy B. *Identity Crisis: "Lookalike" Drugs & "Peashooters"—Identifying Over–the–Counter Drugs*. Richmond, Va.: ADAPTS, 1981.

Schmidt, J. E. *Narcotics: Lingo and Lore*. Springfield, Ill.: Charles C. Thomas, 1959.

Schuckit, M. A. *Drug and Alcohol Abuse: A Clinical Guide to Diagnosis and Treatment*. New York: Plenum Medical Book Co., 1979.

Schulberg, A.; Sheldon, A.; and Baker, F. *Program Evaluation in the Health Fields*. New York: Behavioral Publications, 1969.

Schur, Edwin M. *Narcotic Addiction in Britain and America*. Bloomington: Indiana University Press, 1962.

Schwarzrock, Shirley, and Wrenn, C. Gilbert. *Facts and Fantasies About Drugs*. Circle Pines, Minn.: American Guidance Service, 1970.

_____ . and Wrenn, C. Gilbert. *The Mind Benders*. Circle Pines, Minn.: American Guidance Service, 1971.

Shafer, Raymond P., ed. *Marihuana, A Signal of Misunderstanding: The Official Report of the National Commission on Marihuana and Drug Abuse*. New York: New American Library, 1972.

Shain, Martin, et al. *Influence, Choice and Drugs: Toward a Systematic Approach to the Prevention of Substance Abuse*. Lexington, Mass.: Lexington Books, 1977.

Sharples, Anthony. *The Scorpion's Tail*. New York: Taplinger Publishing Co. Inc., 1976.

Shedd, Charlie W. *Is Your Family Turned On? Coping with the Drug Culture*. Waco, Tex.: Word Books, 1971.

Silverman, Harold L., and Simon, Gilbert I. *The Pill Book*. New York: Bantam Books, 1979.

Silverman, Milton, et al. *Pills and the Public Purse*. Berkeley, Calif.: University of California Press, 1981.

Silverstein, Alvin, and Silverstein, Virginia B. *Alcoholism*. Philadelphia: J. B. Lippincott Co., 1975.

Simmons, J. L. *Marihuana: Myths and Realities*. North Hollywood, Calif.: Brandon House, 1967.

Simmons, Luis R., and Said, Abdul A., eds. *Drugs, Politics and Diplomacy: The International*

Connection. Beverly Hills, Calif.: Sage Publications, Inc., 1974.

Smart, R. E. *LSD in the Treatment of Alcoholism*. Toronto: University of Toronto Press, 1968.

Smart, Reginald G. *The New Drinkers: Teenage Use and Abuse of Alcohol*. 2nd ed. Toronto: Addiction Research Foundation, 1980.

———. et al. *Lysergic Acid Diethylamide (LSD) in the Treatment of Alcoholism: An Investigation of Its Effects on Drinking Behavior, Personality Structure and Social Functioning*. Toronto: University of Toronto Press, 1967.

Smith, David E. *The New Social Drug*. Englewood Cliffs, N.J.: Prentice-Hall, 1970.

———. and Gay, G. R. *It's So Good, Don't Even Try It Once: Heroin in Perspective*. Englewood Cliffs, N.J.: Prentice-Hall, 1972.

———., and Wesson, Donald R. *Uppers and Downers*. Englewood Cliffs, N.J.: Prentice-Hall, 1973.

Snyder, S. *Madness and the Brain*. New York: McGraw-Hill, 1974.

Sobel, Robert. *They Satisfy: The Cigarette in American Life*. Garden City, N.Y.: Doubleday, 1975.

Sobell, Linda Carter; Sobell, Mark B.; and War, Elliott. *Evaluating Alcohol and Drug Abuse Treatment Effectiveness*. New York: Pergamon Press, 1980.

Social Service Publications. *Narcotics and Drug Abuse, A to Z*. Queens Village, N.Y.: Croner Publications, Inc., 1982.

Sokoloff, Boris. *The Permissive Society*. New Rochelle, N.Y.: Arlington House, 1971.

Solomon, D., ed. *LSD: The Consciousness–Expanding Drug*. New York: G. P. Putnam, 1964.

———. ed. *The Marihuana Papers*. Indianapolis: Bobbs-Merrill Company, Inc., 1966.

Souter, John. *The Pleasure Seller*. Wheaton, Ill.: Tyndale Publishers, 1979.

Srimson, G. V. *Heroin and Behavior*. New York: John Wiley and Sons, 1973.

Stafford, P. G., and Golightly, B. H. *LSD: The Problem–Solving Psychedelic*. New York: Universal Publishing, 1967.

Starks, Michael. *Cocaine Fiends and Reefer Madness: An Illustrated History of Drugs in the Movies*. East Brunswick, N.J.: Cornwall Books, 1981.

———. *Marijuana Potency*. Berkeley, Calif.: And/Or Press, 1977.

Stearn, Jess. *The Seekers*. New York: Doubleday, 1969.

Stefanis, C.; Dornbush, R.; and Fink, M., eds. *Hashish—Studies of Long–term Use*. New York: Raven Press, 1977.

Steinmetz, E. F. *Kava–Kava, Famous Drug Plant of the South Sea Islands*. New York: High Times Press, 1973.

Stevenson, G. H. *Drug Addiction in British Columbia*. Vancouver: University of British Columbia, 1956.

Stewart, George R. *American Ways of Life*. New York: Doubleday and Co., 1954.

Strack, Jay. *Drugs and Drinking*. Nashville, Tenn.: Sceptre Books, 1979.

Stwertka, Eve, and Stwertka, Albert. *Marijuana*. New York: Franklin Watts, Inc., 1979.

Sumach, Alexander. *Growing Your Own Stone*. Toronto: Yellow Ford Truck, 1973.

Summers, Marcia, et al. *Our Chemical Culture: Drug Use and Misuse*. Nashville, Tenn.: Nelson Thomas Inc., 1981.

Szasz, Thomas. *Ceremonial Chemistry: The Ritual Persecution of Drugs, Addicts, and Pushers*. Garden City, N.Y.: Anchor Press, 1974.

Talland, George A. *Deranged Memory*. New York: Academic Press, 1965.

———. and Waugh, N. C., eds. *The Pathology of Memory*. New York, Academic Press, 1969.

Task Force Report. *Narcotics, Marijuana and Dangerous Drugs: Findings and Recommendations*. The President's Commission on Law Enforcement and Administration of Justice. Washington, D.C.: Government Printing Office, 1967.

Taylor, Norman. *Narcotics, Nature's Dangerous Gifts*. New York: Dell Publishing Company, 1966.

Tec, Nechame. *The Grass is Green in Suburbia: A Sociological Study of Adolescent Usage of Illicit Drugs*. New York: Libra Books, 1974.

Tenin, Peter. *Taking Your Medicine: Drug Regulation in the United States*. Cambridge, Mass.: Harvard University Press, 1980.

Tessler, Diane Jane. *Drugs, Kids, and Schools: Practical Strategies for Educators and Other Concerned Adults*. Rockville, Md.: National Institute on Drug Abuse, 1980.

The Mayor's Committee on Marihuana. *The Marihuana Problem in the City of New York*. New York: The Ronald Press Company, 1972.

The National Narcotics Intelligence Consumers Committee. *The Supply of Drugs to the U.S. Illicit Market From Foreign and Domestic Sources in 1980 (With Projections Through 1984)*. Washington, D.C.: Drug Enforcement Administration, 1982.

Thompson, J. *Alcohol and Drug Research in Saskatchewan, 1970–78: Subject, Index and Abstracts*. Regina: Saskatchewan Alcoholism Commission, 1978.

Tinklenberg, J. R. *Marihuana and Health Hazards*. New York: Academic Press, 1975.

Tolstoy, Leo. *Why Do Men Stupify Themselves?* Blauvelt, N.Y.: Multimedia Publishing Corp., 1978.

Towery, O. B.; Seidenberg, G. R.; and Santoro, V. *Quality Assurance for Alcohol, Drug Abuse, and Mental Health Services: An Annotated Bibliography*. Rockville, Md.: U.S. Alcohol, Drug Abuse, and Mental Health Administration, 1979.

Towns, Charles B. *Habits That Handicap: The Menace of Opium, Alcohol and Tobacco, and the Remedy*. Reprint of 1915 edition. New York: Arno Press, 1981.

Trice, Harrison M. *Alcoholism in America*. New York: McGraw-Hill, 1966.

——— . *Alcoholism in Industry—Modern Procedures*. New York: Christopher D. Smithers Foundation, 1962.

Truax, Lyle H. *Judge's Guide for Alcohol Offenders*. New York: National Council on Alcoholism, 1972.

Tuell, Jim. *The Drug Scene*. Dallas: Tane Press, 1972.

Turner, W. W., ed. *Drugs and Poisons*. Rochester, N.Y.: Aqueduct Books, 1965.

U.S. Department of Health and Human Services. *Research Issues Series: 1. Drugs and Employment; 2. Drugs and Sex; 3. Drugs and Attitude Change; 4. Drugs and Family; Peer Influence; 5. Drugs and Pregnancy; 6. Drugs and Death; 7. Drugs and Addict Lifestyles; 8. A Cocaine Bibliography; 9. Drug Themes in Science Fiction; 10. Drug Themes in Fiction; 11. Predicting Adolescent Drug Abuse; 12. Drug Abuse Instrument Handbook; 13. Data Analysis Strategies and Designs for Substance Abuse Research; 14. Drugs and Personality; 15. Cocaine—Summaries of Psychosocial Research; 16. The Lifestyles of Nine American Cocaine Users—Summary; 17. Drugs and Crime; 18. Drugs Users and the Criminal Justice System; 19. Drugs and Psychopathology; 20. Drug Users and Driving Behaviors; 21. Drugs and Minorities; 22. Research Issues Update, 1978; 23. International Drug Use; 24. Perspectives on the History of Psychoactive Substance Use; 25. Use and Abuse of Amphetamine and its Substitutes; 26. Guide to Drug Abuse Research Terminology; 27. Guide to the Drug Research Literature; 28. Assessing Marijuana Consequences: Selected Questionnaire Items; 29. Drugs and the Family*. Washington, D.C.: Government Printing Office.

Uhr, L., ed. *Drugs and Behavior*. New York: Wiley, 1960.

Usdin, Earl, and Efron, Daniel H. *Psychotropic Drugs and Related Compounds*. Rockville, Md.: Department of Health, Education and Welfare, 1972.

Vischi, T. R., et al. *The Alcohol, Drug Abuse, and Mental Health National Date Book*. Washington, D.C.: U.S. Alcohol, Drug Abuse and Mental Health Administration, 1980.

Vuylsteek, K. *Health Education: Smoking, Alcoholism, Drugs*. Albany: World Health Organization Publications Centre, 1979.

Waddell, Jack O., and Everett, Michael W. *Drinking Behavior among Southwestern Indians: An Anthropological Perspective*. Tucson: University of Arizona Press, 1980.

————. and Watson, O. Michael. *The American Indian in Urban Society*. Boston: Little, Brown and Company, 1971.

Wakefield, D. *The Addict*. New York: Fawcett Books, 1969.

Walker, Lenore E. *The Battered Woman*. New York: Harper and Row, 1979.

Wallace, Bill C. *Education and the Drug Scene*. Lincoln, Neb.: Cliff's Notes, 1974.

Walton, R. P. *Marihuana: America's New Drug Problem*. Philadelphia: J. B. Lippincott Co., 1938.

Wasson, R. G. *Soma: Divine Mushroom of Immortality*. New York: Harcourt, Brace, Jovanovich, 1971.

Way, Walter L. *The Drug Scene: Help or Hang–Up?* Englewood Cliffs, N.J.: Prentice-Hall, 1970.

Weil, A. *The Natural Mind*. Boston: Houghton Mifflin, 1972.

Weil, R. G., ed. *The Psychedelic Reader*. New York: University Books, 1965.

Weinswig, Melvin H. *Use and Misuse of Drugs Subject to Abuse*. Indianapolis: Pegasus Books, 1973.

Weiss, Kenneth L., and Kurland, David J. *Drug Laws and the Rights that Protect You*. New York: Simon and Schuster, 1979.

Weissman, James C. *Drug Abuse: The Law and Treatment Alternatives*. Cincinnati, Ohio: Anderson Publishing Co., 1978.

————. and DuPont, Robert L., eds. *Criminal Justice and Drugs: The Unresolved Connection*. Port Washington, N.Y.; Kennikat Press, Corp., 1981.

Wesson, D. R., and Smith, D. E. *Barbiturates: Their Use, Misuse and Abuse*. Washington, D.C.: Government Printing Office, 1977.

————. and Adams, Kenneth, eds. *Polydrug Abuse: The Results of a National Collaborative Study*. New York: Academic Press, 1978.

Westermeyer, Joseph. *A Primer on Chemical Dependency*. Baltimore, Md.: Williams and Wilkins Publishers, 1978.

Westman, Wesley. *Drug Epidemic: What It Means and How to Combat It*. New York: Dial Press, 1970.

Whitlock, F. *Drugs, Morality, and the Law*. St. Lawrence, Mass.: University of Queensland Press, 1975.

Wicks, Robert J., and Platt, Jerome J. *Drug Abuse: A Criminal Justice Primer*. Beverly Hills, Calif.: Glencoe Press, 1977.

Wigder, H. Neil. *Wigder's Guide to Over–the–Counter Drugs*. Burlington, Mass.: J. P. Tarcher, 1979.

Wikler, Abraham. *Opioid Dependence—Mechanisms and Treatment*. New York: Plenum Publishing Corp., 1980.

Wilkerson, Don. *Marijuana*. Old Tappan, N.J.: Fleming H. Revell Co., 1980.

Williams, Henry S. *Drugs Against Men*. Reprint of 1935 edition. New York: Arno Press, 1981.

Williams, Melvin H. *Drugs and Athletics*. Springfield, Ill.: Charles C. Thomas, 1974.

Wilner, D. M., and Kassebaum, G. G. *Narcotics*. McGraw-Hill, 1965.

Wilson, Morrow, and Wilson, Suzanne. *Drugs in American Life*. Bronx, N.Y.: H. W. Wilson, 1975.

Windholz, Martha, ed. *The Merck Index*. Ninth edition. Rahway, N.J.: Merck Sharp and Dohme Research Laboratories, 1976.

Winek, Charles. *Everything You Wanted to Know About Drug Abuse But Were Afraid to Ask*. New York: Marcel Dekker Inc., 1974.

Winick, C., and Kinsie, P. *The Lively Commerce: Prostitution in the United States*. Chicago: Quadrangle Books, 1971.

Wittenborn, J. R., ed. *Drugs and Youth*. Springfield, Ill.: Charles C. Thomas, 1969.

———. et al. *Communication and Drug Abuse: Proceedings of the Second Rutgers Symposium on Drug Abuse*. Springfield, Ill.: Charles C. Thomas, 1970.

Witters, Weldon L., and Jones-Witters, Patricia. *Drugs and Sex*. New York: Macmillan, 1974.

Wolfe, T. *The Electric Kool–Aid Acid Test*. New York: Farrar, Straus & Giroux, 1968.

Wolstenholme, G. E. W., and Knight, J., eds. *Hashish: Its Chemistry and Pharmacology*. Boston: Little, Brown and Company, 1965.

Woodley, R. *Dealer: Portrait of a Cocaine Merchant*. New York: Holt, Rinehart, and Winston, 1971.

Worick, W., and Schaller, W. *Alcohol, Tobacco and Drugs: Their Use and Abuse*. Englewood Cliffs, N.J.: Prentice-Hall, 1977.

World Health Organization Study Group. *Youth and Drugs Report*. Geneva, 1971.

World Health Organization. *Alcohol–Related Disabilities*. Geneva, 1977.

———. *Expert Committee on Mental Health, Alcoholism Subcommittee, Second Report*. World Health Organization Technical Report Series, no. 48. Geneva, 1952.

———. *Public Health Aspects of Alcohol and Drug Dependence: Report of a WHO Conference, Dubrovnik, 21–25 August 1978*. Copenhagen: WHO Regional Office for Europe, 1979.

Wrenn, C. Gilbert. *Facts and Fantasies about Drugs*. Circle Pines, Minn.: American Guidance Service, 1970.

Wurmser, Leon. *Drug Abuse: Hidden Dimension*. New York: Jason Aronson, Inc., 1978.

Yablonsky, L. *The Tunnel Back: Synanon*. New York; Macmillan, 1965.

Young, J. *The Drugtakers: The Social Meaning of Drug Use*. London: Paladin Press, 1971.

Young, James H. *American Self–Dosage Medicines: An Historical Perspective*. Lawrence, Kan.: Coronado Press, 1974.

———. *The Toadstool Millionaires*. Princeton: Princeton University Press, 1961.

Young, Lawrence A., et al. *Recreational Drugs*. New York: Macmillan, 1977.

Young, Warren R., and Hixon, Joseph R., eds. *LSD on Campus*. New York: Dell Publishing Co., Inc., 1966.

Zador, P. *Statistical Evaluation of the Effectiveness of Alcohol Safety Action Programs*. Washington, D.C.: Insurance Institute for Highway Safety, 1974.

Zinberg, N. E., and Robertson, J. A. *Drugs and the Public*. New York: Simon and Schuster, 1972.

INDEX

absenteeism 1, 2, 48-49, 76
absinthe 1
absolute alcohol 1
absorption 1
abstainer 1
abstinence 1
abuse 1, 246
abuse potential 2
accidents 2-3, 246-247
acetaldehyde 3
acetone 3
Ackoff's model 3
acne rosea 4
Acquired Immune Deficiency
   Syndrome 4-5
active principle 5
actuarial prediction 5
acupuncture 5
acute 5
acute alcohol intoxication 5-6
acute alcoholic state 6
acute alcoholism 6
adaptive cell metabolism 6
Adaatus® 6
addict subculture 246
addiction 6-7, 131
Addiction Research Foundation 7
addictive personality 211
additive effect 7, 252
Adipex-P® 7
administration 4, 7-9
adrenochrome 9
adulteration 9, 78
adverse drug reaction 9-10
advertising 10-12, 188-189
aerosol sprays 132-134
aging See elderly
agitation 12
agonist 12
AIDS 4-5
airplane glue 132-134, 274
Al-Anon 12-13
Alateen 13
alcohol 1, 4, 5-6, 58-59, 62, 66,
   68-69, 74-77, 80, 82, 83, 88, 89,
   92, 94, 96, 113, 128, 135-136,
   174, 175, 179, 181-182, 192,
   194-195, 200, 215, 216-218,

218-220, 221, 224, 229, 234-
235, 238, 240, 243-244, 246-
247, 250, 253, 268, 269-270,
273-279; accidents related to, 2,
92-93; combined with other
drugs, 26, 37-38, 41, 67, 161-
162, 169-170, 257; consumption
of, 14, 21, 22, 29, 69, 92; costs
related to, 1, 48-50, 97-98, 135-
136, diseases associated with, 13-
14, 15, 16, 53-54, 57, 62, 80, 86,
89, 102-103, 157, 268-269;
effects on body organs, 45, 56-
57, 108, 121, 149-150, 155, 163-
164, 179, 179-181, 182, 203-
204, 245; metabolism of, 3, 6,
52, 55; types of alcoholism, 13,
27, 50, 170, 171, 175; See also
treatment methods and programs;
etiological theories; and testing
for drugs
alcohol amblyopia 13-14, 100
alcohol concentration 14, 43-44
alcohol discharge rate 14
Alcohol Drug Abuse and Mental
   Health Administration 14
alcohol pathology 14
alcohol poisoning 15
alcoholic 14
alcoholic beverage control laws 14-
   15
alcoholic hepatitis 150
alcoholic muscle disease 15
alcoholic myopathy 15, 180
alcoholic poisoning 15
alcoholic polyneuropathy 16
alcoholic psychosis 16
Alcoholic Treatment Center 16
Alcoholics Anonymous 12, 13, 16-
   18, 227, 230
alcoholism 6, 18-19
alcoholist 19
alcoolisation 19
alcoolist 19
alienation 19
alkaloid 5, 19
alkyl nitrites 19
allergy 19

allobarbital 19, 35-38
allopathy 20
allyl isothiocyanate 20
Alpha alcoholism 144
alpha-chloralose 20
alphaprodine 20
altered state of consciousness 20
Alurate® 20
American Council for Drug
   Education 20
American Council on Alcohol
   Problems 20
American Indians 20-22, 212, 219
American Military 22-23, 178, 197
amethystic 23-24
amnesia 24, 43
amobarbital 24, 28, 35-38
amotivational syndrome 24, 160
amphetamines 2, 24-27, 29, 76,
   83, 85, 86, 194-195, 200, 218-
   219, 235, 238, 241-243, 273-279;
   effects on body organs, 46, 56-
   57, 100, 121, 155, 179, 180,
   182, 245, 271
amyl alcohol 27
amyl nitrate 19, 27-28, 120, 129,
   134, 236
Amytal® 28, 35-38
Amytal Sodium® 28, 35-38
anal administration 9
analeptics 28
analgesic 28
anesthetics 28, 61, 52, 99, 133,
   192, 218, 220
Anexsia-D® 28, 66-67
angitis, necrotizing 28
anileridine 28-29
anorectics 24-27, 29
Anstie's Law 29
Antabuse® 3, 29
antagonist, narcotic 84-85
antagonistic 252
anticholinergic 29
antidepressant 29, 83
antihistamines 29-30
Antilirium® 30
antipsychotics 30, 256-258
antitussive 30

anxiety   30
anxiolytic   30
aphrodisiac   30, 234-236
apomorphine   30, 34
approval   See peer pressure
aprobarbital   30, 35-38
arecoline   30
asarone   30
Ascriptin with Codeine®   30
aspergillosis   30
Asthmador   30
ataraxic drugs   31, 256-258
Atropa belladonna   39
atropine   31
attack therapy   31
attitudes of social classes to drug
    use   238-239
Australia   31-34
aversion therapy   30, 34
aversive conditioning   30, 34
ayahuasca   34, 117

BAC   43-44
Bacarate®   35
BAL   35, 43-44
balloon effect   35
banana smoking   35
Bancap®   35
Banisteriopsis caapi   34, 117
bar drinker   35
barbital   35-38
barbiturates   19, 24, 30, 35-38, 50,
    76-77, 85, 195, 200, 218-220,
    235, 239, 246-247, 270, 273-279;
    effects on body organs, 46, 56-
    57, 108, 155, 163, 179-181, 182
behavioral learning theory   38-39
behavioral toxicity   39
beinsa   39
belladonna   39, 245
Benzedrinei   39
benzene   39, 133
benzine   39, 133
benzodiazepine   39-41, 46, 246-
    247
benzoylecgonine   41
benzphetamine   41
benzpyrene   41
Beta alcoholism   144-145
Bible, the   214
biofeedback   41
biological models   214
Biphetamine®   41-42
black Americans   42-43, 219
blackout   43

blood alcohol concentration   43-44
blood alcohol level (BAL)   43-44
blood sugar   44, 86
B'nai B'rith International   44
BNDD   44
B & O Supprettes®   44
Boggs Amendment   44
BOL-148   44
Bolivia   44-45
Bontril PDM®   45
book, the   214
booting   45
bootlegging See moonshine
booze   45
Bowery   45-46
brain   45-46, 56-57, 163-164, 234,
    268
breathalyzers   46
breech births   46
Brevital Sodium®   46
British System, the   46-47, 262-263
bromides   47
Brompton Cocktail   47
bruxism See tooth grinding
Buff-A-Comp®   47
bufotenine   47-48
buprenorphine   48
Bureau of Narcotics, Federal   48
business   1, 2-3, 48-50, 97-98,
    135-136
butabarbital   35-38, 50
butalbital   35-38, 47, 50
Buticaps®   50
Butisol Sodium®   50
butyl alcohol   13, 50
butyl nitrite   50

caffeine   50-52, 66, 245
Caines   52
calabar bean   52
California poppy   52
calorie   52, 55
Canada   52-53
Canary Island broom   53, 78
cancer   53-54, 147, 155-156, 171,
    190
cannabinoids   54
cannabis   54-55 See also marijuana
    and hashish
Capital with Codeine®   55
carbohydrate   55
carbon tetrachloride   55, 132-134
Carbrital®   55
cardiac arrhythmia   120-122
catnip   56

causes of drug abuse   274-279 See
    also etiological theories of drug
    abuse
cement, household   132-134
central nervous system   45-46, 56-
    57
central pontine myelinolysis   57
cephalotropic See psychotropic
charas   57, 131-132
chia seeds   58
child abuse   58-59, 243
children of drug dependent
    individuals   58-59, 276-277
China   59, 196-199
chloral alcoholate   59
chloral betaine   59
chloral derivatives   59-60
chloral hydrate   59-60
chlordiazepoxide   39-41, 60-61,
    149
chlormezanone   61, 255-256
chloroform   28, 61, 132-134
chlorphentermine
    hydrochloride   24-27, 61, 216
chlorpromazine   61, 255, 257
chocolate   50-52, 61
chromatography   61-62
chronic   62
chronic alcohol intoxication   62
chronic alcoholic   62
chronic alcoholism   62
cigarettes See nicotine
cirrhosis   62, 99, 122, 149-150,
    169, 203-204, 216
citronella   62
cleaning fluids   62, 132-134
Client Oriented Data Acquisition
    Program   66
clonidine   62
Clonopin®   62
clorazepate dipotassium   39-41, 62,
    258
clortermine   62
co-alcoholic See para-alcoholic
coca   62-63, 63-65, 67-68, 211
coca paste   63, 211
cocaine   2, 9, 41, 48-49, 62, 63-65,
    67-68, 83, 182, 200, 218-219,
    235, 238, 241-243; effects on
    body organs, 46, 56-57, 100,
    109, 121, 150, 155, 182, 184
cocaine freebase   106-107
cocktail   66
cocktail hour   66
cocoa   50-52, 66
Codalan®   66

CODAP 66
codeine 66-67, 197
coercive therapy 67
coffee *See* caffeine
cola 50-52, 63, 67
cold turkey 85
collapsed veins 67, 124
Colombia 67-68, 237, 255-256
colorines 68
coma 68
Compazine® 68
compulsion 6, 68, 74
confidentiality 68
congener 68, 191
consumption 69
contingency 69
controlled drinking 69-70. 226-228
controlled drugs 70-74
Controlled Substances Act 70-74,
    146-147
convulsions 74, 200-201, 244
cough medicine 67, 74, 254
counseling *See* treatment;
    rehabilitation; and group therapy
counterculture 74, 113, 246
craving 6, 68, 74
crime 48, 74-77, 107, 218-220
crime, organized 77, 107, 222
crisis intervention 77
cross-addiction 77-78
cross-dependence 78
cross-tolerance 78, 82
cultural stress etiological theories
    See sociocultural etiological
    theories
cut 9, 78, 124
cyclazocine 78
cyclobarbital 35-38, 78
Cylert® 78
Cystospaz-SR® 78
cytisine 53, 78, 233, 241

Dalmane® 78-79
damiana 79
Darvocet-N® 79
Darvoni 79
Darvon-N® 79
datura 79
dawamesk 79, 118
DAWN 93
Daytop *See* therapeutic communities
DEA 93
deadly nightshade *See* belladonna
decriminalization 146-148, 185
delirium 80
delirium tremens 80, 269

Delta alcoholism 145
delusions 80
dementia 80
Demerol® 80
denial 80, 204
Denmark 81-82
dentistry 82, 179
dependence 6-7, 82, 223
depressants 56-57, 82
depressed communities 82-83
depression 83, 95-96, 246-247,
    271-273
deprivation 83-84
Deprol® 84
desensitization 84
Desoxyn® 84
DET 84
detoxification 84-86
Dexedrine® 86
dextroamphetamine 24-27, 86
dextromoramide 86
diabetes 86, 203-204
diacetylmorphine 86, 123-127
diazepam 87-88, 256-258, 267
Didrex® 88
diethylpropion 88, 254
diethytryptamine *See* DET
digestion 88, 108-109, 245-246
dihydrocodeine 88, 250
dihydrocodeinone 88, 201
dihydromorphinone 88
Dilaudid® 88
dill 88
dimethyltryptamine 88, 89-90
diphenoxylate 88, 150-151
dipipanone 88
dipsomania 88
disease concept of alcoholism 88-
    89, 144-145
diseases 89
disorientation 89
distillation 89
distribution restrictions on drugs 72
diviner's sage 89
d-lysergic acid diethylamide
    tartrate 25 151-154
DMT 89-90, 114-116
DNA 90
Do It Now Foundation 90
Dolene® 90
Dolonil® 90
Dolophine Hydrochloride® 90,
    167-168
DOM 90-91, 114-116
Dona Ana 91
dopamine 91

Doriden® 91-92
Dover's powder 92
doxepin 92
DPT 92
dram 92
dram shop law 92
Drinamyl® 92
driving and drugs 3, 41, 43, 92-93,
    94, 178-179
dropper 93, 124
drug addiction *See* addiction and
    dependence
drug automatism 93
drug culture 74, 113, 246
Drug Enforcement
    Administratior 70-74, 77, 93,
    120, 205-206
drug interaction *See* synergy
drunk 94
dry drunk 94
DSM III 94
DUI 94
Duradyne DHC® 94
DWI 94
dynorphin 94, 98
dysphoria 94

ebriate 94
ebriety 94
economic impact *See* absenteeism;
    business; accidents; employee
    assistance programs; and
    insurance
Ectasul® 94
ED50 94
effective dose of a drug 94
Eighteenth Amendment 95
Elavil® 95
elderly 82-83, 95-97
electric shock 97
elemicin 97, 194
emetine 97
Empirin Compound with
    Codeine® 97
employee assistance programs 48-
    49, 97-98
enabling 98, 204
encounter groups *See* group therapy
endocrine etiological theories 98
endorphins 94, 98
enkephalins 98
enzyme multiplied imminoassay
    technique 98, 267
epena 98
ephedrine 99
epidemiology 99

Epsilon alcoholism 145
Equanil® 99
Erthroxylon coca 63-65, 99
erogenics 99
Esgic® 99
esophagus 53-54, 99, 157
ethanol 13, 99
ethclorvynol 99, 215
ether 28, 99, 132-134, 139
ethinamate 99, 267
ethnopharmacology 99
ethyl alcohol *See* ethanol
ethylmorphine hydrochloride 99
etiological theories of drug
    abuse 19, 38-39, 83-84, 98,
    101, 110, 135, 199, 209, 211,
    212-213, 214, 223, 239
etiology 99
euphoria 100
ex-addict 100
experimental drug use 100, 275-
    277
eyes 13-14, 100, 182

fake coke 52, 101
false negative, false positive 101
familial etiological theories 101
Families in Action 101
family problems 58-59, 101, 243-
    244
family therapy 101
Fastin® 101
fatty liver 101, 149-150
Federal Bureau of Investigation 93,
    102
fenfluramine hydrochloride 102,
    215-216
fentanyl 102, 246
fetal alcohol syndrome 102-103,
    217
Finland 103-104
Fiorinal® 104
flashback 104, 115, 152, 164
fluorocarbons 104, 132-134
flurazepan 78-79, 104
fly agaric 104-105, 114-116
formaldehyde 105
France 105-106, 107
freebase, cocaine 106
French Connection 106, 107, 139
Freon 107, 132-142
fructose 107, 116
fumo d'Angola 107

Gamma alcoholism 6, 145
gaseous anesthetics 108, 132-134

gasoline 108, 132-134
gastrointestinal tract 108-109, 245-
    246
gay drug users *See* homosexuals
Gaysal® 109
Gemonil® 109
generics 109
genetics *See* heredity
genetotropic etiological theory 110
Germany, West 110-111
glue sniffing 111, 134, 274
glutethimide 91-92, 111
Golden Crescent 111-112, 137-
    138, 202-203
Golden Triangle 112-113
grand mal convulsions 86, 113
grog 113
group therapy 31, 113, 223
gum opium 113

habit 6-7, 113
habit-forming 113
habituation 6-7, 113
Haight-Ashbury, the 113
Haldol® 113-114
half-life of drugs 114, 252
halfway house 114, 250, 258-259
hallucinogens 80, 85, 114-116,
    166-167, 181, 207-209, 212,
    222-223, 235, 239, 247, 271 *See
    also* LSD
hangover 44, 107, 116-117, 269
hard drugs, hard narcotics 117
harmal 117
harmaline 117
harmine 117
Harris-Dodd Act 117
Harrison Narcotics Act 117
haschischins, Le club des 117
hashish 79, 117-119
hash oil 118
Hawaiian wood rose, baby 119
Hawaiian wood rose, large 119
head shop 101, 119-120
heart 120-122
heavy drinker 122
hedonistic 122
hemochromatosis 122
hemp 54-55, 157-162, 264
henbane 122
hepatitis 8, 122, 149-150
hepatoma 122
herbals 122
heredity 122-123
heroin 8, 9, 45, 74-77, 78, 123-
    127, 194, 200-201, 216-217,

218-220, 235, 238, 270-271,
    273-279; *diseases associated
    with,* 28, 67; *deaths related to,*
    250-251; *effects on body organs,*
    46, 56-57, 108-109, 120-121,
    127-128, 150, 155-156, 163,
    179, 179-181, 182, 245;
    *maintenance programs and
    treatments,* 46-47, 78, 84-85,
    167-170, 182-182
hexane 127
hexobarbital 35-38, 127
high 127
high blood pressure 127
highway safety *See* driving and drugs
hippie 127, 246
histamine 127-128
holiday heart syndrome 128
holistic medicine 128
homicide *See* crime
homosexuals 4-5, 128-129
hormones 129, 234-235
hormones, male sex 129, 234-235
hot lines 129
Hughes Act 129
Hycodan® 129
Hycomine® 129-130
hydrocodone 6, 66-67, 130
hydromorphone 130
hyoscine, hyoscyamine *See*
    scopolamine
hyperactive 130
hyperglycemia 130
hypertension 62, 130
hypnosis 130
hypnotic 131
hypodermic administration 8-9,
    124
hypoglycemia 44, 131
hypotension 131

iatrogenic addiction 131
ibogaine 131
illusions 131
impairment 131
impotence 234-236
import and export limitations on
    drugs 73
inability to abstain 131, 145
India 131-132
Indians, American 20-22, 212
inebriate 132
inebriety 132
infancy *See* pregnancy and oral
    fixation
infection 122, 132, 254

inhalants 28, 61, 99, 104, 107, 132-134, 201, 238-239, 273-279; *effects on body organs*, 120, 150
input-output models for treatment 134-135
insomnia 135, 246
instability and crisis etiological theory 135
insurance 135-136
intemperance 136
international drug commissions 74, 136, 273
intervention 137
interviews, structured and unstructured 137
intravenous injection 8-9
intramuscular injection 8-9
Ionamin® 137
ipecac 137
Iran 111-112, 137-138
Ireland 138-139
isocarboxazid 139
isopropyl alcohol 13, 139
Italy 107, 139-140
IV 140

Jamaica 140-141, 228
Japan 141-144
Jellinek, E. M. 144-145

kava 145
kerosene 133
Ketaject® 145
Ketalar® 145
ketamine hydrochloride 145
khat 145
Korsakoff's Syndrome 146, 163

LAMM 146
lacquer thinner 132-134, 146
La Guardia Report 146, 158
laudanum 146, 196
laws and legislation 14, 29, 44, 70-74, 93, 117, 146-148, 158, 183-184, 189
L-dopa 146
legal aspects of drug use 70-74, 146-148
legal high 148
Lemmon Company 148, 226
lesbian drug users 128-129
lethal dose 148
lettuce 148
levallorphan 148, 151
Levo-Dromoran® 148
levorphanol 148

Librax® 148-149
Libritabs® 149
Librium® 60-61, 149
lidocaine 149
lighter fluids 132-134
liquid hashish 118, 149
liquor 149
liver 53-54, 99, 149-150 *See also* cirrhosis
lobelia 150
Lomotil® 150-151
lophophorine 151, 211-212
Lorfan® 151
Lotusate® 151
LSD 61-62, 85, 114-116, 151-154, 182, 201, 217, 218-220, 239, 273-279; *effects on body organs*, 45-46, 56-57, 100, 109, 120, 156, 164, 181
LSM 154
Luminal® 154-155
lungs 155-156, 188-192, 251

mace 156
macromerine 91, 156
macronodular cirrhosis 156
Madagascar periwinkle 156
magic mushrooms 156, 222-223
mainline, mainlining 124, 156
maintenance therapy 46-47, 167-170, 262
major tranquilizer 157, 256-258
malaria 157, 226
Mallory-Weiss Syndrome 157
mandrake 157
Mandrax® 157
manufacturing quotas for drugs 72
MAO inhibitors 175
marijuana 2, 24, 41, 53, 54, 76, 85, 90, 114, 157-162, 181-182, 194, 201, 207, 217, 218-220, 235, 236, 239, 252, 271, 273-279; *accidents related to,* 2-3, 92-93; *effects on body organs,* 46, 57, 100, 109, 120, 150, 156, 163-164, 179, 179-181, 245-246; *legal aspects,* 146-148
mazindol 162
MDA 114-116, 162
Mebaral® 162-163
Mediatric® 163
medical costs 48, 135-136
Medicare 135-136
Melfiat® 163
Mellaril® 163

memory 146, 163-164, 268-269
Menrium® 164
meperidine 164-165
mephobarbital 35-38, 165
meprobamate 165-166, 257
Meprospan® 166
mescal 166
mescaline 114-116, 166-167
metabolism 3, 52, 55, 95, 167, 194-195
methadone 42, 46-47, 76, 84, 167-170, 271
Methadone Hydrochloride Diskettes® 170
methamphetamine 24-27, 170
methanol 170
methaqualone 148, 170-171, 226, 236, 273-279
metharbital 35-38, 171
methyl alcohol 13, 105, 171
methyldihydromorphinone 171
methylmorphine 171
methylphenidate 171-172, 231-232
methyphenobarbital 35-38, 172
methyprylon 172, 192
metopon 172
Mexico 172-173, 237, 256
micronodular cirrhosis 173
milieu therapy 173
Military, American 22-23
milk sugar 173
Milpath® 173-174
Milprem® 174
Miltown® 174
Miltrate® 174
minerals 194-195
minor tranquilizer 174, 256-258
mixed addiction 174
mixed cirrhosis 174
mixing drinks 174
MMDA 174
moderate drinking 29, 175
monoamine oxidase (MAO) inhibitors 175
moonshine 170, 175
morning drinking 175
morning glory seeds 114-116, 175-176
morning shot 176
morphine 176-178, 197
Mothers Against Drunk Driving 178-179
mouth 82, 179
mouthwash 179
multihabituation 179
muscarine 179

muscimol   179
muscles   15, 179-181, 182
mushrooms, sacred   114-116, 181
music and drugs   181-182, 228
mydriasis   182
myoglobinuria   182
myristicin   182, 194

N₂O   192
nail polish remover   132-134, 182
nalbuphine   182, 193
Nalline®   182
Nalline test   182-183
nalorphine   182, 183
naloxone   183, 254
Naloxone Challenge Test   183
naltrexone   183, 254
nanogram   183
Narcan®   183
Narcan Test   183
narcotic   183, 252
Narcotic Addiction Rehabilitation
   Act   183-184
narcotic antagonist   84-85, 182-
   183, 184
Narcotics Anonymous   184
Narcotics Education Inc.   184
nasal administration   9
nasal septum   184
National Association of State
   Alcohol and Drug Abuse
   Directors   184
National Clearinghouse for Drug
   Abuse Information   184
National Commission on Marijuana
   and Drug Abuse   185
National Federation of Parents for
   Drug Free Youth   185
National Institute on Alcohol Abuse
   and Alcoholism   129, 185, 226
National Institute on Drug
   Abuse   160, 185
National Organization for the
   Reform of Marijuana Laws   146,
   185, 206
National Parents Resource Institute
   for Drug Education   186
National Prohibition Act   268
Native American Church   20, 212
needle freak   9
Nembutal®   186
Netherlands, The   186-187
New Zealand   187-188
NIAAA   185
nicotine   7-8, 10, 41, 130, 181,
   188-192, 217, 273; *diseases*

related to, 53-54, 99; *effects on*
   body organs, 109, 121, 155-156,
   179
NIDA   185
niopo   192
nitrous oxide   133, 192
Noctec®   192
nodding   124
Noludar®   192
non-addictive pathological
   drinker   192
North Conway Institute   192
Norway   192-193
noscapine   193
Nubain®   193
Numorphan®   194
nutmeg   194, 220,
nutrition   80, 89, 194-195, 245
nystagmus   100, 195

Obetrol®   195-196
Odyssey Resources, Inc.   196
ololiuqui   175-176
Olympic Games   241-243
opiates   196
opioids   196
opium   57, 59, 109, 179, 146, 196-
   199, 254
oral administration   7-8
oral fixation   199
organic disorder   199
organic solvents   133
organized crime   77, 107, 222
outreach   199
overdose   77, 200-201, 250-251
over-the-counter medications   10-
   11, 74, 201, 240
oxazepam   39-41, 201
Oxford Group   16, 201
oxycodone   201, 210
oxymorphone   194, 202

Pakistan   111-112, 202-203
panaddiction   203
pancreas   203-204
Pantopon®   204
papaverine   204
Papaver somniferum   204
para-alcoholic   58, 98, 204
parahexyl   204
paraldehyde   204-205
paranoia   205
paraquat   205-206
paraphernalia   119-120
paregoric   196, 206, 225

parenteral administration   8-9
Parest®   206
parica   207
passion flower   207
passive inhalation   207
Pathibamate®   207
pathological drinker   207
pathological intoxication   207
PCP   24, 100, 114-116, 207-277
PDR   214
peer pressure   209, 275-277
pemoline   78, 209
pentazocine   210, 253
pentobarbital   35-38, 210
Pentothal®   210
peptides, endogenous   210
Percocet-5®   210
Percodan®   210-211
periodic alcoholism   145, 211
peripheral neuritis   211
personality trait theories   211
Peru   211
pethidine   211
peyote   20-21, 114-116, 166-167,
   211-212
pharmaceutical   212
pharmacogenic orgasm   212
pharmacokinetics   212
pharmacological etiology   212-213
phenacetin   213
Phenaphen with Codeine®   213
phenazocine   213
phencyclidine   207-209
phendimetrazine tartrate   213
phenelzine   175
phenobarbital   35-38, 154-155, 213
phentermine   137, 213
phenylpropanolamine   213-214
phenytoin   214
pholocodine   214
Phrenilin®   214
physical dependence   6-7, 82, 84
Physician's Desk Reference   214
physiological models of
   etiology   214
physostigmine   30, 214
Pil-Anon Family Program   214
Pills Anonymous   214
piloerection   214
pinpoint pupils   100
piptadenia   215
pituri   215
Placidyl®   215
Plegine®   215
Plexonal®   215
PMB-200 & PMB-400®   215

poly-drug use 18, 92, 215
polystyrene cement 215
Pondimin® 215-216

portal cirrhosis 216
postintoxicated state 216
postnecrotic cirrhosis 216
potentiation 216, 252
Pre-Sate® 216
pregnancy 37, 46, 58-59, 123,
    125, 180, 190-191, 216-218, 258
Preludin® 218
prisoners and drug use 218-220
problem drinker 220
procaine 220
progression 220
Prohibition 95, 253, 261, 265, 268
Prolixin® 220-221
proof 221
propoxyphene 79, 221
propoxyphene napsylate 221-222
prostitution 222
protopine 222
psilocybin 114-116, 222-223
psychedelic 223
psychodrama 223
psychological dependence 6-7, 223
psychological models of
    etiology 223
psychosis 223
psychostimulant 223
psychotogenic 223
psychotomimetic 224
psychotropic 224
Public Affairs Committee 224
public drunkenness 224
Puerto Rico 224-225
pyrahexyl 225
pyribenzamine 225

Quaalude® 148, 170-171, 226
Quibron Plus® 226
quinine 124, 226, 251

radioimmunoassay 226
Rand Reports 69-70, 134, 226-
    228, 230-231
Rapid Eye Movement *See* REM
Rastafarians 140-141, 228
Rauwolfia serpentina 228-229,
    256-257
reassurance 229
receptor sites 229
recovery 229
recreational drug use 229
rectal administration 9

red eye 100
rehabilitation 12, 167-170, 229-
    230
reinforcement, positive and
    negative 230
relapse 230
relaxation training 230
Release 230
REM (Rapid Eye Movement) 50,
    60, 230
remission 230-231
Repan® 231
reserpine 231
resin 231
reverse tolerance 162, 231
rhinophyma 4, 231
Ritalin® 231-232
RNA 232
Robitussin A-C® 232
rock groups 181-182
rubbing alcohol 13, 232
rum fits 86, 232, 269

sacred mushrooms 181
Salvia divinorum 232
Sanorex® 232
San Pedro cactus 232
Sansert® 232
sassafras 232-233
S.B.P. Plus® 233
scheduled drugs 70-74
schizophrenia 233, 244
scopolamine 233, 240
Scotch broom 78, 233
Seconal® 233
Sedapap® 233
sedative 233, 256-258
sedative hypnotic 233
sedativism 233
Sed-Tens Ty-Med® 233
seizures 74, 113, 244, 269
self-help groups *See* treatment;
    rehabilitation; halfway houses;
    Narcotics Anonymous; and
    Alcoholics Anonymous
sensitivity 234
Serax® 234
serotonin 45, 234
Sernyl® 234
sex 4-5, 30, 128-129, 234-236
sinsemilla 236
Shiva, Siva 236
SK-Bamate® 236
SK-65® 236
skid row 236

skinning, skin popping 8, 124,
    236-237
smoking *See* nicotine
smuggling 67, 77, 220, 237, 255-
    256
snakeroot 228-229
sniff, sniffing 9, 238
snort, snorting 9, 238
sober 238
sober up, sobering up 238
social class 42, 238-239
social drinking 227, 239
sociocultural etiological
    theories 239
socioeconomic groups *See* social
    class
sodium butabarbital 35-38, 240
Solfoton® 240
solitary drinking 240
solvents 132-134
Sominex® 240
South Africa 240
Spanish broom 78, 241
Special Action Office for Drug
    Abuse Prevention 241
spirits 241
sports 220, 241-243
spouse abuse 243-244
spree 244
Stadol® 244
stall 244
Statobex® 244
status epilepticus 244, 269
stereotypy 244
steroids 241-243
stimulants 244-245
stomach 108-109, 245-246
stramonium 79, 246
strychnine 246
subculture, drug 127, 113, 246
subcutaneous injection 8-9
Sublimaze® 246
substance abuse 246
succinylcholine 246
suicide 77, 83, 85, 87-88, 246-247
suppositories 9
supra-additive 247, 252
Surital® 247
susceptibility 122-123, 247
Sweden 247-250
sympathomimetic amines 250
symptomatic alcoholism 250
symptomatic drinking 250
Synalgos® 250
Synanon 250
Syndrome X 125, 250-251

synergy, synergistic effect   252
synhexyl   252
synesthesia   152, 252
synthetic marijuana   252
synthetic narcotics   252

talbutal   35-38, 253
tachycardia   120, 253
Talwin®   253
Taractan®   253
TASC   259
TCA   29, 253
Tedral®   253
telepathine   253
temperance   253
temposil   254
Tenuate®   254
Tepanil®   254
terpin hydrate   254
testing for drugs   46, 49, 61-62, 98,
    101, 182-183, 226, 244
tetrahydrocannabinol   254
tetanus   8, 254
Thai sticks   254
THC   54-55, 157-162, 254
thebaine   254
theories on the causes of drug abuse
    See etiological theories
therapeutic index   254
therapeutic communities   114, 196,
    250, 258
Thorazine®   255
TM   255
TMA   114-116, 255
tobacco See nicotine
tolerance   6-7, 200, 255
toluene   132-134, 255
tooth grinding   255
topical administration   9
toxic   255
toxic psychosis   223

trafficking   67-68, 73, 77, 111-113,
    255-256
Trancopal®   256
tranquilizers   11-12, 39-41, 60-61,
    92, 95-96, 195, 200, 219, 235,
    239, 246-247, 256-258, 270,
    273-279; effects on body organs,
    45, 56-57, 108, 155, 179-181
Tranxene®   258
tranylcypromine   175, 258
transcendental meditation   255
treatment methods and programs   3,
    16, 23, 29, 31, 34, 41, 67, 68,
    69, 80, 84-86, 97, 114, 130-131,
    134-135, 135-136, 137, 167-170,
    173, 195, 220, 223, 229-230,
    250, 254, 255, 258-259
Treatment Alternatives to Street
    Crimes   259
tremor   80, 259, 269
trichloroethylene   132-134, 259
triclofos sodium   259
Triclos®   259
Trimstat®   259
Trimtabs®   260
Tuinal®   260
Turkey   107, 111, 260
Tussanil®   261
Tussionex®   261
Twenty-first Amendment   261
tybamate   256-258, 261
Tybatran®   261
Tylenol with Codeine®   261

under the influence of alcohol   262
United Kingdom   46-47, 262-264
United States   264-266
urine testing   61-62, 98, 101, 226,
    244, 266-267

Valium®   267
Valmid®   267
vaporous anesthetics   61, 99, 132-
    134, 267
Veronal®   267
Vietnam See American Military
vinbarbital   35-38, 267
vinho de jurumena   267-268
violence   58-59, 74-77, 218-220,
    243-244
virola   268
vitamins   103, 194-195
volatile hydrocarbons and
    solvents   132-134
Volstead Act   268
Voranil®   268

water of life   268
Webb-Canyon Act   268
weight loss and control   24-27, 29
Wernicke's encephalopathy   268-
    269
WHO   273
wild cucumber   269
wild fennel   269
wino   269
withdrawal   269-271
women   128, 191, 216-218, 219,
    222, 234-236, 243-244, 246-247,
    271-273
wood alcohol   170
World Health Organization   6-7,
    160-161
wormwood   1

xylene   132-134

yerba mate   273
yohimbe   235-236, 273
youths   58-59, 134, 189, 209, 273-
    279